ADVENTURE

RAFT THE CANYON.

10% OFF

AAA Members Receive
10% Off All
Grand Canyon West
Tickets & Tours

GRAND CANYON West.COM

888-868-WEST (9378)

Arizona & New Mexico

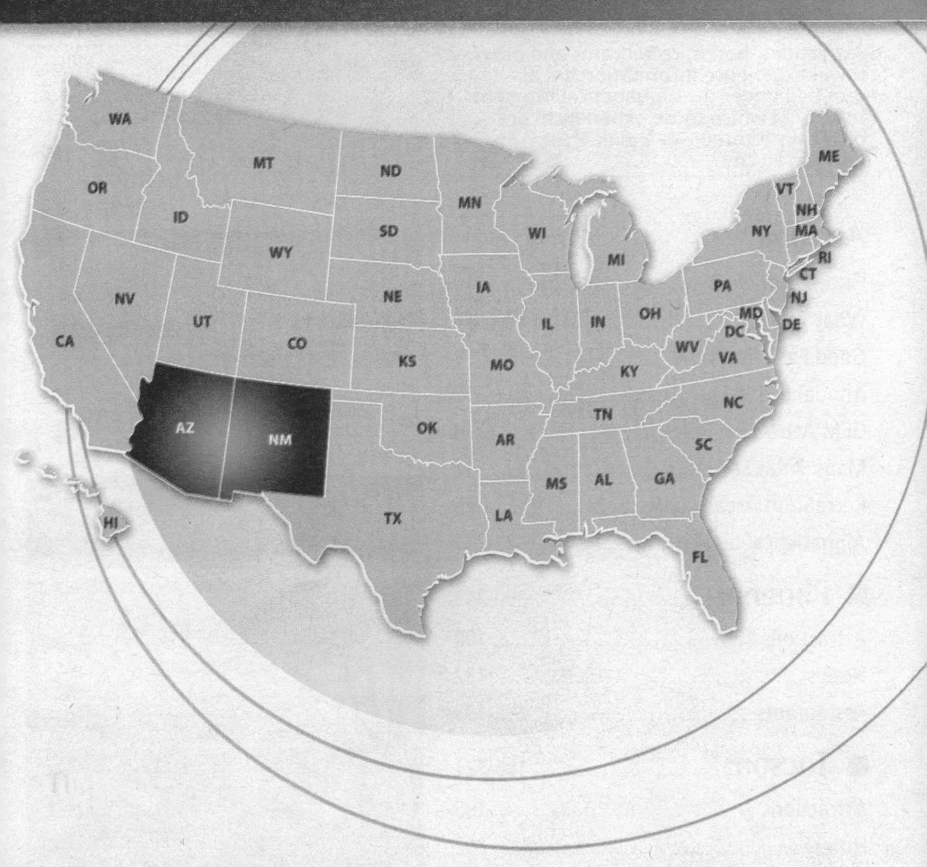

Published by AAA Publishing
1000 AAA Drive, Heathrow, FL 32746-5063

Advertising Rate and Circulation Information: (407) 444-8280

Printed in the USA by Quad/Graphics

This book is printed on paper certified by third-party standards for sustainably managed forestry and production.

Printed on recyclable paper.
Please recycle whenever possible.

Stock #4602

CONTENTS

Get more travel information at AAA.com/travelguides and AAA.com/traveltips

Attractions, hotels, restaurants and other travel experience information are all grouped under the alphabetical listing of the city in which those experiences are physically located—or the nearest recognized city.

Arizona

New Mexico

Featured Information

Using Your Guide

AAA TourBook guides are packed with travel insights, maps and listings of places to stay, play, eat and save. For more listings, more details and online booking, visit **AAA.com/travelguides**.

Helping You Make the Connection

Look for this symbol throughout the guides for direct links to related content.

A to Z City Listings

Cities and places are listed alphabetically within each state or province. Attractions, hotels and restaurants are listed once — under the city in which they are physically located.

Cities that are considered part of a larger destination city or area have an expanded city header. The header identifies the larger region and cross-references pages that contain shared trip-planning resources:

- Destination map – outline map of the cities that comprise a destination city or area
- Attraction spotting map – regional street map marked with attraction locations
- Hotel/restaurant spotting map and index – regional street map numbered with hotel and restaurant locations identified in an accompanying index

Cities that are not considered part of a larger destination city or area but have a significant number of listings may have these resources within the individual city section:

- Attraction spotting map
- Hotel/restaurant spotting map and index

Location Abbreviations

Directions are from the center of town unless otherwise specified, using these highway abbreviations:

Bus. Rte.=business route

CR=county road

FM=farm to market

FR=forest road

Hwy.=Canadian highway

I=interstate highway

LR=legislative route

R.R.=rural route

SR/PR=state or provincial route

US=federal highway

About Listed Establishments

AAA/CAA Inspected & Approved hotels and restaurants are listed on the basis of merit alone after careful evaluation and approval by full-time, professionally trained AAA inspectors. An establishment's decision to advertise in the TourBook guide has no bearing on its evaluation or rating; nor does inclusion of advertising imply AAA endorsement of products and services.

Information in this guide was believed accurate at the time of publication. However, since changes inevitably occur between annual editions, please contact your AAA travel professional, visit **AAA.com/travelguides** or download the free AAA Mobile app to confirm prices and schedules.

Attraction Listing Icons

SAVE AAA Discounts & Rewards® member discount

Electric vehicle charging station on premises. Domestic station information provided by the U.S. Department of Energy. Canadian station information provided by Plug'n Drive Ontario.

GT Guided Tours available

Camping facilities

Food on premises

Recreational activities

Pet friendly (Call for restrictions/fees.)

Picnicking allowed

In select cities only:

Mass transit station within 1 mile. Icon is followed by station name and AAA/CAA designated station number within listing.

GEM AAA/CAA travel experts may designate an attraction of exceptional interest and quality as a AAA GEM — a *Great Experience for Members®*. See GEM Attraction Index (listed on CONTENTS page) for a complete list of locations.

Consult the online travel guides at **AAA.com/travelguides** or visit AAA Mobile for additional things to do if you have time.

Hotel Listing Icons

May be preceded by CALL and/or SOME UNITS.

Member Information:

SAVE Member rates: discounted standard room rate or lowest public rate available at time of booking for dates of stay.

Eco-certified by government or private organization.

Electric vehicle charging station on premises. Domestic station information provided by the U.S. Department of Energy. Canadian station information provided by Plug'n Drive Ontario.

Smoke-free premises

In select cities only:

Mass transit station within 1 mile. Icon is followed by station name and AAA/CAA designated station number within listing.

Services:

Airport transportation

Pet friendly (Call for restrictions/fees.)

Restaurant on premises

Restaurant off premises

Room service for 2 or more meals

Full bar

Child care

Business center

Accessible features (Call property for available services and amenities.)

Activities:

Full-service casino

Pool

Health club or exercise room on premises

In-Room Amenities:

High-speed Internet service

High-speed Internet service (Call property for fees.)

Wireless Internet service

Wireless Internet service (Call property for fees.)

No wireless Internet service

Pay movies

Refrigerator

Microwave

Coffeemaker

No air conditioning

No TV

No telephones

Restaurant Listing Icons

AAA Discounts & Rewards® member discount

Eco-certified by government or private organization.

Electric vehicle charging station on premises. Domestic station information provided by the U.S. Department of Energy. Canadian station information provided by Plug'n Drive Ontario.

No air conditioning

Accessible features (Call property for available services and amenities.)

Designated smoking section

Breakfast

Lunch

Dinner

Open 24 hours

Open after 11 p.m.

Pet friendly (Call for restrictions/fees.)

In select cities only:

Mass transit station within 1 mile. Icon is followed by station name and AAA/CAA designated station number within listing.

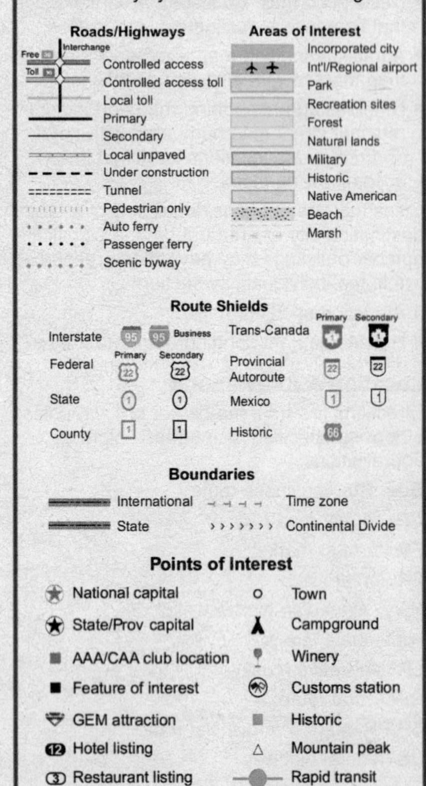

Understanding the Diamond Ratings

Hotel and restaurant inspections are unscheduled to ensure our trained professionals encounter the same unbiased experience members do.

Inspected & Approved

- The first step for every hotel and restaurant is to demonstrate they meet expected standards of cleanliness, comfort and hospitality.
- Only hotels and restaurants that pass AAA's rigorous on-site inspection are designated **AAA Inspected & Approved.**

But all AAA Inspected & Approved properties aren't the same: The difference is in the **Diamonds.** Each additional Diamond means greater comfort, amenities and service. Learn more at **AAA.com/Diamonds**.

Hotels	Restaurants
 Budget-oriented, offering basic comfort and hospitality.	 Simple, economical food, often quick-serve, in a functional environment.
 Affordable, with modestly enhanced facilities, décor and amenities.	 Familiar food, often cooked to order, served in casual surroundings.
 Distinguished, multifaceted with enhanced physical attributes, amenities and guest comforts.	 Trendy cuisine, skillfully prepared and served, with expanded beverage options, in an enhanced setting.
 Refined, stylish with upscale physical attributes, extensive amenities and high degree of hospitality, service and attention to detail.	 Distinctive fine-dining. Creative preparations, skillfully served, often with wine steward, amid upscale ambience.
 Ultimate luxury, sophistication and comfort with extraordinary physical attributes, meticulous personalized service, extensive amenities and impeccable standards of excellence.	 Leading-edge cuisine of the finest ingredients, uniquely prepared by an acclaimed chef, served by expert service staff led by maître d' in extraordinary surroundings.

Guest Safety

Inspectors view a sampling of rooms during hotel evaluations and, therefore, AAA/CAA cannot guarantee working locks and operational fire safety equipment in every guest unit.

Contacting AAA/CAA About the TourBook Guide

Tell us what you think about the TourBook guides or your experience at a listed hotel, restaurant or attraction. If your visit doesn't meet your expectations, please contact us **during your visit or within 30 days**. Be sure to save your receipts. We also welcome your recommendations on places to inspect.

Use the easy online form at **AAA.com/MemberFeedback**, email memberrelations@national.aaa.com or mail your feedback to: AAA Member Comments, 1000 AAA Dr., Box 61, Heathrow, FL 32746.

Monument Valley Navajo Tribal Park

Arizona

Close your eyes and think about Arizona. Chances are the images that first come to mind are those of the Old West—cowboys, Native Americans, deserts, cacti—stuff straight out of TV Westerns.

Cowboys still do exist here, but they're more likely to be found assisting city slickers at modern guest ranches than lassoing cattle on a trail drive.

Native Americans, the first Arizonans, though a small percentage of today's population, are a major influence in everyday life. Reminders of their heritage are evident in national monuments, tribal parks and historic sites that preserve their ancient dwellings, customs and crafts.

As for the deserts, well, the sand and the intricate rock formations are still there, but their expanse is now broken by major metropolitan areas like Phoenix and Tucson and golf courses that seem strangely out of place. And rare species of cactus, such as the organ pipe and saguaro, are protected in their own preserves.

Organ pipe cactus

The Grand Canyon State

"Did the government build it?"

More than one flabbergasted visitor has asked this upon first seeing Arizona's Grand Canyon. Though it may sound preposterous, it's a question you'll find less naive after gazing at these myriad erosion-carved columns, arches and windows—a virtual cityscape of landforms that would make a Manhattanite feel at home.

No doubt Uncle Sam would love to claim responsibility for the Grand Canyon, but only Father Time can take credit for this natural wonder. Over millions of years geologic upheaval forced a former sea bottom into the sky, allowing wind and water to work their rock-sculpting magic. The result: a spectacle so awesome that some 5 million people from all over the world visit each year.

The South Rim area boasts many of the best vantage points from which to gape at the canyon in all its multihued glory. What's more, the tall pine trees here hide the great chasm from view until you are almost at its edge. Confronting this breathtaking scene as you emerge from the forest is an unforgettable experience.

In the early morning and late afternoon, colors dance along canyon walls in the rapidly changing sunlight. If a storm comes your way, don't despair: Shadows of rain clouds can create striking patterns of darkness as they drift across the canyon's depths.

But even after visiting the Grand Canyon, don't think you've seen it all. An equally spectacular play of color and light awaits you at Monument Valley Navajo Tribal Park. Here you just might feel like you're walking through a Hollywood set, and with good reason: The valley, with its rose-tinted buttes and mesas, has served as backdrop for countless Westerns and car commercials.

Grand Canyon visitors frequently overlook another Arizona jewel—Sedona's Red Rock territory. Oak Creek Canyon has its own collection of buttes, spires and sheer rock walls that shimmer with shades of beige, ocher, salmon and scarlet. Beat the heat and go with Oak Creek's flow at Slide Rock State Park, where a waterslide—natural, not man-made—splashes from pool to pool.

"Married to the Ground"

Ancient cliff dwellings at Montezuma Castle, Canyon de Chelly and Navajo national monuments blend with their environs so well, they seem to have sprouted from the precipices they're perched upon.

Centuries after these towns in the sky were abandoned, architect Frank Lloyd Wright designed buildings—notably Taliesin West, his former home and studio in Scottsdale—according to his belief that they should harmoniously coexist with their surroundings.

Wright once encapsulated his design philosophy by saying his buildings were "married to the ground." It's easy to see why he chose Arizona as his studio's setting. Here the terrain seems a willing companion to man's handiwork: mesas rise from the desert like skyscrapers and pinnacles soar like church spires.

Recreation

Canyons. Mountains. Forests. Lakes. The extensive Colorado River. Arizona, derived from the Native American word meaning "little spring," is a veritable fountain of fun for outdoor types.

Hopefully you packed your putter. With more than 350 golf courses to choose from, people drive from all over the country to chip and putt. But watch out for hazards—Mesa, Phoenix, northern Scottsdale and Tucson are chock-full of challenging fairways.

Then there's *the* Canyon, the grandest of them all. For a bird's-eye view, try a helicopter or airplane tour; or capture that Old West spirit of adventure on a train ride from Williams. Peer off the edge while hiking along the South Rim Trail—the panorama will knock your socks off.

If you're more adventurous, follow Bright Angel Trail into the depths of the gorge. The South Kaibab and North Kaibab trails also are good treks on foot or on hoof: Mule rides are available for 2-day jaunts (advance reservations are required). Since it takes a full day to reach the canyon floor, camping is a popular option; contact Trip Planner, phone (928) 638-7888, for a backcountry permit.

Despite Arizona's arid landscape, there are plenty of places to find refreshment. Dip your toes, skis, personal watercraft, sailboard or speedboat into Glen Canyon National Recreation Area's Lake Powell or Lake Mead National Recreation Area's lakes Mead and Mojave. Why not explore the Colorado River on a peaceful float trip or an adrenaline-pumping ride through white-water rapids?

If fishing is your sport, head for the waters of the White Mountains, where you can hook all sorts of trout and bass. For information about hunting trophy elk or other game, contact the Arizona Game and Fish Department.

When it gets chilly, skiing at the Arizona Snowbowl, north of Flagstaff in the Coconino National Forest, is the cool thing to do. Other places to catch a chairlift are Sunrise Park, in Greer; Mount Lemmon, north of Tucson; and Elk Ridge Ski and Outdoor Recreation Area, in Williams.

Montezuma Castle National Monument

Historic Timeline

1539	Franciscan friar Marcos de Niza searches unsuccessfully for the fabled Seven Cities of Cíbola throughout the Southwest.
1853	The Gadsden Purchase brings a portion of present-day southern Arizona and southern New Mexico under U.S. control.
1889	Phoenix is chosen as the territorial capital.
1911	The completion of the Roosevelt Dam on the Salt River delivers much-needed water to the area.
1912	Arizona enters the Union as the 48th state.
1919	Grand Canyon is designated a national park.
1966	The Miranda vs. Arizona ruling stipulates that arrested persons must be informed of their rights before any questioning occurs.
1973	Construction begins on the Central Arizona Project to bring Colorado River water to dry parts of the state.
1981	Arizonan Sandra Day O'Connor is appointed as the first woman member of the U.S. Supreme Court.
1991	Eight scientists researching ecosystem sustainability begin living in the glass-enclosed biomes of Biosphere 2 in Oracle.
2001	In just their fourth season, the Arizona Diamondbacks defeat the New York Yankees in the World Series.

What To Pack

Temperature Averages Maximum/Minimum	JANUARY	FEBRUARY	MARCH	APRIL	MAY	JUNE	JULY	AUGUST	SEPTEMBER	OCTOBER	NOVEMBER	DECEMBER
Flagstaff	43/17	45/19	50/24	58/29	68/35	78/42	81/51	78/50	73/42	62/32	50/23	43/17
Grand Canyon NP	45/18	47/21	53/25	61/29	72/36	82/43	86/51	82/50	76/43	65/33	53/24	45/18
Kingman	54/31	59/35	63/38	71/45	80/53	91/63	96/69	94/68	88/61	77/50	63/38	55/32
Phoenix	67/46	71/49	77/54	85/60	95/69	104/78	106/84	105/83	100/77	89/65	76/53	66/45
Tucson	65/42	68/44	74/48	82/55	91/64	99/72	99/76	97/75	94/71	84/59	73/48	64/41
Yuma	70/46	75/49	80/53	87/58	95/65	104/73	107/81	106/81	101/75	90/64	77/52	69/46

From the records of The Weather Channel Interactive, Inc.

Good Facts To Know

ABOUT THE STATE

POPULATION: 6,392,017.

AREA: 113,990 square miles; ranks 6th.

CAPITAL: Phoenix.

HIGHEST POINT: 12,643 ft., Humphreys Peak.

LOWEST POINT: 70 ft., Colorado River.

TIME ZONE(S): Mountain. DST on Navajo Nation Reservation only.

GAMBLING

MINIMUM AGE FOR GAMBLING: 21.

REGULATIONS

TEEN DRIVING LAWS: No more than one unrelated passenger under age 18 is permitted unless accompanied by a parent or legal guardian. Driving is not permitted midnight-5 a.m. The minimum age for an unrestricted driver's license is 16 years, 6 months. Phone (800) 251-5866.

SEAT BELT/CHILD RESTRAINT LAWS: Seat belts are required for driver and front-seat passengers ages 8 and over. Children ages 8-15 are required to be properly restrained by a seat belt in all seats. Children ages 5-7 and 57 inches or less in height must use a booster seat. Child restraints are required for children under age 5. AAA recommends seat belts/child restraints for driver and all passengers.

CELLPHONE RESTRICTIONS: Hand-held ban is in effect. All drivers are prohibited from holding or supporting a wireless device, text messaging, recording or broadcasting video while driving.

HELMETS FOR MOTORCYCLISTS: Required for riders under age 18.

RADAR DETECTORS: Permitted for passenger vehicles; prohibited for commercial vehicles.

MOVE OVER LAW: Slow down and vacate the lane nearest any stationary vehicle with flashing or warning lights, including emergency vehicles and tow trucks.

FIREARMS LAWS: Varies. Contact the State Library of Arizona, 1700 W. Washington St., Suite 300, Phoenix, AZ 85007; phone (602) 926-3620.

HOLIDAYS

HOLIDAYS: Jan. 1 ▪ Martin Luther King Jr. Day, Jan. (3rd Mon.) ▪ Presidents Day, Feb. (3rd Mon.) ▪ Memorial Day, May (last Mon.) ▪ July 4 ▪ Labor Day, Sept. (1st Mon.) ▪ Columbus Day, Oct. (2nd Mon.) ▪ Veterans Day, Nov. 11 ▪ Thanksgiving, Nov. (4th Thurs.) ▪ Christmas, Dec. 25.

MONEY

TAXES: Arizona's statewide sales tax is 5.6 percent, along with local taxes on goods and services, including lodgings.

VISITOR INFORMATION

INFORMATION CENTERS: Lupton state welcome center, I-40 westbound exit 359, provides details about attractions, accommodations, parks and events.

DAYLIGHT SAVING TIME:
The Navajo Nation Reservation is the only area in the state to observe daylight saving time.

NATIVE AMERICAN RESERVATIONS:
Reservations are regarded as sovereign nations, making and enforcing laws pertaining to their land. The following rules are the most relevant to visitors: Alcoholic beverages (including transportation and use) are prohibited; leaving established roadways and hiking cross-country is prohibited unless permission is obtained from the local tribal office; motorists must wear seat belts; and motorcyclists must wear helmets.

FURTHER INFORMATION FOR VISITORS:
Arizona Office of Tourism
118 N. 7th Ave., Suite 400
Phoenix, AZ 85007
(602) 364-3700
(866) 275-5816

Phoenix Visitor Center
125 N. 2 St., Suite 120
Phoenix, AZ 85004
(602) 254-6500
(877) 225-5749

NATIONAL FOREST INFORMATION:
Southwestern Region
Public Affairs Office
333 Broadway Blvd. S.E.
Albuquerque, NM 87102
(505) 842-3292
(877) 444-6777 (reservations)

FISHING AND HUNTING REGULATIONS:
Arizona Game and Fish Department
5000 W. Carefree Hwy.
Phoenix, AZ 85086-5000
(602) 942-3000

RECREATION INFORMATION:
Arizona State Parks and Trails
23751 N. 23rd Ave., Suite 190
Phoenix, AZ 85085
(602) 542-4174
(877) 697-2757

Arizona BLM Information Center
1 N. Central Ave., Suite 800
Phoenix, AZ 85004
(602) 417-9300

Arizona Annual Events

Please call ahead to confirm event details.

Visit AAA.com/travelguides/events to find AAA-listed events for every day of the year

WINTER

Dec.
- Boat Parade of Lights / Lake Havasu City / 928-486-4159
- Tempe Fall Festival of the Arts Tempe / 480-355-6060
- Pueblo Grande Museum Indian Market / Phoenix / 602-495-0901

Jan.
- Arizona National Horse Show Scottsdale / 602-258-8568
- Brian Lebel's Old West Show & Auction / Mesa / 480-779-9378
- Native American Fine Arts Festival Litchfield Park / 623-935-9040

Feb.
- Cochise Cowboy Poetry and Music Gathering / Sierra Vista / 520-508-9359
- Gold Rush Days / Wickenburg 928-684-5479
- Arizona Matsuri / Phoenix 602-262-5029

SPRING

Mar.
- Bluegrass on the Beach / Lake Havasu City /
- Heard Museum Guild Indian Fair and Market / Phoenix / 602-252-8840
- Midnight at the Oasis Festival / Yuma 928-343-1715

Apr.
- Maricopa County Fair / Phoenix 602-252-0717
- Scottsdale Culinary Festival Scottsdale / 480-945-7193
- Rose Tree Festival / Tombstone 520-457-3326

May
- Wyatt Earp Days / Tombstone 520-457-3451

SUMMER

June
- Flag Wool and Fiber / Flagstaff 928-774-6272
- Made in the Shade Beer Tasting Festival / Flagstaff / 928-779-1775

July
- Hopi Festival of Arts and Culture Flagstaff / 928-774-5213
- July 4th Tempe Town Lake Festival Tempe / 480-350-5189
- Fabulous Phoenix Fourth / Phoenix 602-262-6011

Aug.
- Summer Series Race / Phoenix 602-684-1496
- World's Oldest Continuous Rodeo Payson / 928-472-5110
- Eagar Daze / Eagar / 928-333-4128, ext. 251

FALL

Sept.
- Oktoberfest / Sierra Vista / 520-417-6980
- Navajo Nation Fair / Window Rock / 928-871-6478
- Bisbee Blues Festival / Bisbee 520-227-6547

Oct.
- Arizona Exposition & State Fair Phoenix / 602-252-6771
- Howl-O-Ween / Phoenix 602-286-3200
- Helldorado Days / Tombstone 520-457-3451

Nov.
- Tucson Celtic Festival and Scottish Highland Games / Tucson 520-349-4345
- Can-Am 500 / Avondale 623-463-5400
- Colorado River Crossing Balloon Festival / Yuma / 928-343-1715

Native American Fine Arts Festival, Litchfield Park

Wupatki National Monument

Saguaro cactus

Tombstone

Heard Museum, Phoenix

Index: Great Experience for Members

AAA editor's picks of exceptional note

Hoover Dam

Phoenix Art Museum

Desert Botanical Garden

Navajo National Monument

See Orientation map on p. 24 for corresponding grid coordinates, if applicable.

*Indicates the GEM is temporarily closed.

Mission San Xavier del Bac *(See p. 198.)*

Sabino Canyon *(See p. 199.)*

Tucson Mountain Park *(See p. 200.)*

Tumacácori National Historical Park (G-4)

Tumacácori National Historical Park *(See p. 221.)*

Tuzigoot National Monument (C-3)

Tuzigoot National Monument *(See p. 221.)*

Walnut Canyon National Monument (C-4)

Walnut Canyon National Monument *(See p. 221.)*

Williams (C-3)

Grand Canyon Railway *(See p. 223.)*

Winslow (C-5)

Meteor Crater *(See p. 227.)*

Wupatki National Monument (B-4)

Wupatki National Monument *(See p. 227.)*

Arizona

Atlas Section

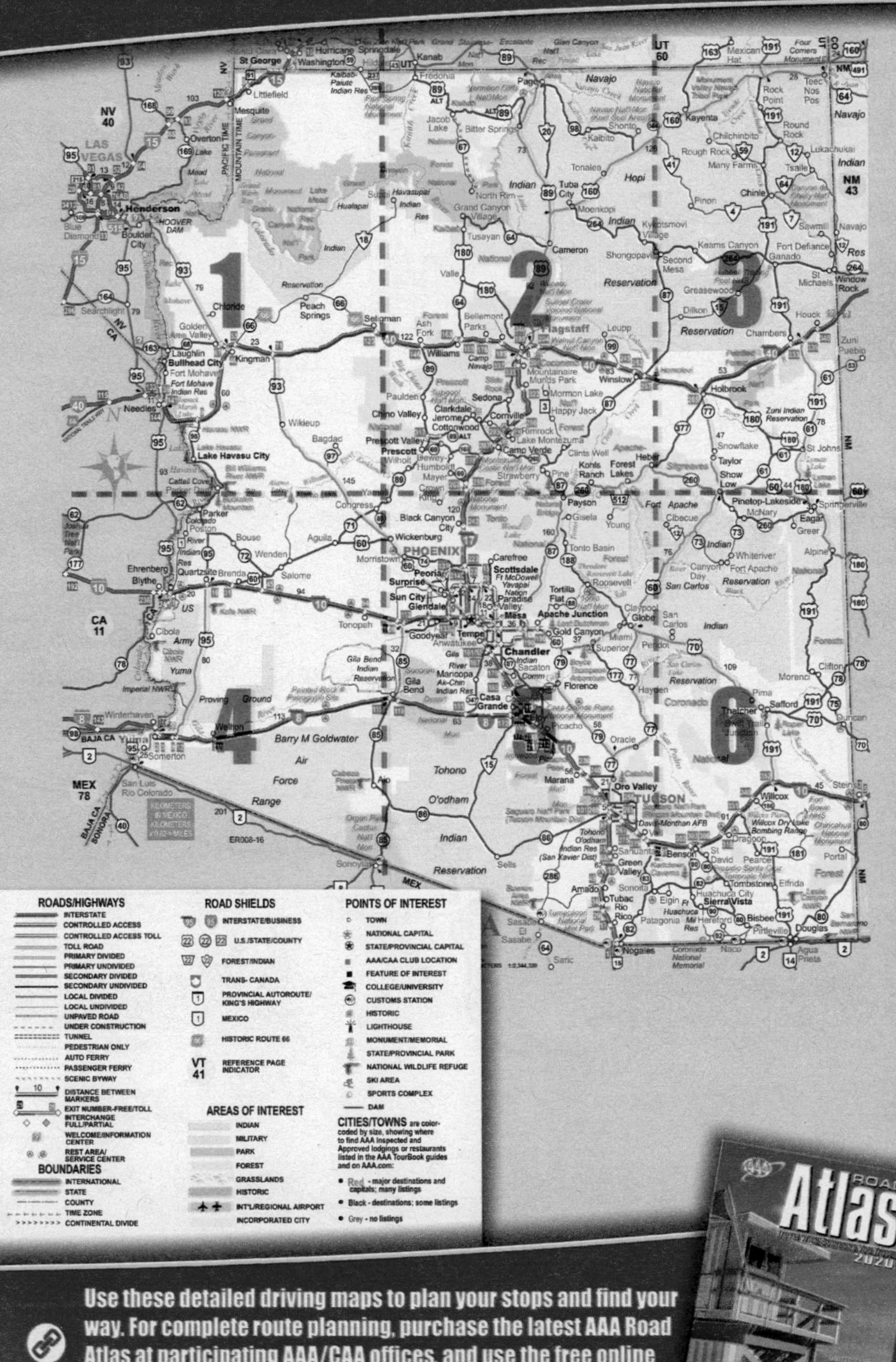

Use these detailed driving maps to plan your stops and find your way. For complete route planning, purchase the latest AAA Road Atlas at participating AAA/CAA offices, and use the free online TripTik Travel Planner at AAA.com/maps

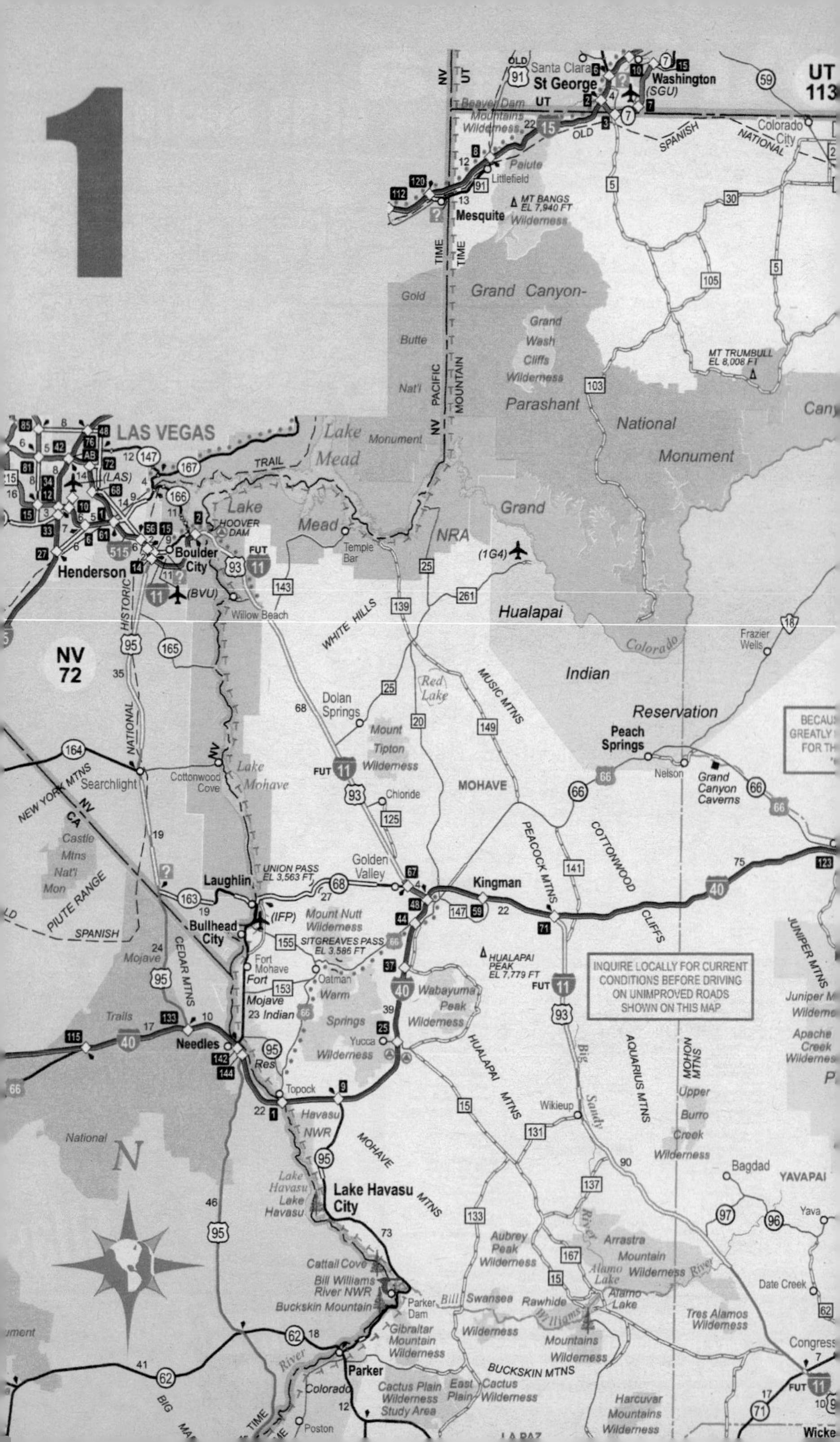

1

NV UT
OLD 91 Santa Clara
St George
Washington
(SGU)
UT 113
59
Beaver Dam Mountains Wilderness
UT
OLD SPANISH NATIONAL
Colorado City
15
Paiute
Littlefield
91
Mesquite
MT BANGS EL 7,940 FT
Wilderness
5
30
105
PACIFIC TIME
MOUNTAIN TIME
Gold Butte Nat'l
Grand Canyon-Grand Wash Cliffs Wilderness
Parashant National Monument
MT TRUMBULL EL 8,008 FT
103
LAS VEGAS
147
167
TRAIL
Lake Mead
Monument
(LAS)
166
Lake Mead
HOOVER DAM
Temple Bar
NRA
Grand
(1G4)
Henderson
Boulder City
515
93
FUT 11
143
25
261
(BVU)
Willow Beach
WHITE HILLS
139
Hualapai
HISTORIC
95
165
NV 72
Colorado
Indian
Reservation
Frazier Wells
18
Dolan Springs
Red Lake
MUSIC MTNS
68
25
20
149
Peach Springs
Nelson
Grand Canyon Caverns
66
164
NATIONAL
Searchlight
NEW YORK MTNS
NV CA
Cottonwood Cove
Lake Mohave
Mount Tipton Wilderness
FUT 11
93
Chloride
125
MOHAVE
PEACOCK MTNS
COTTONWOOD
Castle Mtns Nat'l Mon
PIUTE RANGE
SPANISH
UNION PASS EL 3,563 FT
Laughlin
68
Golden Valley
Kingman
141
147
59
40
123
163
Bullhead City
(IFP)
Mount Nutt Wilderness
155
SITGREAVES PASS EL 3,586 FT
CLIFFS
Mojave
CEDAR MTNS
95
Fort Mohave
Fort Mojave Indian
Oatman
153
Warm Springs Wilderness
40
Wabayuma Peak Wilderness
HUALAPAI PEAK EL 7,779 FT
FUT 11
93
INQUIRE LOCALLY FOR CURRENT CONDITIONS BEFORE DRIVING ON UNIMPROVED ROADS SHOWN ON THIS MAP
JUNIPER MTNS
Juniper M Wilderne
Apache Creek Wilderness
Trails
Needles
40
Res
95
Yucca
HUALAPAI MTNS
Big Sandy
AQUARIUS MTNS
MOHON MTNS
Upper Burro Creek Wilderness
Topock
Havasu NWR
15
Wikieup
131
National
MOHAVE
95
Lake Havasu Lake Havasu
Lake Havasu City
MTNS
137
Bagdad
YAVAPAI
97
96
Yava
95
133
Aubrey Peak Wilderness
River
Arrastra Mountain Wilderness
167
15
Alamo Lake
Cattail Cove
Bill Williams River NWR
Buckskin Mountain
Parker Dam
Bill Williams
Swansea Wilderness
Rawhide Mountains Wilderness
Alamo Lake
Tres Alamos Wilderness
Date Creek
62
Gibraltar Mountain Wilderness
62
Congress
Parker
62
Colorado River
BUCKSKIN MTNS
Cactus Plain Wilderness Study Area
East Cactus Plain Wilderness
Harcuvar Mountains Wilderness
FUT 11
71
Poston
LA PAZ
Wicke

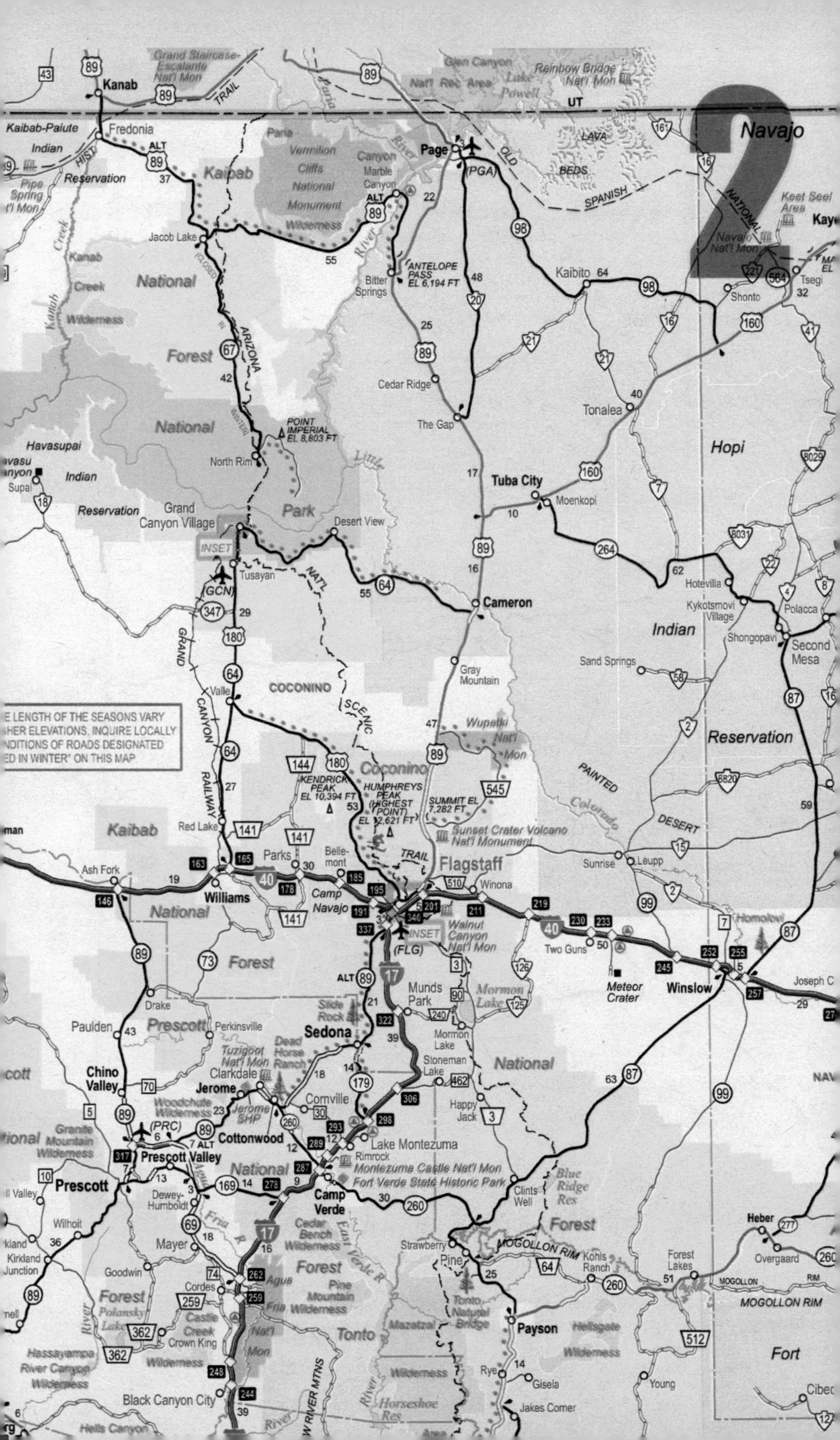

2
Navajo
Kanab
Grand Staircase-Escalante Nat'l Mon
Glen Canyon Nat'l Rec Area
Lake Powell
Rainbow Bridge Nat'l Mon
UT
Kaibab-Paiute Indian Reservation
Fredonia
Pipe Spring Nat'l Mon
Kaibab
Vermilion Cliffs National Monument Wilderness
Marble Canyon
Page
(PGA)
LAVA BEDS
OLD SPANISH NATIONAL
Keet Seel Area
Navajo Nat'l Mon
Jacob Lake
Kanab Creek Wilderness
National Forest
ARIZONA
ANTELOPE PASS EL 6,194 FT
Bitter Springs
Kaibito
Shonto
Tsegi
Cedar Ridge
The Gap
Tonalea
Hopi
POINT IMPERIAL EL 8,803 FT
North Rim
Havasupai Indian Reservation
Supai
Grand Canyon Village
INSET
Park
Desert View
Tuba City
Moenkopi
Tusayan
(GCN)
Cameron
Hotevilla
Kykotsmovi Village
Polacca
Shongopavi
Second Mesa
GRAND CANYON RAILWAY
Valle
COCONINO
SCENIC
Gray Mountain
Sand Springs
Indian Reservation
E LENGTH OF THE SEASONS VARY
HER ELEVATIONS, INQUIRE LOCALLY
NDITIONS OF ROADS DESIGNATED
ED IN WINTER" ON THIS MAP
Wupatki Nat'l Mon
Coconino
KENDRICK PEAK EL 10,394 FT
HUMPHREYS PEAK (HIGHEST POINT) EL 12,621 FT
SUMMIT EL 7,282 FT
PAINTED DESERT
Colorado
Sunset Crater Volcano Nat'l Monument
Red Lake
Kaibab
Parks
Bellemont
TRAIL
Flagstaff
Ash Fork
Williams
Camp Navajo
Winona
Sunrise
Leupp
Walnut Canyon Nat'l Mon
(FLG)
Two Guns
Homolovi
Meteor Crater
Winslow
Joseph C
National Forest
Drake
Munds Park
Mormon Lake
Paulden
Prescott
Perkinsville
Sedona
Slide Rock
Dead Horse Ranch
Tuzigoot Nat'l Mon
Clarkdale
Jerome
Jerome SHP
Woodchute Wilderness
Chino Valley
Stoneman Lake
Happy Jack
National
Cornville
Granite Mountain Wilderness
(PRC)
Cottonwood
Lake Montezuma
Rimrock
Montezuma Castle Nat'l Mon
Fort Verde State Historic Park
Prescott Valley
Prescott
Dewey-Humboldt
Camp Verde
Clints Well
Blue Ridge Res
Forest
Heber
Overgaard
Wilhoit
Kirkland
Kirkland Junction
Mayer
Cedar Bench Wilderness
Strawberry
Pine
MOGOLLON RIM
Kohls Ranch
Forest Lakes
Goodwin
Cordes
Agua Fria Nat'l Mon
Pine Mountain Wilderness
Forest
Tonto Natural Bridge
Payson
Hellsgate Wilderness
Fort
Polansky Lake
Castle Creek
Crown King
Mazatzal Wilderness
Tonto
Rye
Gisela
Young
Hassayampa River Canyon Wilderness
Horseshoe Res
Black Canyon City
Jakes Corner
Hells Canyon

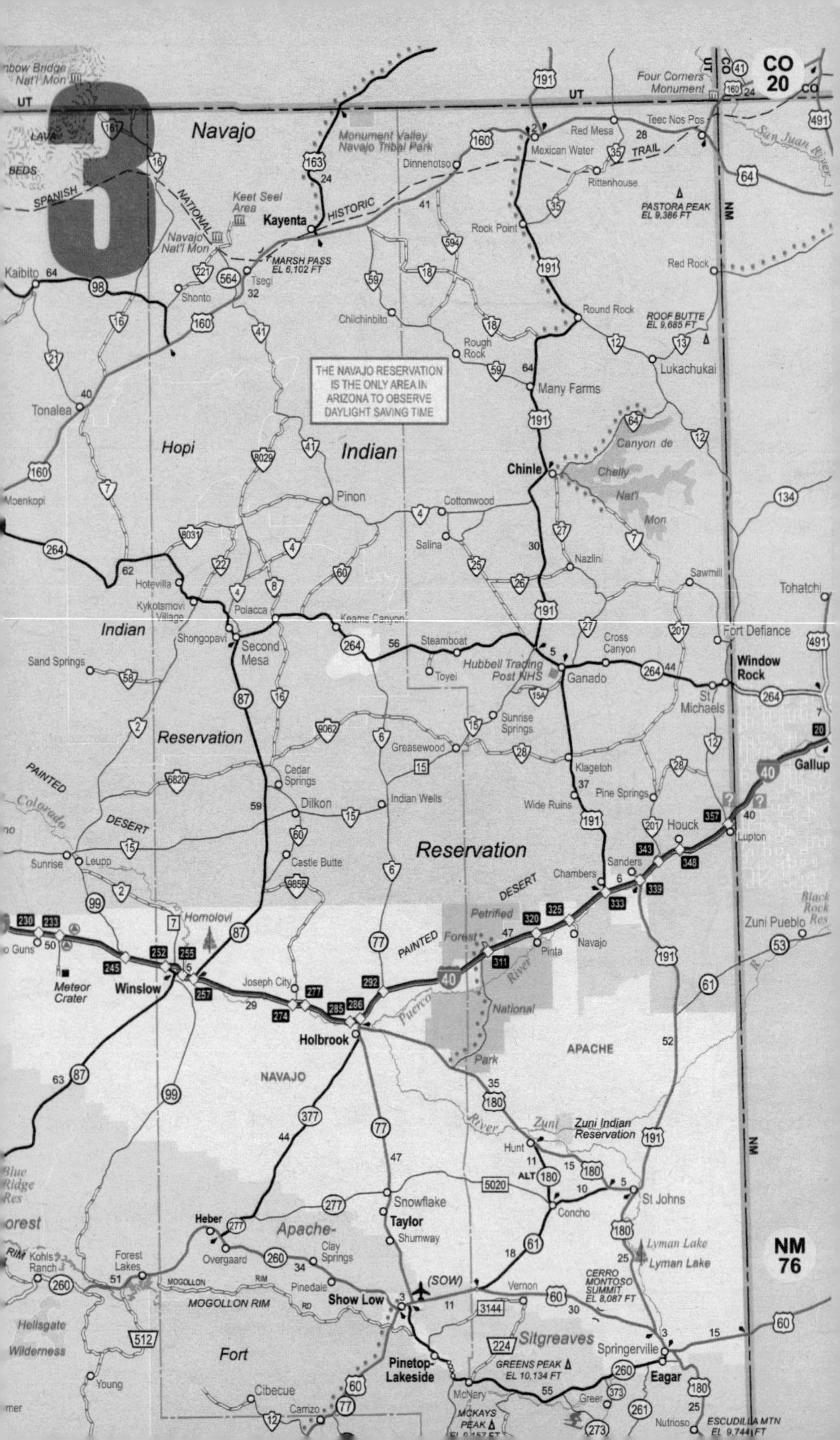

3
CO
20
NM
76
Navajo
Indian
Reservation
Hopi
Indian
Reservation
THE NAVAJO RESERVATION IS THE ONLY AREA IN ARIZONA TO OBSERVE DAYLIGHT SAVING TIME
Monument Valley Navajo Tribal Park
Four Corners Monument
Keet Seel Area
Navajo Nat'l Mon
MARSH PASS EL 6,102 FT
PASTORA PEAK EL 9,386 FT
ROOF BUTTE EL 9,685 FT
Canyon de Chelly Nat'l Mon
Hubbell Trading Post NHS
Petrified Forest National Park
PAINTED DESERT
Colorado
Homolovi
Meteor Crater
Zuni Indian Reservation
Puerco River
Zuni River
San Juan River
Lyman Lake
CERRO MONTOSO SUMMIT EL 8,087 FT
GREENS PEAK EL 10,134 FT
MCKAYS PEAK
ESCUDILLA MTN EL 9,744 FT
Apache-Sitgreaves
Fort
MOGOLLON RIM
Hellsgate Wilderness
Blue Ridge Res
NAVAJO
APACHE
SPANISH NATIONAL HISTORIC TRAIL
Kayenta
Kaibito
Shonto
Tsegi
Tonalea
Moenkopi
Dinnehotso
Mexican Water
Red Mesa
Teec Nos Pos
Rittenhouse
Rock Point
Red Rock
Round Rock
Lukachukai
Chilchinbito
Rough Rock
Many Farms
Chinle
Pinon
Cottonwood
Salina
Nazlini
Sawmill
Tohatchi
Fort Defiance
Window Rock
St Michaels
Gallup
Hotevilla
Kykotsmovi Village
Polacca
Keams Canyon
Shongopavi
Second Mesa
Steamboat
Toyei
Ganado
Cross Canyon
Sand Springs
Sunrise Springs
Greasewood
Klagetoh
Cedar Springs
Dilkon
Indian Wells
Wide Ruins
Pine Springs
Houck
Lupton
Sunrise
Leupp
Castle Butte
Sanders
Chambers
Navajo
Pinta
Zuni Pueblo
Black Rock Res
Two Guns
Winslow
Joseph City
Holbrook
Hunt
Concho
St Johns
Snowflake
Taylor
Shumway
Heber
Overgaard
Clay Springs
Pinedale
Show Low
(SOW)
Vernon
Springerville
Eagar
Forest Lakes
Kohls Ranch
Young
Cibecue
Carrizo
Pinetop-Lakeside
McNary
Greer
Nutrioso
UT
CO
NM

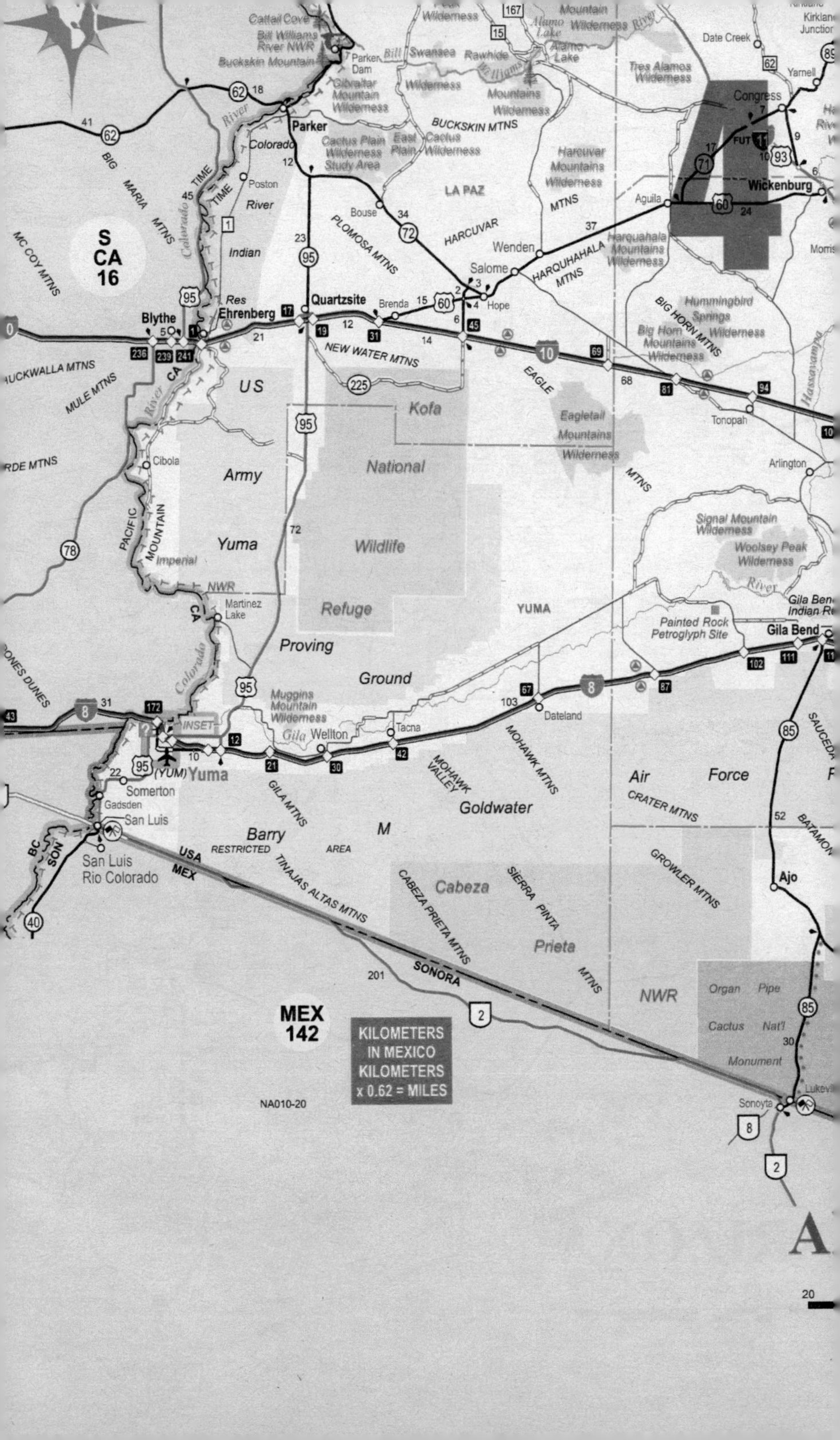

Cattail Cove
Bill Williams River NWR
Buckskin Mountain
Parker Dam
Gibraltar Mountain Wilderness
Swansea Wilderness
Rawhide Mountains Wilderness
Alamo Lake
Tres Alamos Wilderness
Date Creek
Yarnell
Congress
Wickenburg
Aguila
Parker
Cactus Plain Wilderness Study Area
East Cactus Plain Wilderness
BUCKSKIN MTNS
Harcuvar Mountains Wilderness
LA PAZ
Colorado River Indian
Poston
Bouse
PLOMOSA MTNS
HARCUVAR MTNS
Wenden
Salome
Hope
HARQUAHALA MTNS
Harquahala Mountains Wilderness
S CA 16
BIG MARIA MTNS
MC COY MTNS
Blythe
Ehrenberg
Quartzsite
Brenda
NEW WATER MTNS
Hummingbird Springs Wilderness
Big Horn Mountains Wilderness
BIG HORN MTNS
Tonopah
US Army Yuma Proving Ground
Kofa National Wildlife Refuge
EAGLE TAIL MTNS
Eagletail Mountains Wilderness
Arlington
Signal Mountain Wilderness
Woolsey Peak Wilderness
Gila Bend Indian Res
Gila Bend
Painted Rock Petroglyph Site
YUMA
Cibola
PACIFIC MOUNTAIN TIME
Imperial NWR
Martinez Lake
Muggins Mountain Wilderness
Wellton
Tacna
Dateland
Yuma
Somerton
Gadsden
San Luis
San Luis Rio Colorado
MOHAWK VALLEY
MOHAWK MTNS
GILA MTNS
Barry M Goldwater Air Force
RESTRICTED AREA
CRATER MTNS
GROWLER MTNS
Ajo
TINAJAS ALTAS MTNS
CABEZA PRIETA MTNS
SIERRA PINTA MTNS
Cabeza Prieta NWR
Organ Pipe Cactus Nat'l Monument
Sonoyta
Lukeville
SONORA
MEX 142
KILOMETERS IN MEXICO
KILOMETERS x 0.62 = MILES
NA010-20
A

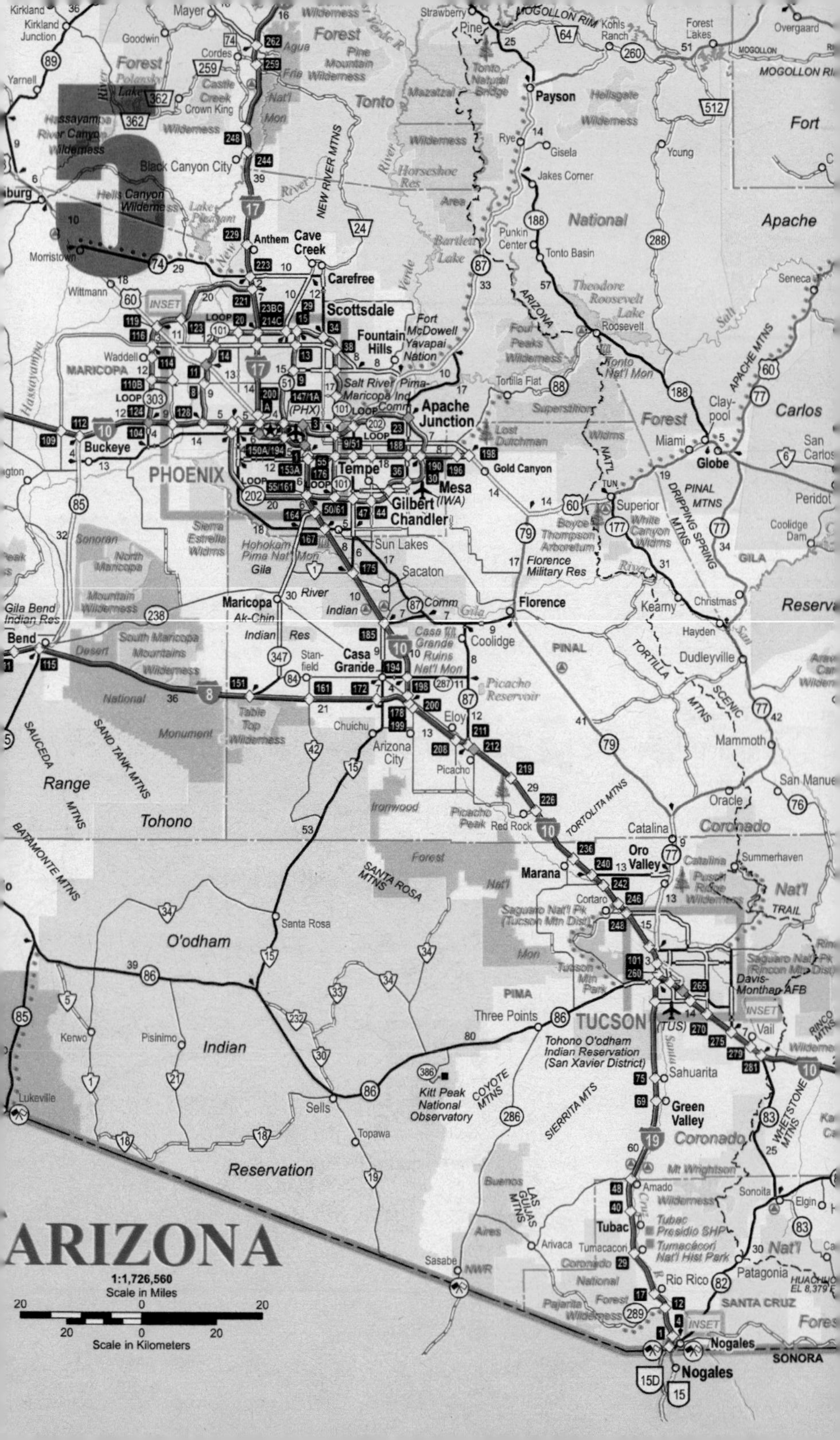

ARIZONA
1:1,726,560
Scale in Miles
20
0
20
Scale in Kilometers
20
0
20
5
PHOENIX
TUCSON
Scottsdale
Tempe
Mesa
Gilbert
Chandler
Apache Junction
Fountain Hills
Fort McDowell Yavapai Nation
Salt River Pima-Maricopa Ind Comm
Carefree
Cave Creek
Anthem
Buckeye
Waddell
Wittmann
Morristown
Black Canyon City
Crown King
Cordes
Mayer
Kirkland
Kirkland Junction
Goodwin
Yarnell
Payson
Pine
Strawberry
Kohls Ranch
Forest Lakes
Overgaard
MOGOLLON RIM
Rye
Gisela
Jakes Corner
Young
Punkin Center
Tonto Basin
Roosevelt
Theodore Roosevelt Lake
Tonto Nat'l Mon
Globe
Miami
Claypool
San Carlos
Peridot
Coolidge Dam
Superior
Kearny
Hayden
Christmas
Dudleyville
Mammoth
Oracle
San Manuel
Summerhaven
Catalina
Oro Valley
Marana
Cortaro
Florence
Coolidge
Casa Grande Ruins Nat'l Mon
Casa Grande
Eloy
Picacho
Picacho Peak
Red Rock
Arizona City
Chuichu
Stanfield
Maricopa
Ak-Chin Indian Res
Gila River Indian Comm
Sacaton
Sun Lakes
Gold Canyon
Florence Military Res
Boyce Thompson Arboretum
Tortilla Flat
Lost Dutchman
Superstition
Four Peaks Wilderness
Gila Bend Indian Res
Bend
Sonoran Desert National Monument
Table Top Wilderness
South Maricopa Mountains Wilderness
North Maricopa Mountain Wilderness
Sierra Estrella Wldrns
Hohokam Pima Nat'l Mon
Ironwood Forest Nat'l Mon
Saguaro Nat'l Pk (Tucson Mtn Dist)
Saguaro Nat'l Pk (Rincon Mtn Dist)
Tucson Mtn Park
Davis-Monthan AFB
Vail
Sahuarita
Green Valley
Three Points
Tohono O'odham Indian Reservation (San Xavier District)
Kitt Peak National Observatory
Santa Rosa
Sells
Topawa
Pisinimo
Kerwo
Lukeville
Sasabe
Arivaca
Amado
Tubac
Tubac Presidio SHP
Tumacacori
Tumacacori Nat'l Hist Park
Rio Rico
Nogales
Patagonia
Sonoita
Elgin
SANTA CRUZ
SONORA
Tohono O'odham Indian Reservation
Buenos Aires NWR
Coronado National Forest
Pajarita Wilderness
Mt Wrightson Wilderness
Pusch Ridge Wilderness
Tonto National Forest
Mazatzal Wilderness
Hellsgate Wilderness
Hassayampa River Canyon Wilderness
Hells Canyon Wilderness
Castle Creek Wilderness
Agua Fria Nat'l Mon
Pine Mountain Wilderness
Tonto Natural Bridge
Lake Pleasant
Horseshoe Res
Bartlett Lake
White Canyon Wldrns
Picacho Reservoir
NEW RIVER MTNS
APACHE MTNS
PINAL MTNS
DRIPPING SPRING MTNS
TORTILLA MTNS
SCENIC
TORTOLITA MTNS
SANTA ROSA MTNS
SAND TANK MTNS
SAUCEDA MTNS
BATAMONTE MTNS
COYOTE MTNS
SIERRITA MTS
LAS GUIJAS MTNS
WHETSTONE MTNS
RINCON MTNS
MARICOPA
PINAL
PIMA
GILA
ARIZONA TRAIL
Fort Apache Reservation
San Carlos Reservation

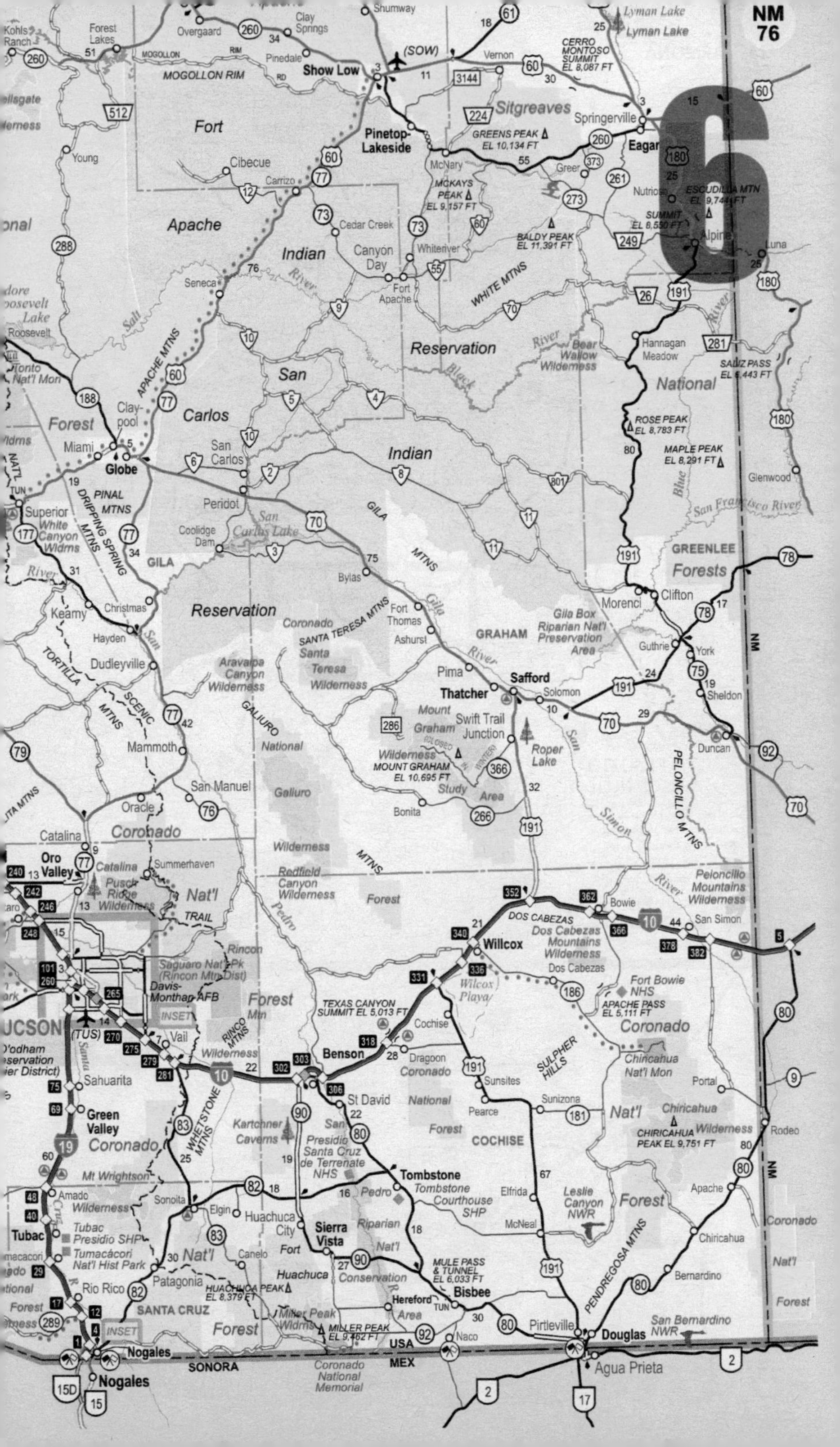

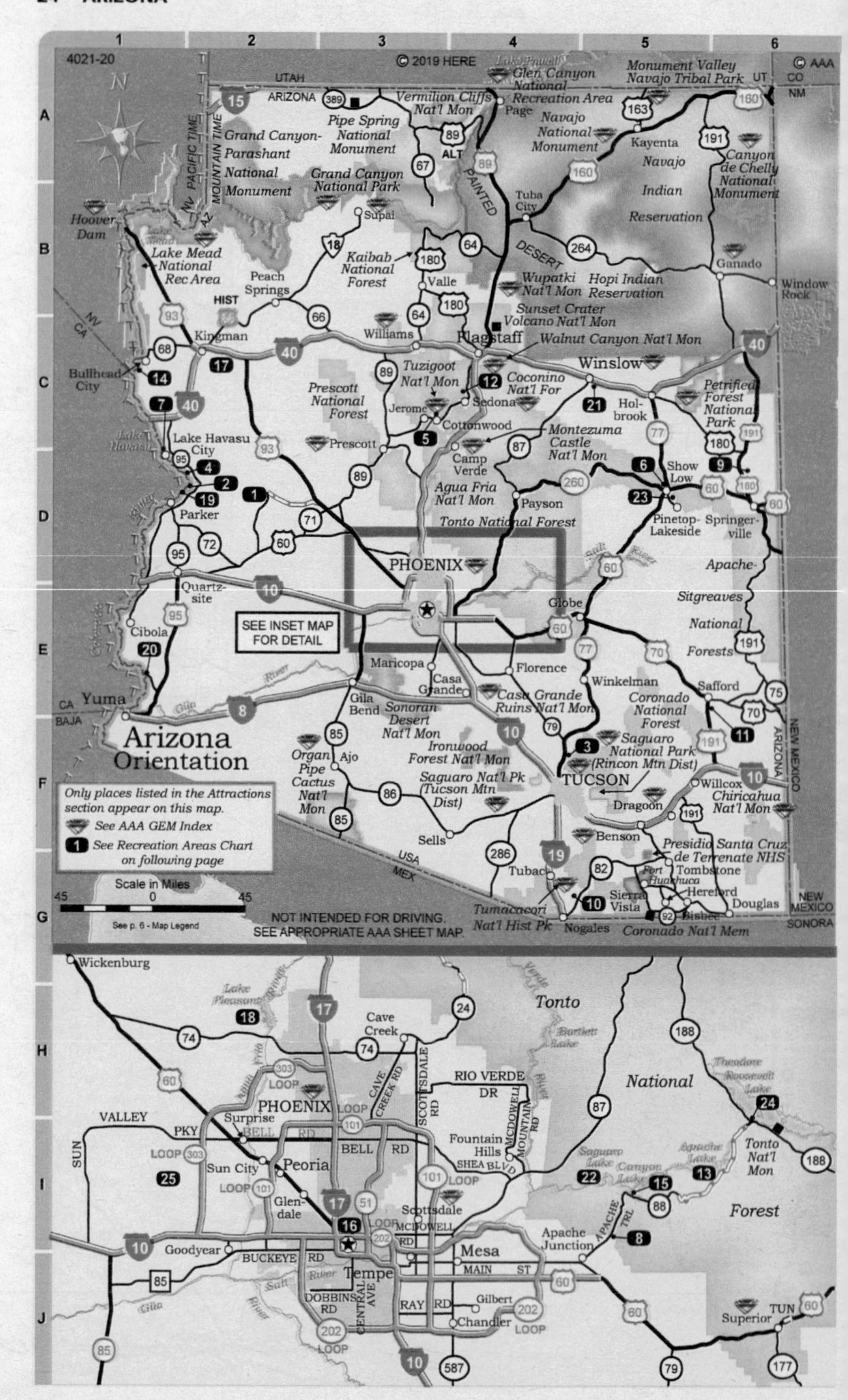

Arizona Orientation
4021-20
© 2019 HERE
© AAA
Only places listed in the Attractions section appear on this map.
See AAA GEM Index
See Recreation Areas Chart on following page
Scale in Miles
See p. 6 - Map Legend
NOT INTENDED FOR DRIVING. SEE APPROPRIATE AAA SHEET MAP.
SEE INSET MAP FOR DETAIL
PHOENIX
TUCSON
Flagstaff
Grand Canyon National Park
Grand Canyon-Parashant National Monument
Pipe Spring National Monument
Vermilion Cliffs Nat'l Mon
Glen Canyon National Recreation Area
Monument Valley Navajo Tribal Park
Navajo National Monument
Canyon de Chelly National Monument
Navajo Indian Reservation
Hopi Indian Reservation
Hoover Dam
Lake Mead National Rec Area
Kaibab National Forest
Wupatki Nat'l Mon
Sunset Crater Volcano Nat'l Mon
Walnut Canyon Nat'l Mon
Petrified Forest National Park
Tuzigoot Nat'l Mon
Coconino Nat'l For
Prescott National Forest
Montezuma Castle Nat'l Mon
Agua Fria Nat'l Mon
Tonto National Forest
Apache-Sitgreaves National Forests
Casa Grande Ruins Nat'l Mon
Sonoran Desert Nat'l Mon
Ironwood Forest Nat'l Mon
Coronado National Forest
Saguaro National Park (Rincon Mtn Dist)
Saguaro Nat'l Pk (Tucson Mtn Dist)
Organ Pipe Cactus Nat'l Mon
Chiricahua Nat'l Mon
Presidio Santa Cruz de Terrenate NHS
Tumacacori Nat'l Hist Pk
Coronado Nat'l Mem
Page
Kayenta
Tuba City
Ganado
Window Rock
Supai
Peach Springs
Valle
Kingman
Williams
Bullhead City
Lake Havasu City
Parker
Quartzsite
Cibola
Yuma
Winslow
Holbrook
Sedona
Jerome
Cottonwood
Prescott
Camp Verde
Payson
Show Low
Pinetop-Lakeside
Springerville
Globe
Maricopa
Casa Grande
Florence
Winkelman
Safford
Gila Bend
Ajo
Sells
Willcox
Dragoon
Benson
Tubac
Tombstone
Sierra Vista
Hereford
Bisbee
Douglas
Nogales
UTAH
ARIZONA
NEW MEXICO
PACIFIC TIME
MOUNTAIN TIME
PAINTED DESERT
USA
MEX
Wickenburg
Lake Pleasant
Cave Creek
Tonto National Forest
Bartlett Lake
Theodore Roosevelt Lake
Tonto Nat'l Mon
Surprise
Sun City
Peoria
Glendale
Fountain Hills
Scottsdale
Goodyear
Tempe
Mesa
Gilbert
Chandler
Apache Junction
Superior
Saguaro Lake
Canyon Lake
Apache Lake
VALLEY PKY
BELL RD
RIO VERDE DR
SHEA BLVD
MCDOWELL RD
BUCKEYE RD
MAIN ST
DOBBINS RD
RAY RD
APACHE TRL

Recreation Areas Chart

The map location numerals in column 2 show an area's location on the preceding map.

Find thousands of places to camp at AAA.com/campgrounds

	MAP LOCATION	CAMPING	PICNICKING	HIKING TRAILS	BOATING	BOAT RAMP	BOAT RENTAL	FISHING	SWIMMING	PET FRIENDLY	BICYCLE TRAILS	WINTER SPORTS	VISITOR CENTER	LODGE/CABINS	FOOD SERVICE
NATIONAL PARKS *(See place listings.)*															
Grand Canyon (A-3) 1,218,376 acres.		•	•	•				•		•		•	•	•	•
Saguaro (F-5) 91,000 acres.		•	•	•						•	•	•	•		
NATIONAL FORESTS *(See place listings.)*															
Apache-Sitgreaves (D-6) 2.1 million acres. East-central Arizona.		•	•	•	•	•	•	•		•	•	•	•		•
Coconino (C-4) 1,821,495 acres. Northern Arizona. Caving, horse-back riding.		•	•	•	•	•	•	•	•	•	•	•		•	•
Coronado (E-5) 1,780,196 acres. Southeastern Arizona.		•	•	•	•	•	•	•		•	•	•	•	•	
Kaibab (B-3) 1.6 million acres. Northern Arizona.		•	•	•	•	•		•		•	•	•	•	•	•
Prescott (C-3) 1,238,154 acres. Central Arizona. Electric boat motors only. Horse rental.		•	•	•	•	•	•	•		•				•	•
Tonto (H-4) 2,900,000 acres. Central Arizona.		•	•	•	•	•	•	•	•	•	•			•	•
NATIONAL RECREATION AREAS *(See place listings.)*															
Glen Canyon (A-4) 1,250,000 acres.		•	•	•	•	•	•	•	•	•	•	•	•	•	•
Lake Mead (B-1) 1,500,000 acres. Southeastern Nevada. Horse-back riding, scuba diving.		•	•	•	•	•	•	•	•	•	•	•	•	•	•
STATE															
Alamo Lake (D-2) 2,858 acres 38 mi. n. of US 60 via a paved road.	1	•	•	•	•	•		•		•	•		•	•	•
Buckskin Mountain (D-2) 1,677 acres 11 mi. n. off SR 95. Arcade, basketball and volleyball courts, playground.	2	•	•	•	•	•		•	•	•	•	•	•		•
Catalina (F-5) 5,500 acres 9 mi. n. off SR 77.	3	•	•	•						•	•	•	•		
Cattail Cove (D-2) 2,375 acres off SR 95.	4	•	•	•	•	•		•	•	•	•	•	•		•
Dead Horse Ranch (C-3) 423 acres off 10th St. Bird-watching; horse rentals, horse trails.	5	•	•	•	•	•	•	•		•	•	•	•	•	
Fool Hollow Lake (D-5) 686 acres 2 mi. n. of US 60 off SR 260, then e. on Old Linden Rd. to 32nd Ave.	6	•	•	•	•	•	•	•		•	•	•	•		•
Lake Havasu (C-1) 928 acres n. of London Bridge off London Bridge Rd.	7	•	•	•	•	•	•	•	•	•			•		
Lost Dutchman (I-5) 320 acres 5 mi. n.e. off SR 88.	8	•	•	•						•	•	•	•		
Lyman Lake (D-6) 1,200 acres 14 mi. n. off US 60 onto US 180/191, then just off SR 81.	9	•	•	•	•	•		•	•	•	•	•	•	•	•
Patagonia Lake (G-5) 2,659 acres 7 mi. s.w. on SR 82, then 5 mi. w. following signs. Equestrian trails.	10	•	•	•	•	•	•	•	•	•	•	•	•		•
Roper Lake (F-6) 339 acres .5 mi. s. off US 191.	11	•	•	•	•	•		•	•	•	•		•	•	
Slide Rock (C-4) 55 acres 7 mi. n. off SR 89A within Oak Creek Canyon.	12		•	•				•	•	•	•	•	•		
OTHER															
Apache Lake (I-5) 2,656 acres 30 mi. n.e. on SR 88.	13	•	•	•	•	•	•	•	•	•				•	•
Bullhead (C-1) 20 acres .25 mi. s. of Bullhead City. No tent camping.	14		•		•	•		•	•	•			•		
Canyon Lake (I-5) 950 acres 16 mi. n.e. on SR 88.	15	•	•	•	•	•	•	•	•	•					•
Encanto (I-3) 222 acres at 2605 N. 15th Ave. Golf (nine and 18 holes).	16		•		•			•	•	•		•			
Hualapai Mountain (C-2) 2,200 acres 12 mi. s.e. of Kingman.	17	•	•	•				•		•	•		•	•	
Lake Pleasant (H-2) 24,500 acres 29 mi. e. on SR 74, then 2 mi. n. off Castle Hot Springs Rd.	18	•	•	•	•	•	•	•	•	•	•		•		•
La Paz County (D-2) 165 acres 8 mi. n. of Parker via SR 95.	19	•	•		•	•		•	•	•	•				•
Martinez Lake (E-1) 600 acres 25 mi. n. of Yuma. Water skiing.	20	•	•		•	•		•	•	•				•	•
McHood (C-5) 160 acres 5 mi. s.e. of Winslow off SR 99.	21	•	•	•	•	•		•	•	•					
Saguaro Lake (I-5) 1,280 acres 25 mi. n.e. of Mesa via US 60 and Bush Hwy.	22		•		•	•	•	•	•	•				•	•

Recreation Areas Chart

The map location numerals in column 2 show an area's location on the preceding map.

Find thousands of places to camp at AAA.com/campgrounds

	MAP LOCATION	CAMPING	PICNICKING	HIKING TRAILS	BOATING	BOAT RAMP	BOAT RENTAL	FISHING	SWIMMING	PET FRIENDLY	BICYCLE TRAILS	WINTER SPORTS	VISITOR CENTER	LODGE/CABINS	FOOD SERVICE
Show Low Lake (D-5) 100 acres 5.5 mi. s.e. of Show Low via SR 260.	23	●	●	●	●	●	●	●	●	●					●
Theodore Roosevelt Lake (H-6) 17,315 acres 29 mi. n.w. of Globe via SR 88.	24	●	●	●	●	●	●	●	●	●		●	●	●	●
White Tank Mountain (I-1) 26,337 acres 8 mi. s. of Surprise via SR 303, then 4 mi. w. on Olive Ave. Horse trails.	25	●	●	●						●	●	●	●		●

AGUA FRIA NATIONAL MONUMENT
(D-4)

North of Phoenix off I-17 exit 259 to Bloody Basin Road or off exit 256 to Badger Springs, Agua Fria National Monument embraces 71,000 acres including the Agua Fria River canyon between Black Canyon City and Cordes Lakes.

The river canyon, at an elevation of 2,150 feet above sea level, and Perry and Black mesas are the primary formations; elevations in the northern hills reach 4,500 feet. The monument preserves thousands of prehistoric sites with more than 450 surveyed and recorded. Petroglyphs, terraced landscapes and pueblo ruins suggest the area was heavily populated A.D. 1250-1450 by an agrarian society skilled at growing food and sustaining life in the desert.

Semidesert grasslands and a riparian forest support abundant wildlife, including pronghorn, mountain lions, javelinas and white-tailed deer.

Camping, hiking and picnicking are permitted. Because the terrain is rugged and rocky, a high-clearance, four-wheel-drive vehicle is recommended in most locations. For further information contact the Monument Manager, Phoenix District, Bureau of Land Management, 21605 N. 7th Ave., Phoenix, AZ 85027; phone (623) 580-5500.

AJO (F-3) pop. 3,304, elev. 1,747'

The name Ajo (ah-ho) comes either from the Tohono O'odham word for "paint" or the Spanish name for "garlic," a fitting moniker for this multicultural community with an emerging arts scene. Home to the first copper mine in the state, Ajo did not boom until ore-refining methods made the mining of low-grade ore profitable in the early 1900s.

In 1906 Col. John Greenway formed the New Cornelia Copper Co., which was eventually purchased by one of the nation's largest copper companies, Dodge Corp., in 1921. Visitors to the town can view the New Cornelia Open Pit Mine on Indian Village Road. The mine, which was shut down in 1984, is nearly 2 miles in diameter and 1,000 feet deep. Open October through May, a visitor center features a video and display of the mining operations as well as an observation area; phone (520) 387-7742.

Organ Pipe Cactus National Monument *(see place listing p. 83)*, 32 miles south of Ajo, preserves a portion of the Sonoran Desert; its inhabitants include the statuesque organ pipe cactus as well as such desert foliage as saguaro, paloverde and ocotillo.

As in much of the southwest, the Spanish and Native American influences can be seen in Ajo's Spanish Colonial Revival town square surrounded by a park, mission churches and Southwestern-style buildings. The Ajo Historical Museum, 160 W. Mission Rd., is housed in a mission church built in the 1930s; phone (520) 387-7105. Other historic buildings include the 1919 Curley School, 201 W. Esperanza Ave., offering live-work lodgings for artists, and the historic 1916 Ajo Train Depot, formerly used by the Tucson, Cornelia and Gila Bend Railroad and now housing the chamber of commerce visitor center, 1 W. Plaza St.

Ajo Chamber of Commerce: 1 W. Plaza St., Ajo, AZ 85321. **Phone:** (520) 387-7742.

GUEST HOUSE INN 520/387-6133

Historic Bed & Breakfast. **Address:** 700 W Guest House Rd 85321

LA SIESTA MOTEL & RV RESORT 520/387-6569

Motel. **Address:** 2561 N Ajo-Gila Bend Hwy 85321

WHERE TO EAT

100 ESTRELLA RESTAURANT & LOUNGE 520/387-3110

American. Casual Dining. **Address:** 100 W Estrella St 85321

AGAVE GRILL 520/387-4235

American. Casual Dining. **Address:** 1051 W Solana Ave 85321

ANTHEM pop. 21,700

HAMPTON INN ANTHEM 623/465-7979

SAVE Hotel. **Address:** 42415 N 41st Dr 85086

AAA Benefit: Members save up to 15%!

WHERE TO EAT

SHANGHAI CLUB 623/465-3225

Chinese. Casual Dining. **Address:** 3434 W Anthem Way 85086

APACHE JUNCTION (J-5) pop. 35,840, elev. 1,715'

- **Hotels p. 29**
- **Part of Phoenix area — see map p. 91**

As its name implies, Apache Junction—the western terminus of the Apache Trail—is at the junction of US 60 and SR 88. The surrounding desert, lakes and mountains make Apache Junction a natural recreation site. Hiking, horseback riding, picnicking, rockhounding and water sports facilities are available.

At the junction of Old West Highway and SR 88 stands a monument to the memory of Jacob Waltz, purported discoverer of the Lost Dutchman Gold Mine, which is said to be in the nearby Superstition Mountains. The Lost Dutchman Days festival in late February celebrates local history with a professional rodeo, carnival activities, live music and a parade.

For eight consecutive weekends from the second Saturday in February through late March or early April, the Arizona Renaissance Festival and Artisan Marketplace is held 7 miles east on US 60. Jousting tournaments, wandering musicians, theatrical productions and demonstrations of period crafts are all part of this event re-creating a 16th-century European village at play.

The Festival of the Superstitions is held over Veterans Day weekend and features a parade, children's activities, gold panning, pie eating contests and a car show.

Apache Junction Chamber of Commerce: 567 W. Apache Tr., Apache Junction, AZ 85120. **Phone:** (480) 982-3141 or (800) 252-3141.

APACHE LAKE, 30 mi. n.e. on SR 88, is part of the Salt River chain of lakes. A popular recreation area, it is surrounded by the Tonto National Forest *(see place listing p. 182)*. To the south lies the Superstition Wilderness. *See Recreation Areas Chart.* **Phone:** (928) 467-3200.

APACHE TRAIL (SR 88) starts at Apache Junction and proceeds for 39 mi., climbing past the famed Superstition Mountains, passing through Fish Creek Canyon and skirting the southern edges of Apache, Saguaro, Canyon and Roosevelt lakes, ending at Globe. The trail was created in 1905 to transport supplies from Phoenix and Globe to the construction site of Roosevelt Dam. The road parallels the ancient route of the Apaches through the canyons of the Salt River.

Note: The 25-mile portion of Apache Trail between Tortilla Flat and Roosevelt is a narrow, winding gravel road. It is not recommended during rainy weather, for inexperienced drivers or for vehicles more than 35 feet. West-to-east travel from Apache Junction to Globe will put you on the inside lane and grant all passengers the security of rock walls rather than the steep cliffs on the other side. **Phone:** (480) 610-3300 or (602) 225-5395.

Fish Creek Canyon is approximately 25 mi. n.e. of Apache Junction on the Apache Trail. The canyon is noted for massive, vividly colored walls rising as much as 2,000 feet above the highway. Formed by Fish Creek, which runs from the center of the Superstition Mountains northwest towards the Salt River, the canyon floor is lush with saguaro cacti, trees, bushes, reeds and waterfalls. **Phone:** (480) 610-3300, (928) 462-4300 or (928) 474-7900.

CANYON LAKE, 16 mi. n.e. on SR 88, is one of a series of lakes on the Salt River. Impounded by the Mormon Flat Dam, Canyon Lake twists for 10 miles through a magnificent gorge to Horse Mesa Dam. *See Recreation Areas Chart.* **Phone:** (480) 610-3300.

GOLDFIELD GHOST TOWN & MINE TOURS, 5 mi. n.e. on SR 88, passing Milepost 200 to 4650 E. Mammoth Mine Rd., offers mine tours, gold panning and specialty shops within view of the spectacular Superstition Mountains. Gunfights are performed November through April. A museum features a large exhibit of antique mining equipment. Of interest is the reptile exhibit. In the Mystery Shack, guests can walk at a 45-degree angle and iron balls roll uphill. A scenic narrow-gauge railroad also encompasses the town. A zipline course is on the grounds.

Hours: Daily 10-5. Gunfights Sat.-Sun. noon-4, Nov.-Apr. Closed Thanksgiving and Christmas. **Cost:** Town free. Mine tour $8; $7 (ages 60+); $5 (ages 6-12). Train ride $8; $7 (ages 60+); $5 (ages 5-12). Gold panning $7; $6 (ages 5-12). Reptile exhibit $5; $4 (ages 6-17). Museum $4; $3 (ages 60+); $1 (ages 5-12). Mystery Shack $5; $4 (ages 60+); $3 (ages 6-12). **Phone:** (480) 983-0333. GT

Apache Trail Tours depart from Goldfield Ghost Town, 5 mi. n.e. on SR 88, passing Milepost 200 to 4650 E. Mammoth Mine Rd. Participants partake in 1- to 4-hour guided jeep tours of the Apache Trail, the Superstition Mountains and the Four Peaks Wilderness. Climate-controlled SUVs are available. Ninety-minute gold-panning experiences also are offered.

Hours: Tours daily by reservation. Closed Thanksgiving and Christmas. **Cost:** One-hour tour $50; $40 (ages 2-15). Ninety-minute tour $65; $55 (ages 2-15). Two-hour tour $85; $75 (ages 2-15). Four-hour tour $120. Phone for other tour rates. One hour and 90-minute tours require a minimum of two people; two- and four-hour tours require a minimum of four people. Reservations are required. **Phone:** (480) 982-7661. GT

LOST DUTCHMAN STATE PARK, 5 mi. n.e. off SR 88 to 6109 N. Apache Tr., offers 320 acres of hiking trails, camping and picnicking areas. Special moonlight hikes are offered monthly and guided hikes and campfire programs are offered weekly November through March. *See Recreation Areas Chart.* **Hours:** Daily dawn-10 p.m. Office daily 7-4; hours vary in summer. **Cost:** $7 (per private vehicle, up to four passengers); $3 (per additional adult passenger in vehicle or person arriving on foot or bicycle). Electric campsites Nov.-Apr. $30 (per private vehicle); rest of year $25. Nonelectric camping Nov.-Apr. $20 (per private vehicle); rest of year $15. **Phone:** (480) 982-4485, or (520) 586-2283 for camping reservations.

SUPERSTITION MOUNTAIN MUSEUM, 4087 N. Apache Tr., contains exhibits and artifacts depicting local history and folklore. You'll find maps of the mythical Lost Dutchman Gold Mine; exhibits about Native Americans, geology and natural history; the Elvis Memorial Chapel and Apacheland Barn, featured in Western movies filmed at the Apacheland Movie Ranch; a military exhibit about the Buffalo Soldiers; and reproductions of 19th-century buildings. The Superstition Mountain Railroad display, housed in its own building, is a G-scale model train set-up that depicts life in late 1800s-early 1900s Arizona, complete with towns, mines and mining camps, brothels, ranches and a working stamp mill.

Nature trails traverse the 12-acre grounds. **Time:** Allow 1 hour minimum. **Hours:** Daily 9-4. Closed Jan. 1, Thanksgiving and Christmas. **Cost:** $5; $4 (ages 55+); free (ages 0-16 with paying adult). **Phone:** (480) 983-4888.

SUPERSTITION MOUNTAINS, e. of town off Apache Trail (SR 88), were named for the many legends surrounding them. The fabled Lost Dutchman Gold Mine lies somewhere in these mountains. Whether the mine really exists is uncertain. At least eight men were killed because of it, and many others died searching for it. Monuments at Roosevelt Dam and Apache Junction commemorate Jacob Waltz, who allegedly discovered the mine.

APACHE JUNCTION MOTEL 480/982-7702

Motel

Address: 1680 W Apache Tr 85120 **Location:** US 60 exit 195, 2 mi n, then just w. **Facility:** 15 units. 1 story, exterior corridors. *Bath:* shower only.

BEST WESTERN APACHE JUNCTION INN 480/982-9200

Hotel

AAA Benefit: Members save up to 15% and earn bonus points!

Address: 1101 W Apache Tr 85220 **Location:** US 60 exit 195, 2 mi n to W Apache Tr, then 0.4 mi e. **Facility:** 40 units. 2 stories (no elevator), interior/exterior corridors. **Pool:** heated outdoor. **Activities:** hot tub. **Guest Services:** coin laundry. **Featured Amenity: full hot breakfast.**

APACHE-SITGREAVES NATIONAL FORESTS (D-6)

Elevations in the forests range from 3,500 ft. in the Upper Sonoran Desert to 11,500 ft. at Mount Baldy. Refer to AAA maps for additional elevation information.

Along the south rim of the Colorado Plateau in east-central Arizona, the Apache-Sitgreaves national forests comprise nearly 2.1 million acres. They are named, respectively, for the Apaches and for Lt. Lorenzo Sitgreaves, who in 1851 led the first military topographical mapping expeditions across Arizona. The forests include the Mount Baldy, Bear Wallow and Escudilla wilderness areas and the Blue Range Primitive Area.

Hunting is permitted in season. Numerous lakes and streams offer trout fishing. Boats with motors larger than 8 horsepower are prohibited; on some lakes only electric motors are permitted. Trails are available for varying interests, including horseback riding, mountain biking, and hiking as well as for off-roading vehicles. Picnic facilities are available in summer. Winter activities include cross-country skiing, snowmobiling, snowshoeing and ice fishing.

Visitor centers are at Big Lake and on the Mogollon Rim near Heber. Visitor information also is available in summer from attendants at developed campgrounds in the forests and district ranger offices.

The Coronado Trail Scenic Byway (US 191), 127 miles long and ranging from 3,500 to 9,000 feet high, connects the cities of Clifton/Morenci to Springerville/Eagar. The present Coronado Trail (US 191) commemorates portions of the historic route followed by Francisco Vázquez de Coronado when he sought the fabled Seven Cities of Cíbola in 1540. The road traverses areas that remain much as they were more than 450 years ago.

From Clifton the road climbs a corkscrew grade up Rose Peak to an elevation of 8,550 feet. Near this point a Forest Service lookout tower affords a magnificent panorama. Continuing northward, the trail rises to an elevation of 9,200 feet at Blue Vista. The steep, narrow road is not recommended for vehicles pulling trailers more than 20 feet long.

From the rim northward the road is noted for its spectacular autumn coloring. The named portion of the trail ends at Springerville, where US 191 joins US 60.

The White Mountains Scenic Byway is a series of connecting roads that forms a loop through the White Mountains of the Apache-Sitgreaves national forests. The 123-mile loop includes parts of SRs 73, 260, 273 and 373.

For more information contact the Forest Supervisor's Office, Apache-Sitgreaves National Forests, 30 S. Chiricahua Dr., P.O. Box 640, Springerville, AZ 85938; phone (928) 333-4301 or (877) 444-6777 for reservations. *See Recreation Areas Chart.*

AVONDALE pop. 76,238

- **Hotels & Restaurants map & index p. 117**
- **Part of Phoenix area — see map p. 91**

HILTON GARDEN INN PHOENIX/AVONDALE
623/882-3351 **32**

Hotel

Hilton Garden Inn **AAA Benefit:** Members save up to 15%!

Address: 11460 W Hilton Way 85323 **Location:** I-10 exit 131 (Avondale Blvd), just s. **Facility:** 123 units. 4 stories, interior corridors. **Terms:** check-in 4 pm. **Pool:** heated outdoor. **Activities:** hot tub, exercise room. **Guest Services:** valet and coin laundry, area transportation.

HOMEWOOD SUITES BY HILTON PHOENIX/AVONDALE
623/882-3315 **33**

Extended Stay Hotel. **Address:** 11450 W Hilton Way 85323

AAA Benefit: Members save up to 15%!

BENSON (F-5) pop. 5,105, elev. 3,581'

- **Hotels p. 30 • Restaurants p. 30**

On the Southern Pacific Railroad route, Benson grew as a distribution center for copper and silver mined in the San Pedro Valley. When railroad transportation began to decline in the 1920s, the town welcomed a new breed of traveler, fledgling motorists out to discover the Southwest. Benson's mining, ranching and railroad history is recalled at the Benson Historical Museum; phone (520) 586-3134.

For a breed of a different kind, visit The Oasis Sanctuary at 5411 N. Teran Rd. Open by appointment only, the facility is an exotic bird sanctuary that permanently houses rescued psittacines (parrot-type) birds; phone (520) 212-4737.

Benson/San Pedro Valley Chamber of Commerce/Visitor Center: 168 E. 4th St., Benson, AZ 85602. **Phone:** (520) 265-8031.

KARTCHNER CAVERNS STATE PARK, 9 mi. s. of I-10 exit 302 off SR 90, contains one of the world's few living wet caves open for viewing. The guided 1.5-hour Rotunda/Throne Room Tour takes visitors through rooms that contain more than 30 types of colorful formations growing for more than 200,000 years out of the limestone beneath the Whetstone Mountains. The guided 1.75-hour Big Room Tour features striking calcite formations and giant boulders. Formations include stalactites, stalagmites, canopies, bacon-colored draperies, helictites and rimstone dams. Turnip shield and birdsnest quartz needle formations also may be found. The guided 1.25-hour Headlight and Helmet Tour allows guests to experience the cave as discoverers did in 1974 using only the light provided by their helmet's headlamp.

Discovered in 1974, the 7-acre cave system holds the world's second-longest soda straw formation and "Kubla Khan," a 58-foot-high column. The skeleton of a Shasta ground sloth from the Pleistocene period is among the fossil finds. Within the 550-acre park are a discovery center with exhibits and interactive displays, an interpretive nature path and 5 miles of hiking trails.

Note: Cameras are not permitted in the cave. **Time:** Allow 2 hours, 30 minutes minimum. **Hours:** Park open daily 6 a.m.-10 p.m. Discovery Center daily 8-6, late Dec.-May 30; 9-5, rest of year. Rotunda/Throne Room tours are offered all year and Big Room tours are offered Oct. 15-Apr. 15. Headlight and Helmet Tour on Sat. Times vary, phone ahead. Closed Christmas.

Cost: $7 (per private vehicle, up to four passengers); $3 (per additional adult passenger in vehicle or person arriving on foot or bicycle); free (with tour reservation). Rotunda/Throne Room tour or Big Room tour $23; $13 (ages 7-13). Ages 0-6 are not permitted on Big Room tour. Headlight and Helmet Tour $30. Ages 0-9 are not permitted on Headlight and Helmet tour. Camping $30. Rates may vary; phone ahead. Reservations are recommended. **Phone:** (520) 586-4100 for information, or (520) 586-2283 for tour and camping reservations. GT

DAYS INN WYNDHAM BENSON 520/586-3000

Hotel. **Address:** 621 Commerce Dr 85602

QUALITY INN 520/586-3646

Hotel. **Address:** 699 N Ocotillo Rd 85602

WHERE TO EAT

G & F PIZZA PALACE 520/586-9449

Italian. Casual Dining. **Address:** 114 E 5th St 85602

MAGALY'S MEXICAN RESTAURANT 520/720-6530

Mexican. Casual Dining. **Address:** 675 W 4th St 85602

BISBEE (G-5) pop. 5,575, elev. 5,300'

Bisbee became internationally renowned during the 1880s mining rush, with the discovery of the Copper Queen Lode. Bisbee mines, nestled in the foothills of the Mule Mountains in southeast Arizona, have produced more than $2 billion in copper, gold, lead, silver and zinc. By 1900 Bisbee was the largest cosmopolitan center between St. Louis and San Francisco. Besides operating several stock exchanges, the town was a major venue for rodeos, circus, vaudeville, theater and lectures.

By the early 1970s most of the mines had closed, and artists' studios replaced the miners' shacks. Bisbee is now home to numerous art galleries and studios and serves as an enclave for more than 100 resident artists and artisans as well as actors, dancers, writers, musicians and photographers. Events and cultural activities are held throughout the year; contact the visitor center for further information.

Artifacts and period furnishings of early Bisbee are displayed at the Muheim Heritage House Museum at 207 Youngblood Hill; phone (520) 432-4815. The house was completed in 1915 by a prominent local businessman. Another museum that preserves Bisbee's past through artifacts, clothing and memorabilia is the Bisbee Restoration Museum at 37 Main St. Historic Warren Ballpark, on Old Bisbee Road, is one of the oldest ballparks in the country; phone (520) 249-5742.

Bisbee Visitor Center: 478 N. Dart Rd., Bisbee, P.O. Box 1642, AZ 85603. **Phone:** (520) 432-3554 or (866) 224-7233.

Shopping: The downtown section known as Old Bisbee has several specialty shops that sell antiques, assorted crafts, gifts, jewelry, turquoise and Western items.

BISBEE BROWNSTONE SUITES 520/422-2317

Condominium. **Address:** 20 Brewery Ave 85603

CANYON ROSE SUITES 520/432-5098

Historic Condominium

Address: 27 Subway St 85603 **Location:** Corner of Shearer Ave; in historic district. **Facility:** This historic building, located just off Main Street, features spacious condo-style rooms with modern conveniences. 7 condominiums. 2 stories (no elevator), interior corridors. **Parking:** street only. **Guest Services:** coin laundry.

LETSON LOFT HOTEL 520/432-3210

Historic Bed & Breakfast. **Address:** 26 Main St 85603

WHERE TO EAT

BISBEE BREAKFAST CLUB 520/432-5885

American. Casual Dining. **Address:** 75A Erie St 85603

BISBEE'S TABLE 520/432-6788

American. Casual Dining. **Address:** 2 Copper Queen Plaza 85603

CAFE CORNUCOPIA 520/432-4820

Deli. Casual Dining. **Address:** 14 Main St 85603

CAFE ROKA 520/432-5153

New American Casual Dining
$14-$28

AAA Inspector Notes: This popular upscale eatery is located in a restored 1907 building with multiple levels and a lively central bar. The chef/owner serves up expertly prepared New American cuisine using fresh, seasonal ingredients. Live jazz is offered every Friday. **Features:** full bar. **Reservations:** suggested. **Address:** 35 Main St 85603 **Location:** SR 80, just n; in historic district. **Parking:** street only. D

HIGH DESERT MARKET & CAFE 520/432-6775

American. Quick Serve. **Address:** 203 Tombstone Canyon 85603

SANTIAGO'S 520/432-1910

Mexican. Casual Dining. **Address:** 1 Howell Ave 85603

SCREAMING BANSHEE PIZZA 520/432-1300

Pizza. Casual Dining. **Address:** 200 Tombstone Canyon 85603

THUY'S NOODLE SHOP 520/366-4479

Vietnamese. Quick Serve. **Address:** 9 Naco Rd 85603

BUCKEYE pop. 50,876

• Part of Phoenix area — see map p. 91

HOLIDAY INN EXPRESS PHOENIX WEST-BUCKEYE 623/386-8550

Hotel. **Address:** 445 S Watson Rd 85326

BULLHEAD CITY (C-1) pop. 39,540, elev. 540'

Established originally as a supply and support base for builders of the Davis Dam, which impounds Lake Mojave in the Lake Mead National Recreation Area *(see place listing p. 75)*, Bullhead City has evolved into a vacation community. The city's accommodations industry thrives on the thousands of visitors drawn to the mild winter weather and the casinos across the river in Laughlin, Nev. Two bridges connect the towns, and a free river ferry is available.

Bullhead Area Chamber of Commerce: 1251 SR 95, Bullhead City, AZ 86429. **Phone:** (928) 754-4121 or (800) 987-7457.

DAYS INN BY WYNDHAM BULLHEAD CITY 928/754-3000

Hotel. **Address:** 1126 Hwy 95 86429

WHERE TO EAT

COLIANNO'S ITALIAN RESTAURANT 928/758-7104

Italian. Casual Dining. **Address:** 2200 Hwy 95 86442

EL PALACIO 928/763-2494

Mexican. Casual Dining. **Address:** 1885 Hwy 95 86442

CAMERON pop. 885

• Part of Grand Canyon National Park area — see map p. 57

CAMERON TRADING POST MOTEL, RESTAURANT & GIFT SHOP 928/679-2231

Motel

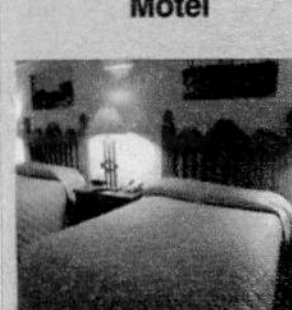

Address: 466 N Hwy 89 86020 **Location:** 1 mi from east gate turn off. **Facility:** 66 units. 2-3 stories (no elevator), exterior corridors. **Terms:** check-in 4 pm. **Dining:** Cameron Trading Post Restaurant, see separate listing. *(See ad p. 63, p. 225.)*

SAVE

/ SOME UNITS

WHERE TO EAT

CAMERON TRADING POST RESTAURANT 928/679-2231

Southwestern Casual Dining
$8-$28

AAA Inspector Notes: Located at a busy intersection outside the Grand Canyon, this restaurant is attached to a trading post and a motel, making it very convenient for travelers. Casual, friendly, helpful staff members deliver steaks, chicken and Mexican cuisine amid Native American decor. Take a chance on an authentic Navajo taco, you won't be disappointed. **Address:** 466 N Hwy 89 86020 **Location:** 1 mi from east gate turn off; in Cameron Trading Post Motel, Restaurant & Gift Shop. B L D

CAMP VERDE (C-4) pop. 10,873, elev. 3,160'

• Hotels p. 32

Camp Verde was founded as Camp Lincoln in 1866 by Arizona Volunteers to defend pioneers from Apache raids. The fort was renamed Fort Verde a few years later by the U.S. Army. As the area became more peaceful, residents turned their energies toward cattle raising and farming, the two major industries in the broad Verde Valley. Native American ruins and cliff dwellings may be seen at nearby Montezuma Castle National Monument *(see place listing p. 80)* and Montezuma Well.

The Fort Verde Days event in October celebrates the town's cowboy and pioneer history with reenactments, parade and live entertainment around Fort Verde State Historic Park.

FORT VERDE STATE HISTORIC PARK is 3 mi. e. of I-17. In one of the four restored structures of the old fort are Native American, pioneer and military artifacts. Officers' quarters, bachelor's housing and the doctor's quarters are furnished in period. Historic reenactments take place in February, April and October. **Time:** Allow 1 hour minimum. **Hours:** Daily 9-4:30. Closed Christmas. **Cost:** $7; $4 (ages 7-13). Hours and rates may vary; phone ahead. **Phone:** (928) 567-3275.

SAVE **OUT OF AFRICA WILDLIFE PARK** is, from I-17 exit 287, 3 mi. w. on SR 260, following signs to park entrance. The Wildlife Preserve features several photography platforms to allow for unobstructed pictures of lions, tigers, wolves, hyenas and more. Visitors may interact with giraffes and camels during the narrated African Bush Safari tour, attend a Predator Feed show, and watch caretakers activate the instinct of play at a Tiger Splash show. Special tour options include a 1-hour Unimog Adventure safari and a 3-hour VIP Behind the Scenes tour. Additional options include the Predator Zip Line over animals.

Time: Allow 1 hour minimum. **Hours:** Park open daily 9:30-5. Predator Feed Sun., Wed. and Fri. at 3. Tiger Splash daily at 1:15. Unimog Adventure departs daily at 11 and 2. VIP Behind the Scenes tour departs daily at 10. Last admission 1 hour before closing. Closed Thanksgiving and Christmas. **Cost:** $33.95; $31.95 (ages 65+); $26.95 (military with ID); $18.95 (ages 3-12). Unimog Adventure $20 (park admission not included for ages 5+). VIP Behind the Scenes tour $175; $145 (ages 3-12). Rates may vary; phone ahead. VIP Behind the Scenes tour and Unimog Adventure reservations must be made 24 hours in advance. Reservations are required. **Phone:** (928) 567-2840. GT

COPPER CANYON INN 928/567-2622
Hotel. **Address:** 1550 W Hwy 260 86322

DAYS INN & SUITES CAMP VERDE 928/567-3700
Hotel. **Address:** 1640 W Hwy 260 86322

CANYON DE CHELLY NATIONAL MONUMENT (B-6)

In the Navajo Nation Reservation 3 miles east of Chinle, Canyon de Chelly (d'-SHAY) National Monument is reached from Gallup or Shiprock, N.M., and Chambers, Holbrook, Winslow or Tuba City, Ariz. Five periods of Native American culture (Archaic, Basket Makers, early Pueblo, Hopi and Navajo), dating from 2500 B.C. to present, are represented within the 83,849-acre monument.

Archaic, Basket Makers and early Pueblo groups successively occupied the canyons until a reduction in population in A.D. 1275. During the 14th and 15th centuries the Hopis utilized the canyons. The Navajo arrived sometime in the 17th century and continue to live in the canyons, growing corn and herding livestock.

The 26-mile-long Canyon de Chelly is joined by the 25-mile-long Canyon del Muerto; red sandstone walls rise from 30 to 1,000 feet in a sheer, remarkably smooth ascent. Pictographs painted on the walls date from the earliest occupation to the Navajo era.

The principal area ruins are White House, Antelope House and Mummy Cave. White House was first explored in 1848, and its architecture may indicate connections with Chaco Canyon. Antelope House is named for the large pictograph of running antelopes that appears there. Mummy Cave, in which some well-preserved human remains were discovered, has a three-story tower. The architecture of these ancient villages suggests connections with Chaco Canyon and Mesa Verde.

Independent companies registered with the Navajo Parks and Recreation Department offer vehicle, horseback and hiking canyon tours led by an authorized guide. Arrangements for tours are made directly with the companies. For individuals with their own four-wheel-drive vehicles, authorized guides are available at the visitor center. Other regulations apply; *see Good Facts To Know.*

Cottonwood Campground is managed by the Navajo Nation and offers primitive campsites for tent and group camping on a first-come, first-served basis. Restroom facilities are on-site; no showers or hookups are available. Limited services are offered in winter. A nightly fee is required. Phone (928) 674-2106.

Except for a self-guiding trail from White House Overlook to the White House Ruin, all visitors within the canyons *must* be accompanied by a park ranger or an authorized guide. Fees and permits are required; phone (928) 674-2016.

Two scenic drives traverse both sides of the canyon, affording views of most major ruins from overlooks. Allow 2 hours for each drive if stopping at seven overlooks; half-day for all 10 overlooks. There are restrooms at Antelope House Overlook and along the rim on South Rim Dr. at White House Overlook. Food and gas are available in Chinle. Pets must be on a leash at all times and are permitted in the parking lots and campground. Pets are not allowed in the canyon or on tours.

Overlooks and trails open daily sunrise-sunset. The visitor center is open daily 8-5; closed Jan. 1, Thanksgiving and Christmas. The Navajo Nation Reservation observes daylight saving time, unlike the rest of the state; times listed reflect this when applicable. Monument admission free. For further information contact Canyon de Chelly National Monument, P.O. Box 588, Chinle, AZ 86503; phone (928) 674-5500.

CAREFREE pop. 3,363

• Part of Phoenix area — see map p. 91

BOULDERS RESORT & SPA, CURIO COLLECTION BY HILTON 480/488-9009
SAVE Resort Hotel. **Address:** 34631 N Tom Darlington Dr 85377

AAA Benefit: Members save up to 15%!

CIVANA 480/653-9000
Resort Hotel

Address: 37220 Mule Train Rd 85377 **Location:** SR 101 exit 36 (Pima Rd), 12.2 mi n to Cave Creek Rd, 1 mi w, then 0.4 mi n. **Facility:** Surrounded by the calming energy of the desert mountains, this property offers a quiet reprieve and a chance to recharge. Guest rooms features clean lines, natural materials, and spacious layouts, all with an outdoor balcony or patio. 176 units. 1-3 stories (no elevator), interior/exterior corridors. **Parking:** on-site and valet. **Terms:** check-in 4 pm. **Amenities:** safes. **Dining:** 2 restaurants. **Pool:** heated outdoor. **Activities:** hot tub, tennis, recreation programs, bicycles, health club, spa. **Guest Services:** valet laundry, rental car service, area transportation.

/ SOME UNITS

WHERE TO EAT

:ONFLUENCE 480/488-9796

American. Casual Dining. **Address:** 36889 N Tom)arlington Dr 85377

:NGLISH ROSE TEA ROOM 480/488-4812

Specialty. Casual Dining. **Address:** 201 Easy St, Unit 03 85377

:ASA GRANDE (E-4) pop. 48,571, elev. 1,387'

Casa Grande, founded in 1879, was named for he Ancestral Desert People Indian ruins *(see Casa Grande Ruins National Monument this page)* 20 niles northeast of town.

Greater Casa Grande Chamber of Commerce: 575 N. Marshall St., Casa Grande, AZ 85122. **Phone:** (520) 836-2125 or (800) 916-1515.

BAYMONT INN & SUITES BY WYNDHAM 520/421-9878

Hotel. **Address:** 2145 E Florence Blvd 85222

FRANCISCO GRANDE HOTEL & GOLF RESORT 520/836-6444

Hotel. **Address:** 12684 W Gila Bend Hwy 85193

HOLIDAY INN EXPRESS & SUITES CASA GRANDE 520/509-6333

Hotel

Address: 805 N Cacheries Ct 85122 **Location:** I-10 exit 194 (SR 287), 0.6 mi w. **Facility:** 77 units. 3 stories, interior corridors. **Pool:** heated outdoor. **Activities:** hot tub, exercise room. **Guest Services:** valet and coin laundry. **Featured Amenity: breakfast buffet.**

SAVE CALL BIZ HS

/ SOME UNITS

HOLIDAY INN HOTEL CASA GRANDE 520/426-3500

Hotel

Address: 777 N Pinal Ave 85122 **Location:** I-10 exit 194 (SR 287), 3.9 mi w. **Facility:** 176 units. 4 stories, interior corridors. **Pool:** heated outdoor. **Activities:** hot tub, exercise room. **Guest Services:** valet and coin laundry. **Featured Amenity: breakfast buffet.**

SAVE BIZ

/ SOME UNITS

QUALITY INN CASA GRANDE 520/836-1600

Hotel. **Address:** 665 N Via del Cielo Rd 85222

SUPER 8 BY WYNDHAM 520/836-8800

Hotel. **Address:** 2066 E Florence Blvd 85222

WHERE TO EAT

A LATTE VINO 520/788-6677

American. Casual Dining. **Address:** 958 E Rodeo Rd 85122

BEDILLON'S CACTUS GARDEN RESTAURANT 520/836-2045

Southwestern. Casual Dining. **Address:** 800 N Park Ave 85222

CAFÉ DE MANUEL 520/421-3199

Mexican. Casual Dining. **Address:** 1300 N Pinal Ave 85222

LEGEND'S RESTAURANT 520/836-6444

Western American. Casual Dining. **Address:** 12684 W Gila Bend Hwy 85293

GEM CASA GRANDE RUINS NATIONAL MONUMENT (E-4)

Off SR 87/287, Casa Grande Ruins National Monument lies within the city limits of Coolidge. The Casa Grande (Big House) was built prior to 1350 A.D. by Ancestral Desert People, the prehistoric peoples formerly known as Hohokam. The four-story structure was constructed of layers of caliche mud and represent the height of the period's architectural advancement. Around the main building are the remains of a walled village. A viewing platform overlooking a prehistoric ball court is behind the picnic area.

The Ancestral Desert People lived in the area for many centuries prior to the construction of the Casa Grande. Sometime around 1450 Casa Grande was abandoned for unknown reasons after the Ancestral Desert People had used it for only a century. The ruins were seen and named in 1694 by Father Eusebio Francisco Kino, a missionary who was led to the site by local Akimel O'odham Indians.

The visitor center features a museum and theater with a 22-minute film. Self-guiding tours and picnic facilities are available year-round. Guided tours are available November through March. Allow 1 hour minimum. Monument open daily 9-5, Oct.-Apr.; 9-4, rest of year; closed July 4, Thanksgiving and Christmas. Admission free. For further information contact the Superintendent, Casa Grande Ruins National Monument, 1100 W. Ruins Dr., Coolidge, AZ 85128; phone (520) 723-3172.

CAVE CREEK (H-3) pop. 5,015, elev. 2,129'

• Part of Phoenix area — see map p. 91

Cave Creek was originally home to the Ancestral Desert People, who irrigated their fields with water from Cave Creek. In 1870 a road was built to link the newly formed town of Cave Creek to Fort McDowell on the Verde River. The late 1800s saw the establishment of numerous mining camps in the surrounding mountains, and permanent settlers who followed took to ranching and farming.

Recreational activities abound in Cave Creek with the Tonto National Forest *(see place listing p. 182)* as its neighbor. Six lakes in the forest offer numerous opportunities for swimming, fishing and boating.

Carefree-Cave Creek Chamber of Commerce: 748 Easy St., Suite 2 and 4, P.O. Box 734, Carefree, AZ 85377. **Phone:** (480) 488-3381.

CARTWRIGHT'S MODERN CUISINE 480/488-8031

Southwestern. Fine Dining. **Address:** 6710 E Cave Creek Rd 85331

EL ENCANTO MEXICAN RESTAURANT 480/488-1752

Mexican. Casual Dining. **Address:** 6248 E Cave Creek Rd 85331

THE HORNY TOAD RESTAURANT 480/488-9542

American. Casual Dining. **Address:** 6738 E Cave Creek Rd 85331

TONTO BAR & GRILL 480/488-0698

American. Casual Dining. **Address:** 5736 E Rancho Mañana Blvd 85331

CHANDLER (J-4) pop. 236,123, elev. 1,214'

- **Restaurants p. 36**
- **Hotels & Restaurants map & index p. 126**
- **Part of Phoenix area — see map p. 91**

Chandler was founded by Dr. Alexander J. Chandler, a veterinary surgeon who bought 80 acres of land in the Salt River Valley in 1891 and created a series of canals. By 1900 his ranch covered 18,000 acres; in 1912, Chandler sold $50,000 worth of land to 300 speculators and the city was born. In the beginning, Chandler's chief industry was agriculture; alfalfa, cotton and grain were common crops. Today agriculture, while still in the picture, takes a back seat to manufacturing and electronics.

With their restored facades and colonnades, buildings in historic downtown Chandler add to the area's original character, giving it a distinct early-1900s ambience. A host of shopping and dining establishments as well as event opportunities are available to visitors year-round.

Shopping: Downtown Chandler, south of Chandler Boulevard on Arizona Avenue, offers an eclectic mix of stores ranging from trendy clothing boutiques to the home and gift items at Sibley's West—The Chandler Arizona Gift Shop, specializing in made-in-Arizona items. Just 3 miles west of downtown, Chandler Fashion Center features such name-brand stores as Eddie Bauer, Nordstrom and Victoria's Secret.

The Shoppes at Casa Paloma, an upscale shopping center east of US 10 on Ray Road, features a combination of national stores and distinctive shops including Francesca's Collections, Pandora's Purse and Sur La Table.

BEST WESTERN INN OF CHANDLER

480/814-8600 75

AAA Benefit: Members save up to 15% and earn bonus points!

Address: 950 N Arizona Ave 85225 **Location:** Just s of Ray Rd. **Facility:** 47 units. 2 stories (no elevator), exterior corridors. **Pool:** outdoor. **Activities:** hot tub. **Featured Amenity: full hot breakfast.**

BEST WESTERN PLUS CHANDLER HOTEL & SUITES

520/796-1350 86

AAA Benefit: Members save up to 15% and earn bonus points!

Address: 7101 W Sundust Rd 85226 **Location:** I-10 exit 162, just e. **Facility:** 87 units, some efficiencies. 4 stories, interior corridors. *Bath:* shower only. **Pool:** heated indoor. **Activities:** picnic facilities, exercise room. **Guest Services:** valet and coin laundry. **Featured Amenity: breakfast buffet.**

CAMBRIA HOTEL PHOENIX CHANDLER/FASHION CENTER

480/899-2203 81

Address: 3165 W Frye Rd 85226 **Location:** SR 101 exit 60 (Chandler Blvd), 0.5 mi s to Price Rd, then just w. **Facility:** 136 units. 5 stories, interior corridors. **Amenities:** safes. **Pool:** heated outdoor. **Activities:** exercise room. **Guest Services:** valet and coin laundry, area transportation.

COMFORT INN CHANDLER-PHOENIX SOUTH

480/857-4969 74

Address: 7400 W Boston St 85226 **Location:** I-10 exit 160 (Chandler Blvd), just e, then just s on Southgate Dr. **Facility:** 129 units. 4 stories, interior corridors. **Pool:** heated outdoor. **Activities:** exercise room. **Guest Services:** valet and coin laundry. **Featured Amenity: full hot breakfast.**

SOME UNITS

COUNTRY INN & SUITES BY RADISSON, CHANDLER

480/940-0099 73

Hotel. **Address:** 7425 W Chandler Blvd 85226

COURTYARD BY MARRIOTT PHOENIX CHANDLER

480/763-9500 69

Hotel. **Address:** 920 N 54th St 85226

AAA Benefit: Members save 5% or more!

COURTYARD BY MARRIOTT PHOENIX CHANDLER/FASHION CENTER

480/855-8600 85

COURTYARD **AAA Benefit:** Members save 5% or more!

Address: 1100 S Price Rd 85286 **Location:** SR 202 exit 50B (Price Rd), just s. **Facility:** 150 units. 6 stories, interior corridors. **Pool:** heated outdoor. **Activities:** hot tub, exercise room. **Guest Services:** valet and coin laundry, boarding pass kiosk, area transportation.

(See map & index p. 126.)

CROWNE PLAZA SAN MARCOS GOLF RESORT 480/812-0900 82

Historic Resort Hotel. **Address:** 1 N San Marcos Pl 85225

DOUBLETREE BY HILTON PHOENIX CHANDLER 480/961-4444 72

Hotel

AAA Benefit: Members save up to 15%!

Address: 7475 W Chandler Blvd 85226 **Location:** I-10 exit 160 (Chandler Blvd), just e, then just s on Southgate Dr. Located in a commercial area. **Facility:** 160 units. 4 stories, interior corridors. **Amenities:** safes. **Pool:** heated outdoor. **Activities:** hot tub, exercise room. **Guest Services:** valet and coin laundry.

/ SOME UNITS

DRURY INN & SUITES PHOENIX CHANDLER FASHION CENTER 480/899-8100 87

Hotel. **Address:** 1205 S Price Rd 85286

ELEMENT BY WESTIN CHANDLER FASHION CENTER 480/553-7277 79

Hotel. **Address:** 44 S Chandler Village Dr N 85226

AAA Benefit: Members save 5% or more!

FAIRFIELD INN & SUITES BY MARRIOTT PHOENIX CHANDLER/FASHION CENTER 480/963-5300 84

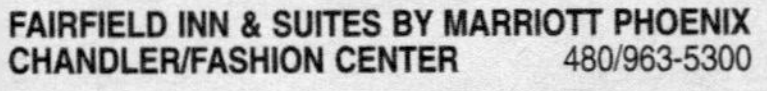

Hotel

Fairfield

AAA Benefit: Members save 5% or more!

Address: 1100 S Price Rd 85286 **Location:** SR 202 exit 50B (Price Rd), just s. **Facility:** 110 units. 6 stories, interior corridors. **Pool:** heated outdoor. **Activities:** hot tub, exercise room. **Guest Services:** valet and coin laundry, area transportation. **Featured Amenity: full hot breakfast.**

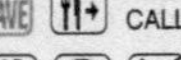

/ SOME UNITS

HAMPTON INN & SUITES PHOENIX/CHANDLER FASHION CENTER 480/917-9500 89

Hotel. **Address:** 1231 S Spectrum Blvd 85286

AAA Benefit: Members save up to 15%!

HAMPTON INN PHOENIX-CHANDLER 480/753-5200 71

Hotel. **Address:** 7333 W Detroit St 85226

AAA Benefit: Members save up to 15%!

HILTON PHOENIX CHANDLER 480/899-7400 80

Hotel

AAA Benefit: Members save up to 15%!

Address: 2929 W Frye Rd 85224 **Location:** SR 202 exit 50B (Price Rd), 0.4 mi n, then just e. **Facility:** 197 units. 6 stories, interior corridors. **Amenities:** safes. **Pool:** heated outdoor. **Activities:** hot tub, exercise room. **Guest Services:** valet laundry, area transportation.

/ SOME UNITS

HOLIDAY INN PHOENIX-CHANDLER 480/203-2121 93

Hotel

Address: 1200 W Ocotillo Rd 85248 **Location:** I-10 exit 164 (Queen Creek Rd), 5.5 mi e, 1.1 mi s on Alma School Rd, then just w. **Facility:** 106 units. 4 stories, interior corridors. **Pool:** heated outdoor. **Activities:** hot tub, exercise room. **Guest Services:** valet and coin laundry, area transportation. **Featured Amenity: full hot breakfast.**

HOME2 SUITES BY HILTON PHOENIX CHANDLER 480/659-2090 91

Extended Stay Contemporary Hotel

AAA Benefit: Members save up to 15%!

Address: 2490 W Queen Creek Rd 85248 **Location:** I-10 exit 164 (Queen Creek Rd), 3.8 mi e. **Facility:** 126 units. 4 stories, interior corridors. **Terms:** check-in 4 pm. **Pool:** heated outdoor. **Activities:** hot tub, picnic facilities, exercise room. **Guest Services:** valet and coin laundry, area transportation. **Featured Amenity: breakfast buffet.**

/ SOME UNITS

HOMEWOOD SUITES BY HILTON PHOENIX-CHANDLER 480/753-6200 70

Extended Stay Hotel. **Address:** 7373 W Detroit St 85226

AAA Benefit: Members save up to 15%!

HOMEWOOD SUITES BY HILTON-PHOENIX/CHANDLER FASHION CENTER 480/963-5700 88

Extended Stay Hotel. **Address:** 1221 S Spectrum Blvd 85286

AAA Benefit: Members save up to 15%!

RESIDENCE INN BY MARRIOTT-CHANDLER FASHION CENTER 480/782-1551 77

Extended Stay Hotel. **Address:** 200 N Federal St 85226

AAA Benefit: Members save 5% or more!

(See map & index p. 126.)

RESIDENCE INN BY MARRIOTT PHOENIX CHANDLER/ SOUTH 480/210-2727 92

SAVE Extended Stay Hotel. **Address:** 2727 W Queen Creek Rd 85248

AAA Benefit: Members save 5% or more!

SHERATON GRAND AT WILD HORSE PASS 602/225-0100 90

SAVE Resort Hotel. **Address:** 5594 W Wild Horse Pass Blvd 85226

AAA Benefit: Members save 5% or more!

SPRINGHILL SUITES BY MARRIOTT PHOENIX/CHANDLER FASHION CENTER 480/726-7666

SAVE Hotel. **Address:** 225 N Metro Blvd 85226

AAA Benefit: Members save 5% or more!

TOWNEPLACE SUITES BY MARRIOTT PHOENIX CHANDLER FASHION CENTER 480/525-8898

SAVE Extended Stay Hotel. **Address:** 3635 W Chandler Blvd 85226

AAA Benefit: Members save 5% or more!

WILD HORSE PASS HOTEL & CASINO 520/796-7777 83

Contemporary Hotel

Address: 5040 W Wild Horse Pass Blvd 85226 **Location:** I-10 exit 162, 2.4 mi w. **Facility:** Located within the Gila River Indian Community, this upscale hotel boasts comfortable guest rooms and many entertainment options, including a nightclub, theater, upscale dining and 36 holes of golf. 242 units. 10 stories, interior corridors. **Parking:** on-site and valet. **Terms:** check-in 4 pm. **Amenities:** safes. **Dining:** 5 restaurants, also, Ling & Louie's Asian Bar & Grill, Shula's America's Steak House, see separate listings, entertainment. **Pool:** heated outdoor. **Activities:** hot tub, regulation golf, exercise room. **Guest Services:** valet laundry, area transportation. *(See ad this page.)*

WHERE TO EAT

CHOU'S KITCHEN 480/821-2888 48

Northern Chinese. Casual Dining. **Address:** 910 N Alma School Rd 85224

CYCLO VIETNAMESE CUISINE 480/963-4490 50

Vietnamese. Casual Dining. **Address:** 1919 W Chandler Blvd, Suite 2 85224

DC STEAKHOUSE 480/899-4400 52

Steak. Casual Dining. **Address:** 98 S San Marcos Pl 85225

EASTWIND SUSHI & GRILL 480/855-7451 51

Asian. Casual Dining. **Address:** 58 W Buffalo St 85225

FLEMING'S PRIME STEAKHOUSE & WINE BAR 480/940-1900 45

Steak. Fine Dining. **Address:** 905 N 54th St 85226

KAI 602/385-5726 55

Southwestern Fine Dining $35-$175

AAA Inspector Notes: Using Native American indigenous foods, this elegant and understated eatery's renowned chefs have created unique seasonally-changing tasting menus, along with intriguing a la carte selections. Meats, game and seafood are enhanced by vegetable and herb sauces developed from native seeds. Sunset views against the mountain backdrop and wild horses roaming the area create a breathtaking scene. **Features:** full bar, patio dining. **Reservations:** suggested. Semiformal attire. **Address:** 5594 W Wild Horse Pass Blvd 85226 **Location:** I-10 exit 162, 2.4 mi w; in Sheraton Grand at Wild Horse Pass. **Parking:** on-site and valet. D

KEEGAN'S GRILL 480/814-0003

American. Casual Dining. **Address:** 1095 W Queen Creek Rd 85248

(See map & index p. 126.)

LING & LOUIE'S ASIAN BAR & GRILL 520/796-7281 (53)
Asian. Casual Dining. **Address:** 5040 Wild Horse Pass Blvd 85226

MIKADO SUSHI 480/726-0255 (56)
Sushi. Casual Dining. **Address:** 3125 S Alma School Rd 85248

P.F. CHANG'S CHINA BISTRO 480/899-0472 (49)
Chinese. Fine Dining. **Address:** 3255 W Chandler Blvd 85226

PITA JUNGLE 480/855-3232 (47)
Mediterranean. Casual Dining. **Address:** 1949 W Ray Rd 85224

ROY'S 480/705-7697 (44)
Hawaiian Fusion. Casual Dining. **Address:** 7151 W Ray Rd 85226

SAIGON PHO & SEAFOOD 480/786-8828 (46)
Vietnamese. Casual Dining. **Address:** 1381 N Alma School Rd 85224

SERRANO'S MEXICAN RESTAURANT 480/899-3318
Mexican. Casual Dining. **Address:** 141 S Arizona Ave 85225

SHULA'S AMERICA'S STEAK HOUSE 520/796-1972 (54)
Steak. Fine Dining. **Address:** 5040 Wild Horse Pass Blvd 85226

Z'TEJAS SOUTHWESTERN GRILL 480/893-7550 (43)
Southwestern. Casual Dining. **Address:** 7221 W Ray Rd 85226

CHINLE pop. 4,518

BEST WESTERN CANYON DE CHELLY INN 928/674-5874

Motel

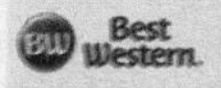

AAA Benefit: Members save up to 15% and earn bonus points!

Address: 100 Main St, Indian Rt 7 86503 **Location:** US 191, just e. **Facility:** 104 units. 2 stories (no elevator), exterior corridors. **Dining:** Junction Restaurant, see separate listing. **Pool:** heated indoor. **Activities:** sauna, exercise room.

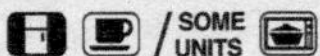

HOLIDAY INN CANYON DE CHELLY 928/674-5000

Hotel

Address: Indian Rt 7 86503 **Location:** US 191, 2.5 mi e; at entrance to Canyon de Chelly National Monument. **Facility:** 108 units. 2 stories (no elevator), interior corridors. **Dining:** Garcia's Restaurant, see separate listing. **Pool:** heated outdoor. **Activities:** exercise room. **Guest Services:** coin laundry.

THUNDERBIRD LODGE 928/674-5841

Motel

Address: Indian Rt 7 86503 **Location:** US 191, 3.5 mi e; just e of visitor center. Located in Canyon de Chelly National Monument. **Facility:** 69 units. 1 story, exterior corridors. **Dining:** Thunderbird Cafeteria, see separate listing.

SOME UNITS

WHERE TO EAT

GARCIA'S RESTAURANT 928/674-2511
American. Casual Dining. **Address:** Indian Rt 7 86503

JUNCTION RESTAURANT 928/674-8443
American. Casual Dining. **Address:** 100 Main St, Indian Rt 7 86503

THUNDERBIRD CAFETERIA 928/674-5841
American. Buffet Style. **Address:** Indian Rt 7 86503

CHINO VALLEY pop. 10,817

DAYS INN CHINO VALLEY 928/636-0311
Hotel. **Address:** 688 Fletcher Ct 86323

GEM CHIRICAHUA NATIONAL MONUMENT (F-6)

Approximately 70 miles northeast of Douglas via US 191 and SR 181 or 36 miles southeast of Willcox via SR 186 and SR 181, Chiricahua (cheer-ee-KAH-wah) National Monument, also called the "Wonderland of Rocks," is in the Chiricahua Mountains at an elevation ranging from 5,180 to 7,310 feet. Nine miles of the 21-mile county road that runs south from Bowie across Apache Pass to SR 186 are unpaved and rough in places. Unseasoned mountain drivers and cars pulling trailers should avoid the narrow, winding route from Portal; it is closed in winter.

The 11,985-acre area encompasses lands once controlled by the Chiricahua Apaches under Cochise, who led the Native Americans' resistance to the white man during the 1860s.

The Chiricahua Mountains rise above the surrounding grasslands, providing shady forests and glens that harbor Mexican chickadees, raccoon-like coatimundis, javelinas and a number of other wildlife species. Among the monument's outstanding features are gigantic, erosion-sculptured monoliths of volcanic ash.

Current research indicates that about 27 million years ago violent eruptions from the nearby Turkey Creek caldera took place, covering the area with white-hot ash. After the ash fused and cooled into an almost

2,000-foot layer of rock, the forces of erosion sculpted it into the odd array of shapes that can be seen.

Formations include the Totem Pole, 137 feet high and only a yard thick at its narrowest point; the Mushroom; and Big Balanced Rock, weighing 1,000 tons and resting on a base about 4 feet thick. In some places canyon walls rise as much as 1,000 feet. Many areas can be reached only on foot.

Among the first pioneers to settle in the area were Ja Hu Stafford and Neil and Emma Erickson. By the 1920s one of the Erickson daughters, Lillian, and her husband, Ed Riggs, had turned the homestead into a guest ranch, built trails into the rocks and were the driving force in the creation of Chiricahua National Monument. Today Faraway Ranch is preserved as a historic site with tours offered *(see attraction listing this page).*

Picnicking, camping and parking areas are available near the visitor center in Bonita Canyon. Reached from the visitor center by 6 miles of paved mountain road, 6,780-foot Massai Point offers an overlook and an exhibit building. More than 17 miles of trails lead to all parts of the monument. Campground programs are conducted in spring and fall. Contact the visitor center, (520) 824-3560, ext. 302, for an updated schedule.

Vehicles longer than 29 feet are not permitted beyond the visitor center. A hiker's shuttle departs to the high country daily; phone for schedule. Visitor center daily 8:30-4:30; closed Christmas. Park entrance and shuttle free. Campers must register at the campground. Camping fee per night $20; $10 (ages 62+). Fees may vary; phone ahead. Campgrounds will not accommodate travel trailers or motor homes more than 29 feet long.

For further information contact the Superintendent, Chiricahua National Monument, 12856 E. Rhyolite Creek Rd., Willcox, AZ 85643; phone (520) 824-3560.

FARAWAY RANCH, 1.5 mi. w. of the monument visitor center, is the homestead of pioneers Neil and Emma Erickson. The home was built in 1888 and additions were made through 1915. By the 1920s the Ericksons' daughter Lillian and her husband had turned the homestead into a working cattle and guest ranch.

Time: Allow 1 hour minimum. **Hours:** Homestead site accessible daily dawn-dusk. Guided tours of the home are given Thurs.-Sun. at 11 and 2, when staff is available; phone ahead to confirm schedule. **Cost:** Free. **Phone:** (520) 824-3560. GT

CIBOLA (E-1) pop. 250, elev. 240'

CIBOLA NATIONAL WILDLIFE REFUGE is 17 mi. s. on Neighbors Blvd., across the Cibola Bridge, then 3.5 mi. s. to 66600 Cibola Lake Rd. Home to many wildlife species including more than 288 species of birds as well as desert tortoises, mule deer and bobcats, the refuge has a visitor center with interpretive displays. A 1-mile nature trail winds through three native habitats: cottonwood, mesquite and willow.

From an elevated observation deck, winter visitors can view flocks of geese, ducks and sandhill cranes on a 20-acre pond. **Time:** Allow 30 minutes minimum. **Hours:** Refuge daily 30 minutes before sunrise-30 minutes after sunset. Visitor center daily 8-4:30, Nov. 1 to mid-Mar.; hours vary, rest of year. Wildlife is best viewed Nov.-Feb. Closed major holidays. **Cost:** Free. **Phone:** (928) 857-3253.

COCONINO NATIONAL FOREST (C-4)

Elevations in the forest range from 2,600 ft. at Fossil Creek in the Verde Valley to 12,643 ft. at the San Francisco Peaks. Refer to AAA maps for additional elevation information.

Surrounding Flagstaff and Sedona, Coconino National Forest covers 1,821,495 acres. In the south the forest is cut by deep canyons; in the north the San Francisco Peaks attain the highest elevation in Arizona. These peaks, including Mount Humphreys, the state's highest point, and Mount Agassiz, are some of the places in Arizona where alpine conditions exist. Many roads provide scenic drives.

Outstanding features include the Mogollon Rim, at an altitude of 7,600 feet, and Oak Creek Canyon *(see Sedona p. 161)*. Among the recreational facilities within the forest is the Arizona Snowbowl winter sports area *(see Flagstaff p. 42)*. Lake Mary offers good fishing, boating and waterfowl hunting. Camping facilities are available in the area Memorial Day-Labor Day, with some facilities open throughout the year; a $14-$22 per night fee is charged. Campfire restrictions may be in effect.

For additional information contact the Forest Service, 1824 S. Thompson St., Flagstaff, AZ 86001, phone (928) 527-3600; or the Flagstaff Ranger District Office, 5075 N. SR 89, Flagstaff, AZ 86004, phone (928) 526-0866. *See Recreation Areas Chart.*

CORONADO NATIONAL FOREST (E-5)

• Attractions map p. 197

Elevations in the forest range from 3,000 ft. in the Santa Catalina Mountains to 10,720 ft. in the Pinaleno Mountains. Refer to AAA maps for additional elevation information.

In southeastern Arizona and southwestern New Mexico, Coronado National Forest's 12 widely scattered sections cover 1,780,000 acres. Named for Spanish explorer Francisco Vázquez de Coronado, who journeyed through southern Arizona in 1540, the forest's varied plant and animal life reflects the area's extremes of elevation: Flat deserts of cacti and paloverde give way to rugged, heavily forested mountains known as the Madrean Sky Islands that are covered with oak, juniper, pine, fir and spruce, depending on the elevation.

Within the forest's boundaries are five fishing lakes. Mount Lemmon, northeast of Tucson, is one of the southernmost ski areas in the continental United States. More than 1,100 miles of trails offer hiking opportunities.

Madera Canyon, nestled in the Santa Rita Moun- ains, is a popular bird-watching spot with more than 00 species, including hummingbirds, woodpeckers nd swallows. Hiking trails, a nature trail, picnic reas and campgrounds complete the area.

Scenic drives include Swift Trail in the Pinaleno Aountains (Mount Graham), Ruby Road in the Tu- nacácori Mountains, Onion Saddle Road and Rucker Canyon Road in the Chiricahua Mountains and SRs 32 and 83. The winding 28-mile Sky Island Scenic Byway begins at Tanque Verde Road in the desert ust outside the Tucson city limits and extends to the op of Mount Lemmon in the Santa Catalina Moun- ains. Pullouts provide opportunities to observe the ontrasts of the lower and upper regions.

Legend has it that Cochise's grave is somewhere within the Cochise Stronghold Recreation Area in he Dragoon Mountains. A natural rock fortress, the stronghold is where the Chiricahua Apache leader nid from his enemies. Camping and picnicking are permitted, and interpretive trails are available.

Picnicking and camping fees range from $10 to $20. Day pass $5. Further information can be ob- ained at district offices in Douglas, (520) 364-3468; Nogales, (520) 281-2296; Safford, (928) 428-4150; Santa Catalina, (520) 749-8700; Sierra Vista, (520) 378-0311; and Tucson, (520) 202-2700; or contact the Supervisor, Coronado National Forest, Federal Building, 300 W. Congress St., Tucson, AZ 85701; phone (520) 388-8300. *See Recreation Areas Chart.*

CORONADO NATIONAL MEMORIAL (G-5)

Lying 22 miles south of Sierra Vista and 5 miles off SR 92, Coronado National Memorial was established to commemorate Francisco Vázquez de Coronado's exploration of the Southwest. The expedition, the first European venture across what is now the U.S.-Mexican border, began in February 1540 when the viceroy of Mexico sent young Coronado northward in search of gold from the fabled Seven Cities of Cíbola.

Coronado led an expedition of more than 1,400 soldiers and natives as well as 1,500 animals. Five months of hard travel brought the party not to the gold of the fabled cities but to the rock and adobe pueblos of the Zuni Indians near Zuni, N.M. After traveling as far east as central Kansas, the expedition gave up its search and retraced the route to Mexico in 1542.

Although they never found the city of gold, Coronado and his men found the Grand Canyon as well as many Hopi, Zuni and other villages. Besides paying tribute to Coronado's journey, the memorial's 4,750 acres provide a natural habitat for a variety of plants and animals.

The park, at the southern end of the Huachuca Mountains, is mostly oak woodland sprinkled with yucca, cholla and bear grass, which bloom from April to August. The mountains and canyons harbor wildlife ranging from bobcats to golden eagles. Three miles west of the visitor center, an overlook provides a sweeping view of the San Rafael Valley, the San Pedro Valley and the San Jose Peak in Mexico.

An alternative to driving to the pass is the 3-mile-long Joe's Canyon Trail, which begins near the visitor center. A half-mile hiking trail, with benches for resting and exhibits explaining the significance of Coronado's expedition extends from the pass to Coronado Peak. The visitor center has a 14-foot-long window wall for viewing birds and wildlife. Picnic facilities are available dawn-dusk.

The visitor center is open daily 8-4; closed Christmas. Free. For further information contact the Visitor Center, Coronado National Memorial, 4101 E. Montezuma Canyon Rd., Hereford, AZ 85615; phone (520) 366-5515.

CORONADO CAVE is accessible via a steep half-mile trail w. of the visitor center. The cave, which remains in its natural state with no lighting or guardrails, features two chambers connected by a narrow passageway. Several short tunnels branch from the main cavern and require some crawling. **Note:** Visitors must be equipped with one flashlight per person. Comfortable walking shoes, water, a backup light source, extra batteries and a whistle also are recommended. **Hours:** Daily dawn-dusk. **Cost:** Free. **Phone:** (520) 366-5515.

COTTONWOOD (C-3) pop. 11,265, elev. 3,314'

• Hotels p. 40 • Restaurants p. 40

One of two Arizona towns called Cottonwood, this Cottonwood is in the center of the 1,500-square-mile Verde Valley, which contributed to its development as a commerce center for the area. In 1874 soldiers from nearby Camp Verde were quartered in town. Settlers eventually arrived and named the community for a nearby stand of 16 large cottonwood trees. Cottonwood is about 2 miles southeast of Tuzigoot National Monument *(see place listing p. 221).*

Cottonwood Chamber of Commerce: 1010 S. Main St., Cottonwood, AZ 86326. **Phone:** (928) 634-7593.

WINERIES

- **Alcantara Vineyards** is at 3445 S. Grapevine Way. **Hours:** Tours Fri.-Sat. at 11:30 and by appointment. Tastings daily 11-5. **Phone:** (928) 649-8463. GT

AZ PINES MOTEL 928/634-9975

Motel. **Address:** 920 S Camino Real 86326

BEST WESTERN COTTONWOOD INN 928/634-5575

Hotel

AAA Benefit: Members save up to 15% and earn bonus points!

Address: 993 S Main St 86326 **Location:** On SR 89A, at SR 260. Across from a shopping center. **Facility:** 77 units. 1-2 stories (no elevator), exterior corridors. **Pool:** heated outdoor. **Activities:** hot tub. **Guest Services:** coin laundry. **Featured Amenity: breakfast buffet.**

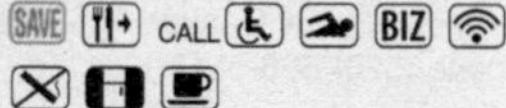

SUPER 8 COTTONWOOD 928/639-1888

Hotel. **Address:** 800 S Main St 86326

THE VIEW MOTEL 928/634-7581

Motel

Address: 818 S Main St 86326 **Location:** On SR 89A, 0.4 mi nw of jct SR 260. **Facility:** 34 units, some efficiencies. 1 story, exterior corridors. **Pool:** heated outdoor. **Activities:** hot tub.

WHERE TO EAT

MAI THAI ON MAIN 928/649-2999

Thai. Casual Dining. **Address:** 157 S Main St 86326

NIC'S ITALIAN STEAK & CRAB HOUSE 928/634-9626

Steak Seafood. Casual Dining. **Address:** 925 N Main St 86326

PIZZERIA BOCCE 928/202-3597

Italian Pizza. Casual Dining. **Address:** 1060 N Main St 86326

THE TAVERN GRILLE 928/634-6669

American. Gastropub. **Address:** 914 N Main St 86326

DOUGLAS (G-6) pop. 17,378, elev. 3,955'

Douglas, on the Mexican border, began as the site of annual roundups for surrounding ranches. The town was founded in 1901 by a copper-smelting company and is now a center for commerce, manufacturing, agriculture and tourism.

The Gadsden Hotel, 1046 G Ave., was built in 1906 and has a high-ceilinged lobby with a mural of Tiffany stained glass and a curving staircase. Of interest in the vicinity are many ghost towns and mining camps as well as shopping and sightseeing opportunities in nearby Agua Prieta, Mexico.

Douglas Visitors Center: 345 16th St., Douglas, AZ 85607. **Phone:** (520) 417-7344.

Self-guiding tours: Maps detailing self-guiding historical tours of Douglas are available at the visitor center.

BEST WESTERN DOUGLAS INN & SUITES 520/364-5000

Hotel

AAA Benefit: Members save up to 15% and earn bonus points!

Address: 199 E 7th St 85607 **Location:** Jct SR 80, 0.6 mi s on Pan American Ave. **Facility:** 69 units. 3 stories, interior corridors. **Pool:** heated outdoor. **Activities:** hot tub, exercise room. **Guest Services:** coin laundry. **Featured Amenity: breakfast buffet.**

DRAGOON (F-5) pop. 209, elev. 4,615'

AMERIND MUSEUM AND RESEARCH CENTER, I-10, exit 318, 1 mi. s. on Dragoon Rd. to 2100 N. Amerind Rd., is an extension of the Amerind (an amalgamated name formed from the words American and Indian) Foundation's archeological research facility. Featured are artifacts, crafts, art and photographs documenting Native American peoples from Alaska to South America.

An art gallery contains works with Western themes by such well-known artists as Carl Oscar Borg, William Leigh and Frederic Remington as well as a variety of contemporary paintings and furnishings dating from the 17th century. **Time:** Allow 1 hour, 30 minutes minimum. **Hours:** Tues.-Sun. 10-4. Closed major holidays. **Cost:** $10; $9 (ages 62+ and college students with ID); $8 (ages 10-17). **Phone:** (520) 586-3666.

EAGAR pop. 4,885

BEST WESTERN SUNRISE INN 928/333-2540

Motel

AAA Benefit: Members save up to 15% and earn bonus points!

Address: 128 N Main St 85925 **Location:** Jct SR 260, just n; jct US 60, 1.5 mi s. **Facility:** 41 units. 2 stories (no elevator), exterior corridors. **Activities:** sauna, exercise room. **Guest Services:** coin laundry. **Featured Amenity: continental breakfast.** *(See ad this page.)*

/ SOME UNITS

EHRENBERG pop. 1,470

BEST WESTERN DESERT OASIS 928/923-9711

Hotel

AAA Benefit: Members save up to 15% and earn bonus points!

Address: Exit 1 S Frontage Rd 85334 **Location:** I-10 exit 1, just s; 0.5 mi e of Colorado River. Located at Flying J Travel Plaza. **Facility:** 81 units. 2 stories (no elevator), interior corridors. **Pool:** outdoor. **Activities:** picnic facilities, exercise room. **Guest Services:** coin laundry. **Featured Amenity: full hot breakfast.**

   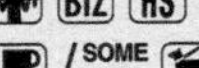

/ SOME UNITS

FLAGSTAFF (C-4) pop. 65,870, elev. 6,905'

• Hotels p. 46 • Restaurants p. 48
• Hotels & Restaurants map & index p. 44
• Part of Grand Canyon National Park area — see map p. 57

Flagstaff rests on the Colorado Plateau under the gaze of the San Francisco Peaks amid ponderosa pine forests, high deserts and lakes. Dusted with snow in winter and wildflowers in summer, the mountains provide a scenic backdrop for what was once a mere rest stop.

The town was established in 1881. The name Flagstaff is believed to refer to a ponderosa pine tree that was stripped of its branches and used as a flagstaff by members of an exploration party during Fourth of July celebrations in 1876. The flagstaff, visible from afar, remained in place to serve as a landmark for wagon trains bound for California; transients knew that they would find a good place to camp when they spotted it.

Shepherd Thomas F. McMillan, said to be the town's first permanent resident, deemed the land perfect for raising sheep when he arrived in 1876. Early industry revolved around timber, sheep and cattle, but when the Atlantic and Pacific Railway Co. (now the Santa Fe) decided to merge with the Southern Pacific line, settlers again put out their welcome mats, providing water and supplies to the railroad crews. The railroad reached Flagstaff in 1882. The Flagstaff Railroad Depot, on SR 66 between S. San Francisco and S. Beaver streets, opened in 1926. Impressive with its

(See map & index p. 44.)

Revival Tudor style, it now houses the Flagstaff Visitor Center and an Amtrak station.

Downtown Flagstaff, which grew up around the railroad depot, contains many historic buildings dating from the late 1800s to early 1900s. Plaques and seasonal tours give insight to buildings' former functions.

The Northern Arizona Normal School, established in 1899, was renamed Northern Arizona University in 1966. The university contributes to Flagstaff's college town feel. NAU's north campus, which encompasses 140 acres, boasts numerous restored buildings constructed 1894-1935 of local sandstone. This area reputedly contains the largest number of restored sandstone buildings in the Southwest.

In the 1920s, Route 66 brought travelers through town; they stayed briefly yet contributed to the economy. Money from tourism helped Flagstaff become an incorporated city in 1928, and the route continues to attract visitors.

Another popular drive is the 54-mile scenic stretch of SR 89A that begins in Flagstaff, winds its way south through Oak Creek Canyon and ends in Jerome. (The steep, narrow road is not recommended for vehicles pulling trailers more than 40 feet long.)

The city remains a good home base for many day trips. Within the boundaries of Coconino County, the second largest in the country, visitors will find Grand Canyon National Park *(see place listing p. 57)*, Meteor Crater *(see attraction listing p. 227)*, Oak Creek Canyon *(see Sedona p. 161)*, Sunset Crater Volcano National Monument *(see place listing p. 175)*, Walnut Canyon National Monument *(see place listing p. 221)*, and Wupatki National Monument *(see place listing p. 227)*. The landscape varies from deep green woodlands to rugged, rocky escarpments and provides for nearly every recreational pursuit, from skiing and hiking to camping, hunting and fishing.

Flagstaff Convention & Visitors Bureau: 323 W. Aspen Ave., Flagstaff, AZ 86001. **Phone:** (928) 213-2910 or (800) 217-2367.

Flagstaff Visitor Center: 1 E. Rte. 66, Historic Train Station, Flagstaff, AZ 86001. **Phone:** (928) 213-2951 or (800) 379-0065.

Self-guiding tours: Maps outlining walking tours of Flagstaff's historic downtown area, Route 66 and supposedly haunted locations are available at the Flagstaff Visitor Center in the historic train station on Route 66. The center also sells Grand Canyon Park entry passes.

Shopping: Flagstaff Mall & The Marketplace, 6 miles east at 4650 SR 89N, has more than 60 stores, including Dillard's, JCPenney and Sears. Flagstaff's downtown historic district also offers shopping opportunities.

LOWELL OBSERVATORY is 1 mi. w. of downtown via Santa Fe Ave. to 1400 W. Mars Hill Rd., following signs. The observatory was founded in 1894 by Percival Lowell. Discoveries made here include Lowell's observations about the planet Mars, the basis for the theory of the expanding universe and the discovery of Pluto in 1930. The Putnam Collection Center houses equipment and archives. Traveling exhibits change every few months.

Daytime tours explore the Rotunda Museum and the Pluto Discovery Telescope, the instrument used when Pluto was first identified here in 1930. At night, you can use the observatory's telescopes to catch a glimpse of planets, the moon and other celestial wonders. Research continues at the observatory with the operation of seven modern telescopes, including the Discovery Channel Telescope.

Hours: Mon.-Sat. 10-10, Sun. 10-5 (also Sun. before Mon. holidays 5-10). Closed major holidays. **Cost:** $15; $14 (ages 65+ and military and college students with ID); $8 (ages 5-17). **Phone:** (928) 774-3358 or (928) 255-5059. GT

NORTHERN ARIZONA UNIVERSITY ART MUSEUM is at 620 S. Knoles Dr., building No. 10 on campus. Five galleries, two with permanent collections and three with changing exhibits, feature oil paintings on canvas, sculptures, contemporary art and American antiques. **Time:** Allow 30 minutes minimum. **Hours:** Tues.-Sat. noon-5. Closed university holidays; phone ahead. **Cost:** Donations. **Phone:** (928) 523-3471.

(See map & index p. 44.)

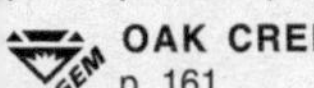

OAK CREEK CANYON—see Sedona p. 161.

RECREATIONAL ACTIVITIES

Skiing

- **Arizona Snowbowl,** in the San Francisco Peaks, is 7 mi. n. on Fort Valley Rd. (US 180), then 7 mi. n. on Snowbowl Rd. Other activities are offered. **Hours:** Skiing is available daily 9-4, late Nov.-early Apr. Chairlift daily 10-4, Memorial Day-Labor Day; Fri.-Sun. and holidays 10-4, day after Labor Day to mid-Oct. **Phone:** (928) 779-1951.
- **Flagstaff Nordic Village,** in the San Francisco Peaks, is on US 180 at mile marker 232. Other activities are offered. **Hours:** Trails open daily 24 hours (weather permitting). Store open Fri.-Sun. 9-2. Phone ahead to confirm schedule. **Phone:** (928) 220-0550.
- **Wing Mountain Snow Play Area,** in the San Francisco Peaks, is on US 180 n. to mile marker 226, then left on FR 222B. Other activities are offered. **Hours:** Daily 9-4, Dec.-Mar. (weather permitting). Phone ahead to confirm schedule. **Phone:** (602) 923-3555.

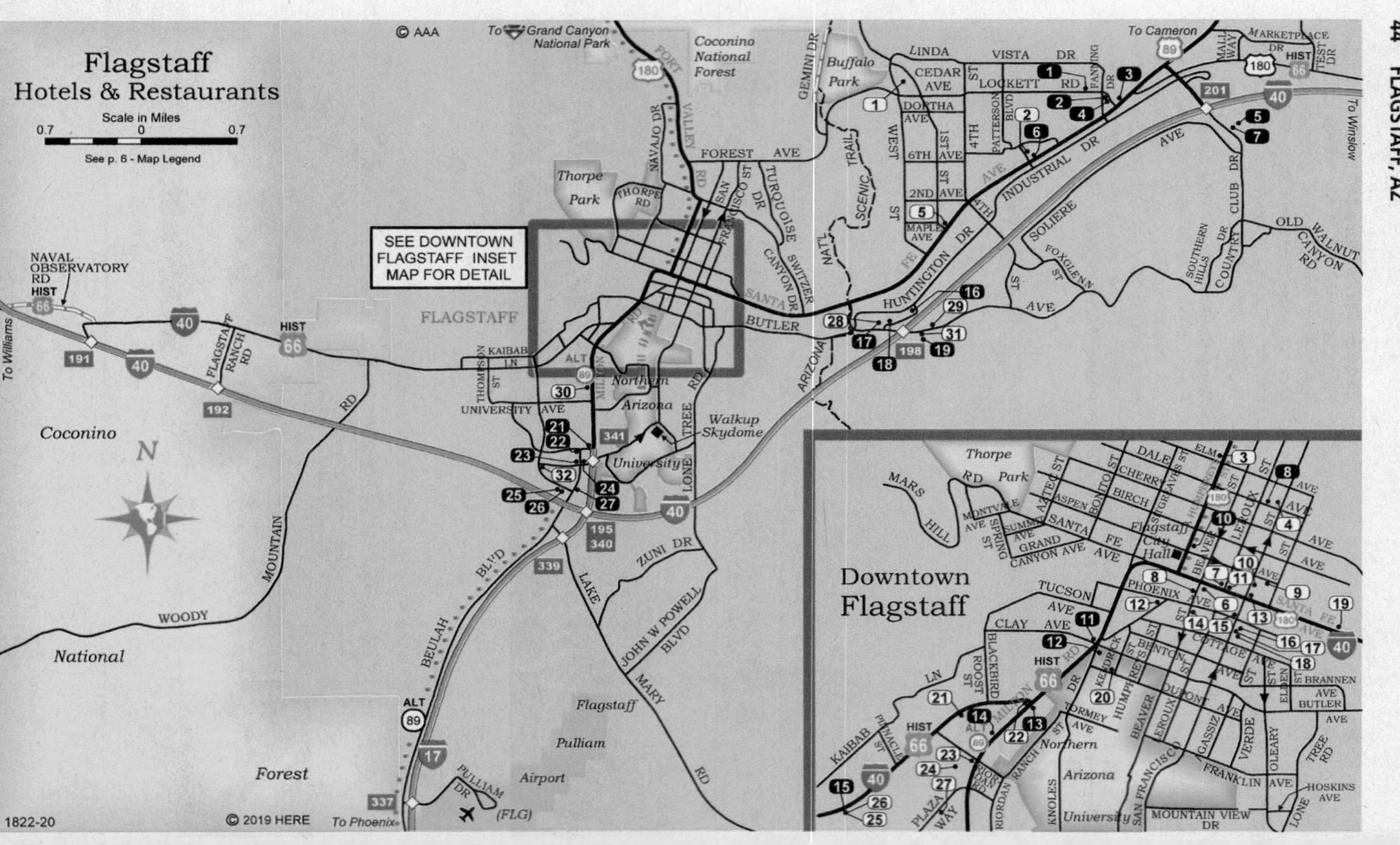
Flagstaff
Hotels & Restaurants
Scale in Miles
0.7 0 0.7
See p. 6 - Map Legend
SEE DOWNTOWN FLAGSTAFF INSET MAP FOR DETAIL
Downtown Flagstaff
© AAA
© 2019 HERE
1822-20
To Grand Canyon National Park
To Cameron
To Winslow
To Williams
To Phoenix
Coconino National Forest
Buffalo Park
Thorpe Park
FLAGSTAFF
Northern Arizona University
Walkup Skydome
Flagstaff Pulliam Airport (FLG)
Coconino
National
Forest
NAVAL OBSERVATORY RD
FLAGSTAFF RANCH RD
WOODY MOUNTAIN RD
BEULAH BLVD
LAKE MARY RD
JOHN W POWELL BLVD
ZUNI DR
LONE TREE RD
PULLIAM DR
UNIVERSITY AVE
THOMPSON ST
KAIBAB LN
MILTON RD
BUTLER AVE
HUNTINGTON DR
INDUSTRIAL DR
SANTA FE AVE
FOREST AVE
FORT VALLEY RD
NAVAJO DR
THORPE RD
SAN FRANCISCO ST
TURQUOISE DR
SWITZER CANYON DR
GEMINI DR
ARIZONA NAT'L SCENIC TRAIL
LINDA VISTA DR
CEDAR AVE
LOCKETT RD
FANNING DR
DORTHA AVE
PATTERSON BLVD
WEST ST
MAPLE AVE
SOLIERE AVE
FOXGLENN ST
SOUTHERN HILLS DR
COUNTRY CLUB DR
OLD WALNUT CANYON RD
MALL WAY
MARKETPLACE DR
TEST DR
MARS HILL RD
MONTVALE AVE
SPRING ST
SUMMIT AVE
GRAND CANYON AVE
AZTEC ST
ASPEN AVE
BONITO ST
CHERRY AVE
BIRCH AVE
DALE AVE
ELM
SITGREAVES ST
HUMPHREYS ST
LEROUX ST
BEAVER ST
Flagstaff City Hall
PHOENIX AVE
TUCSON AVE
CLAY AVE
BLACKBIRD ROOST ST
KENDRICK ST
BENTON AVE
COTTAGE AVE
DUPONT AVE
AGASSIZ ST
VERDE ST
OLEARY ST
ELDEN ST
BRANNEN AVE
BUTLER AVE
TREE RD
HOSKINS AVE
LONE
FRANKLIN AVE
MOUNTAIN VIEW DR
SAN FRANCISCO
KNOLES
RIORDAN RANCH ST
RIORDAN RD
TORMEY AVE
PLAZA WAY
PINNACLE ST
KAIBAB LN

Flagstaff

This index helps you "spot" where approved hotels and restaurants are located on the corresponding detailed maps. Restaurant price range is a combination of lunch and/or dinner. Turn to the listing page for more information and consult display ads for special promotions.

For more details, rates and reservations: AAA.com/travelguides/hotels

FLAGSTAFF

Map Page	Hotels	Diamond Rated	Member Savings	Page
1 p. 44	Starlight Pines, A Bed & Breakfast	♦♦♦		48
2 p. 44	Country Inn & Suites by Radisson, Flagstaff	♦♦		47
3 p. 44	**Super 8 Flagstaff**	♦♦	✔	48
4 p. 44	**Days Inn & Suites**	♦♦	✔	47
5 p. 44	Fairfield Inn & Suites by Marriott Flagstaff East	♦♦♦	✔	47
6 p. 44	**Best Western Pony Soldier Inn & Suites**	♦♦	✔	46
7 p. 44	Hampton Inn & Suites Flagstaff East	♦♦♦	✔	47
8 p. 44	The Inn at 410 Bed & Breakfast	♦♦♦		48
10 p. 44	Residence Inn by Marriott Flagstaff	♦♦♦	✔	48
11 p. 44	**Highland Country Inn**	♦	✔	47
12 p. 44	Drury Inn & Suites-Flagstaff	♦♦♦		47
13 p. 44	Embassy Suites by Hilton Flagstaff	♦♦♦	✔	47
14 p. 44	**Budget Inn**	♦	✔	46
15 p. 44	**DoubleTree by Hilton Flagstaff**	♦♦♦	✔	47
16 p. 44	**Comfort Inn Lucky Lane**	♦♦	✔	47
17 p. 44	**Days Hotel Flagstaff**	♦♦	✔	47
18 p. 44	Holiday Inn Express	♦♦♦		47
19 p. 44	**Little America Hotel**	♦♦♦♦	✔	48
21 p. 44	**Hilton Garden Inn**	♦♦♦	✔	47
22 p. 44	Comfort Inn I-17/I-40	♦♦♦		47
23 p. 44	SpringHill Suites by Marriott	♦♦♦	✔	48
24 p. 44	Hampton Inn & Suites	♦♦	✔	47
25 p. 44	**GreenTree Inn Flagstaff**	♦♦	✔	47
26 p. 44	Sleep Inn Flagstaff	♦♦		48
27 p. 44	Courtyard by Marriott-Flagstaff	♦♦♦	✔	47

Map Page	Restaurants	Diamond Rated	Cuisine	Price Range	Page
1 p. 44	**Brandy's Restaurant & Bakery**	♦♦	Breakfast Sandwiches	$6-$12	48
2 p. 44	Mamma Luisa	♦♦	Italian	$12-$21	49
3 p. 44	**Josephine's Modern American Bistro**	♦♦	American	$11-$33	49
4 p. 44	Brix Restaurant & Wine Bar	♦♦♦	American	$15-$36	48
5 p. 44	Salsa Brava	♦♦	Mexican	$7-$17	49
6 p. 44	La Bellavia	♦	Breakfast Sandwiches	$5-$12	49

Map Page	Restaurants (cont'd)	Diamond Rated	Cuisine	Price Range	Page
7 p. 44	The McMillan Bar & Kitchen	◆◆	American	$10-$27	49
8 p. 44	Beaver Street Brewery	◆◆	American	$9-$25	48
9 p. 44	Swaddee Authentic Thai Cuisine	◆◆	Thai	$11-$16	49
10 p. 44	Criollo Latin Kitchen	◆◆	Latin American	$13-$28	49
11 p. 44	**Karma Sushi Bar Grill**	◆◆	Japanese Sushi	$9-$26	49
12 p. 44	Pizzicletta	◆◆	Italian Pizza	$11-$16	49
13 p. 44	Majerle's Sports Grill	◆◆	American	$10-$14	49
14 p. 44	Macy's European Coffee House & Bakery	◆	Coffee/Tea Vegetarian	$7-$8	49
15 p. 44	Lumberyard Brewing Company	◆◆	American	$8-$18	49
16 p. 44	Cornish Pasty Co	◆◆	English Specialty	$10-$14	48
17 p. 44	Dara Thai Restaurant	◆◆	Thai	$7-$14	49
18 p. 44	Tinderbox Kitchen	◆◆◆	New American	$16-$34	49
19 p. 44	Kachina Restaurant	◆	Mexican	$7-$26	49
20 p. 44	**1899 Bar & Grill**	◆◆◆	American	$10-$22	48
21 p. 44	Galaxy Diner	◆◆	Comfort Food	$8-$12	49
22 p. 44	Bun Huggers	◆	American	$5-$8	48
23 p. 44	Little Thai Kitchen	◆	Thai	$6-$14	49
24 p. 44	YogurtU	◆	Desserts	$5-$10	49
25 p. 44	**Woodlands Restaurant**	◆◆	American	$7-$24	49
26 p. 44	**Sakura Restaurant**	◆◆	Japanese	$10-$29	49
27 p. 44	Hiro's Sushi Bar & Japanese Restaurant	◆◆	Japanese Sushi	$10-$25	49
28 p. 44	**The Northern Pines Restaurant**	◆◆	American	$10-$28	49
29 p. 44	**Black Bart's Steak House & Musical Revue**	◆◆	Steak	$17-$52	48
30 p. 44	Hickory's Smokehouse BBQ	◆	Barbecue	$9-$22	49
31 p. 44	Silver Pine Restaurant and Bar	◆◆	American	$12-$30	49
32 p. 44	Delhi Palace	◆◆	Indian	$9-$20	49

BEST WESTERN PONY SOLDIER INN & SUITES

928/526-2388 6

Hotel

AAA Benefit: Members save up to 15% and earn bonus points!

Address: 3030 E Route 66 86004 **Location:** I-40 exit 201, just n, then 1 mi w. Next to railroad tracks. **Facility:** 75 units, some two bedrooms. 2 stories (no elevator), interior corridors. **Pool:** heated indoor. **Activities:** hot tub. **Featured Amenity: full hot breakfast.**

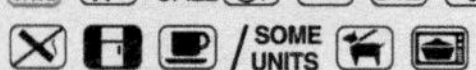

BUDGET INN

928/774-5038 14

Motel

Address: 913 S Milton Rd 86001 **Location:** I-40 exit 195, 1.2 mi n. **Facility:** 38 units. 2 stories (no elevator), exterior corridors.

(See map & index p. 44.)

COMFORT INN I-17/I-40 928/774-2225 22

Hotel. **Address:** 2355 S Beulah Blvd 86001

COMFORT INN LUCKY LANE 928/774-7701 16

Hotel

Address: 2480 E Lucky Ln 86004 **Location:** I-40 exit 198 (Butler Ave), just n, then just e. **Facility:** 66 units. 3 stories, interior corridors. **Pool:** heated indoor. **Activities:** sauna, hot tub, limited exercise equipment. **Guest Services:** coin laundry. **Featured Amenity: breakfast buffet.**

SAVE / SOME UNITS

COUNTRY INN & SUITES BY RADISSON, FLAGSTAFF 928/526-1878 2

Hotel. **Address:** 3501 E Lockett Rd 86004

COURTYARD BY MARRIOTT-FLAGSTAFF 928/774-5800 27

SAVE Hotel. **Address:** 2650 S Beulah Blvd 86001

AAA Benefit: Members save 5% or more!

DAYS HOTEL FLAGSTAFF 928/779-6944 17

Hotel

Address: 2200 E Butler Ave 86004 **Location:** I-40 exit 198 (Butler Ave), just n. **Facility:** 100 units. 3 stories, interior corridors. **Amenities:** safes. **Dining:** The Northern Pines Restaurant, see separate listing. **Pool:** heated indoor. **Activities:** sauna, hot tub, exercise room. **Guest Services:** coin laundry.

SAVE BIZ / SOME UNITS

DAYS INN & SUITES 928/527-1477 4

Hotel

Address: 3601 E Lockett Rd 86004 **Location:** I-40 exit 201, 0.5 mi w on I-40 business loop, then just n on Fanning Dr. **Facility:** 54 units. 3 stories, interior corridors. **Pool:** heated indoor. **Activities:** hot tub. **Guest Services:** coin laundry. **Featured Amenity: full hot breakfast.**

SAVE BIZ / SOME UNITS

DOUBLETREE BY HILTON FLAGSTAFF 928/773-8888 15

Hotel

AAA Benefit: Members save up to 15%!

Address: 1175 W Route 66 86001 **Location:** I-40 exit 195, 1.5 mi n on SR 89A (Milton Rd), then 0.5 mi w. **Facility:** 183 units. 3-4 stories, interior corridors. **Terms:** check-in 4 pm. **Amenities:** safes. **Dining:** Sakura Restaurant, Woodlands Restaurant, see separate listings. **Pool:** heated outdoor. **Activities:** sauna, hot tub, exercise room. **Guest Services:** valet and coin laundry, area transportation.

DRURY INN & SUITES-FLAGSTAFF 928/773-4900 12

Hotel. **Address:** 300 S Milton Rd 86001

EMBASSY SUITES BY HILTON FLAGSTAFF 928/774-4333 13

SAVE Hotel. **Address:** 706 S Milton Rd 86001

AAA Benefit: Members save up to 15%!

FAIRFIELD INN & SUITES BY MARRIOTT FLAGSTAFF EAST 928/707-7800 5

SAVE Hotel. **Address:** 1000 N Country Club Dr 86004

AAA Benefit: Members save 5% or more!

GREENTREE INN FLAGSTAFF 928/773-1111 25

Hotel

Address: 2755 S Woodlands Village Blvd 86001 **Location:** I-40 exit 195, just n to Forest Meadows St, w to Beulah Blvd, just s, then w. **Facility:** 90 units. 2 stories (no elevator), exterior corridors. *Bath:* shower only. **Pool:** heated outdoor. **Activities:** hot tub. **Featured Amenity: breakfast buffet.**

SAVE BIZ / SOME UNITS

HAMPTON INN & SUITES 928/913-0900 24

SAVE Hotel. **Address:** 2400 S Beulah Blvd 86001

AAA Benefit: Members save up to 15%!

HAMPTON INN & SUITES FLAGSTAFF EAST 928/433-1234 7

SAVE Hotel. **Address:** 990 N Country Club Dr 86004

AAA Benefit: Members save up to 15%!

HIGHLAND COUNTRY INN 928/774-5041 11

Motel

Address: 223 S Milton Rd 86001 **Location:** I-40 exit 195, 1.8 mi n on SR 89A (Milton Rd). **Facility:** 42 units. 2 stories (no elevator), exterior corridors. **Guest Services:** coin laundry.

SAVE

HILTON GARDEN INN 928/226-8888 21

Hotel

AAA Benefit: Members save up to 15%!

Address: 350 W Forest Meadows St 86001 **Location:** I-40 exit 195, 0.5 mi n on SR 89A (Milton Rd), then just w. **Facility:** 90 units. 3 stories, interior corridors. **Pool:** heated indoor. **Activities:** hot tub, exercise room. **Guest Services:** valet and coin laundry, area transportation.

SAVE CALL BIZ HS

HOLIDAY INN EXPRESS 928/714-1000 18

Hotel. **Address:** 2320 E Lucky Ln 86004

(See map & index p. 44.)

THE INN AT 410 BED & BREAKFAST 928/774-0088 8

Historic Bed & Breakfast. **Address:** 410 N Leroux St 86001

LITTLE AMERICA HOTEL 928/779-7900 19

Hotel

Address: 2515 E Butler Ave 86004 **Location:** I-40 exit 198 (Butler Ave), just s. **Facility:** This hotel has a convenient location along the interstate and offers many large rooms and bathrooms. The property is surrounded by lawns and pine forest for added tranquility. 247 units, some two bedrooms and kitchens. 2 stories (no elevator), interior corridors. **Terms:** check-in 4 pm. **Amenities:** safes. **Dining:** Silver Pine Restaurant and Bar, see separate listing. **Pool:** heated outdoor. **Activities:** hot tub, playground, trails, exercise room. **Guest Services:** valet laundry, area transportation.

RESIDENCE INN BY MARRIOTT FLAGSTAFF 928/440-5499 10

SAVE Extended Stay Hotel. **Address:** 100 N Humphreys St 86001

AAA Benefit: Members save 5% or more!

SLEEP INN FLAGSTAFF 928/556-3000 26

Motel. **Address:** 2765 S Woodlands Village Blvd 86001

SPRINGHILL SUITES BY MARRIOTT 928/774-8042 23

SAVE Contemporary Hotel. **Address:** 2455 S Beulah Blvd 86001

AAA Benefit: Members save 5% or more!

STARLIGHT PINES, A BED & BREAKFAST 928/527-1912 1

Bed & Breakfast. **Address:** 3380 E Lockett Rd 86004

SUPER 8 FLAGSTAFF 928/526-0818 3

Hotel

Address: 3725 N Kaspar Dr 86004 **Location:** I-40 exit 201, just n, 0.5 mi w on I-40 business loop, then just n. Located on a busy commercial street. **Facility:** 89 units. 2 stories (no elevator), interior corridors. **Guest Services:** coin laundry. **Featured Amenity: continental breakfast.**

SOME UNITS

TWIN ARROWS NAVAJO CASINO RESORT 928/856-7200

Contemporary Resort Hotel

Address: 22181 Resort Blvd 86004 **Location:** I-40 exit 219, 0.5 mi ne. **Facility:** Influenced by Navajo culture, this desert hotel is bright and vibrant. Large rooms offer elegant amenities, including online streaming through the televisions. A trucker's lounge is available. 199 units. 5 stories, interior corridors. **Parking:** on-site and valet. **Terms:** check-in 4 pm. **Amenities:** safes. **Dining:** 5 restaurants, entertainment. **Pool:** heated indoor. **Activities:** hot tub, game room, exercise room. **Guest Services:** area transportation.

SAVE CALL BIZ SOME UNITS

WHERE TO EAT

1899 BAR & GRILL 928/523-1899 20

American Fine Dining $10-$22

AAA Inspector Notes: Named after the opening year of the Arizona College, this large and impressive dining room gives a visual surprise as each guest enters. The food goes right along with the contemporary decor by offering such vibrant items as summer salads, filet mignon, red trout and shrimp scampi. Check the schedule for entertainment some evenings. **Features:** full bar, patio dining, happy hour. **Address:** 307 W Dupont Ave 86001 **Location:** I-40 exit 195, 1.8 mi n on SR 89A (Milton Rd), then just e.

L D CALL

BEAVER STREET BREWERY 928/779-0079 8

American. Brewpub. **Address:** 11 S Beaver St, Suite 1 86001

BLACK BART'S STEAK HOUSE & MUSICAL REVUE 928/779-3142 29

Steak Dinner Theatre $17-$52

AAA Inspector Notes: A musical revue provides nightly entertainment in this rustic, casual restaurant. Oak-broiled steak, seafood, chicken and prime rib delight the palate. Located adjacent to an RV park, the freeway and a lodging, Black Bart's is convenient for those looking for diners. Full service is provided by an attentive staff casually attired fitting the theme of the restaurant. The staff doubles as entertainers providing the nightly musical revue. **Features:** full bar. **Reservations:** suggested, weekends. **Address:** 2760 E Butler Ave 86004 **Location:** I-40 exit 198 (Butler Ave), just se. D

BRANDY'S RESTAURANT & BAKERY 928/779-2187 1

Breakfast Sandwiches Casual Dining $6-$12

AAA Inspector Notes: Operating since 1993, this popular establishment serves breakfast dishes including 10 variations of eggs Benedict, 3-egg omelets and made-from-scratch pancakes. Lunch stand-outs are albacore tuna melts, Reubens, burgers, grilled salmon and grilled Portobello sandwiches. **Features:** beer & wine. **Address:** 1500 E Cedar Ave, Suite 40 86004 **Location:** Route 66, 0.8 mi n on 4th St, then just w; in strip mall.

B L

BRIX RESTAURANT & WINE BAR 928/213-1021 4

American. Fine Dining. **Address:** 413 N San Francisco St 86001

BUN HUGGERS 928/779-3743 22

American. Quick Serve. **Address:** 901 S Milton Rd 86001

CORNISH PASTY CO 928/440-5196 16

English Specialty. Gastropub. **Address:** 26 S San Francisco St 86001

(See map & index p. 44.)

CRIOLLO LATIN KITCHEN 928/774-0541 (10)

Latin American. Casual Dining. **Address:** 16 N San Francisco St 86001

DARA THAI RESTAURANT 928/774-8390 (17)

Thai. Casual Dining. **Address:** 14 S San Francisco St 86001

DELHI PALACE 928/556-0019 (32)

Indian. Casual Dining. **Address:** 2700 S Woodlands Village Blvd 86001

GALAXY DINER 928/774-2466 (21)

Comfort Food. Casual Dining. **Address:** 931 W Route 66 86001

HICKORY'S SMOKEHOUSE BBQ 928/774-2278 (30)

Barbecue. Quick Serve. **Address:** 1435 S Milton Rd 86001

HIRO'S SUSHI BAR & JAPANESE RESTAURANT 928/226-8030 (27)

Japanese Sushi. Casual Dining. **Address:** 1312 S Plaza Way 86001

JOSEPHINE'S MODERN AMERICAN BISTRO 928/779-3400 (3)

American Casual Dining
$11-$33

AAA Inspector Notes: This renovated historic home provides a casually comfortable setting. The eclectic menu is a showcase for steak, seafood, chicken, lamb and pork dishes prepared with European, Asian, Pan American and Southwestern influences. **Features:** full bar, patio dining, Sunday brunch. **Reservations:** suggested. **Address:** 503 N Humphrey's St 86001 **Location:** Just n of jct Old Route 66. L D

KACHINA RESTAURANT 928/779-1944 (19)

Mexican. Casual Dining. **Address:** 522 E Route 66 86001

KARMA SUSHI BAR GRILL 928/774-6100 (11)

Japanese Sushi Casual Dining
$9-$26

AAA Inspector Notes: This downtown restaurant is popular for its specialty rolls. I really enjoyed the tuna poke appetizer and the albacore nigiri. The décor is fun and contemporary. **Features:** full bar, happy hour. **Address:** 6 E Route 66 86001 **Location:** Downtown. **Parking:** street only.

L D

LA BELLAVIA 928/774-8301 (6)

Breakfast Sandwiches. Casual Dining. **Address:** 18 S Beaver St 86001

LITTLE THAI KITCHEN 928/226-9422 (23)

Thai. Casual Dining. **Address:** 1051 S Milton Rd 86001

LUMBERYARD BREWING COMPANY 928/779-2739 (15)

American. Brewpub. **Address:** 5 S Francisco St 86001

MACY'S EUROPEAN COFFEE HOUSE & BAKERY 928/774-2243 (14)

Coffee/Tea Vegetarian. Quick Serve. **Address:** 14 S Beaver St 86001

MAJERLE'S SPORTS GRILL 928/774-6463 (13)

American. Casual Dining. **Address:** 102 E Route 66 86001

MAMMA LUISA 928/526-6809 (2)

Italian. Casual Dining. **Address:** 2710 N Steves Blvd 86004

THE MCMILLAN BAR & KITCHEN 928/774-3840 (7)

American. Gastropub. **Address:** 2 W Route 66 86001

THE NORTHERN PINES RESTAURANT 928/266-1929 (28)

American Casual Dining
$10-$28

AAA Inspector Notes: This inviting diner boasts several stack stone walls and tasty, traditional food. The casual and friendly staff members joke with the locals as they serve hearty items such as french toast, chicken-fried steak and even filet mignon. **Features:** full bar. **Address:** 2200 E Butler Ave 86004 **Location:** I-40 exit 198 (Butler Ave), just n; in Days Hotel Flagstaff.

B L D CALL

PIZZICLETTA 928/774-3242 (12)

Italian Pizza. Casual Dining. **Address:** 203 W Phoenix Ave 86001

SAKURA RESTAURANT 928/773-9118 (26)

Japanese Casual Dining
$10-$29

AAA Inspector Notes: Teppanyaki-style cooking is prepared in a traditional Japanese steakhouse atmosphere. A sushi bar also is offered. **Features:** full bar. **Address:** 1175 W Route 66 86001 **Location:** I-40 exit 195, 1.5 mi n on SR 89A (Milton Rd), then 0.5 mi w; in DoubleTree by Hilton Flagstaff. D

SALSA BRAVA 928/779-5293 (5)

Mexican. Casual Dining. **Address:** 2220 E Route 66 86004

SILVER PINE RESTAURANT AND BAR 928/779-7950 (31)

American. Casual Dining. **Address:** 2515 E Butler Ave 86004

SWADDEE AUTHENTIC THAI CUISINE 928/773-1122 (9)

Thai. Casual Dining. **Address:** 115 E Aspen Ave 86001

TINDERBOX KITCHEN 928/226-8400 (18)

New American. Casual Dining. **Address:** 34 S San Francisco St 86001

WOODLANDS RESTAURANT 928/773-9118 (25)

American Casual Dining
$7-$24

AAA Inspector Notes: This casual restaurant shares a kitchen with a Japanese restaurant. Although there are several Asian influences, the menu consists of mainly American cuisine such as basic steak cuts, salmon and halibut cakes. Great for a casual and relaxing meal. **Features:** full bar, Sunday brunch. **Address:** 1175 W Route 66 86001 **Location:** I-40 exit 195, 1.5 mi n on SR 89A (Milton Rd), then 0.5 mi w; in DoubleTree by Hilton Flagstaff.

B L D LATE CALL

YOGURTU 928/213-0777 (24)

Desserts. Quick Serve. **Address:** 1061 S Plaza Way 86001

FLORENCE (E-4) pop. 25,536, elev. 1,493'

• **Restaurants p. 50**

One of Arizona's oldest towns and the seat of Pinal County, Florence was founded by Levi Ruggles in 1866. Many historic homes and buildings perpetuate its frontier atmosphere.

Scenic desert highways from Florence include Kelvin Highway, a county road running east to Kelvin, and the Pinal Pioneer Parkway, a part of SR 79 leading southeast to Oracle Junction. Markers along the parkway identify desert wildlife.

RANCHO SONORA INN 520/868-8000

Country Inn. **Address:** 9198 N Hwy 79 85232

WHERE TO EAT

LB CANTINA 520/868-9981
Mexican. Casual Dining. **Address:** 695 S Main St 85132

FORT HUACHUCA (G-5)

In southeastern Arizona, Fort Huachuca (wa-CHOO-ka) was founded in 1877 to combat raids by Native Americans and outlaws. In 1954 the fort became the site of the Army Electronic Proving Ground. The 73,272-acre fort is headquarters of the U.S. Army Information Systems Command, the U.S. Army Intelligence Center and various other military organizations. The Old Post retains many of the original buildings constructed in the late 19th century.

Note: Each visitor must be a U.S. citizen and present photo identification to gain admittance to the fort. Foreign nationals must be escorted by public affairs personnel. Proof of vehicle registration and insurance must be provided for each vehicle entering the premises.

FORT HUACHUCA HISTORICAL MUSEUM is 3.6 mi. n.w. of Fort Huachuca's main gate in the Old Post area at Boyd and Grierson aves. Southwest history and the U.S. Army's activities in the area are depicted through exhibits in three buildings. **Hours:** Mon.-Thurs. 9:30-6:30, Fri. 9:30-4:30, Sat. 10-4. Closed major holidays. **Cost:** Donations. **Phone:** (520) 533-3638.

FOUNTAIN HILLS (I-4) pop. 22,489, elev. 1,600'

• Part of Phoenix area — see map p. 91

The community features rolling terrain as well as a number of recreation and vacation opportunities.

Fountain Hills Chamber of Commerce: 16837 E. Palisades Blvd., Fountain Hills, AZ 85268. **Phone:** (480) 837-1654.

RIVER OF TIME MUSEUM, adjacent to the library at 12901 N. La Montana Blvd., includes multimedia displays, historical and cultural programs, and activities educating visitors about the vital role of water in the Lower Verde River Valley. Conditions in this part of the High Sonoran Desert forced such inhabitants as Native American tribes and early ranchers to invent ways to control water. Visitors learn about ancient canals and more recent dam projects as well as the area's developments in housing. The museum also houses a scale model of Fort McDowell.

Time: Allow 30 minutes minimum. **Hours:** Tues.-Sat. 10-4, Oct.-Apr.; Tues.-Sat. 10-2, rest of year. Closed major holidays. Phone ahead to confirm schedule. **Cost:** $5; $4 (ages 65+); $3 (ages 6-12 and students with ID). **Phone:** (480) 837-2612. GT

INN AT EAGLE MOUNTAIN 480/816-3000

Hotel

Address: 9800 N Summer Hill Blvd 85268 **Location:** Loop 101 exit 41, 7.3 mi e on Shea Blvd, 0.3 mi e on Eagle Mountain Pkwy, then just w. **Facility:** 37 units. 2 stories (no elevator), exterior corridors. **Pool:** heated outdoor. **Activities:** hot tub, spa. **Guest Services:** coin laundry.

GANADO (B-6) pop. 1,210, elev. 6,386'

Ganado is one of the traditional meeting and trading centers of the Pueblo Colorado Valley. For centuries the valley has been a favored Native American gathering place, first for the Ancestral Puebloans and now for the Navajo. When John Hubbell bought the original trading post, he christened it Ganado to honor his Navajo friend Ganado Mucho and to distinguish the community from Pueblo, Colo.

Visitors to the reservation should be aware of certain travel restrictions; *see Good Facts To Know.*

HUBBELL TRADING POST NATIONAL HISTORIC SITE, .5 mi. w. via SR 264, is the oldest continuously operated trading post in the Navajo Nation. In 1878 John L. Hubbell bought the trading post and established himself as a leading trader. Hubbell's collection of Western art and Native American crafts is displayed in his furnished house on the site.

The trading post and the Hubbell home depict the role of trading in the history of the Southwest and the life of a trader's family. The trading post conducts business much as it did when the Hubbell family ran it. Members of the Navajo, Hopi, Zuni and other tribes sell and trade such crafts as handwoven rugs, jewelry, baskets and pottery. Ranger-led programs, guided house tours and weaving demonstrations are offered.

Time: Allow 1 hour minimum. **Hours:** Park daily 8-6, May-Oct.; 8-5, rest of year. **Note:** In summer the reservation observes daylight saving time, which is an hour later than outside the reservation. Closed Jan. 1, Thanksgiving and Christmas. **Cost:** Donations. Hubbell home tour free. **Phone:** (928) 755-3475. GT

GILA BEND (E-3) pop. 1,922, elev. 735'

Gila Bend is the center for a prosperous stock-raising and farming region in the Gila River Valley. The first farms were established in 1699 by Jesuit missionary Father Eusebio Francisco Kino. Just west of town is the site of the infamous 1851 Oatman Massacre, where all but three children of a westward-bound family were killed by Apaches. Exhibits about area history are displayed in a museum at the information center.

Gila Bend Tourist Information Center and Chamber of Commerce: 644 W. Pima, P.O. Box CC, Gila Bend, AZ 85337. **Phone:** (928) 420-1964.

BEST WESTERN SPACE AGE LODGE 928/683-2273

Motel

AAA Benefit: Members save up to 15% and earn bonus points!

Address: 401 E Pima St 85337 **Location:** Business Loop I-8; center. **Facility:** 41 units. 1 story, exterior corridors. **Dining:** Space Age Restaurant, see separate listing. **Pool:** outdoor. **Activities:** hot tub. **Featured Amenity: full hot breakfast.**

SAVE / SOME UNITS

WHERE TO EAT

SPACE AGE RESTAURANT 928/683-2761

American Casual Dining
$5-$15

AAA Inspector Notes: Friendly servers dish up good food at this kitschy diner with a hard-to-miss spaceship design outside and a unique atmosphere inside. **Address:** 401 E Pima St 85337 **Location:** Business Loop I-8; center; in Best Western Space Age Lodge. B L D

GILBERT (J-4) pop. 208,453, elev. 1,237'

• **Hotels & Restaurants map & index p. 126**
• **Part of Phoenix area — see map p. 91**

THE RIPARIAN PRESERVE AT WATER RANCH is at 2757 E. Guadalupe Rd. The 110-acre preserve features interpretive exhibits, an observatory, a floating boardwalk, trails and children's play areas. A great spot for bird-watching, the area is home to more than 200 species. Visitors can also fish (with a license) and camp on the grounds.

Ramadas can be rented by the hour. **Time:** Allow 1 hour minimum. **Hours:** Preserve daily 5:30 a.m.-10 p.m. Fishing lake daily dawn-10 p.m. Phone for observatory hours. **Cost:** Free. Camping $30-$40. Phone for other activity fees. Campsites must be reserved. **Phone:** (480) 503-6234, or (480) 503-6200 for camping reservations.

HYATT PLACE PHOENIX/GILBERT 480/899-5900 (65)

Hotel

HYATT PLACE **AAA Benefit:** Members save up to 10%!

Address: 3275 S Market St 85297 **Location:** Loop 202 exit 42 (Val Vista Dr), just n, then just e. **Facility:** 127 units. 6 stories, interior corridors. **Pool:** heated outdoor. **Activities:** exercise room. **Guest Services:** valet laundry, area transportation. **Featured Amenity: breakfast buffet.**

SAVE CALL BIZ / SOME UNITS HS

PHOENIX/GILBERT HAMPTON INN & SUITES BY HILTON 480/543-1500 (66)

SAVE Hotel. **Address:** 3265 S Market St 85297

AAA Benefit: Members save up to 15%!

RESIDENCE INN BY MARRIOTT PHOENIX/GILBERT 480/699-4450 (64)

SAVE Extended Stay Hotel. **Address:** 3021 E Banner Gateway Dr 85234

AAA Benefit: Members save 5% or more!

WHERE TO EAT

CANTINA LAREDO 480/782-6777

Mexican. Casual Dining. **Address:** 2150 E Williams Field Rd 85295

CLEVER KOI 480/306-4237 (35)

Asian. Casual Dining. **Address:** 384 N Gilbert Rd 85234

THE FARMHOUSE RESTAURANT 480/926-0676 (40)

Breakfast Sandwiches. Casual Dining. **Address:** 228 N Gilbert Rd 85234

JOE'S REAL BBQ 480/503-3805 (38)

Barbecue Quick Serve
$8-$19

AAA Inspector Notes: Pecan-grilled meats, barbecue beans, root beer made on site and fresh desserts are favorites at this family joint. The quick counter service setting and optional patio seating lend to a fun atmosphere. **Features:** patio dining. **Address:** 301 N Gilbert Rd 85234 **Location:** US 60 (Superstition Frwy) exit 182 (Gilbert Rd), 2.1 mi s. **Parking:** street only. L D

LIBERTY MARKET 480/892-1900 (39)

American. Quick Serve. **Address:** 230 N Gilbert Rd 85234

NICO HEIRLOOM KITCHEN 480/584-4760 (36)

Italian. Casual Dining. **Address:** 366 N Gilbert Rd 85234

POSTINO WINECAFE 480/632-6363 (37)

Italian Small Plates. Casual Dining. **Address:** 302 N Gilbert Rd 85234

RANCHO DE TIA ROSA 480/396-8787 (34)

Mexican. Casual Dining. **Address:** 891 N Higley Rd 85234

GLEN CANYON NATIONAL RECREATION AREA (A-4)

Along the Colorado River from Grand Canyon National Park in far north-central Arizona to Canyonlands National Park in southeastern Utah, Glen Canyon National Recreation Area is home to one of the highest dams in the United States. Part of the Colorado River storage project, the Glen Canyon Dam generates hydroelectric power that is distributed to cities and industries throughout the West; the dam's main purpose is water storage.

Reaching out to hidden canyons, sandy coves and inlets, and winding through towering red cliffs, 186-mile-long Lake Powell presents an ever-changing array of scenery and such recreational opportunities as water skiing, boating and fishing. Amenities include campsites, marinas, and boat rentals and tours. A copy of fishing regulations can be obtained at the Carl Hayden Visitor Center, the Navajo Bridge Interpretive Center, the Bullfrog Visitor Center or at the administration offices in Page, Ariz.; phone (928) 608-6200.

The Bullfrog Visitor Center, at the Bullfrog Marina in Utah, exhibits the natural and cultural history of Glen Canyon and includes a life-size slot canyon model. The visitor center is open seasonally as staffing allows; phone (435) 684-7423. The Navajo Bridge Interpretive Center, on US 89A near Lees Ferry, Ariz., features a historic pedestrian bridge over the Colorado River at Marble Canyon and outdoor exhibits highlighting the early river crossings. The interpretive center is open daily 9-5, Apr.-Oct., as staffing allows; phone (928) 355-2319.

Exhibits in the Carl Hayden Visitor Center, next to US 89, Glen Canyon Dam and Glen Canyon Bridge in Page illustrate the construction of the dam and bridge and include a relief model of the canyon country. Guided tours of the dam are available throughout the year. The center is open daily 8-6, Memorial Day-Labor Day; 8-5, Mar. 1-day before Memorial Day; 8-4, rest of year. Closed Jan. 1, Thanksgiving and Christmas. Phone (928) 608-6200.

Ranger-led interpretive programs are offered Memorial Day through Labor Day; phone ahead or stop by the Carl Hayden Visitor Center for program times and locations.

Arrangements for boat tours on Lake Powell can be made at Wahweap Lodge and Marina; facilities, including public launching ramps, boat rentals, camping and boat and automobile fuel, are provided at Wahweap and at four other marinas on the lake. All facilities may not be available year-round. A boat ramp providing access to 15 miles of the Colorado River below Glen Canyon Dam is available at Lees Ferry, 5 miles north of Marble Canyon.

Boat excursions, which last from 4 to 6.5 hours, are available through Colorado River Discovery; phone (928) 645-9175 or (888) 522-6644. The tours

▼ See AAA listing p. 85 ▼

begin near the Glen Canyon Dam and conclude at Lees Ferry. One-day raft trips on the Colorado River below the dam can be arranged in Page. Half-day and full-day trips are available to Rainbow Bridge National Monument, Utah, which is about 50 miles from Wahweap. Trips on the San Juan River leave from Mexican Hat and Bluff, Utah.

Admission, valid for up to 7 days, is $30 (per private vehicle); $25 (per motorcycle); $15 (per person ages 16+ arriving by foot or bicycle). An annual pass is $55. An additional use fee of $30 is charged for one motorized water vessel and is valid for up to 7 days. Tours of the Glen Canyon Dam, departing from the Carl Hayden Visitor Center, are $5.

For further information contact the Superintendent, Glen Canyon National Recreation Area; phone (928) 608-6200. *See Recreation Areas Chart.*

GLENDALE (I-2) pop. 226,721, elev. 1,154'

- **Restaurants p. 55**
- **Hotels & Restaurants map & index p. 117**
- **Part of Phoenix area — see map p. 91**

Established in 1892, Glendale retains much of its turn-of-the-20th-century charm. A tree-lined town square, red brick sidewalks and gaslights form an appropriate setting for the abundance of boutique and antique shops around shady Murphy Park in the city's historic downtown. Cerreta Candy Company, about half a mile east of Murphy Park at 5345 W. Glendale Ave., provides behind-the-scenes guided tours of its candy- and chocolate-making operations; phone (623) 930-9000.

In early January, the Fiesta Bowl, one of the nation's largest college bowl games, is played at State Farm Stadium, which also is the home stadium for the National Football League's Arizona Cardinals. In early February, chocoholics flock to Murphy Park for the Glendale Chocolate Affaire, which features chocolate purveyors from across the country.

In a more modern vein, Glendale also is home to Thunderbird School of Global Management and the jet fighter wing at Luke Air Force Base, purportedly the world's largest F-16 training base. Major League Baseball's Los Angeles Dodgers and Chicago White Sox play their spring training games at Camelback Ranch-Glendale, while the Arizona Cardinals football and Arizona Coyotes hockey teams call the city home.

During the holiday season, Glendale Glitters jazzes up downtown in festive multicolored lights.

Glendale Visitor Center: 5800 W. Glenn Dr., Suite 140, Glendale, AZ 85301. **Phone:** (623) 930-4500 or (877) 800-2601.

Shopping: Known as the Antique Capital of Arizona, more than 90 antique stores, specialty shops and restaurants are concentrated around Glendale's town square, Murphy Park, at the intersection of Glendale and 58th avenues. Old Towne Glendale and the Historic Catlin Court Shops District specialize in arts, crafts, furniture, dolls, jewelry, period clothing and Western memorabilia. Arrowhead Towne Center contains more than 170 stores, including Dillard's and JCPenney. More than 90 stores draw deal-seekers to SAVE Tanger Outlets Westgate, off Loop 101 at Glendale Avenue exit.

SAHUARO RANCH PARK HISTORIC AREA is 2.5 mi. n. of Glendale Ave. to 9802 N. 59th Ave.; or take I-10 exit 138, then go n. 7.6 mi. on N. 59th Ave. Seventeen acres of a model fruit and animal farm developed by William Henry Bartlett in 1885 feature 13 historic structures, including an adobe house, a foreman's house, a barnyard, the main house and a fruit packing shed. A lavish rose garden planted in 1890, several citrus groves and free-roaming peacocks enhance the fenced grounds.

Time: Allow 1 hour minimum. **Hours:** Grounds daily 6 a.m.-dusk. Phone for guided tour schedule. Closed major holidays. Phone ahead to confirm schedule. **Cost:** Grounds free. Tours by donation. Admission is charged for some special events. **Phone:** (623) 930-4200. GT

SAVE **SIX FLAGS HURRICANE HARBOR PHOENIX,** 4243 W. Pinnacle Peak Rd., is a 30-plus-acre water park featuring more than 30 attractions. Slides include the Bahama Blaster and the high-speed Anaconda raft ride as well as the Tornado, which catapults guests through a swirling 45-foot tunnel. Hurricane Bay is a 700,000-gallon wave pool. A children's water park features miniature versions of the park's most popular attractions for youngsters.

Changing rooms and showers are on the premises; lockers, cabanas and tubes can be rented. **Hours:** Open mid-May to mid-Oct. Times and operating days vary; phone ahead to confirm schedule. **Cost:** $45.99; $35.99 (ages 65+ and under 42 inches tall); free (ages 0-2). Ticket discounts are available online. **Parking:** $15. **Phone:** (623) 201-2000.

COMFORT INN & SUITES AT TALAVI 602/896-8900 14

Hotel. **Address:** 5511 W Bell Rd 85308

COMFORT SUITES STATE FARM STADIUM AREA 623/271-9005 22

Hotel. **Address:** 9824 W Camelback Rd 85305

HAMPTON INN & SUITES BY HILTON GLENDALE/WESTGATE 623/271-7771 20

Hotel

Hampton by HILTON

AAA Benefit: Members save up to 15%!

Address: 6630 N 95th Ave 85305 **Location:** SR 101 exit 7 (Glendale Ave), just e, then 0.4 mi s. **Facility:** 149 units. 4 stories, interior corridors. **Pool:** heated outdoor. **Activities:** hot tub, exercise room. **Guest Services:** complimentary and valet laundry, area transportation.

(See map & index p. 117.)

HOLIDAY INN EXPRESS & SUITES PHOENIX/GLENDALE 623/939-8888 **18**

Hotel

Address: 9310 W Cabela Dr 85305 **Location:** SR 101 exit 7 (Glendale Ave), 0.6 mi e to N Zanjero Blvd, then just n. **Facility:** 96 units. 3 stories, interior corridors. **Pool:** heated outdoor. **Activities:** hot tub, picnic facilities, exercise room. **Guest Services:** valet laundry, area transportation. **Featured Amenity: breakfast buffet.**

SAVE BIZ HS / SOME UNITS

▼ See AAA listing p. 77 ▼

HOME2 SUITES BY HILTON PHOENIX GLENDALE WESTGATE 623/877-4600 **21**

Extended Stay Contemporary Hotel

AAA Benefit: Members save up to 15%!

Address: 6620 N 95th Ave 85305 **Location:** SR 101 exit 7 (Glendale Ave), just e, then 0.4 mi s; adjacent to University of Phoenix Stadium. **Facility:** 127 units. 4 stories, interior corridors. **Pool:** heated outdoor. **Activities:** hot tub, game room, picnic facilities, exercise room. **Guest Services:** complimentary and valet laundry, area transportation. **Featured Amenity: continental breakfast.**

RENAISSANCE GLENDALE HOTEL & SPA 623/937-3700 **19**

SAVE Hotel. **Address:** 9495 W Coyotes Blvd 85305

AAA Benefit: Members save 5% or more!

RESIDENCE INN BY MARRIOTT PHOENIX GLENDALE SPORTS & ENTERTAINMENT DISTRICT 623/772-8900 **15**

SAVE Extended Stay Hotel. **Address:** 7350 W Zanjero Blvd 85305

AAA Benefit: Members save 5% or more!

SPRINGHILL SUITES BY MARRIOTT PHOENIX GLENDALE/PEORIA 623/878-6666 **13**

Hotel

SPRINGHILL SUITES MARRIOTT

AAA Benefit: Members save 5% or more!

Address: 7810 W Bell Rd 85308 **Location:** SR 101 exit 14 (Bell Rd), 0.3 mi e. Adjacent to Arrowhead Towne Center. **Facility:** 88 units. 4 stories, interior corridors. **Pool:** heated outdoor. **Activities:** hot tub, exercise room. **Guest Services:** valet and coin laundry. **Featured Amenity: breakfast buffet.**

SPRINGHILL SUITES BY MARRIOTT PHOENIX GLENDALE SPORTS & ENTERTAINMENT DISTRICT 623/772-9200 **16**

SAVE Hotel. **Address:** 7370 N Zanjero Blvd 85305

AAA Benefit: Members save 5% or more!

STAYBRIDGE SUITES PHOENIX/GLENDALE 623/842-0000 **17**

Extended Stay Hotel

Address: 9340 W Cabela Dr 85305 **Location:** SR 101 exit 7 (Glendale Ave), 0.6 mi e to N Zanjero Blvd, then just n. **Facility:** 116 efficiencies, some two bedrooms. 4 stories, interior corridors. **Pool:** heated outdoor. **Activities:** hot tub, picnic facilities, exercise room. **Guest Services:** complimentary and valet laundry, area transportation. **Featured Amenity: breakfast buffet.**

HS / SOME UNITS

(See map & index p. 117.)

WHERE TO EAT

HAUS MURPHY'S 623/939-2480 (12)

German. Casual Dining. **Address:** 5739 W Glendale Ave 85301

MACAYO'S MEXICAN TABLE 602/298-8080

Mexican. Casual Dining. **Address:** 6012 W Bell Rd 85308

MAMA GINA'S PIZZERIA 623/872-0300 (10)

Italian. Casual Dining. **Address:** 9380 W Westgate Blvd, Suite D101 85305

PITA JUNGLE 623/486-2615 (8)

Mediterranean. Casual Dining. **Address:** 7530 W Bell Rd, Suite 106 85308

SAKANA SUSHI & GRILL 623/566-3595 (7)

Japanese. Casual Dining. **Address:** 20250 N 59th Ave 85308

SOLEIL 623/937-3700 (11)

Regional American. Casual Dining. **Address:** 9495 W Coyotes Blvd 85305

THEE PITT'S "AGAIN" 602/996-7488 (9)

Barbecue. Casual Dining. **Address:** 5558 W Bell Rd 85308

GLOBE (E-5) pop. 7,532, elev. 3,517'

Named for a globe-shaped piece of almost pure silver reputedly found nearby, Globe has a colorful history punctuated by mining discoveries. It began as a mining community in 1876. The town's first boom was silver; the second was copper, which is still mined in large quantities. Globe also serves as a trading center for the San Carlos Apache Reservation 4 miles east.

Salt River Canyon, traversed by US 60 about 45 miles northeast, is 1,500 to 2,000 feet deep. About 5 miles wide at the top, the vertical-walled canyon winds for many miles with sedimentary rock layers visible from the road. At the foot of the canyon is a state roadside park. Running westward from Globe, scenic US 60 traverses Devil's Canyon before reaching Superior *(see place listing p. 176)*.

Globe is the eastern terminus of yet another scenic highway, the Apache Trail (SR 188). The road runs northwest to Roosevelt and Theodore Roosevelt Lake Recreation Area *(see Recreation Areas Chart)* before turning southwest (SR 88) toward Apache Junction *(see attraction listing p. 28 for an advisory about driving this route)*.

Globe-Miami Regional Chamber of Commerce: 1360 N. Broad St., Globe, AZ 85501. **Phone:** (928) 425-4495 or (800) 804-5623.

BESH-BA-GOWAH ARCHAEOLOGICAL PARK, 1324 Jesse Hayes Rd., is a 300-room pueblo inhabited 1225-1400 by Salado Indians. Several rooms are restored and furnished in period. Artifacts from the ruins are displayed in the museum, and an ethnobotanical garden illustrating how native plants were used by the Salado is featured. A video presentation also is available. **Hours:** Daily 9-4:30, Oct.-June; Wed.-Sun. 9-4:30, rest of year. Closed Jan. 1, Thanksgiving and Christmas. **Cost:** $5; $4 (ages 65+); free (ages 0-12 with adult). **Phone:** (928) 425-0320.

BEST WESTERN COPPER HILLS INN 928/425-7575

AAA Benefit: Members save up to 15% and earn bonus points!

Address: 1565 E South St 85501 **Location:** On US 60, 1 mi e of town. Adjacent to Round Mountain Park. **Facility:** 52 units. 2 stories, exterior corridors. **Amenities:** *Some:* safes. **Pool:** outdoor. **Activities:** hot tub, exercise room. **Guest Services:** coin laundry. **Featured Amenity: full hot breakfast.**

WHERE TO EAT

GUAYO'S ON THE TRAIL 928/425-9969

Mexican. Casual Dining. **Address:** 14239 S Hwy 188 85501

GOLD CANYON elev. 1,839'

BEST WESTERN GOLD CANYON INN & SUITES 480/671-6000

Hotel

AAA Benefit: Members save up to 15% and earn bonus points!

Address: 8333 E Sunrise Sky Dr 85118 **Location:** US 60 exit Kings Ranch Rd, just n, then just e; 7 mi e of Apache Junction. **Facility:** 68 units. 2 stories, interior corridors. **Pool:** heated outdoor. **Activities:** hot tub, exercise room. **Guest Services:** coin laundry. **Featured Amenity: full hot breakfast.**

GOODYEAR (I-2) pop. 65,275, elev. 1,000'

• **Hotels p. 56 • Restaurants p. 56**
• **Hotels & Restaurants map & index p. 117**
• **Part of Phoenix area — see map p. 91**

In the early 1900s Goodyear Tire & Rubber Company obtained tracts of land in the Salt River Valley, with the intent of growing Egyptian cotton, a component in tire cords. The small farms established on this land evolved into company towns, including one named for its originator. Just 14 miles west of Phoenix, the town is now a suburban residential community. Goodyear Ballpark, 1933 S. Ballpark Way, is the spring training center for Major League Baseball's Cleveland Indians and Cincinnati Reds.

Southwest Valley Chamber of Commerce: 289 N. Litchfield Rd., Goodyear, AZ 85338. **Phone:** (623) 932-2260.

(See map & index p. 117.)

BEST WESTERN PHOENIX GOODYEAR INN
623/932-3210 45

Hotel

Best Western. **AAA Benefit:** Members save up to 15% and earn bonus points!

Address: 55 N Litchfield Rd 85338 **Location:** I-10 exit 128, 0.8 mi s. **Facility:** 85 units. 1-2 stories (no elevator), interior/exterior corridors. **Pool:** heated outdoor. **Guest Services:** valet and coin laundry. **Featured Amenity: breakfast buffet.**

SAVE BIZ / SOME UNITS

COMFORT SUITES GOODYEAR 623/266-2884 41
Hotel. **Address:** 15575 W Roosevelt St 85338

HAMPTON INN & SUITES BY HILTON GOODYEAR
623/536-1313 40
SAVE Hotel. **Address:** 2000 N Litchfield Rd 85395

AAA Benefit: Members save up to 15%!

HOLIDAY INN & SUITES GOODYEAR 623/547-1313 43
Hotel. **Address:** 1188 N Dysart Rd 85395

RED LION INN & SUITES GOODYEAR 623/535-1313 42
Hotel. **Address:** 1313 N Litchfield Rd 85395

RESIDENCE INN BY MARRIOTT 623/866-1313 39
SAVE Extended Stay Hotel. **Address:** 2020 N Litchfield Rd 85395

AAA Benefit: Members save 5% or more!

TOWNEPLACE SUITES BY MARRIOTT PHOENIX/GOODYEAR
623/535-5009 44
SAVE Extended Stay Hotel. **Address:** 13971 W Celebrate Life Way 85338

AAA Benefit: Members save 5% or more!

WHERE TO EAT

BELLA LUNA RISTORANTE 623/535-4642 25
Italian. Casual Dining. **Address:** 14175 W Indian School Rd 85338

MACAYO'S MEXICAN TABLE 623/209-7000
Mexican. Casual Dining. **Address:** 1474 N Litchfield Rd 85338

P.F. CHANG'S CHINA BISTRO 623/536-3222 26
Chinese. Fine Dining. **Address:** 14681 W McDowell Rd 85395

ROYAL JASMINE THAI 623/236-3362 24
Thai. Casual Dining. **Address:** 14970 W Indian School Rd 85395

TOMO JAPANESE CUISINE 623/935-2031 27
Japanese. Casual Dining. **Address:** 1550 N Dysart Rd, Suite A7-9 85338

GRAND CANYON NATIONAL PARK (A-3)

• Hotels p. 62 • Restaurants p. 67
• Attractions map p. 59

Elevations in the park range from 1,100 ft. in the lower part of the canyon to about 9,000 ft. at the North Rim. Refer to AAA maps for additional elevation information.

The Grand Canyon of the Colorado River is so magnificent, so humbling, you'll never forget the sensation you feel at first sight. And yes, if you visit in summer, the South Rim is so crowded you'll be griping about the crush of tourists for years to come. But this 277-mile-long canyon, sculpted by the mighty Colorado, is without question America's number one natural wonder.

Viewing aerial IMAX footage simply can't compare to finding a solitary spot somewhere, anywhere, in this mile-deep gorge, and silently watching a raven glide on the breeze above a vast panorama of pyramidal buttes, lonely mesas, rust-colored cliffs and shadowy side canyons.

Of course, not everyone who visits the canyon is compelled to wax poetic like a talking head in a Ken Burns documentary. In the early 19th century, James Ohio Pattie, the first American to lay eyes on the immense chasm, called it "horrid." Following an 1857 Army expedition, Lt. Joseph Ives deemed it a "profitless locality." If he could only witness the 6 million visitors a year who fill the hotels, ride the mules to Phantom Ranch, light up the gift shop cash registers and buzz over the canyon on helicopter tours.

As the raven flies, it's 10 miles from the South Rim Village to the North Rim lodge. To grasp the canyon's geologic scope, a bit of textbook-speak is necessary. Eons of time are on display in the layer-cake-like strata of the canyon walls. Though scientists estimate the canyon is relatively young (6 million years old), the rock layers at the bottom, near the Colorado River, date back some 2 billion years. Put in perspective, the 270-million-year-old Permian Period layer (formed just prior to the age of the dinosaurs) is what you're standing on at the rim. No wonder they call the canyon "grand."

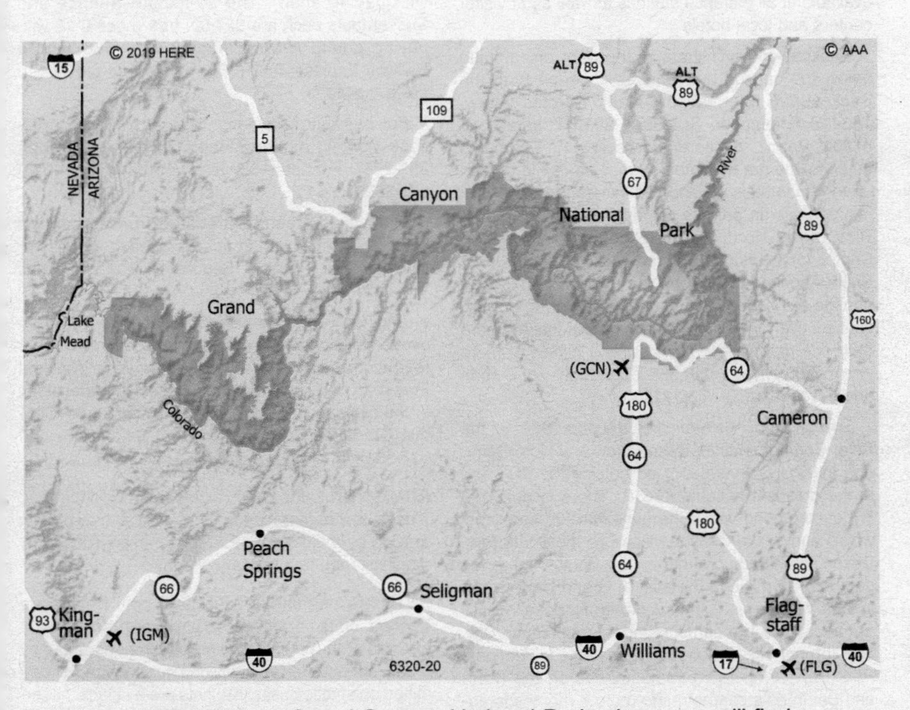

This map shows cities in Grand Canyon National Park where you will find attractions, hotels and restaurants. Cities are listed alphabetically in this book on the following pages.

General Information and Activities

North Rim visitor services and facilities are open mid-May to late October; heavy snow closes the road to the North Rim during the winter (November 1 to mid-May). For road conditions and weather information phone (928) 638-7888.

South Rim visitor services and facilities are open all year. During the winter South Rim trails into the canyon are open; however, they can be dangerously icy from November through April. Trail conditions should be verified at the Backcountry Information Center or at Grand Canyon Visitor Center. Hikers are advised not to hike from the rim to the river and back in one day. If you attempt to do so, you may find yourself stranded overnight, or at the very least, exhausted. Since nights are cool even in summer, pack warm clothing. However, be prepared for high daytime summer temperatures within the canyon. The area also is subject to monsoon weather with dangerous lightning in July and August.

Maps, trail descriptions, lists of ranger-led activities, seasonal information and shuttle schedules are available at all entrance stations as well as at visitor centers and local hotels.

Backpacking anywhere in the park or camping below the canyon rim requires a permit from the Backcountry Information Center, Permits Office, 1824 S. Thompson St., Suite 201, Flagstaff, AZ 86001. Permit requests and backcountry camping reservations are accepted by mail, fax or in person up to 4 months in advance. A limited number of last minute walk-up permits are available at the South Rim and/or North Rim Backcountry Information Center for Corridor Campgrounds (Indian Garden, Bright Angel and Cottonwood campgrounds). These permits are issued in person only, are for one or two consecutive nights and cannot be purchased more than one day prior to the start of a hike. For more information phone (928) 638-7875, Mon.-Fri. 8-noon and 1-5 or fax (928) 638-2125.

Six campgrounds are inside the park (three in the River Corridor, Mather, Desert View and North Rim), and there are several located outside the park and in the adjacent national forests. There is only one RV campground within the park with full hook-ups, which is in Grand Canyon Village on the South Rim. Desert View Campground, on the South Rim of the park and 25 miles to the east of Grand Canyon Village, is first-come, first-served only. No reservations are accepted. The campground is open seasonally, May through mid-October. Reservations for National Park Service-operated campgrounds on the North and South rims can be made up to 6 months in advance by phoning (877) 444-6777 or TTY (877) 833-6777. *See Recreation Areas Chart.*

Trans-Canyon Shuttle provides one-way and round-trip van transportation between the canyon's two rims. From mid-May to mid-October the 4.5-hour shuttle ride departs the North Rim at 7 a.m. and 2 p.m. and the South Rim at 8 a.m. and 1:30 p.m. From mid-October to mid-November, the shuttle departs the South Rim at 8 a.m. and the North Rim at 2 p.m. The fare is $90 for a one-way trip. Shuttle service also is available from the South Rim to Marble Canyon. Reservations are required; phone (928) 638-2820 for information and reservations.

Flagstaff Shuttle, Charter and Tours offers transportation to and from the park and its environs from Sedona, Flagstaff and Phoenix. From Flagstaff to the South Rim, the fare is $150 for up to three people ($35 each additional person); $595 from Phoenix to the South Rim for up to three ($45 each additional person); and $450 for up to three ($45 each additional person) to the North Rim from Flagstaff or the South Rim. Fare for children ages 0-6 is half off with a paying adult. Fare does not include admission to Grand Canyon National Park. Prices may vary; phone (888) 215-3105 for information and reservations.

Buses departing from Yavapai Lodge, Maswik Lodge and Bright Angel Lodge & Cabins take visitors on a variety of sightseeing tours and are a good option for group travel. The 2-hour Hermits Rest Tour is $36; free (ages 0-16 with paying adult). The 3.75-hour Desert View Tour is $65; free (ages 0-16 with paying adult). The 90-minute Sunrise and Sunset tours each are $27.50; free (ages 0-16 with paying adult). A Combination Tour ($80) and a Railway Express Tour ($65); $37 (ages 0-16) also are available.

For bus tour information and advance reservations, contact Xanterra Parks & Resorts at (888) 297-2757. For same-day reservations, phone (928) 638-2631.

Flightseeing tours are offered from the airport south of Tusayan and from several nearby cities, including Page, Phoenix, Sedona, Williams and Las Vegas, Nev.

Another way to glimpse the Grand Canyon from overlooks is on a four-wheel-drive tour. These backroad sightseeing trips through the Kaibab National Forest are led by guides well versed in the ecology of the canyon, its history, wildlife and legends. Contact Grand Canyon Jeep Tours & Safaris at (928) 638-5337 or (800) 320-5337.

ADMISSION to the park, valid for both rims for up to 7 days, is $35 (per private vehicle); $30 (per person arriving by motorcycle); $20 (per person arriving by other means); free (military with ID).

PETS are permitted in the park only if they are leashed, crated or otherwise physically restrained at all times. Pets are excluded entirely from backcountry areas, are not allowed below the rim and are not permitted on shuttle buses. Kennels are available; reservations are recommended. Restrictions do not apply to service animals. Phone (928) 638-0534.

ADDRESS inquiries to the Superintendent, Grand Canyon National Park, P.O. Box 129, Grand Canyon, AZ 86023; phone (928) 638-7888. Information also is available from the Grand Canyon South Rim Chamber of Commerce and Visitors Bureau, P.O. Box 3007, Grand Canyon, AZ 86023; phone (844) 638-2901

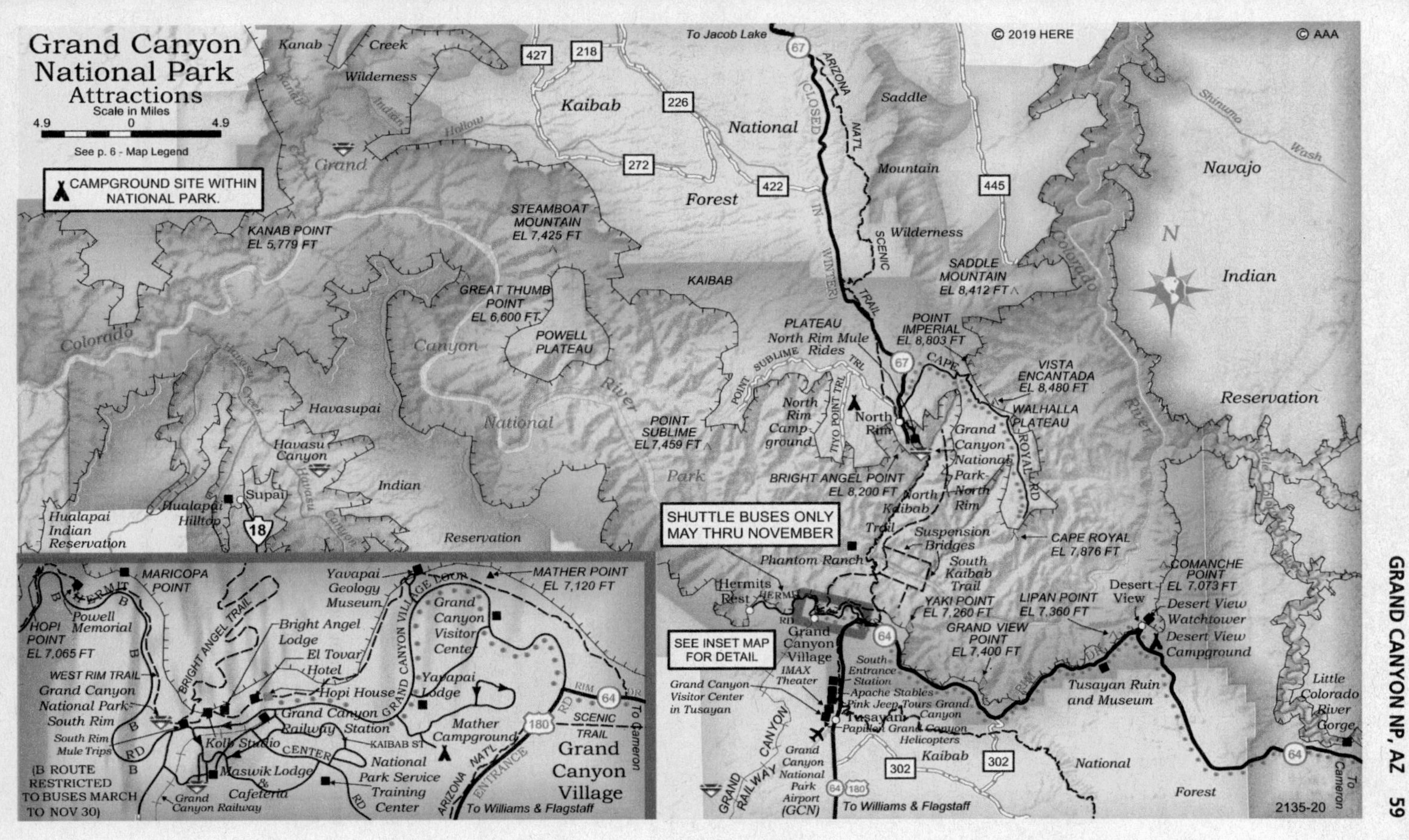
Grand Canyon National Park Attractions
Scale in Miles
4.9 0 4.9
See p. 6 - Map Legend
CAMPGROUND SITE WITHIN NATIONAL PARK.
© 2019 HERE
© AAA
2135-20
To Jacob Lake
To Cameron
To Williams & Flagstaff
Kanab Creek Wilderness
Kaibab National Forest
Saddle Mountain Wilderness
Navajo Indian Reservation
Havasupai Indian Reservation
Hualapai Indian Reservation
Grand Canyon National Park
ARIZONA NAT'L SCENIC TRAIL
(CLOSED IN WINTER)
KAIBAB PLATEAU
STEAMBOAT MOUNTAIN EL 7,425 FT
KANAB POINT EL 5,779 FT
GREAT THUMB POINT EL 6,600 FT
POWELL PLATEAU
POINT SUBLIME EL 7,459 FT
POINT SUBLIME TRL
TIYO POINT TRL
North Rim Mule Rides
North Rim Campground
North Rim
SADDLE MOUNTAIN EL 8,412 FT
POINT IMPERIAL EL 8,803 FT
CAPE ROYAL RD
VISTA ENCANTADA EL 8,480 FT
WALHALLA PLATEAU
Grand Canyon National Park-North Rim
BRIGHT ANGEL POINT EL 8,200 FT
North Kaibab Trail
Suspension Bridges
South Kaibab Trail
CAPE ROYAL EL 7,876 FT
SHUTTLE BUSES ONLY MAY THRU NOVEMBER
Phantom Ranch
Hermits Rest
Grand Canyon Village
SEE INSET MAP FOR DETAIL
YAKI POINT EL 7,260 FT
LIPAN POINT EL 7,360 FT
GRAND VIEW POINT EL 7,400 FT
COMANCHE POINT EL 7,073 FT
Desert View
Desert View Watchtower
Desert View Campground
Tusayan Ruin and Museum
Little Colorado River Gorge
Colorado River
Havasu Canyon
Havasu Creek
Supai
Hualapai Hilltop
South Entrance Station
IMAX Theater
Grand Canyon Visitor Center in Tusayan
Apache Stables
Pink Jeep Tours Grand Canyon
Tusayan
Papillon Grand Canyon Helicopters
Grand Canyon National Park Airport (GCN)
GRAND CANYON RAILWAY
MARICOPA POINT
HOPI POINT EL 7,065 FT
Powell Memorial
HERMIT RD
BRIGHT ANGEL TRAIL
WEST RIM TRAIL
Grand Canyon National Park South Rim
South Rim Mule Trips
(B ROUTE RESTRICTED TO BUSES MARCH TO NOV 30)
Bright Angel Lodge
El Tovar Hotel
Hopi House
Grand Canyon Railway Station
Kolb Studio
Maswik Lodge & Cafeteria
Grand Canyon Railway
Yavapai Geology Museum
GRAND CANYON VILLAGE LOOP
Grand Canyon Visitor Center
Yavapai Lodge
Mather Campground
KAIBAB ST
CENTER RD
National Park Service Training Center
MATHER POINT EL 7,120 FT
RIM DR
SCENIC TRAIL
ARIZONA NAT'L ENTRANCE
Grand Canyon Village

GRAND CANYON NATIONAL PARK - SOUTH RIM (A-3)

• Hotels p. 62 • Restaurants p. 67
• Attractions map p. 59

One superb canyon vista after another is what you'll see along the South Rim's paved roads. The 25-mile Desert View Drive (open year-round to private vehicles) connects the East Entrance Station with Grand Canyon Village, winding through a ponderosa pine forest and passing a half-dozen viewpoints (Grandview is a standout) along the way.

West of the village, Hermit Road leads to more overlooks (including the phenomenal Hopi Point) on its way to Hermit's Rest, where you'll find restrooms, a snack bar and a gift shop. The road is closed to private vehicles March through November but can be accessed by the park's free shuttle bus during these months.

In peak summer travel season, brace yourself for crowds. In most areas of Grand Canyon Village, parking is scarce. Free shuttles run year round at the village, and it's often wise to park at the visitor center and use the shuttle to get around. To avoid parking headaches all together, consider riding the free shuttle from Tusayan (the park's gateway town); service is available June through September.

If you're driving into the park through the South Entrance Station (near Tusayan), take note: There are five entry gates with one gate dedicated to prepaid passes. This is a very popular point of entry and crowds can be large, so paying admission outside the park at the Grand Canyon Visitor Center in Tusayan *(see attraction listing p. 61)* is a smart move when traffic is heavy. Passes also can be purchased at most Tusayan hotels and at visitor centers in Williams and Flagstaff. Of course, the most obvious way to avoid possible delays is to get an early start.

Both helicopter and airplane tours of the canyon are available from the Grand Canyon National Park Airport in Tusayan, 5 miles south of the park headquarters. For information and reservations contact Grand Canyon Airlines, (866) 235-9422; Grand Canyon Helicopters, (928) 638-2764; Maverick Helicopters, (928) 638-2622 or (800) 962-3869; or Papillon Grand Canyon Helicopters, (928) 638-2419 or (800) 528-2418.

BRIGHT ANGEL TRAIL starts just w. of Bright Angel Lodge & Cabins. Descending 4,460 feet to the Colorado River, the trail leads 9 miles to the river and Phantom Ranch. From Indian Garden, 4.4 miles below the trailhead, a branch trail leads 1.5 miles across the Tonto Platform to Plateau Point, offering a grand view of the Colorado River. To view the depths from the rim, telescopes are available near Bright Angel Lodge & Cabins.

Note: Hikers should check park publications for the latest information about the trail. Overnight hikers must obtain a camping permit. Water and other hiking necessities must be carried on all canyon trails. **Phone:** (928) 638-7888.

DESERT VIEW WATCHTOWER is 25 mi. e. of Grand Canyon Village at Desert View. Built in 1932, the 70-ft. tower built of stone and mortar was inspired by prehistoric towers found in the Four Corners region. From the brink of the canyon wall, the tower commands views of the river, the canyon, the Painted Desert and Kaibab National Forest *(see place listing p. 70)*.

Also at Desert View are food concessions, an information desk, a seasonal campground and a gas station. **Hours:** Daily 8-7, day before Memorial Day-Labor Day; 9-6, day after Labor Day-Nov. 30; 9-5, Dec.-Feb.; 8-6, rest of year. **Cost:** Free.

GRAND CANYON RAILWAY—see Williams p. 223.

GRAND CANYON SKYWALK—see Kingman p. 71.

GRAND CANYON VISITOR CENTER is 5 mi. n. of the South Entrance Station near Mather Point. The center can be reached via a free shuttle bus from various locations in Grand Canyon Village. The visitor center is at an altitude of 6,950 feet and features indoor displays, a theater with a film, outdoor exhibits, an information center and views of the canyon from nearby observation points.

Note: Inquire at the center about local road conditions. **Hours:** Daily 9-7. Ranger programs are presented. Hours may vary; consult park publications for details. **Cost:** Free. **Phone:** (928) 638-7888.

HAVASU CANYON—see Supai p. 176.

KOLB STUDIO, just w. of Bright Angel Lodge & Cabins, was built as a photography studio in 1904 for brothers Ellsworth and Emery Kolb, who took photos of tourists descending Bright Angel Trail *(see attraction listing)* on mules. The building now serves as both a bookstore and a gallery with changing Grand Canyon-related exhibits. Antique photographic equipment used by the Kolb brothers is on display, and you can snap your own photos from a small outdoor viewing area. **Time:** Allow 30 minutes minimum. **Hours:** Daily 8-8, Memorial Day-Labor Day; 8-6, day after Labor Day-Oct. 31 and Feb. 1-day before Memorial Day; 8-5, rest of year. Phone ahead to confirm schedule. **Cost:** Free. **Phone:** (928) 638-2481.

LIPAN POINT, along Desert View Dr., has an elevation of 7,360 feet and offers a fine view of the river, the Unkar Delta and the San Francisco Peaks.

GRAND CANYON VISITOR CENTER IN TUSAYAN, 9 mi. s. of Grand Canyon Village at 450 SR 64, features exhibits about Grand Canyon history, explorers, geology and wildlife. Visitors wishing to visit Grand Canyon National Park can obtain trip-planning information, purchase park passes and book tours. **Hours:** Daily 8 a.m.-10 p.m., Mar.-Oct.; 10-8, rest of year. **Cost:** Free. **Phone:** (928) 638-2468. ***(See ad this page.)*** 🍴

IMAX Theater is within the Grand Canyon Visitor Center, 9 mi. s. of Grand Canyon Village at 450 SR 64 in Tusayan. Equipped with a six-story screen and surround system, the theater presents "Grand Canyon: The Hidden Secrets," a 34-minute IMAX film that depicts the beauty of this geologic formation and 4,000 years of its history. The film also shows parts of the canyon that can't be seen on tours.

Time: Allow 45 minutes minimum. **Hours:** The film is shown daily every hour on the half-hour 8:30-8:30, Mar.-Oct.; 9:30-6:30, rest of year. **Cost:** Film $13.59; $12.50 (ages 55+ and military with ID); $10.33 (ages 6-10). **Phone:** (928) 638-2468. ***(See ad this page.)***

PINK JEEP TOURS GRAND CANYON depart from the IMAX Theater, 9 mi. s. of Grand Canyon Village at 450 SR 64 in Tusayan. Board a distinctively colored jeep for a professionally guided ride along the South Rim with several stops during the tour to take photos of the Grand Canyon's incredible vistas. **Time:** Allow 2 hours minimum. **Hours:** Tours depart daily every half-hour 8:30-6. Departures may be reduced in winter; phone ahead to confirm schedule. Closed Christmas. **Cost:** Grand Entrance Tour $99; $90 (ages 18 months-15 years). Other tours are available. All tours include admission to IMAX Theater for the "Grand Canyon: The Hidden Secrets" IMAX film. Reservations are recommended. **Phone:** (800) 873-3662. GT

PHANTOM RANCH, at the bottom of the Grand Canyon, is reached by hiking *(see Bright Angel Trail)* or mule ride *(see South Rim Mule Trips)*. The only lodging available below the rim, it provides dormitory accommodations, cabins and a dining room. Dormitories and cabins are available to hikers; cabin lodging is included with overnight mule trips. **Cost:** Dorm space $52.92 per person. Cabins $154.80 (for two people); $13 (additional person in cabin). Reservations are required for lodging and meals and must be made well in advance, especially during summer and holidays. **Phone:** (303) 297-2757 or (888) 297-2757.

RIM TRAIL extends 13 mi. along the rim of the canyon from Hermits Rest to South Kaibab Trailhead (near Yaki Point). A paved section starting at Pima Point and extending east for about 1.7 miles accommodates wheelchairs and is suitable for walking and biking. The trail is steeply downhill from Maricopa Point to Grand Canyon Village, then relatively flat. The paved 5.4-mile section from Maricopa Point to Pipe Creek Vista is better for children and casual hikers than the park's other more strenuous canyon trails. Pamphlets about the biology and geology of the canyon can be obtained from boxes along the trail. The Trail of Time is a 2.83-mile interpretive geologic walking timeline. Bronze markers indicate your location in time; every tenth marker is labeled in millions of years. Along the timeline trail are a series of rocks and exhibits that explain how the Grand Canyon and its rocks were formed.

SOUTH KAIBAB TRAIL begins near Yaki Point, 3.5 mi. e. of Grand Canyon Village. This is a steep, 7-mile trail to a Colorado River suspension bridge. A good 3-mile round-trip day hike leads from the head of South Kaibab Trail to Cedar Ridge, where beautiful views of the canyon may be seen.

Note: Visitors should not attempt to hike from the South Rim to the river and back in 1 day. The Kaibab Trail is strenuous and not recommended for hiking out of the canyon. The trip is recommended only for hardy individuals. Hikers should carry water (1 gallon per person per day), since none is available along the trail. The road to the trailhead is closed to private vehicles and may be reached by shuttle bus. **Hours:** Conducted hikes to Cedar Ridge are scheduled early on summer mornings.

SOUTH RIM MULE TRIPS depart from a point near the trailhead of the Bright Angel Trail. Offered through Grand Canyon National Parks Lodges, guided overnight mule trips take visitors along the Bright Angel Trail to Phantom Ranch in the bottom of the canyon. There also is the 3-hour Canyon Vistas mule ride through Kaibab Forest along the canyon rim.

Note: For safety purposes, riders must be fluent in English, be taller than 4 feet 7 inches, and weigh no more than 200 pounds when fully dressed (including equipment) for the Phantom Ranch ride or 225 pounds for the Canyon Vistas ride. The trips are strenuous and should be undertaken only by those in good physical condition; pregnant women are not permitted on the trips.

Hours: Trips depart daily at 8 and noon, Mar. 15-Nov. 30; at 9, rest of year. **Cost:** $142.83. Prices may vary; phone ahead. Reservations are required and must be made well in advance, particularly during summer and holidays. **Phone:** (888) 297-2757. GT

TUSAYAN RUIN AND MUSEUM is 22 mi. e. of Grand Canyon Village on a short spur leading off Desert View Dr. The ruin is a U-shaped, prehistoric pueblo inhabited 1185-1225 by two generations of Ancestral Puebloans; it contains about 15 rooms and about 30 people lived there. The Ancestral Puebloans are believed to be the ancestors of the Hopi as well as other Pueblo tribes.

The museum traces the development of the Native American culture at the canyon. Exhibits include a painting of the ruin, displays about modern tribes and such Ancestral Puebloan artifacts as pottery, twig figurines and rock drawings.

An adjacent .1-mile paved trail runs around the pueblo. A self-guiding brochure is available at the trailhead. **Note:** Inclement weather may result in winter closures; phone ahead. **Hours:** Daily 9-5. **Cost:** Free. **Phone:** (928) 638-7888. GT

YAVAPAI GEOLOGY MUSEUM, 1.5 mi. e. of Grand Canyon Village, offers exhibits and programs that explain the geologic history of the region. A panoramic view of the canyon is visible through the building's windows. **Hours:** Daily 8-8, Memorial Day-Labor Day; 8-7, Mar. 1-Wed. before Memorial Day and day after Labor Day-Nov. 30; 8-6, rest of year. **Cost:** Free.

RECREATIONAL ACTIVITIES

Bicycling

- **Bright Angel Bicycles** is next door to the Grand Canyon Visitor Center. Tours and rentals are offered. **Hours:** Daily 8-6, May 1-Sept. 15. Otherwise varies; phone ahead. **Phone:** (928) 679-0992. GT

Horseback Riding

- **Apache Stables** is 1 mi. n. of Tusayan off SR 64, then .25 mi. w. on FR 328/Moqui Dr. **Hours:** Daily, Mar.-Nov. (weather permitting). Phone for schedule details. **Phone:** (928) 638-2891. GT

White-water Rafting

- **Rivers & Oceans** is on the Colorado River. **Hours:** Trips operate mid-Mar. through Oct. 31. **Phone:** (928) 440-1646 or (800) 473-4576. GT

BEST WESTERN PREMIER GRAND CANYON SQUIRE INN 928/638-2681

Hotel

AAA Benefit: Members save up to 15% and earn bonus points!

Address: 74 SR 64 86023 **Location:** 2 mi s of South Rim entrance. **Facility:** 321 units. 1-3 stories, interior/exterior corridors. **Terms:** check-in 4 pm. **Amenities:** safes. **Dining:** 3 restaurants, also, Coronado Room, see separate listing. **Pool:** heated outdoor, heated indoor. **Activities:** hot tub, game room, exercise room. **Guest Services:** coin laundry.

▼ See AAA listing p. 31 ▼

EL TOVAR HOTEL 303/297-2757

Classic Historic Resort Hotel. **Address:** South Rim 86023

GRAND CANYON PLAZA HOTEL 928/638-2673

Hotel

Address: 406 Canyon Plaza Ln 86023 **Location:** On SR 64; 2 mi s of South Rim entrance. Located behind IMAX Theater. **Facility:** 232 units. 3 stories, interior/exterior corridors. **Pool:** heated outdoor. **Activities:** hot tub, exercise room. **Guest Services:** coin laundry.

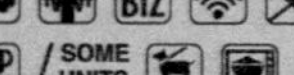
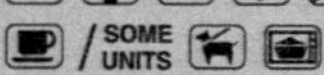
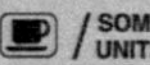
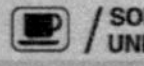

THE GRAND HOTEL AT THE GRAND CANYON
928/638-3333

Hotel

Address: 149 State Hwy 64 86023 **Location:** 2 mi s of South Rim entrance. **Facility:** 121 units. 3 stories, interior corridors. **Terms:** check-in 4 pm. **Amenities:** safes. **Dining:** Canyon Star Steakhouse, see separate listing, entertainment. **Pool:** heated indoor. **Activities:** hot tub, exercise room.

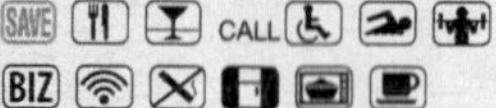
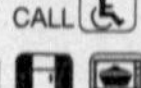

HOLIDAY INN EXPRESS HOTEL & SUITES-GRAND CANYON
928/638-3000

Hotel. **Address:** 226 SR 64 86023 *(See ad p. 65.)*

▼ See AAA listing p. 64 ▼

KACHINA LODGE 303/297-2757

Hotel. **Address:** South Rim 86023

MASWIK LODGE 303/297-2757

Motel. **Address:** South Rim 86023

For complete hotel, dining and attraction listings: AAA.com/travelguides

RED FEATHER LODGE 928/638-2414

Hotel

Address: 300 SR 64 86023 **Location:** 1 mi s of South Rim entrance. **Facility:** 226 units. 2-3 stories, interior/exterior corridors. **Terms:** check-in 4 pm. **Pool:** heated outdoor. **Activities:** hot tub. **Guest Services:** coin laundry. *(See ad this page.)*

SAVE CALL BIZ / SOME UNITS

THUNDERBIRD LODGE 303/297-2757

Hotel. **Address:** South Rim 86023

▼ *See AAA listing this page* ▼

AVAPAI LODGE 928/638-4001

Motel. **Address:** 11 Yavapai Rd 86023

WHERE TO EAT

ARIZONA STEAKHOUSE 928/638-2631

American. Casual Dining. **Address:** 10 Albright Ave 86023

BIG E STEAKHOUSE & SALOON 928/638-0333

American Casual Dining $14-$36

AAA Inspector Notes: Hungry guests flock to this Western-style steakhouse after a long day at the Grand Canyon. It's hard to go wrong with the rib-eye, but the Atlantic salmon and the crab cakes are great as well. **Features:** full bar, patio dining. **Address:** 395 SR 64 86023 **Location:** 1 mi s of South Rim entrance.

L D

BRIGHT ANGEL RESTAURANT 928/638-2631

American. Casual Dining. **Address:** Hwy 64, South Rim 86023

CANYON STAR STEAKHOUSE 928/638-3333

Steak Casual Dining $10-$45

AAA Inspector Notes: Featuring a Southwestern menu with steaks and a seasonal buffet, the restaurant also entertains guests with Native American dancers and singing cowboys. **Features:** full bar. **Address:** Hwy 64 86023 **Location:** 2 mi s of South Rim entrance; in The Grand Hotel at the Grand Canyon. L D

CORONADO ROOM 928/638-2681

Steak Seafood. Casual Dining. **Address:** 74 SR 64 86023

EL TOVAR HOTEL DINING ROOM 928/638-2631

Continental. Fine Dining. **Address:** South Rim 86023

WE COOK PIZZA & PASTA 928/638-2278

Italian Pizza Quick Serve $12-$29

AAA Inspector Notes: After a long day exploring the canyon, locals and visitors congregate here for beer and pizza. Although specialty pizzas are the most popular choices, the menu also lists sandwiches, simple pasta dishes, calzones and a salad bar. **Features:** beer & wine, patio dining. **Address:** 605 N Hwy 64 86023 **Location:** 2 mi s of South Rim entrance.

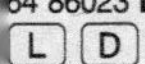

L D

GRAND CANYON NATIONAL PARK - NORTH RIM (A-3)

• Attractions map p. 59

Less visited than the South Rim, the North Rim is not as extensively developed. The views from the North and South rims differ considerably. Observers at Bright Angel Point on the North Rim can see the San Francisco Peaks, which are 80 miles south of the South Rim.

From Grand Canyon Village on the South Rim, it is 215 miles to Grand Canyon North Rim Lodge via SR 64 to Cameron, US 89 to its junction with US 89A at Bitter Springs, US 89A to Jacob Lake and scenic SR 67 to the North Rim Entrance Station. The 5-hour drive passes through the Navajo Nation Reservation, the Painted Desert and Kaibab National Forest.

A road runs 22 miles southeast from the Grand Canyon North Rim Lodge road to Point Imperial, Vista Encantada and Cape Royal. **NOTE:** The road to Point Imperial and Cape Royal was damaged by the winter weather; phone ahead to confirm its status. Point Imperial, at 8,803 feet, is the highest point on the canyon rim. These points all afford splendid views. Reservations for the North Rim Campground can be made up to 6 months in advance by phoning Reserve America at (877) 444-6777. *See Recreation Areas Chart.*

GRAND CANYON RAILWAY—see Williams p. 223.

GRAND CANYON SKYWALK—see Kingman p. 71.

MARBLE CANYON, at the n.e. end of the park, is traversed by US 89A via the Navajo Bridge, which is 616 feet long and 467 feet high. The Colorado River lies in a 500-foot-deep gorge that cuts across the level plain on which the highway sits.

NORTH KAIBAB TRAIL starts at the head of Roaring Springs Canyon. This 14.2-mile trail descends 5,850 feet to the river and Phantom Ranch, following Bright Angel Creek. **Note:** Only experienced hikers in good physical condition should use the trail. Check park publications, for the latest information about the trail. Overnight hikers must obtain a camping permit and make camping reservations.

NORTH RIM MULE RIDES depart from a point near the trailhead of the North Kaibab Trail. Offered through Grand Canyon Trail Rides, 3-hour muleback trips take visitors through the canyon to the Supai Tunnel. A 1-hour trip along the North Rim and a 3-hour trip to Uncle Jim's Point also are available. Trips do not go to the Colorado River.

Note: For safety purposes, riders must be fluent in English; they also must weigh no more than 220 pounds when fully dressed (including equipment) for the trip to the Supai Tunnel and no more than 200 pounds when fully dressed for the 1-hour rim trip and the 3-hour trip to Uncle Jim's Point. All riding levels can participate.

Hours: Three-hour trips depart daily at 7:30 and 12:30, May 15-Oct. 15. One-hour trips depart daily 8:30-2:30, May 15-Oct. 15. **Cost:** Three-hour trips $90. One-hour trip $45. Ages 0-9 are not permitted on 3-hour trips; ages 0-6 are not permitted on 1-hour trip. **Phone:** (435) 679-8665. GT

TUWEEP AREA is in the n.w. corner, via SR 389 and a 60-mile dirt road west of Fredonia. Also known as Toroweap, the remote area embraces 40 miles of the Grand Canyon between Kanab Creek and the Uinkaret Mountains. Toroweap Overlook offers exceptional views of the Grand Canyon's inner gorge and of Lava Falls rapids. Vulcans Throne, a cinder cone, is on the Esplanade just west of Toroweap Overlook.

Note: Due to a lack of accommodations, the trip should not be attempted without adequate preparation and equipment. Water, gasoline and camping supplies are not available. Limited camping is offered south of the Tuweep Ranger Station; electricity and water are not available. The 60-mile dirt road is impassable when wet. A high-clearance, four-wheel-drive vehicle is required at all times.

GRAND CANYON-PARASHANT NATIONAL MONUMENT (A-2)

In the northwestern corner of the state, Grand Canyon-Parashant National Monument comprises more than 1 million undeveloped acres bordered on the west by Nevada and on the south by Grand Canyon National Park *(see place listing p. 57)*.

Exposed in the remote, unspoiled canyons and mesas are layers representing nearly 1.7 billion years of the earth's formation. Human occupation can be traced through such archeological finds as petroglyphs, pit houses and villages, with evidence pointing to habitation by hunter-gatherers as early as the Paleo-Indian and Archaic periods, and later by Puebloan and Southern Paiute cultures. Abandoned homesteads, ranches and mining camps are among the 19th- and 20th-century ruins preserved.

Wildlife is as diverse as the scenery. Two extreme ecological regions, the Mojave Desert and the Colorado Plateau, intersect within the boundaries of the monument, which is inhabited by bighorn sheep, coyotes, mule deer, turkeys and Kaibab squirrels as well as the endangered California condor.

Hiking, picnicking and primitive camping are permitted. There are no paved roads, services or developed recreation sites. Graded dirt roads are passable by two-wheel drive vehicles when dry but become impassable when wet. Use four-wheel drive vehicles with full-sized spare tires to travel alternative routes. Be prepared for adverse and isolated conditions; most of the monument has no cellphone coverage. For maps and further information contact the Arizona Strip District Field Office, Bureau of Land Management, 345 E. Riverside Dr., St. George, UT 84790; phone (435) 688-3200.

GREEN VALLEY pop. 21,391

• Hotels & Restaurants map & index p. 212
• Part of Tucson area — see map p. 187

BEST WESTERN GREEN VALLEY INN 520/625-2250 2

Hotel

AAA Benefit: Members save up to 15% and earn bonus points!

Address: 111 S La Canada Dr 85614 **Location:** I-19 exit 65, just w, then just s. **Facility:** 105 units. 2 stories, interior corridors. **Pool:** heated outdoor. **Activities:** hot tub, exercise room. **Guest Services:** coin laundry. **Featured Amenity: full hot breakfast.**

SOME UNITS

CANOA RANCH GOLF RESORT 520/382-0450

Resort Condominium

Address: 5775 S Camino Del Sol 85622 **Location:** I-19 exit 56 (Canoa Rd), just w, 0.5 mi n on Frontage Rd to Calle Tres, just w, then 1 mi s. **Facility:** Located across from the golf club and restaurant, the property's well-appointed rooms offer views of the mountains and valleys. 98 condominiums. 3 stories, interior corridors. **Pool:** heated outdoor. **Activities:** hot tub, regulation golf, picnic facilities, exercise room. **Featured Amenity: breakfast buffet.**

SOME UNITS

COMFORT INN 520/399-3736 1

Hotel

Address: 90 W Esperanza Blvd 85614 **Location:** I-19 exit 65, just w. **Facility:** 55 units. 2 stories, interior corridors. **Pool:** outdoor. **Activities:** hot tub, exercise room. **Guest Services:** coin laundry. **Featured Amenity: full hot breakfast.**

SOME UNITS

WHERE TO EAT

AGAVE AT DESERT DIAMOND CASINO 520/342-2328 1
Regional American. Casual Dining. **Address:** 1100 W Pima Mine Rd 85629

GRILL AT QUAIL CREEK 520/393-5806 2
American. Casual Dining. **Address:** 1490 N Quail Range Loop, Bldg 3 85614

GRILL ON THE GREEN AT CANOA RANCH GOLF CLUB 520/393-1933 3
American. Casual Dining. **Address:** 5800 S Camino Del Sol 85614

HEBER

BEST WESTERN SAWMILL INN 928/535-5053

Hotel

AAA Benefit: Members save up to 15% and earn bonus points!

Address: 1877 Hwy 260 85928 **Location:** 0.5 mi e of center. **Facility:** 42 units. 2 stories (no elevator), exterior corridors. **Activities:** exercise room. **Guest Services:** coin laundry, area transportation. **Featured Amenity: full hot breakfast.**

SOME UNITS

WHERE TO EAT

RED ONION LOUNGE 928/535-4433
American. Casual Dining. **Address:** 1931 Hwy 260 85933

HEREFORD (G-5) elev. 7,587'

THE NATURE CONSERVANCY'S RAMSEY CANYON PRESERVE is 5.9 mi. s. on SR 92 from jct. SR 90, then 3.5 mi. w. to 27 E. Ramsey Canyon Rd. The 380-acre preserve serves as a sanctuary or more than 400 species of plants; 170 species of birds, including hummingbirds and painted redstarts; various species of butterflies; and other wildlife, including black bears and Yarrow's spiny lizards. A natural history interpretive center is available.

Note: Parking is limited. Picnicking is permitted only at the headquarters. Pets and firearms are not permitted. **Hours:** Thurs.-Mon. 8-5, Mar.-Oct.; 9-4, rest of year. Guided tours depart Mon., Thurs. and Sat. at 9. Closed Jan. 1, Thanksgiving and Christmas. **Cost:** Admission, valid for 7 days, $6; free (ages 0-16). **Phone:** (520) 378-2785. GT

PIZZERIA MIMOSA 520/378-0022

Italian. Casual Dining. **Address:** 4755 E Neapolitan Way 85615

HOLBROOK (C-5) pop. 5,053, elev. 5,080'

Holbrook was founded in 1881 when the Atlantic and Pacific Railroad reached this point. Once called the "town too tough for women and churches," the community was named for Henry R. Holbrook, chief engineer of the railroad project. The seat of Navajo County, Holbrook is close to Petrified Forest National Park *(see place listing p. 88)* and several reservations.

The Little Colorado River's sweeping turns traverse westward through town, and the terrain consists of flat plains, rugged hills and small buttes. Official U.S. mail is delivered to Scottsdale in early February when the Pony Express rides from Holbrook.

The Navajo County Historic Courthouse, 100 E. Arizona St., is the center of Wild West Days the second weekend in July. Native American and Mexican folkloric dances are held Mon.-Sat. evenings in June and July at Gillespie Park, at the junction of Navajo and Hopi blvds. Phone the chamber of commerce to confirm schedule. A parade of lights is held the second weekend in December.

Holbrook Chamber of Commerce: 100 E. Arizona St., Holbrook, AZ 86025. **Phone:** (928) 524-6558.

Self-guiding tours: A self-guiding tour including the Navajo County Courthouse/Museum is available. Brochures can be obtained at the chamber of commerce.

BEST WESTERN ARIZONIAN INN 928/524-2611

Hotel

AAA Benefit: Members save up to 15% and earn bonus points!

Address: 2508 Navajo Blvd 86025 **Location:** I-40 exit 289, 0.5 mi w. **Facility:** 72 units. 2 stories (no elevator), exterior corridors. **Pool:** heated outdoor. **Featured Amenity: breakfast buffet.**

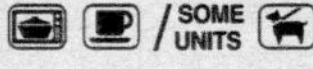

DAYS INN 928/524-6949

Motel. **Address:** 2601 Navajo Blvd 86025

ECONO LODGE 928/297-0292

Motel. **Address:** 2211 Navajo Blvd 86025

HOWARD JOHNSON 928/524-2566

Hotel. **Address:** 2608 E Navajo Blvd 86025

QUALITY INN 928/524-6131

Hotel

Address: 2602 Navajo Blvd 86025 **Location:** I-40 exit 289, just w. **Facility:** 59 units. 2 stories (no elevator), exterior corridors. **Pool:** outdoor. **Featured Amenity: breakfast buffet.**

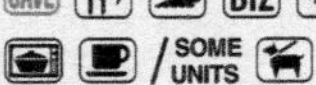

WHERE TO EAT

BUTTERFIELD STAGE STEAK HOUSE AT THE PETRIFIED FOREST 928/524-3447

Steak. Casual Dining. **Address:** 609 W Hopi Dr 86025

MESA ITALIANA RESTAURANT 928/524-6696

Italian. Casual Dining. **Address:** 2318 E Navajo Blvd 86025

IRONWOOD FOREST NATIONAL MONUMENT (F-3)

Northwest of Tucson 25 miles via I-10 to Avra Valley Road, Ironwood Forest National Monument contains the highest density of ironwood trees in the Sonoran Desert. The diverse ironwood provides food and shelter for a variety of wildlife, including desert bighorn sheep, tortoises and hawks.

For further information contact the Tucson Field Office, Bureau of Land Management, 3201 E. Universal Way, Tucson, AZ 85756; phone (520) 258-7200.

JEROME (C-3) pop. 444, elev. 5,435'

• Hotels p. 70 • Restaurants p. 70

In 1582 Spanish missionaries exploring the Verde Valley recorded that natives were using the copper mines near what is now Jerome. The missionaries' description of the mines was identical to the workings found in 1883 by the United Verde Co. Eugene Jerome of New York agreed to finance the mining project on condition the camp be named for him. In 1886 a smelter arrived by rail from Ash Fork and operations began in earnest.

Once a city with a population of 15,000, Jerome became a virtual ghost town when the United Verde Branch copper mines of the Phelps Dodge Corp. closed in 1953. Since then, shops, galleries, studios and museums, some housed in former brothels and saloons, have been established in the restored town which clings to Cleopatra Hill on the side of Mingus Mountain. Some of the restored homes are open during the Home Tour in May.

A 54-mile scenic stretch of SR 89A begins in Flagstaff and winds its way south through Oak Creek Canyon *(see Sedona p. 162)* and ends in Jerome. The steep, narrow road is not recommended for vehicles pulling trailers more than 40 feet long. The nearby mountains are ideal for camping, fishing and hunting.

Jerome Chamber of Commerce: 310 Hull Ave., P.O. Box K, Jerome, AZ 86331. **Phone:** (928) 634-2900.

CONNOR HOTEL OF JEROME 928/634-5006

Historic Hotel. **Address:** 160 S Main St 86331

WHERE TO EAT

THE ASYLUM RESTAURANT 928/639-3197

American Casual Dining

$10-$32

AAA Inspector Notes: *Historic.* Billed as fun, fine dining, the experience at this cozy restaurant includes relaxed service and spectacular views. The wide selection of wines, interesting sauces and creative combinations, such as roast maple leaf duck breast on green chili brown rice with plum serrano salsa, add up to fine dining. **Features:** full bar, patio dining. **Reservations:** suggested. **Address:** 200 Hill St 86331 **Location:** 0.3 mi s on SR 89A, just s on Cobblestone Rd; center; in Jerome Grand Hotel. L D

GRAPES 928/639-8477

Pizza. Casual Dining. **Address:** 111 Main St 86331

HAUNTED HAMBURGER 928/634-0554

American. Casual Dining. **Address:** 410 Clark St 86331

KAIBAB NATIONAL FOREST (B-3)

• Attractions map p. 59

Elevations in the forest range from 3,000 ft. to 10,418 ft. at Kendrick Peak. Refer to AAA maps for additional elevation information.

Comprised of three districts north and south of Grand Canyon National Park *(see place listing p. 57)*, Kaibab National Forest covers 1.6 million acres. The portion north of the canyon includes Grand Canyon National Game Preserve, a thickly forested, domed limestone plateau. The Kaibab Plateau is the only known home of the Kaibab squirrel, a dark gray squirrel with a white tail and tufted ears. The southernmost of the three districts contains volcanic cones and scattered forested peaks.

Big game animals can be seen in roadside meadows and throughout the forest. Fishing can be enjoyed at several lakes. Recreational opportunities within the national forest include camping, hiking, mountain biking, horseback riding and cross-country skiing.

The Kaibab Plateau-North Rim Scenic Byway has been described as the most beautiful 42 miles in the United States. The scenic parkway begins at Jacob Lake and winds through dense forests and alpine meadows to culminate at the North Rim of the Grand Canyon; the road is closed mid-October through May.

For further information contact the Kaibab Plateau Visitor Center (mid-May through Sept. 30), US 89A and SR 67, Jacob Lake, AZ 86022, phone (928) 643-7298; or the Williams Visitor Center, 200 W. Railroad Ave., Williams, AZ 86046; phone (928) 635-1418. *See Recreation Areas Chart.*

KAYENTA (A-5) pop. 5,189, elev. 5,641'

Kayenta grew from a trading post that John Wetherill established in 1910. He first called it Oljeto, but eventually changed the name to Kayenta after a deep spring nearby. The area's uranium and coal deposits are important in the town's economy. Scenic US 163, beginning at US 160, passes through Kayenta before running 22 miles north to the Utah border and the entrance to Monument Valley Navajo Tribal Park *(see place listing p. 81)*.

Crawley's Monument Valley Tours offers backcountry trips into areas of the park. For further information about the tours and the area contact Crawley's Monument Valley Tours, P.O. Box 187, Kayenta, AZ 86033; phone (928) 429-6833.

HAMPTON INN OF KAYENTA 928/697-3170

 Hotel. **Address:** Hwy 160 86033

AAA Benefit: Members save up to 15%!

WETHERILL INN 928/697-3231

Hotel

Address: US Hwy 163 86033 **Location:** 1 mi n of jct US 160. **Facility:** 54 units. 2 stories (no elevator), exterior corridors. **Pool:** heated indoor. **Guest Services:** coin laundry. **Featured Amenity: continental breakfast.**

WHERE TO EAT

REUBEN HEFLIN RESTAURANT 928/697-3170

Regional American. Casual Dining. **Address:** Hwy 160 86033

KINGMAN (C-2) pop. 28,068, elev. 3,334'

• Hotels p. 72 • Restaurants p. 73
• Part of Grand Canyon National Park area — see map p. 57

Kingman, the county seat of Mohave County, is located between Las Vegas and the Grand Canyon and was established in the early 1880s with the arrival of the railroad. It also serves as a transportation corridor to Grand Canyon National Park South Rim *(see place listing p. 60)* as well as the Grand Canyon Skywalk *(see attraction listing)* in the western area.

Kingman's popularity is maintained as the main stop on the longest existing stretch of Historic Route 66—the first completely paved national highway in the country. Linking hundreds of towns and cities between Chicago and Los Angeles, Route 66 formed the main street of towns along its route, thus its nickname "Main Street of America." Today travelers can traverse some 158 miles of historic roadway beginning west of Ashfork, continuing through Seligman, Peach Springs, Valentine, Truxton, Hackberry and on to Kingman and through Oatman to Topock.

Some 800 classic cars start their engines in Seligman and head 140 miles to Topock/Golden Shores during the Historic Route 66 Fun Run, held the first weekend in May. Communities along the route celebrate with food and entertainment.

At the junction of I-40 and US 93, Kingman is an access point to lakes Mead, Mohave and Havasu. Ghost towns surround this former gold-mining community. Towns such as Oatman and Chloride were business and social centers for surrounding mining camps during the early 20th century. With many of their original buildings still standing, Oatman and Chloride draw both filmmakers and tourists. In Oatman, visitors may even hand-feed the burros—descendants of those left behind by early-day miners—that roam the town's streets. From Kingman, Oatman is reached by SR 66 (Old Route 66). Chloride is north of Kingman on SR 93 at mile marker 53, 4 miles off the highway on CR 125.

Hualapai Mountain Park (pronounced Wal-lah-pie) is 12 miles southeast. It is named for the Native Americans who inhabited the mountains until the 1870s. Mountain elevations range from 5,000 to 8,500 feet, and a variety of native wildlife lives here, including deer, eagles, elk, foxes, hawks, rabbits and squirrels. *See Recreation Areas Chart.*

City of Kingman Visitor Center: 120 W. Andy Devine Ave., Kingman, AZ 86401. **Phone:** (928) 753-6106 or (866) 427-7866.

GRAND CANYON SKYWALK is at the far western end of the Grand Canyon; from Kingman, go north on CR 20 (Stockton Hill Rd.) about 42 mi. to CR 25 (Pierce Ferry Rd.), CR 25 n. about 7 mi. to CR 261 (Diamond Bar Rd.) and Diamond Bar Rd. 21 mi. to Grand Canyon West (the Hualapai Indian tribe's recreation area), an approximate 100-minute drive. Drivers should follow the road to the parking lot by Grand Canyon West Airport.

Staunch environmentalists protested when the Hualapai tribe built this horseshoe-shaped, glass-floored "sky bridge" on their reservation land in 2007. Extending 70 feet out from the canyon rim, the skywalk is suspended 4,000 feet above the canyon bottom and the Colorado River far, far below. Weighing 1.2 million pounds, it's unquestionably an architectural wonder and a unique engineering feat, and the views—as long as you don't suffer from acrophobia—are jaw-dropping. Grand Canyon National Park visitors should keep in mind that the location is remote, easily a 4.5-hour drive from the park's South Rim.

Note: To stroll on the skywalk you must first purchase a Grand Canyon West tour package; the fee includes hop-on, hop-off bus transportation to the skywalk, a faux Native American village, a mock cowboy town and the Guano Point overlook. Personal items are not permitted on the skywalk (free lockers are available for storage). Cameras are strictly prohibited; you will be searched. Allow 2-4 hours minimum to view the skywalk and take the Grand Canyon West tour.

Hours: Daily 7-7, Apr.-Sept.; 8-5, rest of year (weather permitting). Last admission 2 hours before closing. **Cost:** Grand Canyon West Legacy Gold Package (includes skywalk admission, permitting fee and hop-on, hop-off shuttle transportation to the Native American village, Hualapai Ranch and the Guano Point overlook) $82.37. **Phone:** (928) 769-2636 or (888) 868-9378. GT

HISTORIC ROUTE 66 MUSEUM is at 120 W. Andy Devine Ave. Dioramas, murals and photos depict the history of historic Route 66 from its early use by Native Americans and pioneers to the travelers of the 1950s. The Route 66 EV (electric vehicle) Museum is on the first floor. A reading room and archive are available. **Time:** Allow 30 minutes minimum. **Hours:** Mon.-Fri. 9-5, Sat. 1-5. Closed Jan. 1, Easter, Thanksgiving and Christmas. **Cost:** (includes pass to Bonelli House and Mohave Museum of History and Arts) $4; $3 (ages 60+); free (ages 0-11 with adult). **Phone:** (928) 753-3195.

BEST WESTERN PLUS A WAYFARER'S INN & SUITES 928/753-6271

Hotel

AAA Benefit: Members save up to 15% and earn bonus points!

Address: 2815 E Andy Devine Ave 86401 **Location:** I-40 exit 53, 0.5 mi w on Route 66. **Facility:** 100 units. 2 stories, exterior corridors. **Pool:** heated outdoor. **Activities:** hot tub, exercise room. **Guest Services:** valet and coin laundry. **Featured Amenity:** breakfast buffet. *(See ad this page.)*

BEST WESTERN PLUS KING'S INN & SUITES 928/753-6101

Hotel

AAA Benefit: Members save up to 15% and earn bonus points!

Address: 2930 E Andy Devine Ave 86401 **Location:** I-40 exit 53, just w on Route 66. **Facility:** 100 units, some two bedrooms and efficiencies. 2 stories, exterior corridors. **Pool:** heated outdoor. **Activities:** hot tub, exercise room. **Guest Services:** valet and coin laundry. **Featured Amenity:** breakfast buffet.

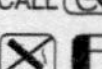

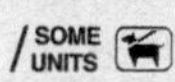

▼ See AAA listing this page ▼

LARION INN 928/718-1717

Hotel

Address: 3129 E Andy Devine Ave 86401 **Location:** I-40 exit 53, just w on Route 66. **Facility:** 60 units. 3 stories, interior corridors. **Pool:** heated indoor. **Activities:** hot tub, exercise room. **Guest Services:** coin laundry. **Featured Amenity: full hot breakfast.**

AMPTON INN & SUITES 928/692-0200

Hotel. **Address:** 1791 ycamore Ave 86409

AAA Benefit: Members save up to 15%!

OLIDAY INN EXPRESS HOTEL & SUITES 928/718-4343

Hotel

Address: 3031 E Andy Devine Ave 86401 **Location:** I-40 exit 53, just w on Route 66. **Facility:** 75 units, some two bedrooms. 3 stories, interior corridors. **Pool:** heated indoor. **Activities:** hot tub, exercise room. **Guest Services:** valet and coin laundry. **Featured Amenity: full hot breakfast.**

IOME2 SUITES BY HILTON KINGMAN 928/529-5500

Extended Stay Hotel. **Address:** 1121 Sunrise Ave 86401

AAA Benefit: Members save up to 15%!

A QUINTA INN & SUITES 928/529-5070

Hotel. **Address:** 3419 Hotel Way 86401

SPRINGHILL SUITES BY MARRIOTT 928/753-8766

Hotel

SPRINGHILL SUITES MARRIOTT **AAA Benefit:** Members save 5% or more!

Address: 3101 E Andy Devine Ave 86401 **Location:** I-40 exit 53, just w on Route 66. **Facility:** 73 units. 4 stories, interior corridors. **Pool:** heated indoor. **Activities:** exercise room. **Guest Services:** valet and coin laundry.

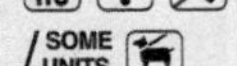

WHERE TO EAT

EL PALACIO 928/718-0018

Mexican. Casual Dining. **Address:** 401 E Andy Devine Ave 86401

FLOYD & CO REAL PIT BBQ 928/757-8227

Southern Barbecue. Quick Serve. **Address:** 420 E Beale St 86401

THE GARLIC CLOVE RESTAURANT & CATERING 928/753-4100

Italian. Casual Dining. **Address:** 509 E Beale St 86401

MATTINA'S RISTORANTE & STEAKHOUSE 928/753-7504

Italian. Casual Dining. **Address:** 318 E Oak St 86401

MR. D'Z ROUTE 66 DINER 928/718-0066

American. Casual Dining. **Address:** 105 E Andy Devine Ave 86401

RICKETY CRICKET BREWING 928/263-8444

American. Brewpub. **Address:** 312 E Beale St 86401

LAKE HAVASU CITY (D-1) pop. 52,527, elev. 482'

• Hotels p. 74 • Restaurants p. 74

Lake Havasu City takes its name from the lake by which it lies. (Havasu is a Mohave Indian word meaning "blue-green water.") Formed by the impoundment of Parker Dam in 1938, Lake Havasu is fed by the Colorado River. The 45-mile-long lake has a maximum width of 3 miles and supplies water to Arizona, Los Angeles and intermediate cities.

In 1963 industrialist Robert P. McCulloch Sr. purchased a 3,500-acre former Army Air Corps landing strip and rest camp on Pittsburg Point, a peninsula jutting into the Colorado River. After expanding the area by another 13,000 acres, McCulloch teamed up with Disneyland developer C.V. Wood to create a planned community and tourist destination.

The new town captured the world's attention in 1968 when McCulloch bought the London Bridge *(see attraction listing)*. Originally built in 1831 by architect John Rennie, the multi-arch bridge resided over the Thames River until 1968, when it began to sink into the river. Dismantled stone by stone, the bridge was brought over from London and reconstructed on Pittsburg Point. A man-made canal (known today as Bridgewater Channel) was dug underneath, separating Pittsburg Point from the land and forming an island.

Just over the bridge and along the island side of Bridgewater Channel, London Bridge Beach (1340 McCulloch Blvd.) has basketball and sand volleyball courts, playgrounds, picnicking facilities and a dog park. On the opposite side of the channel, Rotary Community Park (1400 S. Smoketree Ave.) features volleyball and bocce courts, a skate park, playgrounds, picnicking facilities, a buoyed swimming area and a shaded walkway.

Lake Havasu provides a setting for all types of water-related activities. Fishing is excellent, especially for striped and large-mouth bass, catfish and panfish; several public fishing docks and piers are available. Numerous companies rent canoes, kayaks, houseboats, pontoon boats, sailboats and other watercraft for use on the lake; contact the convention and visitors bureau for more information.

Believe it or not, lighthouses exist in landlocked Arizona. Twenty-four functioning one-third-scale replicas of famous U.S. lighthouses stand along the shoreline of Lake Havasu, providing navigational aid *and* a conversation piece.

On the last day in November and the first day in December a fleet of illuminated boats on the lake makes the Boat Parade of Lights a dazzling sight spectators won't soon forget.

Lake Havasu City Convention and Visitors Bureau: 314 London Bridge Rd., Lake Havasu City, AZ 86403. **Phone:** (928) 453-3444 or (800) 242-8278.

Shopping: The English Village, Island Fashion Mall, Havasu Downtown District and Shops at Lake Havasu all provide shopping opportunities in the London Bridge area.

HAMPTON INN BY HILTON LAKE HAVASU 928/855-4071

SAVE Hotel. **Address:** 245 London Bridge Rd 86403

AAA Benefit: Members save up to 15%!

HOLIDAY INN EXPRESS & SUITES 928/733-6388

Hotel. **Address:** 40 London Bridge Rd 86403

ISLAND SUITES 928/855-7333

Extended Stay Hotel. **Address:** 236 S Lake Havasu Ave 86403

LONDON BRIDGE RESORT 928/855-0888

Resort Hotel

Address: 1477 Queens Bay 86403 **Location:** Waterfront. SR 95, just sw on Swanson Ave. **Facility:** Located adjacent to London Bridge, this waterfront hotel offers many recreational facilities and large, comfortable suites which vary in size; some offer lake views. 122 efficiencies, some two bedrooms. 3 stories, interior corridors. **Terms:** check-in 4 pm. **Amenities:** safes. **Dining:** 2 restaurants, also, Martini Bay, see separate listing, nightclub. **Pool:** heated outdoor. **Activities:** hot tub, boat dock, regulation golf, tennis, recreation programs, picnic facilities, exercise room, massage. **Guest Services:** valet and coin laundry, area transportation. **Featured Amenity: breakfast buffet.** *(See ad this page.)*

SAVE BIZ

THE NAUTICAL BEACHFRONT RESORT 928/855-2141

Resort Hotel. **Address:** 1000 McCulloch Blvd N 86403

QUALITY INN & SUITES 928/855-1111

Hotel. **Address:** 271 S Lake Havasu Ave 86403

RODEWAY INN & SUITES 928/453-4656

Hotel. **Address:** 335 London Bridge Rd 86403

WHERE TO EAT

ANGELINA'S ITALIAN KITCHEN 928/680-3868

Italian. Casual Dining. **Address:** 1530 El Camino Dr 86403

BARLEY BROS. RESTAURANT & BREWERY 928/505-7837

American. Brewpub. **Address:** 1425 McCulloch Blvd N 86403

CASA SERRANO 928/854-5500

Mexican. Casual Dining. **Address:** 150 Swanson Ave 86403

▼ *See AAA listing this page* ▼

CHA' BONES 928/854-5554

American. Casual Dining. **Address:** 112 London Bridge Rd 86403

FARRELL'S GOLDEN HORSESHOE STEAKHOUSE 928/764-3800

Steak. Casual Dining. **Address:** 4501 N London Bridge Rd 86404

JAVELINA CANTINA 928/855-8226

Mexican. Casual Dining. **Address:** 1420 N McCulloch Blvd 86403

JUICY'S RIVER CAFE 928/855-8429

American. Casual Dining. **Address:** 42 Smoketree Ave S 86403

MARIO'S ITALIAN RESTAURANT & LOUNGE 928/854-3223

Italian. Casual Dining. **Address:** 350 London Bridge Rd 86403

MARTINI BAY 928/855-0888

International Casual Dining
$14-$36

AAA Inspector Notes: High-gloss decor and fun music make this a happening place. Thankfully, the food is just as enjoyable as the surroundings. Mediterranean-inspired dishes include plates of freshly grilled steaks and seafood as well as cold, crisp salads. Plenty of hearty appetizers await, including marinated beef filet skewers to lighter options like smoked chicken quesadillas. **Features:** full bar, patio dining, happy hour. **Address:** 1477 Queens Bay 86403 **Location:** SR 95, just sw on Swanson Ave; in London Bridge Resort. *(See ad p. 74.)* D

MONTANA STEAK HOUSE 928/855-3736

Steak. Casual Dining. **Address:** 3301 Maricopa Ave 86406

MUDSHARK BREWING CO 928/453-2981

American. Brewpub. **Address:** 210 Swanson Ave 86403

THE RED ONION 928/505-0302

American. Casual Dining. **Address:** 2013 McCulloch Blvd N 86403

SCOTTY'S BROASTED CHICKEN & RIBS 928/680-4441

Chicken. Quick Serve. **Address:** 410 El Camino Way 86403

SHO-GUN JAPANESE CUISINE 928/680-6668

Japanese. Casual Dining. **Address:** 90 Swanson Ave 86403

SHUGRUE'S 928/453-1400

Steak. Casual Dining. **Address:** 1425 McCulloch Blvd N 86403

THE TURTLE GRILL 928/855-1897

American. Casual Dining. **Address:** 1000 McCulloch Blvd N 86403

GEM LAKE MEAD NATIONAL RECREATION AREA (B-1)

• **Restaurants p. 77**

This 1.5 million-acre recreation area, established in 1964, was created around Lake Mead, the massive Colorado River reservoir resulting from the construction of Hoover Dam. Exit wild river rapids. Enter motorboating, water skiing and fishing on a placid lake. Further downstream, the completion of Davis Dam in 1951 impounded Lake Mohave, another popular spot with the boat and Jet Ski set. In all, the recreation area extends about 140 miles along the Colorado River from the west end of Grand Canyon National Park, Ariz., down to Bullhead City, Ariz., and its neighbor across the river, Laughlin, Nev.

Though man remodeled nature to suit his thirst for water and hydroelectric power, that doesn't mean the native desert bighorn sheep, mountain lions, mule deer, coyotes, foxes, bobcats, lizards, snakes and tortoises were going to take a hike. Not by a long shot. They're all still here, where three of America's four desert ecosystems—the Mojave, the Great Basin and the Sonoran deserts—meet against a starkly beautiful backdrop of desert mountains, cliffs, canyons and plateaus.

If you're here on a day trip from Vegas and water sports aren't in the cards, point your ride down scenic Lakeshore Road. A good starting point is at the junction of Lakeshore and US 93, next to the Alan Bible Visitor Center. Skirting the shores of Lake Mead, the road winds through desert terrain, passing beaches, boat marinas and several nice viewpoints, some with sheltered picnic tables. From the suggested starting point to the Lake Mead Parkway entrance station, with a few short stops, budget about 30 to 40 minutes.

From fall through spring (soaring summer temps can spell heat stroke), go for a hike. One of the area's best hiking paths is the Redstone Trail, off the Northshore Road at Mile Marker 27. From the Lake Mead Parkway entrance station, it's a good half-hour drive, but well worth it. Sandy walking trails snake past huge, jumbled red rock formations similar to what you'll see at nearby Valley of Fire State Park. The difference is this hidden gem usually lacks the crowds you'll find up the road. Rock scrambling and photography opportunities are outstanding. Pack plenty of water, and perhaps, a lunch; there's a picnic area with shaded tables.

Back at the lakes, whip out your rod and reel. Striped and largemouth bass are the chief catches in Lake Mead; crappie and catfish are common in the waters of Callville Bay. Wherever you cast off, remember that either a Nevada or an Arizona fishing license is required.

If boats, kayaks and personal watercraft are too much fuss, go for a swim. There's a long, kid-friendly strand at Lake Mead's Boulder Beach. The lake bottom here is a bit rocky; those with sensitive tootsies should wear water shoes or sport sandals. **Note:** No lifeguards are on duty at Boulder Beach or anywhere else in the recreation area. Life jackets are recommended.

Most areas are open daily 24 hours; signs are posted for areas that close earlier. Alan Bible Visitor Center daily 9-4:30. Closed Jan. 1, Thanksgiving and Christmas. Food is available. Admission $20 (per private vehicle); $15 (per motorcycle); $10 (per person arriving by other means). Lake-use fee $16 (per boat). Passes are valid for up to 7 days. For further information contact Lake Mead National Recreation Area, 601 Nevada Way, Boulder City, NV 89005. Phone (702) 293-8990 for the Alan Bible Visitor Center. *See Recreation Areas Chart.*

GEM **HOOVER DAM** is along SR 172 (Hoover Dam Access Rd.), about 8 mi. n.e. of Boulder City. Soaring 726 feet high (about 60 stories), this curved wall of concrete is one of the highest arched-gravity dams ever constructed. It's also a hugely popular day trip from Vegas, and with good reason. The Depression-era engineering marvel (built 1931-35) sits in Black Canyon, a ruggedly dramatic Colorado River chasm that's home to the dam, its mega-wattage hydroelectric powerplant and a visitor center/tourist complex with all the bells and whistles.

Hoover Dam was lucky enough to be born in the 1930s, the peak of the Art Deco craze. Witness the dam's main plaza, a Deco-style beauty graced with terrazzo floor-embedded celestial diagrams and the twin, 30-foot-high bronze sculptures, the Winged Figures of the Republic (luck seekers take note: rubbing the statues' toes will reputedly bring you good luck). Walking across the top of the dam, take time to admire the beautiful bas-relief panels adorning the elevator towers, and stop in the center at the Arizona-Nevada state line to grab a selfie as you stand in two states at once.

The Hoover Dam Visitor Center is a glass-and-steel building perched on the upper cliffs of Black Canyon; feel free to wander the excellent, upper level exhibits, many of them high-tech, interactive affairs. Once you tire of learning about turbines, transformers and penstocks, step out on the top level's outdoor observation platform for dizzying photo-ops, both of the dam and the downstream Mike O'Callaghan-Pat Tillman Memorial Bridge *(see attraction listing this page)*. The Original Exhibit Building, built in the 1940s and located across the dam roadway, displays a vintage, raised-relief topographical map of the entire desert Southwest, a must-see for cartography geeks.

For the full, in-depth experience, the guided 30-minute Powerplant Tour begins 537 feet underground and views eight of the plant's 17 generators. The Dam Tour is a behind-the-scenes 1-hour guided experience which visits the Powerplant leg of the tour followed by tunnels and inspection points.

Note: Before reaching the dam you'll pass through a vehicle inspection station. Upon entering the visitor center, expect an airport-style security inspection. Food, weapons, knives and oversize backpacks and purses are prohibited; however, bottled water is permitted.

Hours: Visitor center daily 9-5. Last admission 1 hour 15 minutes minutes before closing. Parking structure daily 8-5:15. Closed Thanksgiving and Christmas. **Cost:** Dam Tour $30. Powerplant Tour $15; $12 (ages 4-16, ages 62+ and military with ID); free (ages 0-3 and active military in uniform). Visitor center $10; free (ages 0-3). The availability of either guided tour is subject to elevator malfunctions and power plant maintenance; phone ahead for updates. The Dam Tour is conducted on a first-come, first-served basis; a maximum of 30 people are allowed on each tour. Under 8 and the physically impaired are not permitted on the Dam Tour. **Parking:** $10. **Phone:** (702) 494-2517 or (866) 730-9097. GT YI

LAKE MEAD, extending behind Hoover Dam, is 110 miles long, averages 200 feet deep at normal capacity and has a 550-mile shoreline. Due to recent drought conditions, the lake's surface elevation is 1,080 feet (1,229 feet is considered a full pool).

Nevada recreational areas with marinas and launch facilities include Hemenway Harbor, 4 miles northeast of Boulder City; and Callville Bay, 22 miles east of North Las Vegas. An additional Arizona center is about 80 miles north of Kingman at Temple Bar. The lake also offers numerous primitive launch ramps without services.

Exhibits and a film about natural and cultural history are offered at the Alan Bible Visitor Center, 4 miles east of Boulder City at US 93 and Lakeshore Road, overlooking Lake Mead. A botanical and cactus garden surrounds the visitor center. *See Recreation Areas Chart.*

Hours: Alan Bible Visitor Center daily 9-4:30. Closed Jan. 1, Thanksgiving and Christmas. **Cost:** Admission, valid for up to 7 days, $20 (per private vehicle); $16 (per motorized boat); $15 (per motorcycle); $10 (per person arriving by other means). **Phone:** (702) 293-8990 for the Alan Bible Visitor Center.

Lake Mead Cruises depart from the Lake Mead Cruises Landing at Hemenway Harbor at 490 Horsepower Rd., just off Lakeshore Rd. Excursion cruises on a Mississippi-style paddlewheeler include a narration about area history and the construction of Hoover Dam. Brunch and dinner cruises also are available April through October.

Note: Visitors traveling to Hemenway Harbor must pay the Lake Mead National Recreation Area access fee of $20 per private vehicle; $15 per motorcycle or $10 per person arriving by other means. **Hours:** Ninety-minute round-trip excursion cruises depart daily at noon and 2, Apr.-Oct.; daily at noon (also Mon., Wed. and Sat. at 2), Feb.-Mar. and in Nov. **Cost:** $26; $13 (ages 2-11). Reservations are recommended. **Phone:** (702) 293-6180 or (866) 292-9191. GT YI

LAKE MOHAVE extends 67 mi. s. from Hoover Dam to Davis Dam. Launching ramps, trailer sites, refreshment concessions, boat rentals and overnight accommodations are available at Katherine Landing, about 35 miles west of Kingman, Ariz., and at Cottonwood Cove, 14 miles east of Searchlight. Accommodations also are available a short distance away in Needles, Calif., and Bullhead City, Ariz. Willow Beach, 28 miles east of Boulder City on US 93, offers a launch ramp and concession facilities. Information about recreational facilities is available at all three sites.

MIKE O'CALLAGHAN-PAT TILLMAN MEMORIAL BRIDGE is along US 93, about 5.5 mi. n.e. of Boulder City. Linking Nevada and Arizona, this arched, 1,900-foot-long concrete-and-steel span is some 1,500 feet downstream from Hoover Dam.

pened in 2010, the bridge was built to replace a ngstanding traffic bottleneck: the two-lane section f US 93 that crossed the Colorado River atop oover Dam (now SR 172).

Thanks to a 6-foot-wide pedestrian sidewalk running its length, the bridge—which honors former Neada Governor Mike O'Callaghan and Afghanistan ar hero Pat Tillman—has become a major attracon. Lined with etched information panels, the sidealk is accessible only from the Nevada side (it ead-ends at the Arizona side); follow signs to the oover Dam Access Road (SR 172) exit. The arking lot for visitors is about 2 miles down the oad; if the bridge lot is full, an overflow lot is a ouple hundred yards further down.

From this lofty perch you'll have a grand view of e Hoover Dam, not to mention a jaw-dropping and stomach-churning, for those afraid of heights) erspective of the turquoise Colorado River 900 feet elow, wedged between the rock cliffs that form lack Canyon. Prime time for photography is mid- to ate-afternoon.

Note: Before reaching the bridge and Hoover)am area you'll pass through a vehicle inspection ecurity station. A switchback trail with 70 steps (and aved, wheelchair-accessible ramps) provides acess to the pedestrian sidewalk. **Time:** Allow 45 ninutes minimum. **Hours:** Pedestrian sidewalk pen daily dawn-dusk. **Cost:** Free.

OX SMOKEHOUSE BBQ 702/489-2211

Barbecue. Quick Serve. **Address:** 1007 Elm St 89005

AVEEN

VEE QUIVA HOTEL 520/946-4452

Hotel

Address: 15091 S Komatke Ln 85339 **Location:** I-10 exit 139 (51st Ave), 10 mi s. **Facility:** Located in the foothills just south of the city, this boutique-style property offers upscale state-of-the-art guest rooms along with multiple dining and entertainment options. 90 units. 3 stories, interior corridors. *Bath:* shower only. **Parking:** on-site and valet. **Terms:** check-in 4 pm. **Dining:** 5 restaurants, nightclub, entertainment. **Pool:** heated outdoor. **Activities:** hot tub, exercise room. **Guest Services:** valet laundry. *(See ad p. 54.)*

LITCHFIELD PARK pop. 5,476, elev. 1,030'

• Hotels & Restaurants map & index p. 117
• Part of Phoenix area — see map p. 91

THE WIGWAM 623/935-3811 48

Historic Resort Hotel

Address: 300 E Wigwam Blvd 85340 **Location:** I-10 exit 128 (Litchfield Rd), 2.4 mi n, then 0.4 mi e. **Facility:** This gracious resort, which opened in 1929, offers beautifully renovated public areas, two of their three golf courses by Robert Trent Jones Sr., lushly landscaped grounds and oversize rooms. 331 units, some two bedrooms. 1-2 stories (no elevator), exterior corridors. **Parking:** on-site (fee) and valet. **Terms:** check-in 4 pm. **Amenities:** safes. **Dining:** 3 restaurants, also, Litchfield's, see separate listing. **Pool:** heated outdoor. **Activities:** sauna, hot tub, steamroom, regulation golf, tennis, recreation programs, bicycles, game room, lawn sports, health club, spa. **Guest Services:** valet laundry, boarding pass kiosk, area transportation.

WHERE TO EAT

LITCHFIELD'S 623/935-3811 30

New American. Casual Dining. **Address:** 300 E Wigwam Blvd 85340

MARANA pop. 34,961

• Restaurants p. 78
• Hotels & Restaurants map & index p. 204
• Part of Tucson area — see map p. 187

BEST WESTERN GOLD POPPY INN 520/579-7202 44

Hotel

AAA Benefit: Members save up to 15% and earn bonus points!

Address: 4930 W Ina Rd 85743 **Location:** I-10 exit 248 (Ina Rd), just w. **Facility:** 60 units. 3 stories, interior corridors. **Pool:** outdoor. **Activities:** hot tub, exercise room. **Featured Amenity:** breakfast buffet.

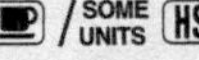

COMFORT INN & SUITES 520/579-1099 41

Hotel. **Address:** 8425 N Cracker Barrel Rd 85743

(See map & index p. 204.)

HOLIDAY INN EXPRESS & SUITES TUCSON NORTH-MARANA
520/572-4777 43

Hotel. **Address:** 8373 N Cracker Barrel Rd 85743

LA QUINTA INN & SUITES NW TUCSON MARANA
520/572-4235 42

Hotel. **Address:** 6020 W Hospitality Rd 85743

THE RITZ-CARLTON, DOVE MOUNTAIN 520/572-3000

AAA Benefit: Unequaled service at special member savings!

Address: 15000 N Secret Springs Dr 85658 **Location:** I-10 exit 240 (Tangerine Rd), 5 mi e to Dove Mountain Dr, then 4.5 mi n, follow signs. **Facility:** Nestled into the Tortolita Mountains, this elegant resort features guest rooms with expansive views and luxurious baths as well as world-class golf and spa facilities. 253 units. 1-5 stories, interior corridors. **Parking:** on-site and valet. **Terms:** check-in 4 pm. **Amenities:** safes. **Dining:** 4 restaurants, also, Core Kitchen & Wine Bar, see separate listing. **Pool:** heated outdoor. **Activities:** sauna, hot tub, steamroom, regulation golf, tennis, recreation programs, kids club, bicycles, game room, lawn sports, trails, health club, spa. **Guest Services:** valet laundry, area transportation.

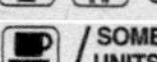
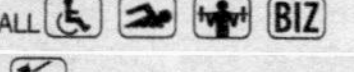

WHERE TO EAT

CORE KITCHEN & WINE BAR 520/572-3000

Regional American. Fine Dining. **Address:** 15000 N Secret Springs Dr 85658

LA OLLA MEXICAN CAFE 520/579-0950 68

Mexican. Casual Dining. **Address:** 8553 N Silverbell Rd 85743

LI'L ABNER'S STEAKHOUSE 520/744-2800 69

Steak. Casual Dining. **Address:** 8500 N Silverbell Rd 85743

MARICOPA (E-3) pop. 43,482, elev. 1,177'

Prevalent clear blue skies beckon fans of soaring to Maricopa. This area at the foot of the Sierra Estrella Mountains is noted for its thermal conditions. Arizona Soaring, (520) 568-2318, is at 22548 N. Sailport Way.

HARRAH'S AK-CHIN CASINO RESORT 480/802-5000

Hotel. **Address:** 15406 Maricopa Rd 85239

MESA (J-4) pop. 439,041, elev. 1,234'

- **Restaurants p. 80**
- **Hotels & Restaurants map & index p. 126**
- **Part of Phoenix area — see map p. 91**

Mesa (Spanish for "tabletop") is in the center of the Salt River Valley on a plateau. The area has long been inhabited by Native Americans, including the Ancestral Desert People, or "the Departed Ones." The resourceful tribe realized the need for water for irrigation and dug some 125 miles of canals around 700 B.C. Some of these irrigation ditches are still in use and can be seen at the Park of the Canals and Mesa Grande Ruins.

In 1883 the founding Mormon community discovered the ancient canal system and used it to irrigate the thousands of fertile acres of farmland above the Salt River. Alfalfa, cotton, wheat and grapes were the major crops; citrus was introduced in 1897. Agriculture carried the town into the 20th century; today, the aviation, education and health care industries play a big role in Mesa's economy.

Recreation areas, mostly east and north of the city are easily accessible from bike-friendly Mesa. Rafting and other water sports on the Salt River are popular as are varied activities available within the Apache Lake and Canyon Lake recreation areas *(see attraction listings p. 28)* and on Theodore Roosevelt Lake and Saguaro Lake. *See Recreation Areas Chart.*

Mesa also hosts major league baseball at two stadiums: Sloan Park, the spring training home of the Chicago Cubs, and Hohokam Stadium, home of the Oakland A's.

Visit Mesa: 120 N. Center St., Mesa, AZ 85201. **Phone:** (480) 827-4700 or (800) 283-6372.

Shopping: The largest indoor shopping centers in the city are Fiesta Mall, US 60 and Alma School Road, which offers Dillard's Clearance Center; and Superstition Springs Center, at US 60 and Superstition Springs Boulevard, which offers Dillard's, JC-Penney, Macy's and Sears. When it comes to open-air destination shopping, Village Square at Dana Park, at Val Vista Drive and Baseline Road, offers such stores as Ann Taylor Loft, Anthropologie, Chico's and Talbot's. Mesa Riverview, at Dobson Road and Loop 202 Freeway, includes Bass Pro Shops Outdoor World and Marshalls.

Bargain hunters can find discounted name-brand merchandise at Power Square Mall, a half-mile south of US 60 at Power and Baseline roads. The Mesa Market Place Swap Meet boasts more than 1,500 vendors offering new and used merchandise at its shaded facility at 10550 E. Baseline Rd.

ARIZONA MUSEUM OF NATURAL HISTORY, 53 N. Macdonald St., covers the history of Arizona from the days of the dinosaurs to the 21st century. Permanent and temporary exhibits focus on Arizona's prehistoric life, featuring animated dinosaurs, dinosaur skeletons and other fossil specimens. Archeology displays highlight the life of Arizona's ancient Ancestral Desert People, while reminders of old Mesa's past include territorial jail cells and the Lost Dutchman's Gold Mine.

Time: Allow 1 hour minimum. **Hours:** Tues.-Fri. 10-5, Sat. 11-5, Sun. 1-5; closed city and major holidays. **Cost:** $12; $10 (ages 65+); $8 (students ages 13+ with ID); $7 (ages 3-12). **Phone:** (480) 644-2230.

GOLFLAND/SUNSPLASH, 155 W. Hampton Ave., is a 15-acre miniature golf and water park complex that offers more than 30 attractions, including the Master Blaster, the four-person Stormrider, a wave pool and a lazy river. Year-round attractions include

ee map & index p. 126.)

ree miniature golf courses, bumper boats, go-arts, a video arcade and laser tag. Changing rooms nd lockers are available.

Hours: Sunsplash Sun.-Thurs. 11-6, Fri.-Sat. 11-11, lemorial Day-Labor Day; Sat.-Sun., day after Labor ay through mid-Sept.; phone for opening and closing mes. Golfland Mon.-Thurs. 11-10, Fri.-Sat. 11 a.m.-idnight, Sun. 11-9. Phone ahead to confirm chedule. **Cost:** Sunsplash $29.99; $19.99 (ages 55+, nder 48 inches tall, active military and after 4 p.m.); 3 (ages 0-2). Golfland free. Fees apply for golf, go-arts, bumper boats and other activities. Prices may ary; phone ahead. **Phone:** (480) 834-8319.

D.E.A. MUSEUM, 150 W. Pepper Pl., offers chil-ren the opportunity to view, create and explore arious forms of art. Six new exhibitions are intro-uced each year, and workshops teach a variety of kills from cartooning to printmaking. ArtVille, a per-nanent gallery, highlights art activities for children ges 0-4. **Time:** Allow 1 hour minimum. **Hours:** ues.-Sat. 9-4 (also Fri. 4-6), Sun. noon-4. The main allery is closed periodically for exhibit installation. losed Jan. 1, Martin Luther King Jr. Day, July 4, abor Day, Veterans Day, Thanksgiving and hristmas. Phone ahead to confirm schedule. **Cost:** 9; free (ages 0-1). **Phone:** (480) 644-2467.

BEST WESTERN LEGACY INN & SUITES
480/457-8181 59

Hotel

AAA Benefit: Members save up to 15% and earn bonus points!

Address: 4470 S Power Rd 85212 **Location:** Santan Frwy (Loop 202) exit Power Rd, just n. **Facility:** 110 units. 3 stories, interior corridors. **Pool:** heated outdoor. **Activities:** hot tub, exercise room. **Guest Services:** coin laundry, area transportation. **Featured Amenity:** breakfast buffet.

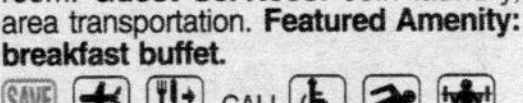

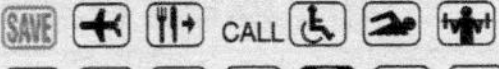

BEST WESTERN PLUS MESA 480/926-3600 54

Hotel

AAA Benefit: Members save up to 15% and earn bonus points!

Address: 1563 S Gilbert Rd 85204 **Location:** US 60 (Superstition Frwy) exit 182 (Gilbert Rd), just n. **Facility:** 115 units. 4 stories, interior corridors. **Pool:** heated outdoor. **Activities:** hot tub, exercise room. **Guest Services:** coin laundry. **Featured Amenity:** breakfast buffet.

BEST WESTERN SUPERSTITION SPRINGS INN
480/641-1164 56

Hotel

AAA Benefit: Members save up to 15% and earn bonus points!

Address: 1342 S Power Rd 85206 **Location:** Just n of US 60 (Superstition Frwy) exit 188 (Power Rd); northwest corner of Power Rd and Hampton Ave. Next to Superstition Springs Mall and Leisure World. **Facility:** 59 units, some kitchens. 2 stories (no elevator), exterior corridors. **Pool:** heated outdoor. **Activities:** hot tub, picnic facilities, limited exercise equipment. **Guest Services:** coin laundry. **Featured Amenity: full hot breakfast.**

COUNTRY INN & SUITES BY RADISSON 480/641-8000 58
Hotel. **Address:** 6650 E Superstition Springs Blvd 85206

COURTYARD BY MARRIOTT PHOENIX MESA
480/461-3000 47
Hotel. **Address:** 1221 S Westwood 85210

AAA Benefit: Members save 5% or more!

COURTYARD BY MARRIOTT PHOENIX MESA GATEWAY AIRPORT
480/351-7088 60

Hotel

COURTYARD **AAA Benefit:** Members save 5% or more!

Address: 6907 E Ray Rd 85212 **Location:** SR 202 exit 36 (Power Rd), 0.5 mi s to Ray Rd, then just e. **Facility:** 99 units. 4 stories, interior corridors. **Pool:** heated outdoor. **Activities:** hot tub, exercise room. **Guest Services:** valet and coin laundry, boarding pass kiosk.

DAYS HOTEL MESA NEAR PHOENIX 480/844-8900 53
Hotel. **Address:** 333 W Juanita Ave 85210

DELTA HOTELS BY MARRIOTT PHOENIX MESA
480/898-8300 45

Hotel

DELTA HOTELS **AAA Benefit:** Members save 5% or more!

Address: 200 N Centennial Way 85201 **Location:** US 60 (Superstition Frwy) exit 180 (Mesa Dr), 2 mi n, just w on Main St, then just n. **Facility:** 272 units. 12 stories, interior corridors. **Terms:** check-in 4 pm. **Amenities:** safes. **Pool:** heated outdoor. **Activities:** hot tub, exercise room. **Guest Services:** valet and coin laundry, boarding pass kiosk.

(See map & index p. 126.)

FOUR POINTS BY SHERATON AT PHOENIX MESA GATEWAY AIRPORT 480/579-2100 61

SAVE Hotel. **Address:** 6850 E Williams Field Rd 85212

AAA Benefit: Members save 5% or more!

GREENTREE INN & SUITES MESA 480/668-8000 50

Hotel. **Address:** 1405 S Westwood 85210

HILTON PHOENIX/MESA 480/833-5555 51

Hotel

Hilton HOTELS & RESORTS **AAA Benefit:** Members save up to 15%!

Address: 1011 W Holmes Ave 85210 **Location:** US 60 (Superstition Frwy) exit 178 (Alma School Rd), just n, then just e. Across from Fiesta Mall. **Facility:** 262 units. 8 stories, interior corridors. **Terms:** check-in 4 pm. **Amenities:** safes. **Pool:** heated outdoor. **Activities:** hot tub, exercise room. **Guest Services:** valet laundry, area transportation.

SAVE CALL

BIZ / SOME UNITS

HOLIDAY INN & SUITES PHOENIX-MESA/CHANDLER 480/964-7000 52

Hotel. **Address:** 1600 S Country Club Dr 85210

HYATT PLACE PHOENIX/MESA 480/969-8200 43

Hotel

HYATT PLACE **AAA Benefit:** Members save up to 10%!

Address: 1422 W Bass Pro Dr 85201 **Location:** Loop 202 exit 10 (Dobson Rd), just s, then just e. **Facility:** 152 units. 4 stories, interior corridors. **Pool:** heated outdoor. **Activities:** hot tub, exercise room. **Guest Services:** valet and coin laundry, area transportation. **Featured Amenity: breakfast buffet.**

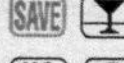
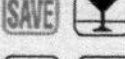

SAVE CALL BIZ

HS

/ SOME UNITS

LA QUINTA INN & SUITES MESA SUPERSTITION SPRINGS 480/654-1970 57

Hotel. **Address:** 6530 E Superstition Springs Blvd 85206

LA QUINTA INN & SUITES PHOENIX MESA WEST 480/844-8747 48

Hotel. **Address:** 902 W Grove Ave 85210

RAMADA MESA-MEZONA HOTEL 480/834-9233 46

Hotel. **Address:** 250 W Main St 85201

RESIDENCE INN BY MARRIOTT PHOENIX MESA 480/610-0100 49

SAVE Extended Stay Hotel. **Address:** 941 W Grove Ave 85210

AAA Benefit: Members save 5% or more!

SHERATON MESA HOTEL AT WRIGLEYVILLE WEST 480/664-1221

SAVE Hotel. **Address:** 860 N Riverview Dr 85201

AAA Benefit: Members save 5% or more!

SLEEP INN MESA 480/807-7760

Hotel. **Address:** 6347 E Southern Ave 85206

WHERE TO EAT

FLANCER'S 480/396-0077

Pizza. Casual Dining. **Address:** 1902 N Higley Rd 8520

MACAYO'S MEXICAN TABLE 480/820-02

Mexican. Casual Dining. **Address:** 1920 S Dobson 85202

MI AMIGOS MEXICAN GRILL 480/892-6822

Mexican. Casual Dining. **Address:** 1264 S Gilbert 85204

NANDO'S MEXICAN CAFE 480/830-8181

Mexican. Casual Dining. **Address:** 6715 E McDowell 85215

THE ORIGINAL BLUE ADOBE GRILLE 480/962-1000

Mexican. Casual Dining. **Address:** 144 N Country Cl Dr 85201

P.F. CHANG'S CHINA BISTRO 480/218-4900

Chinese. Fine Dining. **Address:** 6610 E Superstiti Springs Blvd 85206

SAKANA SUSHI & GRILL 480/218-1023

Sushi. Casual Dining. **Address:** 1853 S Power Rd 8520

SERRANO'S MEXICAN RESTAURANT

Mexican. Casual Dining.

LOCATIONS:

Address: 1021 S Power Rd 85205 **Phone:** 480/854-7455

Address: 1964 E McKellips Rd 85203 **Phone:** 480/649-3503

SHAANXI GARDEN 480/733-8888

Chinese. Casual Dining. **Address:** 67 N Dobson 85201

GEM MONTEZUMA CASTLE NATIONAL MONUMENT (C-4)

Off I-17 exit 289 on Montezuma Castle Hwy., Montezuma Castle National Monument contains remains of an early cliff dwelling. Built in the 12th and 13th centuries, it is among the best preserved dwellings of its type. The foundation is in a vertical cliff 46 feet above the talus slope. The five-story castle, believed to be inhabited by the Ancestral Puebloan people referred to as the Sinagua, contains 20 rooms and was once accessible only by ladders. Other pueblos dot the cliffs and hilltops around Beaver Creek.

As a preservative measure, tours into Montezuma Castle are not allowed, but a self-guiding trail offers good views of the castle and displays a scale model of its interior. The .34-mile trail is handicap accessible. The visitor center contains artifacts found in the area. Picnicking is permitted in designated areas. Allow 1 hour minimum. Visitor center and monument open daily 8-5. Closed Christmas. Admission (valid 7 days, includes admission to Tuzigoot National Monument) $10; free (ages 0-15).

Prices may vary; phone ahead. Phone (928) 567-3322, ext. 221.

MONTEZUMA WELL, about 11 mi. n.e., is a detached portion of the monument. The limestone sinkhole, 470 feet wide and more than 55 feet deep, is rimmed by pueblos and cliff dwellings. A source of water to the fields of ancient peoples, some of the ditches dug A.D. 1200-1300 are still visible. A self-guiding trail is available (not recommended for wheelchairs). **Time:** Allow 1 hour minimum. **Hours:** Daily 8-5. **Cost:** Free. **Phone:** (928) 567-4521.

MONUMENT VALLEY NAVAJO TRIBAL PARK (A-5)

Reached via scenic US 163, Monument Valley Navajo Tribal Park is a colorful region covering several thousand square miles within the Navajo Nation Reservation. The park contains Mystery Valley, where isolated monoliths of red sandstone tower as much as 1,000 feet above the valley floor.

The visitor center, 4 miles southeast of US 163, provides information about self-guiding tours. Guided tours from the center are offered daily; picnicking is permitted.

Horseback and four-wheel-drive trips through the vicinity can be arranged through agencies in Arizona at Kayenta and in Utah at Bluff, Mexican Hat and Monument Valley. Overnight accommodations also are available in Kayenta, Mexican Hat and Monument Valley; reservations are recommended.

Visitors should not photograph the Navajo people, their homes or their possessions without asking permission; a gratuity is usually requested. Other restrictions apply. For more information contact Monument Valley Navajo Tribal Park, P.O. Box 360289, Monument Valley, UT 84536.

The park is open daily 6 a.m.-8 p.m., Apr.-Sept.; 8-5, rest of year (weather permitting). Closed Jan. 1, Thanksgiving (at noon) and Christmas. Last admission 30 minutes before closing. Recreational vehicles more than 25 feet long and motorcycles are not permitted on the self-guiding tour. A 4-day pass is $20 (per vehicle with 1-4 people; $6 each additional person); $10 (per person on foot, bicycle or motorcycle). Phone (435) 727-5870.

VISITOR CENTER is 4 mi. s.e. of US 163 near the Arizona/Utah border. In addition to an impressive panoramic view of the Mitten and Merrick buttes, it has exhibits about Native Americans, an auditorium, an outdoor amphitheater, a patio, a library and a Navajo hogan, the traditional Navajo housing structure.

Guided tours led by Navajo tour operators explore Monument Valley and the surrounding backcountry. **Time:** Allow 2 hours, 30 minutes minimum. **Hours:** Daily 6 a.m.-8 p.m., Apr.-Sept.; 8-5, rest of year. Closed Jan. 1, Thanksgiving (at noon) and Christmas. **Cost:** Free. **Phone:** (435) 727-5870. GT

NAVAJOLAND

Encompassing some 27,000 square miles, Navajoland includes parts of Arizona, Utah and New Mexico. Larger than the state of West Virginia, the sovereign nation is the largest Native American nation in the country.

From the stark monoliths of Monument Valley Navajo Tribal Park *(see place listing this page)* and the sheer walls of Canyon de Chelly National Monument *(see place listing p. 32)* to the ancient ruins of Navajo National Monument *(see place listing this page)*, Navajoland is home to more than a dozen national monuments. The area also contains the Petrified Forest National Park *(see place listing p. 88)*, 186-mile-long Lake Powell and various tribal parks and historic sites.

Heritage is important to the Navajo, and singing and dancing give the Navajo a chance to wear their traditional attire. Tribal dress includes knee-high moccasins, velvet vests, concho belts and silver and turquoise jewelry for both men and women. Powwows often are performed throughout the Navajo nation and visitors are invited to observe.

The Navajo, or Dineh, consider themselves an extension of Mother Earth and therefore treat nature with great respect. Not only rich in culture, the Navajo live in an area rich in minerals; oil, gas, coal and uranium lie beneath the arid desert. The discovery of oil in the 1920s prompted the Navajo to form their own tribal government to help handle the encroachment of mining companies.

Reorganized in 1991, the Navajo government consists of an elected president, vice president and 88 council delegates representing 110 local units of government. Council meetings take place four times a year in Window Rock *(see place listing p. 226)*; visitors are welcome.

Tradition also can be seen in the Navajo's arts and crafts, particularly the distinctive style of their vibrantly-colored rugs and blankets as well silver pieces, basketry and sand paintings. Visitors to the area can purchase Navajo wares at various shops throughout the area.

The following places in Navajoland are listed separately under their individual names: Fort Defiance, Ganado, Kayenta, Keams Canyon, Page, Second Mesa, Tuba City and Window Rock. Visitors should be aware of certain restrictions while in Navajoland*; see Good Facts To Know.*

Navajo Tourism Department-Navajoland: P.O. Box 663, Window Rock, AZ 86515. **Phone:** (928) 810-8501.

NAVAJO NATIONAL MONUMENT (A-4)

Reached via US 160 and a 9-mile paved road (SR 564), Navajo National Monument preserves some of the largest and most intact of Arizona's known cliff dwellings in perhaps the most awe-inspiring area in the Southwest. There are two areas that can be visited by ranger-guided tours, each of which contains a remarkable 13th-century Pueblo ruin.

The monument lies within the Navajo Nation Reservation. Traveling off paved roads is not permitted. Most of the unmarked dirt-surfaced roads on the reservation are private driveways; private Navajo property is not open to visitors. Visitors should be aware of certain restrictions*; see Good Facts To Know.*

Free year-round camping and picnicking are permitted near the monument headquarters. The 41 campsites are available on a first-come first-served basis and are usually filled by dusk during the summer; vehicles must be no longer than 30 feet in length. Accommodations are available at Kayenta; reservations are recommended. Gas and grocery services are not available in the park; the nearest services are 9 miles south at the junction of SR 564 and US 160.

Note: In summer the Navajo Nation Reservation observes daylight saving time, which is an hour later than outside the reservation.

At an elevation of approximately 7,300 feet, the visitor center at the monument headquarters offers exhibits of ancestral Native American artifacts, a 20-minute video tour of the Betatakin ruins, and a 25-minute video about the prehistoric culture. Check for fire restrictions at the campgrounds. Visitor center open daily 8-5:30, Memorial Day-Labor Day; 9-5, rest of year. Closed Jan. 1, Thanksgiving and Christmas. Free. Phone (928) 672-2700.

BETATAKIN AREA is 2.5 mi. from monument headquarters by way of a strenuous 5-mi. round-trip trail. This is the monument's most accessible area. Ranger-guided tours depart daily at 8:15 a.m. and 10 a.m. from Memorial Day through Labor Day (weather permitting). Hikers should arrive early to ensure a spot on these popular tours. The early tour is limited to 25 people per day on a first-come, first-served basis. The second tour at 10 a.m., which takes a different trail, also is limited to 25 people. The cliff dwelling also can be viewed across the canyon from the end of the Sandal Trail year-round via a 1-mile round-trip self-guiding walk.

Note: Sturdy shoes and 2 quarts of water are recommended; the high altitude, heat and steep grade of the trail make good physical condition a requirement. Allow 3-5 hours for tour. **Hours:** Daily 8-5:30, Memorial Day-Labor Day; 9-5, rest of year. **Cost:** Tour free. **Phone:** (928) 672-2700 for information and schedule updates. GT

KEET SEEL AREA is accessible by hiking a difficult 17-mi. round-trip trail (with a daily limit of 20 people). The area contains the largest and best-preserved cliff dwellings in the vicinity, which date 1250-1300. To protect these fragile ruins there is a daily limit of 20 people.

Note: This trip is not recommended for inexperienced hikers. Hikers are required to attend a trail briefing to receive a permit and are advised to bring sufficient bottled water. Primitive campgrounds are available for hikers. **Hours:** Trail open Memorial Day-Labor Day. Schedules for tours of the ruins vary. **Cost:** Free. Check with rangers at the visitor center for reservations, which can be confirmed 1 week prior. Reservations are required and can be made beginning in January for the year. **Phone:** (928) 672-2700 for reservations, information and schedule updates.

NOGALES (G-4) pop. 20,837, elev. 3,865'

Nogales (noh-GAH-lehs) is rich in history; Franciscan missionary Fray Marcos de Niza entered Santa Cruz County as early as 1539. Hollywood actors made cowboy films in the area during the 1940s.

Mexico's Pacific Highway, a four-lane divided highway, starts in Nogales and continues through Guadalajara, Mexico, with connecting roads to Mexico City. Nogales is a popular port of entry for U.S. travelers as well as for more than 75 percent of winter fruits and vegetables shipped throughout the United States and Canada. Retail and wholesale trade with northern Mexico also is an important industry in the town. Passports are required for visitors planning to cross into Mexico.

Nogales-Santa Cruz County Chamber of Commerce and Visitor Center: 123 W. Kino Park Pl., Nogales, AZ 85621. **Phone:** (520) 287-3685.

BEST WESTERN SONORA INN & SUITES 520/375-6500

Hotel

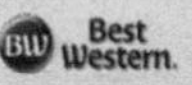

AAA Benefit: Members save up to 15% and earn bonus points!

Address: 750 W Shell Rd 85621 **Location:** I-19 exit 4, just w to Frank Reed Rd, then just nw. **Facility:** 65 units. 3 stories, interior corridors. **Pool:** outdoor. **Activities:** hot tub, picnic facilities, exercise room. **Guest Services:** valet and coin laundry. **Featured Amenity: full hot breakfast.**

CANDLEWOOD SUITES 520/281-1111

Extended Stay Hotel. **Address:** 875 N Frank Reed Rd 85621

HOLIDAY INN EXPRESS HOTEL NOGALES 520/281-0123

Hotel. **Address:** 850 W Shell Rd 85621

WHERE TO EAT

LAS VIGAS STEAK RANCH 520/287-6641

Mexican Steak. Casual Dining. **Address:** 180 W Loma St 85621

MR. C'S RESTAURANT & SUPPER CLUB 520/281-9000

Steak. Casual Dining. **Address:** 282 W View Point Dr 85621

RAGAZZI NORTHERN ITALIAN CUISINE 520/281-1020

Italian. Casual Dining. **Address:** 204 W Mariposa Rd 85621

isiting Mexico

ersonal Safety

Thousands of Americans routinely cross the rder into Mexico on a daily basis for business and rsonal reasons without incident, and crimes di-cted at tourists are unlikely. The possibility does ist, however, particularly in cities that are centers activity for Mexican drug cartels. This violence abs news headlines and adversely affects the ily lives of many Mexicans.

But for the casual visitor, safety almost always ils down to good old common sense. Stash checks d cash in different places; for example, in money lts and extra pockets sewn inside clothing. Keep otocopies of passports, credit cards and other cuments in a separate place from the originals. se parking lots or garages whenever possible. gal parking is designated by a sign showing a red rcle with a capital "E" inside; no-parking zones have gns with a diagonal red line through the "E."

Nearby Mexico

OGALES, SONORA pop. 220,292, ev. 3,674'

Note: For current information about safety/security sues in Nogales, refer to the U.S. State Department ebsite (travel.state.gov).

The border city of Nogales (noh-GAH-lehs) is ometimes referred to as Ambos Nogales ("both No-ales") in recognition of the sister city of Nogales, riz. on the other side of the international boundary nce. Established in 1882, the city is not only sig-ficantly larger than its U.S. counterpart but also re-ins a strong sense of Mexican identity.

The gateway into northwestern mainland Mexico nd points south is primarily a day visit for tourists. A urist permit is not needed for in-town stays of less an 72 hours, but proof of citizenship is required.

Mexican and U.S. Customs and Border Protection ffices are open 24 hours daily. For southbound motor-ts, the official immigration checkpoint is 21 kilometers 3 miles) south of Nogales on Mex. 15. You can obtain tourist permit here if you don't already have one, and ust present a federal temporary vehicle importation ermit or an "Only Sonora" temporary vehicle importa-on permit (if you intend to stay within the state of So-ora) and accompanying windshield sticker.

A vehicle permit is not required for travel to the fol-wing destinations in the state of Sonora: Rocky Point Puerto Peñasco), Guaymas, San Carlos, Bahía Kino nd other locations west of Mex. 15, as well as cities long Mex. 15 (Magdalena, Santa Ana, Hermosillo). n "Only Sonora" permit is required if driving within onora east of Mex. 15 as well as south of Empalme bout 350 miles south of the U.S. border). The permit an be obtained at Banjercito offices in Agua Prieta pposite Douglas, Ariz.), Cananea (southwest of gua Prieta on Mex. 2) and Empalme (on Mex. 15 at m marker 98, just south of the Guaymas bypass).

From Tucson, I-19 south ends at Nogales, Ariz.; signs point the way to the border crossing. Mex. 15 begins at the border, but the downtown Nogales crossing passes through the most congested part of the city. Motorists intending to bypass Nogales for points south can save time by using the international truck crossing, known as the Mariposa crossing; take exit 4 off I-19, then proceed west on SR 189 (Mariposa Road), following signs that say "Border Truck Route" and "International Border." This route reconnects with Mex. 15 south of Nogales at the 21-kilometer (13-mile) immigration checkpoint. The charge at the toll booth approximately 6 miles south of the border is about $2 (U.S.).

If you're driving through downtown Nogales back to the United States, watch for the sign that says "Linea International"; follow the directions for the road that leads to the border crossing.

Since almost all of the tourist-oriented shopping is within easy walking distance of the border, it is recommended that day visitors park on the Arizona side and head into Mexico on foot. From the Nogales-Santa Cruz County Chamber of Commerce and Visitor Center, 123 W. Kino Park Way (just off the intersection of Grand Avenue and US 82) in Nogales, Ariz., it's about a 1.5-mile drive south to a series of guarded lots; all-day parking fees average about $8, and cash is expected. The turnstiles to Mexico are at the foot of the Port of Entry.

Shops and vendor stalls catering to tourists are concentrated along north-south Avenida Obregón. They sell pottery, baskets, fabrics, ceramics, leather goods, glassware, carved pine furniture, rugs, jewelry and more. Most business is conducted in English, bargaining is acceptable and even expected, and American currency is preferred. More exclusive establishments have fixed prices and carry crafts and gift items from all over Mexico. When buying at stalls or from street vendors, always check for quality.

Along with shopping, Nogales offers such standard tourist experiences as having your picture taken astride a donkey and listening to mariachi bands. And like other Mexican border cities, it's a place to get prescriptions filled at a cost that is often far less than stateside.

This ends the Nogales section and resumes the alphabetical city listings for Arizona.

OAK CREEK CANYON—See Sedona p. 159.

ORGAN PIPE CACTUS NATIONAL MONUMENT (F-2)

In southwestern Arizona, Organ Pipe Cactus National Monument preserves a diverse and relatively undisturbed sample of the Sonoran Desert of particular interest to desert aficionados. The organ pipe cactus thrives within the United States primarily in this 517-square-mile preserve. The spectacular saguaro cacti, along with the paloverde, ironwood and ocotillo, also contribute to the desert landscape.

The monument contains two scenic drives. The 21-mile Ajo Mountain Drive begins near the visitor center, and conditions are generally good for car travel. The drive is closed occasionally because of adverse weather conditions or construction; phone ahead. No trailers or recreational vehicles more than 25 feet are permitted on this park road. A high-clearance vehicle is recommended for the 41-mile Puerto Blanco Loop. Check conditions at the visitor center.

The Kris Eggle Visitor Center, at Milepost 75 on scenic SR 85 (34 miles south of Ajo), is open daily 8-5; closed Thanksgiving and Christmas. Exhibits interpret the monument's flora, fauna and cultural history. A 15-minute introductory slide program is shown upon request. Ranger-led interpretive programs are offered January through March. Self-guiding interpretive trails are near the visitor center and the campground area ($16 per night).

Admission is by 7-day permit. The cost is $25 (per private vehicle); $15 (per person arriving by other means). Fees may vary; phone ahead. For further information contact the Superintendent, Organ Pipe Cactus National Monument, 10 Organ Pipe Dr., Ajo, AZ 85321; phone (520) 387-6849, ext. 7302.

ORO VALLEY pop. 41,011, elev. 2,543'

• **Hotels & Restaurants map & index p. 204**
• **Part of Tucson area — see map p. 187**

FAIRFIELD INN & SUITES BY MARRIOTT TUCSON NORTH/ ORO VALLEY 520/202-4000 (48)
Hotel. **Address:** 10150 N Oracle Rd 85737
AAA Benefit: Members save 5% or more!

HOLIDAY INN EXPRESS HOTEL & SUITES ORO VALLEY-TUCSON NORTH 520/544-2100 (47)
Hotel. **Address:** 11075 N Oracle Rd 85737

WHERE TO EAT

CAFFE TORINO RISTORANTE ITALIANO 520/297-3777 (75)
Italian. Casual Dining. **Address:** 10325 N La Cañada Dr, Suite 151 85739

DRAGON VILLAGE RESTAURANT 520/229-0388 (72)
Chinese. Casual Dining. **Address:** 12152 N Rancho Vistoso Blvd, Suite 180 85737

GMG CHINESE BISTRO 520/797-8383 (74)
Chinese. Casual Dining. **Address:** 10370 N La Cañada Dr 85737

HARVEST 520/731-1100 (73)
Regional American. Casual Dining. **Address:** 10355 N La Cañada Dr 85737

PAGE (A-4) pop. 7,247, elev. 4,281'

Established to provide housing and facilities for workers on the Glen Canyon Dam project, Page was named for John Chatfield Page, the commissioner of reclamation who devoted many years to the development of the upper Colorado River. The town is a center for outfitters who provide trips i Antelope Canyon and the Glen Canyon Natio Recreation Area *(see place listing p. 52)*.

Scenic flights over Lake Powell and the s rounding Navajo country as well as to the Gra Canyon depart from the Page airport.

Page-Lake Powell Chamber of Commerce Lake Powell Blvd., Unit #3, P.O. Box 727, Page, 86040. **Phone:** (928) 645-2741.

GLEN CANYON NATIONAL RECREATI AREA—see place listing p. 52.

LAKE POWELL NAVAJO TRIBAL PARK, 1 mi. on SR 98, comprises two slot canyons with grace swirling red sandstone walls carved by wind a rain over thousands of years. Visitors are driven miles to the canyons and must tour the canyons w a licensed guide. Access to Lower Antelope Cany requires a climb down ladders bolted to the cany walls. On the Upper Antelope Canyon tour visit walk right into the canyon.

Time: Allow 1 hour minimum. **Hours:** Entran fee station daily 8-5, late Mar.-Nov. 1; 9-3, rest year. Phone ahead to confirm schedule. **Cost:** free (ages 0-7). Guided tour fees vary; pho ahead. **Phone:** (928) 698-2808. GT

BAYMONT INN & SUITES 928/645-5
Hotel. **Address:** 677 Scenic View Dr 86040

BEST WESTERN PLUS AT LAKE POWELL

928/645-59

AAA Benefit: Members save up t 15% and earn bonu points!

Address: 208 N Lake Powell Blvd 860 **Location:** 0.8 mi e of US 89 via Loop **Facility:** 130 units. 4 stories, interior c ridors. **Terms:** check-in 4 pm. **Po** heated outdoor. **Activities:** hot tub, ex cise room. **Guest Services:** coin launc **Featured Amenity: breakfast buffet.**

BEST WESTERN VIEW OF LAKE POWELL HOTEL

928/645-88

AAA Benefit: Members save up t 15% and earn bonu points!

Address: 716 Rimview Dr 86040 **Loc tion:** 0.7 mi e of US 89 via Loop 89. **F cility:** 102 units. 3 stories, inter corridors. *Bath:* shower only. **Term** check-in 4 pm. **Pool:** heated outdo **Activities:** hot tub, exercise room. **Fe tured Amenity: breakfast buffet.**

COUNTRY INN & SUITES BY RADISSON 928/484-1
Hotel. **Address:** 880 Haul Rd 86040

COURTYARD BY MARRIOTT 928/645-5000

Hotel

COURTYARD **AAA Benefit:** Members save 5% or more!

Address: 600 Clubhouse Dr 86040 **Location:** On Loop 89, jct US 89. **Facility:** 153 units. 2-4 stories, interior corridors. **Amenities:** safes. **Pool:** heated outdoor. **Activities:** hot tub, exercise room. **Guest Services:** valet and coin laundry.

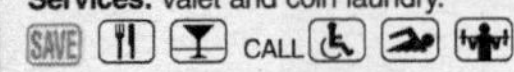

/SOME UNITS

HAMPTON INN & SUITES PAGE-LAKE POWELL AZ 928/645-0075

Hotel. **Address:** 294 Sandhill Rd 86040

AAA Benefit: Members save up to 15%!

HOLIDAY INN EXPRESS & SUITES PAGE-LAKE POWELL AREA 928/645-9900

Hotel. **Address:** 643 S Lake Powell Blvd 86040

HYATT PLACE PAGE/LAKE POWELL 928/212-2200

Hotel

HYATT PLACE **AAA Benefit:** Members save up to 10%!

Address: 1126 N Navajo Dr 86040 **Location:** 0.8 mi e of US 89 via Loop 89, 0.4 mi n, then just w. **Facility:** 102 units. 3 stories, interior corridors. **Pool:** heated outdoor. **Activities:** exercise room. **Guest Services:** coin laundry.

/SOME UNITS

LAKE POWELL DAYS INN & SUITES 928/645-2800

Hotel. **Address:** 961 N Hwy 89 86040

LAKE POWELL RESORT AND MARINA 928/645-2433

Resort Hotel. **Address:** 100 Lakeshore Dr 86040 ***(See ad p. 52.)***

LA QUINTA INN & SUITES 928/645-9898

Hotel. **Address:** 70 Kaibab Rd 86040

SLEEP INN & SUITES 928/645-2020

Hotel

Address: 673 Scenic View Rd 86040 **Location:** On US 89, just n. **Facility:** 98 units. 3 stories, interior corridors. **Pool:** heated indoor. **Activities:** hot tub, exercise room. **Guest Services:** coin laundry. **Featured Amenity: full hot breakfast.**

WINGATE BY WYNDHAM PAGE/LAKE POWELL 928/484-1115

Hotel. **Address:** 671 Scenic View Rd 86040

WHERE TO EAT

BIG JOHN'S TEXAS BBQ 928/645-3300

Barbecue. Quick Serve. **Address:** 153 S Lake Powell Blvd 86040

BIRDHOUSE 928/645-4087

Chicken. Quick Serve. **Address:** 707 N Navajo Blvd 86040

BLUE BUDDHA SUSHI & TEPPANYAKI 928/645-0007

Japanese Casual Dining

$8-$34

AAA Inspector Notes: From the alley entrance, you will find a trendy ultra-lounge décor with fun Japanese favorites. Some items include shrimp tempura, chicken teriyaki, pork dumplings, and, of course, fresh sushi. Specialty drinks are a big hit. **Features:** full bar. **Address:** 644 N Navajo Dr, Suite G 86040 **Location:** 0.6 mi n of US 89 via Loop 89; in shopping center. D

BONKERS RESTAURANT 928/645-2706

American. Casual Dining. **Address:** 810 N Navajo Dr 86040

THE DAM BAR & GRILLE 928/645-2161

American Casual Dining

$10-$35

AAA Inspector Notes: Located in a small shopping center, this casual, sports-bar restaurant is convenient to other eateries and lodgings. The dining room is separated from the sports bar by a half-wall and hallway. On the menu is a nice selection of steak, chicken, seafood and pasta dishes, as well as an assortment of sandwiches. The staff provides full service in a cordial and attentive fashion. **Features:** full bar, patio dining, happy hour. **Address:** 644 N Navajo Dr, Suite C 86040 **Location:** 0.6 mi n of US 89 via Loop 89.

L D

EL TAPATIO 928/645-4055

Mexican. Casual Dining. **Address:** 25 S Lake Powell Blvd 86040

MANDARIN GOURMET CHINESE CUISINE 928/645-5516

Chinese. Casual Dining. **Address:** 683 S Lake Powell Blvd 86040

RAINBOW ROOM 928/645-1162

American. Casual Dining. **Address:** 100 Lakeshore Dr 86040

RANCH HOUSE GRILLE 928/645-1420

Breakfast Sandwiches. Casual Dining. **Address:** 819 N Navajo Dr 86040

STATE 48 TAVERN 928/645-1912

American. Gastropub. **Address:** 614 N Navajo Dr 86040

STROMBOLLI'S ITALIAN RESTAURANT & PIZZERIA 928/645-2605

Italian. Casual Dining. **Address:** 711 N Navajo Dr 86040

PARADISE VALLEY pop. 12,820, elev. 1,340'

• Hotels & Restaurants map & index p. 120
• Part of Phoenix area — see map p. 91

THE HERMOSA INN 602/955-8614 (58)

Boutique Hotel

Address: 5532 N Palo Cristi Rd 85253 **Location:** 1 mi s of Lincoln Dr; corner of Stanford Dr. Located in a quiet residential area. **Facility:** This historic home of cowboy artist Lon Megargee offers a variety of intimate guest rooms housed in different buildings scattered throughout the beautifully landscaped grounds. 43 units. 1 story, exterior corridors. **Parking:** on-site and valet. **Terms:** check-in 4 pm. **Amenities:** safes. **Dining:** Lon's at the Hermosa, see separate listing. **Pool:** heated outdoor. **Activities:** hot tub, bicycles, lawn sports, trails, exercise room, massage. **Guest Services:** valet laundry.

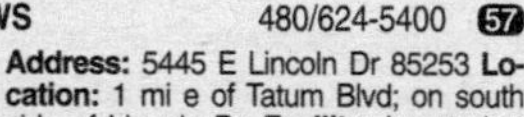

MOUNTAIN SHADOWS 480/624-5400 (57)

Contemporary Resort Hotel

Address: 5445 E Lincoln Dr 85253 **Location:** 1 mi e of Tatum Blvd; on south side of Lincoln Dr. **Facility:** Located at the base of Camelback Mountain, this minimalist, modern resort offers upscale guest rooms, many with a patio or balcony. The lobby features sweeping views and a rotating art gallery. 198 units, some two bedrooms, three bedrooms and condominiums. 3 stories, interior corridors. **Parking:** valet only. **Terms:** check-in 4 pm. **Amenities:** safes. **Dining:** 3 restaurants. **Pool:** heated outdoor. **Activities:** hot tub, steamroom, regulation golf, par 3 golf, recreation programs, health club, massage. **Guest Services:** valet laundry, area transportation.

OMNI SCOTTSDALE RESORT & SPA AT MONTELUCIA 480/627-3200 (56)

Resort Hotel

Address: 4949 E Lincoln Dr 85253 **Location:** Southeast corner of Lincoln Dr and Tatum Blvd, enter from Lincoln Dr. **Facility:** The resort features large, luxurious guest rooms and baths along with attractive, spacious grounds located at the foot of Camelback Mountain. A man-made cave and waterfall enhance the main pool. 293 units, some two bedrooms. 1-3 stories, interior/exterior corridors. **Parking:** on-site (fee) and valet. **Terms:** check-in 4 pm. **Amenities:** safes. **Dining:** 3 restaurants, also, Prado, see separate listing. **Pool:** heated outdoor. **Activities:** sauna, hot tub, steamroom, recreation programs, bicycles, lawn sports, health club, spa. **Guest Services:** valet laundry.

SANCTUARY CAMELBACK MOUNTAIN 480/948-2100 (59)

Resort Hotel

Address: 5700 E McDonald Dr 85253 **Location:** SR 101 exit McDonald Dr, 3.9 mi w; 1.8 mi w of jct Scottsdale Rd. **Facility:** This quiet retreat offers luxurious amenities in the spacious suites and casitas. Some units feature fireplaces and most provide panoramic views of the surrounding mountains and desert valley below. 116 units, some efficiencies, kitchens and houses. 1 story, exterior corridors. **Parking:** on-site and valet. **Terms:** check-in 4 pm. **Amenities:** safes. **Dining:** Elements, see separate listing. **Pool:** heated outdoor. **Activities:** hot tub, steamroom, tennis, recreation programs, bicycles, health club, spa. **Guest Services:** valet laundry, area transportation.

SAVE CALL / SOME UNITS

WHERE TO EAT

EL CHORRO 480/948-5170 (81)

Continental. Fine Dining. **Address:** 5550 E Lincoln Dr 85253

ELEMENTS 480/607-2300 (84)

Fusion. Fine Dining. **Address:** 5700 E McDonald Dr 85253

HEARTH 61 480/624-5400 (82)

New American. Casual Dining. **Address:** 5445 E Lincoln Dr 85253

LON'S AT THE HERMOSA 602/955-7878 (83)

American Fine Dining
$27-$70

AAA Inspector Notes: Coming here for dinner is like returning to the 'home ranch' in Arizona territorial days. The excellent menu selection centers on natural and organic foods, some grown on the premises. Choices include seafood, steak and fowl preparations, delivered with casual yet attentive service. **Features:** full bar, patio dining, Sunday brunch, happy hour. **Reservations:** suggested. **Address:** 5532 N Palo Cristi Rd 85253 **Location:** 1 mi s of Lincoln Dr; corner of Stanford Dr; in Hermosa Inn. **Parking:** on-site and valet. B L D

PRADO 480/627-3004 (80)

Italian Fine Dining
$13-$30

AAA Inspector Notes: The menu is inspired by old world Spain, with a healthy tapas selection. Savory, fresh, local ingredients are used with a Mediterranean influence. If weather permits, dine al fresco with a stunning view of Camelback Mountain. **Features:** full bar, patio dining. **Reservations:** suggested. **Address:** 4949 E Lincoln Dr 85253 **Location:** Southeast corner of Lincoln Dr and Tatum Blvd, enter from Lincoln Dr; in Omni Scottsdale Resort & Spa at Montelucia. **Parking:** on-site and valet. B L D CALL

PARKER (D-1) pop. 3,083, elev. 1,642'

Parker, founded in 1908, was named for Ely Parker, the first Native American commissioner for the U.S. government. The city originally was south of its current location but was moved to accommodate the Santa Fe Railroad. Parker is a trade center for the surrounding Native American communities and a water recreation destination attracting nearly 1 million visitors each year.

The Parker Dam and Power Plant, 17 miles north on SR 95, is considered the world's deepest because 65 percent of its structural height is below the riverbed. Overlooks on top of the dam provide views of Lake Havasu and the Colorado River. Just north of town on SR 95 is La Paz County Park *(see Recreation Areas Chart)*.

Parker Area Chamber of Commerce: 1217 California Ave., Parker, AZ 85344. **Phone:** (928) 669-2174.

BEST WESTERN PARKER INN 928/669-6060

Hotel

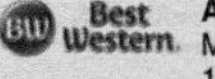

AAA Benefit: Members save up to 15% and earn bonus points!

Address: 1012 Geronimo Ave 85344 **Location:** Jct SR 95, just e. **Facility:** 44 units. 2 stories (no elevator), interior corridors. **Pool:** outdoor. **Activities:** picnic facilities, exercise room. **Guest Services:** coin laundry. **Featured Amenity:** continental breakfast.

HAMPTON INN BY HILTON PARKER 928/669-1000

Hotel. **Address:** 1110 S Geronimo Ave 85344

AAA Benefit: Members save up to 15%!

WHERE TO EAT

STROKE'S BAR & GRILL 928/667-2366

American. Casual Dining. **Address:** 8010 Riverside Dr 85344

PAYSON (D-4) pop. 15,301, elev. 4,887'

Known by such names as Green Valley, Long Valley, Big Valley and Union City, Payson was first settled by prospectors who came to the area seeking wealth. Payson's mines produced little, and cattle and lumber soon became the community's livelihood. With the help of Senator Payson of Chicago, the early residents helped establish a post office and named it and the town in his honor.

Surrounded by the lakes and dense woodlands of Tonto National Forest *(see place listing p. 182)* and the nearby Mogollon Rim, Payson has become a convenient getaway for visitors, with Phoenix only 90 minutes away.

Rim Country Regional Chamber of Commerce: 100 W. Main St., P.O. Box 1380, Payson, AZ 85547. **Phone:** (928) 474-4515.

RIM COUNTRY MUSEUM, 1 mi. w. on Main St. from jct. SR 87, then just n. to 700 S. Green Valley Pkwy., is comprised of several historic structures. A replica of the turn-of-the-20th-century Herron Hotel contains exhibits about the ancient cultures that developed around the Mogollon Rim as well as a 1908 kitchen, blacksmith shop and gold mine. Payson's original forest ranger's station and residence, built in 1907, depict the life of the forest ranger. Firefighting equipment also is featured. The 40-acre Green Valley Park neighbors the museum.

Time: Allow 30 minutes minimum. **Hours:** Mon. and Wed.-Sat. 10-4, Sun. 1-4. Closed Jan. 1, Thanksgiving and Christmas. **Cost:** (includes admittance to the Zane Grey Cabin) $5; $4 (ages 55+); $3 (ages 12-18). **Phone:** (928) 474-3483.

Zane Grey Cabin is at 700 S. Green Valley Pkwy. The replica cabin and the adjoining Rim Country Museum house the personal belongings and memorabilia of adventurer and "Riders of the Purple Sage" author Zane Grey. The original cabin was destroyed in the 1990 Dude Fire; exhibits in the museum focus on Grey's literary contributions and career achievements. Displays also document the history of the Payson community, which Grey frequented from 1918-29.

Hours: Mon. and Wed.-Sat. 10-4, Sun. 1-4. Closed Jan. 1, Thanksgiving and Christmas. **Cost:** (includes admittance to the Rim Country Museum) $5; $4 (ages 55+); $3 (ages 12-18). **Phone:** (928) 474-3483.

TONTO NATURAL BRIDGE STATE PARK, 10 mi. n.w. off SR 87, is bordered by Tonto National Forest. The bridge, among the world's largest natural travertine structures, reaches a height of 183 feet; the opening beneath is 150 feet wide and 400 feet long. A historic lodge (available for overnight stays) is furnished with antiques that were lowered into the canyon using ropes and mules. There are four easily accessible viewpoints from which to see the bridge; the walk to each is less than a half-mile.

Note: Four trails lead into the canyon; all are steep and difficult for many persons to negotiate. Pets are not permitted on canyon trails but are permitted at viewpoints. **Hours:** Daily 8-6. Last admission 1 hour before closing. Closed Christmas. **Cost:** $7; $3 (ages 7-13). **Phone:** (928) 476-4202.

COMFORT INN PAYSON 928/472-7484

Hotel. **Address:** 206 S Beeline Hwy 85541

QUALITY INN PAYSON 928/474-3241

Hotel. **Address:** 801 N Beeline Hwy 85541

RIM COUNTRY INN 928/474-2283

Motel. **Address:** 811 S Beeline Hwy 85541

SUPER 8 INN & SUITES OF PAYSON 928/474-5241

Motel. **Address:** 809 E Hwy 260 85541

WOODEN NICKEL CABINS 928/478-4519

Cabin. **Address:** 1022 S Hunter Creek Dr 85541

WHERE TO EAT

CROSSWINDS RESTAURANT 928/474-1613

American. Casual Dining. **Address:** 800 W Airport Rd 85541

FARGO'S STEAKHOUSE 928/474-7455

Steak. Casual Dining. **Address:** 620 E Hwy 260 85541

GERARDO'S FIREWOOD CAFE 928/468-6500

Italian. Casual Dining. **Address:** 512 N Beeline Hwy 85541

MACKY'S GRILL 928/474-7411

American. Casual Dining. **Address:** 201 W Main St 85541

PEACH SPRINGS pop. 1,090, elev. 4,788'

• Part of Grand Canyon National Park area — see map p. 57

Peach Springs is the trading center and headquarters for the Hualapai Indian Reservation, which covers nearly a million acres between the town and the Colorado River. The town serves as one of the transportation corridors to the western parts of Grand Canyon National Park *(see place listing p. 57)*. Fishing is allowed on the river and at small ponds on the reservation. Primitive camping also is available.

GRAND CANYON SKYWALK—see Kingman p. 71.

HUALAPAI LODGE 928/769-2230

Hotel

Address: 900 Route 66 86434 **Location:** Center. Located near railroad tracks. **Facility:** 54 units. 2 stories, interior corridors. **Dining:** Diamond Creek Restaurant, see separate listing. **Pool:** heated outdoor. **Activities:** hot tub, exercise room. **Guest Services:** coin laundry. **Featured Amenity: continental breakfast.**

/ SOME UNITS

WHERE TO EAT

DIAMOND CREEK RESTAURANT 928/769-2800

Regional American Casual Dining

$6-$19

AAA Inspector Notes: Although this restaurant serves traditional American offerings, there are Native American-influenced options as well. Items include a Hualapai taco (a traditional taco served on fry bread), Hualapai stew and an Indian fry bread dessert. Equally loved are the half-pound charbroiled hamburgers, sandwiches and pizza. The homemade desserts are a huge hit. **Address:** 900 Route 66 86434 **Location:** Center; in Hualapai Lodge. B L D

PEORIA (I-2) pop. 154,065, elev. 1,138'

• Hotels & Restaurants map & index p. 117
• Part of Phoenix area — see map p. 91

CHALLENGER SPACE CENTER is 3.2 mi. n. on 91st Ave., 1 mi. e. on Lake Pleasant Blvd., then .3 mi. n. to 21170 N. 83rd Ave. An affiliate of the Smithsonian Institution, the center features permanent and temporary space exhibits as well as stargazing events, Lego building workshops, rocket-launching events and classes and camps. A highlight is the 2-hour simulated space mission, including launching and docking. The mission control room is based on the design of the Johnson Space Center; the spacecraft simulates a room on the International Space Station.

Time: Allow 1 hour minimum. **Hours:** Mon.-Sat. 10-4. Space missions are held monthly; phone for schedule. Closed Jan. 1, Thanksgiving, Christmas Eve, Christmas and Dec. 31. Other holiday hours vary; phone ahead. **Cost:** $8; $7 (ages 55+ and military with ID); $6 (ages 4-12). Space mission $20; $17 (ages 55+, seventh grade-age 14 for Voyage to Mars mission and fifth grade-age 14 for Rendezvous with a Comet mission); $16 (ages 0-12 with adult). Students below sixth grade must be with a ticketed adult on space mission. The space mission Rendezvous with a Comet is not recommended for students below fifth grade. The space mission Voyage to Mars is not recommended for students below seventh grade. Reservations are required for space mission. **Phone:** (623) 322-2001.

BLUEGREEN VACATION CIBOLA VISTA RESORT AND SPA, AN ASCEND RESORT COLLECTION MEMBER 623/889-6700

Condominium. **Address:** 27501 N Lake Pleasant Pkwy 85383

COMFORT SUITES BY CHOICE HOTELS/PEORIA SPORTS COMPLEX 623/334-3993 25

Hotel. **Address:** 8473 W Paradise Ln 85382

HAMPTON INN PEORIA 623/486-9918 29

SAVE Hotel. **Address:** 8408 W Paradise Ln 85382

AAA Benefit: Members save up to 15%!

HOLIDAY INN EXPRESS HOTEL PEORIA NORTH-GLENDALE 623/853-1313 26

Hotel. **Address:** 16771 N 84th Ave 85382

LA QUINTA INN & SUITES BY WYNDHAM PHOENIX WEST PEORIA 623/487-1900 27

Hotel. **Address:** 16321 N 83rd Ave 85382

RESIDENCE INN BY MARRIOTT GLENDALE/PEORIA 623/979-2074 28

SAVE Extended Stay Hotel. **Address:** 8435 W Paradise Ln 85382

AAA Benefit: Members save 5% or more!

WHERE TO EAT

AH-SO STEAK & SUSHI 623/487-8862 17

Japanese. Casual Dining. **Address:** 16610 N 75th Ave, Suite 104 85381

FLEMING'S PRIME STEAKHOUSE & WINE BAR 623/772-9463 18

Steak. Fine Dining. **Address:** 9712 W Northern Ave 85345

GOOD CHINA 623/572-8838 15

Chinese. Casual Dining. **Address:** 9180 W Union Hills Dr 85382

P.F. CHANG'S CHINA BISTRO 623/412-3335 16

Chinese. Fine Dining. **Address:** 16170 N 83rd Ave 85382

SQUID INK SUSHI 623/561-7747

Japanese Sushi. Casual Dining. **Address:** 9947 W Happy Valley Rd 85383

PETRIFIED FOREST NATIONAL PARK (C-6)

Elevations in the park range from 5,300 ft. at the Puerco River to 6,235 ft. at Pilot Rock. Refer to AAA maps for additional elevation information.

East of Holbrook, Petrified Forest National Park contains an abundance of petrified logs. Most of the brilliantly colored trees in the 140,000-acre park are prone, and many are in fragments. Early dinosaurs and other reptiles once roamed the area, and numerous fossil bones and fossil plants have been discovered in the park.

More than 200 million years ago trees clinging to eroding riverbanks fell into streams and were buried in the floodplains. The trees were buried under river sediments in ground water that included volcanic ash rich in silica; a replacement process began to take place. Silica replaced the wood until the logs were virtually turned to stone. Iron oxide and other minerals stained the silica to produce rainbow colors.

In more recent times, the area was uplifted as part of the Colorado Plateau, and erosion exposed some logs; many more probably remain buried to a depth of 300 feet. There are five areas with heavy concentrations of petrified wood in the park: Blue Mesa, Jasper Forest, Crystal Forest, Rainbow Forest (comprising Long Logs and Giant Logs near US 180) and Black Forest. The first four are accessible by the park road. Black Forest, in a designated wilderness area, can be reached from the parking lot at Kachina Point, down a switchback unimproved trail to the desert floor. The Rainbow Forest area contains the most colorful concentration of petrified wood.

General Information and Activities

The park opens daily at 7, early Mar.-late Oct.; at 8, rest of year. Hours may vary due to season; phone ahead to confirm schedule.

The 28-mile drive through the park offers breathtaking views of the Painted Desert from Pintado Point and Kachina Point. Other scenic overlooks include Chinde, Nizhoni, Tawa, Tiponi and Whipple points. Petrified logs are common in the southern part of the park.

Westbound motorists on I-40 should use the northern entrance to avoid backtracking. Visitors can view the Painted Desert *(see attraction listing this page)*, ancient pueblos and petroglyphs, petrified log deposits and the Rainbow Forest Museum *(see attraction listing this page)*. Motorists should exit on US 180 and continue west to Holbrook. Eastbound motorists can use the southern (Rainbow Forest) entrance off US 180, 19 miles from Holbrook, to see the same attractions in reverse order, then exit onto I-40 east. Allow 3 hours minimum.

Within the park it is unlawful to gather plants, sand, rocks or specimens of petrified wood of any size whatsoever; archeological and other paleontological material is likewise protected. Violations are punishable by heavy fines and imprisonment. Curio stores sell a variety of polished specimens collected from privately owned land outside the park.

There are no overnight accommodations in the park; backpack camping is allowed by free permit only for hikers staying overnight in one of the park's two designated wilderness areas. Picnic sites are near the Rainbow Forest Museum and on the Painted Desert rim at Chinde Point. Gas, oil and food services are available next to the Painted Desert Visitor Center.

ADMISSION to the park is $20 (per private vehicle), $10 (per person arriving by other means).

PETS are permitted in the park only if they are leashed, crated or otherwise physically restricted at all times. With the exception of service animals, pets are not permitted in park buildings.

ADDRESS inquiries to the Superintendent, Petrified Forest National Park, P.O. Box 2217, Petrified Forest National Park, AZ 86028; phone (928) 524-6228.

AGATE BRIDGE, at a stopping point on the park road in Petrified Forest National Park, is a nearly 140-foot-long petrified log that spans a 40-foot-wide ravine. **Hours:** Park opens daily at 7, late Feb.-late Oct.; at 8, rest of year. Closing hours may vary due to season; phone ahead to confirm schedule. Closed Christmas. Phone ahead to confirm schedule. **Cost:** Included in Petrified Forest National Park admission of $20 (per private vehicle); $10 (per person arriving by other means). **Phone:** (928) 524-6228.

NEWSPAPER ROCK, via a short side road 1 mi. s. of Puerco Pueblo in Petrified Forest National Park, bears prehistoric petroglyphs that can be viewed through spotting scopes from an overlook. **Hours:** Park opens daily at 7, late Feb.-late Oct.; at 8, rest of year. Closing hours may vary due to season; phone ahead to confirm schedule. Closed Christmas. **Cost:** Included in park admission of $20 (per private vehicle); $10 (per person arriving by other means). **Phone:** (928) 524-6228.

GEM **PAINTED DESERT,** partially contained in the northern part of Petrified Forest National Park, is an area of colorful badlands that displays a variety of hues. Representing more than 200-million-year-old-soil layers and river channels turned red from oxidation of iron minerals and then to stone, the desert's colorful erosion effects were created over the millennia by sculpturing from wind and water. Overlooks with an especially scenic view include Chinde Point, Kachina Point, Pintado Point, Tawa Point and Tiponi Point.

The Painted Desert Visitor Center, located in the Painted Desert Community Complex off I-40, offers restrooms, a short loop walking trail, a gas station, exhibits and an 18-minute film that explains park resources, including how wood is petrified. **Hours:** Visitor center is open daily at 7, late Feb.-late Oct.; at 8, rest of year. Closing hours may vary due to the season; phone ahead to confirm schedule. Closed Christmas. Phone ahead to confirm schedule. **Cost:** Free. **Phone:** (928) 524-6228.

PUERCO PUEBLO, s. of the Puerco River in Petrified Forest National Park, is the visible remains of a Native American village that was utilized more than 6 centuries ago. Petroglyphs can be seen along a short (.3-mile), paved loop trail.

RAINBOW FOREST MUSEUM, near the s. entrance of Petrified Forest National Park, contains fossils and exhibits telling the story of the early dinosaurs, giant reptiles and the Triassic forest ecosystem. An 18-minute film explains park resources, including how wood is petrified. **Time:** Allow 30 minutes minimum. **Hours:** Open daily at 7, late Feb.-late Oct.; at 8, rest of year. Closing hours may vary due to season; phone ahead to confirm schedule. Closed Christmas. **Cost:** Free. **Phone:** (928) 524-6822.

Phoenix

Then & Now

In Phoenix, if you don't drink plenty of water, a golf stroke is promptly followed by heat stroke. Precious H_20. Piped in from the Colorado, Salt and Verde rivers, it's what makes this ultrahot metropolis possible. Lush resorts, posh spas, superb museums and excellent local restaurants surrounded by a starkly beautiful landscape, Phoenix is Arizona's big city-vacation destination.

If your mental picture of Arizona is one of a Marlboro man riding merrily across the saguaro cactus-studded desert, that's here, too. Rising behind the downtown skyscrapers is Camelback Mountain, the go-to spot for desert-style hiking. East of the city, beyond the spill of cookie-cutter suburbs, are the rugged Superstition Mountains.

Of course, from late spring to late summer when daytime temps spike past the century mark for weeks on end, the only hiking you'll be doing is from Nordstrom to Neiman Marcus at the Scottsdale Fashion Square mall. Located about 10 miles northeast of downtown, Scottsdale—with its golf resorts, upscale eateries, hip nightlife and art galleries galore—is the state capital's tourist hot spot.

Downtown Phoenix, which has been spruced up over the past few decades, is where you can see the Arizona Diamondbacks turn double plays in their retractable-roofed stadium, listen to a Brahms concerto at Symphony Hall or watch a Phoenix Suns point guard hit an outside jump shot at Talking Stick Resort Arena.

Heritage Square

The downtown core is loaded with restaurants, lively bars and fun places to go, especially in the streets surrounding sports venues. But unless you get a charge out of staring up at modern glass-and-steel towers inhabited by banks, this isn't exactly the stuff of walking tour brochures. A few exceptions include the 1929 Art Deco-style Luhrs Tower (at the corner of First Avenue and Jefferson Street) and Heritage Square, where the city's original Victorian brick buildings house small museums and a pair of popular restaurants.

Greater Phoenix, often maligned for its housing tracts full of stucco schlock, boasts many architectural jewels. Frank Lloyd Wright chose Scottsdale for the site of his gorgeous Taliesin West winter retreat, which started out as a rustic camp in the desert but over the remaining years of Wright's life evolved into a renowned and exclusive architecture school. And as

(Continued on p. 92.)

Destination Phoenix

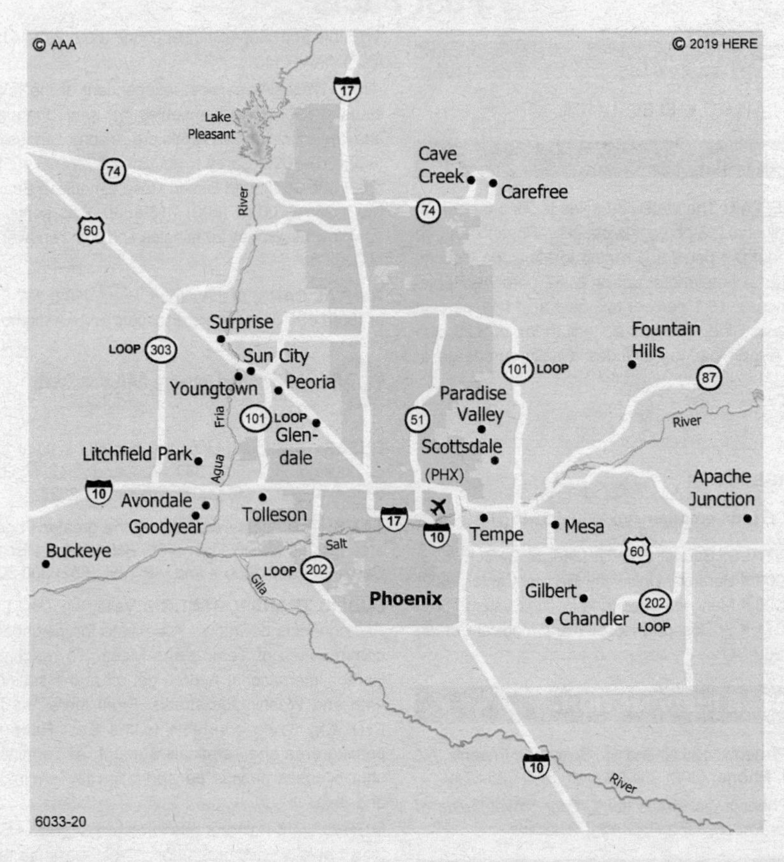

This map shows cities in the Phoenix vicinity where you will find attractions, hotels and restaurants. Cities are listed alphabetically in this book on the following pages.

Fast Facts

ABOUT THE CITY

POP: 1,445,632 ▪ **ELEV:** 1,117 ft.

MONEY

SALES TAX: The statewide sales tax is 5.6 percent; an additional 2.3 percent is added in Phoenix and an additional 0.7 percent is added in Maricopa County. There is a hotel/motel tax of 12.57 percent. Rental cars incur a 15.1 percent tax, plus an 11.11 percent concession fee. There is a stadium tax of 3.25 percent. Airport parking includes a daily surcharge of $4.50.

WHOM TO CALL

EMERGENCY: 911

POLICE (non-emergency): (602) 262-6151

HOSPITALS: Banner Estrella Medical Center, (623) 327-4000 ▪ Banner—University Medical Center, (602) 839-2000 ▪ Maricopa Integrated Health System, (602) 344-5011 ▪ St. Joseph's Hospital and Medical Center, (844) 369-5479.

VISITOR INFORMATION

Visit Phoenix: 125 N. 2nd St., Suite 120, Phoenix, AZ 85004. **Phone:** (602) 254-6500 or (877) 225-5749.

Visit Phoenix distributes the *Official Travel Guide to Greater Phoenix* and *Phoenix Trail Guide.*

TRANSPORTATION

AIR TRAVEL: Phoenix Sky Harbor International Airport (PHX), 4 miles southeast of downtown, is served by 17 major airlines. SuperShuttle is a 24-hour shared-ride service; phone (602) 244-9000 in metro Phoenix, or (800) 258-3826 outside Arizona. ExecuCar also is available from SuperShuttle; phone (602) 232-4610 or (800) 410-4444.

Airport limousine service, independent of the hotels, starts at $90. Some companies that serve the airport and certain downtown hotels are Arizona Limousines, (602) 267-7097; Carey Limousine, (602) 996-1955 or (800) 336-4646; and Desert Rose Limousine Service, (602) 256-7200 or (800) 716-8660. Cab service to downtown averages 20 minutes and costs an average of $20.

RENTAL CARS: At the airport, Hertz, (602) 267-8822 or (800) 654-3131, offers discounts to AAA members.

BUSES: Greyhound Lines Inc. has terminals at 2115 E. Buckeye Rd., (602) 389-4200, and 2647 W. Glendale Ave., (602) 246-0907 or (800) 231-2222.

TAXIS: Taxi companies serving the greater Phoenix area include Yellow Cab, (480) 888-8888 ▪ Discount Cab, (602) 200-2000 ▪ and VIP Taxi, (602) 300-3000.

PUBLIC TRANSPORTATION: Valley METRO Light Rail connects downtown Phoenix to the neighboring communities of Tempe and Mesa. To reach Sky Harbor International Airport, get off at the station at 44th and Washington streets. From there, the free PHX Sky Train connects to the East Economy parking area and Terminals 3 and 4. At Terminal 4, shuttle buses provide transportation to Terminals 2 and 3.

METRO Light Rail and bus fares are $2 per ride, $4 for an all-day pass or $20 for a 7-day pass; an additional $1.25 is charged for Express/RAPID per ride. Self-serve ticket machines located at all stations accept cash and credit cards. The light rail operates 4:30 a.m.-midnight, with extended hours on Friday and Saturday. More information and printed route maps are available at downtown's Central Station (300 N. Central Ave.), or by phoning (602) 253-5000.

(Continued from p. 90.)

a consulting architect working with a former student, Wright also influenced the Mayan textile block design of the beautiful Arizona Biltmore, A Waldorf Astoria Resort, which opened its doors in 1929.

In the older neighborhoods surrounding the downtown core you'll take a trip down sunbaked boulevards lined with ranch-style homes and aging strip malls. In these areas you'll find several outstanding Mexican eateries and a handful of small joints dishing up cheap and tasty Native American food.

The Ancestral Desert People were the first to settle in the Valley of the Sun (as the Phoenix area is known). They built a network of irrigation canals, farmed the beautiful wasteland and created a great city. But around the mid-1400s, they mysteriously vanished. The 1860s saw a new frontier town begin to take shape atop the old site. This rebirth, like the mythical Phoenix rising from the ashes, is what gives the city its name.

Now crisscrossed by a network of wide L.A.-style freeways, the greater metro area is home to some 4.3 million residents, making it the largest city in the desert Southwest. One reason behind the explosive growth of the past 20 years is that the weather isn't always comparable to an oven set on broil. In the often warm, mild months of late fall, winter and early spring, Phoenix residents are wearing shorts and reserving tee times.

Must Do: AAA Editor's Picks

- Touch scarlet cactus fruit and watch butterflies settle on wildflowers and giant saguaro cacti at the **Desert Botanical Garden** (1201 N. Galvin Pkwy.), where you'll find plenty of Sonoran Desert wonders to admire during your vacation.
- Hike up Camelback Mountain, the double-humped peak that soars above Paradise Valley and Arcadia. A strenuous trail beginning in **Echo Canyon Recreation Area** (4925 E. McDonald Dr.) is called—for good reason—the "Scenic Stairmaster." At the top, scan the spectacular panorama of metropolitan Phoenix and the Sonoran Desert beyond.
- Pamper yourself in one of the spa capitals of the world. Walking through the tranquil lobby of the **Arizona Biltmore, A Waldorf Astoria Resort** (2400 E. Missouri Ave.)—with architecture inspired by Frank Lloyd Wright—is a great way to begin your luxurious experience. At the spa, delight in a massage with warm basalt stones, and enjoy other fun things to do.
- Go power shopping in Scottsdale. In the **Scottsdale Arts District** (along Main Street between 69th Street and Brown Avenue and Marshall Way from 5th Avenue to 1st Street) you can browse art galleries galore. Nearby in **Old Town Scottsdale** (bordered by N. Scottsdale and E. Indian School roads, E. 2nd Street and N. Drinkwater Boulevard)—with its Wild West-themed wooden storefronts—you'll find touristy trinket emporiums, local restaurants and dealers of authentic Native American crafts. Funky clothing boutiques and one-of-a-kind shops line 5th Avenue. And for those addicted to brand-name designer threads, there's the behemoth, three-story **Scottsdale Fashion Square** mall (7014 E. Camelback Rd.).
- Be a cowpoke for a day and ride a horse through Sonoran Desert country. In the foothills of **South Mountain Park** (109019 S. Central Ave.) you can trot and canter along more than 40 miles of trails. Hire horses and guides through Ponderosa Stables (10215 S. Central Ave.).
- Take an art walk on **Roosevelt Row,** aka RoRo, the stretch of Roosevelt Street between 7th Street and Grand Avenue, on the first Friday of the month. If you're wondering what to do in the evening, galleries and art studios stay open late, and sidewalks are crowded with families, hipsters and street performers.
- "Batter up!" If it's late February or March, catch **spring training** with Major League Baseball's Cactus League. In the autumn, check out the Arizona Fall League, a proving ground for Major League farm teams. Phoenix has plenty of interesting things to do for sports fans—this is the hometown of the **NBA Suns, NHL Coyotes, NFL Cardinals** and **MLB Diamondbacks.**
- Hear bells at **Cosanti** (6433 E. Doubletree Ranch Rd.) in Paradise Valley. Paolo Soleri, an architect, sculptor and protégé of Frank Lloyd Wright, founded this site to further his organically inspired architecture. An hour north of Phoenix in Mayer is Soleri's experimental community, Arcosanti (13555 S. Cross L Rd.), where you can see his distinctive spiraling, swooping buildings.
- Search for the fabled Lost Dutchman Gold Mine in the rugged **Superstition Mountains** east of the city. Even if you don't find the mine (no one has in more than 110 years), the scenery alone is a rich payoff. For groups in search of fun things to do with friends, stop at **Goldfield Ghost Town & Mine Tours** (4650 N. Mammoth Mine Rd.) for some cheesy Wild West adventure. Go hiking in nearby **Lost Dutchman State Park** (6109 N. Apache Tr.). Then drive the winding but incredibly scenic **Apache Trail** road (SR 88) to **Canyon Lake** and beyond; the road is unpaved but suitable for cars.
- Up, up and away—in a **hot air balloon.** From high in the clouds, marvel at the immensity of metro Phoenix and the stark beauty of its desert surroundings. The convention and visitors bureau can provide a list of ballooning companies.

Desert Botanical Garden

Phoenix 1-day Itinerary

AAA editors suggest these activities for a great short vacation experience. Those staying in the area for a longer visit can access a 3-day itinerary at AAA.com/TravelGuides.

Morning

- Start your trip by communing with nature at the **Desert Botanical Garden** (1201 N. Galvin Pkwy.) in 1,200-acre **Papago Park** on the east side of town. This is where visitors really come to understand the majesty of the Sonoran Desert and Phoenix's arid climate. You'll see native and exotic cacti, aloes and other plant species that thrive in desertlike conditions. Take the loop trail leading to the wildflower exhibits. This area is lovely no matter what time of year you visit, but it's bursting with color in March and April.
- Next, drive south in Papago Park and enjoy the scenery—sandstone buttes dramatically jut skyward. Stop at the **Phoenix Zoo** (455 N. Galvin Pkwy.) and meet a Galapagos tortoise, a reticulated giraffe, a Grevy's zebra, a ring-tailed lemur and other heat-loving animals that live in replicas of their own natural habitats. Visitors craving up-close animal encounters can touch stingrays, feed a giraffe or ride a camel.

Afternoon

- For lunch, head west toward downtown, where you'll spend the rest of the day. North of town, inhale a barbecue sandwich or a slab of ribs slathered in a special, spicy tomato-based sauce at **Honey Bear's BBQ** (2824 N. Central Ave.). The tasty side dishes complete the Honey Bear's experience, so try the mac & cheese or the chunky potato salad, and if you love sweet potato fries, this is the place!
- Now duck indoors away from the desert heat at the **Heard Museum** (2301 N. Central Ave.) and immerse yourself in Native American culture and arts. Stroll through the museum's 10 exhibit galleries and view baskets, drawings, paintings, photographs, pottery, jewelry, Kachina dolls, sculpture and textiles of the past and present. You can try your hand at bead looming, watch audiovisual presentations and unwind in the serene courtyards. Hit up the Heard Museum Shop on your way out if you're in the market for authentic Native American arts and crafts.
- You can peruse the masters: Boucher, Rodin and Monet. Stop at the **Phoenix Art Museum** (1625 N. Central Ave.) for some high art. You'll find more than 17,000 works from many art periods, ancient to contemporary. If you have a passion for high fashion, the Fashion Design collection is a must-see; if architecture and interior design interest you, don't miss the Thorne Miniature Rooms exhibit. Even the kids will enjoy this place—there's a family-friendly, hands-on gallery, and elementary schoolers are given packs stuffed with puzzles and other activities that correspond with art displays.

Heard Museum

- A visit to the **Arizona Capitol Museum** (1700 W. Washington St.), about 3 miles southwest of the N. Central Avenue museums, will definitely satisfy history buffs who want to learn more about the state's fascinating beginnings. The museum is housed in the old state capitol building, built of tuff stone and granite and capped with a copper dome. Inside you'll explore former government officials' offices and the House and Senate chambers and view all sorts of historical and political memorabilia.

Evening

- For dinner in the area, check out **Pizzeria Bianco** (623 E. Adams St.). It may take awhile to be seated, but the wood-fired oven pizza is worth the wait. When it comes time to order your pie, opt for the Rosa, topped with Parmigiano-Reggiano cheese, red onion, rosemary and Arizona pistachios; or the Wiseguy, which has a tasty combination of fennel sausage, smoked mozzarella and roasted onion on top.
- Need something different? Check out the restaurant and bar scene in the Mill Avenue District of nearby Tempe. With Arizona State University (ASU) a short jaunt away, Mill Avenue mainly courts the college crowd and the young at heart, but there's more here than greasy pizza-by-the-slice spots and sports bars. For an upscale evening, make reservations at the **Top of the Rock Restaurant** (10 minutes from Mill Avenue in **Marriott Phoenix Tempe at the Buttes,** 2000 W. Westcourt Way), where your rib-eye and martini come with fabulous city views.

Top Picks for Kids

Under 13

- Start the day with a fun-filled trip to the **Arizona Science Center** (600 E. Washington St.). Five themed galleries feature more than 300 hands-on exhibits, including a rock-climbing wall and the Evans Family SkyCycle, which allows riders to pedal along a 90-foot cable suspended in midair. There's also a giant screen theater and a planetarium, giving you enough choices to fill an entire afternoon with educational activities!
- Fans of G.I. Joe and antique dolls alike should head to the **Arizona Doll and Toy Museum** (5847 W. Myrtle Ave.). There are figurines and even a classroom filled with porcelain students. Meanwhile, parents should get a kick out of seeing toys they recognize, such as a rare Vinyl Cape Jawa from "Star Wars."
- At the **Phoenix Art Museum** (1625 N. Central Ave.), kids can frame their art experiences easily; just ask for a children's pack, which includes activities and other fun things to do that capture the imagination and explain a thing or two about art.
- In the South Mountain foothills, the butte-top, cowboy-themed **Rustler's Rooste** steakhouse (8383 S. 48th St.) offers an entertaining spot for a family night out. A live longhorn steer next to the front entrance? Check. An indoor waterfall and children's slide? Check. Live country music nightly? Check. Fried rattlesnake appetizer? Naturally. Unabashedly touristy? Of course, but that's part of the fun.

Phoenix Zoo

Teens

- Walk down **Roosevelt Row** (RoRo), the stretch of Roosevelt Street between 7th Street and Grand Avenue, which is the hip heart of the Downtown Arts District. Showcasing galleries, boutiques, restaurants and many additional fun places to go, it's a walkable, artsy epicenter for gathering those hard-to-find objects you never knew you needed.
- The renowned **Heard Museum** (2301 N. Central Ave.) highlights Native American culture and art. With audiovisual guides and interactive exhibits, you can develop a greater appreciation for the region's culture. You can even step inside a traditional Navajo hogan and think about how different it is from your own home.
- Continue time-traveling during your vacation by visiting the **Deer Valley Petroglyph Preserve** (3711 W. Deer Valley Rd.), a 30-minute drive to the Hedgpeth Hills, to see firsthand examples of Native American heritage. More than 1,500 petroglyphs, or carved symbols, cover the black basalt boulders. Walk the quarter-mile Petroglyph Trail, visit the museum to learn about the people and culture behind the petroglyphs or just enjoy the scenery. You may even see roadrunners and coyotes (not necessarily giving chase).
- The nearby **Pioneer Arizona Living History Museum** (3901 W. Pioneer Rd.) adds to the state's story with a pioneer village from the late 19th century. Costumed interpreters fill the old buildings—complete with an opera house, blacksmith shop and jail—with new life by reenacting historical events.

All Ages

- Closer to the airport, there's **Pueblo Grande Museum** (4619 E. Washington St.) with its ruins of a 1,500-year-old Hohokam village. Along with an ancient ball court and platform mound, this destination sports an updated theater and galleries, including a hands-on children's section.
- The **Phoenix Zoo** (455 N. Galvin Pkwy.) shows off more than 3,000 animals across 125 acres in the area known as Papago Park. With four trails—or themed areas—explaining the different zoo environments, it offers things to do for both adults and children. The Children's Trail, for example, displays kid-friendly farming methods and a petting zoo.
- The **Desert Botanical Garden** (1201 N. Galvin Pkwy.) features collections of the growing sort, including Australian, Baja California and South American areas—all artistically arranged. Kids may enjoy following the main trail's discovery stations, while parents can enjoy the photo opportunities as they travel along the path.

Arriving

By Car

Major highways make Phoenix readily accessible from all directions. The main route from Flagstaff and other points north is I-17, while the main route from the south and southeast is I-10. US 60, coming from the east, joins I-10 just north of Baseline Road.

In Phoenix I-10 intersects I-17 at 20th Street and leads west to Los Angeles. West of Phoenix, SR 85 intersects with I-10 and continues south to Gila Bend; I-8 can then be followed to Yuma and San Diego.

Getting Around

Street System

The streets in Phoenix form an orderly grid. Numbered streets run north and south, intersected by named streets going east and west. The axis is formed by Washington Street, which divides the city north and south, and Central Avenue, which determines the east and west sections. All avenues run west of Central; all streets, east.

Unless otherwise posted the speed limit on most streets is 25 mph. A right turn on red after a complete stop is legal unless otherwise posted. During rush hours the center turn lanes of 7th Avenue and 7th Street are reverse traffic flow lanes: morning rush hour one way into the city and evening rush hour one way out of the city. Try to avoid rush hours, 7-9 a.m. and 4-6 p.m.

Parking

Parking is regulated by meters, which are enforced daily 8 a.m.-10 p.m. with an hourly rate of $1 to $1.50. Most parking meters accept credit and debit cards as well as coins. During business hours and in the downtown area certain one-way streets have restricted parking hours. Rates at public lots start at $1.50 per hour.

Mojave Coffee & Records

Shopping

If your monthly credit card statements read like shopping mall directories, this is your kinda town. The metro Phoenix phone book lists some two dozen major shopping malls.

At the high end is **Biltmore Fashion Park,** 2502 E. Camelback Rd., an open-air affair loaded with budget-busting names like Saks Fifth Avenue and Ralph Lauren. **Desert Sky Mall,** west of downtown at 7611 W. Thomas Rd., is more akin to the all-purpose suburban center you'll find back home (think Dillard's, Hot Topic and Sunglass Hut). Try **Desert Ridge Marketplace,** 21001 N. Tatum Blvd., for an open-air shopping center.

The **Outlets at Anthem,** SR 17 and Anthem Way, are a good 30 minutes north of the city center, but if you're crazy for Ann Taylor and Calvin Klein at cut-rate prices, it's worth the drive.

In the shadow of office buildings, downtown's open-air **Arizona Center,** 455 N. 3rd St., offers apparel and a handful of tourist souvenir stores. Even if you keep the Visa card holstered, it's worth wandering around the nicely landscaped courtyards and fountains.

CityScape Phoenix, bounded by Washington and Jefferson streets and First Avenue, features an entertainment complex filled with hip dining and shopping options. Plus, after you exercise your buying power, you can get a workout in the on-site gym.

For authentic Native American arts and crafts, there's no topping the **Heard Museum Shop,** 2301 N. Central Ave. From high-quality jewelry and weavings to pottery and Kachina dolls, everything is purchased directly from Native American artists. The shop also stocks an extensive selection of books on the Southwest.

Mojave Coffee & Records, 4747 E. Thomas Rd., offers a holistic arts experience with coffee, books and films as well as records.

The pedestrian-friendly **Roosevelt Row (RoRo),** Roosevelt Street between 7th Avenue and 16th Street, is the heart of the **Downtown Arts District.** Once a run-down part of town, it's now home to several indie art galleries. If cutting-edge art is your thing, it's a must. If not, stick to Scottsdale *(see p. 147)*, where you'll find galleries of all kinds, as well as the valley's best shopping in general.

Nightlife

You'll find most of the valley's nocturnal action in Scottsdale *(see p. 147)* and Tempe *(see p. 177)*, but Phoenix proper is no slouch when it comes to fun things to do. With live music, cocktail lounges and casual bars happening all over town, pick up the free weekly *Phoenix New Times* or view it online for a comprehensive roundup of club and concert listings if you need help figuring out what to do today.

The downtown streets are brimming with sports bars and local restaurants that get wild on big game nights. Located between **Talking Stick Resort Arena** and **Chase Field, Crown Public House**, 333 E. Jefferson St., is loaded with flat-screen TVs and sports memorabilia. The beer is cold and the menu features chicken wings, hamburgers and sandwiches as well as elevated pub grub.

Stand Up Live at **CityScape Phoenix** is the latest place to catch top comedy acts in the CityScapes complex. Nearby **Lucky Strike** combines state-of-the-art bowling with an upscale menu and full-service bar—definitely not your daddy's bowling alley.

Everyone knows what to expect from **Hard Rock Cafe,** 3 S. 2nd St., and the Phoenix branch near **Talking Stick Resort Arena** holds no surprises. But it's still a fun spot to grab a pre- or post-game brew. If you're looking for places to eat, **Majerle's Sports Grill,** 24 N. 2nd St., is owned by ex-Suns great Dan Majerle and draws big crowds during the NBA season.

If suds and ESPN SportsCenter aren't part of your vacation scene, the city has several classy cocktail bars where you can sip a $12 appletini and chill in style. SoHo meets the Southwest at **MercBar,** 2525 E. Camelback Rd., a dark, sexy lounge across the street from Biltmore Fashion Park. A short trip northwest of downtown is **SideBar,** 1514 N. 7th Ave., a snug watering hole with swank décor and bartenders who know their business.

When the kids are in bed and you're in search of things for couples to do, Chivas Regal on the rocks is best enjoyed while gazing out at twinkling city lights. The upscale **Jade Bar,** 5700 E. McDonald Dr., obliges with outstanding nighttime views from its lofty locale at the Sanctuary on Camelback Mountain resort.

The Rhythm Room, 1019 E. Indian School Rd., is the place to catch live blues, roots rock and R&B. In the **Downtown Arts District,** the **Crescent Ballroom,** 308 N. 2nd Ave., hosts live jazz several nights a week. For country music and line dancing, you'll need to saddle up and travel to Scottsdale *(see p. 147).*

Big Events

What are New Year's festivities without college football? Pregame fun for the **Cactus Bowl**, held the day after Christmas, includes a party near Chase Stadium with marching bands, pep rallies and live music. Starting in mid-November enjoy a hole-in-one golf tournament and a block party that leads up to the **PlayStation Fiesta Bowl,** held at State Farm Stadium in **Glendale**, in early January. The excitement continues with **Phoenix's** annual **Desert Financial Fiesta Bowl Parade**, one of the country's largest. It proceeds down Central Avenue and includes marching bands that travel from around the country, gussied-up horses, lavish floats and colorful balloons.

In March, the **Heard Museum Guild Indian Fair and Market** brings together the finest Native American artists in the Southwest. You'll see pottery,

Hard Rock Cafe

carved Kachina dolls, baskets, jewelry, photography and paintings—along with talented musicians, drummers and feather-costumed dancers. If you're wondering where to eat, be sure to try the fry bread and posole stew.

The Valley of the Sun knows how to put on a party for Independence Day, and the **Fabulous Phoenix Fourth** lives up to its name. Enjoy live entertainment by local acts, amusement rides, a classic car exhibit and lots of food from local restaurants. The party wraps up with a spectacular fireworks display at Steele Indian School Park.

After a long, sizzling summer the heat finally breaks in October, just in time for the **Arizona Exposition & State Fair.** If you're into livestock shows, carnival games, live tunes, handmade quilts, homemade jellies and unique places to eat, you'll love this family-friendly destination. The grandstand is home to rodeos, a stunt show and a demolition derby. Ride the Ferris wheel, test your aim at the shooting gallery or visit the Home Arts Building to see if you agree with the judges' blue ribbon choices.

The bratwurst's steaming, the accordion's jamming and the tap's open at Tempe's annual **Four Peaks Oktoberfest.** Knockwurst and potato latkes are on the menu, and so is your favorite brew. Sitting is verboten, so boogie to an R&B band, feel irie with a reggae outfit or oompah into the night with polka players.

In December, more than 3.5 million lights transform the **Phoenix Zoo** into a twinkling holiday wonderland that's one of the most magical things to do in Phoenix. **ZooLights** features fantastic creatures and light sculptures, including an 18-foot-long rattlesnake and a life-size talking giraffe. For holiday shopping, don't miss the **Pueblo Grande Museum Indian Market,** held on the museum grounds. One-of-a-kind crafts by more than 100 top artisans make perfect gifts for friends and family.

From late November to late December you can experience Christmas lights the old-fashioned way at the Desert Botanical Garden's **Las Noches de las Luminarias.** A Southwestern Christmas tradition, luminarias are sand-weighted paper bags holding a candle, and they're typically spaced along walkways and rooflines. In the botanical garden, thousands of luminarias light the paths and cast a radiant glow on beautiful desert flora. Stroll the garden and enjoy musical entertainment, and sip on a glass of wine or warm cider to keep the December chill at bay.

Sports & Rec

Phoenix's mild winters make it an all-year sports paradise. For spectators the winter months mean **horse racing** at Turf Paradise from October through early May; phone (602) 942-1101.

Note: Policies vary concerning admittance of children to pari-mutuel betting facilities. Phone for information.

During **baseball** season the Arizona Diamondbacks, 2001 World Series champs, play at the retractable-roofed Chase Field, 401 E. Jefferson St. in downtown Phoenix; phone (602) 514-8400. Both the Diamondbacks and the Colorado Rockies conduct spring training at Salt River Fields at Talking Stick in Scottsdale; phone (480) 270-5000 or (480) 362-9467 for ticket information.

Pueblo Grande Museum Indian Market

Other teams with spring training sites in the Phoenix area include the Milwaukee Brewers at American Family Fields of Phoenix in Phoenix, (623) 245-5500; Oakland Athletics at Hohokam Stadium in Mesa, (480) 644-4452; the Los Angeles Angels of Anaheim at Tempe Diablo Stadium in Tempe, (480) 350-5205; the Kansas City Royals and the Texas Rangers at Surprise Stadium in Surprise, (623) 222-2222; the San Diego Padres and the Seattle Mariners at Peoria Sports Complex in Peoria, (623) 773-8700 or (623) 773-8720; the Los Angeles Dodgers and the Chicago White Sox at Camelback Ranch in Glendale, (623) 302-5000; the Cleveland Indians and the Cincinnati Reds at the Goodyear Ballpark in Goodyear, (623) 882-3120; and the San Francisco Giants at Scottsdale Stadium in Scottsdale, (480) 312-3111; and the Chicago Cubs at Sloan Park in Mesa, (480) 668-0500.

Talking Stick Resort Arena, 201 E. Jefferson St., is the site of many of Phoenix's sporting events. It is the home court of the NBA Phoenix Suns **basketball** team November through April; phone (602) 379-7867. The WNBA's Phoenix Mercury take over the arena's court May through September; phone (602) 252-9622. April through August the arena also houses the Arizona Rattlers, Phoenix's professional **arena football** team; phone (602) 514-8383. September through April the Gila River Arena, 9400 W. Maryland Ave., is the home of the Arizona Coyotes, the city's National **Hockey** League team; phone (480) 563-7825.

Professional **football** is played in Glendale, where the NFL Arizona Cardinals take the field at State Farm Stadium, 1 Cardinals Dr.; phone (602) 379-0102. The GEM Fiesta Bowl football classic at the stadium is an early January highlight.

Drift and drag racing are at Wild Horse Pass Motorsports Park, about 8 miles south of Phoenix at Maricopa Road and I-10; phone (520) 796-5601. Indy cars, NASCAR **stock cars and trucks,** and Grand Am sports cars race at ISM Raceway; phone (866) 408-7223.

Licensed drivers can experience race car driving at The Official Performance Driving School of Dodge//SRT, I-10 and Maricopa Road; phone (800) 842-7223.

Play **golf** all year in Arizona. There are more than 300 golf courses in the state, both public and private, appealing to all levels of proficiency. Phone (602) 534-4653 to reserve a tee time at one of six city courses.

Public and private courses include Encanto, (602) 534-4653, at 2745 N. 15th Ave.; The Foothills, (480) 460-4653, at 2201 E. Clubhouse Dr.; Grand Canyon University Golf Course, (623) 846-4022, at 5902 W. Indian School Rd.; Papago, (602) 275-8428, in Papago Park at 5595 E. Moreland St.; The Arizona Grand Golf Resort, (602) 431-6480, at 8000 S. Arizona Grand Pkwy.; Lookout Mountain Golf Club,

(602) 866-6356, at 11111 N. 7th St.; and Stonecreek, (602) 953-9111, at 4435 E. Paradise Village Pkwy. S.

Golf courses in nearby Mesa include: Dobson Ranch, (480) 644-2291, at 2155 S. Dobson Rd.; Red Mountain Ranch Country Club, (480) 981-6501, at 6425 E. Teton Cir.; and Superstition Springs, (480) 985-5622, at 6542 E. Baseline Rd.

Courses in Scottsdale include: Marriott's Camelback, (480) 596-7050, at 7847 N. Mockingbird Ln.; McCormick Ranch, (480) 948-0260, at 7505 E. McCormick Pkwy.; Starfire at Scottsdale Country Club, (480) 948-6000, at 11500 N. Hayden Rd.; TPC Scottsdale, (480) 585-4334, at 17020 N. Hayden Rd.; and Troon North, (480) 585-5300, at 10320 E. Dynamite Blvd.

Other area courses include: Gold Canyon, (480) 982-9090, at 6100 S. Kings Ranch Rd. in Apache Junction; Hillcrest, (623) 584-1500, at 20002 N. Star Ridge Dr. in Sun City West; The Legend at Arrowhead, (623) 561-1902, at 21027 N. 67th Ave. in Glendale; Ocotillo, (480) 917-6660, at 3751 S. Clubhouse Dr. in Chandler; We-Ko-Pa, (480) 836-9000, at 18200 East Toh Vee Cir. in Fort McDowell; and The Wigwam Resort, (800) 909-4224, at 300 E. Wigwam Blvd. in Litchfield Park. In Tempe is Ken McDonald, (480) 350-5250, at 800 E. Divot Dr.

Tennis courts open to the public are plentiful at several high schools and park areas, including Encanto Park, 2121 N. 15th Ave., and Granada Park, 6505 N. 20th St. The Phoenix Tennis Center, (602) 249-3712, at 6330 N. 21st Ave., has 25 lighted courts and reasonable rates; reservations are accepted.

The valley's beautiful desert country lends itself to **horseback riding.** Ponderosa Stables, (602) 268-1261, at 10215 S. Central Ave., offers trail rides.

Trails for **hiking** and **biking** are plentiful. A favorite hike is the 1-mile scenic trek to the summit of Piestewa Peak. Formerly known as Squaw Peak, the peak was renamed in honor of Lori Piestewa, an American servicewoman and Hopi who was killed in combat during Operation Iraqi Freedom in 2003. Guided hiking trips along several mountain trails in Phoenix and Scottsdale are offered by 360 Adventures; phone (480) 722-0360 or (877) 445-3749.

The Phoenix Parks and Recreation Department, (602) 534-6587, operates a number of parks; some have municipal **swimming** pools. Saguaro Lake and Canyon Lake *(see Recreation Areas Chart)* offer **water skiing, boating** and **fishing.** The Salt River is popular with **tubing** enthusiasts. Salt River Tubing and Recreation, (480) 984-3305, rents tubes and also provides shuttle-bus service along the Salt River.

For the **shooting** enthusiast, the Ben Avery Shooting Range, (623) 582-8313, 25 miles north of Phoenix off I-17 exit 223, offers pistol, rifle and archery ranges and trap and skeet fields.

The suburb of Tempe boasts inland **surfing** at Big Surf, (480) 994-2297; and **ice skating** at the Oceanside Ice Arena, (480) 941-0944, at 1520 N. McClintock Dr.

Horseback riding

Hot air balloon rides over the metropolitan area and the Sonora Desert are available through several companies. Balloon rides average 1 hour and are usually followed by a champagne brunch. Many companies operate October through May, but some offer flights year-round. Prices range from $149 to $219 per person. Companies include: Aerogelic Ballooning, (866) 359-8329, Hot Air Expeditions, (480) 502-6999 or (800) 831-7610, and Rainbow Ryders, Inc. Hot Air Balloon Ride Co., (480) 299-0154 or (800) 725-2477.

Performing Arts

Phoenix's rapid growth has been cultural as well as industrial, and it's quickly becoming a vacation destination for fans of performing arts. The following theaters present many fun things to do with a mix of classic and contemporary drama: **Herberger Theater Center,** (602) 254-7399, 222 E. Monroe; **Phoenix Theatre,** (602) 254-2151, 1825 N. Central Ave.; **Greasepaint Youtheatre,** (480) 949-7529, 7020 E. 2nd St. in Scottsdale; and **TheaterWorks,** (623) 815-7930, at 10580 N. 83rd Dr. in Peoria. Arizona's professional state theater group, the **Arizona Theater Co.,** (602) 256-6995, performs at the **Herberger Theater Center** during its October to June season.

The historic **Orpheum Theatre,** (800) 282-4842, at 203 W. Adams St., was originally built for vaudeville acts and movies in 1929. Scheduled to be condemned, the city bought the theater and in 1997 reopened it as a 1,400-seat performing arts center offering unique things to do in Phoenix throughout the year.

For music and dance lovers, the **Arizona Opera, Ballet Arizona** and **Phoenix Symphony** offer performances throughout the year. The symphony performs in the striking **Symphony Hall,** Phoenix Civic Plaza, 75 N. Second St.; phone (602) 495-1999.

Cabarets, special concerts, big-name entertainment, shows and lectures travel from all over the world to perform at the Herberger Theater Center, (602) 252-7399, 222 E. Monroe; and the **ASU Gammage,** (480) 965-3434, on the campus of Arizona State University at Mill Avenue and Apache Boulevard in Tempe.

Other special performance areas to see during your trip include **Talking Stick Resort Arena,** (602) 379-7800, 201 E. Jefferson St.; **Arizona Veterans Memorial Coliseum,** (602) 252-6771, 1826 W. McDowell Rd.; **Celebrity Theatre,** (602) 267-1600, 440 N. 32nd St.; **Ak-Chin Pavilion,** (602) 254-7200, 2121 N. 83rd Ave.; and the **Comerica Theatre,** (602) 379-2800, 400 W. Washington St. In Mesa are the **Mesa Arts Center,** (480) 644-6500, 1 E. Main St.; and the **Mesa Amphitheater,** (480) 644-2560, 263 N. Center St. Many venues are close to local restaurants if you're looking for places to eat before a show.

ATTRACTIONS

For a complete list of attractions, visit AAA.com/travelguides/attractions

ARIZONA CAPITOL MUSEUM is in the Arizona Capitol building at 1700 W. Washington St. The Capitol is built of tuff stone from Kirkland Junction and granite from the Salt River Mountains. Opened in 1901, the four-story building served as the territorial capitol until statehood came in 1912; it then became the state capitol.

The museum, located in the center of the Capitol Complex, is designed to connect Arizonans to their state government and reveals how Arizona was established as a territory, how it transitioned to a state and how the people continue to shape their government after more than 100 years of statehood.

Hours: Mon.-Fri. 9-4 (also Sat. 10-2, Sept.-May). Closed state holidays. Guided tours are available by reservation. **Cost:** Donations. **Parking:** Free at Wesley Bolin Park. **Phone:** (602) 926-3620. GT

CHASE FIELD is at 401 E. Jefferson St. Opened in 1998, this multipurpose ballpark is home to the Arizona Diamondbacks, the state's first Major League Baseball team. The facility also serves as a venue for other sporting events as well as concerts, temporary exhibitions and trade shows.

A 75-minute guided tour of the Diamondbacks' stadium encompasses the rotunda, a luxury suite, the dugout, and the visiting team's clubhouse or press box. **Hours:** Tours Mon.-Sat. at 9:30, 11 and 12:30. **Cost:** $7; $5 (ages 65+); $3 (ages 4-6). **Phone:** (602) 514-8400, or (602) 462-6799 for tour information. GT 3rd St/Jefferson, 16

HEARD MUSEUM, 2301 N. Central Ave., is a museum of native cultures and art. Among the exhibits in its 12 galleries are contemporary, ethnological and historical materials of Southwestern Native Americans; Native American basketry, jewelry and pottery; and Kachina dolls.

Visitors are greeted with colorful images as they enter the exhibit area. The architecture, foods, culture and spirituality of more than 20 tribes from desert, uplands and the Colorado Plateau regions are examined. Interactive exhibits allow visitors to work on a bead loom and experience re-created geographic

▼ See AAA listing p. 149 ▼

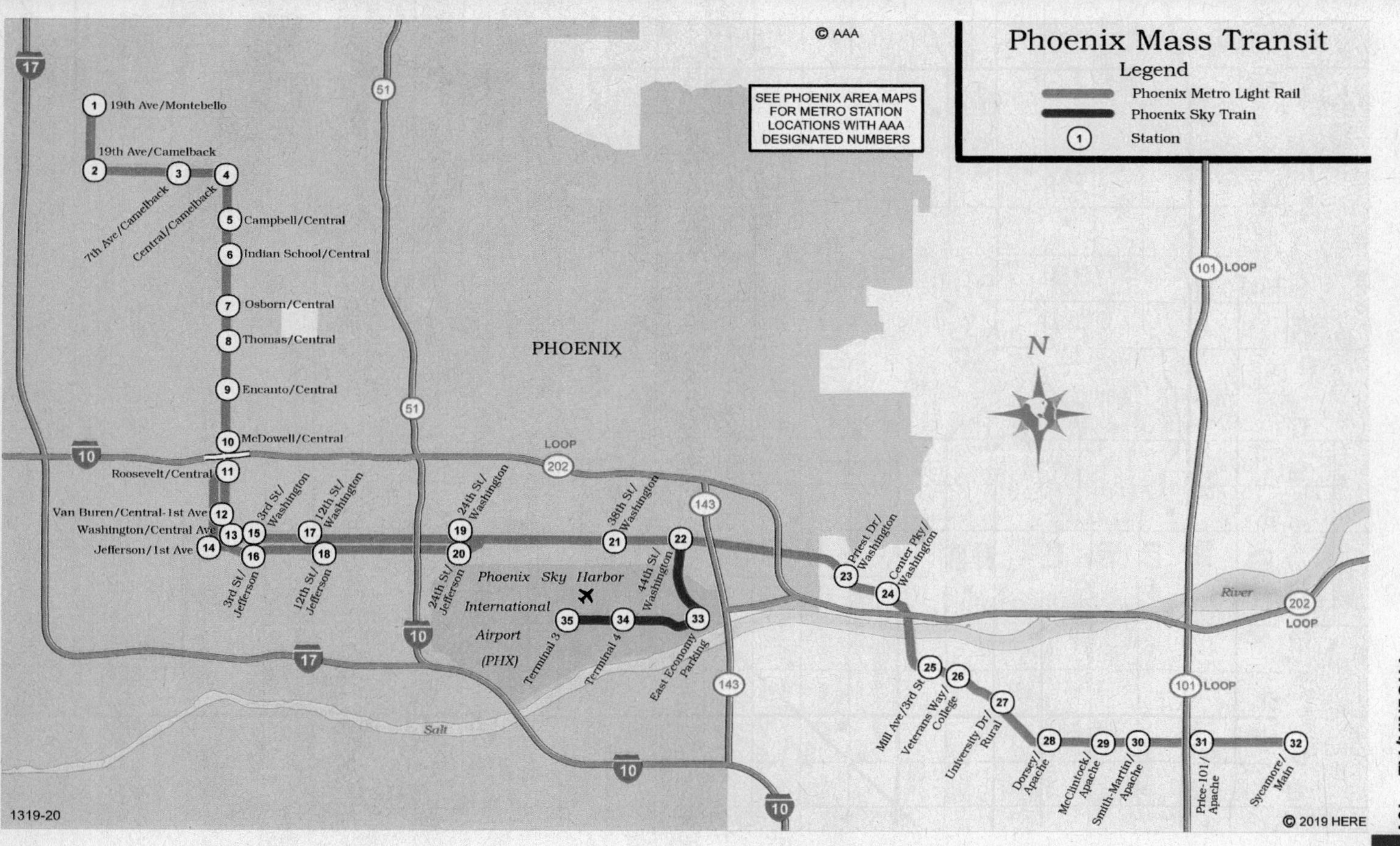
Phoenix Mass Transit
Legend
Phoenix Metro Light Rail
Phoenix Sky Train
Station
© AAA
SEE PHOENIX AREA MAPS FOR METRO STATION LOCATIONS WITH AAA DESIGNATED NUMBERS
N
PHOENIX
1 19th Ave/Montebello
2 19th Ave/Camelback
3 7th Ave/Camelback
4 Central/Camelback
5 Campbell/Central
6 Indian School/Central
7 Osborn/Central
8 Thomas/Central
9 Encanto/Central
10 McDowell/Central
11 Roosevelt/Central
12 Van Buren/Central-1st Ave
13 Washington/Central Ave
14 Jefferson/1st Ave
15 3rd St/Washington
16 3rd St/Jefferson
17 12th St/Washington
18 12th St/Jefferson
19 24th St/Washington
20 24th St/Jefferson
21 38th St/Washington
22 44th St/Washington
23 Priest Dr/Washington
24 Center Pky/Washington
25 Mill Ave/3rd St
26 Veterans Way/College
27 University Dr/Rural
28 Dorsey/Apache
29 McClintock/Apache
30 Smith-Martin/Apache
31 Price-101/Apache
32 Sycamore/Main
33 East Economy Parking
34 Terminal 4
35 Terminal 3
Phoenix Sky Harbor International Airport (PHX)
Salt
River
101 LOOP
202 LOOP
17
10
51
143
© 2019 HERE
1319-20

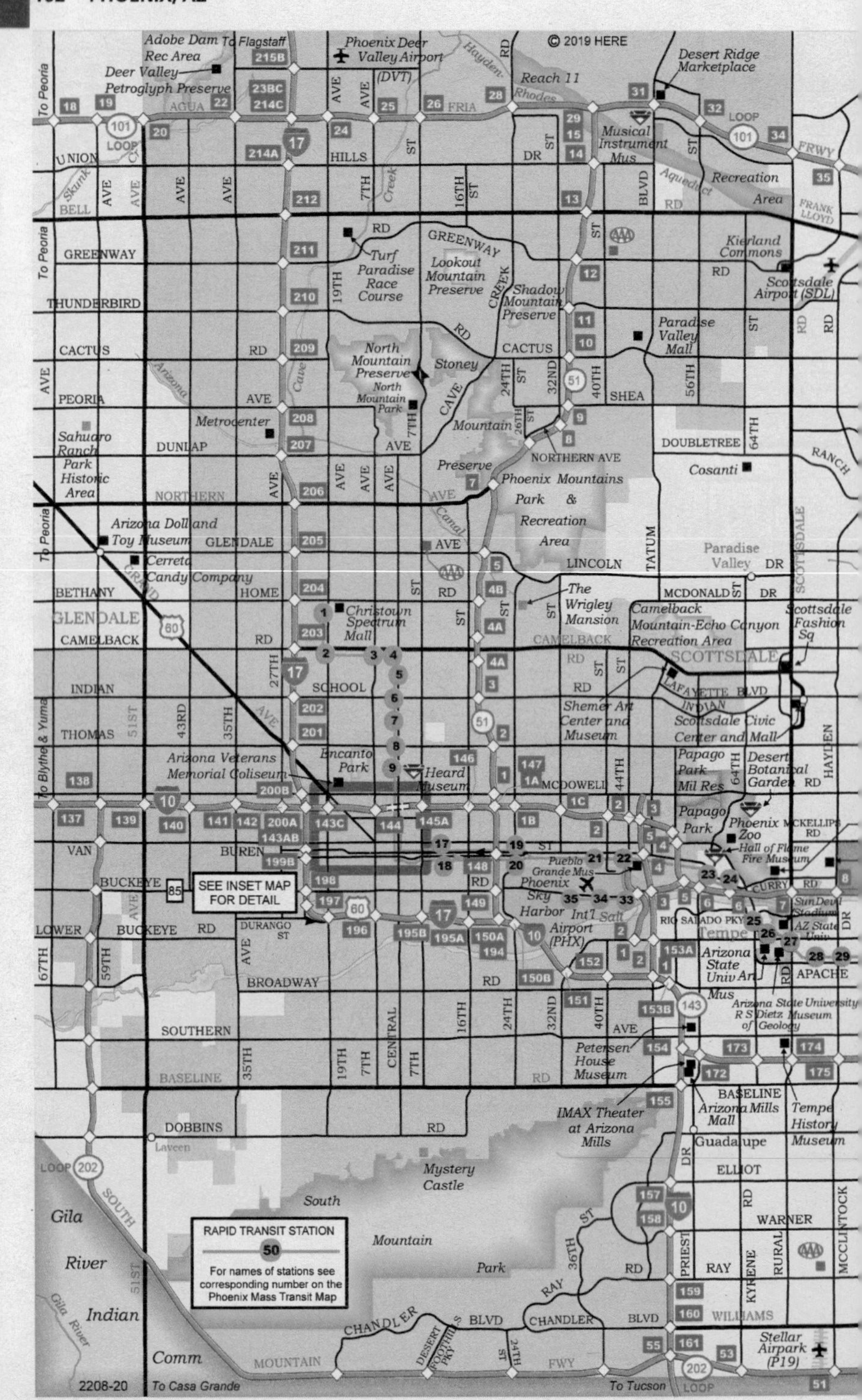
© 2019 HERE
Adobe Dam Rec Area
To Flagstaff
Deer Valley Petroglyph Preserve
Phoenix Deer Valley Airport (DVT)
Reach 11
Desert Ridge Marketplace
Musical Instrument Mus
Recreation Area
Turf Paradise Race Course
Lookout Mountain Preserve
Shadow Mountain Preserve
Kierland Commons
Scottsdale Airport (SDL)
Paradise Valley Mall
North Mountain Preserve
North Mountain Park
Stoney
Mountain
Preserve
Metrocenter
Sahuaro Ranch Park Historic Area
Phoenix Mountains Park & Recreation Area
Cosanti
Arizona Doll and Toy Museum
Cerreta Candy Company
Paradise Valley
The Wrigley Mansion
Camelback Mountain-Echo Canyon Recreation Area
Scottsdale Fashion Sq
GLENDALE
SCOTTSDALE
Christown Spectrum Mall
Shemer Art Center and Museum
Scottsdale Civic Center and Mall
Arizona Veterans Memorial Coliseum
Encanto Park
Heard Museum
Papago Park Mil Res
Desert Botanical Garden
Papago Park
Phoenix Zoo
Hall of Flame Fire Museum
Pueblo Grande Mus
Phoenix Sky Harbor Int'l Airport (PHX)
SEE INSET MAP FOR DETAIL
Tempe
Arizona State Univ Art Mus
Arizona State University R S Dietz Museum of Geology
Petersen House Museum
IMAX Theater at Arizona Mills
Arizona Mills Mall
Tempe History Museum
Guadalupe
Laveen
Mystery Castle
South Mountain Park
Gila River Indian Comm
RAPID TRANSIT STATION
50
For names of stations see corresponding number on the Phoenix Mass Transit Map
Stellar Airpark (P19)
To Peoria
To Blythe & Yuma
To Casa Grande
To Tucson
2208-20

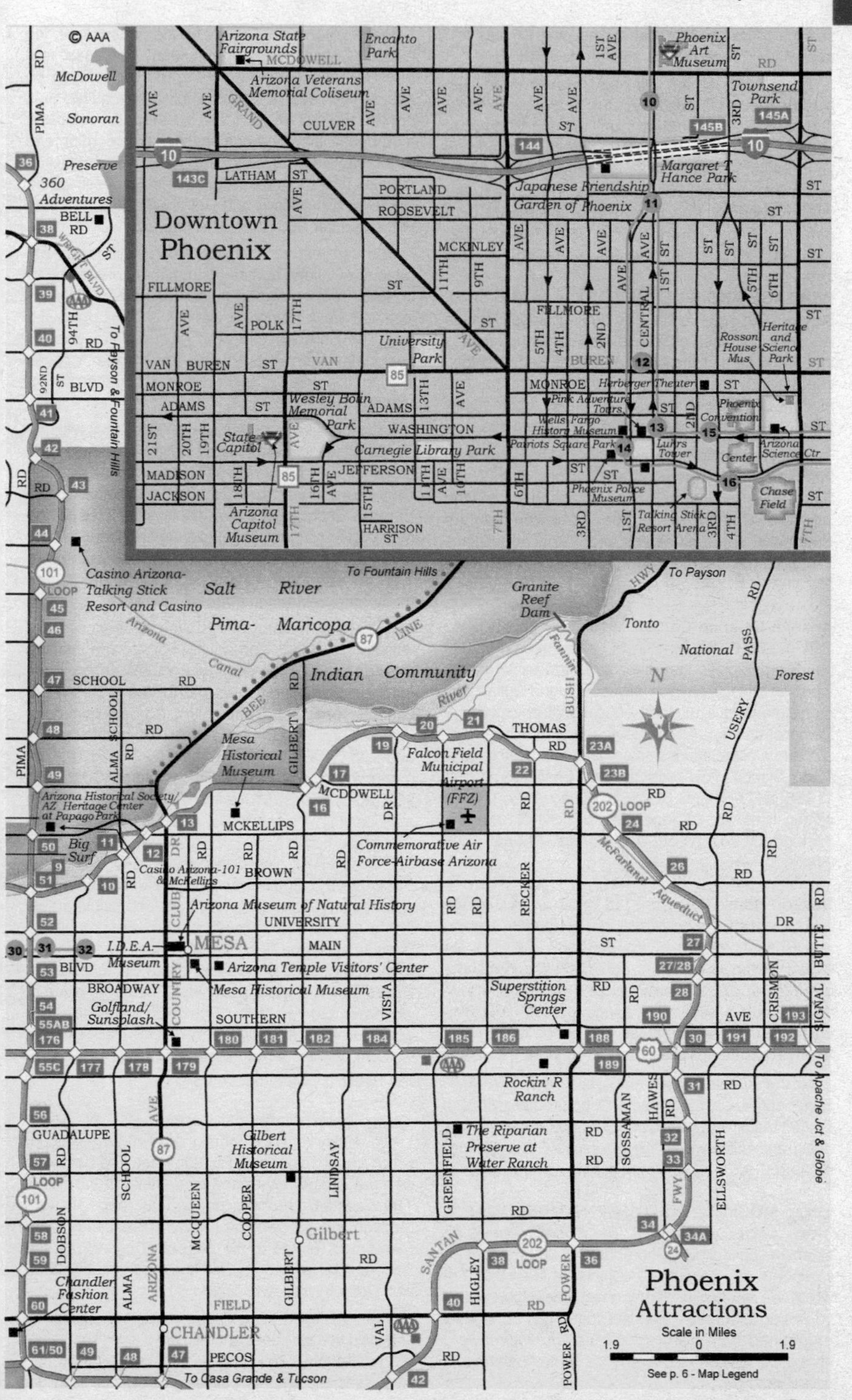
© AAA
Downtown Phoenix
Arizona State Fairgrounds
Encanto Park
Phoenix Art Museum
Arizona Veterans Memorial Coliseum
Townsend Park
Margaret T. Hance Park
Japanese Friendship Garden of Phoenix
University Park
Wesley Bolin Memorial Park
State Capitol
Carnegie Library Park
Arizona Capitol Museum
Herberger Theater
Pink Adventure Tours
Wells Fargo History Museum
Patriots Square Park
Phoenix Police Museum
Talking Stick Resort Arena
Luhrs Tower
Rosson House Mus
Heritage and Science Park
Phoenix Convention Center
Arizona Science Ctr
Chase Field
McDowell Sonoran Preserve
360 Adventures
To Payson & Fountain Hills
Casino Arizona-Talking Stick Resort and Casino
Salt River Pima-Maricopa Indian Community
To Fountain Hills
To Payson
Granite Reef Dam
Tonto National Forest
Mesa Historical Museum
Falcon Field Municipal Airport (FFZ)
Commemorative Air Force-Airbase Arizona
Arizona Historical Society/AZ Heritage Center at Papago Park
Big Surf
Casino Arizona-101 & McKellips
Arizona Museum of Natural History
I.D.E.A. Museum
MESA
Arizona Temple Visitors' Center
Mesa Historical Museum
Golfland/Sunsplash
Superstition Springs Center
Rockin' R Ranch
Gilbert Historical Museum
The Riparian Preserve at Water Ranch
Gilbert
Chandler Fashion Center
CHANDLER
To Casa Grande & Tucson
To Apache Jct & Globe
Phoenix Attractions
Scale in Miles
1.9 0 1.9
See p. 6 - Map Legend

settings of Native Americans. Changing exhibits and audiovisual presentations also are featured.

Time: Allow 1 hour minimum. **Hours:** Mon.-Sat. 9:30-5, Sun. 11-5 (also First Fri. of the month 6-10 p.m. Apr.-Feb.). Guided tours are given daily at noon, 2 and 3. Closed Easter, July 4, Thanksgiving and Christmas. **Cost:** $18; $15 (ages 65+); $7.50 (ages 6-17 and college students with ID); free (Native Americans); free (First Fri. of the month 6-10 p.m. Apr.-Feb.). **Phone:** (602) 252-8848 or (602) 252-8840. GT Encanto/Central, 9

HERITAGE AND SCIENCE PARK is on Monroe St. between 5th and 7th sts. The park includes Heritage Square, comprised of 10 late 19th-century structures that were part of the original site of Phoenix; they contain exhibits, museums and restaurants. The modern Lath House Pavilion serves as a community meeting area, botanical garden and festival site.

Validated parking is available in the garage at Fifth and Monroe sts. **Hours:** Buildings open Wed.-Sat. 10-5, Sun. noon-5. Phone ahead to confirm schedule. **Cost:** Grounds free. Admission fees are charged at some museums and historical buildings $10; $5 (ages 6-12). **Parking:** $1-$12. **Phone:** (602) 262-5029. 3rd St/Washington, 15

Arizona Science Center, in Heritage and Science Park at 600 E. Washington St., offers more than 300 hands-on displays that allow guests to explore such topics as biology, physics, psychology and digital communications in a fun and educational environment. Demonstrations, a SkyCycle ride, a giant screen theater and a planetarium also are featured. **Hours:** Daily 10-5. Closed Thanksgiving and Christmas. **Cost:** $19.95; $17.95 (ages 62+); $14.95 (ages 3-17). Giant screen films $9; $8 (ages 3-17). SkyCycle ride $5. **Parking:** $1-$12 on 5th and Monroe. **Phone:** (602) 716-2000. 3rd St/Jefferson, 16

Rosson House Museum, 113 N. 6th St. in Heritage and Science Park, was built in 1895 for Dr. Roland Lee Rosson, mayor of Phoenix 1895-96. The restored Victorian mansion, constructed in 6 months at a cost of $7,525, features lathe-worked posts on the veranda, pressed-tin ceilings, parquet floors, an elaborately carved staircase and period furnishings. Various events are presented throughout the year.

Hours: Guided tours are given Wed.-Sat. 10-4, Sun. noon-4. Last tour begins 1 hour before closing. Closed major holidays. **Cost:** $10; $9 (ages 62+, students and military with ID); $5 (ages 6-12). **Phone:** (602) 262-5070. GT 3rd St/Washington, 15

GEM **MUSICAL INSTRUMENT MUSEUM** is at 4725 E. Mayo Blvd. The museum boasts an extensive collection of more than 16,000 musical instruments and associated objects, at least 6,500 of which are on display at any given time. Upon arrival you'll don a wireless headset that picks up signals transmitted from each exhibit; as you walk toward an exhibit you'll hear the sounds of the instruments displayed.

In the Orientation Gallery on the ground floor, the exhibit "Guitars. Many Forms, Many Countries" features 22 wall-mounted guitars and 8 displayed on stands, including an 1800 English lute guitar. Just beyond the guitars you'll see a 12-foot tall octobass, a sūrbahār, an alphorn, a saxello, an accordion and other instruments accompanied by identification plaques that explain each instrument's construction. Upstairs in the Rock and Roll exhibit is a 12-string Rickenbacker 360 (think The Beatles).

You can test your music-making skills in the Experience Gallery, admire instruments donated by or on loan from renowned musicians in the Artist Gallery and view temporary exhibits in the Target Gallery. The Elvis exhibit in the Artist Gallery, done in conjunction with Elvis Presley Enterprises, features a changing array of instruments and artifacts centering on The King.

Upstairs, five galleries are divided almost continentally: Africa and the Middle East, Asia and Oceania, Latin America (including Mexico and the Caribbean), North America (U.S. and Canada) and Europe. Each gallery has displays devoted to the music of individual countries. Asian *dombras* and *dutars* (long-necked lutes), Guatemalan *marimbas*, Tibetan *dungchen* (giant copper trumpets), and many other instruments are all on display.

A 300-seat theater brings live performances and workshops to kids and adults. For a more intimate experience, however, find a musician giving a teaching demonstration as part of the Museum Encounters program. **Time:** Allow 2 hours minimum. **Hours:** Daily 9-5, Christmas 11-5. Guided tours Sat. and Sun. 11 and 2; Mon. and Fri. 2. Closed Thanksgiving. Phone ahead to confirm schedule. **Cost:** $20; $15 (ages 13-19); $10 (ages 4-12). Special exhibits additional $7. **Phone:** (480) 478-6000. GT

PAPAGO PARK, jct. Galvin Pkwy. and Van Buren St., covers 1,200 acres and features fishing lagoons, bicycle paths, nature trails and picnic areas. There also is a golf course on the park grounds. A popular attraction is Hole-in-the-Rock, a sandstone formation offering good views of the city to the west. Hunt's Tomb, a white pyramid, is the burial place of Governor George Wiley Paul Hunt, Arizona's first governor. **Hours:** Daily 5 a.m.-7 p.m. Trails close at 11 p.m. **Cost:** Free. **Phone:** (602) 495-5458. Priest Dr/Washington, 23

GEM **Desert Botanical Garden,** 1201 N. Galvin Pkwy., covers more than 140 acres, 55 of which are developed, in Papago Park. The garden is devoted exclusively to arid land plants of the world. The paved Desert Discovery Trail leads visitors through the garden; other walkways include the Plants and People of the Sonoran Desert Trail, the Sonoran Desert Nature Trail and the Harriet K. Maxwell Desert Wildflower Trail.

The majority of the garden's plants are succulents and include cacti, aloes and century plants. The height of the wildflower blooming season is March through May. Special programs, including bird walks, flashlight tours and children's ecology camps, are offered. **Time:** Allow 2 hours minimum. **Hours:** Daily 7 a.m.-8 p.m. Closed July 4, Thanksgiving and Christmas. **Cost:** $24.95; $12.95 (ages 3-17). Phone ahead to confirm rates. **Phone:** (480) 941-1225. GT

GEM **Hall of Flame Fire Museum,** in Papago Park at 6101 E. Van Buren St., houses one of the largest collections of firefighting equipment dating from 1725. A 10-minute video presentation introduces visitors to the museum's exhibits, which include hand- and horse-drawn pumpers, hook-and-ladder wagons and vehicles dating 1800-1969.

A wildland firefighting gallery explains the history and techniques of fighting wildfires. Other displays include fire marks, helmets, badges, patches, an interactive fire safety exhibit and play area for children, and artwork depicting major events in the history of fire service.

The National Firefighting Hall of Heroes recognizes firefighters who died in the line of duty and were decorated for bravery. **Time:** Allow 2 hours, 30 minutes minimum. **Hours:** Mon.-Sat. 9-5, Sun. noon-4. Closed Jan. 1, Thanksgiving and Christmas. **Cost:** $10; $8 (ages 6-17 and 62+); $4 (ages 3-5). **Phone:** (602) 275-3473. Priest Dr/Washington, 23

Phoenix Zoo, off N. Galvin Pkwy. in Papago Park, is home to more than 3,000 mammals, birds and reptiles. The 125-acre zoo features four trails and is home to Southwestern animals, African lions, Sumatran tigers, Bornean orangutans, Asian elephants, Masai giraffes and Komodo dragons. Encounters, tours and experiences include Monkey Village, Stingray Bay, Giraffe Encounter, 4-D Theater, Discovery Farm and the Safari Cruiser. Feel the Difference, an exhibit for the visually impaired, includes life-size sculptures of such animals as elephants, fish and insects. The displays are labeled in Braille.

Time: Allow 2 hours minimum. **Hours:** Daily 7-2, June-Aug.; 9-5, rest of year. Phone ahead to confirm schedule and admission. Closed Christmas. **Cost:** $24.95; $16.95 (ages 3-13). **Phone:** (602) 286-3800. GT Priest Dr/Washington, 23

GEM **PHOENIX ART MUSEUM,** 1625 N. Central Ave., features more than 18,000 works of American, European, Asian, Latin American, Western American and contemporary art as well as photography and fashion design. Changing exhibits may include works by such renowned artists as Pablo Picasso, Frida Kahlo, Claude Monet, Kehinde Wiley, Yayoi Kusama and Louisa McElwain. Among the highlights are photography exhibitions from the Center for Creative Photography at the University of Arizona as well as traveling national and international exhibits and the Dorrance Sculpture Garden. Families can enjoy PhxArtKids, an interactive gallery filled with hands-on exhibits. Also featured are the Thorne Miniature Rooms of historic interiors and a collection of works by Arizona artist Philip C. Curtis.

Time: Allow 1 hour minimum. **Hours:** Tues.-Sat. 10-5 (also Wed. 5-9 and first Fri. of the month 5-10), Sun. noon-5. Closed major holidays. **Cost:** Admission includes special exhibitions. $18-$23; $15-$20 (ages 65+); $13-$18 (full-time college students with ID); $9-$14 (ages 6-17); free (ages 0-5, members and Military Access Program). **Phone:** (602) 257-1880. GT McDowell/Central, 10

SHEMER ART CENTER AND MUSEUM, 5005 E. Camelback Rd., is located in the first house built in the Arcadia neighborhood of Phoenix. Building began in 1919, and after two remodels, was completed in 1928. The restored Santa Fe Mission-style building with adobe walls contains changing exhibits of fine art by Arizona artists; seasonal classes and workshops also are available. A highlight is the outdoor sculpture garden set amidst a citrus orchard. **Hours:** Tues.-Sat. 10-3. Closed city and major holidays. Schedule varies seasonally; phone ahead. **Cost:** Donations. A fee is charged for special events. **Phone:** (602) 262-4727.

SOUTH MOUNTAIN PARK, 8 mi. s. at 10919 S. Central Ave., contains more than 16,000 acres of peaks, canyons and strange rock formations as well as native Arizona flora. The park also features Native American petroglyphs. There are some 50 miles of trails for hiking, horseback riding and mountain biking. Dobbins Lookout, accessible by road and trail, affords an excellent view. The Pima Canyon park entrance (9904 S. 4th St.) offers convenient access to many of the hiking trails. **Note:** Park roads are closed to motorists on the fourth Sunday of every month; trailhead access points outside the park remain open. **Hours:** Parking lot open daily 5 a.m.-7 p.m. Trails close at 11 p.m. **Cost:** Free. **Phone:** (602) 262-7393.

WELLS FARGO HISTORY MUSEUM is at 145 W. Adams St. Exhibits portray Arizona stagecoach history beginning in the mid-1850s. An 1860 stagecoach and Western art by such artists as Frederic Remington and N.C. Wyeth are on display. **Time:** Allow 1 hour minimum. **Hours:** Mon.-Fri. 9-5. Closed major holidays. **Cost:** Free. **Phone:** (602) 378-1852. Jefferson/1st Ave, 14

Sightseeing

Bus, Four-wheel-drive and Van Tours

A tour is the best way to get an overall view of the city during your trip, especially if you have an interest in adventure travel. Several companies offer travel packages with fun things to do such as four-wheel-drive or van tours of the desert: Open Road Tours, (602) 997-6474 or (800) 766-7117; Vaughan's Southwest Custom Tours, (602) 971-1381 or (800) 513-1381; and Wayward Wind Tours Inc., (602) 867-7825 or (800) 804-0480.

Plane Tours

For one of the more unique things to do in Phoenix during your vacation, Westwind Air Service provides scenic flights of the Grand Canyon as well as Valley of the Sun tours of the Sonoran Desert. For travel arrangements, phone (480) 991-5557 or (888) 869-0866.

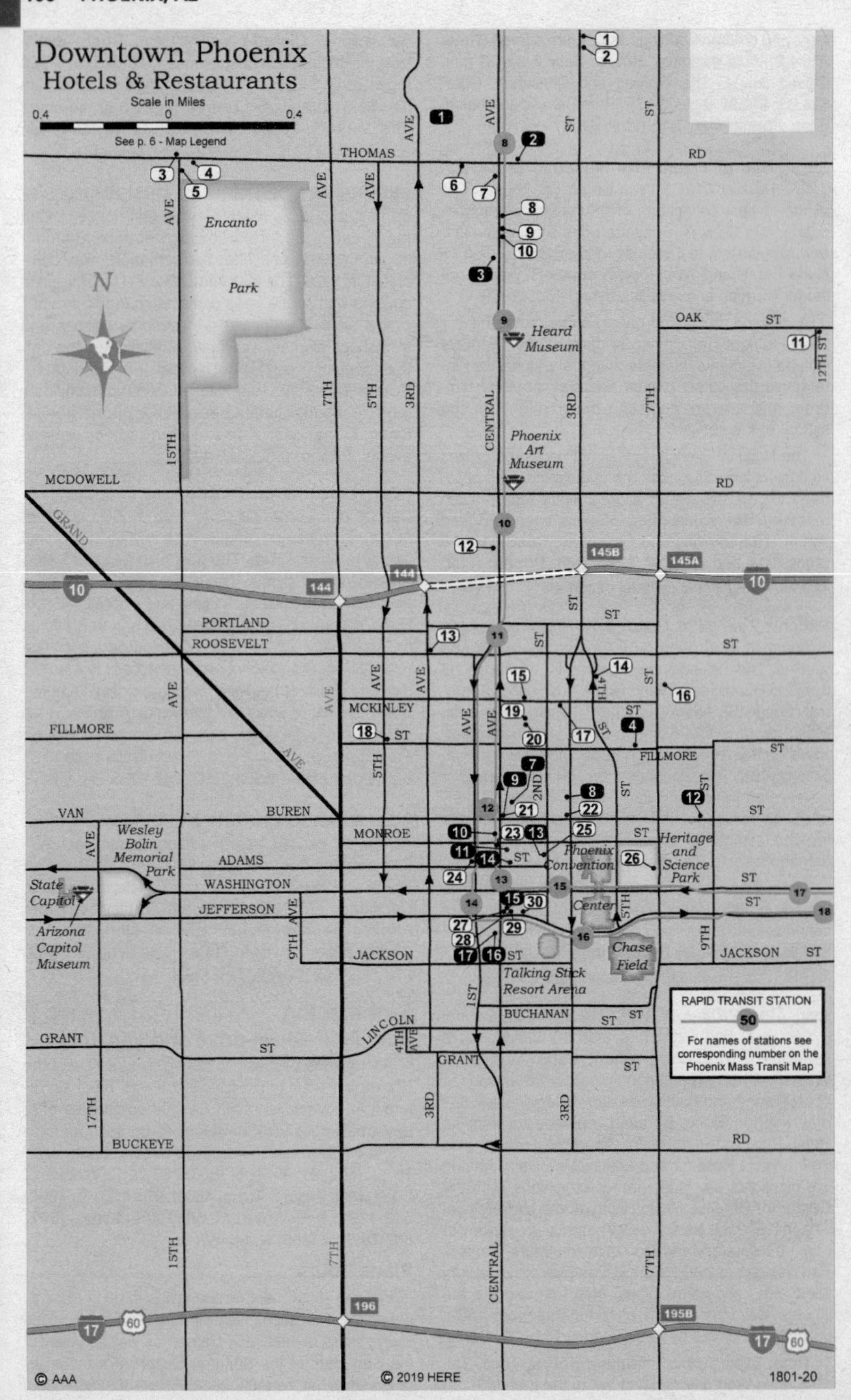

Downtown Phoenix
Hotels & Restaurants
Scale in Miles
0.4 0 0.4
See p. 6 - Map Legend
Encanto
Park
Heard
Museum
Phoenix
Art
Museum
Wesley
Bolin
Memorial
Park
State
Capitol
Arizona
Capitol
Museum
Phoenix
Convention
Center
Heritage
and
Science
Park
Chase
Field
Talking Stick
Resort Arena
THOMAS RD
OAK ST
MCDOWELL RD
GRAND AVE
PORTLAND ST
ROOSEVELT ST
MCKINLEY ST
FILLMORE ST
VAN BUREN ST
MONROE ST
ADAMS ST
WASHINGTON ST
JEFFERSON ST
JACKSON ST
BUCHANAN ST
LINCOLN ST
GRANT ST
BUCKEYE RD
15TH AVE
7TH AVE
5TH AVE
3RD AVE
CENTRAL AVE
3RD ST
7TH ST
12TH ST
17TH AVE
9TH AVE
1ST AVE
2ND ST
4TH ST
5TH ST
9TH ST
4TH AVE
RAPID TRANSIT STATION
50
For names of stations see corresponding number on the Phoenix Mass Transit Map
© AAA
© 2019 HERE
1801-20

Downtown Phoenix

This index helps you "spot" where approved hotels and restaurants are located on the corresponding detailed maps. Restaurant price range is a combination of lunch and/or dinner. Turn to the listing page for more information and consult display ads for special promotions.

For more details, rates and reservations: AAA.com/travelguides/hotels

DOWNTOWN PHOENIX

Map Page	Hotels	Diamond Rated	Member Savings	Page
1 p. 106	Hampton Inn-Phoenix/Midtown (Downtown Area)	◆◆◆	✔	132
2 p. 106	Embassy Suites by Hilton Phoenix Downtown North	◆◆◆	✔	132
3 p. 106	**Fairfield Inn & Suites by Marriott Phoenix Midtown**	◆◆◆	✔	132
4 p. 106	**Holiday Inn Express Hotel & Suites Phoenix Downtown-Ball Park**	◆◆◆	✔	132
7 p. 106	**Hampton Inn & Suites Phoenix Downtown**	◆◆◆	✔	132
8 p. 106	**Sheraton Grand Phoenix**	◆◆◆◆	✔	133
9 p. 106	**The Westin Phoenix Downtown**	◆◆◆◆	✔	133
10 p. 106	Historic Hotel San Carlos	◆◆		132
11 p. 106	Hilton Garden Inn Phoenix Downtown	◆◆◆	✔	132
12 p. 106	**SpringHill Suites by Marriott Phoenix Downtown**	◆◆◆	✔	133
13 p. 106	**Hyatt Regency Phoenix**	◆◆◆	✔	132
14 p. 106	**Renaissance Phoenix Downtown**	◆◆◆	✔	132
15 p. 106	**Kimpton Hotel Palomar Phoenix**	◆◆◆◆	✔	132
16 p. 106	Courtyard by Marriott Phoenix Downtown	◆◆◆	✔	132
17 p. 106	Residence Inn by Marriott Phoenix Downtown	◆◆◆	✔	133

Map Page	Restaurants	Diamond Rated	Cuisine	Price Range	Page
1 p. 106	China Chili	◆◆	Chinese	$7-$26	133
2 p. 106	Ocotillo	◆◆◆	New American	$16-$32	133
3 p. 106	Mu Shu Asian Grill	◆◆	Asian	$9-$17	133
4 p. 106	Persian Garden Café	◆◆	Middle Eastern	$10-$35	133
5 p. 106	The Original Hamburger Works	◆	American	$4-$7	133
6 p. 106	Pino's Pizza Al Centro	◆◆	Italian	$6-$17	134
7 p. 106	Honey Bear's BBQ	◆	Barbecue	$7-$25	133
8 p. 106	**The Wild Thaiger**	◆◆	Thai	$9-$29	134
9 p. 106	**Durant's**	◆◆◆	Steak	$14-$64	133
10 p. 106	Switch Restaurant & Wine Bar	◆◆◆	Comfort Food	$9-$25	134
11 p. 106	Tuck Shop	◆◆◆	Regional Comfort Food	$12-$32	134
12 p. 106	Pizza People Pub	◆◆	Pizza	$8-$15	134
13 p. 106	Lola Coffee	◆	Coffee/Tea	$2-$6	133
14 p. 106	Bliss	◆◆	American	$9-$17	133
15 p. 106	Matt's Big Breakfast	◆◆	American	$5-$9	133
16 p. 106	Mother Bunch Brewing	◆◆	American	$10-$18	133
17 p. 106	Moira Sushi Bar & Kitchen	◆◆	Japanese	$10-$15	133
18 p. 106	Cibo Urban Pizzeria Cafe	◆◆	Italian	$9-$20	133

Map Page	Restaurants (cont'd)	Diamond Rated	Cuisine	Price Range	Page
19 p. 106	Pomo Pizzeria Napoletana	◆◆	Italian	$12-$17	134
20 p. 106	The Breadfruit & Rum Bar	◆◆	Jamaican	$14-$38	133
21 p. 106	Province Urban Kitchen & Bar	◆◆◆	American	$18-$35	134
22 p. 106	District American Kitchen & Wine Bar	◆◆◆	American	$12-$48	133
23 p. 106	Cornish Pasty Co.	◆◆	English	$10-$12	133
24 p. 106	Noodle Bar	◆◆	International Noodles	$10-$14	133
25 p. 106	Compass Arizona Grill	◆◆◆	American	$23-$60	133
26 p. 106	Pizzeria Bianco	◆◆	Pizza	$13-$18	134
27 p. 106	Squid Ink Sushi	◆◆	Sushi	$11-$24	134
28 p. 106	Blue Hound Kitchen & Cocktails	◆◆◆	American	$10-$36	133
29 p. 106	The Breakfast Club	◆◆	American	$7-$14	133
30 p. 106	The Arrogant Butcher	◆◆◆	American	$13-$39	133

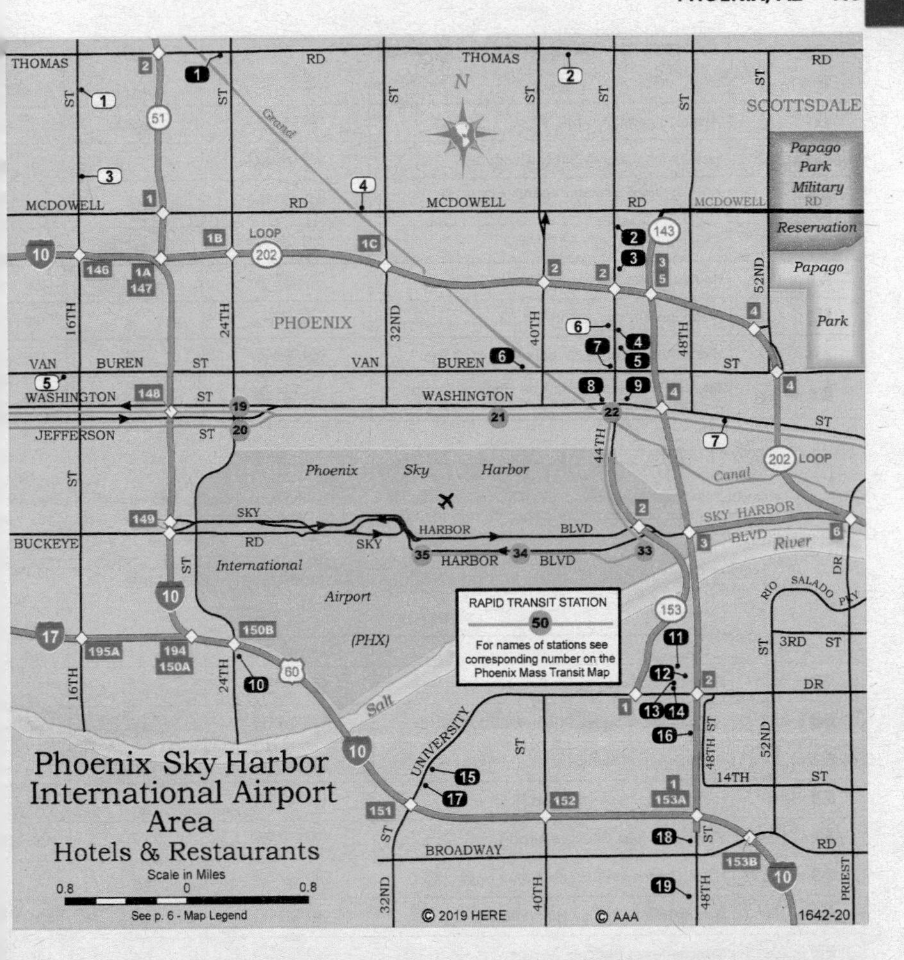

Airport Hotels

Map Page	PHOENIX SKY HARBOR INTERNATIONAL (Maximum driving distance from airport: 4.6 mi)	Diamond Rated	Member Savings	Page
9 this page	**Aloft Phoenix Airport Hotel, 2.6 mi**	◆◆◆	✔	134
10 this page	**Best Western Airport Inn, 2.5 mi**	◆◆	✔	135
14 this page	**Country Inn & Suites by Radisson Phoenix Airport, 3.0 mi**	◆◆◆	✔	135
13 this page	Courtyard by Marriott Phoenix Airport, 3.0 mi	◆◆◆	✔	135
8 this page	**Crowne Plaza Phoenix Airport, 2.4 mi**	◆◆◆	✔	136
7 this page	**DoubleTree Suites by Hilton Phoenix, 3.1 mi**	◆◆◆	✔	136
17 this page	Drury Inn & Suites Phoenix Airport, 4.6 mi	◆◆◆		136
4 this page	Hampton Inn Phoenix Airport North, 3.0 mi	◆◆◆	✔	137
15 this page	Hilton Garden Inn Phoenix Airport, 4.4 mi	◆◆◆	✔	137
6 this page	Hilton Garden Inn Phoenix Airport North, 3.2 mi	◆◆◆	✔	137

Map Page	**PHOENIX SKY HARBOR INTERNATIONAL** (Maximum driving distance from airport: 4.6 mi) (cont'd)	Diamond Rated	Member Savings	Page
11 p. 109	**Hilton Phoenix Airport, 3.2 mi**	◆◆◆	✔	137
16 p. 109	Holiday Inn & Suites Phoenix Airport, 3.3 mi	◆◆◆		137
2 p. 109	**Holiday Inn & Suites Phoenix Airport North, 3.6 mi**	◆◆◆	✔	137
3 p. 109	Phoenix Airport Marriott, 3.3 mi	◆◆◆	✔	138
5 p. 109	**Radisson Hotel Phoenix Airport, 2.8 mi**	◆◆◆	✔	139
12 p. 109	Sleep Inn Phoenix Airport, 3.1 mi	◆◆		139
7 p. 126	**Hyatt Place Tempe/Phoenix Airport, 3.7 mi**	◆◆◆	✔	179
5 p. 126	**SpringHill Suites by Marriott Phoenix Tempe Airport, 3.6 mi**	◆◆◆	✔	180

Phoenix Sky Harbor International Airport

This index helps you "spot" where approved hotels and restaurants are located on the corresponding detailed maps. Restaurant price range is a combination of lunch and/or dinner. Turn to the listing page for more information and consult display ads for special promotions.

For more details, rates and reservations: AAA.com/travelguides/hotels

PHOENIX

Map Page	Hotels	Diamond Rated	Member Savings	Page
1 p. 109	Embassy Suites by Hilton Phoenix Airport	◆◆◆	✔	136
2 p. 109	**Holiday Inn & Suites Phoenix Airport North**	◆◆◆	✔	137
3 p. 109	Phoenix Airport Marriott	◆◆◆	✔	138
4 p. 109	Hampton Inn Phoenix Airport North	◆◆◆	✔	137
5 p. 109	**Radisson Hotel Phoenix Airport**	◆◆◆	✔	139
6 p. 109	Hilton Garden Inn Phoenix Airport North	◆◆◆	✔	137
7 p. 109	**DoubleTree Suites by Hilton Phoenix**	◆◆◆	✔	136
8 p. 109	**Crowne Plaza Phoenix Airport**	◆◆◆	✔	136
9 p. 109	**Aloft Phoenix Airport Hotel**	◆◆◆	✔	134
10 p. 109	**Best Western Airport Inn**	◆◆	✔	135
11 p. 109	**Hilton Phoenix Airport**	◆◆◆	✔	137
12 p. 109	Sleep Inn Phoenix Airport	◆◆		139
13 p. 109	Courtyard by Marriott Phoenix Airport	◆◆◆	✔	135
14 p. 109	**Country Inn & Suites by Radisson Phoenix Airport**	◆◆◆	✔	135
15 p. 109	Hilton Garden Inn Phoenix Airport	◆◆◆	✔	137
16 p. 109	Holiday Inn & Suites Phoenix Airport	◆◆◆		137
17 p. 109	Drury Inn & Suites Phoenix Airport	◆◆◆		136
18 p. 109	**GreenTree Inn & Suites Phoenix Sky Harbor**	◆◆◆	✔	136
19 p. 109	Homewood Suites by Hilton Phoenix Airport South	◆◆◆	✔	138

Map Page	Restaurants	Diamond Rated	Cuisine	Price Range	Page
1 p. 109	Casa Corazon	◆◆	Mexican	$8-$20	140

Map Page	Restaurants (cont'd)	Diamond Rated	Cuisine	Price Range	Page
2 p. 109	Sa Bai Modern Thai	♦♦	Thai	$10-$18	142
3 p. 109	La Santisima Gourmet Taco Shop	♦	Mexican	$4-$9	141
4 p. 109	Red Devil Restaurant & Pizzeria	♦♦	Italian	$9-$23	142
5 p. 109	Roland's Cafe Market Bar	♦♦	Regional American	$6-$15	142
6 p. 109	Szechwan Palace	♦♦	Chinese	$7-$20	142
7 p. 109	Stockyards Restaurant & 1889 Saloon	♦♦♦	Steak	$8-$75	142

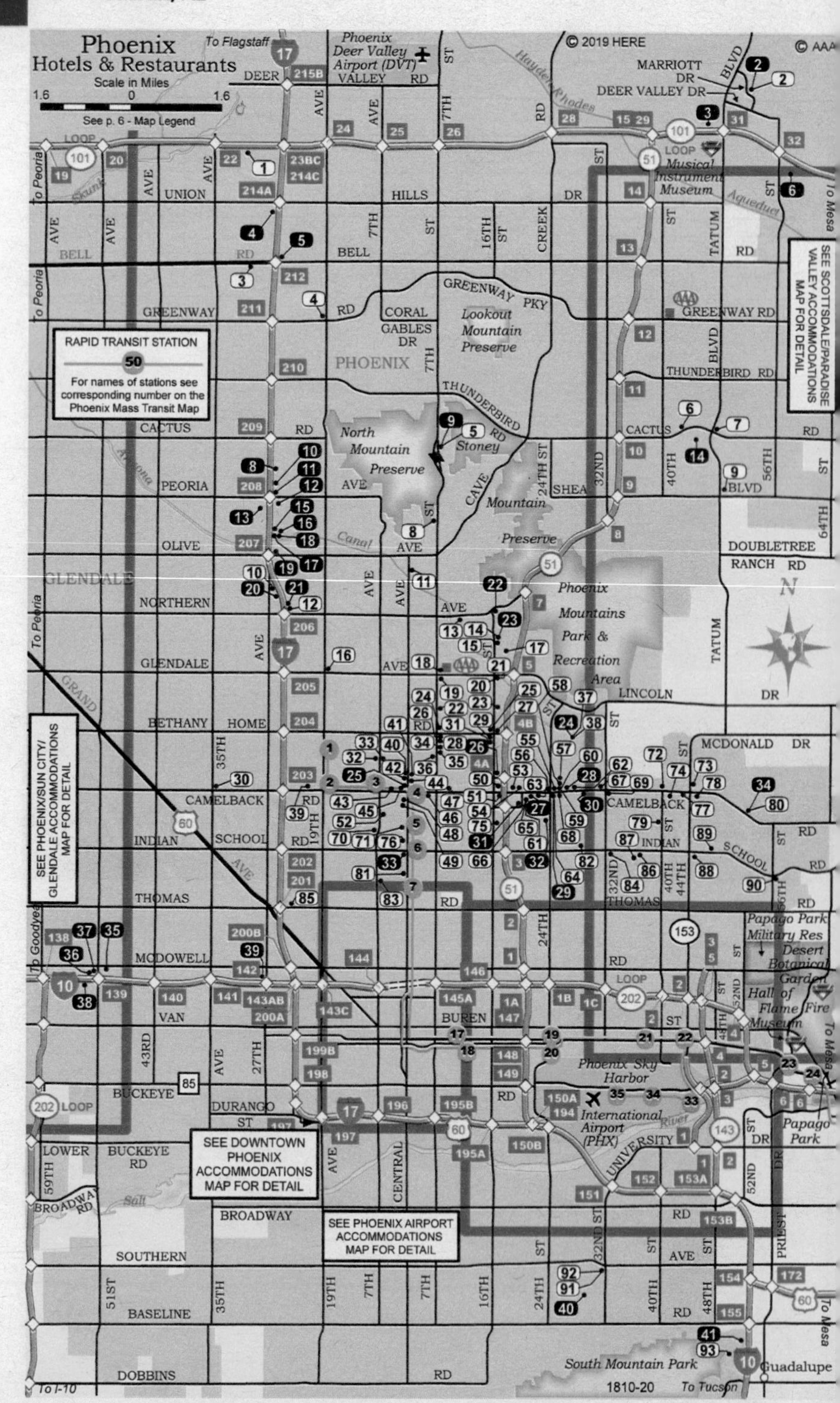
Phoenix
Hotels & Restaurants
Scale in Miles
1.6 0 1.6
See p. 6 - Map Legend
© 2019 HERE
RAPID TRANSIT STATION
50
For names of stations see corresponding number on the Phoenix Mass Transit Map
SEE SCOTTSDALE/PARADISE VALLEY ACCOMMODATIONS MAP FOR DETAIL
SEE PHOENIX/SUN CITY/GLENDALE ACCOMMODATIONS MAP FOR DETAIL
SEE DOWNTOWN PHOENIX ACCOMMODATIONS MAP FOR DETAIL
SEE PHOENIX AIRPORT ACCOMMODATIONS MAP FOR DETAIL
Phoenix Deer Valley Airport (DVT)
Musical Instrument Museum
North Mountain Preserve
Lookout Mountain Preserve
Stoney Mountain Preserve
Phoenix Mountains Park & Recreation Area
PHOENIX
GLENDALE
Papago Park Military Res
Desert Botanical Garden
Hall of Flame Fire Museum
Papago Park
Phoenix Sky Harbor International Airport (PHX)
South Mountain Park
Guadalupe
To Flagstaff
To Peoria
To Goodyear
To Mesa
To Tucson
To I-10
1810-20

Phoenix

This index helps you "spot" where approved hotels and restaurants are located on the corresponding detailed maps. Restaurant price range is a combination of lunch and/or dinner. Turn to the listing page for more information and consult display ads for special promotions.

For more details, rates and reservations: AAA.com/travelguides/hotels

PHOENIX

Map Page	Hotels	Diamond Rated	Member Savings	Page
2 p. 112	**JW Marriott Phoenix Desert Ridge Resort & Spa**	♦♦♦♦	✔	138
3 p. 112	Holiday Inn Express & Suites Phoenix North-Scottsdale	♦♦♦		138
4 p. 112	**Sleep Inn Phoenix North**	♦♦	✔	140
5 p. 112	Comfort Inn & Suites	♦♦♦		135
6 p. 112	**Residence Inn by Marriott Phoenix Desert View at Mayo Clinic**	♦♦♦	✔	139
8 p. 112	Candlewood Suites Phoenix	♦♦		135
9 p. 112	Pointe Hilton Tapatio Cliffs Resort	♦♦♦	✔	139
10 p. 112	**Hyatt Place Phoenix-North**	♦♦♦	✔	138
11 p. 112	Four Points by Sheraton Phoenix North	♦♦♦	✔	136
12 p. 112	Homewood Suites by Hilton Phoenix Metrocenter	♦♦♦	✔	138
13 p. 112	DoubleTree by Hilton Phoenix North	♦♦♦	✔	136
14 p. 112	**Embassy Suites by Hilton Phoenix-Scottsdale**	♦♦♦	✔	136
15 p. 112	Courtyard by Marriott Phoenix North	♦♦♦	✔	135
16 p. 112	**Best Western North Phoenix Hotel**	♦♦♦	✔	135
17 p. 112	SpringHill Suites by Marriott Phoenix North	♦♦♦	✔	140
18 p. 112	TownePlace Suites by Marriott Phoenix North	♦♦♦	✔	140
19 p. 112	Sheraton Crescent Hotel	♦♦♦	✔	139
20 p. 112	Residence Inn by Marriott Phoenix	♦♦♦	✔	139
21 p. 112	Quality Inn Phoenix North I-17	♦♦		139
22 p. 112	**Best Western InnSuites Phoenix/Biltmore**	♦♦♦	✔	135
23 p. 112	**Pointe Hilton Squaw Peak Resort**	♦♦♦	✔	139
24 p. 112	**Arizona Biltmore, A Waldorf Astoria Resort**	♦♦♦♦	✔	134
25 p. 112	Maricopa Manor Bed & Breakfast Inn	♦♦♦		138
26 p. 112	Extended Stay America Phoenix-Biltmore	♦♦		136
27 p. 112	Courtyard by Marriott-Camelback	♦♦♦	✔	135
28 p. 112	Embassy Suites by Hilton Phoenix Biltmore	♦♦♦	✔	136
29 p. 112	The Camby, Autograph Collection	♦♦♦♦	✔	135
30 p. 112	**AC Hotel by Marriott Phoenix Biltmore**	♦♦♦	✔	134
31 p. 112	Homewood Suites by Hilton Phoenix-Biltmore	♦♦♦	✔	138
32 p. 112	**Hampton Inn by Hilton Phoenix Biltmore**	♦♦♦	✔	137
33 p. 112	Hilton Garden Inn Phoenix Midtown	♦♦♦	✔	137
34 p. 112	**Royal Palms Resort and Spa**	♦♦♦♦	✔	139
35 p. 112	La Quinta Inn & Suites Phoenix I-10 West	♦♦♦		138
36 p. 112	**Red Roof PLUS+ Phoenix West**	♦♦	✔	139

PHOENIX (cont'd)

Map Page	Hotels (cont'd)	Diamond Rated	Member Savings	Page
37 p. 112	Holiday Inn Phoenix West	◆◆◆		138
38 p. 112	Baymont by Wyndham Phoenix I-10	◆◆		135
39 p. 112	Comfort Inn I-10 West/Central	◆◆		135
40 p. 112	**The Legacy Golf Resort**	◆◆◆	✔	138
41 p. 112	**Arizona Grand Resort & Spa**	◆◆◆◆	✔	134

Map Page	Restaurants	Diamond Rated	Cuisine	Price Range	Page
1 p. 112	George & Son's	◆◆	Chinese	$8-$40	140
2 p. 112	Roy's Desert Ridge	◆◆◆	Hawaiian	$20-$59	142
3 p. 112	India Palace	◆◆	Indian	$11-$16	141
4 p. 112	Chino Bandido	◆	Fusion	$7-$10	140
5 p. 112	**Different Pointe of View**	◆◆◆◆	New American	$29-$42	140
6 p. 112	Yasu Sushi Bistro	◆◆◆	Japanese	$9-$42	143
7 p. 112	Marigold Maison	◆◆	Indian	$10-$26	141
8 p. 112	Scramble	◆	American	$11-$12	142
9 p. 112	Rusconi's American Kitchen	◆◆◆	New American	$12-$28	142
10 p. 112	Bobby Q	◆◆	Barbecue	$12-$47	140
11 p. 112	Ladera Taverna y Cocina	◆◆	Regional Mexican	$10-$22	141
12 p. 112	Akaihana Sushi & Grill	◆◆	Sushi	$11-$17	140
13 p. 112	RedThai Southeast Asian Kitchen	◆◆	Asian	$12-$18	142
14 p. 112	Rico's American Grill	◆◆◆	American	$12-$32	142
15 p. 112	Tutti Santi Ristorante	◆◆◆	Italian	$14-$27	142
16 p. 112	Restaurant Atoyac Estilo Oaxaca	◆	Mexican	$4-$9	142
17 p. 112	Aunt Chilada's Hideaway	◆◆	Mexican	$6-$18	140
18 p. 112	Scott's Generations Deli	◆◆	Deli	$12-$18	142
19 p. 112	Sierra Bonita Grill	◆◆◆	Southwestern	$12-$28	142
20 p. 112	Babbo Italian Eatery	◆◆	Italian	$9-$15	140
21 p. 112	Moto	◆◆	Asian Fusion	$7-$19	141
22 p. 112	Christo's	◆◆	Italian	$11-$33	140
23 p. 112	Richardson's of New Mexico	◆◆	Southwestern	$13-$50	142
24 p. 112	Otro Cafe	◆◆	Mexican	$8-$15	141
25 p. 112	George Yang's Chinese Cuisine	◆◆	Chinese	$10-$25	141
26 p. 112	Pubblico Italian Eatery	◆◆◆	Italian	$12-$38	142
27 p. 112	The Vig Uptown	◆◆	American	$13-$22	142
28 p. 112	Fuego Bistro	◆◆	Latin American	$12-$30	140
29 p. 112	Zipps Sports Grill	◆◆	American	$9-$18	143
30 p. 112	Great Wall Hong Kong Cuisine	◆◆	Chinese	$8-$25	141
31 p. 112	Phoenix City Grille	◆◆◆	American	$14-$39	141

Map Page	Restaurants (cont'd)	Diamond Rated	Cuisine	Price Range	Page
32 p. 112	Hana Japanese Eatery	♦♦	Japanese	$12-$36	141
33 p. 112	La Pinata	♦♦	Mexican	$9-$19	141
34 p. 112	Mora Italian	♦♦♦	Italian	$13-$39	141
35 p. 112	Cold Beers & Cheeseburgers	♦♦	American	$11-$19	140
36 p. 112	Stock & Stable	♦♦♦	American	$13-$28	142
37 p. 112	Frank & Albert's	♦♦♦	American	$16-$42	140
38 p. 112	Wright's at the Biltmore	♦♦♦♦	American	$29-$46	142
39 p. 112	Pepe's Taco Villa	♦♦	Mexican	$7-$16	141
40 p. 112	Federal Pizza	♦♦	Italian	$10-$18	140
41 p. 112	Windsor	♦♦	American	$12-$20	142
42 p. 112	Postino Central WineCafe	♦♦	Small Plates Sandwiches	$10-$14	141
43 p. 112	Southern Rail	♦♦♦	Southern American	$7-$27	142
44 p. 112	Flower Child	♦♦	Natural/Organic	$9-$13	140
45 p. 112	The Prime Chinese Restaurant	♦♦	Chinese	$10-$20	142
46 p. 112	St. Francis	♦♦♦	New American	$12-$28	142
47 p. 112	Cherryblossom Noodle Cafe	♦♦	Noodles	$7-$15	140
48 p. 112	Yama Sushi House	♦♦	Sushi	$9-$21	142
49 p. 112	Hula's Modern Tiki	♦♦	Polynesian	$10-$26	141
50 p. 112	Blue Water Grill	♦♦♦	Seafood	$15-$49	140
51 p. 112	Duck and Decanter	♦	Deli	$7-$12	140
52 p. 112	The Fry Bread House	♦	Regional Specialty	$3-$10	140
53 p. 112	The Parlor Pizzeria	♦♦	Pizza	$12-$31	141
54 p. 112	Greekfest	♦♦♦	Greek	$7-$30	141
55 p. 112	True Food Kitchen	♦♦♦	American	$10-$26	142
56 p. 112	Over Easy - Biltmore	♦♦	Breakfast	$7-$12	141
57 p. 112	Seasons 52 Fresh Grill	♦♦♦	New American	$11-$32	142
58 p. 112	The Capital Grille	♦♦♦	Steak	$19-$110	140
59 p. 112	Zinburger	♦♦	Burgers	$10-$17	143
60 p. 112	Blanco Tacos & Tequila	♦♦	Mexican	$8-$21	140
61 p. 112	Snooze an A.M. Eatery	♦♦	Breakfast	$7-$12	142
62 p. 112	Hillstone Restaurant	♦♦♦	American	$15-$54	141
63 p. 112	The Gladly	♦♦♦	New American	$14-$45	141
64 p. 112	Artizen	♦♦♦	New American	$22-$44	140
65 p. 112	Pizzeria Bianco	♦♦♦	Italian Pizza	$13-$23	141
66 p. 112	Tratto	♦♦♦	Italian	$12-$30	142
67 p. 112	Matt's Big Breakfast	♦♦	American	$10-$14	141

Map Page	Restaurants (cont'd)	Diamond Rated	Cuisine	Price Range	Page
68 p. 112	TEN - Handcrafted American Fare and Spirits	♦♦♦	American	$9-$22	142
69 p. 112	Tarbell's	♦♦♦	American	$12-$39	142
70 p. 112	Restaurant Progress	♦♦♦	New American	$15-$35	142
71 p. 112	Pane Bianco	♦♦	Specialty Sandwiches	$9-$16	141
72 p. 112	Chelsea's Kitchen	♦♦♦	American	$15-$36	140
73 p. 112	Steak 44	♦♦♦	Steak	$33-$69	142
74 p. 112	North Italia	♦♦♦	Italian	$13-$38	141
75 p. 112	Miracle Mile Delicatessen	♦	Deli	$9-$17	141
76 p. 112	The Clever Koi	♦♦	Asian	$10-$18	140
77 p. 112	Buck & Rider	♦♦♦	Seafood	$16-$38	140
78 p. 112	The Henry	♦♦♦	New American	$13-$29	141
79 p. 112	Postino WineCafe	♦♦	American	$10-$14	142
80 p. 112	T. Cook's	♦♦♦♦	Mediterranean	$28-$59	142
81 p. 112	Alexi's Grill	♦♦♦	Northern Italian	$9-$31	140
82 p. 112	Giuseppe's on 28th	♦♦	Italian	$9-$29	141
83 p. 112	Mi Patio Mexican Food	♦♦	Mexican	$5-$14	141
84 p. 112	Desert Jade	♦♦	Chinese	$11-$26	140
85 p. 112	Pizza a Metro	♦♦	Italian	$13-$36	141
86 p. 112	Nook Kitchen	♦♦♦	American	$11-$28	141
87 p. 112	Ocean Poke Co.	♦	Hawaiian Fusion	$7-$12	141
88 p. 112	Sushi Brokers	♦♦	Japanese	$11-$16	142
89 p. 112	Over Easy Cafe	♦♦	American	$5-$12	141
90 p. 112	Kitchen 56	♦♦♦	American	$10-$26	141
91 p. 112	**Farm Kitchen at The Farm at South Mountain**	♦	American	$10-$14	140
92 p. 112	Quiessence	♦♦♦♦	New American	$20-$40	142
93 p. 112	Rustler's Rooste	♦♦	Steak	$16-$36	142

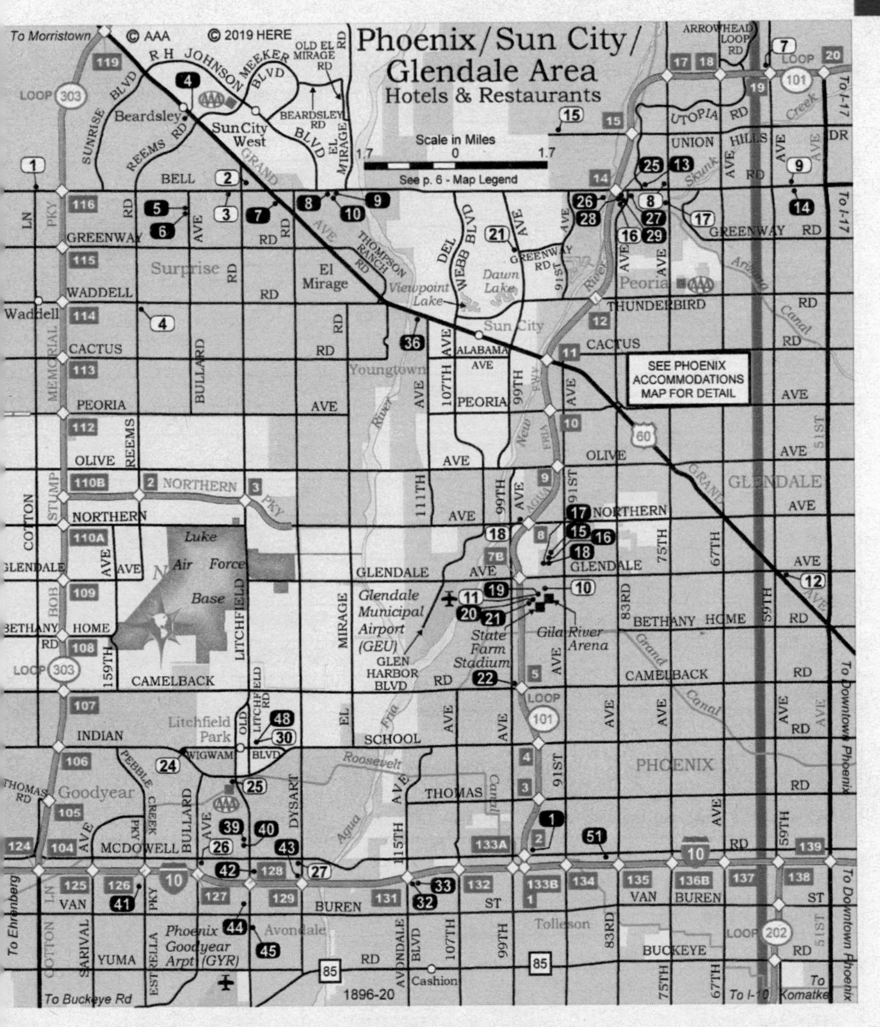

Phoenix/Sun City/Glendale Area

This index helps you "spot" where approved hotels and restaurants are located on the corresponding detailed maps. Restaurant price range is a combination of lunch and/or dinner. Turn to the listing page for more information and consult display ads for special promotions.

For more details, rates and reservations: AAA.com/travelguides/hotels

PHOENIX

Map Page	Hotel	Diamond Rated	Member Savings	Page
1 this page	**Courtyard by Marriott Phoenix West-Avondale**	◆◆◆	✔	135

SURPRISE

Map Page	Hotels	Diamond Rated	Member Savings	Page
4 this page	**Hampton Inn & Suites by Hilton Surprise**	◆◆◆	✔	176
5 this page	Holiday Inn Express & Suites	◆◆◆		176
6 this page	Residence Inn by Marriott Phoenix NW Surprise	◆◆◆	✔	177
7 this page	Comfort Inn & Suites Surprise-Phoenix NW	◆◆◆		176

SURPRISE (cont'd)

Map Page	Hotels (cont'd)	Diamond Rated	Member Savings	Page
8 p. 117	Windmill Suites Surprise, an Ascend Hotel Collection Member	◆◆◆		177
9 p. 117	Days Inn & Suites Surprise	◆◆		176
10 p. 117	Quality Inn & Suites of Surprise near Sun City	◆◆		176

Map Page	Restaurants	Diamond Rated	Cuisine	Price Range	Page
1 p. 117	Amuse Bouche	◆◆	American	$12-$34	177
2 p. 117	Uni Sushi & Steak	◆◆	Japanese Sushi	$10-$38	177
3 p. 117	Saigon Kitchen	◆◆	Vietnamese	$8-$25	177
4 p. 117	Vogue Bistro	◆◆◆	New American	$8-$26	177

GLENDALE

Map Page	Hotels	Diamond Rated	Member Savings	Page
13 p. 117	**SpringHill Suites by Marriott Phoenix Glendale/ Peoria**	◆◆◆	✔	54
14 p. 117	Comfort Inn & Suites at Talavi	◆◆		53
15 p. 117	Residence Inn by Marriott Phoenix Glendale Sports & Entertainment District	◆◆◆	✔	54
16 p. 117	SpringHill Suites by Marriott Phoenix Glendale Sports & Entertainment District	◆◆◆	✔	54
17 p. 117	**Staybridge Suites Phoenix/Glendale**	◆◆◆	✔	54
18 p. 117	**Holiday Inn Express & Suites Phoenix/Glendale**	◆◆◆	✔	54
19 p. 117	Renaissance Glendale Hotel & Spa	◆◆◆◆	✔	54
20 p. 117	**Hampton Inn & Suites by Hilton Glendale/ Westgate**	◆◆◆	✔	53
21 p. 117	**Home2 Suites by Hilton Phoenix Glendale Westgate**	◆◆◆	✔	54
22 p. 117	Comfort Suites State Farm Stadium Area	◆◆◆		53

Map Page	Restaurants	Diamond Rated	Cuisine	Price Range	Page
7 p. 117	Sakana Sushi & Grill	◆◆	Japanese	$8-$34	55
8 p. 117	Pita Jungle	◆◆	Mediterranean	$8-$16	55
9 p. 117	Thee Pitt's "Again"	◆◆	Barbecue	$10-$22	55
10 p. 117	Mama Gina's Pizzeria	◆◆	Italian	$8-$21	55
11 p. 117	Soleil	◆◆◆	Regional American	$12-$40	55
12 p. 117	Haus Murphy's	◆◆	German	$8-$20	55

PEORIA

Map Page	Hotels	Diamond Rated	Member Savings	Page
25 p. 117	Comfort Suites by Choice Hotels/Peoria Sports Complex	◆◆		88
26 p. 117	Holiday Inn Express Hotel Peoria North-Glendale	◆◆◆		88
27 p. 117	La Quinta Inn & Suites by Wyndham Phoenix West Peoria	◆◆◆		88
28 p. 117	Residence Inn by Marriott Glendale/Peoria	◆◆◆	✔	88
29 p. 117	Hampton Inn Peoria	◆◆◆	✔	88

Map Page	Restaurants	Diamond Rated	Cuisine	Price Range	Page
15 p. 117	Good China	◆◆	Chinese	$8-$20	88
16 p. 117	P.F. Chang's China Bistro	◆◆◆	Chinese	$10-$28	88
17 p. 117	Ah-So Steak & Sushi	◆◆	Japanese	$7-$38	88

Map Page	Restaurants (cont'd)	Diamond Rated	Cuisine	Price Range	Page
18 p. 117	Fleming's Prime Steakhouse & Wine Bar	💎💎💎	Steak	$38-$90	88

AVONDALE

Map Page	Hotels	Diamond Rated	Member Savings	Page
32 p. 117	**Hilton Garden Inn Phoenix/Avondale**	💎💎💎	✔	29
33 p. 117	Homewood Suites by Hilton Phoenix/Avondale	💎💎💎	✔	29

YOUNGTOWN

Map Page	Hotel	Diamond Rated	Member Savings	Page
36 p. 117	**Quality Inn & Suites Phoenix NW-Sun City**	💎💎	✔	229

GOODYEAR

Map Page	Hotels	Diamond Rated	Member Savings	Page
39 p. 117	Residence Inn by Marriott	💎💎💎	✔	56
40 p. 117	Hampton Inn & Suites by Hilton Goodyear	💎💎💎	✔	56
41 p. 117	Comfort Suites Goodyear	💎💎💎		56
42 p. 117	Red Lion Inn & Suites Goodyear	💎💎		56
43 p. 117	Holiday Inn & Suites Goodyear	💎💎💎		56
44 p. 117	TownePlace Suites by Marriott Phoenix/Goodyear	💎💎💎	✔	56
45 p. 117	**Best Western Phoenix Goodyear Inn**	💎💎	✔	56

Map Page	Restaurants	Diamond Rated	Cuisine	Price Range	Page
24 p. 117	Royal Jasmine Thai	💎💎	Thai	$10-$18	56
25 p. 117	Bella Luna Ristorante	💎💎💎	Italian	$10-$26	56
26 p. 117	P.F. Chang's China Bistro	💎💎💎	Chinese	$9-$28	56
27 p. 117	Tomo Japanese Cuisine	💎💎	Japanese	$8-$27	56

LITCHFIELD PARK

Map Page	Hotel	Diamond Rated	Member Savings	Page
48 p. 117	**The Wigwam**	💎💎💎💎	✔	77

Map Page	Restaurant	Diamond Rated	Cuisine	Price Range	Page
30 p. 117	Litchfield's	💎💎💎	New American	$22-$45	77

TOLLESON

Map Page	Hotel	Diamond Rated	Member Savings	Page
51 p. 117	**Best Western Tolleson**	💎💎	✔	181

SUN CITY

Map Page	Restaurant	Diamond Rated	Cuisine	Price Range	Page
21 p. 117	Little Bite of Italy	💎💎	Italian	$8-$20	175

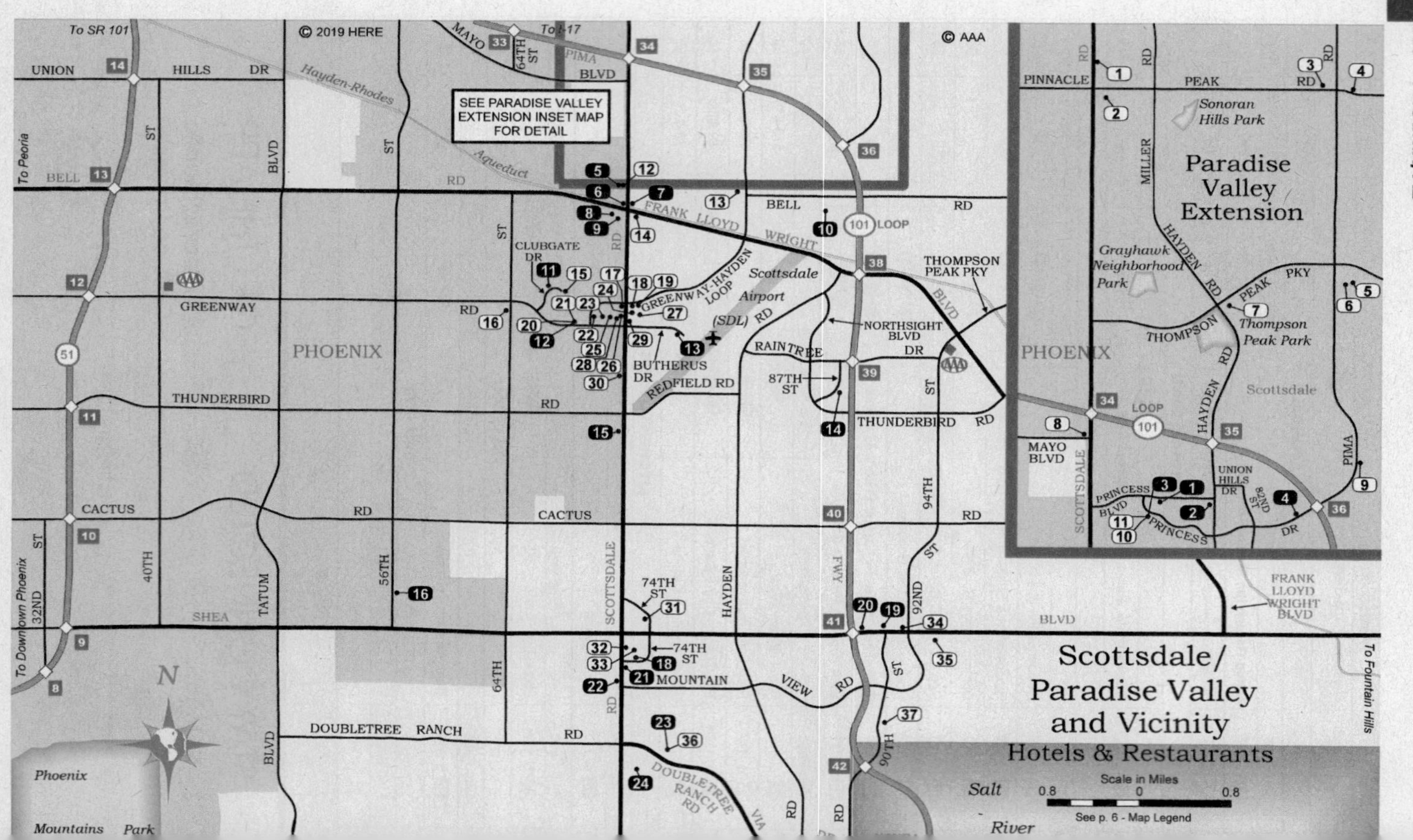
Scottsdale / Paradise Valley and Vicinity
Hotels & Restaurants
Scale in Miles
0.8 0 0.8
See p. 6 - Map Legend
Paradise Valley Extension
SEE PARADISE VALLEY EXTENSION INSET MAP FOR DETAIL
© 2019 HERE
© AAA
To SR 101
To I-17
To Peoria
To Downtown Phoenix
To Fountain Hills
PHOENIX
Scottsdale
Scottsdale Airport (SDL)
Sonoran Hills Park
Grayhawk Neighborhood Park
Thompson Peak Park
Phoenix Mountains Park
Salt River
Hayden-Rhodes Aqueduct
UNION HILLS DR
BELL RD
GREENWAY RD
THUNDERBIRD RD
CACTUS RD
SHEA BLVD
MOUNTAIN VIEW RD
DOUBLETREE RANCH RD
FRANK LLOYD WRIGHT BLVD
THOMPSON PEAK PKY
GREENWAY-HAYDEN LOOP
NORTHSIGHT BLVD
RAINTREE DR
BUTHERUS DR
REDFIELD RD
CLUBGATE DR
MAYO BLVD
PIMA RD
SCOTTSDALE RD
HAYDEN RD
TATUM BLVD
PINNACLE PEAK RD
MILLER RD
PRINCESS BLVD
PRINCESS DR
LOOP 101 FWY
32ND ST
40TH ST
56TH ST
64TH ST
74TH ST
82ND ST
87TH ST
90TH ST
92ND ST
94TH ST

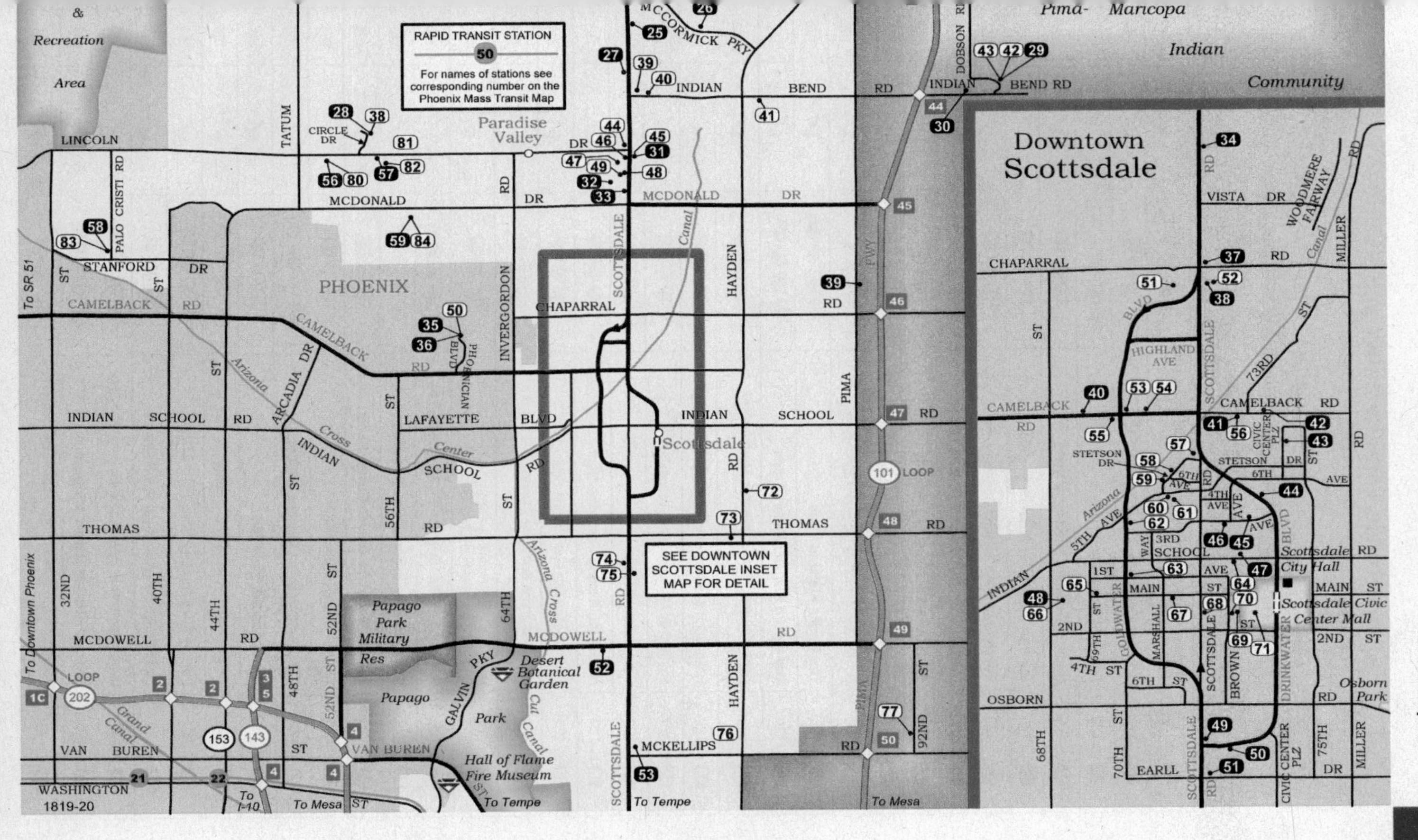

Downtown Scottsdale
RAPID TRANSIT STATION
50
For names of stations see corresponding number on the Phoenix Mass Transit Map
SEE DOWNTOWN SCOTTSDALE INSET MAP FOR DETAIL
Pima- Maricopa Indian Community
& Recreation Area
Paradise Valley
PHOENIX
Scottsdale
Papago Park Military Res
Papago Park
Desert Botanical Garden
Hall of Flame Fire Museum
Scottsdale City Hall
Scottsdale Civic Center Mall
Osborn Park
To Mesa
To Tempe
To Downtown Phoenix
To SR 51
To I-10
WASHINGTON
1819-20
VAN BUREN
MCDOWELL
THOMAS
INDIAN SCHOOL RD
CAMELBACK RD
LINCOLN
MCDONALD DR
INDIAN BEND RD
CHAPARRAL
OSBORN
MCKELLIPS
SCOTTSDALE RD
HAYDEN RD
PIMA RD
TATUM
INVERGORDON
LAFAYETTE BLVD
ARCADIA DR
PHOENICIAN BLVD
STANFORD DR
PALO CRISTI RD
CIRCLE DR
DOBSON RD
MCCORMICK PKY
32ND
40TH
44TH ST
48TH
52ND ST
56TH ST
64TH ST
68TH ST
70TH ST
75TH DR
92ND ST
MILLER RD
VISTA DR
WOODMERE FAIRWAY
HIGHLAND AVE
73RD ST
STETSON DR
DRINKWATER BLVD
GOLDWATER BLVD
MARSHALL WAY
BROWN
EARLL
CIVIC CENTER PLZ
Arizona Canal
Arizona Cross Cut Canal
Cross Center
Grand Canal
GALVIN PKY
101 LOOP
202 LOOP
143
153

Scottsdale/Paradise Valley and Vicinity

This index helps you "spot" where approved hotels and restaurants are located on the corresponding detailed maps. Restaurant price range is a combination of lunch and/or dinner. Turn to the listing page for more information and consult display ads for special promotions.

For more details, rates and reservations: AAA.com/travelguides/hotels

SCOTTSDALE

Map Page	Hotels	Diamond Rated	Member Savings	Page
1 p. 120	**Holiday Inn Club Vacations Scottsdale Resort** *(See ad p. 153.)*	♦♦♦	✔	153
2 p. 120	Sheraton Desert Oasis	♦♦♦	✔	156
3 p. 120	**Fairmont Scottsdale Princess**	♦♦♦♦♦	✔	152
4 p. 120	**Hilton Garden Inn Scottsdale North**	♦♦♦	✔	152
5 p. 120	**SpringHill Suites by Marriott-Scottsdale North**	♦♦♦	✔	156
6 p. 120	**Courtyard by Marriott/Scottsdale North**	♦♦♦	✔	151
7 p. 120	Residence Inn by Marriott Scottsdale North	♦♦♦	✔	155
8 p. 120	Sleep Inn North Scottsdale/Phoenix	♦♦		156
9 p. 120	Hampton Inn & Suites Phoenix/Scottsdale	♦♦♦	✔	152
10 p. 120	Scottsdale Marriott at McDowell Mountains	♦♦♦	✔	156
11 p. 120	**The Westin Kierland Villas**	♦♦♦♦	✔	157
12 p. 120	**The Westin Kierland Resort & Spa**	♦♦♦♦	✔	157
13 p. 120	**Best Western Plus Scottsdale Thunderbird Suites**	♦♦♦	✔	150
14 p. 120	Holiday Inn & Suites Scottsdale North-Airpark	♦♦♦		153
15 p. 120	Fairfield by Marriott North Scottsdale	♦♦♦	✔	151
16 p. 120	Orange Tree Resort	♦♦♦		155
18 p. 120	Holiday Inn Express Scottsdale North	♦♦♦		153
19 p. 120	TownePlace Suites by Marriott Scottsdale	♦♦♦	✔	156
20 p. 120	La Quinta Inn & Suites by Wyndham Phoenix Scottsdale	♦♦♦		154
21 p. 120	Hampton Inn & Suites by Hilton Phoenix/Scottsdale on Shea Blvd	♦♦♦	✔	152
22 p. 120	Homewood Suites by Hilton Phoenix/Scottsdale	♦♦♦	✔	153
23 p. 120	**Hyatt Regency Scottsdale Resort & Spa**	♦♦♦♦	✔	154
24 p. 120	**Sonesta Suites Scottsdale Gainey Ranch**	♦♦♦	✔	156
25 p. 120	The McCormick Scottsdale	♦♦♦		154
26 p. 120	**Scottsdale Resort & Conference Center**	♦♦♦♦	✔	156
27 p. 120	**The Scottsdale Plaza Resort**	♦♦♦	✔	156
28 p. 120	**JW Marriott Camelback Inn Resort & Spa**	♦♦♦♦	✔	154
29 p. 120	**Talking Stick Resort**	♦♦♦♦	✔	156
30 p. 120	Hampton Inn & Suites Scottsdale Riverwalk	♦♦♦	✔	152
31 p. 120	**Hilton Scottsdale Resort & Villas**	♦♦♦♦	✔	152
32 p. 120	**Andaz Scottsdale Resort & Bungalows**	♦♦♦♦	✔	149
33 p. 120	**Residence Inn by Marriott, Scottsdale/Paradise Valley**	♦♦♦	✔	155

SCOTTSDALE (cont'd)

Map Page	Hotels (cont'd)	Diamond Rated	Member Savings	Page
34 p. 120	**DoubleTree Resort by Hilton Paradise Valley-Scottsdale**	◆◆◆◆	✔	151
35 p. 120	**The Canyon Suites at The Phoenician, A Luxury Collection Resort, Scottsdale** *(See ad p. 150.)*	◆◆◆◆◆	✔	151
36 p. 120	**The Phoenician, A Luxury Collection Resort, Scottsdale** *(See ad p. 155.)*	◆◆◆◆◆	✔	155
37 p. 120	**Embassy Suites by Hilton Scottsdale Resort**	◆◆◆	✔	151
38 p. 120	**The Scott Resort & Spa**	◆◆◆◆	✔	156
39 p. 120	Courtyard by Marriott Scottsdale Salt River	◆◆◆	✔	151
40 p. 120	Motel 6 Scottsdale #29	◆		155
41 p. 120	W Scottsdale	◆◆◆◆	✔	157
42 p. 120	**Best Western Plus Sundial**	◆◆◆	✔	150
43 p. 120	**Aloft Scottsdale**	◆◆◆	✔	149
44 p. 120	**Hyatt House Scottsdale/Old Town**	◆◆◆	✔	154
45 p. 120	**Hyatt Place Scottsdale/Old Town**	◆◆◆	✔	154
46 p. 120	Scottsdale Marriott Suites Old Town	◆◆◆	✔	156
47 p. 120	Hilton Garden Inn Scottsdale Old Town	◆◆◆	✔	152
48 p. 120	**Hotel Valley Ho**	◆◆◆◆	✔	154
49 p. 120	**Courtyard by Marriott Scottsdale Old Town**	◆◆◆	✔	151
50 p. 120	Comfort Suites Old Town	◆◆		151
51 p. 120	**Holiday Inn Express Hotel & Suites-Scottsdale Old Town** *(See ad p. 153.)*	◆◆◆	✔	153
52 p. 120	Magnuson Hotel Papago Inn	◆◆		154
53 p. 120	Hotel Bixby Scottsdale, BW Signature Collection by Best Western	◆◆	✔	153

Map Page	Restaurants	Diamond Rated	Cuisine	Price Range	Page
1 p. 120	Jade Palace	◆◆	Chinese	$15-$39	158
2 p. 120	Eddie Merlot's	◆◆◆	Steak	$25-$103	158
3 p. 120	Preston's Steakhouse	◆◆◆	Steak	$29-$80	159
4 p. 120	Mastro's Steakhouse	◆◆◆	Steak	$27-$90	158
5 p. 120	All American Modern Sports Grill	◆◆	American	$13-$34	157
6 p. 120	Fleming's Prime Steakhouse & Wine Bar	◆◆◆	Steak	$38-$90	158
7 p. 120	Pure Sushi Bar & Dining	◆◆◆	Japanese Sushi	$12-$26	159
8 p. 120	The White Chocolate Grill	◆◆◆	American	$13-$36	159
9 p. 120	Lush Burger	◆◆	American	$9-$14	158
10 p. 120	**Bourbon Steak**	◆◆◆◆	Steak	$22-$175	157
11 p. 120	La Hacienda	◆◆◆	Mexican	$14-$45	158
12 p. 120	Persian Room	◆◆◆	Middle Eastern	$12-$35	159
13 p. 120	Toro Latin Restaurant and Rum Bar	◆◆◆	Latin American Fusion	$24-$45	159
14 p. 120	The Capital Grille	◆◆◆	Steak	$18-$85	157

Map Page	Restaurants (cont'd)	Diamond Rated	Cuisine	Price Range	Page
15 p. 120	Brittlebush Bar & Grill	◆◆◆	American	$12-$16	157
16 p. 120	Tutti Santi Ristorante	◆◆◆	Italian	$16-$33	159
17 p. 120	Morton's The Steakhouse	◆◆◆	Steak	$29-$64	158
18 p. 120	Eddie V's Prime Seafood	◆◆◆	Seafood	$28-$96	158
19 p. 120	Kona Grill	◆◆◆	Asian	$10-$30	158
20 p. 120	Deseo	◆◆◆◆	New Latin American	$27-$38	158
21 p. 120	Nellie Cashman's Monday Club Cafe	◆◆◆	New American	$9-$28	158
22 p. 120	Mastro's Ocean Club	◆◆◆	Seafood	$35-$87	158
23 p. 120	NoRTH Italia	◆◆◆	New Italian	$13-$38	158
24 p. 120	True Food Kitchen	◆◆	Continental Natural/Organic Vegan	$12-$26	159
25 p. 120	Zinc Bistro	◆◆◆	French	$14-$45	159
26 p. 120	Snooze an A.M. Eatery	◆◆	American	$8-$12	159
27 p. 120	Zinburger	◆◆	Burgers	$10-$17	159
28 p. 120	P.F. Chang's China Bistro	◆◆◆	Chinese	$11-$28	159
29 p. 120	Dominick's Steakhouse	◆◆◆	Steak	$28-$58	158
30 p. 120	Kasai Asian Grill	◆◆◆	Pacific Rim Sushi	$10-$55	158
31 p. 120	Pita Jungle	◆◆	Mediterranean	$7-$16	159
32 p. 120	Razz's Restaurant	◆◆◆	New American	$28-$47	159
33 p. 120	Takeda Thai	◆◆	Thai	$14-$43	159
34 p. 120	Jade Palace	◆◆	Chinese	$11-$45	158
35 p. 120	Ling & Louie's Asian Bar & Grill	◆◆	Asian	$10-$20	158
36 p. 120	Alto Ristorante & Bar	◆◆◆	Italian	$20-$32	157
37 p. 120	Hiro Sushi	◆◆	Sushi	$10-$21	158
38 p. 120	Lincoln Restaurant	◆◆◆	Southwestern	$29-$48	158
39 p. 120	Sushi Sen	◆◆	Sushi	$10-$30	159
40 p. 120	Ruth's Chris Steak House	◆◆◆	Steak	$31-$40	159
41 p. 120	Sakana Sushi & Grill	◆◆	Sushi	$8-$17	159
42 p. 120	Orange Sky	◆◆◆	Seafood Steak	$30-$70	158
43 p. 120	Ocean Trail	◆◆	Creole	$15-$23	158
44 p. 120	Sumo Maya Mexican Asian Kitchen	◆◆◆	Fusion	$10-$32	159
45 p. 120	Fleming's Prime Steakhouse & Wine Bar	◆◆◆	Steak	$38-$90	158
46 p. 120	Fat Ox	◆◆◆	Italian	$15-$65	158
47 p. 120	Tottie's Asian Fusion 2	◆◆	Asian Fusion	$12-$19	159
48 p. 120	Rancho Pinot	◆◆◆	American	$22-$38	159
49 p. 120	Blanco Tacos + Tequila	◆◆	Mexican	$11-$21	157
50 p. 120	**J&G Steakhouse**	◆◆◆◆	Steak	$17-$66	158

Map Page	Restaurants (cont'd)	Diamond Rated	Cuisine	Price Range	Page
51 p. 120	Roaring Fork	◆◆◆	Western American	$14-$48	159
52 p. 120	The Canal Club	◆◆◆	Caribbean	$15-$32	157
53 p. 120	P.F. Chang's China Bistro	◆◆◆	Chinese	$10-$28	159
54 p. 120	Kona Grill	◆◆◆	Pacific Rim Fusion	$10-$30	158
55 p. 120	Mastro's City Hall Steakhouse	◆◆◆	Steak	$27-$78	158
56 p. 120	Sushi Roku	◆◆◆	Japanese	$10-$42	159
57 p. 120	The Breakfast Club	◆◆	Breakfast	$7-$16	157
58 p. 120	The Herb Box	◆◆◆	American	$13-$28	158
59 p. 120	Marcellino Ristorante	◆◆◆	Italian	$21-$44	158
60 p. 120	Citizen Public House	◆◆◆	American	$12-$38	157
61 p. 120	FnB Restaurant	◆◆◆	New American	$22-$35	158
62 p. 120	EVO	◆◆◆	Italian	$11-$30	158
63 p. 120	Arcadia Farms	◆◆	American	$14-$19	157
64 p. 120	Tommy V's Urban Kitchen and Bar	◆◆◆	Italian	$16-$37	159
65 p. 120	Old Town Tortilla Factory	◆◆	Mexican	$14-$29	158
66 p. 120	Cafe Zu Zu	◆◆◆	American	$10-$30	157
67 p. 120	Malee's Thai Bistro	◆◆	Regional Thai	$12-$21	158
68 p. 120	Bandera	◆◆◆	American	$16-$43	157
69 p. 120	Jewel of the Crown	◆◆	Indian	$13-$20	158
70 p. 120	The Mission	◆◆◆	Latin American	$23-$32	158
71 p. 120	Sasaki Sushi & Bar	◆◆	Sushi	$10-$20	159
72 p. 120	Carlsbad Tavern	◆◆	Southwestern	$12-$37	157
73 p. 120	Tottie's Asian Fusion	◆◆	Asian	$8-$14	159
74 p. 120	Los Sombreros	◆◆	Mexican	$8-$23	158
75 p. 120	Atlas Bistro	◆◆◆	International	$25-$35	157
76 p. 120	The Salt Cellar Restaurant	◆◆◆	Seafood	$30-$80	159
77 p. 120	Cholla Prime Steakhouse	◆◆◆	Regional Steak	$10-$29	157

PARADISE VALLEY

Map Page	Hotels	Diamond Rated	Member Savings	Page
56 p. 120	**Omni Scottsdale Resort & Spa at Montelucia**	◆◆◆◆	✔	86
57 p. 120	**Mountain Shadows**	◆◆◆◆	✔	86
58 p. 120	**The Hermosa Inn**	◆◆◆◆	✔	86
59 p. 120	**Sanctuary Camelback Mountain**	◆◆◆◆	✔	86

Map Page	Restaurants	Diamond Rated	Cuisine	Price Range	Page
80 p. 120	**Prado**	◆◆◆	Italian	$13-$30	86
81 p. 120	El Chorro	◆◆◆	Continental	$29-$59	86
82 p. 120	Hearth 61	◆◆◆	New American	$15-$46	86
83 p. 120	**Lon's at the Hermosa**	◆◆◆◆	American	$27-$70	86
84 p. 120	Elements	◆◆◆◆	Fusion	$16-$45	86

SEE SCOTTSDALE/PARADISE VALLEY ACCOMMODATIONS MAP FOR DETAIL
SEE PHOENIX ACCOMMODATIONS MAP FOR DETAIL
Papago Park
Desert Botanical Garden
Hall of Flame Fire Museum
Sun Devil Stadium
Wells Fargo Arena
Arizona State Univ
Tempe
Salt River Pima-Maricopa Indian Community
Mesa Convention and Visitors Bureau
Phoenix Sky Harbor International Airport (PHX)
South Mountain Park
Pecos Park
Stellar Airpark (P19)
Gila River Indian Community
To Scottsdale
To Payson
To Downtown Phoenix
To Laveen
To Maricopa
To Tucson
To Casa Grande
1827-20
© AAA

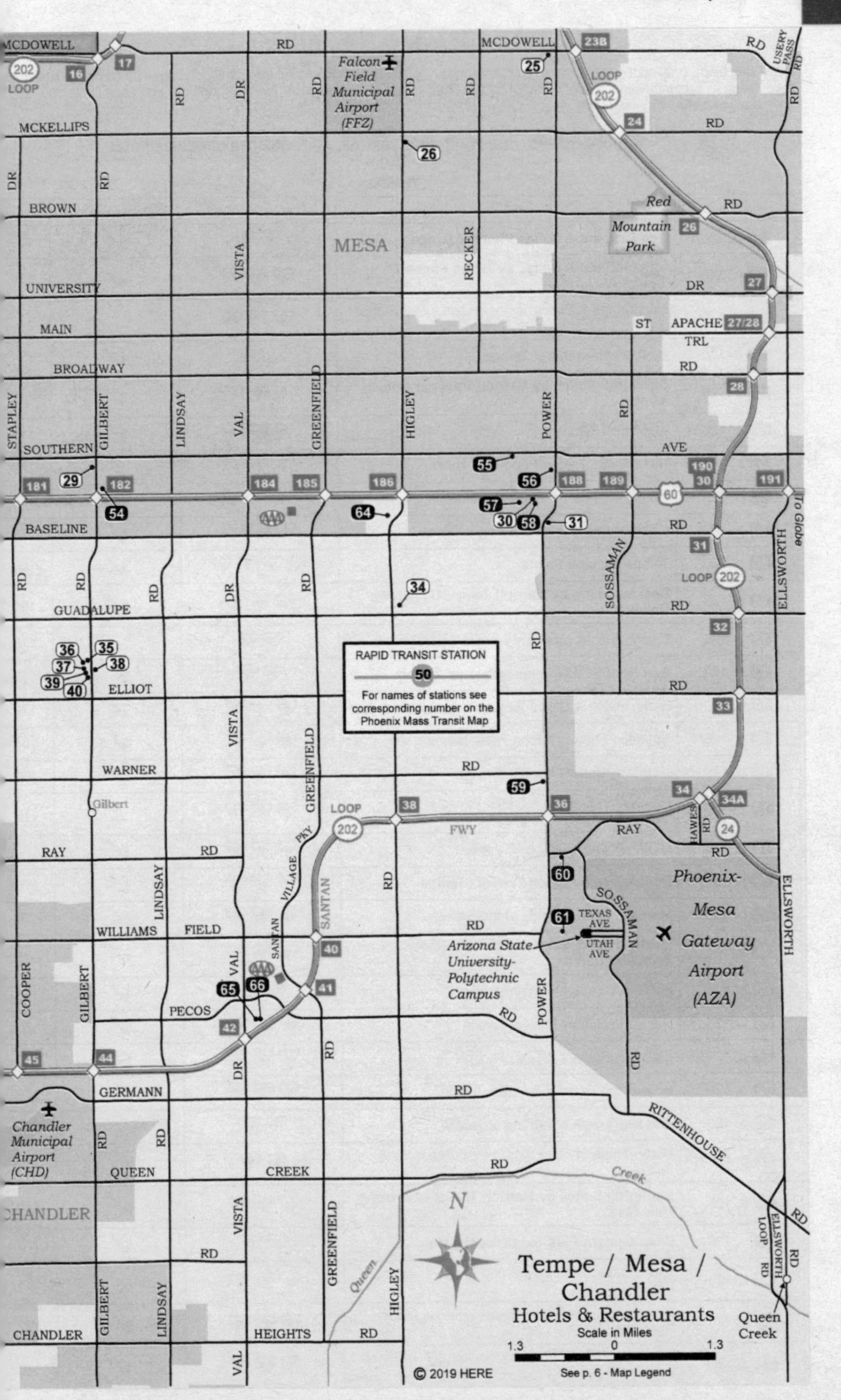
Tempe / Mesa / Chandler
Hotels & Restaurants
Scale in Miles
1.3
0
1.3
See p. 6 - Map Legend
© 2019 HERE
RAPID TRANSIT STATION
50
For names of stations see corresponding number on the Phoenix Mass Transit Map
MESA
CHANDLER
Falcon Field Municipal Airport (FFZ)
Red Mountain Park
Phoenix-Mesa Gateway Airport (AZA)
Chandler Municipal Airport (CHD)
Arizona State University-Polytechnic Campus
MCDOWELL
MCKELLIPS
BROWN
UNIVERSITY
MAIN
BROADWAY
SOUTHERN
BASELINE
GUADALUPE
ELLIOT
WARNER
RAY
WILLIAMS
FIELD
PECOS
GERMANN
QUEEN
CREEK
HEIGHTS
RITTENHOUSE
APACHE
TRL
STAPLEY
GILBERT
LINDSAY
VAL
VISTA
GREENFIELD
HIGLEY
RECKER
POWER
SOSSAMAN
ELLSWORTH
COOPER
SANTAN
VILLAGE
PKY
USERY PASS
HAWES
TEXAS AVE
UTAH AVE
LOOP
FWY
To Globe
Gilbert
Queen Creek
N

Tempe/Mesa/Chandler

This index helps you "spot" where approved hotels and restaurants are located on the corresponding detailed maps. Restaura price range is a combination of lunch and/or dinner. Turn to the listing page for more information and consult display ads f special promotions.

For more details, rates and reservations: AAA.com/travelguides/hotels

TEMPE

Map Page	Hotels	Diamond Rated	Member Savings	Page
1 p. 126	**Red Lion Inn & Suites Phoenix/Tempe**	◆◆	✔	179
2 p. 126	**Hampton Inn & Suites by Hilton Phoenix/ Tempe-ASU Area**	◆◆◆	✔	179
3 p. 126	Comfort Inn & Suites Tempe Phoenix Sky Harbor Airport	◆◆◆		178
4 p. 126	**Best Western Inn of Tempe**	◆◆	✔	178
5 p. 126	**SpringHill Suites by Marriott Phoenix Tempe Airport**	◆◆◆	✔	180
6 p. 126	Aloft Hotel Tempe	◆◆◆	✔	178
7 p. 126	**Hyatt Place Tempe/Phoenix Airport**	◆◆◆	✔	179
8 p. 126	AC Hotel Phoenix Tempe/Downtown	◆◆◆	✔	178
9 p. 126	Courtyard by Marriott-Downtown Tempe	◆◆◆	✔	178
10 p. 126	**Tempe Mission Palms**	◆◆◆◆	✔	180
11 p. 126	**Residence Inn by Marriott Tempe Downtown/ University**	◆◆◆	✔	180
12 p. 126	Extended Stay America-Phoenix/Airport/Tempe	◆◆		178
13 p. 126	**Red Roof PLUS+ Tempe-Phoenix Airport**	◆◆	✔	179
14 p. 126	Hampton Inn & Suites Tempe Phoenix Airport	◆◆◆	✔	179
15 p. 126	Sheraton Phoenix Airport Hotel Tempe	◆◆◆	✔	180
16 p. 126	**Comfort Suites Phoenix Airport**	◆◆◆	✔	178
17 p. 126	Holiday Inn Express & Suites Phoenix Tempe-University	◆◆◆		179
18 p. 126	MOXY Phoenix Tempe/ASU Area	◆◆◆	✔	179
19 p. 126	**DoubleTree by Hilton Phoenix-Tempe**	◆◆◆	✔	178
20 p. 126	Marriott Phoenix Tempe at the Buttes	◆◆◆	✔	179
21 p. 126	**Fairfield Inn & Suites by Marriott Phoenix Tempe/Airport**	◆◆◆	✔	179
22 p. 126	**Hawthorn Suites by Wyndham**	◆◆	✔	179
23 p. 126	Residence Inn by Marriott Tempe	◆◆◆	✔	180
24 p. 126	Embassy Suites by Hilton Phoenix-Tempe	◆◆◆	✔	178
25 p. 126	Holiday Inn Express & Suites Tempe	◆◆◆		179
26 p. 126	Ramada Tempe at Arizona Mills Mall	◆◆		179
27 p. 126	Hotel Tempe Phoenix Airport InnSuites Hotel & Suites	◆◆		179
28 p. 126	**SpringHill Suites by Marriott Tempe at Arizona Mills Mall**	◆◆◆	✔	180
29 p. 126	**Best Western Plus Tempe by the Mall**	◆◆	✔	178
30 p. 126	TownePlace Suites by Marriott Tempe at Arizona Mills Mall	◆◆◆	✔	180
31 p. 126	Home2 Suites by Hilton Phoenix-Tempe ASU Research Park	◆◆◆	✔	179
32 p. 126	Hilton Garden Inn Phoenix-Tempe ASU Research Park	◆◆◆	✔	179

TEMPE (cont'd)

Map Page	Hotels (cont'd)	Diamond Rated	Member Savings	Page
33 p. 126	Drury Inn & Suites Phoenix Tempe	♦♦♦		178

Map Page	Restaurants	Diamond Rated	Cuisine	Price Range	Page
1 p. 126	La Bocca	♦♦	Pizza	$8-$16	180
2 p. 126	House of Tricks	♦♦♦	American	$23-$49	180
3 p. 126	Snooze an A.M. Eatery	♦♦	Breakfast	$7-$12	181
4 p. 126	Cafe Lalibela	♦♦	Ethiopian	$6-$17	180
5 p. 126	P.F. Chang's China Bistro	♦♦♦	Chinese	$10-$28	180
6 p. 126	Casey Moore's Oyster House	♦♦	American	$6-$28	180
7 p. 126	Sushi 101	♦♦	Sushi	$6-$41	181
8 p. 126	Republic Ramen & Noodles	♦♦	Asian Noodles	$9-$12	181
9 p. 126	Chou's Kitchen	♦♦	Regional Chinese	$9-$19	180
10 p. 126	Tasty Kabob	♦♦	Middle Eastern	$7-$31	181
11 p. 126	Haji Baba Middle Eastern Food	♦♦	Middle Eastern	$8-$16	180
12 p. 126	**The Dhaba**	♦♦	Indian	$10-$24	180
13 p. 126	Top of the Rock Restaurant	♦♦♦	American	$14-$35	181
14 p. 126	Lemon Grass Thai Cafe	♦♦	Thai	$9-$17	180
15 p. 126	Byblos Restaurant	♦♦	Greek	$10-$20	180
16 p. 126	Tom's BBQ Chicago Style	♦	Barbecue	$7-$28	181

PHOENIX

Map Page	Hotels	Diamond Rated	Member Savings	Page
36 p. 126	Four Points by Sheraton Phoenix South Mountain	♦♦♦	✔	136
37 p. 126	Extended Stay America-Phoenix-Chandler	♦♦		136
38 p. 126	**Holiday Inn Express & Suites Phoenix-Chandler**	♦♦♦	✔	137
39 p. 126	La Quinta Inn & Suites Phoenix Chandler	♦♦♦		138
40 p. 126	Extended Stay America Phoenix-Chandler-E Chandler Blvd	♦♦		136

Map Page	Restaurants	Diamond Rated	Cuisine	Price Range	Page
19 p. 126	Sakana Sushi and Grill	♦♦	Sushi	$8-$34	142
20 p. 126	Caffe Boa	♦♦♦	Italian	$11-$27	140
21 p. 126	La Stalla Cucina Rustica	♦♦♦	Italian	$10-$30	141
22 p. 126	Trattoria D'Amico	♦♦♦	Italian	$17-$39	142

MESA

Map Page	Hotels	Diamond Rated	Member Savings	Page
43 p. 126	**Hyatt Place Phoenix/Mesa**	♦♦♦	✔	80
44 p. 126	Sheraton Mesa Hotel at Wrigleyville West	♦♦♦	✔	80
45 p. 126	**Delta Hotels by Marriott Phoenix Mesa**	♦♦♦	✔	79
46 p. 126	Ramada Mesa-Mezona Hotel	♦♦		80
47 p. 126	Courtyard by Marriott Phoenix Mesa	♦♦♦	✔	79
48 p. 126	La Quinta Inn & Suites Phoenix Mesa West	♦♦		80
49 p. 126	Residence Inn by Marriott Phoenix Mesa	♦♦♦	✔	80
50 p. 126	GreenTree Inn & Suites Mesa	♦♦		80

MESA (cont'd)

Map Page	Hotels (cont'd)	Diamond Rated	Member Savings	Page
51 p. 126	**Hilton Phoenix/Mesa**	◆◆◆	✔	80
52 p. 126	Holiday Inn & Suites Phoenix-Mesa/Chandler	◆◆◆		80
53 p. 126	Days Hotel Mesa Near Phoenix	◆◆		79
54 p. 126	**Best Western Plus Mesa**	◆◆◆	✔	79
55 p. 126	Sleep Inn Mesa	◆◆		80
56 p. 126	**Best Western Superstition Springs Inn**	◆◆	✔	79
57 p. 126	La Quinta Inn & Suites Mesa Superstition Springs	◆◆◆		80
58 p. 126	Country Inn & Suites by Radisson	◆◆◆		79
59 p. 126	**Best Western Legacy Inn & Suites**	◆◆	✔	79
60 p. 126	**Courtyard by Marriott Phoenix Mesa Gateway Airport**	◆◆◆	✔	79
61 p. 126	Four Points by Sheraton at Phoenix Mesa Gateway Airport	◆◆◆	✔	80

Map Page	Restaurants	Diamond Rated	Cuisine	Price Range	Page
25 p. 126	Nando's Mexican Cafe	◆◆	Mexican	$10-$19	80
26 p. 126	Flancer's	◆◆	Pizza	$7-$18	80
27 p. 126	Shaanxi Garden	◆◆	Chinese	$10-$30	80
28 p. 126	The Original Blue Adobe Grille	◆◆	Mexican	$9-$20	80
29 p. 126	Mi Amigos Mexican Grill	◆◆	Mexican	$10-$24	80
30 p. 126	P.F. Chang's China Bistro	◆◆◆	Chinese	$10-$28	80
31 p. 126	Sakana Sushi & Grill	◆◆	Sushi	$8-$34	80

GILBERT

Map Page	Hotels	Diamond Rated	Member Savings	Page
64 p. 126	Residence Inn by Marriott Phoenix/Gilbert	◆◆◆	✔	51
65 p. 126	**Hyatt Place Phoenix/Gilbert**	◆◆◆	✔	51
66 p. 126	Phoenix/Gilbert Hampton Inn & Suites by Hilton	◆◆◆	✔	51

Map Page	Restaurants	Diamond Rated	Cuisine	Price Range	Page
34 p. 126	Rancho de Tia Rosa	◆◆	Mexican	$10-$33	51
35 p. 126	Clever Koi	◆◆◆	Asian	$12-$18	51
36 p. 126	Nico Heirloom Kitchen	◆◆◆	Italian	$13-$25	51
37 p. 126	Postino WineCafe	◆◆	Italian Small Plates	$11-$16	51
38 p. 126	**Joe's Real BBQ**	◆	Barbecue	$8-$19	51
39 p. 126	Liberty Market	◆◆	American	$11-$23	51
40 p. 126	The Farmhouse Restaurant	◆◆	Breakfast Sandwiches	$8-$12	51

CHANDLER

Map Page	Hotels	Diamond Rated	Member Savings	Page
69 p. 126	Courtyard by Marriott Phoenix Chandler	◆◆◆	✔	34
70 p. 126	Homewood Suites by Hilton Phoenix-Chandler	◆◆◆	✔	35
71 p. 126	Hampton Inn Phoenix-Chandler	◆◆◆	✔	35
72 p. 126	**DoubleTree by Hilton Phoenix Chandler**	◆◆◆	✔	35
73 p. 126	Country Inn & Suites by Radisson, Chandler	◆◆◆		34

CHANDLER (cont'd)

Map Page	Hotels (cont'd)	Diamond Rated	Member Savings	Page
74 p. 126	**Comfort Inn Chandler-Phoenix South**	◆◆◆	✔	34
75 p. 126	**Best Western Inn of Chandler**	◆◆	✔	34
76 p. 126	SpringHill Suites by Marriott Phoenix/Chandler Fashion Center	◆◆◆	✔	36
77 p. 126	Residence Inn by Marriott-Chandler Fashion Center	◆◆◆	✔	35
78 p. 126	TownePlace Suites by Marriott Phoenix Chandler Fashion Center	◆◆◆	✔	36
79 p. 126	Element by Westin Chandler Fashion Center	◆◆◆	✔	35
80 p. 126	**Hilton Phoenix Chandler**	◆◆◆	✔	35
81 p. 126	**Cambria Hotel Phoenix Chandler/Fashion Center**	◆◆◆	✔	34
82 p. 126	Crowne Plaza San Marcos Golf Resort	◆◆◆		35
83 p. 126	**Wild Horse Pass Hotel & Casino** *(See ad p. 36.)*	◆◆◆◆	✔	36
84 p. 126	**Fairfield Inn & Suites by Marriott Phoenix Chandler/Fashion Center**	◆◆◆	✔	35
85 p. 126	**Courtyard by Marriott Phoenix Chandler/ Fashion Center**	◆◆◆	✔	34
86 p. 126	**Best Western Plus Chandler Hotel & Suites**	◆◆◆	✔	34
87 p. 126	Drury Inn & Suites Phoenix Chandler Fashion Center	◆◆◆		35
88 p. 126	Homewood Suites by Hilton-Phoenix/Chandler Fashion Center	◆◆◆	✔	35
89 p. 126	Hampton Inn & Suites Phoenix/Chandler Fashion Center	◆◆◆	✔	35
90 p. 126	Sheraton Grand at Wild Horse Pass	◆◆◆◆	✔	36
91 p. 126	**Home2 Suites by Hilton Phoenix Chandler**	◆◆◆	✔	35
92 p. 126	Residence Inn by Marriott Phoenix Chandler/South	◆◆◆	✔	36
93 p. 126	**Holiday Inn Phoenix-Chandler**	◆◆◆	✔	35

Map Page	Restaurants	Diamond Rated	Cuisine	Price Range	Page
43 p. 126	Z'Tejas Southwestern Grill	◆◆◆	Southwestern	$12-$35	37
44 p. 126	Roy's	◆◆◆	Hawaiian Fusion	$26-$55	37
45 p. 126	Fleming's Prime Steakhouse & Wine Bar	◆◆◆	Steak	$38-$90	36
46 p. 126	Saigon Pho & Seafood	◆◆	Vietnamese	$7-$13	37
47 p. 126	Pita Jungle	◆◆	Mediterranean	$7-$16	37
48 p. 126	Chou's Kitchen	◆◆	Northern Chinese	$5-$13	36
49 p. 126	P.F. Chang's China Bistro	◆◆◆	Chinese	$9-$25	37
50 p. 126	Cyclo Vietnamese Cuisine	◆◆	Vietnamese	$6-$13	36
51 p. 126	Eastwind Sushi & Grill	◆◆	Asian	$7-$20	36
52 p. 126	DC Steakhouse	◆◆	Steak	$15-$52	36
53 p. 126	Ling & Louie's Asian Bar & Grill	◆◆	Asian	$11-$23	37
54 p. 126	Shula's America's Steak House	◆◆◆	Steak	$25-$68	37
55 p. 126	**Kai**	◆◆◆◆◆	Southwestern	$35-$175	36
56 p. 126	Mikado Sushi	◆◆	Sushi	$9-$20	37

DOWNTOWN PHOENIX

• Hotels & Restaurants map & index p. 106

COURTYARD BY MARRIOTT PHOENIX DOWNTOWN
602/603-2001 **16**

Hotel. **Address:** 132 S Central Ave 85003

AAA Benefit: Members save 5% or more!

EMBASSY SUITES BY HILTON PHOENIX DOWNTOWN NORTH
602/222-1111 **2**

Hotel. **Address:** 10 E Thomas Rd 85012

AAA Benefit: Members save up to 15%!

FAIRFIELD INN & SUITES BY MARRIOTT PHOENIX MIDTOWN
602/716-9900 **3**

Hotel

Fairfield **AAA Benefit:** Members save 5% or more!

Address: 2520 N Central Ave 85004 **Location:** I-10 exit 145 (7th St), 0.8 mi n to Virginia Ave, 0.4 mi w, then 0.7 mi n. Located in a commercial area. Encanto/Central, 9. **Facility:** 107 units. 4 stories, interior corridors. **Amenities:** safes. **Pool:** heated outdoor. **Activities:** hot tub, picnic facilities, exercise room. **Guest Services:** valet and coin laundry. **Featured Amenity: breakfast buffet.**

HAMPTON INN & SUITES PHOENIX DOWNTOWN
602/710-1240 **7**

Hotel

AAA Benefit: Members save up to 15%!

Address: 77 E Polk St 85004 **Location:** SW corner of Polk and 1st sts. Van Buren/Central-1st Ave, 12. **Facility:** 210 units. 11 stories, interior corridors. **Parking:** valet only. **Amenities:** safes. **Activities:** exercise room. **Guest Services:** valet laundry. **Featured Amenity: breakfast buffet.**

CALL / SOME UNITS

HAMPTON INN-PHOENIX/MIDTOWN (DOWNTOWN AREA)
602/200-0990 **1**

Hotel. **Address:** 160 W Catalina Dr 85013

AAA Benefit: Members save up to 15%!

HILTON GARDEN INN PHOENIX DOWNTOWN
602/343-0006 **11**

Historic Hotel. **Address:** 15 E Monroe St 85004

AAA Benefit: Members save up to 15%!

HISTORIC HOTEL SAN CARLOS 602/253-4121 **10**

Historic Hotel. **Address:** 202 N Central Ave 85004

HOLIDAY INN EXPRESS HOTEL & SUITES PHOENIX DOWNTOWN-BALL PARK
602/452-2020 **4**

Hotel

Address: 620 N 6th St 85004 **Location:** I-10 exit 145 (7th St), 0.5 mi s, then 1 blk w on Fillmore St. 3rd St/Washington, 15. **Facility:** 90 units. 3 stories, interior corridors. **Pool:** heated outdoor. **Activities:** hot tub, exercise room. **Guest Services:** valet and coin laundry.

HYATT REGENCY PHOENIX
602/252-1234 **13**

Hotel

HYATT REGENCY **AAA Benefit:** Members save up to 10%!

Address: 122 N 2nd St 85004 **Location:** Just n of Washington St; at Phoenix Convention Center. 3rd St/Washington, 15. **Facility:** 693 units, some two bedrooms. 24 stories, interior corridors. **Parking:** on-site and valet. **Amenities:** safes. **Dining:** 2 restaurants, also, Compass Arizona Grill, see separate listing. **Pool:** heated outdoor. **Activities:** hot tub, exercise room. **Guest Services:** valet laundry, boarding pass kiosk, rental car service.

CALL / SOME UNITS

KIMPTON HOTEL PALOMAR PHOENIX
602/253-6633 **15**

Contemporary Hotel

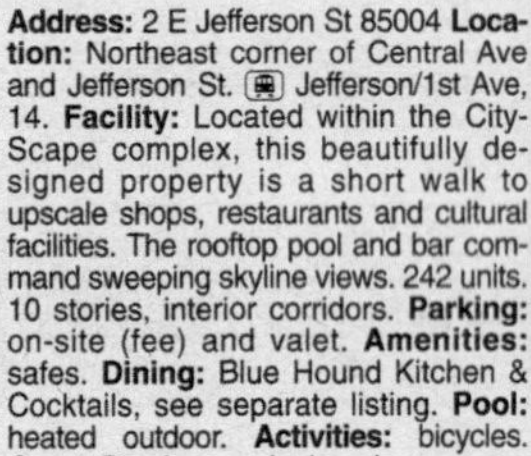

Address: 2 E Jefferson St 85004 **Location:** Northeast corner of Central Ave and Jefferson St. Jefferson/1st Ave, 14. **Facility:** Located within the CityScape complex, this beautifully designed property is a short walk to upscale shops, restaurants and cultural facilities. The rooftop pool and bar command sweeping skyline views. 242 units. 10 stories, interior corridors. **Parking:** on-site (fee) and valet. **Amenities:** safes. **Dining:** Blue Hound Kitchen & Cocktails, see separate listing. **Pool:** heated outdoor. **Activities:** bicycles. **Guest Services:** valet laundry.

CALL / SOME UNITS

RENAISSANCE PHOENIX DOWNTOWN
602/333-0000 **14**

Hotel

R RENAISSANCE® HOTELS **AAA Benefit:** Members save 5% or more!

Address: 100 N 1st St 85004 **Location:** Just w of 1st St; between 1st St and Central Ave. Washington/Central Ave, 13. **Facility:** 519 units. 18 stories, interior corridors. **Parking:** valet only. **Terms:** check-in 4 pm. **Amenities:** safes. **Dining:** 3 restaurants. **Pool:** heated outdoor. **Activities:** exercise room. **Guest Services:** valet laundry, boarding pass kiosk.

(See map & index p. 106.)

RESIDENCE INN BY MARRIOTT PHOENIX DOWNTOWN 602/603-2000 **17**

Extended Stay Hotel. **Address:** 132 S Central Ave 85003

AAA Benefit: Members save 5% or more!

SHERATON GRAND PHOENIX 602/262-2500 **8**

Hotel

AAA Benefit: Members save 5% or more!

Address: 340 N 3rd St 85004 **Location:** I-10 exit 145A (7th St), 0.5 mi s to Fillmore St, just w, then just s. Van Buren/Central-1st Ave, 12. **Facility:** Upscale and spacious public areas, refined service and well-appointed guest rooms make this downtown property a good choice for either business or leisure travel. 1000 units. 31 stories, interior corridors. **Parking:** on-site (fee) and valet. **Amenities:** safes. **Dining:** 3 restaurants, also, District American Kitchen & Wine Bar, see separate listing, entertainment. **Pool:** heated outdoor. **Activities:** hot tub, exercise room. **Guest Services:** valet laundry.

SPRINGHILL SUITES BY MARRIOTT PHOENIX DOWNTOWN 602/307-9929 **12**

Hotel

AAA Benefit: Members save 5% or more!

Address: 802 E Van Buren St 85006 **Location:** I-10 exit 145 (7th St), just s, then just e. 12th St/Washington, 17. **Facility:** 121 units. 6 stories, interior corridors. **Pool:** heated outdoor. **Activities:** hot tub, exercise room. **Guest Services:** valet and coin laundry. **Featured Amenity: breakfast buffet.**

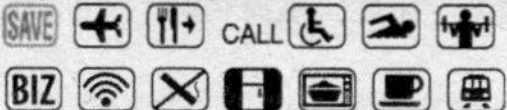

THE WESTIN PHOENIX DOWNTOWN 602/429-3500 **9**

Hotel

AAA Benefit: Members save 5% or more!

Address: 333 N Central Ave 85004 **Location:** Northeast corner of Central Ave and Van Buren St. Van Buren/Central-1st Ave, 12. **Facility:** Spacious, modern and elegant guest rooms with sweeping views are the showcase of this downtown property. 242 units. 26 stories, interior corridors. **Parking:** valet and street only. **Amenities:** safes. **Dining:** Province Urban Kitchen & Bar, see separate listing. **Pool:** heated outdoor. **Activities:** exercise room, massage. **Guest Services:** valet laundry.

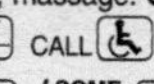

WHERE TO EAT

THE ARROGANT BUTCHER 602/324-8502 **30**
American. Gastropub. **Address:** 2 E Jefferson St, #150 85004

BLISS 602/795-1792 **14**
American. Casual Dining. **Address:** 901 N 4th St 85004

BLUE HOUND KITCHEN & COCKTAILS 602/258-0231 **28**
American. Casual Dining. **Address:** 2 E Jefferson St 85004

THE BREADFRUIT & RUM BAR 602/267-1266 **20**
Jamaican. Casual Dining. **Address:** 108 E Pierce St 85004

THE BREAKFAST CLUB 602/354-7284 **29**
American. Casual Dining. **Address:** 2 E Jefferson St, Suite 213 85004

CHINA CHILI 602/266-4463 **1**
Chinese. Casual Dining. **Address:** 302 E Flower St 85012

CIBO URBAN PIZZERIA CAFE 602/441-2697 **18**
Italian. Casual Dining. **Address:** 603 N 5th Ave 85003

COMPASS ARIZONA GRILL 602/440-3166 **25**
American. Fine Dining. **Address:** 122 N 2nd St 85004

CORNISH PASTY CO. 602/374-8500 **23**
English. Casual Dining. **Address:** 7 W Monroe St 85003

DISTRICT AMERICAN KITCHEN & WINE BAR 602/817-5400 **22**
American. Casual Dining. **Address:** 320 N 3rd St 85004

DURANT'S 602/264-5967 **9**

Steak
Casual Dining
$14-$64

AAA Inspector Notes: *Classic.* For great steaks, a classic club atmosphere and accomplished service, this restaurant fits the bill. The well-trained staff strives to provide guests a special dining experience. When entering from the parking area, diners may meet the grill chef as they walk through the kitchen. **Features:** full bar. **Reservations:** suggested. **Address:** 2611 N Central Ave 85004 **Location:** 0.8 mi n of McDowell Rd. Thomas/Central, 8. **Parking:** on-site and valet. L D

HONEY BEAR'S BBQ 602/279-7911 **7**
Barbecue. Quick Serve. **Address:** 2824 N Central Ave 85004

LOLA COFFEE 602/252-2265 **13**
Coffee/Tea. Quick Serve. **Address:** 1001 N 3rd Ave 85003

MATT'S BIG BREAKFAST 602/254-1074 **15**
American. Casual Dining. **Address:** 825 N 1st St 85004

MOIRA SUSHI BAR & KITCHEN 602/254-5085 **17**
Japanese. Casual Dining. **Address:** 215 E McKinley St 85004

MOTHER BUNCH BREWING 602/368-3580 **16**
American. Casual Dining. **Address:** 825 N 7th St 85006

MU SHU ASIAN GRILL 602/277-9867 **3**
Asian. Casual Dining. **Address:** 1502 W Thomas Rd 85015

NOODLE BAR 480/454-7905 **24**
International Noodles. Casual Dining. **Address:** 114 W Adams St 85003

OCOTILLO 480/390-7794 **2**
New American. Casual Dining. **Address:** 3243 N 3rd St 85012

THE ORIGINAL HAMBURGER WORKS 602/263-8693 **5**
American. Casual Dining. **Address:** 2801 N 15th Ave 85013

PERSIAN GARDEN CAFÉ 602/263-1915 **4**
Middle Eastern. Casual Dining. **Address:** 1335 W Thomas Rd 85013

(See map & index p. 106.)

PINO'S PIZZA AL CENTRO 602/279-3237 (6)

Italian. Casual Dining. **Address:** 139 W Thomas Rd 85013

PIZZA PEOPLE PUB 602/795-7954 (12)

Pizza. Casual Dining. **Address:** 1326 N Central Ave 85004

PIZZERIA BIANCO 602/258-8300 (26)

Pizza. Casual Dining. **Address:** 623 E Adams St 85004

POMO PIZZERIA NAPOLETANA 602/795-2555 (19)

Italian. Casual Dining. **Address:** 705 N 1st St, Suite 120 85004

PROVINCE URBAN KITCHEN & BAR 602/429-3600 (21)

American. Fine Dining. **Address:** 333 N Central Ave 85004

SQUID INK SUSHI 602/258-0510 (27)

Sushi. Casual Dining. **Address:** 2 E Jefferson St 85004

SWITCH RESTAURANT & WINE BAR 602/264-2295 (10)

Comfort Food. Casual Dining. **Address:** 2603 N Central Ave 85004

TUCK SHOP 602/354-2980 (11)

Regional Comfort Food. Casual Dining. **Address:** 2245 N 12th St 85006

THE WILD THAIGER 602/241-8995 (8)

Thai Casual Dining $9-$29

AAA Inspector Notes: The friendly staff at this eatery presents classic, made-to-order dishes that are marked by attractive presentations. Popular choices include hot pots that serve two, a variety of curries and many vegetarian options. The intimate, casual setting is located along the Central Corridor and offers streetside dining. **Features:** full bar, patio dining, happy hour. **Address:** 2631 N Central Ave 85004 **Location:** Just s of Thomas Rd. Thomas/Central, 8.

PHOENIX

- **Restaurants p. 140**
- **Hotels & Restaurants map & index p. 109, 112, 117, 120, 126**

AC HOTEL BY MARRIOTT PHOENIX BILTMORE 602/852-6500 (30)

Hotel

AAA Benefit: Members save 5% or more!

Address: 2811 E Camelback Cir 85016 **Location:** Jct 24th St, 0.5 mi e. **Facility:** 160 units. 5 stories, interior corridors. *Bath:* shower only. **Amenities:** safes. **Pool:** heated outdoor. **Activities:** exercise room. **Guest Services:** valet and coin laundry.

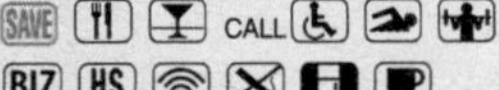

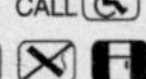

ALOFT PHOENIX AIRPORT HOTEL 602/275-6300 (9)

Hotel

AAA Benefit: Members save 5% or more!

Address: 4450 E Washington St 85034 **Location:** SR 143 exit Washington St, just w. 44th St/Washington, 22. **Facility:** 143 units. 6 stories, interior corridors. *Bath:* shower only. **Amenities:** safes. **Pool:** heated outdoor. **Activities:** exercise room. **Guest Services:** valet and coin laundry, area transportation.

SOME UNITS

ARIZONA BILTMORE, A WALDORF ASTORIA RESORT 602/955-6600 (24)

Historic Retro Resort Hotel

WALDORF ASTORIA HOTELS & RESORTS

AAA Benefit: Members save up to 15%!

Address: 2400 E Missouri Ave 85016 **Location:** Jct Camelback Rd, 0.5 mi n on 24th St, then 0.4 mi e. Located in a residential area. **Facility:** This venerable valley resort is noted for its attentive staff, Frank Lloyd Wright-inspired design, elegant guest rooms and expansive grounds with lush landscaping. 720 units, some kitchens and condominiums. 2-4 stories, interior/exterior corridors. **Parking:** on-site (fee) and valet. **Terms:** check-in 4 pm. **Amenities:** safes. **Dining:** 3 restaurants, also, Frank & Albert's, Wright's at the Biltmore, see separate listings. **Pool:** heated outdoor. **Activities:** sauna, hot tub, steamroom, regulation golf, tennis, recreation programs, kids club, bicycles, playground, lawn sports, health club, spa. **Guest Services:** valet laundry, boarding pass kiosk, area transportation.

SOME UNITS

ARIZONA GRAND RESORT & SPA 602/438-9000 (41)

Resort Hotel

Address: 8000 S Arizona Grand Pkwy 85044 **Location:** I-10 exit 155 (Baseline Rd), just w, then just s. **Facility:** Water plays a key role at this six-acre property, which features fountains, adult and children's pools, a waterslide and a simulated lazy river. Guest rooms all feature separate sitting rooms. 744 units, some kitchens. 2-5 stories, exterior corridors. **Parking:** on-site and valet. **Terms:** check-in 4 pm. **Amenities:** video games, safes. **Dining:** 4 restaurants, also, Rustler's Rooste, see separate listing, entertainment. **Pool:** heated outdoor. **Activities:** hot tub, steamroom, regulation golf, recreation programs, bicycles, trails, health club, spa. **Guest Services:** valet and coin laundry, boarding pass kiosk, area transportation.

(See maps & indexes p. 109, 112, 117, 120, 126.)

BAYMONT BY WYNDHAM PHOENIX I-10 602/585-0555 38
Hotel. **Address:** 1242 N 53rd Ave 85043

BEST WESTERN AIRPORT INN 602/273-7251 10

Hotel

AAA Benefit: Members save up to 15% and earn bonus points!

Address: 2425 S 24th St 85034 **Location:** I-10 exit 150B (24th St) westbound, just s; exit 151 (University Dr) eastbound, just n to I-10 westbound, 1 mi w to exit 150B (24th St), then just s. **Facility:** 117 units. 2 stories (no elevator), interior/exterior corridors. **Terms:** check-in 4 pm. **Amenities:** *Some:* safes. **Pool:** heated outdoor. **Activities:** sauna, hot tub, exercise room. **Guest Services:** coin laundry, area transportation.

SOME UNITS HS

BEST WESTERN INNSUITES PHOENIX/BILTMORE 602/997-6285 22

Hotel

AAA Benefit: Members save up to 15% and earn bonus points!

Address: 1615 E Northern Ave 85020 **Location:** SR 51 exit 7, 0.6 mi w. **Facility:** 120 units. 2 stories (no elevator), exterior corridors. **Terms:** check-in 4 pm. **Pool:** heated outdoor. **Activities:** hot tub, picnic facilities, exercise room. **Guest Services:** valet and coin laundry. **Featured Amenity: breakfast buffet.**

SOME UNITS HS

BEST WESTERN NORTH PHOENIX HOTEL 602/395-0900 16

Hotel

AAA Benefit: Members save up to 15% and earn bonus points!

Address: 9455 N Black Canyon Hwy 85021 **Location:** I-17 exit 207 (Dunlap Ave), just e to frontage road, then 0.4 mi n. **Facility:** 87 units, some efficiencies. 3 stories, interior corridors. **Pool:** outdoor. **Activities:** hot tub, picnic facilities, exercise room. **Guest Services:** valet and coin laundry. **Featured Amenity: breakfast buffet.**

CALL BIZ SOME UNITS HS

THE CAMBY, AUTOGRAPH COLLECTION 602/468-0700 29
Hotel. **Address:** 2401 E Camelback Rd 85016

AAA Benefit: Members save 5% or more!

CANDLEWOOD SUITES PHOENIX 602/861-4900 8
Extended Stay Hotel. **Address:** 11411 N Black Canyon Hwy 85029

COMFORT INN & SUITES 602/548-8888 5
Hotel. **Address:** 17017 N Black Canyon Hwy 85023

COMFORT INN I-10 WEST/CENTRAL 602/415-1623 39
Hotel. **Address:** 1344 N 27th Ave 85009

COUNTRY INN & SUITES BY RADISSON PHOENIX AIRPORT 480/829-0700 14

Hotel

Address: 4702 E University Dr 85034 **Location:** I-10 exit 151 (University Dr), 2 mi n, then e. East Economy Parking, 33. **Facility:** 88 units. 3 stories, interior corridors. **Pool:** heated outdoor. **Activities:** hot tub, exercise room. **Guest Services:** valet and coin laundry. **Featured Amenity: continental breakfast.**

SAVE CALL BIZ SOME UNITS

COURTYARD BY MARRIOTT-CAMELBACK 602/955-5200 27
SAVE Hotel. **Address:** 2101 E Camelback Rd 85016

AAA Benefit: Members save 5% or more!

COURTYARD BY MARRIOTT PHOENIX AIRPORT 480/966-4300 13
SAVE Hotel. **Address:** 2621 S 47th St 85034

AAA Benefit: Members save 5% or more!

COURTYARD BY MARRIOTT PHOENIX NORTH 602/944-7373 15
SAVE Hotel. **Address:** 9631 N Black Canyon Hwy 85021

AAA Benefit: Members save 5% or more!

COURTYARD BY MARRIOTT PHOENIX NORTH/HAPPY VALLEY 623/580-8844

Hotel

COURTYARD **AAA Benefit:** Members save 5% or more!

Address: 2029 W Whispering Wind Dr 85085 **Location:** I-17 exit 218 (Happy Valley Rd), 0.4 mi e to 23rd Ave, just s, then just e. **Facility:** 164 units. 5 stories, interior corridors. **Pool:** heated outdoor. **Activities:** hot tub, exercise room. **Guest Services:** valet and coin laundry, boarding pass kiosk.

SAVE BIZ SOME UNITS

COURTYARD BY MARRIOTT PHOENIX WEST-AVONDALE 623/271-7660 1

Hotel

COURTYARD **AAA Benefit:** Members save 5% or more!

Address: 1650 N 95th Ln 85037 **Location:** I-10 exit 133 (99th Ave) eastbound, just n to McDowell Rd, 0.5 mi e, then just n; exit 134 (91st Ave) westbound, just n to McDowell Rd, just w, then just n. **Facility:** 127 units. 4 stories, interior corridors. **Pool:** heated outdoor. **Activities:** hot tub, exercise room. **Guest Services:** valet and coin laundry, boarding pass kiosk.

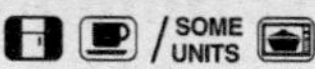

SAVE CALL BIZ HS SOME UNITS

(See maps & indexes p. 109, 112, 117, 120, 126.)

CROWNE PLAZA PHOENIX AIRPORT
602/273-7778 8

Hotel

Address: 4300 E Washington St 85034 **Location:** SR 202 exit 2 (44th St), 0.7 mi s. 44th St/Washington, 22. **Facility:** 290 units. 10 stories, interior corridors. **Parking:** on-site and valet. **Amenities:** *Some:* safes. **Pool:** heated outdoor. **Activities:** hot tub, exercise room. **Guest Services:** valet and coin laundry.

SAVE BIZ

/ SOME UNITS

DOUBLETREE BY HILTON PHOENIX NORTH
602/997-5900 13

SAVE Hotel. **Address:** 10220 N Metro Pkwy E 85051

AAA Benefit:
Members save up to 15%!

DOUBLETREE SUITES BY HILTON PHOENIX
602/225-0500 7

Hotel

AAA Benefit:
Members save up to 15%!

Address: 320 N 44th St 85008 **Location:** SR 202 exit 2 (44th St), 0.5 mi s. 44th St/Washington, 22. **Facility:** 242 units. 6 stories, exterior corridors. **Amenities:** safes. **Pool:** heated outdoor. **Activities:** hot tub, exercise room. **Guest Services:** valet and coin laundry, area transportation. **Featured Amenity:** breakfast buffet.

SAVE CALL

/ SOME UNITS HS

DRURY INN & SUITES PHOENIX AIRPORT
602/437-8400 17

Hotel. **Address:** 3333 E University Dr 85034

DRURY INN & SUITES PHOENIX HAPPY VALLEY
623/879-8800

Hotel. **Address:** 2335 W Pinnacle Peak Rd 85027

EMBASSY SUITES BY HILTON PHOENIX AIRPORT
602/957-1910 1

SAVE Hotel. **Address:** 2333 E Thomas Rd 85016

AAA Benefit:
Members save up to 15%!

EMBASSY SUITES BY HILTON PHOENIX BILTMORE
602/955-3992 28

SAVE Hotel. **Address:** 2630 E Camelback Rd 85016

AAA Benefit:
Members save up to 15%!

EMBASSY SUITES BY HILTON PHOENIX-SCOTTSDALE
602/765-5800 14

Hotel

AAA Benefit:
Members save up to 15%!

Address: 4415 E Paradise Village Pkwy S 85032 **Location:** Just s of Cactus Rd; just w of Tatum Blvd. **Facility:** 270 units. 6 stories, interior corridors. **Amenities:** safes. **Pool:** heated outdoor. **Activities:** hot tub, exercise room. **Guest Services:** valet and coin laundry, area transportation. **Featured Amenity:** full hot breakfast.

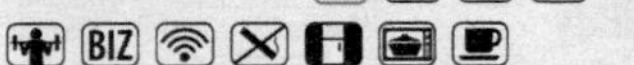

EXTENDED STAY AMERICA PHOENIX-BILTMORE
602/265-6800 26

Extended Stay Hotel. **Address:** 5235 N 16th St 85016

EXTENDED STAY AMERICA-PHOENIX-CHANDLER
480/785-0464 37

Extended Stay Hotel. **Address:** 14245 S 50th St 85044

EXTENDED STAY AMERICA PHOENIX-CHANDLER-E CHANDLER BLVD
480/753-6700 40

Extended Stay Hotel. **Address:** 5035 E Chandler Blvd 85048

FOUR POINTS BY SHERATON PHOENIX NORTH
602/943-2341 11

SAVE Hotel. **Address:** 2532 W Peoria Ave 85029

AAA Benefit:
Members save 5% or more!

FOUR POINTS BY SHERATON PHOENIX SOUTH MOUNTAIN
480/893-3000 36

SAVE Hotel. **Address:** 10831 S 51st St 85044

AAA Benefit:
Members save 5% or more!

GREENTREE INN & SUITES PHOENIX SKY HARBOR
602/438-8688 18

Hotel

Address: 4234 S 48th St 85040 **Location:** I-10 exit 153 (48th St/Broadway Rd) eastbound, just s; exit 153B (52nd St/Broadway Rd) westbound, 0.4 mi w. **Facility:** 106 units. 4 stories, interior corridors. **Pool:** heated outdoor. **Activities:** hot tub, exercise room. **Guest Services:** valet and coin laundry, area transportation. **Featured Amenity:** breakfast buffet.

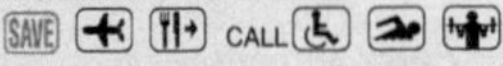

(See maps & indexes p. 109, 112, 117, 120, 126.)

HAMPTON INN & SUITES PHOENIX NORTH/HAPPY VALLEY

623/516-9300

AAA Benefit: Members save up to 15%!

Address: 2550 W Charlotte Dr 85085 **Location:** I-17 exit 217 (Pinnacle Peak Rd), 0.6 mi n on Frontage Rd. **Facility:** 125 units. 4 stories, interior corridors. **Pool:** heated outdoor. **Activities:** hot tub, exercise room. **Guest Services:** valet and coin laundry, area transportation. **Featured Amenity: breakfast buffet.**

SAVE CALL BIZ HS / SOME UNITS

HAMPTON INN BY HILTON PHOENIX BILTMORE

602/956-5221 32

AAA Benefit: Members save up to 15%!

Address: 2310 E Highland Ave 85016 **Location:** Just sw of Camelback Rd and 24th St. **Facility:** 120 units. 4 stories, interior corridors. **Pool:** heated outdoor. **Activities:** hot tub, exercise room. **Guest Services:** valet laundry, area transportation. **Featured Amenity: breakfast buffet.**

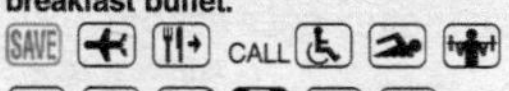

SAVE CALL BIZ

HAMPTON INN PHOENIX AIRPORT NORTH

602/267-0606 4

SAVE Hotel. **Address:** 601 N 44th St 85008

AAA Benefit: Members save up to 15%!

HILTON GARDEN INN PHOENIX AIRPORT

602/470-0500 15

SAVE Hotel. **Address:** 3422 E Elwood St 85040

AAA Benefit: Members save up to 15%!

HILTON GARDEN INN PHOENIX AIRPORT NORTH

602/306-2323 6

SAVE Hotel. **Address:** 3838 E Van Buren St 85008

AAA Benefit: Members save up to 15%!

HILTON GARDEN INN PHOENIX MIDTOWN

602/279-9811 33

SAVE Hotel. **Address:** 4000 N Central Ave 85012

AAA Benefit: Members save up to 15%!

HILTON GARDEN INN PHOENIX NORTH /HAPPY VALLEY

623/434-5556

Hilton Garden Inn

AAA Benefit: Members save up to 15%!

Address: 1940 W Pinnacle Peak Rd 85027 **Location:** I-17 exit 217 (Pinnacle Peak Rd), 0.8 mi e. **Facility:** 126 units. 4 stories, interior corridors. **Pool:** heated outdoor. **Activities:** hot tub, exercise room. **Guest Services:** valet and coin laundry, area transportation.

SAVE BIZ HS

HILTON PHOENIX AIRPORT

480/894-1600 11

Hilton HOTELS & RESORTS

AAA Benefit: Members save up to 15%!

Address: 2435 S 47th St 85034 **Location:** I-10 exit 151 (University Dr), 2 mi n, then just w. East Economy Parking, 33. **Facility:** 259 units. 4 stories, interior corridors. **Amenities:** safes. **Pool:** heated outdoor. **Activities:** hot tub, exercise room. **Guest Services:** valet laundry.

SAVE BIZ / SOME UNITS

HOLIDAY INN & SUITES PHOENIX AIRPORT

480/543-1700 16

Hotel. **Address:** 3220 S 48th St 85040

HOLIDAY INN & SUITES PHOENIX AIRPORT NORTH

602/244-8800 2

Hotel

Address: 1515 N 44th St 85008 **Location:** SR 202 exit 2 (44th St), 0.3 mi n. **Facility:** 228 units, some efficiencies. 4 stories, exterior corridors. **Pool:** heated outdoor. **Activities:** hot tub, exercise room. **Guest Services:** valet and coin laundry, area transportation.

SAVE CALL BIZ / SOME UNITS HS

HOLIDAY INN EXPRESS & SUITES PHOENIX-CHANDLER

480/785-8500 38

Hotel

Address: 15221 S 50th St 85044 **Location:** I-10 exit 160 (Chandler Blvd), just w, then just n. **Facility:** 125 units. 4 stories, interior corridors. **Pool:** heated outdoor. **Activities:** hot tub, exercise room. **Guest Services:** valet and coin laundry. **Featured Amenity: continental breakfast.**

SAVE BIZ

(See maps & indexes p. 109, 112, 117, 120, 126.)

HOLIDAY INN EXPRESS & SUITES PHOENIX NORTH-SCOTTSDALE 480/473-3400 **3**

Hotel. **Address:** 4575 E Irma Ln 85050

HOLIDAY INN PHOENIX WEST 602/484-9009 **37**

Hotel. **Address:** 1500 N 51st Ave 85043

HOMEWOOD SUITES BY HILTON PHOENIX AIRPORT SOUTH 602/470-2100 **19**

Extended Stay Hotel. **Address:** 4750 E Cotton Center Blvd 85040

AAA Benefit: Members save up to 15%!

HOMEWOOD SUITES BY HILTON PHOENIX-BILTMORE 602/508-0937 **31**

Extended Stay Hotel. **Address:** 2001 E Highland Ave 85016

AAA Benefit: Members save up to 15%!

HOMEWOOD SUITES BY HILTON PHOENIX METROCENTER 602/674-8900 **12**

Extended Stay Hotel. **Address:** 2536 W Beryl Ave 85021

AAA Benefit: Members save up to 15%!

HOMEWOOD SUITES PHOENIX NORTH/HAPPY VALLEY 623/580-1800

Extended Stay Hotel

AAA Benefit: Members save up to 15%!

Address: 2470 W Charlotte Dr 85085 **Location:** I-17 exit 217 (Pinnacle Peak Rd), 0.6 mi n on Frontage Rd. **Facility:** 134 efficiencies, some two bedrooms. 4 stories, interior corridors. *Bath:* shower only. **Pool:** heated outdoor. **Activities:** hot tub, picnic facilities, exercise room. **Guest Services:** valet and coin laundry, area transportation. **Featured Amenity:** **breakfast buffet.**

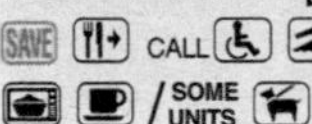

HYATT PLACE PHOENIX-NORTH 602/997-8800 **10**

Hotel

HYATT PLACE

AAA Benefit: Members save up to 10%!

Address: 10838 N 25th Ave 85029 **Location:** I-17 exit 208 (Peoria Ave), just e, then 0.3 mi n. **Facility:** 127 units. 4 stories, interior corridors. **Pool:** heated outdoor. **Activities:** exercise room. **Guest Services:** valet laundry, area transportation. **Featured Amenity:** **breakfast buffet.**

JW MARRIOTT PHOENIX DESERT RIDGE RESORT & SPA 480/293-5000 **2**

Resort Hotel

AAA Benefit: Members save 5% or more!

Address: 5350 E Marriott Dr 85054 **Location:** SR 101 exit 31 (Tatum Blvd), 0.4 mi n to Deer Valley Dr, then 0.5 mi e. **Facility:** This expansive destination resort has activities for families or groups. A tri-level lobby opens to a courtyard with pools, water play areas and a flowing lazy river. 950 units. 6 stories, interior corridors. **Parking:** on-site and valet. **Terms:** check-in 4 pm. **Amenities:** safes. **Dining:** 3 restaurants, also, Roy's Desert Ridge, see separate listing. **Pool:** heated outdoor. **Activities:** sauna, hot tub, steamroom, regulation golf, tennis, recreation programs, kids club, bicycles, lawn sports, health club, spa. **Guest Services:** complimentary and valet laundry, boarding pass kiosk, rental car service, area transportation.

LA QUINTA INN & SUITES PHOENIX CHANDLER 480/961-7700 **39**

Hotel. **Address:** 15241 S 50th St 85044

LA QUINTA INN & SUITES PHOENIX I-10 WEST 602/595-7601 **35**

Hotel. **Address:** 4929 W McDowell Rd 85035

THE LEGACY GOLF RESORT 602/305-5500 **40**

Resort Condominium

Address: 6808 S 32nd St 85042 **Location:** I-10 exit 155 (Baseline Rd), 2.4 mi w, then 0.4 mi n. **Facility:** Spacious rooms and baths, along with a golf course designed by Gary Panks, await you in this contemporary desert setting. 328 condominiums. 2 stories (no elevator), exterior corridors. **Terms:** check-in 4 pm. **Amenities:** safes. **Pool:** heated outdoor. **Activities:** hot tub, regulation golf, tennis, recreation programs, playground, lawn sports, picnic facilities, exercise room, massage. **Guest Services:** complimentary laundry. Affiliated with Wyndham Extra Holidays.

MARICOPA MANOR BED & BREAKFAST INN 602/264-9200 **25**

Classic Bed & Breakfast. **Address:** 15 W Pasadena Ave 85013

PHOENIX AIRPORT MARRIOTT 602/273-7373 **3**

Hotel. **Address:** 1101 N 44th St 85008

AAA Benefit: Members save 5% or more!

(See maps & indexes p. 109, 112, 117, 120, 126.)

POINTE HILTON SQUAW PEAK RESORT
602/997-2626 **23**

Resort Hotel

AAA Benefit:
Members save up to 15%!

Address: 7677 N 16th St 85020 **Location:** SR 51 exit Glendale Ave, 0.4 mi w, then 0.6 mi n. **Facility:** The resort's suites and large casitas are scattered throughout extensive grounds featuring shaded pool areas and courtyards with tiered fountains. 563 units, some houses. 3-4 stories, exterior corridors. **Parking:** on-site and valet. **Terms:** check-in 4 pm. **Amenities:** safes. **Dining:** 2 restaurants, also, Rico's American Grill, see separate listing. **Pool:** heated outdoor. **Activities:** sauna, hot tub, steamroom, miniature golf, tennis, recreation programs, kids club, playground, health club, spa. **Guest Services:** valet and coin laundry, area transportation.

SOME UNITS

POINTE HILTON TAPATIO CLIFFS RESORT
602/866-7500 **9**

SAVE Resort Hotel. **Address:** 11111 N 7th St 85020

AAA Benefit:
Members save up to 15%!

QUALITY INN PHOENIX NORTH I-17 602/864-6233 **21**

Hotel. **Address:** 8101 N Black Canyon Hwy 85021

RADISSON HOTEL PHOENIX AIRPORT
602/220-4400 **5**

Hotel

Address: 427 N 44th St 85008 **Location:** SR 202 exit 2 (44th St), 0.5 mi s. 44th St/Washington, 22. **Facility:** 204 units. 7 stories, interior corridors. **Parking:** on-site (fee). **Amenities:** *Some:* safes. **Pool:** heated outdoor. **Activities:** hot tub, exercise room. **Guest Services:** valet and coin laundry.

RED ROOF PLUS+ PHOENIX WEST 602/233-8004 **36**

Hotel

Address: 5215 W Willetta St 85043 **Location:** I-10 exit 139 (51st Ave), just n, just e on McDowell Rd, then just s. **Facility:** 133 units. 4 stories, interior corridors. **Amenities:** safes. **Pool:** heated outdoor.

RESIDENCE INN BY MARRIOTT PHOENIX
602/864-1900 **20**

SAVE Extended Stay Hotel. **Address:** 8242 N Black Canyon Hwy 85051

AAA Benefit:
Members save 5% or more!

RESIDENCE INN BY MARRIOTT PHOENIX DESERT VIEW AT MAYO CLINIC
480/563-1500 **6**

Extended Stay Hotel

Residence INN. **AAA Benefit:**
Members save 5% or more!

Address: 5665 E Mayo Blvd 85054 **Location:** SR 101 exit 32 (56th St), just s, then just e. **Facility:** 208 units, some two bedrooms, efficiencies and kitchens. 6 stories, interior corridors. **Parking:** on-site (fee). **Pool:** heated outdoor. **Activities:** picnic facilities, exercise room. **Guest Services:** valet and coin laundry, boarding pass kiosk, area transportation. **Featured Amenity:** continental breakfast.

SOME UNITS

RESIDENCE INN BY MARRIOTT PHOENIX NORTH/ HAPPY VALLEY
623/580-8833

Extended Stay Hotel

Residence INN. **AAA Benefit:**
Members save 5% or more!

Address: 2035 W Whispering Wind Dr 85085 **Location:** I-17 exit 128 (Happy Valley Rd), 0.4 mi e to 23rd Ave, just s, then just e. **Facility:** 129 units, some two bedrooms, efficiencies and kitchens. 5 stories, interior corridors. **Pool:** heated outdoor. **Activities:** hot tub, picnic facilities, exercise room. **Guest Services:** valet and coin laundry.

SAVE BIZ SOME UNITS

ROYAL PALMS RESORT AND SPA 602/283-1234 **34**

Historic Boutique Hotel

AAA Benefit:
Members save up to 10%!

Address: 5200 E Camelback Rd 85018 **Location:** Just e of 52nd St. Located in a quiet residential area. **Facility:** Originally built as a private residence in the 1920s, this nine-acre hideaway nestled into the base of Camelback Mountain has extensive grounds dotted with fountains and outdoor fireplaces. 119 units. 1-2 stories, interior/exterior corridors. **Parking:** valet only. **Terms:** check-in 4 pm. **Amenities:** safes. **Dining:** 2 restaurants, also, T. Cook's, see separate listing. **Pool:** heated outdoor. **Activities:** hot tub, steamroom, recreation programs, lawn sports, exercise room, spa. **Guest Services:** valet laundry, area transportation. Affiliated with The Unbound Collection by Hyatt.

SAVE ECO CALL BIZ HS SOME UNITS

SHERATON CRESCENT HOTEL 602/943-8200 **19**

SAVE Hotel. **Address:** 2620 W Dunlap Ave 85021

AAA Benefit:
Members save 5% or more!

SLEEP INN PHOENIX AIRPORT 480/967-7100 **12**

Hotel. **Address:** 2621 S 47th Pl 85034

(See maps & indexes p. 109, 112, 117, 120, 126.)

SLEEP INN PHOENIX NORTH 602/504-1200 **4**

Hotel

Address: 18235 N 27th Ave 85053 **Location:** I-17 exit 214A (Union Hills Dr), just w, then just s. **Facility:** 61 units. 2 stories, interior corridors. *Bath:* shower only. **Amenities:** safes. **Pool:** heated outdoor. **Activities:** hot tub, limited exercise equipment. **Guest Services:** valet and coin laundry. **Featured Amenity:** full hot breakfast.

SAVE CALL BIZ / SOME UNITS

SPRINGHILL SUITES BY MARRIOTT PHOENIX NORTH 602/943-0010 **17**

SAVE Hotel. **Address:** 9425 N Black Canyon Frwy 85021

AAA Benefit: Members save 5% or more!

TOWNEPLACE SUITES BY MARRIOTT PHOENIX NORTH 602/943-9510 **18**

SAVE Extended Stay Hotel. **Address:** 9425 N Black Canyon Frwy 85021

AAA Benefit: Members save 5% or more!

WHERE TO EAT

AH-SO SUSHI & STEAK 623/869-7700

Japanese. Casual Dining. **Address:** 2450 W Happy Valley Rd 85085

AKAIHANA SUSHI & GRILL 602/864-9202 (12)

Sushi. Casual Dining. **Address:** 8041 N Black Canyon Hwy, Suite 112 85021

ALEXI'S GRILL 602/279-0982 (81)

Northern Italian. Casual Dining. **Address:** 3550 N Central Ave 85012

ARTIZEN 602/522-6655 (64)

New American. Fine Dining. **Address:** 2401 E Camelback Rd 85016

AUNT CHILADA'S HIDEAWAY 602/944-1286 (17)

Mexican. Casual Dining. **Address:** 7330 N Dreamy Draw Dr 85020

BABBO ITALIAN EATERY 602/279-1500 (20)

Italian. Casual Dining. **Address:** 6855 N 16th St 85016

BLANCO TACOS & TEQUILA 602/429-8000 (60)

Mexican. Casual Dining. **Address:** 2502 E Camelback Rd 85016

BLUE WATER GRILL 602/277-3474 (50)

Seafood. Casual Dining. **Address:** 1720 E Camelback Rd 85016

BOBBY Q 602/995-5982 (10)

Barbecue. Casual Dining. **Address:** 8501 N 27th Ave 85051

BUCK & RIDER 602/346-0110 (77)

Seafood. Casual Dining. **Address:** 4225 E Camelback Rd 85018

CAFFE BOA 480/893-3331 (20)

Italian. Casual Dining. **Address:** 5063 E Elliot Rd 85044

THE CAPITAL GRILLE 602/952-8900 (58)

Steak. Fine Dining. **Address:** 2502 E Camelback Rd, Suite 199 85016

CASA CORAZON 602/334-1917 (1)

Mexican. Casual Dining. **Address:** 2637 N 16th St 85006

CHELSEA'S KITCHEN 602/957-2555 (72)

American. Casual Dining. **Address:** 5040 N 40th St 85018

CHERRYBLOSSOM NOODLE CAFE 602/248-9090 (47)

Noodles. Casual Dining. **Address:** 914 E Camelback Rd 85014

CHINO BANDIDO 602/375-3639 (4)

Fusion. Quick Serve. **Address:** 15414 N 19th Ave 85023

CHRISTO'S 602/264-1784 (22)

Italian. Fine Dining. **Address:** 6327 N 7th St 85014

THE CLEVER KOI 602/222-3474 (76)

Asian. Casual Dining. **Address:** 4236 N Central Ave 85012

COLD BEERS & CHEESEBURGERS 602/354-8093 (35)

American. Casual Dining. **Address:** 5625 N 7th St 85014

DESERT JADE 602/954-0048 (84)

Chinese. Casual Dining. **Address:** 3215 E Indian School Rd 85018

DIFFERENT POINTE OF VIEW 602/866-6350 (5)

New American Fine Dining
$29-$42

AAA Inspector Notes: The panoramic views of the valley are truly spectacular at this mountain-top restaurant, which offers indoor and outdoor dining areas. The menu, created by chef Anthony DeMuro reflects New American cuisine, incorporating natural and organic ingredients. The restaurant boasts an award-winning, international wine list. **Features:** full bar, patio dining. **Reservations:** suggested. **Address:** 11111 N 7th St 85020 **Location:** I-17 exit 207 (Dunlap Ave), 3 mi e, then 2 mi n; in Pointe Hilton Tapatio Cliffs Resort. **Parking:** on-site and valet. D

DUCK AND DECANTER 602/274-5429 (51)

Deli. Quick Serve. **Address:** 1651 E Camelback Rd 85016

FARM KITCHEN AT THE FARM AT SOUTH MOUNTAIN 602/276-6545 (91)

American Quick Serve
$10-$14

AAA Inspector Notes: Dining outdoors is a picnic, with meals in a basket given to patrons who can seek refuge under canvas awnings or shady trees. Take a seat at one of the checkered-cloth covered picnic tables scattered among the brick-covered patio and enjoy cool salads and warming soups along with homemade pies, cookies and cakes. **Features:** patio dining. **Address:** 6106 S 32nd St 85042 **Location:** I-10 exit 151 (University Dr/32nd St), 1.4 mi s, then just s of Southern Ave. L

FEDERAL PIZZA 602/795-2520 (40)

Italian. Casual Dining. **Address:** 5210 N Central Ave 85012

FLOWER CHILD 480/212-0180 (44)

Natural/Organic. Quick Serve. **Address:** 100 E Camelback Rd 85012

FRANK & ALBERT'S 602/381-7632 (37)

American. Casual Dining. **Address:** 2400 E Missouri Ave 85016

THE FRY BREAD HOUSE 602/351-2345 (52)

Regional Specialty. Quick Serve. **Address:** 4545 N 7th Ave 85014

FUEGO BISTRO 602/277-1151 (28)

Latin American. Casual Dining. **Address:** 713 E Palo Verde Dr 85014

GEORGE & SON'S 623/434-1888 (1)

Chinese. Casual Dining. **Address:** 3049 W Agua Fria Frwy 85027

(See maps & indexes p. 109, 112, 117, 120, 126.)

GEORGE YANG'S CHINESE CUISINE 602/368-2688 25
Chinese. Casual Dining. **Address:** 6048 N 16th St 85016

GIUSEPPE'S ON 28TH 602/381-1237 82
Italian. Casual Dining. **Address:** 2824 E Indian School Rd 85016

THE GLADLY 602/759-8132 63
New American. Casual Dining. **Address:** 2201 E Camelback Rd 85016

GREAT WALL HONG KONG CUISINE 602/973-1112 30
Chinese. Casual Dining. **Address:** 3446 W Camelback Rd 85017

GREEKFEST 602/265-2990 54
Greek. Casual Dining. **Address:** 1940 E Camelback Rd 85016

HANA JAPANESE EATERY 602/973-1238 32
Japanese. Casual Dining. **Address:** 5524 N 7th Ave 85013

THE HENRY 602/429-8020 78
New American. Casual Dining. **Address:** 4455 E Camelback Rd 85018

HILLSTONE RESTAURANT 602/957-9700 62
American. Casual Dining. **Address:** 2650 E Camelback Rd 85016

HULA'S MODERN TIKI 602/265-8454 49
Polynesian. Casual Dining. **Address:** 5114 N 7th St 85014

INDIA PALACE 602/942-4224 3
Indian. Casual Dining. **Address:** 2941 W Bell Rd 85032

KEEGAN'S GRILL
American. Casual Dining.
LOCATIONS:
Address: 3114 E Camelback Rd 85016 **Phone:** 602/955-6616
Address: 4723 E Ray Rd 85044 **Phone:** 480/705-0505

KITCHEN 56 480/994-5656 90
American. Casual Dining. **Address:** 3433 N 56th St 85018

LADERA TAVERNA Y COCINA 602/606-2258 11
Regional Mexican. Casual Dining. **Address:** 8729 N Central Ave 85020

LA PINATA 602/279-1763 33
Mexican. Casual Dining. **Address:** 5521 N 7th Ave 85013

LA SANTISIMA GOURMET TACO SHOP 602/254-6330 3
Mexican. Quick Serve. **Address:** 1919 N 16th St 85006

LA STALLA CUCINA RUSTICA 480/855-9990 21
Italian. Casual Dining. **Address:** 4855 E Warner Rd 85044

MACAYO'S MEXICAN TABLE
Mexican. Casual Dining.
LOCATIONS:
Address: 7829 W Thomas Rd 85033 **Phone:** 623/873-0313
Address: 12637 S 48th St 85044 **Phone:** 480/598-5101

MARIGOLD MAISON 602/795-0020 7
Indian. Casual Dining. **Address:** 4720 E Cactus Rd 85032

MATT'S BIG BREAKFAST 602/840-3450 67
American. Casual Dining. **Address:** 3118 E Camelback Rd 85016

MI PATIO MEXICAN FOOD 602/277-4831 83
Mexican. Casual Dining. **Address:** 3347 N 7th Ave 85013

MIRACLE MILE DELICATESSEN 602/776-0992 75
Deli. Quick Serve. **Address:** 4433 N 16th St 85016

MORA ITALIAN 602/795-9943 34
Italian. Fine Dining. **Address:** 5651 N 7th St 85014

MOTO 602/263-5444 21
Asian Fusion. Casual Dining. **Address:** 6845 N 16th St 85016

NOOK KITCHEN 602/651-1390 86
American. Casual Dining. **Address:** 3623 E Indian School Rd 85018

NORTH ITALIA 602/324-5600 74
Italian. Casual Dining. **Address:** 4929 N 40th St 85018

OCEAN POKE CO. 602/283-5153 87
Hawaiian Fusion. Quick Serve. **Address:** 3619 E Indian School Rd 85018

OREGANO'S PIZZA BISTRO 602/241-0707
Italian Pizza. Casual Dining. **Address:** 1008 E Camelback Rd 85014

OTRO CAFE 602/266-0831 24
Mexican. Casual Dining. **Address:** 6035 N 7th St 85014

OVER EASY - BILTMORE 602/687-7456 56
Breakfast. Casual Dining. **Address:** 2398 E Camelback Rd 85016

OVER EASY CAFE 602/468-3447 89
American. Casual Dining. **Address:** 4730 E Indian School Rd 85018

PANE BIANCO 602/234-2100 71
Specialty Sandwiches. Casual Dining. **Address:** 4404 N Central Ave 85012

PAPPADEAUX SEAFOOD KITCHEN 602/331-3434
Cajun Seafood. Casual Dining. **Address:** 11051 N Black Canyon Hwy 85029

THE PARLOR PIZZERIA 602/248-2480 53
Pizza. Casual Dining. **Address:** 1916 E Camelback Rd 85016

PEPE'S TACO VILLA 602/242-0379 39
Mexican. Casual Dining. **Address:** 2108 W Camelback Rd 85015

P.F. CHANG'S CHINA BISTRO 623/707-4495
Chinese. Fine Dining. **Address:** 2420 W Happy Valley Rd 85085

PHOENIX CITY GRILLE 602/266-3001 31
American. Casual Dining. **Address:** 5816 N 16th St 85016

PITA JUNGLE 623/587-5572
Mediterranean. Casual Dining. **Address:** 2530 W Happy Valley Rd 85085

PITA JUNGLE 602/277-7482
Mediterranean. Casual Dining. **Address:** 5505 N 7th St 85014

PIZZA A METRO 602/262-9999 85
Italian. Casual Dining. **Address:** 2336 W Thomas Rd 85015

PIZZERIA BIANCO 602/368-3273 65
Italian Pizza. Casual Dining. **Address:** 4743 N 20th St 85016

POSTINO CENTRAL WINECAFE 602/274-5144 42
Small Plates Sandwiches. Casual Dining. **Address:** 5144 N Central Ave 85012

(See maps & indexes p. 109, 112, 117, 120, 126.)

POSTINO WINECAFE 602/852-3939 (79)

American. Casual Dining. **Address:** 3939 E Campbell Ave 85018

THE PRIME CHINESE RESTAURANT 602/274-7219 (45)

Chinese. Casual Dining. **Address:** 24 W Camelback Rd 85013

PUBBLICO ITALIAN EATERY 602/601-5651 (26)

Italian. Casual Dining. **Address:** 5813 N 7th St 85014

QUIESSENCE 602/276-0601 (92)

New American. Fine Dining. **Address:** 6106 S 32nd St 85042

RA SUSHI BAR RESTAURANT 480/940-1111

Japanese Sushi. Casual Dining. **Address:** 4921 E Ray Rd, Suite B1 85044

RED DEVIL RESTAURANT & PIZZERIA 602/267-1036 (4)

Italian. Casual Dining. **Address:** 3102 E McDowell Rd 85008

REDTHAI SOUTHEAST ASIAN KITCHEN 602/870-3015 (13)

Asian. Casual Dining. **Address:** 7822 N 12th St 85020

RESTAURANT ATOYAC ESTILO OAXACA 602/246-1111 (16)

Mexican. Quick Serve. **Address:** 1830 W Glendale Ave 85021

RESTAURANT PROGRESS 602/441-0553 (70)

New American. Casual Dining. **Address:** 702 W Montecito Ave 85013

RICHARDSON'S OF NEW MEXICO 602/265-5886 (23)

Southwestern. Casual Dining. **Address:** 6335 N 16th St 85016

RICO'S AMERICAN GRILL 602/997-5850 (14)

American. Casual Dining. **Address:** 7677 N 16th St 85020

ROLAND'S CAFE MARKET BAR 602/441-4749 (5)

Regional American. Casual Dining. **Address:** 1505 E Van Buren St 85006

ROY'S DESERT RIDGE 480/419-7697 (2)

Hawaiian. Casual Dining. **Address:** 5350 E Marriott Dr 85054

RUSCONI'S AMERICAN KITCHEN 480/483-0009 (9)

New American. Casual Dining. **Address:** 10637 Tatum Blvd 85028

RUSTLER'S ROOSTE 602/431-6474 (93)

Steak. Casual Dining. **Address:** 8383 S 48th St 85044

SA BAI MODERN THAI 602/954-8774 (2)

Thai. Casual Dining. **Address:** 4121 E Thomas Rd 85018

ST. FRANCIS 602/200-8111 (46)

New American. Casual Dining. **Address:** 111 E Camelback Rd 85012

SAKANA SUSHI AND GRILL 480/598-0506 (19)

Sushi. Casual Dining. **Address:** 5061 E Elliot Rd 85044

SAUCE 602/216-2400

Italian. Casual Dining. **Address:** 742 E Glendale Ave 85020

SCOTT'S GENERATIONS DELI 602/277-5662 (18)

Deli. Casual Dining. **Address:** 742 E Glendale Ave, Suite 142 85020

SCRAMBLE 602/374-2294 (8)

American. Quick Serve. **Address:** 9832 N 7th St 85020

SEASONS 52 FRESH GRILL 602/840-5252 (57)

New American. Fine Dining. **Address:** 2502 E Camelback Rd 85016

SIERRA BONITA GRILL 602/264-0700 (19)

Southwestern. Casual Dining. **Address:** 6933 N 7th St 85014

SNOOZE AN A.M. EATERY 480/725-8000 (61)

Breakfast. Casual Dining. **Address:** 2045 E Camelback Rd 85016

SOUTHERN RAIL 602/200-0085 (43)

Southern American. Casual Dining. **Address:** 300 W Camelback Rd 85013

STEAK 44 602/271-4400 (73)

Steak. Fine Dining. **Address:** 5101 N 44th St 85018

STOCK & STABLE 602/313-1001 (36)

American. Gastropub. **Address:** 5538 N 7th St 85014

STOCKYARDS RESTAURANT & 1889 SALOON 602/273-7378 (7)

Steak. Casual Dining. **Address:** 5009 E Washington St, Suite 115 85034

SUSHI BROKERS 480/515-5000 (88)

Japanese. Casual Dining. **Address:** 4419 E Indian School Rd 85018

SZECHWAN PALACE 602/685-0888 (6)

Chinese. Casual Dining. **Address:** 668 N 44th St, Suite 108 85008

TARBELL'S 602/955-8100 (69)

American. Casual Dining. **Address:** 3213 E Camelback Rd 85018

T-BONE STEAKHOUSE 602/276-0945

Steak. Casual Dining. **Address:** 10037 S 19th Ave 85041

T. COOK'S 602/808-0766 (80)

Mediterranean. Fine Dining. **Address:** 5200 E Camelback Rd 85018

TEN - HANDCRAFTED AMERICAN FARE AND SPIRITS 602/374-2611 (68)

American. Casual Dining. **Address:** 2501 E Camelback Rd 85016

TRATTO 602/296-7761 (66)

Italian. Casual Dining. **Address:** 4743 N 20th St 85016

TRATTORIA D'AMICO 480/893-8544 (22)

Italian. Fine Dining. **Address:** 4902 E Warner Rd 85044

TRUE FOOD KITCHEN 602/774-3488 (55)

American. Casual Dining. **Address:** 2502 E Camelback Rd 85016

TUTTI SANTI RISTORANTE 602/216-0336 (15)

Italian. Casual Dining. **Address:** 7575 N 16th St, Suite 5 85254

THE VIG UPTOWN 602/633-1187 (27)

American. Casual Dining. **Address:** 6015 N 16th St 85014

WINDSOR 602/279-1111 (41)

American. Casual Dining. **Address:** 5223 N Central Ave 85012

WRIGHT'S AT THE BILTMORE 602/381-7668 (38)

American. Fine Dining. **Address:** 2400 E Missouri Ave 85016

YAMA SUSHI HOUSE 602/264-4260 (48)

Sushi. Casual Dining. **Address:** 4750 N Central Ave 85012

(See maps & indexes p. 109, 112, 117, 120, 126.)

YASU SUSHI BISTRO 602/787-9181 (6)

Japanese. Casual Dining. **Address:** 4316 E Cactus Rd 85032

ZINBURGER 602/424-9500 (59)

Burgers. Casual Dining. **Address:** 2502 E Camelback Rd 85016

ZIPPS SPORTS GRILL 602/266-1600 (29)

American. Casual Dining. **Address:** 1515 E Bethany Home Rd 85014

PINETOP-LAKESIDE (D-5) pop. 4,282, elev. 6,960'

Lakeside originally was named Fairview in 1880 by Mormon pioneers. Pinetop, also founded by Mormons, began in 1878 with a sawmill and ranching on the open range of the White Mountains. Before tourism, logging and ranching were the mainstays of the area. The twin towns were incorporated in 1984 as a resort area.

Pinetop-Lakeside, on the edge of the White Mountain Apache Reservation, is 10 miles southeast of Show Low on SR 260 on the edge of Mogollon Rim. The elevation makes the area cool in summer for trout fishing, camping and other activities. Winter sports such as snowmobiling, skiing and ice fishing are popular in the Apache-Sitgreaves National Forests *(see place listing p. 29)* and on the reservation. Fishing also is permitted by fee on the reservation.

Pinetop-Lakeside Chamber of Commerce: 518 W. White Mountain Blvd. in Lakeside, P.O. Box 4220, Pinetop, AZ 85935. **Phone:** (928) 367-4290.

BEST WESTERN INN OF PINETOP 928/367-6667

AAA Benefit: Members save up to 15% and earn bonus points!

Address: 404 E White Mountain Blvd 85935 **Location:** On SR 260, east end of town. Located in Pinetop. **Facility:** 41 units. 2 stories (no elevator), exterior corridors. **Activities:** hot tub. **Guest Services:** coin laundry. **Featured Amenity: full hot breakfast.**

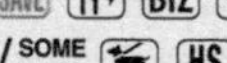

COMFORT INN & SUITES 928/368-6600

Hotel. **Address:** 1637 W White Mountain Blvd 85929

HON-DAH RESORT CASINO AND CONFERENCE CENTER 928/369-0299

Address: 777 Hwy 260 85935 **Location:** Jct SR 260 and 73; east end of town. Located in White Mountain Apache Reservation of Pinetop. **Facility:** The surrounding acres of the wooded reservation, cool weather and outdoor sports are as enticing here as the casino. Guest rooms are spacious with recently renovated, contemporary-style bathrooms. 128 units. 2 stories, interior corridors. **Terms:** check-in 4 pm. **Dining:** 2 restaurants, nightclub, entertainment. **Pool:** heated outdoor. **Activities:** sauna, hot tub, game room.

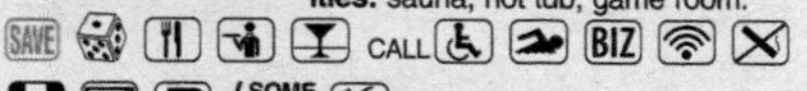

NORTHWOODS RESORT 928/367-2966

Cabin. **Address:** 165 E White Mountain Blvd 85935

QUALITY INN PINETOP 928/367-3636

Motel. **Address:** 458 E White Mountain Blvd 85935

WHERE TO EAT

THE CHALET RESTAURANT & SHARKY'S SUSHI BAR 928/367-1514

American. Casual Dining. **Address:** 348 W White Mountain Blvd 85929

CHARLIE CLARK'S STEAK HOUSE 928/367-4900

Steak. Casual Dining. **Address:** 1701 E White Mountain Blvd 85935

DARBI'S CAFE 928/367-6556

American. Casual Dining. **Address:** 235 E White Mountain Blvd 85935

EL RANCHO RESTAURANT 928/367-4557

Mexican. Casual Dining. **Address:** 1523 E White Mountain Blvd 85935

MOUNTAIN THAI RESTAURANT 928/368-4166

Thai. Casual Dining. **Address:** 2741 Hwy 260 85929

THE PASTA HOUSE BAR & GRILL 928/367-2782

Italian. Casual Dining. **Address:** 2188 E White Mountain Blvd 85935

VILLAGE GRILL 928/368-2424

Burgers. Quick Serve. **Address:** 1477 W White Mountain Blvd, Suite 4 85929

PIPE SPRING NATIONAL MONUMENT (A-3)

Off SR 389 15 miles west of Fredonia, Pipe Spring National Monument preserves a life-sustaining water source that Paiute Indians called Mu-tum-wa-va, or Dripping Rock. In the early 1870s, Mormon pioneers built a compound over the springs consisting of a sandstone fort and ranch house. Tours of the fort, named Winsor Castle, are offered. Pipe Spring has long served as a way station for weary travelers. The visitor center and cultural museum offers exhibits and a movie about Kaibab and pioneer culture and history.

Allow 1 hour minimum. Daily 8:30-4:30. Closed Jan. 1, Thanksgiving and Christmas. Tours of Winsor Castle are given daily generally on the half-hour in summer; otherwise varies. Admission, valid for 7 days, $7; free (ages 0-15). Phone (928) 643-7105.

PRESCOTT (C-3) pop. 39,843, elev. 5,346'

• Hotels p. 145 • Restaurants p. 145

The area around Prescott was first settled in 1864 by miners prospecting for gold. It was the presence of gold that prompted the cash-poor Union to designate Arizona as a territory in 1863. In 1867 the capitol was moved south to Tucson. However, Prescott briefly became capital again in 1877, a title it lost to Phoenix in 1889.

Named to honor historian William Hickling Prescott, the town was incorporated in 1883. Because of the surrounding pine forests, wooden structures rather than the typical adobe buildings were built. Fire devastated Prescott in 1900, but determined townsfolk rebuilt and developed a water system utilizing Del Rio Springs.

Surrounded by mountain ranges and nearly encircled by the 1.2-million-acre Prescott National Forest, the mile-high town is now a resort community. Outdoor enthusiasts can indulge in more than 450 miles of multiuse groomed trails, four lakes and five golf courses. Camping, horseback riding, hiking, fishing, rockhounding and picnicking are popular activities. A robust arts community helps facilitate year-round activities, events and festivals, many of which are held on Prescott's charming, tree-lined Courthouse Plaza.

Prescott Chamber of Commerce and Visitor Information Center: 117 W. Goodwin St., Prescott, AZ 86303. **Phone:** (928) 445-2000 or (800) 266-7534.

Self-guiding tours: Maps of mountain biking areas along with a leaflet outlining a self-guiding walking tour of Prescott's Victorian-era neighborhoods can be obtained at the chamber of commerce and visitor information center.

Shopping: Dillard's, JCPenney and Sears anchor the Prescott Gateway Mall, 3250 Gateway Blvd. near SR 69 and Lee Boulevard. Whiskey Row/Courthouse Square, downtown off SR 89 and Cortez Street, offers antique, souvenir and clothes shopping opportunities as well as several eateries.

PHIPPEN MUSEUM—ART AND HERITAGE OF THE AMERICAN WEST, 6 mi. n.e. at 4701 SR 89 N., displays permanent and changing exhibitions by prominent Western artists. The 16,900-square-foot facility also displays contemporary artwork depicting the American West. **Time:** Allow 30 minutes minimum. **Hours:** Tues.-Sat. 10-4, Sun. 1-4. Closed Jan. 1, Thanksgiving, Christmas Eve and Christmas. **Cost:** $7; $5 (students with ID); free (ages 0-12). **Phone:** (928) 778-1385.

GEM **SHARLOT HALL MUSEUM,** downtown at 415 W. Gurley St., contains 4 acres of exhibits, historic buildings and gardens. The highlight is the Territorial Governor's Mansion, which was the home and center of government for Arizona's first territorial officials. It was later restored by poet and historian Sharlot M. Hall. Hall filled the mansion with Native American and pioneer artifacts and opened it as a museum in 1928.

Additional historic buildings and several exhibits trace the area's heritage including Fort Misery, the oldest surviving log cabin in Arizona (1864), which was used as a store, boarding house and residence; a replica of the first school house in Prescott which began operation in 1867; the John C. Frémont and the William Bashford houses both classic Victorian-style homes built in the 1870s; the Lawler Exhibit Center featuring exhibits tracing Arizona history from prehistoric beasts to the Clovis native people through territorial days to U.S. statehood; the Sharlot Hall Building, built in 1936 as a CWA project, and housing many of the museum's historical exhibits and dioramas; and the library and archives for historical and academic research.

Time: Allow 1 hour minimum. **Hours:** Mon.-Sat. 10-5, Sun. noon-4, May-Sept.; Mon.-Sat. 10-4, Sun. noon-4, rest of year. Weekend events are held May-Oct.; phone ahead for information. Closed Jan. 1, Thanksgiving and Christmas. **Cost:** $12; $10 (ages 65+ and active and retired military with ID); $6 (college students ages 18-25 with ID); $5 (ages 13-17); free (ages 0-12). **Phone:** (928) 445-3122.

Governor's Mansion, part of the Sharlot Hall Museum complex at 415 W. Gurley St., was completed in 1864 for John N. Goodwin, Arizona's first territorial governor. The mansion's furnishings and artifacts depict the period 1864-67. The exhibit Behind Whiskey Row tells the story of Prescott's second-class citizens, including its Chinese workers, during the late 1800s. **Hours:** Mon.-Sat. 10-5, Sun. noon-4, May-Sept.; Mon.-Sat. 10-4, Sun. noon-4, rest of year. Weekend events are held May-Oct.; phone ahead for information. Closed Jan. 1, Thanksgiving and Christmas. **Cost:** $12; $10 (ages 65+, and active and retired military with ID); $6 (college students ages 18-25 with ID); $5 (ages 13-17); free (ages 0-12). **Phone:** (928) 445-3122.

John C. Frémont House, part of the Sharlot Hall Museum complex at 415 W. Gurley St., was built in 1875 from locally milled lumber. It served as the home of the celebrated "Pathfinder" during his term as fifth territorial governor of Arizona. The furnishings and memorabilia represent the period 1875-81. **Hours:** Mon.-Sat. 10-5, Sun. noon-4, May-Sept.; Mon.-Sat. 10-4, Sun. noon-4, rest of year. Weekend events are held May-Oct.; phone ahead for information. Closed Jan. 1, Thanksgiving and Christmas. **Cost:** $12; $10 (ages 65+, and active and retired military with ID); $6 (college students ages 18-25 with ID); $5 (ages 13-17); free (ages 0-12). **Phone:** (928) 445-3122.

William C. Bashford House, part of the Sharlot Hall Museum complex at 415 W. Gurley St., was built in 1877 and represents the late Victorian style. The home is furnished in period. **Hours:** Mon.-Sat. 10-5, Sun. noon-4, May-Sept.; Mon.-Sat. 10-4, Sun. noon-4, rest of year. Weekend events are held May-Oct.; phone ahead for information. Closed Jan. 1, Thanksgiving and Christmas. **Cost:** $12; $10 (ages 65+, and active and retired military with ID); $6 (college students ages 18-25 with ID); $5 (ages 13-17); free (ages 0-12). **Phone:** (928) 445-3122.

GAMBLING ESTABLISHMENTS

- **Bucky's Casino,** in the Prescott Resort at 1500 E. SR 69, just e. of jct. SR 89. **Hours:** Daily 24 hours. **Phone:** (928) 778-7909 or (800) 756-8744.

BEST WESTERN PRESCOTTONIAN 928/445-3096

Motel

Best Western **AAA Benefit:** Members save up to 15% and earn bonus points!

Address: 1317 E Gurley St 86301 **Location:** On SR 89, just s of jct SR 69. **Facility:** 121 units, some two bedrooms. 2-3 stories (no elevator), exterior corridors. **Pool:** heated outdoor. **Guest Services:** coin laundry. **Featured Amenity: breakfast buffet.**

SAVE BIZ / SOME UNITS

HAMPTON INN PRESCOTT 928/443-5500

SAVE Hotel. **Address:** 3453 Ranch Dr 86303

AAA Benefit: Members save up to 15%!

HASSAYAMPA INN 928/778-9434

Historic Hotel. **Address:** 122 E Gurley St 86301

HOLIDAY INN EXPRESS PRESCOTT 928/445-8900

Hotel. **Address:** 3454 Ranch Dr 86303

HOTEL ST. MICHAEL 928/776-1999

Historic Hotel. **Address:** 205 W Gurley St 86301

HOTEL VENDOME 928/776-0900

Historic Hotel. **Address:** 230 S Cortez St 86303

PRESCOTT RESORT & CONFERENCE CENTER 928/776-1666

Hotel

Address: 1500 Hwy 69 86301 **Location:** Jct SR 69, just e. **Facility:** 161 units. 4 stories, interior corridors. **Amenities:** safes. **Pool:** heated indoor. **Activities:** sauna, hot tub, exercise room, spa. **Guest Services:** valet laundry.

SAVE CALL BIZ HS

QUALITY INN 928/776-1282

Motel. **Address:** 1105 E Sheldon St 86301

RESIDENCE INN BY MARRIOTT 928/775-2232

Extended Stay Hotel

Residence INN **AAA Benefit:** Members save 5% or more!

Address: 3599 Lee Cir 86301 **Location:** Jct SR 69, just n on Lee Blvd, then just e. **Facility:** 93 kitchen units, some two bedrooms. 3 stories, interior corridors. **Pool:** heated outdoor. **Activities:** hot tub, exercise room. **Guest Services:** valet and coin laundry. **Featured Amenity: breakfast buffet.**

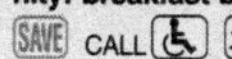

SAVE CALL BIZ / SOME UNITS

WHERE TO EAT

BARBUDOS MEXICAN GRILL & CANTINA 928/443-0102

Mexican. Casual Dining. **Address:** 1042 Willow Creek Rd, Suite 107 86301

THE BARLEY HOUND 928/237-4506

American. Gastropub. **Address:** 234 S Cortez St 86303

BISTRO ST. MICHAEL 928/778-2500

American. Casual Dining. **Address:** 100 S Montezuma St 86301

EL GATO AZUL 928/445-1070

Mediterranean Small Plates. Casual Dining. **Address:** 316 W Goodwin St 86303

FARM PROVISIONS 928/776-3001

American. Casual Dining. **Address:** 148 N Montezuma St 86301

GENOVESE'S 928/771-9032

Italian. Casual Dining. **Address:** 217 W Gurley St 86301

MURPHY'S RESTAURANT 928/445-4044

American. Casual Dining. **Address:** 201 N Cortez St 86301

OFFICE CANTINA RESTAURANT & BAR 928/445-1211

Southwestern. Casual Dining. **Address:** 128 N Cortez St 86301

THE PALACE RESTAURANT AND SALOON 928/541-1996

American. Casual Dining. **Address:** 120 S Montezuma St 86301

PAPA'S ITALIAN RESTAURANT 928/776-4880

Italian. Casual Dining. **Address:** 129-1/2 N Cortez St 86303

PEACOCK DINING ROOM 928/778-9434

American. Fine Dining. **Address:** 122 E Gurley St 86301

PRESCOTT BREWING COMPANY 928/771-2795

American Brewpub
$9-$17

AAA Inspector Notes: This place is always packed for the freshly brewed beer, nightly specials and freshly baked items. The in-house baked pizza is always amazing, but I would recommend visiting on Tuesday for the BBQ beef brisket special. **Features:** full bar, happy hour. **Address:** 130 W Gurley St, Suite A 86301 **Location:** Between Cortez and Montezuma sts; downtown. **Parking:** street only. L D

RAVEN CAFE 928/717-0009

European Natural/Organic Sandwiches. Casual Dining. **Address:** 142 N Cortez St 86301

SHANNON'S GOURMET CHEESECAKES 928/776-0133

American. Casual Dining. **Address:** 208 W Gurley St 86301

TAJ MAHAL 928/445-5752

Northern Indian. Casual Dining. **Address:** 124 N Montezuma St 86301

THE WAFFLE IRON 928/445-9944

Breakfast Sandwiches. Casual Dining. **Address:** 420 E Sheldon St 86301

ZEKE'S EATIN' PLACE 928/776-4602

American. Casual Dining. **Address:** 1781 E Hwy 69, Suite 35 86301

PRESCOTT NATIONAL FOREST (C-3)

Elevations in the forest range from 3,071 ft. in the Verde Valley to 7,971 ft. at Mount Union. Refer to AAA maps for additional elevation information.

Accessed via SR 89, SR 89A and SR 69 off I-17 in central Arizona, Prescott National Forest encompasses two long mountain ranges with varying elevations. In addition to its major access routes, other scenic but primitive roads not recommended for low-clearance vehicles penetrate the 1,238,154-acre forest. Phone ahead for current road condition updates.

Developed recreation areas are at Mingus Mountain and in Prescott Basin. The forest also contains Granite Mountain Trail (a National Recreation Trail), and Lynx Lake where boating and fishing take place all year. Camping, picnicking, hiking, backpacking, mountain biking and horseback riding are popular recreational pursuits in the forest; many trails can be enjoyed year-round. Groom Creek is an equestrian-only campground. Most campgrounds are first-come, first-served; Lynx Campground and Groom Creek accept reservations. Some popular day-use areas in Prescott have a $5 parking fee. Hunting is permitted in season with the appropriate state game license obtained from the Game and Fish Department (Kingman office); phone (928) 692-7700.

For further information contact Prescott National Forest, Bradshaw Ranger District, 344 S. Cortez St., Prescott, AZ 86303; phone (928) 443-8000 Mon.-Fri. 8-4:30. *See Recreation Areas Chart.*

PRESCOTT VALLEY pop. 38,822

COMFORT SUITES PRESCOTT VALLEY 928/771-2100

Hotel

Address: 2601 N Crownpointe Dr 86314 **Location:** Just w on SR 69, just n on Market St. **Facility:** 100 units. 4 stories, interior corridors. **Pool:** heated outdoor. **Activities:** hot tub, exercise room. **Guest Services:** valet and coin laundry. **Featured Amenity: full hot breakfast.**

SAVE CALL BIZ HS

/SOME UNITS

HAMPTON INN & SUITES BY HILTON PRESCOTT VALLEY 928/772-1800

SAVE Hotel. **Address:** 2901 N Glassford Hill Rd 86314

AAA Benefit: Members save up to 15%!

WHERE TO EAT

GARCIA'S MEXICAN RESTAURANT 928/759-9499

Mexican. Casual Dining. **Address:** 2992 N Park Ave, Suite B 86314

PRESIDIO SANTA CRUZ DE TERRENATE NATIONAL HISTORIC SITE (F-5)

Presidio Santa Cruz de Terrenate National Historic Site is 4 miles north of Tombstone on SR 80, 6 miles west on SR 82 to Fairbank, .75 miles west to In Balance Ranch Road, then 2 miles north in the San Pedro Riparian National Conservation Area. Established by the Spanish in 1776 on the banks of the San Pedro River, the presidio was built to protect the overland route east of Tucson. Because of the frequent Apache raids as well as the lack of proper supplies, Terrenate was abandoned less than 5 years after its establishment.

The site, once consisting of seven structures built around a central courtyard, contains signs showing what each of the structures originally looked like. Many of the adobe walls that surrounded the presidio are eroded and only a few remain. They were planned to be 15 feet tall, but were built to only 12 feet due to lack of funds. In addition, the bastion/gunpowder storehouse was never completed, and less than one-fourth of the planned barracks were never constructed because of insufficient funding.

The historic site is fragile, and visitors are instructed by signs to stay on the trails and not to touch the remaining structures. A 1.2-mile dirt trail leads from the parking lot to the presidio. Camping is permitted. Visitors should bring their own food and water as no facilities are available. Site admission free. Camping $2 per person per night. Phone (520) 439-6400.

QUARTZSITE (D-1) pop. 3,677, elev. 876'

A settler named Charles Tyson built a fort on this site in 1856 for protection against Native Americans. Because of a good water supply it soon became a stagecoach stop on the Ehrenburg-to-Prescott route. As the stage lines vanished, Fort Tyson, or Tyson's Wells (as it became known), was abandoned. A small mining boom in 1897 revitalized the area, and the settlement revived as Quartzsite.

The winter population of this desert town swells to 1 million during January and February because of the gem and mineral shows in the area. The Pow Wow Rock and Mineral Show began the rockhound winter migration to town in 1965; now 10 major shows entice gem enthusiasts, collectors and jewelers to Quartzsite to buy and sell. In an event that has attained international scope, thousands of dealers offer raw and handcrafted merchandise throughout January and February.

Quartzsite Area Chamber of Commerce & Tourism Center: 1240 W. Main St., P.O. Box 640, Quartzsite, AZ 85346. **Phone:** (928) 927-5200.

SAFFORD (E-6) pop. 9,566, elev. 2,920'

The first American colony in the Gila Valley, Safford was founded in 1874 by farmers whose previous holdings had been washed away by the Gila River. From Safford the Swift Trail winds 36 miles to the top of 10,720-foot Mount Graham. En route the trail traverses five of the seven ecological zones in Western North America. Camping, hiking and picnicking are permitted. Gila Box Riparian National Conservation Area, 15 miles northeast, offers seasonal river floating opportunities.

The region south of Safford is known for its hot mineral water baths. Information about area spas is available from the chamber of commerce. One popular spot is Hot Well Dunes, which has two artesian mineral wells now turned into hot tubs. The area also is popular with off-road enthusiasts.

For seekers of fire agates and other semiprecious stones, there are two rockhound areas administered and maintained by the U.S. Bureau of Land Management. Black Hills Back Country Byway is a 21-mile scenic drive through the Black Hills. The drive is a graded dirt road with sharp turns and steep drops.

Round Mountain Rockhound Area, featuring chalcedony roses and fire agates, is 12 miles south of Duncan on US 70, west at Milepost 5.6, 7.1 miles to the BLM sign, then 2.5 miles south to the first collection area. A second collection area is 4.5 miles south using the left fork in the road. **Note:** The road is not maintained and is very rough. Because of the area's remote location, visitors should bring along plenty of water and gasoline. Phone ahead for road conditions. Information about these areas can be obtained by contacting the Bureau of Land Management, 711 14th Ave., Safford, AZ 85546; phone (928) 348-4400.

Graham County Chamber of Commerce: 1111 Thatcher Blvd., Safford, AZ 85546. **Phone:** (928) 428-2511 or (888) 837-1841.

EASTERN ARIZONA COLLEGE DISCOVERY PARK CAMPUS is at 1651 W. Discovery Park Blvd. Located at the base of Mount Graham, this site offers both nature and science enthusiasts an interactive experience. Trail paths with viewing areas feature diverse wildlife and ponds while the Gov Aker Observatory contains exhibits relating to time and space. A Space Shuttle Polaris simulator takes visitors on a virtual tour of the solar system. . **Note:** Rattlesnakes and Gila monsters roam the trails; use caution when walking. **Time:** Allow 30 minutes minimum. **Hours:** Campus open Mon.-Fri. 8-5, Sat. 4-9:30. Simulator Mon.-Thurs. 8-4, Sat. 4-9. Closed major holidays. **Cost:** Free. A fee may apply during special events. **Phone:** (928) 428-6260.

BEST WESTERN DESERT INN 928/428-0521

Motel

AAA Benefit: Members save up to 15% and earn bonus points!

Address: 1391 W Thatcher Blvd 85546 **Location:** US 191, 1 mi w on US 70. **Facility:** 66 units. 2 stories (no elevator), exterior corridors. **Pool:** outdoor. **Guest Services:** coin laundry. **Featured Amenity: breakfast buffet.**

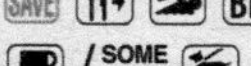

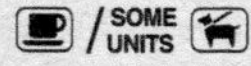

WHERE TO EAT

CASA MAÑANA 928/428-3170

Mexican. Casual Dining. **Address:** 502 S 1st Ave 85546

COPPER STEER STEAKHOUSE 928/348-8400

Steak. Casual Dining. **Address:** 1206 E US Hwy 70 85546

MANOR HOUSE 928/428-7148

American. Casual Dining. **Address:** 415 E Hwy 70 85546

SAGUARO NATIONAL PARK (F-5)

• **Attractions map p. 197**
• **Part of Tucson area — see map p. 187**

Elevations in the park range from 2,500ft. on the desert floor along the loop roads to 8,666 ft. at Mica Mountain. Refer to AAA maps for additional elevation information.

Separated by the city of Tucson *(see place listing p. 186)*, Saguaro National Park is divided into two districts: Rincon Mountain (Saguaro East) is about 15 miles east of Tucson via Old Spanish Trail, and Tucson Mountain (Saguaro West) is 15 miles west via Speedway Boulevard. Both districts typify the Sonoran arboreal desert and contain stands of saguaro cacti, known for their sometimes humanlike shapes.

The saguaro grows only in southern Arizona, in California along the Colorado River and in the northern Mexican state of Sonora. It can live more than 200 years, attaining heights of 30 to 40 feet; a few exceptional ones exceed 50 feet. Its blossom, the state flower, appears in May and June. Native Americans use its fruit for food and as a beverage base.

In addition to protecting the saguaro and other desert vegetation of the Sonoran Desert, the park's Saguaro West district has rock formations decorated with Native American petroglyphs and designs.

At the park headquarters in Saguaro East a visitor center contains plant and animal exhibits and offers nature programs; phone (520) 733-5153. The 8-mile Cactus Forest Drive begins at the visitor center parking lot. Picnic facilities are available. Saguaro West's unpaved 5-mile Bajada Loop Drive winds through dense stands of saguaro cacti. A visitor center has exhibits, a slide show and interpretive programs; phone (520) 733-5158.

Saguaro East and Saguaro West are open to vehicles daily 7 a.m.-dusk; 24 hours for visitors on foot or bicycle. Visitor centers open daily 9-5; closed Thanksgiving and Christmas. Admission to Saguaro East or Saguaro West is by 7-day or annual permit. A 7-day permit costs $20 (per private vehicle); $15 (per motorcycle); $10 (for ages 16+ arriving by other means). Backcountry backpacking is by permit only in Saguaro East; no drive-in camping permitted. For additional information contact the Superintendent, Saguaro National Park, 3693 S. Old Spanish Tr., Tucson, AZ 85730-5601; phone (520) 733-5153. *See Recreation Areas Chart.*

SCOTTSDALE (I-3) pop. 217,385, elev. 1,259'

• **Hotels p. 149 • Restaurants p. 157**
• **Hotels & Restaurants map & index p. 120**
• **Part of Phoenix area — see map p. 91**

Scottsdale was named for Chaplain Winfield Scott, Civil War veteran and retired military man who in 1888 purchased some farmland near the center of present-day Scottsdale. The city's slogan, "The West's Most Western Town," certainly applies to the wooden storefronts and hitching posts of Old Town Scottsdale. But the rest of the city is better described as "South Beach meets the Sonoran Desert."

(See map & index p. 120.)

Chic and sophisticated, Scottsdale is home to more than 100 art galleries, an array of specialty stores, fine dining, hip nightlife, plush resorts and golf courses galore. In short, this is the Valley of the Sun's tourist hot spot.

Indian Bend Wash Greenbelt along Hayden Road offers 7 miles of trails for bicyclists and runners. McCormick-Stillman Railroad Park, 7301 E. Indian Bend Rd., (480) 312-2312, offers 1-mile rides on a scale train. Several full-size railroad cars, a 1907 locomotive, playgrounds and an operating 1950s carousel are in the park. Picnic facilities are available.

The free Scottsdale trolley is a handy way to get around the downtown area. Following a route that includes stops at Old Town, the Arts District and Scottsdale Fashion Square, the trolley operates daily (except January 1, Memorial Day, July 4, Labor Day, Thanksgiving and Christmas) 11-9 and runs every 10 minutes. For route maps and more information check hotel brochure racks, or phone (480) 312-7250 or (800) 782-1117.

Experience Scottsdale Tourist Information Center: 7014 E. Camelback Rd., Scottsdale, AZ 85251. **Phone:** (480) 421-1004 or (800) 782-1117.

Self-guiding tours: Maps detailing self-guiding walking tours of Scottsdale's Old Town are available from the convention and visitors bureau. There's also a self-serve information kiosk loaded with maps and brochures at the corner of Main Street and Brown Avenue.

Shopping: Arizona's answer to Santa Fe, New Mexico, downtown Scottsdale is one of the biggest art gallery centers in the Southwest. Fine art collectors armed with high-limit plastic will want to head for the Arts District, along palm-lined Main Street (just w. of Scottsdale Rd.) and Marshall Way (between Main St. and 5th Ave.)

The Knox Artifacts & David Stock Native Art (7056 E. Main St.) is a must for collectors of Pre-Columbian and Native American art.

If your taste leans more toward abstract squiggles on a huge white canvas, the Gebert Contemporary Art Gallery (7160 E. Main St.) deals in cutting-edge paintings and sculptures by established international artists. For modern art that's a bit more accessible to the masses, Xanadu Gallery (7039 E. Main St., #101) sells beautiful glass art, jewelry, paintings, photography and intriguing contemporary sculptures; some of it is surprisingly affordable.

The weekly Scottsdale ArtWalk (held Thursday 7 p.m.-9 p.m., except Thanksgiving) is a fun way to get acquainted with the area. Many of the galleries stay open late for this "open house" event, which occasionally features live music and artist demonstrations.

If souvenirs are more your speed, Old Town Scottsdale (a four-block area bounded by Scottsdale Road, Indian School Road, Brown Avenue and 2nd Street) is loaded with trinket shops selling everything from fridge magnets to toy tomahawks. For authentic Native American crafts, try Bischoff's Shades of the West (7247 E. Main St.) or Gilbert Ortega Galleries (3925 N. Scottsdale Rd.).

Old Town's wooden storefronts may very well put you in the mood to don Western duds. Saba's Famous Texas Boots (7254 Main St.) stocks brand names like Tony Lama and Nocona. Az-Tex Hats & Gifts (3903 N. Scottsdale Rd.) has a nice selection of quality cowboy hats and straw sun hats but, beware, prices are steep.

For clothes you might actually wear back home, head for the funky boutiques and shops lining 5th Avenue (between Scottsdale Rd. and Marshall Way). A relaxed shady lane, the 5th Avenue shopping district also has jewelry stores, art galleries and a sprinkling of casual sidewalk cafés.

Just north of 5th Avenue is the Scottsdale Waterfront, a 5-acre mixed-use development spread along the banks of the Arizona Canal. The complex features a handful of mall stores (High Point, Urban Outfitters), restaurants and the Ellie & Michael Ziegler Fiesta Bowl Museum (7135 E. Camelback Rd., #190), a must-visit for college football fans; phone (480) 350-0900.

A massive three-story mall, Scottsdale Fashion Square (at the corner of Camelback and Scottsdale roads) has more than 250 stores, including upscale anchor Neiman Marcus. Scottsdale Quarter (15059 N. Scottsdale Rd.) is a 28-acre shopping district featuring retail, restaurant and entertainment options as well as office space. Retailers include Apple Store, H & M, Lululemon, Nike, Pottery Barn and Sephora.

Shopping Tours: Spree! The Art of Shopping is an upscale shopping service and experience for those who want to channel their inner Carrie Bradshaw. Several round-trip tour packages are available and power shoppers have the choice of being picked up in either a limousine or luxury sedan. Tours run approximately 3 hours and advance reservations of at least 24 hours are required; phone (480) 201-5480 for more information or to make reservations.

Nightlife: Scottsdale lays claim to the valley's hottest dance club scene. You'll find the trendiest spots in the dozen-or-so city blocks southeast of the intersection of Scottsdale and Camelback roads.

For those with country in their hearts and a love of live music, there's the Rusty Spur Saloon (7245 E. Main St.). Scottsdale's last real cowboy saloon is housed in the former Farmers Bank of Scottsdale. Celebrities including Clint Eastwood, John Wayne, Vince Vaughn and Jennifer Aniston have walked through its swinging doors.

For a good old Budweiser-fueled, boot-scootin' night on the town, head for Handlebar J (7116 E. Becker Ln.). A Scottsdale landmark since 1966, the club has live country music nightly, plus free country dance lessons every Thursday at 6:45. Line dancing lessons are offered Tuesday at 6:30. Phone (480) 948-0110.

(See map & index p. 120.)

SCOTTSDALE CIVIC CENTER MALL, 3939 N. Drinkwater Blvd., includes a library, municipal buildings, a park, fountains, sculptures, a pond and landscaped lawns. Also on the mall is the Scottsdale Center for the Performing Arts, a forum for the visual and performing arts. **Cost:** Free. **Phone:** (480) 312-3111, or (480) 499-8587 for performing arts center.

Scottsdale Historical Museum, 7333 E. Scottsdale Mall, is housed in a 1909 red brick grammar school furnished in period. A replica of a barbershop, complete with a barber chair and tools, and an old-fashioned kitchen are featured. Other exhibits include a display of town memorabilia and a replica of a 1900 schoolroom. Rotating exhibits change every 2 to 3 months. **Time:** Allow 30 minutes minimum. **Hours:** Wed.-Sat. 10-5, Sun. noon-4, Oct.-May; Wed.-Sat. 10-2, Sun. noon-4, in Sept. Closed major holidays. **Cost:** Free. **Phone:** (480) 945-4499.

Scottsdale Museum of Contemporary Art, 7374 E. 2nd St. in the Scottsdale Civic Center Mall, features contemporary art, architecture and design from Arizona and around the world. Exhibitions rotate throughout the year and are accompanied by programs and events. **Hours:** Tues.-Sun. noon-5 (also Thurs.-Sat. 5-9). Closed major holidays. **Cost:** $10; $7 (students with ID); free (ages 0-15 and for all Thurs. noon-9 and Fri.-Sat. 5-9). **Phone:** (480) 874-4666.

GEM **TALIESIN WEST,** 12345 N. Taliesin Dr., was the winter home and studio of architect Frank Lloyd Wright. On nearly 500 acres of Sonoran Desert at the foothills of the McDowell Mountains, the complex of buildings is connected by gardens, terraces and walkways. Taliesin West is the international headquarters for the Frank Lloyd Wright Foundation.

Tours include a 1-hour Panorama Tour, a 2-hour Details Tour, a 90-minute Insights Tour, a 2.5-hour Behind the Scenes Tour and a 2-hour Night Lights Tour. The Panorama Tour provides a basic introduction to the complex and Wright's theories of architecture. The Insights Tour encompasses the famed Living Room and Wright's private living quarters. The Details Tour is identical to the Insights Tour but proceeds at a leisurely pace. The Behind the Scenes Tour includes tea in the colorful dining room. The Night Lights Tour shows visitors the home at night. Other tours are available.

Note: Tours may be canceled due to inclement weather; phone ahead to confirm. Walking shoes and sun protection are recommended. **Time:** Allow 1 hour minimum. **Hours:** Panorama Tour departs daily at 10:15 and 2:15, Sept.-May; Thurs.-Mon. at 10:15, rest of year. Insights Tour departs every 30 minutes daily 9-4, Nov.-Apr.; every hour daily 9-4 in May and Sept.-Oct.; every 30 minutes Thurs.-Mon. 9-1, rest of year. Details Tour departs Thurs.-Mon. at 11:30 a.m. Behind the Scenes Tour departs Mon., Thurs. and Sat. at 9:15. Night Lights Tour departs Fri. at 6:30, 7 and 7:15 p.m., in May and Oct.; Fri. at 6, 6:30 and 7 p.m., Feb.-Apr.; Fri. at 6:30, June-Sept. Closed Easter, Thanksgiving and Christmas. Phone ahead to confirm schedule.

Cost: Panorama Tour $30; $25 (ages 60+ and students and active military with ID); $12 (ages 4-12). Insights Tour $40; $35 (ages 60+ and students and active military with ID); $19 (ages 6-12). Details Tour (Fri.-Sun.) $45; (Mon. and Thurs.) $40. Behind the Scenes Tour $70; reservations are required. Night Lights Tour $45; reservations are required. Rates may vary and combination rates may be available; phone ahead. Tours not recommended for children ages 0-5, unless in strollers or parents' arms. Reservations are highly recommended. **Phone:** (480) 860-2700, ext. 5462 for recorded tour information, or (888) 516-0811 for reservations. GT

RECREATIONAL ACTIVITIES

Hot Air Ballooning

- **Rainbow Ryders, Inc. Hot Air Balloon Ride Co.** departs from various locations for flights over the Sonoran Desert. **Hours:** Daily at dawn and dusk (weather permitting), Nov.-Mar.; daily at dawn, rest of year. **Phone:** (480) 299-0154 or (800) 725-2477. ***(See ad p. 100.)*** GT

ALOFT SCOTTSDALE 480/253-3700 43

Hotel

AAA Benefit: Members save 5% or more!

Address: 4415 N Civic Center Plaza 85251 **Location:** Scottsdale Rd, just e on Camelback Rd, just s on 75th St. **Facility:** 126 units. 5 stories, interior corridors. *Bath:* shower only. **Amenities:** safes. **Pool:** heated outdoor. **Activities:** exercise room. **Guest Services:** valet laundry.

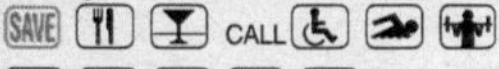

/SOME UNITS

ANDAZ SCOTTSDALE RESORT & BUNGALOWS 480/368-1234 32

Resort Hotel

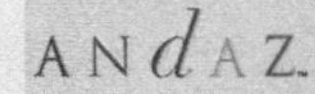

AAA Benefit: Members save up to 10%!

Address: 6114 N Scottsdale Rd 85253 **Location:** Jct Lincoln Dr, just s. **Facility:** This resort's secluded location, at the base of Camelback Mountain near the heart of the city, can't be beat. Guest rooms feature a private terrace, beautiful furnishings and a unique, modern décor. 201 units, some two bedrooms and houses. 1 story, exterior corridors. *Bath:* shower only. **Parking:** on-site and valet. **Terms:** check-in 4 pm. **Amenities:** safes. **Pool:** heated outdoor. **Activities:** hot tub, steamroom, cabanas, recreation programs, health club, spa. **Guest Services:** valet laundry, area transportation.

(See map & index p. 120.)

BEST WESTERN PLUS SCOTTSDALE THUNDERBIRD SUITES
480/951-4000 13

AAA Benefit: Members save up to 15% and earn bonus points!

Address: 7515 E Butherus Dr 85260 **Location:** 0.5 mi e of jct Scottsdale Rd. Located at Scottsdale Municipal Airport. **Facility:** 120 units. 4 stories, interior/exterior corridors. **Pool:** heated outdoor. **Activities:** hot tub, exercise room. **Guest Services:** valet and coin laundry, area transportation. **Featured Amenity: breakfast buffet.**

/ SOME UNITS

BEST WESTERN PLUS SUNDIAL
480/994-4170 42

AAA Benefit: Members save up to 15% and earn bonus points!

Address: 7320 E Camelback Rd 85251 **Location:** Just e of Scottsdale Rd. **Facility:** 54 units. 3 stories, exterior corridors. **Amenities:** safes. **Pool:** heated outdoor. **Activities:** hot tub, exercise room. **Guest Services:** valet and coin laundry. **Featured Amenity: breakfast buffet.**

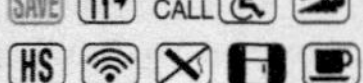
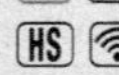

/ SOME UNITS

▼ See AAA listing p. 151 ▼

(See map & index p. 120.)

THE CANYON SUITES AT THE PHOENICIAN, A LUXURY COLLECTION RESORT, SCOTTSDALE
480/423-2880 35

THE LUXURY COLLECTION **AAA Benefit:** Members save 5% or more!

Address: 6000 E Camelback Rd 85251 **Location:** 0.5 mi w of 64th St; in The Phoenician, A Luxury Collection Resort, Scottsdale. **Facility:** This elegant resort is nestled at the base of Camelback Mountain. Ambassadors tend to every guest's needs with such comforts as nightly wine tastings and a "tub turn down" with scented bath water. 60 units, some kitchens. 2 stories, interior corridors. **Parking:** on-site and valet. **Terms:** check-in 4 pm. **Amenities:** safes. **Pool:** heated outdoor. **Activities:** hot tub, kids club, bicycles, lawn sports, trails, health club, spa. **Guest Services:** valet laundry, rental car service, luggage security pick-up, area transportation. **Featured Amenity: full hot breakfast.** *(See ad p. 150.)*

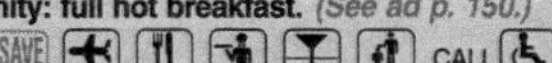

COMFORT SUITES OLD TOWN 480/946-1111 50
Hotel. **Address:** 3275 N Drinkwater Blvd 85251

COURTYARD BY MARRIOTT SCOTTSDALE AT MAYO CLINIC 480/860-4000
Hotel. **Address:** 13444 E Shea Blvd 85259

AAA Benefit: Members save 5% or more!

COURTYARD BY MARRIOTT/SCOTTSDALE NORTH
480/922-8400 6

COURTYARD **AAA Benefit:** Members save 5% or more!

Address: 17010 N Scottsdale Rd 85255 **Location:** Just n of Frank Lloyd Wright Blvd. **Facility:** 153 units. 3 stories, interior corridors. **Amenities:** safes. **Pool:** heated outdoor. **Activities:** hot tub, exercise room. **Guest Services:** valet and coin laundry, boarding pass kiosk, area transportation.

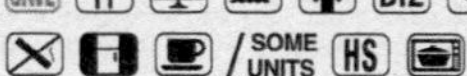

COURTYARD BY MARRIOTT SCOTTSDALE OLD TOWN
480/429-7785 49

COURTYARD **AAA Benefit:** Members save 5% or more!

Address: 3311 N Scottsdale Rd 85251 **Location:** Jct Drinkwater Blvd. **Facility:** 180 units. 5 stories, interior corridors. **Parking:** on-site (fee). **Pool:** heated outdoor. **Activities:** hot tub, exercise room. **Guest Services:** valet and coin laundry, boarding pass kiosk.

COURTYARD BY MARRIOTT SCOTTSDALE SALT RIVER
480/745-8200 39
Hotel. **Address:** 5201 N Pima Rd 85250

AAA Benefit: Members save 5% or more!

DOUBLETREE RESORT BY HILTON PARADISE VALLEY-SCOTTSDALE
480/947-5400 34

Resort Hotel

AAA Benefit: Members save up to 15%!

Address: 5401 N Scottsdale Rd 85250 **Location:** Just n of Chaparral Rd; on east side of Scottsdale Rd. **Facility:** Guests will enjoy beautiful manicured grounds, luxurious pool areas, a basketball court and spacious guest rooms. All rooms have great views from a balcony or patio. 378 units. 2 stories, exterior corridors. **Parking:** on-site and valet. **Terms:** check-in 4 pm. **Amenities:** safes. **Dining:** 4 restaurants. **Pool:** heated outdoor. **Activities:** sauna, hot tub, steamroom, tennis, bicycles, health club, massage. **Guest Services:** valet laundry, rental car service, area transportation.

EMBASSY SUITES BY HILTON SCOTTSDALE RESORT
480/949-1414 37

Hotel

AAA Benefit: Members save up to 15%!

Address: 5001 N Scottsdale Rd 85250 **Location:** At Chaparral Rd. **Facility:** 312 units, some two bedrooms. 4 stories, exterior corridors. **Amenities:** safes. **Pool:** heated outdoor. **Activities:** hot tub, tennis, bicycles, exercise room. **Guest Services:** valet and coin laundry, area transportation. **Featured Amenity: breakfast buffet.**

FAIRFIELD BY MARRIOTT NORTH SCOTTSDALE
480/483-0042 15
Hotel. **Address:** 13440 N Scottsdale Rd 85254

AAA Benefit: Members save 5% or more!

(See map & index p. 120.)

FAIRMONT SCOTTSDALE PRINCESS
480/585-4848 **3**

Resort Hotel

Address: 7575 E Princess Dr 85255 **Location:** SR 101 exit 34 (Scottsdale Rd), 0.8 mi s, then just e; 0.6 mi n of Bell Rd. **Facility:** Each spacious unit at this expansive 64-acre luxury resort features a balcony or terrace. A world-class spa and elaborate pool areas add to the abundance of recreational and leisure activities. 750 units. 1-4 stories, interior/exterior corridors. **Parking:** on-site (fee) and valet. **Terms:** check-in 4 pm. **Amenities:** safes. **Dining:** 2 restaurants, also, Bourbon Steak, La Hacienda, Toro Latin Restaurant and Rum Bar, see separate listings. **Pool:** heated outdoor. **Activities:** sauna, hot tub, steamroom, fishing, regulation golf, recreation programs, kids club, bicycles, game room, lawn sports, trails, health club, spa. **Guest Services:** valet laundry, area transportation.

Scottsdale's perfect playcation destination turning moments into memories for over 30 years.

FOUR SEASONS RESORT SCOTTSDALE AT TROON NORTH
480/515-5700

Resort Hotel

Address: 10600 E Crescent Moon Dr 85262 **Location:** SR 101 exit 36 (Pima Rd), 4.7 mi n, 2 mi e on Happy Valley Rd, then 1.5 mi n on Alma School Rd. **Facility:** Well-designed landscaping seamlessly blends with the desert surroundings, allowing for striking views from the territorial-style casitas, each with a fireplace and terrace. 210 units, some two bedrooms. 1-3 stories, exterior corridors. **Parking:** on-site and valet. **Terms:** check-in 4 pm. **Amenities:** safes. **Dining:** 3 restaurants, also, Talavera, see separate listing. **Pool:** heated outdoor. **Activities:** sauna, hot tub, steamroom, regulation golf, tennis, recreation programs, kids club, lawn sports, trails, health club, spa. **Guest Services:** valet laundry, boarding pass kiosk, area transportation.

HAMPTON INN & SUITES BY HILTON PHOENIX/SCOTTSDALE ON SHEA BLVD
480/443-3233 **21**

SAVE Hotel. **Address:** 10101 N Scottsdale Rd 85253

AAA Benefit: Members save up to 15%!

HAMPTON INN & SUITES PHOENIX/SCOTTSDALE
480/348-9280 **9**

SAVE Hotel. **Address:** 16620 N Scottsdale Rd 85254

AAA Benefit: Members save up to 15%!

HAMPTON INN & SUITES SCOTTSDALE RIVERWALK
480/270-5393 **30**

SAVE Hotel. **Address:** 9550 E Talking Stick Way 85256

AAA Benefit: Members save up to 15%!

HILTON GARDEN INN SCOTTSDALE NORTH
480/515-4944 **4**

Hotel

Hilton Garden Inn **AAA Benefit:** Members save up to 15%!

Address: 8550 E Princess Dr 85255 **Location:** SR 101 exit 36 (Princess Dr/Pima Rd), just w. **Facility:** 122 units. 3 stories, interior corridors. **Terms:** check-in 4 pm. **Pool:** heated outdoor. **Activities:** hot tub, exercise room. **Guest Services:** valet and coin laundry, area transportation.

SAVE CALL BIZ HS

HILTON GARDEN INN SCOTTSDALE OLD TOWN
480/481-0400 **47**

SAVE Hotel. **Address:** 7324 E Indian School Rd 85251

AAA Benefit: Members save up to 15%!

HILTON SCOTTSDALE RESORT & VILLAS
480/948-7750 **31**

Hotel

Hilton HOTELS & RESORTS **AAA Benefit:** Members save up to 15%!

Address: 6333 N Scottsdale Rd 85250 **Location:** SR 101 exit 45, 2.1 mi w on McDonald Dr, then 0.3 mi n. **Facility:** Rooms feature chic, stylish décor that is highlighted by large TVs and high headboards. Relax and enjoy the tropical pool area, complete with a lounge and poolside food and beverage service. 235 units, some two bedrooms and kitchens. 2-3 stories, interior corridors. **Parking:** on-site and valet. **Terms:** check-in 4 pm. **Amenities:** safes. **Dining:** 3 restaurants. **Pool:** heated outdoor. **Activities:** sauna, hot tub, steamroom, exercise room, spa. **Guest Services:** valet laundry, rental car service, area transportation.

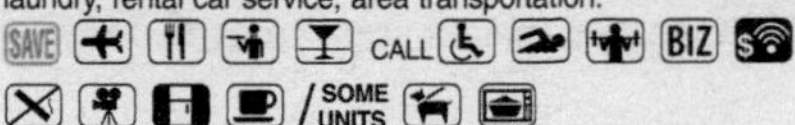

SOME UNITS

(See map & index p. 120.)

HOLIDAY INN & SUITES SCOTTSDALE NORTH-AIRPARK
480/922-6500 **14**

Hotel. **Address:** 14255 N 87th St 85260

HOLIDAY INN CLUB VACATIONS SCOTTSDALE RESORT 480/248-9001 **1**

Resort Condominium

Address: 7677 E Princess Blvd 85255 **Location:** SR 101 exit 34 (Scottsdale Rd), 0.8 mi s, then just e; 0.6 mi n of Bell Rd. **Facility:** This resort features lush landscaping with multiple pool areas and spacious guest rooms with fully equipped kitchens that are perfect for family getaways or long romantic weekends. 213 condominiums. 2-3 stories (no elevator), exterior corridors. **Terms:** check-in 4 pm. **Amenities:** safes. **Pool:** heated outdoor. **Activities:** hot tub, game room, picnic facilities, exercise room. **Guest Services:** complimentary laundry. *(See ad this page.)*

HOLIDAY INN EXPRESS HOTEL & SUITES-SCOTTSDALE OLD TOWN 480/675-7665 **51**

Hotel

Address: 3131 N Scottsdale Rd 85251 **Location:** Northeast corner of Scottsdale Rd and Earll Dr. **Facility:** 169 units. 3 stories, interior corridors. **Pool:** heated outdoor. **Activities:** hot tub, exercise room. **Guest Services:** valet and coin laundry, area transportation. **Featured Amenity: breakfast buffet.** *(See ad this page.)*

/ SOME UNITS HS

HOLIDAY INN EXPRESS SCOTTSDALE NORTH
480/596-6559 **18**

Hotel. **Address:** 7350 E Gold Dust Ave 85258

HOMEWOOD SUITES BY HILTON PHOENIX/SCOTTSDALE
480/368-8705 **22**

SAVE Extended Stay Hotel. **Address:** 9880 N Scottsdale Rd 85253

AAA Benefit: Members save up to 15%!

HOTEL BIXBY SCOTTSDALE, BW SIGNATURE COLLECTION BY BEST WESTERN 480/949-5115 **53**

SAVE Hotel. **Address:** 409 N Scottsdale Rd 85257

AAA Benefit: Members save up to 15% and earn bonus points!

(See map & index p. 120.)

HOTEL VALLEY HO

480/248-2000 48

Boutique Contemporary Retro Hotel

Address: 6850 E Main St 85251 **Location:** 0.4 mi w of Scottsdale Rd, just s of Indian School Rd; on north side of Main St. **Facility:** Maintaining the flavor of its 1950s origins, this classic gem offers fully retro-fitted trendy rooms with oversize posh baths. The tower suites offer full kitchens and balconies with sweeping views. 241 units, some kitchens and condominiums. 2-6 stories, interior/exterior corridors. **Parking:** on-site (fee) and valet. **Terms:** check-in 4 pm. **Amenities:** safes. **Dining:** Cafe Zu Zu, see separate listing. **Pool:** heated outdoor. **Activities:** sauna, hot tub, health club, spa. **Guest Services:** valet laundry, area transportation. Affiliated with Preferred Hotels & Resorts.

SAVE ECO BIZ HS / SOME UNITS

HYATT HOUSE SCOTTSDALE/OLD TOWN

480/946-7700 44

Extended Stay Hotel

HYATT house™ **AAA Benefit:** Members save up to 10%!

Address: 4245 N Drinkwater Blvd 85251 **Location:** 0.3 mi e of Scottsdale Rd. **Facility:** 164 units, some two bedrooms, efficiencies and kitchens. 3 stories (no elevator), exterior corridors. **Terms:** check-in 4 pm. **Pool:** heated outdoor. **Activities:** hot tub, picnic facilities, exercise room. **Guest Services:** valet and coin laundry, area transportation. **Featured Amenity: breakfast buffet.**

/ SOME UNITS

HYATT PLACE SCOTTSDALE/OLD TOWN

480/423-9944 45

Hotel

HYATT PLACE™ **AAA Benefit:** Members save up to 10%!

Address: 7300 E 3rd Ave 85251 **Location:** Just e of Scottsdale Rd. **Facility:** 126 units. 6 stories, interior corridors. **Amenities:** safes. **Pool:** heated outdoor. **Activities:** exercise room. **Guest Services:** valet laundry. **Featured Amenity: breakfast buffet.**

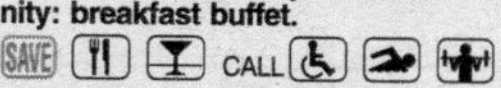

BIZ / SOME UNITS

HYATT REGENCY SCOTTSDALE RESORT & SPA

480/444-1234 23

Resort Hotel

AAA Benefit: Members save up to 10%!

Address: 7500 E Doubletree Ranch Rd 85258 **Location:** SR 101 exit 43, 2.6 mi w on Via de Ventura. **Facility:** This sprawling property offers something to please all family members with a three-story waterslide and a luxurious spa. Guests will love the stylish and spacious rooms with oversize televisions. 493 units, some two bedrooms. 4 stories, interior/exterior corridors. **Parking:** on-site (fee) and valet. **Terms:** check-in 4 pm. **Amenities:** safes. **Dining:** 3 restaurants, also, Alto Ristorante & Bar, see separate listing, entertainment. **Pool:** heated outdoor. **Activities:** sauna, hot tub, steamroom, regulation golf, tennis, recreation programs, kids club, bicycles, playground, lawn sports, health club, spa. **Guest Services:** valet laundry, boarding pass kiosk, rental car service, area transportation.

SAVE ECO CALL BIZ HS / SOME UNITS

JW MARRIOTT CAMELBACK INN RESORT & SPA

480/948-1700 28

Resort Hotel

AAA Benefit: Members save 5% or more!

Address: 5402 E Lincoln Dr 85253 **Location:** 0.5 mi e of Tatum Blvd; on north side of Lincoln Dr. **Facility:** This lovely resort, dating back to 1936, occupies 125 scenic acres and boasts elegant Southwestern décor with mountain views. Some of the Pueblo-style casitas have a private pool. 453 units, some efficiencies. 1-2 stories (no elevator), exterior corridors. **Parking:** on-site and valet. **Terms:** check-in 4 pm. **Amenities:** safes. **Dining:** 6 restaurants, entertainment. **Pool:** heated outdoor. **Activities:** sauna, hot tub, steamroom, regulation golf, tennis, recreation programs, bicycles, playground, lawn sports, exercise room, spa. **Guest Services:** complimentary and valet laundry, boarding pass kiosk, area transportation.

SAVE CALL BIZ HS / SOME UNITS

LA QUINTA INN & SUITES BY WYNDHAM PHOENIX SCOTTSDALE 480/614-5300 20

Hotel. **Address:** 8888 E Shea Blvd 85260

MAGNUSON HOTEL PAPAGO INN 480/947-7335 52

Hotel. **Address:** 7017 E McDowell Rd 85257

THE MCCORMICK SCOTTSDALE 480/948-5050 25

Hotel. **Address:** 7421 N Scottsdale Rd 85253

(See map & index p. 120.)

MOTEL 6 SCOTTSDALE #29 480/946-2280 **40**

Motel. **Address:** 6848 E Camelback Rd 85251

ORANGE TREE RESORT 480/948-6100 **16**

Resort Hotel. **Address:** 10601 N 56th St 85254

THE PHOENICIAN, A LUXURY COLLECTION RESORT, SCOTTSDALE 480/941-8200 **36**

Resort Hotel

THE LUXURY COLLECTION **AAA Benefit:** Members save 5% or more!

Address: 6000 E Camelback Rd 85251 **Location:** 0.5 mi w of 64th St. **Facility:** Tucked at the base of Camelback Mountain, this venerable resort features extensive landscaping, sweeping valley views, world-class dining and golf, a tropical lagoon and newly renovated elegant rooms. 585 units, some two bedrooms and kitchens. 3-4 stories, interior/exterior corridors. **Parking:** on-site (fee) and valet. **Terms:** check-in 4 pm. **Amenities:** safes. **Dining:** 5 restaurants, also, J&G Steakhouse, see separate listing, entertainment. **Pool:** heated outdoor. **Activities:** sauna, hot tub, steamroom, regulation golf, tennis, recreation programs, kids club, bicycles, playground, lawn sports, health club, spa. **Guest Services:** valet laundry, rental car service, luggage security pick-up, area transportation. **Featured Amenity: full hot breakfast.** *(See ad this page.)*

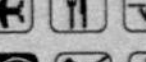

CALL

/ SOME UNITS

RESIDENCE INN BY MARRIOTT SCOTTSDALE NORTH 480/563-4120 **7**

SAVE Extended Stay Hotel. **Address:** 17011 N Scottsdale Rd 85255

AAA Benefit: Members save 5% or more!

RESIDENCE INN BY MARRIOTT, SCOTTSDALE/PARADISE VALLEY 480/948-8666 **33**

Extended Stay Hotel

Residence INN. **AAA Benefit:** Members save 5% or more!

Address: 6040 N Scottsdale Rd 85253 **Location:** Just n of McDonald Dr. **Facility:** 122 efficiencies, some two bedrooms. 2 stories (no elevator), interior/exterior corridors. **Pool:** heated outdoor. **Activities:** hot tub, picnic facilities, exercise room. **Guest Services:** valet and coin laundry. **Featured Amenity: continental breakfast.**

SAVE CALL BIZ

/ SOME UNITS

▼ *See AAA listing this page* ▼

(See map & index p. 120.)

THE SCOTT RESORT & SPA 480/945-7666 38

Hotel

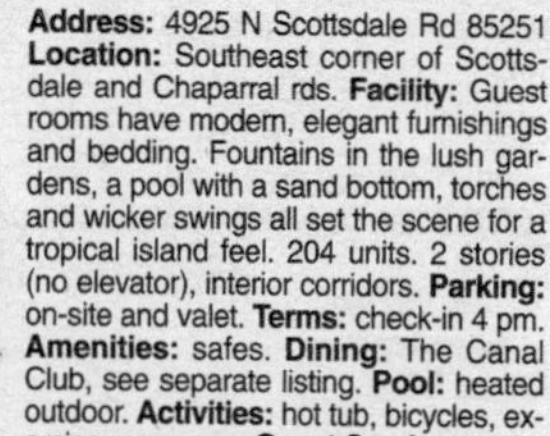

Address: 4925 N Scottsdale Rd 85251 **Location:** Southeast corner of Scottsdale and Chaparral rds. **Facility:** Guest rooms have modern, elegant furnishings and bedding. Fountains in the lush gardens, a pool with a sand bottom, torches and wicker swings all set the scene for a tropical island feel. 204 units. 2 stories (no elevator), interior corridors. **Parking:** on-site and valet. **Terms:** check-in 4 pm. **Amenities:** safes. **Dining:** The Canal Club, see separate listing. **Pool:** heated outdoor. **Activities:** hot tub, bicycles, exercise room, spa. **Guest Services:** valet laundry, area transportation.

SAVE ECO CALL BIZ / SOME UNITS

SCOTTSDALE MARRIOTT AT MCDOWELL MOUNTAINS 480/502-3836 10

SAVE Hotel. **Address:** 16770 N Perimeter Dr 85260

AAA Benefit: Members save 5% or more!

SCOTTSDALE MARRIOTT SUITES OLD TOWN 480/945-1550 46

SAVE Hotel. **Address:** 7325 E 3rd Ave 85251

AAA Benefit: Members save 5% or more!

THE SCOTTSDALE PLAZA RESORT 480/948-5000 27

Hotel

Address: 7200 N Scottsdale Rd 85253 **Location:** Just n of Indian Bend Rd. **Facility:** 404 units. 1-2 stories (no elevator), exterior corridors. **Parking:** on-site and valet. **Terms:** check-in 4 pm. **Amenities:** safes. **Dining:** 4 restaurants. **Pool:** heated outdoor. **Activities:** sauna, hot tub, tennis, health club, spa. **Guest Services:** valet laundry, area transportation.

SAVE BIZ / SOME UNITS

SCOTTSDALE RESORT & CONFERENCE CENTER 480/991-9000 26

Resort Hotel

Address: 7700 E McCormick Pkwy 85258 **Location:** Just w of Hayden Rd; 0.7 mi e of Scottsdale Rd. **Facility:** This sprawling property features lovely pools and a unique variety of room types. The hacienda-style rooms are luxuriously appointed, featuring patios, shaded courtyards and spacious public areas. 326 units. 2-3 stories, interior/exterior corridors. **Parking:** on-site and valet. **Terms:** check-in 4 pm. **Amenities:** safes. **Dining:** 3 restaurants. **Pool:** heated outdoor. **Activities:** sauna, bicycles, health club, spa. **Guest Services:** valet laundry. Affiliated with Destination Hotels.

SAVE ECO CALL BIZ / SOME UNITS

SHERATON DESERT OASIS 480/515-5888 2

SAVE Condominium. **Address:** 17700 N Hayden Rd 85255

AAA Benefit: Members save 5% or more!

SLEEP INN NORTH SCOTTSDALE/PHOENIX 480/998-9211 8

Hotel. **Address:** 16630 N Scottsdale Rd 85254

SONESTA SUITES SCOTTSDALE GAINEY RANCH 480/922-6969 24

Boutique Contemporary Hotel

Address: 7300 E Gainey Suites Dr 85258 **Location:** Just e of Scottsdale Rd. **Facility:** Suites are decorated with a southwestern contemporary flair. A wonderful courtyard lined with towering palm trees surrounds the pool and spa area. A complimentary evening reception is offered nightly. 162 efficiencies, some two bedrooms. 2-3 stories, interior corridors. **Amenities:** safes. **Pool:** heated outdoor. **Activities:** hot tub, exercise room. **Guest Services:** valet laundry, area transportation. **Featured Amenity: full hot breakfast.**

SAVE BIZ / SOME UNITS

SPRINGHILL SUITES BY MARRIOTT-SCOTTSDALE NORTH 480/922-8700 5

Hotel

AAA Benefit: Members save 5% or more!

Address: 17020 N Scottsdale Rd 85255 **Location:** Just n of Frank Lloyd Wright Blvd. Located in a commercial area. **Facility:** 121 units. 4 stories, interior corridors. **Amenities:** safes. **Pool:** heated outdoor. **Activities:** hot tub, exercise room. **Guest Services:** valet and coin laundry, area transportation. **Featured Amenity: full hot breakfast.**

SAVE CALL BIZ / SOME UNITS

TALKING STICK RESORT 480/850-7777 29

Resort Hotel

Address: 9800 E Talking Stick Way 85256 **Location:** SR 101 exit 44 (E Indian Bend Rd), just e. **Facility:** This expansive, upscale resort and casino combines outstanding entertainment, fine dining and luxurious guest rooms to bring a taste of Vegas to the Valley of the Sun. 496 units. 15 stories, interior corridors. **Parking:** on-site and valet. **Terms:** check-in 4 pm. **Amenities:** safes. **Dining:** 4 restaurants, also, Ocean Trail, Orange Sky, see separate listings, nightclub, entertainment. **Pool:** heated outdoor. **Activities:** hot tub, steamroom, regulation golf, game room, exercise room, spa. **Guest Services:** valet laundry, boarding pass kiosk, area transportation.

SAVE CALL BIZ HS

TOWNEPLACE SUITES BY MARRIOTT SCOTTSDALE 480/551-1100 19

SAVE Extended Stay Hotel. **Address:** 10740 N 90th St 85260

AAA Benefit: Members save 5% or more!

(See map & index p. 120.)

WE-KO-PA RESORT AND CONFERENCE CENTER 480/789-5300

Resort Hotel

Address: 10438 N Ft. McDowell Rd 85264 **Location:** Jct Shea Blvd, 1.6 mi ne on SR 87. Located in a rural area. **Facility:** Situated on Fort McDowell Yavapai Nation land, this property boasts newly refreshed guest rooms and baths reflecting an elegant southwest design. An abundance of outdoor activities are available. 246 units. 5 stories, interior corridors. **Parking:** on-site and valet. **Terms:** check-in 4 pm. **Amenities:** safes. **Dining:** 7 restaurants, also, Ahnala, see separate listing, entertainment. **Pool:** heated outdoor. **Activities:** hot tub, regulation golf, lawn sports, picnic facilities, trails, exercise room, spa. **Guest Services:** valet laundry, area transportation.

SAVE CALL BIZ / SOME UNITS

THE WESTIN KIERLAND RESORT & SPA 480/624-1000 12

Resort Hotel

WESTIN HOTELS & RESORTS **AAA Benefit:** Members save 5% or more!

Address: 6902 E Greenway Pkwy 85254 **Location:** 0.5 mi w of Scottsdale Rd. **Facility:** Located adjacent to two high-end shopping areas in North Scottsdale, this upscale resort offers spectacular golf course and mountain views. Guest rooms are spacious and feature patios or balconies. 732 units. 11 stories, interior corridors. **Parking:** on-site (fee) and valet. **Terms:** check-in 4 pm. **Amenities:** safes. **Dining:** 2 restaurants, also, Brittlebush Bar & Grill, Deseo, Nellie Cashman's Monday Club Cafe, see separate listings, entertainment. **Pool:** heated outdoor. **Activities:** sauna, hot tub, steamroom, regulation golf, tennis, recreation programs, kids club, bicycles, lawn sports, trails, health club, spa. **Guest Services:** valet laundry, area transportation.

SAVE ECO CALL BIZ sHS / SOME UNITS

THE WESTIN KIERLAND VILLAS 480/624-1700 11

Vacation Rental Condominium

AAA Benefit: Members save 5% or more!

Address: 15620 N Clubgate Dr 85254 **Location:** Jct Scottsdale Rd, 0.6 mi w on Greenway Pkwy, then just n. **Facility:** Elegant, attractively furnished rooms offer kitchens and balconies or patios; some overlook the golf course. Public space is limited, but privileges are offered at the nearby affiliated hotel. 298 condominiums. 3-4 stories, exterior corridors. **Terms:** check-in 4 pm. **Amenities:** safes. **Pool:** heated outdoor. **Activities:** sauna, hot tub, steamroom, regulation golf, recreation programs, kids club, bicycles, lawn sports, picnic facilities, trails, exercise room, massage. **Guest Services:** complimentary and valet laundry, area transportation.

W SCOTTSDALE 480/970-2100 41

Hotel. **Address:** 7277 E Camelback Rd 85251

AAA Benefit: Members save 5% or more!

WHERE TO EAT

AHNALA 480/836-5305

Regional Southwestern. Casual Dining. **Address:** 10438 N Ft. McDowell Rd 85264

ALL AMERICAN MODERN SPORTS GRILL 480/887-0652 5

American. Sports Bar. **Address:** 20751 N Pima Rd 85255

ALTO RISTORANTE & BAR 480/444-1234 36

Italian. Casual Dining. **Address:** 7500 E Doubletree Ranch Rd 85258

ARCADIA FARMS 480/941-5665 63

American. Casual Dining. **Address:** 7014 E 1st Ave 85251

ATLAS BISTRO 480/990-2433 75

International. Fine Dining. **Address:** 2515 N Scottsdale Rd 85257

BANDERA 480/994-3524 68

American. Casual Dining. **Address:** 3821 N Scottsdale Rd 85251

BLANCO TACOS + TEQUILA 480/305-6692 49

Mexican. Casual Dining. **Address:** 6166 N Scottsdale Rd 85253

BOURBON STEAK 480/513-6002 10

Steak Fine Dining $22-$175

AAA Inspector Notes: Acclaimed chef Michael Mina's Bourbon Steak offers a diverse range of delectable menu selections. Along with the tender Kobe and all-natural USDA Prime beef, diners will find Colorado lamb, Kurobuta pork, Maine lobster, ahi tuna and Scottish salmon, to name a few. An incredible dining experience awaits. **Features:** full bar, patio dining, happy hour. **Reservations:** suggested. **Address:** 7575 E Princess Dr 85255 **Location:** SR 101 exit 34 (Scottsdale Rd), 0.8 mi s, then just e; 0.6 mi n of Bell Rd; in Fairmont Scottsdale Princess. **Parking:** on-site and valet.

D CALL

THE BREAKFAST CLUB 480/222-2582 57

Breakfast. Casual Dining. **Address:** 4400 N Scottsdale Rd 85251

BRITTLEBUSH BAR & GRILL 480/624-1000 15

American. Casual Dining. **Address:** 6902 E Greenway Pkwy 85254

CAFE ZU ZU 480/421-7997 66

American. Casual Dining. **Address:** 6850 E Main St 85251

THE CANAL CLUB 480/424-6095 52

Caribbean. Casual Dining. **Address:** 4925 N Scottsdale Rd 85251

THE CAPITAL GRILLE 480/348-1700 14

Steak. Fine Dining. **Address:** 16489 N Scottsdale Rd 85254

CARLSBAD TAVERN 480/970-8164 72

Southwestern. Casual Dining. **Address:** 3313 N Hayden Rd 85251

CHOLLA PRIME STEAKHOUSE 480/850-7736 77

Regional Steak. Fine Dining. **Address:** 524 N 92nd St 85256

CITIZEN PUBLIC HOUSE 480/398-4208 60

American. Gastropub. **Address:** 7111 E 5th Ave 85251

(See map & index p. 120.)

DESEO 480/624-1202 (20)
New Latin American. Fine Dining. **Address:** 6902 E Greenway Pkwy 85254

DOMINICK'S STEAKHOUSE 480/272-7271 (29)
Steak. Fine Dining. **Address:** 15169 N Scottsdale Rd 85254

EDDIE MERLOT'S 480/699-0480 (2)
Steak. Fine Dining. **Address:** 23207 N Scottsdale Rd 85255

EDDIE V'S PRIME SEAFOOD 480/730-4800 (18)
Seafood. Fine Dining. **Address:** 15323 N Scottsdale Rd 85254

EVO 480/265-9814 (62)
Italian. Casual Dining. **Address:** 4175 N Goldwater Blvd 85251

FAT OX 480/307-6900 (46)
Italian. Fine Dining. **Address:** 6316 N Scottsdale Rd 85253

FLEMING'S PRIME STEAKHOUSE & WINE BAR
Steak. Fine Dining.
LOCATIONS:
Address: 6333 N Scottsdale Rd 85250
Phone: 480/596-8265 (45)
Address: 20753 N Pima Rd 85255 **Phone:** 480/538-8000 (6)

FNB RESTAURANT 480/284-4777 (61)
New American. Casual Dining. **Address:** 7125 E 5th Ave 85251

THE HERB BOX 480/289-6160 (58)
American. Casual Dining. **Address:** 7134 E Stetson Dr 85251

HIRO SUSHI 480/314-4215 (37)
Sushi. Casual Dining. **Address:** 9393 N 90th St 85258

JADE PALACE 480/391-0607 (34)
Chinese. Casual Dining. **Address:** 9160 E Shea Blvd 85260

JADE PALACE 480/585-6630 (1)
Chinese. Casual Dining. **Address:** 23623 N Scottsdale Rd 85255

JEWEL OF THE CROWN 480/949-8000 (69)
Indian. Casual Dining. **Address:** 7373 E Scottsdale Mall, Suite 1 85251

J&G STEAKHOUSE 480/214-8000 (50)

Steak
Fine Dining
$17-$66

AAA Inspector Notes: The first of many upscale steakhouses from chef Jean-Georges Vongerichten, this restaurant has commanding views of the valley. Fresh, local ingredients combine with premium cuts of meat and global seafood selections to create a memorable experience. **Features:** full bar, patio dining, happy hour. **Reservations:** suggested. **Address:** 6000 E Camelback Rd 85251 **Location:** 0.5 mi w of 64th St; in The Phoenician, A Luxury Collection Resort, Scottsdale. **Parking:** on-site and valet. D CALL

KASAI ASIAN GRILL 480/607-1114 (30)
Pacific Rim Sushi. Casual Dining. **Address:** 14344 N Scottsdale Rd 85254

KONA GRILL
Pacific Rim Fusion. Casual Dining.
LOCATIONS:
Address: 7014 E Camelback Rd 85251
Phone: 480/429-1100 (54)
Address: 15345 N Scottsdale Rd 85254
Phone: 480/378-8186 (19)

LA HACIENDA 480/585-4848 (11)
Mexican. Fine Dining. **Address:** 7575 E Princess Dr 85255

LINCOLN RESTAURANT 480/905-7979 (38)
Southwestern. Casual Dining. **Address:** 5402 E Lincoln Dr 85253

LING & LOUIE'S ASIAN BAR & GRILL 480/767-5464 (35)
Asian. Casual Dining. **Address:** 9397 E Shea Blvd 85260

LOS SOMBREROS 480/994-1799 (74)
Mexican. Casual Dining. **Address:** 2534 N Scottsdale Rd 85257

LUSH BURGER 480/686-8908 (9)
American. Casual Dining. **Address:** 18251 N Pima Rd 85255

MALEE'S THAI BISTRO 480/947-6042 (67)
Regional Thai. Casual Dining. **Address:** 7131 E Main St 85251

MARCELLINO RISTORANTE 480/990-9500 (59)
Italian. Fine Dining. **Address:** 7114 E Stetson Dr 85251

MASTRO'S CITY HALL STEAKHOUSE 480/941-4700 (55)
Steak. Fine Dining. **Address:** 6991 E Camelback Rd 85251

MASTRO'S OCEAN CLUB 480/443-8555 (22)
Seafood. Fine Dining. **Address:** 15045 N Kierland Blvd 85254

MASTRO'S STEAKHOUSE 480/585-9500 (4)
Steak. Fine Dining. **Address:** 8852 E Pinnacle Peak Rd 85260

THE MISSION 480/636-5005 (70)
Latin American. Casual Dining. **Address:** 3815 N Brown Ave 85251

MORTON'S THE STEAKHOUSE 480/951-4440 (17)
Steak. Fine Dining. **Address:** 15233 N Kierland Blvd 85254

NELLIE CASHMAN'S MONDAY CLUB CAFE 480/624-1000 (21)
New American. Casual Dining. **Address:** 6902 E Greenway Pkwy 85254

NORTH ITALIA 480/948-2055 (23)
New Italian. Casual Dining. **Address:** 15024 N Scottsdale Rd 85254

OCEAN TRAIL 480/850-7777 (43)
Creole. Casual Dining. **Address:** 9800 E Indian Bend Rd 85256

OLD TOWN TORTILLA FACTORY 480/945-4567 (65)
Mexican. Casual Dining. **Address:** 6910 E Main St 85251

ORANGE SKY 480/850-7777 (42)
Seafood Steak. Fine Dining. **Address:** 9800 E Talking Stick Way 85256

(See map & index p. 120.)

OREGANO'S PIZZA BISTRO 480/348-0500

Italian Pizza. Casual Dining. **Address:** 7215 E Shea Blvd 85260

PERSIAN ROOM 480/614-1414 (12)

Middle Eastern. Fine Dining. **Address:** 17040 N Scottsdale Rd 85255

P.F. CHANG'S CHINA BISTRO

Chinese. Fine Dining.

LOCATIONS:

Address: 7135 E Camelback Rd, Suite 101 85251
Phone: 480/949-2610 (53)

Address: 7132 E Greenway Pkwy 85254
Phone: 480/367-2999 (28)

PITA JUNGLE 480/922-7482 (31)

Mediterranean. Casual Dining. **Address:** 7366 E Shea Blvd 85260

PRESTON'S STEAKHOUSE 480/629-5087 (3)

Steak. Fine Dining. **Address:** 8700 E Pinnacle Peak Rd 85255

PURE SUSHI BAR & DINING 480/355-0999 (7)

Japanese Sushi. Casual Dining. **Address:** 20567 N Hayden Rd 85255

RANCHO PINOT 480/367-8030 (48)

American. Fine Dining. **Address:** 6208 N Scottsdale Rd 85253

RA SUSHI BAR RESTAURANT 480/990-9256

Japanese Sushi. Casual Dining. **Address:** 3815 N Scottsdale Rd 85251

RA SUSHI BAR RESTAURANT 480/951-5888

Japanese Sushi. Casual Dining. **Address:** 13802 N Scottsdale Rd, Suite 176 85254

RAZZ'S RESTAURANT 480/905-1308 (32)

New American. Casual Dining. **Address:** 10315 N Scottsdale Rd 85254

ROARING FORK 480/947-0795 (51)

Western American. Casual Dining. **Address:** 4800 N Scottsdale Rd, Suite 1700 85251

RUTH'S CHRIS STEAK HOUSE 480/991-5988 (40)

Steak. Fine Dining. **Address:** 7001 N Scottsdale Rd 85253

SAKANA SUSHI & GRILL 480/609-3850 (41)

Sushi. Casual Dining. **Address:** 6989 N Hayden Rd 85250

THE SALT CELLAR RESTAURANT 480/947-1963 (76)

Seafood. Casual Dining. **Address:** 550 N Hayden Rd 85257

SASAKI SUSHI & BAR 480/659-9023 (71)

Sushi. Casual Dining. **Address:** 7373 E Scottsdale Rd 85251

SAUCE 480/321-8800

Italian. Quick Serve. **Address:** 14418 N Scottsdale Rd 85254

SNOOZE AN A.M. EATERY 480/664-3133 (26)

American. Casual Dining. **Address:** 15054 N Scottsdale Rd 85254

SUMO MAYA MEXICAN ASIAN KITCHEN 480/397-9520 (44)

Fusion. Casual Dining. **Address:** 6560 N Scottsdale Rd 85253

SUSHI ROKU 480/970-2121 (56)

Japanese. Casual Dining. **Address:** 7277 E Camelback Rd 85251

SUSHI SEN 480/483-7000 (39)

Sushi. Casual Dining. **Address:** 7001 N Scottsdale Rd, Suite 154 85253

TAKEDA THAI 480/483-5006 (33)

Thai. Casual Dining. **Address:** 10271 N Scottsdale Rd 85253

TALAVERA 480/513-5086

American Fine Dining
$28-$72

AAA Inspector Notes: The talented chefs have created a forum for dining that is exceptional. Using the freshest ingredients and specialty items, they offer Arizona grass-fed and Australian Wagyu beef prepared with regional flavors such as chorizo bread pudding and chipotle honeycomb polenta. Tasting menus change weekly. **Features:** full bar, patio dining. **Reservations:** suggested. **Address:** 10600 E Crescent Moon Dr 85262 **Location:** SR 101 exit 36 (Pima Rd), 4.7 mi n, 2 mi e on Happy Valley Rd, then 1.5 mi n on Alma School Rd; in Four Seasons Resort Scottsdale at Troon North. **Parking:** valet only. D CALL

TOMMY V'S URBAN KITCHEN AND BAR 480/427-2264 (64)

Italian. Casual Dining. **Address:** 7303 E Indian School Rd 85251

TORO LATIN RESTAURANT AND RUM BAR 480/585-4848 (13)

Latin American Fusion. Casual Dining. **Address:** 17020 N Hayden Rd 85255

TOTTIE'S ASIAN FUSION 480/970-0633 (73)

Asian. Casual Dining. **Address:** 7901 E Thomas Rd 85251

TOTTIE'S ASIAN FUSION 2 480/998-8220 (47)

Asian Fusion. Casual Dining. **Address:** 6204 N Scottsdale Rd 85253

TRUE FOOD KITCHEN 480/265-4500 (24)

Continental Natural/Organic Vegan. Casual Dining. **Address:** 15191 N Scottsdale Rd 85254

TUTTI SANTI RISTORANTE 480/951-3775 (16)

Italian. Fine Dining. **Address:** 6339 E Greenway Rd 85254

THE WHITE CHOCOLATE GRILL 480/563-3377 (8)

American. Casual Dining. **Address:** 7000 E Mayo Blvd 85251

ZINBURGER 480/285-0690 (27)

Burgers. Casual Dining. **Address:** 15257 N Scottsdale Rd 85254

ZINC BISTRO 480/603-0922 (25)

French. Casual Dining. **Address:** 15034 N Scottsdale Rd, Suite 140 85254

SEDONA (C-4) pop. 10,031, elev. 4,400'

• **Hotels p. 167 • Restaurants p. 171**
• **Hotels & Restaurants map & index p. 164**

Sedona is nestled between the massive, fire-hued rocks of Red Rock State Park and the lush gorges of Oak Creek Canyon *(see attraction listing p. 161)*. The dusty, semi-arid topography is the base for giant, striped monoliths that take on shades from bright red to pale sand and seem to change color with each passing cloud or ray of sunshine. Since most of the rock is sedimentary, the portrait is constantly eroding and changing shape. Verdant Oak

(See map & index p. 164.)

Creek Canyon, with juniper and cypress trees lining a clear stream, provides a sharp contrast.

So prominent are the buttes and pinnacles that locals have named them. Some of the more popular rock stars are Bell Rock, Cathedral Rock, Chimney Rock, Coffeepot Rock, Courthouse Butte and Snoopy Rock. Formations in the shape of a castle or merry-go-round also can be spotted. Conveniently, two nuns overlook a chapel. And close by, a submarine surfaces near a mushroom cap.

Sedona's rugged red rocks and canyons have even shared the screen with Hollywood movie stars. The area has served as a backdrop for dozens of Western movies. Some popular titles filmed here include "Angel and the Badman," "Broken Arrow," "Firecreek," "Midnight Run" and "The Quick and the Dead."

Mother Nature was kind to Sedona, blessing her with sharp light, bright blue skies, colorful terrain, picturesque sunsets and animated clouds. Inspired painters, sculptors and other creative souls flocked to Sedona and now call the area home. In 1965 the Cowboy Artists of America, a successful art organization, was founded in what is now Uptown; its goals remain to ensure accurate portrayal of Western scenes in art. An established art colony, Sedona boasts ubiquitous galleries and studios that display residents' artistic endeavors: Pottery, sculpture, paintings and jewelry embody a variety of styles, from Western and Southwestern to modern.

Tlaquepaque Arts and Crafts Village, on SR 179 just south of SR 89A, is a shopping village modeled after a small Mexican village. Notable for its architectural features alone, it houses a theater, a collection of galleries and restaurants as well as a chapel; musicians often perform in the courtyards.

Alongside artists live spiritualists, who embrace the energy set forth by such natural splendor. Sedona is purportedly home to several vortices, specific fields that emit energy upward or inward from or to the earth. First channeled and defined by Page Bryant in 1980, a vortex is said to emanate three types of energy: electrical (masculine), magnetic (feminine) or electromagnetic (neutral). Found at various locations, these natural power fields are thought to energize and inspire.

Sedona is said to contain a curiously high number of vortexes and is one of the few places in the world that possesses all three types of energy. Countless businesses in Sedona specialize in alternative medicine, and many offer vortex or spiritual tours. Visitors may find vortexes at Bell Rock, Cathedral Rock and Boynton Canyon. At Airport Mesa, the attraction is twofold: Guests may locate an electric force as well as a great spot from which to view a spectacular sunset.

The town received its name in 1902 from T. Carl Schnebly, one of the first settlers in the area. Schnebly wanted to establish a post office, yet both names he submitted to the postmaster general—Schnebly Station and Oak Creek Crossing—were deemed too long for a cancellation stamp. At the suggestion of his brother, he suggested his wife's name, and it stuck.

The Schneblys weren't the first ones to reside in Sedona. Ancient cliff dwellings found in the area were constructed by the Southern Sinagua people (Spanish for "without water") around A.D. 1130-1300. Two of the largest cliff dwellings, Honanki and Palatki *(see attraction listings)*, still retain a number of pictographs in the shapes of animals, people and various designs.

Sedona is the starting point for hikes and scenic drives through the Red Rock Country. From the vista point on the Mogollon Rim to Sedona, Oak Creek Canyon Drive (SR 89A) winds through the canyon, offering a continuous display of natural beauty, including the area's signature colored rock formations as well as sudden changes in vegetation. Oak Creek flows between 1,200-foot-tall canyon walls toward the red rocks of Sedona.

A Red Rock Pass is required for parking when visiting or hiking the many scenic areas in Sedona. Passes may be purchased at the Sedona Chamber of Commerce. A daily pass is $5; a weekly pass is $15; an annual pass is $20. Federal Inter-agency passes are available at self-serve machines at various trailheads, at the Sedona Chamber of Commerce Visitor Center, the Red Rock Ranger Station Visitor Center and Oak Creek Overlook. Some restrictions may apply; phone (928) 203-2900.

Red Rock Country is just the spot for an exhilarating, hang-on-tight jeep adventure. Guided tours of the backcountry are offered by Red Rock Western Jeep Tours; phone (928) 282-6667 or (800) 848-7728.

Great West Adventure Co. provides transportation and tours to the Grand Canyon and the Hopi Reservation as well as scenic tours of Sedona via 14-passenger buses; Colorado River rafting trips also are available. Phone (928) 204-5506 or (877) 367-2383.

Sedona Chamber of Commerce and Tourism Bureau: 331 Forest Rd., Sedona, AZ 86336. **Phone:** (928) 282-7722 or (800) 288-7336.

Shopping: Art galleries and restaurants intermingle with specialty shops at Tlaquepaque Arts and Crafts Village, just south of Uptown on SR 179. Oakcreek Factory Outlets, 7 miles south on SR 179, offers 16 outlet stores. Other areas featuring galleries and shops are Hillside Sedona, Hozho Center and along SR 89A near the Village of Oak Creek.

ARIZONA SAFARI JEEP TOURS, .3 mi. n. of jct. SRs 179 and 89A to 335 Jordan Rd., offers a variety of tours of Sedona, the Colorado Plateau and the Sonoran Desert. All tours include narration by educated guides with backgrounds in biology, geology and game and range management; hands-on animal demonstrations are featured. **Time:** Allow 2 hours minimum. **Hours:** Daily dawn-dusk. **Cost:** $55-$169; $41.25-$129 (ages 0-12). **Phone:** (928) 282-3012. GT

A DAY IN THE WEST JEEP TOURS is at 252 N. SR 89A, .3 mi. n.e. from jct. SR 179. Comprehensive

▼ See AAA listing p. 162 ▼

(See map & index p. 164.)

jeep tours of Sedona's red rock canyons, rock formations and trails are offered. Guides in old-fashioned cowboy garb dispense photography tips and provide information about local animals, geology, history and vegetation. Winery tours and horseback rides also are offered.

Note: Comfortable walking shoes are recommended. Inquire about weather policies. **Time:** Allow 1 hour minimum. **Hours:** Tours daily 8-dusk. **Cost:** Tours $55-$85; $43-$66 (ages 18 months-12 years). Phone ahead for specialty tour prices. Ages 0-18 months and pregnant women are not permitted. Reservations are recommended. **Phone:** (928) 282-4320 or (800) 973-3662. GT 🍴

GREAT VENTURE TOURS, with pickup from hotels in Phoenix, Sedona and Flagstaff, offers narrated coach tours into the south rim of the Grand Canyon. Highlights include the Painted Desert and the Navajo Nation Reservation. Colorado River float trips and white-water adventures also are offered; phone for information. **Hours:** Daily 7-7. Phone ahead to confirm schedule. **Cost:** $44-$99; $34-$70 (ages 2-16). Fares may vary; phone ahead to confirm. Reservations are required. **Phone:** (928) 282-4451 or (800) 578-2643. GT

GEM **OAK CREEK CANYON,** n. on SR 89A, is traversed by a scenic stretch of that road. About 12 miles long and rarely more than 1 mile wide, the canyon is known for its spectacularly colored white, yellow and red cliffs dotted with pine, cypress and juniper. Rocky gorges, unusual rock formations and buttes add interest to the drive.

Oak Creek is noted for trout fishing; throughout the canyon are Forest Service camping and picnicking grounds. Area maps are available from the chambers of commerce in Flagstaff and Sedona. **Phone:** (928) 204-1123 or (800) 288-7336.

PINK JEEP TOURS is at 204 N. SR 89A, .4 mi. n.e. from jct. SR 179. Passengers experience a

true four-wheel-drive adventure on and over Sedona red rocks. Well-trained guides share lore about local flora, fauna, geology and Native American history and legends. Other tours are available.

Time: Allow 1 hour, 30 minutes minimum. **Hours:** Departures require a minimum of 2 people. Tours daily 7-dusk, Mar.-Sept.; 8-dusk, rest of year. Closed Christmas. **Cost:** Fare $75; $68 (ages 18 months-12 years). Children ages 0-17 months are not permitted. Rates may vary; phone ahead. **Phone:** (928) 282-5000 or (800) 873-3662. *(See ad p. 61.)* GT

SEDONA AIR TOURS, 1 mi. w. of SR 179 on SR 89A, then s. to 1225 Airport Rd., offers various aerial tours over Sedona and the Grand Canyon as well as destination tours. Passengers can view from the air ancient Native American dwellings not accessible by foot or vehicle. **Hours:** Bi-plane, helicopter and sky safari tours daily 8-6. **Cost:** Fare $99-$215. **Phone:** (928) 204-5939 or (888) 866-7433. GT

SEDONA HERITAGE MUSEUM is .1 mi. n. of jct. SR 179 and SR 89A, then .6 mi. n. to 735 N. Jordan Rd. in Jordan Park. The museum features a restored one-room cabin built in 1931; additional rooms were added 1937-47. One exhibit is dedicated to more than 80 movies made in Sedona (mainly Westerns) and another depicts the lifestyle of the cowboy. A restored telegraph office used in the John Wayne movie "Angel and the Bad Man" is outside the museum in Jordan Park. A 1940 apple grading machine and a 1942 fire truck are on display. **Time:** Allow 1 hour minimum. **Hours:** Daily 11-3. Closed major holidays. **Cost:** $5; free (ages 0-12). Audio tour $2. **Phone:** (928) 282-7038.

SEDONA OFFROAD ADVENTURES is at Tlaquepaque Arts and Crafts Village, 336 SR 179, Suite F-103, and at Sinagua Plaza, 320, Suite T, SR 89A N. Experienced guides take passengers on jeep excursions to Bear Wallow Canyon, the Red Rock Outback or Sedona vortexes. Hummer tours go to the Colorado Plateau and the Western and Cliffhanger trails. **Time:** Allow 1 hour minimum. **Hours:** Daily 8-8, May 1-Labor Day; 8-6, rest of year. **Cost:** $39-$99; $29-$85 (ages 1-12). **Phone:** (928) 282-6656. GT

RECREATIONAL ACTIVITIES

Hot Air Ballooning

- **Northern Light Balloon Expeditions** provides transportation to the departure point. **Hours:** Tours depart daily at dawn (weather permitting). **Phone:** (928) 282-2274 or (800) 230-6222. ***(See ad p. 161.)*** GT
- **Red Rock Balloon Adventures,** 273 N. Hwy 89A, Suites M & N in the Uptown Mall, picks up from local hotels. **Hours:** Tours depart daily at dawn (weather permitting). **Phone:** (928) 284-0040 or (800) 258-3754. ***(See ad p. 163.)*** GT

▼ See AAA listing p. 162 ▼

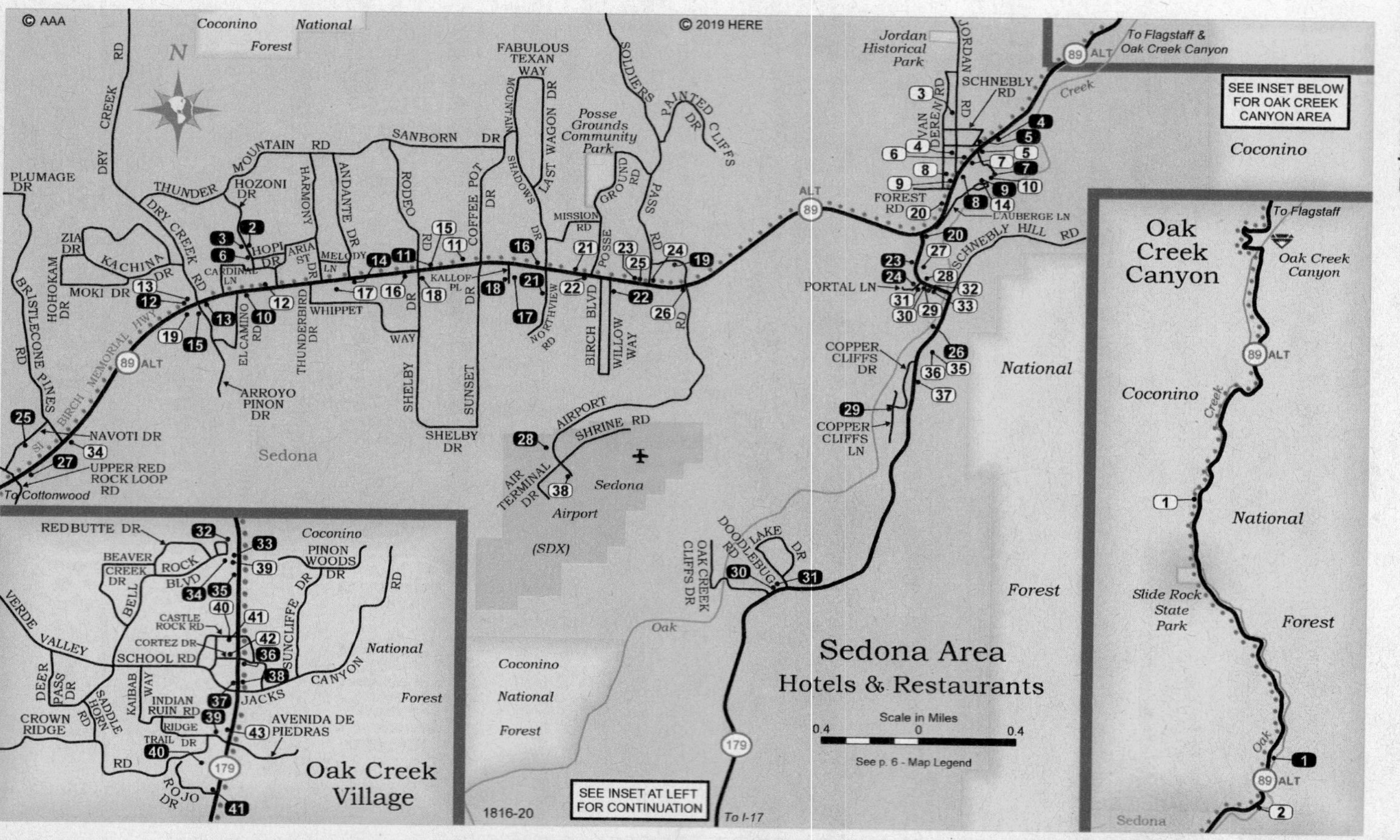
Sedona Area
Hotels & Restaurants
Scale in Miles
0.4
0
0.4
See p. 6 - Map Legend
SEE INSET BELOW FOR OAK CREEK CANYON AREA
SEE INSET AT LEFT FOR CONTINUATION
Oak Creek Canyon
Oak Creek Village
Coconino National Forest
Slide Rock State Park
Jordan Historical Park
Posse Grounds Community Park
Sedona Airport (SDX)
To Flagstaff & Oak Creek Canyon
To Flagstaff
To I-17
To Cottonwood
© AAA
© 2019 HERE
1816-20

Sedona Area

This index helps you "spot" where approved hotels and restaurants are located on the corresponding detailed maps. Restaurant price range is a combination of lunch and/or dinner. Turn to the listing page for more information and consult display ads for special promotions.

For more details, rates and reservations: AAA.com/travelguides/hotels

SEDONA

Map Page	Hotels	Diamond Rated	Member Savings	Page
1 p. 164	Briar Patch Inn Bed & Breakfast	◆◆◆		167
2 p. 164	Alma de Sedona Inn B&B	◆◆◆		167
3 p. 164	Casa Sedona Inn	◆◆◆		167
4 p. 164	**Best Western Plus Arroyo Roble Hotel & Creekside Villas**	◆◆◆	✔	167
5 p. 164	Matterhorn Inn	◆◆		169
6 p. 164	**Adobe Grand Villas**	◆◆◆◆	✔	167
7 p. 164	Amara Resort and Spa	◆◆◆◆		167
8 p. 164	**Orchards Inn of Sedona**	◆◆◆	✔	169
9 p. 164	**L'Auberge de Sedona**	◆◆◆◆	✔	168
10 p. 164	**GreenTree Inn**	◆◆	✔	168
11 p. 164	Sedona Rouge Hotel & Spa, Trademark Collection by Wyndham	◆◆◆		170
12 p. 164	**Southwest Inn at Sedona**	◆◆	✔	171
13 p. 164	**Arroyo Pinion Hotel, an Ascend Hotel Collection Member**	◆◆	✔	167
14 p. 164	Andante Inn of Sedona	◆◆		167
15 p. 164	**Sedona Real Inn & Suites** *(See ad p. 170.)*	◆◆◆	✔	170
16 p. 164	Hampton Inn	◆◆	✔	168
17 p. 164	Villas of Sedona	◆◆◆		171
18 p. 164	The Lodge at Sedona	◆◆◆		169
19 p. 164	**Sky Rock Inn of Sedona** *(See ad p. 171.)*	fyi	✔	170
20 p. 164	Cedars Resort	◆◆		167
21 p. 164	Sedona Springs Resort	◆◆◆		170
22 p. 164	Baby Quail Inn	◆◆		167
23 p. 164	Sedona Hilltop Inn	◆◆		169
24 p. 164	**El Portal Sedona Hotel**	◆◆◆◆	✔	168
25 p. 164	Sedona Summit Resort	◆◆◆		170
26 p. 164	The Inn Above Oak Creek	◆◆◆		168
27 p. 164	**Courtyard by Marriott-Sedona**	◆◆◆	✔	168
28 p. 164	Sky Ranch Lodge	◆◆		170
29 p. 164	Creekside Inn at Sedona	◆◆◆		168
30 p. 164	Villas at Poco Diablo	◆◆◆		171
31 p. 164	**Poco Diablo Resort** *(See ad p. 169.)*	◆◆◆	✔	169
32 p. 164	**Canyon Villa Bed & Breakfast Inn of Sedona**	◆◆◆	✔	167
33 p. 164	**Wildflower Inn at BellRock**	◆◆	✔	171
34 p. 164	Sedona Village Lodge	◆		170
35 p. 164	Holiday Inn Express-Sedona	◆◆◆		168

SEDONA (cont'd)

Map Page	Hotels (cont'd)	Diamond Rated	Member Savings	Page
36 p. 164	The Views Inn Sedona	♦♦		171
37 p. 164	Desert Quail Inn	♦♦		168
38 p. 164	Days Inn Sedona by Wyndham	♦		168
39 p. 164	**Hilton Sedona Resort at Bell Rock**	♦♦♦	✔	168
40 p. 164	Diamond Resorts International-The Ridge on Sedona Golf Resort	♦♦♦		168
41 p. 164	Adobe Hacienda Bed & Breakfast	♦♦♦		167

Map Page	Restaurants	Diamond Rated	Cuisine	Price Range	Page
1 p. 164	The Table at Junipine	♦♦	American	$13-$25	172
2 p. 164	India Palace Cuisine	♦	Indian	$11-$17	172
3 p. 164	Takashi Japanese Restaurant	♦♦	Japanese	$9-$25	172
4 p. 164	Sedona Memories Bakery & Cafe	♦	Breads/Pastries Sandwiches	$7-$10	172
5 p. 164	Open Range Grill & Tavern	♦♦	American	$11-$30	172
6 p. 164	Oaxaca Restaurant	♦♦	Mexican	$12-$21	172
7 p. 164	89Agave Cantina	♦♦	Mexican	$17-$27	171
8 p. 164	Thai Palace Uptown	♦♦	Thai	$11-$21	172
9 p. 164	Cowboy Club	♦♦	American	$15-$39	171
10 p. 164	SaltRock Southwest Kitchen	♦♦♦	Southwestern	$12-$52	172
11 p. 164	Coffee Pot Restaurant	♦	Breakfast Comfort Food	$7-$14	171
12 p. 164	Nick's on the West Side	♦♦	American	$8-$23	172
13 p. 164	Famous Pizza	♦	Pizza	$8-$22	172
14 p. 164	Cress on Oak Creek	♦♦♦♦	New American	$95-$145	171
15 p. 164	**Red's**	♦♦♦	American	$8-$34	172
16 p. 164	Dahl & DiLuca Ristorante Italiano	♦♦♦	Italian	$13-$32	172
17 p. 164	Thai Spices Natural Restaurant	♦♦	Thai	$13-$18	173
18 p. 164	Pisa Lisa	♦♦	Italian Pizza	$10-$25	172
19 p. 164	Relics Restaurant at Rainbow's End	♦♦	Steak	$22-$36	172
20 p. 164	Wildflower Bread Company	♦	Breads/Pastries Sandwiches	$8-$13	173
21 p. 164	The Heartline Cafe	♦♦♦	American	$8-$30	172
22 p. 164	ChocolaTree Organic Eatery	♦♦	Vegetarian Natural/Organic	$6-$18	171
23 p. 164	Szechuan Chinese Restaurant & Sushi Bar	♦♦	Asian	$10-$21	172
24 p. 164	Judi's Restaurant & Lounge	♦♦	American	$9-$34	172
25 p. 164	New York Bagels and Deli	♦	Breads/Pastries Deli	$4-$9	172
26 p. 164	Mariposa Latin Inspired Grill	♦♦♦	Latin American	$22-$58	172
27 p. 164	Creekside Restaurant	♦♦♦	American	$12-$37	171
28 p. 164	Pump House Urban Eatery and Market	♦♦♦	American	$18-$29	172
29 p. 164	Oak Creek Brewery & Grill	♦♦	American	$11-$28	172
30 p. 164	El Rincon Restaurante Mexicano	♦♦	Mexican	$8-$22	172

Map Page	Restaurants (cont'd)	Diamond Rated	Cuisine	Price Range	Page
31 p. 164	Spoke & Wheel Tavern and Eatery	◆◆	American	$12-$39	172
32 p. 164	**Rene At Tlaquepaque**	◆◆◆	French	$12-$55	172
33 p. 164	The Secret Garden Cafe	◆◆	American	$14-$28	172
34 p. 164	Bella Vita Restorante	◆◆◆	Italian	$19-$45	171
35 p. 164	Dellepiane Sedona	◆◆	Burgers	$10-$32	172
36 p. 164	The Hudson	◆◆◆	American	$18-$43	172
37 p. 164	Elote Cafe	◆◆◆	Mexican	$20-$30	172
38 p. 164	Mesa Grill	◆◆	American	$10-$39	172
39 p. 164	Tara Thai	◆◆	Thai	$10-$18	172
40 p. 164	Maria's Restaurant & Cantina	◆◆	Mexican	$8-$19	172
41 p. 164	Pago's Pizzeria & Italian Cuisine	◆◆	Italian	$7-$20	172
42 p. 164	PJ's Village Pub	◆◆	American	$9-$17	172
43 p. 164	**Cucina Rustica**	◆◆◆	Italian	$20-$34	172

ADOBE GRAND VILLAS 928/203-7616 **6**

◆◆◆◆ **Boutique Bed & Breakfast**

Address: 35 Hozoni Dr 86336 **Location:** Jct SR 179, 2 mi w on SR 89A, just nw on Tortilla and Southwest drs, then just nw. Located in West Sedona residential area. **Facility:** This boutique-style B&B has spacious villas offering luxurious appointments; rooms have custom-designed furnishings and a private balcony or patio. 16 units, some two bedrooms and kitchens. 2 stories (no elevator), exterior corridors. **Amenities:** safes. **Pool:** outdoor. **Activities:** hot tub, spa. **Guest Services:** valet laundry. **Featured Amenity: full hot breakfast.**

SAVE BIZ HS

ADOBE HACIENDA BED & BREAKFAST 928/284-2020 **41**

◆◆◆ Bed & Breakfast. **Address:** 10 Rojo Dr 86351

ALMA DE SEDONA INN B&B 928/282-2737 **2**

◆◆◆ Bed & Breakfast. **Address:** 50 Hozoni Dr 86336

AMARA RESORT AND SPA 928/282-4828 **7**

◆◆◆◆ Hotel. **Address:** 100 Amara Ln 86336

ANDANTE INN OF SEDONA 928/282-1533 **14**

◆◆ Hotel. **Address:** 2545 W Hwy 89A 86336

ARROYO PINION HOTEL, AN ASCEND HOTEL COLLECTION MEMBER 928/204-1146 **13**

◆◆ **Hotel**

Address: 3119 W Hwy 89A 86336 **Location:** Jct SR 179, 3 mi w. Located in business section of West Sedona. **Facility:** 47 units. 2 stories (no elevator), exterior corridors. **Amenities:** safes. **Pool:** heated outdoor. **Activities:** hot tub, limited exercise equipment. **Guest Services:** coin laundry. **Featured Amenity: breakfast buffet.**

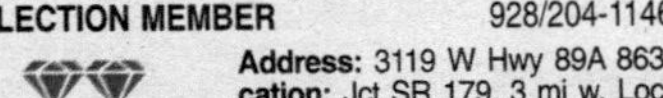

SAVE CALL BIZ / SOME UNITS

BABY QUAIL INN 928/282-2835 **22**

◆◆ Motel. **Address:** 50 Willow Way 86336

BEST WESTERN PLUS ARROYO ROBLE HOTEL & CREEKSIDE VILLAS 928/282-4001 **4**

◆◆◆ **Hotel**

Best Western PLUS **AAA Benefit:** Members save up to 15% and earn bonus points!

Address: 400 N SR 89A 86336 **Location:** Jct SR 179, 0.5 mi ne. **Facility:** 66 units, some two bedrooms, kitchens and cottages. 5 stories, exterior corridors. **Amenities:** safes. **Pool:** heated outdoor, heated indoor. **Activities:** sauna, hot tub, steamroom, tennis, playground, game room, exercise room. **Guest Services:** coin laundry. **Featured Amenity: full hot breakfast.**

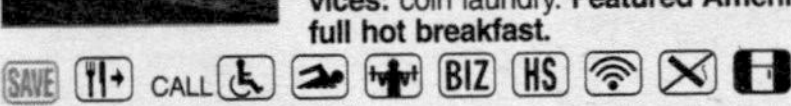

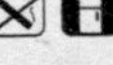

SAVE CALL BIZ HS / SOME UNITS

BRIAR PATCH INN BED & BREAKFAST 928/282-2342 **1**

◆◆◆ Cottage. **Address:** 3190 N SR 89A 86336

CANYON VILLA BED & BREAKFAST INN OF SEDONA 928/284-1226 **32**

◆◆◆ **Bed & Breakfast**

Address: 40 Canyon Circle Dr 86351 **Location:** Jct SR 179, just w on Bell Rock Blvd, then just n. Located in Village of Oak Creek. **Facility:** A nearby desert provides outdoor interest at this upscale Spanish-Mission compound overlooking the red rocks. The Southwestern-style building houses spacious guest rooms and common areas. 11 units. 2 stories (no elevator), interior/exterior corridors. **Pool:** heated outdoor. **Featured Amenity: full hot breakfast.**

SAVE BIZ

CASA SEDONA INN 928/282-2938 **3**

◆◆◆ Boutique Hotel. **Address:** 55 Hozoni Dr 86336

CEDARS RESORT 928/282-7010 **20**

◆◆ Hotel. **Address:** 20 N SR 89A 86339

(See map & index p. 164.)

COURTYARD BY MARRIOTT-SEDONA
928/325-0055 27

Hotel

COURTYARD **AAA Benefit:** Members save 5% or more!

Address: 4105 W SR 89A 86336 **Location:** Jct SR 179, 4.5 mi w on SR 89A. **Facility:** 121 units. 2 stories, interior corridors. **Terms:** check-in 4 pm. **Pool:** heated outdoor. **Activities:** hot tub, exercise room. **Guest Services:** coin laundry, boarding pass kiosk, area transportation.

CREEKSIDE INN AT SEDONA 928/282-4992 29
Bed & Breakfast. **Address:** 99 Copper Cliffs Dr 86336

DAYS INN SEDONA BY WYNDHAM 928/284-1100 38
Hotel. **Address:** 6465 SR 179 86351

DESERT QUAIL INN 928/284-1433 37
Hotel. **Address:** 6626 SR 179 86351

DIAMOND RESORTS INTERNATIONAL-THE RIDGE ON SEDONA GOLF RESORT 928/284-1200 40
Condominium. **Address:** 55 Sunridge Cir 86351

EL PORTAL SEDONA HOTEL 928/203-9405 24

Hotel

Address: 95 Portal Ln 86336 **Location:** Jct SR 89A, just s on SR 179, just w. Adjacent to Tlaquepaque Plaza. **Facility:** Built to replicate early 1900s Southwestern buildings, the hotel features elegantly appointed guest rooms that surround a courtyard. All guests have access to the neighboring Sedona Spa. 12 units. 2 stories (no elevator), interior/exterior corridors. **Amenities:** safes. **Activities:** massage. **Guest Services:** valet laundry, area transportation.

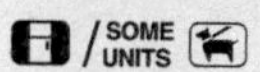

ENCHANTMENT RESORT AND MII AMO SPA
928/282-2900

Resort Hotel

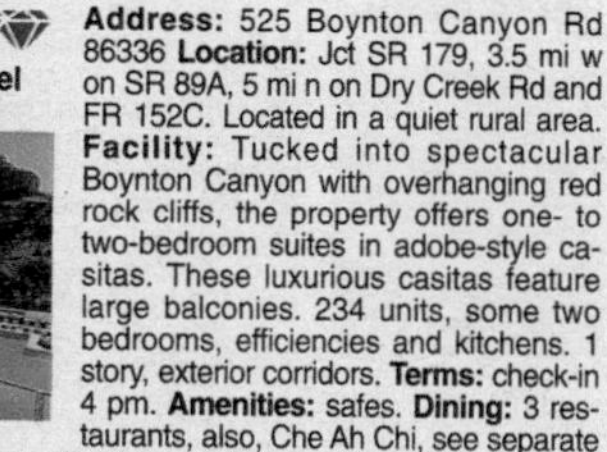

Address: 525 Boynton Canyon Rd 86336 **Location:** Jct SR 179, 3.5 mi w on SR 89A, 5 mi n on Dry Creek Rd and FR 152C. Located in a quiet rural area. **Facility:** Tucked into spectacular Boynton Canyon with overhanging red rock cliffs, the property offers one- to two-bedroom suites in adobe-style casitas. These luxurious casitas feature large balconies. 234 units, some two bedrooms, efficiencies and kitchens. 1 story, exterior corridors. **Terms:** check-in 4 pm. **Amenities:** safes. **Dining:** 3 restaurants, also, Che Ah Chi, see separate listing, entertainment. **Pool:** heated outdoor, heated indoor. **Activities:** sauna, hot tub, tennis, recreation programs, kids club, bicycles, lawn sports, trails, health club, spa. **Guest Services:** complimentary and valet laundry, area transportation.

GREENTREE INN 928/282-9166 10

Motel

Address: 2991 W SR 89A 86336 **Location:** Jct SR 179, 3 mi w. **Facility:** 66 units, some two bedrooms. 2 stories (no elevator), exterior corridors. **Pool:** heated outdoor. **Activities:** hot tub. **Featured Amenity: breakfast buffet.**

HAMPTON INN 928/282-4700 16
Hotel. **Address:** 1800 W Hwy 89A 86336

AAA Benefit: Members save up to 15%!

HILTON SEDONA RESORT AT BELL ROCK
928/284-4040 39

Resort Hotel

AAA Benefit: Members save up to 15%!

Address: 90 Ridge Trail Dr 86351 **Location:** Jct SR 89A, 7.3 mi s on SR 179. Located in Village of Oak Creek. **Facility:** Beautiful red rock views can be enjoyed from some of these well-appointed guest rooms with a patio and fireplace. 221 units. 3 stories, interior corridors. **Parking:** on-site (fee). **Terms:** check-in 4 pm. **Amenities:** safes. **Dining:** 2 restaurants. **Pool:** heated outdoor. **Activities:** hot tub, regulation golf, tennis, health club, spa. **Guest Services:** complimentary laundry.

Hilton
SEDONA RESORT AT BELL ROCK

A resort for adventure seekers offering an array of amenities & expert vacation planning assistance.

HOLIDAY INN EXPRESS-SEDONA 928/284-0711 35
Hotel. **Address:** 6176 SR 179 86351

THE INN ABOVE OAK CREEK 928/282-7896 26
Boutique Hotel. **Address:** 556 SR 179 86336

L'AUBERGE DE SEDONA 928/282-1661 9

Hotel

Address: 301 L'Auberge Ln 86336 **Location:** Jct SR 179, just n on SR 89A, then ne; down the hill. Located in a secluded area. **Facility:** A lodge and individual cottages are nestled on several acres of landscaped and tree-shaded grounds along Oak Creek. A country French décor, impressive beds and fireplaces are offered in the cottages. 88 units, some two bedrooms and cottages. 1-2 stories (no elevator), interior/exterior corridors. **Parking:** valet only. **Terms:** check-in 4 pm. **Amenities:** safes. **Dining:** 2 restaurants. **Pool:** heated outdoor. **Activities:** hot tub, exercise room, spa. **Guest Services:** valet laundry, area transportation. Affiliated with Destination Hotels.

(See map & index p. 164.)

THE LODGE AT SEDONA 928/204-1942 18

Bed & Breakfast. **Address:** 125 Kallof Pl 86336

MATTERHORN INN 928/282-7176 5

Motel. **Address:** 230 Apple Ave 86336

ORCHARDS INN OF SEDONA 928/282-2405 8

Hotel

Address: 254 N SR 89A 86336 **Location:** Jct SR 179, just ne. Located in Uptown Sedona shopping area. **Facility:** 70 units. 2-3 stories (no elevator), exterior corridors. **Terms:** check-in 4 pm. **Dining:** 89Agave Cantina, see separate listing. **Pool:** heated outdoor. **Activities:** hot tub. **Guest Services:** coin laundry. Affiliated with Destination Hotels.

SAVE BIZ

POCO DIABLO RESORT 928/282-7333 31

Resort Hotel

Address: 1752 State Route 179 86336 **Location:** Jct SR 179, 2 mi s of SR 89A. **Facility:** The resort's multiple buildings are spread across several acres featuring ponds, cool streams, lush landscape and an outdoor fireplace. Some of the spacious rooms have either a patio or balcony. 137 units. 2 stories (no elevator), exterior corridors. **Terms:** check-in 4 pm. **Pool:** heated outdoor. **Activities:** hot tub, regulation golf, tennis, bicycles, exercise room, spa. **Guest Services:** valet and coin laundry.

(See ad this page.)

SAVE CALL BIZ sHS / SOME UNITS

SEDONA HILLTOP INN 928/282-7187 23

Motel. **Address:** 218 SR 179 86336

(See map & index p. 164.)

SEDONA REAL INN & SUITES 928/282-1414 **15**

Hotel

Address: 95 Arroyo Pinon Dr 86336 **Location:** Jct SR 179, 3.4 mi w on SR 89A, just sw. Located in West Sedona. **Facility:** 89 units. 2 stories (no elevator), exterior corridors. **Amenities:** safes. **Pool:** heated outdoor. **Activities:** hot tub, picnic facilities, exercise room. **Guest Services:** valet and coin laundry. **Featured Amenity: breakfast buffet.** *(See ad this page.)*

SAVE CALL BIZ

/ SOME UNITS

SEDONA ROUGE HOTEL & SPA, TRADEMARK COLLECTION BY WYNDHAM 928/203-4111 **11**

Hotel. **Address:** 2250 W Hwy 89A 86336

SEDONA SPRINGS RESORT 928/204-3400 **21**

Condominium. **Address:** 55 Northview Rd 86336

SEDONA SUMMIT RESORT 928/204-3100 **25**

Condominium. **Address:** 4055 Navoti Dr 86336

SEDONA VILLAGE LODGE 928/284-3626 **34**

Motel. **Address:** 105 Bell Rock Plaza 86351

SKY RANCH LODGE 928/282-6400 **28**

Motel. **Address:** 1105 Airport Rd 86336

SKY ROCK INN OF SEDONA 928/282-3072 **19**

fyi

Hotel

Under major renovation, call for details. **Last Rated:** **Address:** 1200 W SR 89A 86336 **Location:** Jct SR 179, 1.2 mi w. **Facility:** 110 units. 1-3 stories (no elevator), exterior corridors. **Terms:** check-in 4 pm. **Pool:** heated outdoor. **Activities:** hot tub, exercise room. **Guest Services:** coin laundry, area transportation. **Featured Amenity: breakfast buffet.** *(See ad p. 171.)*

SAVE ECO CALL BIZ

/ SOME UNITS

▼ *See AAA listing this page* ▼

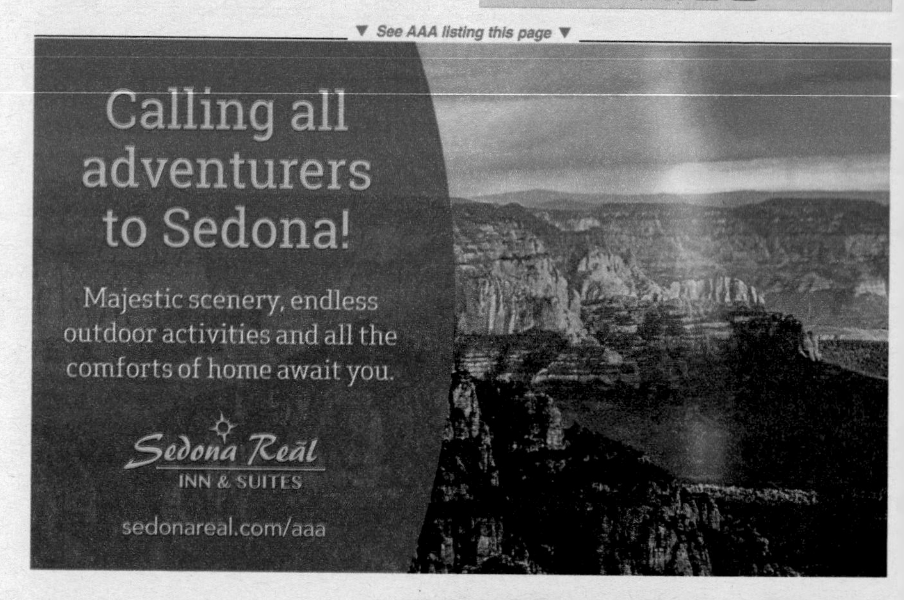

(See map & index p. 164.)

SOUTHWEST INN AT SEDONA 928/282-3344 **12**

Hotel

Address: 3250 W Hwy 89A 86336 **Location:** Jct SR 179, 3.5 mi w. Located in West Sedona. **Facility:** 28 units. 2 stories (no elevator), exterior corridors. **Pool:** heated outdoor. **Activities:** hot tub, exercise room. **Featured Amenity:** breakfast buffet.

SAVE BIZ / SOME UNITS

THE VIEWS INN SEDONA 928/284-2487 **36**
Hotel. **Address:** 65 E Cortez Dr 86351

VILLAS AT POCO DIABLO 928/204-3300 **30**
Condominium. **Address:** 1752 SR 179 86336

VILLAS OF SEDONA 928/204-3400 **17**
Condominium. **Address:** 120 Kallof Pl 86336

WILDFLOWER INN AT BELLROCK 928/284-3937 **33**

Hotel

Address: 6086 SR 179 86351 **Location:** Jct SR 179 and Bell Rock Blvd. Located in Village of Oak Creek. **Facility:** 29 units. 2 stories (no elevator), exterior corridors. **Guest Services:** coin laundry.

SAVE

WHERE TO EAT

89AGAVE CANTINA 928/282-7200 (7)
Mexican. Casual Dining. **Address:** 254 N SR 89A 86336

BELLA VITA RESTORANTE 928/282-4540 (34)
Italian. Fine Dining. **Address:** 6701 W SR 89A 86336

CHE AH CHI 928/204-6000

American Fine Dining
$26-$52

AAA Inspector Notes: While taking in stunning views of Boynton Canyon, patrons can savor contemporary dishes. The elegant service and décor complete a truly distinguished dining experience. **Features:** full bar, patio dining. **Reservations:** suggested. **Address:** 525 Boynton Canyon Rd 86336 **Location:** Jct SR 179, 3.5 mi w on SR 89A, 5 mi n on Dry Creek Rd and FR 152C; in Enchantment Resort and Mii amo Spa. B D

CHOCOLATREE ORGANIC EATERY 928/282-2997 (22)
Vegetarian Natural/Organic. Casual Dining. **Address:** 1595 W SR 89A 86336

COFFEE POT RESTAURANT 928/282-6626 (11)
Breakfast Comfort Food. Casual Dining. **Address:** 2050 W Hwy 89A 86336

COWBOY CLUB 928/282-4200 (9)
American. Casual Dining. **Address:** 241 N Hwy 89A 86336

CREEKSIDE RESTAURANT 928/282-1705 (27)
American. Casual Dining. **Address:** 251 Hwy 179 86336

CRESS ON OAK CREEK 928/282-1661 (14)
New American. Fine Dining. **Address:** 301 L'Auberge Ln 86336

▼ See AAA listing p. 170 ▼

(See map & index p. 164.)

CUCINA RUSTICA 928/284-3010 (43)

Italian Fine Dining $20-$34

AAA Inspector Notes: Boasting décor akin to that of an elegant villa, this restaurant serves fresh cuisine in several small dining rooms. The homemade fettuccine and linguine pastas are incredible and cannot be passed up. **Features:** full bar, patio dining, happy hour. **Reservations:** suggested. **Address:** 7000 Hwy 179, Suite 126A 86351 **Location:** Just s of Bell Rock Blvd. D

DAHL & DILUCA RISTORANTE ITALIANO 928/282-5219 (16)
Italian. Fine Dining. **Address:** 2321 W Hwy 89A 86336

DELLEPIANE SEDONA 928/828-4129 (35)
Burgers. Gastropub. **Address:** 671 SR 179 86336

ELOTE CAFE 928/203-0105 (37)
Mexican. Casual Dining. **Address:** 771 SR 179 86336

EL RINCON RESTAURANTE MEXICANO 928/282-4648 (30)
Mexican. Casual Dining. **Address:** 336 S Hwy 179 86336

FAMOUS PIZZA 928/282-5464 (13)
Pizza. Quick Serve. **Address:** 3190 W Hwy 89A, Suite 300 86336

THE HEARTLINE CAFE 928/282-0785 (21)
American. Fine Dining. **Address:** 1600 W Hwy 89A 86336

THE HUDSON 928/862-4099 (36)
American. Gastropub. **Address:** 671 SR 179 86336

INDIA PALACE CUISINE 928/204-2300 (2)
Indian. Casual Dining. **Address:** 1910 W SR 89A, Suite 102 86336

JAVELINA CANTINA 928/282-1313
Mexican. Casual Dining. **Address:** 671 Hwy 179 86336

JUDI'S RESTAURANT & LOUNGE 928/282-4449 (24)
American. Casual Dining. **Address:** 40 Soldier's Pass Rd 86336

MARIA'S RESTAURANT & CANTINA 928/284-3739 (40)
Mexican. Casual Dining. **Address:** 6446 Hwy 179, #212 86351

MARIPOSA LATIN INSPIRED GRILL 928/862-4444 (26)
Latin American. Fine Dining. **Address:** 700 W SR 89A 86336

MESA GRILL 928/282-2400 (38)
American. Casual Dining. **Address:** 1185 Airport Rd 86336

NEW YORK BAGELS AND DELI 928/204-1242 (25)
Breads/Pastries Deli. Quick Serve. **Address:** 1650 W SR 89A 86336

NICK'S ON THE WEST SIDE 928/204-2088 (12)
American. Casual Dining. **Address:** 2920 W Hwy 89A 86336

OAK CREEK BREWERY & GRILL 928/282-3300 (29)
American. Brewpub. **Address:** 336 Hwy 179, Suite D201 86336

OAXACA RESTAURANT 928/282-4179 (6)
Mexican. Casual Dining. **Address:** 321 N SR 89A 86336

OPEN RANGE GRILL & TAVERN 928/282-0002 (5)
American. Casual Dining. **Address:** 320 N SR 89A 86336

PAGO'S PIZZERIA & ITALIAN CUISINE 928/284-1939 (41)
Italian. Casual Dining. **Address:** 6446 SR 179 86351

PICAZZO'S HEALTHY ITALIAN KITCHEN 928/282-4140
Italian. Casual Dining. **Address:** 1855 W Hwy 89A 86336

PISA LISA 928/282-5472 (18)
Italian Pizza. Casual Dining. **Address:** 2245 W Hwy 89A 86336

PJ'S VILLAGE PUB 928/284-2250 (42)
American. Casual Dining. **Address:** 40 W Cortez Dr 86351

PUMP HOUSE URBAN EATERY AND MARKET 928/862-4141 (28)
American. Gastropub. **Address:** 313 SR 179 86336

RED'S 928/203-4111 (15)

American Casual Dining $8-$34

AAA Inspector Notes: The trendy California décor fits well in this red rock town and attentive staff watch over the tables. Chef Ron Moler creates his own delectable version of meatloaf, grilled seafood and salads such as grilled endive with pear and honey-spiced pecans that will simply delight. **Features:** full bar, patio dining, happy hour. **Address:** 2250 W Hwy 89A 86336 **Location:** Jct SR 179, 2 mi w; in Sedona Rouge Hotel & Spa. B L D

RELICS RESTAURANT AT RAINBOW'S END 928/282-1593 (19)
Steak. Fine Dining. **Address:** 3235 W SR 89A 86336

RENE AT TLAQUEPAQUE 928/282-9225 (32)

French Fine Dining $12-$55

AAA Inspector Notes: *Classic.* Tucked into an upscale, art-filled shopping plaza, this quietly elegant dining room is where diners are treated to attentive service and Continental and American favorites. Entertainers perform on weekends and the efficient staff works as a team to quietly meet all dining needs. The antelope tenderloin and the tableside flambé are amazing. **Features:** full bar, patio dining. **Reservations:** suggested. **Address:** 336 Hwy 179, B-118 86336 **Location:** SR 89A, 0.3 mi s; in Tlaquepaque Arts & Crafts Village. L D

SALTROCK SOUTHWEST KITCHEN 928/340-8821 (10)
Southwestern. Casual Dining. **Address:** 100 Amara Ln 86336

THE SECRET GARDEN CAFE 928/203-9564 (33)
American. Casual Dining. **Address:** 336 Hwy 179, Suite F101 86336

SEDONA MEMORIES BAKERY & CAFE 928/282-0032 (4)
Breads/Pastries Sandwiches. Quick Serve. **Address:** 321 Jordan Rd 86336

SPOKE & WHEEL TAVERN AND EATERY 928/203-5334 (31)
American. Casual Dining. **Address:** 160 Portal Ln 86336

SZECHUAN CHINESE RESTAURANT & SUSHI BAR 928/282-9288 (23)
Asian. Casual Dining. **Address:** 1350 W Hwy 89A, Suite 21 86336

THE TABLE AT JUNIPINE 928/282-7406 (1)
American. Casual Dining. **Address:** 8351 N SR 89A 86336

TAKASHI JAPANESE RESTAURANT 928/282-2334 (3)
Japanese. Casual Dining. **Address:** 465 Jordan Rd 86336

TARA THAI 928/284-9167 (39)
Thai. Casual Dining. **Address:** 34 Bell Rock Plaza 86351

THAI PALACE UPTOWN 928/282-8424 (8)
Thai. Casual Dining. **Address:** 260 Van Deren Rd 86336

(See map & index p. 164.)

THAI SPICES NATURAL RESTAURANT 928/282-0599 (17)

Thai. Casual Dining. **Address:** 2611 W SR 89A 86336

WILDFLOWER BREAD COMPANY 928/204-2223 (20)

Breads/Pastries Sandwiches. Quick Serve. **Address:** 101 N Hwy 89A 86336

SELIGMAN pop. 445

• Part of Grand Canyon National Park area — see map p. 57

DELUXE INN MOTEL 928/422-3244

Vintage Motel. **Address:** 22295 Old Hwy 66 86337

HISTORIC ROUTE 66 MOTEL 928/422-3204

Vintage Motel

Address: 22750 W Hwy 66 86337 **Location:** I-40 exit 121, 1 mi n, then just e. **Facility:** A throwback to lodging from a bygone era, the property offers varied-size guest units with many homey niceties and décor of the famous historic highway. You can't miss the Route 66 neon sign! 16 units. 1 story, exterior corridors. *Bath:* shower only.

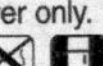

SUPAI MOTEL 928/422-4153

Vintage Motel

Address: 22450 Old Hwy 66 86337 **Location:** I-40 exit 121, 1 mi n, then 0.7 mi e. **Facility:** Screaming historic Route 66 charm, this property features a restored neon sign that has become a popular photo spot. This basic motel offers very small rooms and some large rooms with three beds. 16 units. 1 story, exterior corridors. **Featured Amenity: continental breakfast.**

WHERE TO EAT

ROADKILL 66 CAFE AND OK SALOON 928/422-3554

American Casual Dining $10-$25

AAA Inspector Notes: Enjoy this distinctive eatery with animal trophies and Route 66 charm. Casual American items, served with fun, local attitudes, include sandwiches, burgers and basic cuts of steak. **Features:** full bar. **Address:** 22830 W Hwy 66 86337 **Location:** I-40 exit 121, 1 mi n, then just e. B L D

SELLS (F-4) pop. 2,495, elev. 2,379'

Originally known as Indian Oasis, Sells was renamed in 1918 in honor of Indian commissioner Cato Sells. The dependable water supply made the area a popular stop for travelers, even in prehistoric times.

Sells is the headquarters of the Tohono O'odham Indian Reservation. In addition to this vast reservation west of Tucson, a smaller tract is south of Tucson at the site of Mission San Xavier del Bac *(see Tucson p. 198)*. Mainly farmers and ranchers, the Tohono O'odham are known for their handcrafted baskets and pottery.

KITT PEAK NATIONAL OBSERVATORY is 20 mi. e. on SR 86, then 12 mi. s. on SR 386, within the Tohono O'odham reservation in the Quinlan Mountains. The facility conducts astronomical research and contains 27 telescopes, including the world's largest solar telescope and the Mayall 4-meter telescope. Exhibits, special programs and a nightly stargazing program are featured.

Travelers are advised to check on weather and road conditions. **Hours:** Visitor center daily 9-3:45. Guided tours of the facility are offered at 10, 11:30 and 1:30. Three types of stargazing programs are available only with reservations and begin at dusk, Sept. to mid-July. Phone to confirm holiday closure and schedule. Closed Jan. 1, Thanksgiving and Christmas.

Cost: Visitor center free. Guided tours $7.75; $3 (ages 7-12). All-day pass $9.75; $3.25 (ages 7-12). Intro-level Nightly Observation Program $55; $52 (ages 5-17, ages 62+ and students and military with ID). Reservations are required for all night observation programs and should be made 1 month in advance. **Phone:** (520) 318-8726. GT

SHOW LOW (D-5) pop. 10,660, elev. 6,347'

• Restaurants p. 174

Show Low took its name from the winning hand in a poker game between Native American scout Col. Croyden E. Cooley and his friend Marion Clark. The town's main street, Deuce of Clubs, was named after the winning card.

On the edge of the Mogollon Rim, the town offers numerous recreational pursuits, including fishing, camping, hiking and horseback riding.

Show Low Chamber of Commerce: 81 E. Deuce of Clubs, Show Low, AZ 85901. **Phone:** (928) 537-2326.

SHOW LOW HISTORICAL SOCIETY MUSEUM is at 561 E. Deuce of Clubs. The 17-room museum is housed in Show Low's former city hall, police department and jail building. You'll see an original jail cell, a railroad display, a quilt room, a kitchen filled with items from the 1800s and early 1900s, and photos of the town and its well-known residents and visitors. **Time:** Allow 30 minutes minimum. **Hours:** Wed.-Sat. 10-3 (weather permitting), Mar.-Dec. **Cost:** Donations. **Phone:** (928) 532-7115.

BEST WESTERN PAINT PONY LODGE 928/537-5773

Motel

AAA Benefit: Members save up to 15% and earn bonus points!

Address: 581 W Deuce of Clubs Ave 85901 **Location:** On US 60 and SR 260. **Facility:** 50 units. 2 stories (no elevator), exterior corridors. **Guest Services:** coin laundry. **Featured Amenity: full hot breakfast.**

/ SOME UNITS HS

DAYS INN 928/537-4356
Motel. **Address:** 480 W Deuce of Clubs Ave 85901

HAMPTON INN & SUITES (SHOW LOW/PINETOP) 928/532-4444
SAVE Hotel. **Address:** 1501 E Woolford Rd 85902

AAA Benefit: Members save up to 15%!

HOLIDAY INN EXPRESS 928/537-5115
Hotel. **Address:** 151 W Deuce of Clubs Ave 85901

K C MOTEL 928/537-4433

Motel

Address: 60 W Deuce of Clubs Ave 85901 **Location:** On US 60 and SR 260. **Facility:** 35 units. 1-2 stories (no elevator), exterior corridors. **Guest Services:** coin laundry. **Featured Amenity:** continental breakfast.

/ SOME UNITS

KIVA MOTEL 928/537-4542
Motel. **Address:** 261 E Deuce of Clubs 85901

WHERE TO EAT

CATTLEMEN'S STEAKHOUSE AND LOUNGE 928/537-9797
Steak. Casual Dining. **Address:** 1231 E Deuce of Clubs Ave 85901

LICANO'S MEXICAN FOOD & STEAK HOUSE 928/537-8220
Mexican. Casual Dining. **Address:** 573 W Deuce of Clubs Ave 85902

SIERRA VISTA pop. 43,888, elev. 4,600'

Sierra Vista has been built upon the historic past of Fort Huachuca *(see place listing p. 50)*, established in 1877. The fort is now the largest single employer in southern Arizona, and most of its personnel live in the area. The scenery makes Sierra Vista special: The city is nestled on the eastern slopes of the Huachuca Mountains and overlooks the San Pedro River Valley. Nature lovers are attracted to nearby Coronado National Memorial *(see place listing p. 39)*, San Pedro Riparian National Conservation Area (6 miles east) and Ramsey Canyon Preserve.

Sierra Vista Visitor Center: 3020 E. Tacoma St. in the Oscar Yrun Community Center, Sierra Vista, AZ 85635. **Phone:** (520) 417-6960 or (800) 288-3861.

FORT HUACHUCA HISTORICAL MUSEUM—see Fort Huachuca p. 50.

CANDLEWOOD SUITES 520/439-8200
Extended Stay Hotel. **Address:** 1904 S Hwy 92 85635

COMFORT INN & SUITES 520/459-0515
Hotel. **Address:** 3500 E Fry Blvd 85635

DAYS INN 520/458-8500
Hotel. **Address:** 3460 E Fry Blvd 85635

FAIRFIELD INN & SUITES BY MARRIOTT 520/439-5900

Hotel

Fairfield **AAA Benefit:** Members save 5% or more!

Address: 3855 El Mercado Loop 85635 **Location:** Jct SR 90, 1.5 mi s on SR 92. Located at Sierra Vista Mall. **Facility:** 67 units. 3 stories, interior corridors. **Pool:** heated outdoor. **Activities:** hot tub, picnic facilities, exercise room. **Guest Services:** valet and coin laundry.

GARDEN PLACE SUITES 520/439-3300
Extended Stay Hotel. **Address:** 100 N Garden Ave 85635

GATEWAY STUDIO SUITES 520/458-5555
Extended Stay Hotel. **Address:** 203 S Garden Ave 85635

HAMPTON INN BY HILTON SIERRA VISTA 520/439-5400

Hotel

AAA Benefit: Members save up to 15%!

Address: 4100 Snyder Blvd 85635 **Location:** On SR 92, 1 mi s of SR 90. **Facility:** 58 units. 3 stories, interior corridors. **Pool:** heated indoor. **Activities:** hot tub, exercise room. **Guest Services:** valet and coin laundry.

HOLIDAY INN EXPRESS 520/439-8800
Hotel. **Address:** 1902 S Hwy 92 85635

QUALITY INN 520/458-7900
Hotel. **Address:** 1631 S Hwy 92 85635

SIERRA SUITES 520/459-4221
Hotel. **Address:** 391 E Fry Blvd 85635

TOWNEPLACE SUITES BY MARRIOTT 520/515-9900

Extended Stay Hotel

TOWNEPLACE SUITES MARRIOTT **AAA Benefit:** Members save 5% or more!

Address: 3399 Rodeo Dr 85635 **Location:** Jct SR 90, 1.5 mi s on SR 92, just w on Avenida Cochise, just s on Oakmont Dr, then just e. **Facility:** 71 efficiencies, some two bedrooms. 3 stories, interior corridors. **Pool:** heated outdoor. **Activities:** picnic facilities, exercise room. **Guest Services:** valet and coin laundry.

/ SOME UNITS

WINDEMERE HOTEL & CONFERENCE CENTER 520/459-5900
Hotel. **Address:** 2047 S Hwy 92 85635

WHERE TO EAT

THE GERMAN CAFE 520/456-1705

German. Casual Dining. **Address:** 1232 E Fry Blvd 85635

GOLDEN DRAGON 520/458-7575

Chinese. Casual Dining. **Address:** 2151 S Hwy 92, Suite 112 85635

HANA TOKYO JAPANESE RESTAURANT 520/458-1993

Japanese. Casual Dining. **Address:** 1633 S Hwy 92 85635

LA CASITA MEXICAN RESTAURANT & CANTINA 520/458-2376

Mexican. Casual Dining. **Address:** 465 E Fry Blvd 85635

THE OUTSIDE INN 520/378-4645

International. Casual Dining. **Address:** 4907 S Hwy 92 85650

TANUKI JAPANESE RESTAURANT & SUSHI BAR 520/459-6853

Japanese. Casual Dining. **Address:** 1221 E Fry Blvd 85635

SONORAN DESERT NATIONAL MONUMENT (E-3)

South of Phoenix in south-central Arizona, Sonoran Desert National Monument comprises mountain ranges, wide valleys and several saguaro cactus forests on 486,000 acres. The functioning desert ecosystem is a habitat for an array of wildlife, including desert bighorn sheep, mule deer, bobcats, desert tortoises, raptors, owls and bats.

It is believed that ancestors of the O'odham, Quechan, Cocopah and other tribes occupied villages in the area, which contains archeological and historical sites. Among the highlights for hikers are remnants of historic trails used by Juan Bautista de Anza, the Mormons and the Overland Stage, which can be found along a well-worn 20-mile corridor. For further information contact the Bureau of Land Management, Phoenix District, 21605 N. 7th Ave., Phoenix, AZ 85027; phone (623) 580-5500.

SPRINGERVILLE (D-6) pop. 1,961, elev. 6,862'

Springerville is in a cattle-ranching area of eastern Arizona. Created by shield volcanoes, the White Mountains neighbor the town, making it a convenient place to stay while enjoying the many outdoor activities offered by the area.

Springerville-Eagar Regional Chamber of Commerce: 7 W. Main St. (in the Springerville Heritage Center), P.O. Box 31, Springerville, AZ 85938. **Phone:** (928) 333-2123 or (866) 733-2123.

SPRINGERVILLE HERITAGE CENTER is at 418 E. Main St. Housed in a restored school building, the center offers a gallery of local art; a sketch by Rembrandt; European antiques dating from the Renaissance to the 18th century; dinosaur fossils found in the area; and access to the ancient ruins at Casa Malpais Pueblo *(see attraction listing)*. **Hours:** Mon.-Sat. 8-4. Closed major holidays. **Cost:** Free. **Phone:** (928) 333-2656, ext. 230.

Casa Malpais Museum, in the Springerville Heritage Center at 418 E. Main St., showcases pottery, artifacts and baskets unearthed at Casa Malpais Archaeological Park, a 15-acre restoration project of Mogollon and ancient pueblo ruins occupied 1250-1400. After watching an orientation film, visitors are driven to the pueblo site for a guided walking tour (self-guiding tours are not permitted).

Time: Allow 1 hour, 30 minutes minimum. **Hours:** Museum Mon.-Sat. 9-4. Site tours depart Tues.-Sat. at 9 and 1 (weather permitting), Mar.-Nov. Closed Jan. 1, Thanksgiving and Christmas. **Cost:** Free. Tours $10; $8 (ages 60+); $5 (ages 5-18 and students with ID). **Phone:** (928) 333-5375. GT

SUN CITY (I-2) pop. 37,499, elev. 1,140'

- **Hotels & Restaurants map & index p. 117**
- **Part of Phoenix area — see map p. 91**

Twelve miles northwest of Phoenix but part of the metropolitan area of the capital city, Sun City is one of the largest and most popular retirement communities in the country. By 1978 it had reached its population goal of more than 40,000, with most residential property in use. Sun City West, 2.5 miles west via Grand Avenue, offers a similar array of golf courses, stores, restaurants, recreation areas and other services.

Sun City Visitors Center: 16824 N. 99th Ave., Sun City, AZ 85351. **Phone:** (623) 977-5000 or (844) 478-6248.

LITTLE BITE OF ITALY 623/972-3311 (21)

Italian. Casual Dining. **Address:** 15456 N 99th Ave 85351

SUNSET CRATER VOLCANO NATIONAL MONUMENT (B-4)

Lying approximately 12 miles north of Flagstaff via US 89, then 2 miles east on Sunset Crater-Wupatki Loop Road, the 1,000-foot-high cinder cone of Sunset Crater Volcano dominates the surrounding fields of cinders, lava flows and spatter cones. The bright-reddish hues of the decomposed, water-stained sulfuric rock at the summit are in stark contrast with the black basalt of the adjacent rocks. From a distance the mountain appears to be on fire.

Dark at the base, the volcano also has shades of red, orange and yellow leading to the summit and takes on a rosy tint during the hour before sunset. In 1892 John Wesley Powell noted the phenomenon and purportedly gave the cone its name.

Sunset Crater Volcano may have first erupted A.D. 1064-65 and was active intermittently for nearly 200 years. Recent research indicates that the eruption may not have occurred until 1088 and may have lasted only a year. A self-guiding trail leads over the Bonito lava flow; sturdy walking shoes are recommended. A paved road crosses the lava flow and connects the monument with Wupatki National Monument *(see place listing p. 227)*. Picnicking is permitted. The

Lenox Crater Trail is a steep 1-mile round-trip hike to the top of a nearby volcanic summit.

Fire restrictions may apply. Allow 30 minutes minimum. Visitor center daily 8-5, June-Oct.; 9-5, rest of year. Closed Christmas. Admission (includes Wupatki National Monument), valid for 7 days, is $20 (per private vehicle); $15 (per motorcycle); $10 (per person arriving by foot or bicycle); free (ages 0-15). Phone (928) 526-0502.

SUPAI (B-3) pop. 208, elev. 3,195'

HAVASU CANYON is accessible from Hualapai Hilltop, which is reached from SR 66 via a turnoff 5 miles e. of Peach Springs. There are no services after the turnoff. Most of the 65-mile road from Peach Springs is in good condition.

Havasu Canyon is home to the village of Supai, which serves as the governmental center of the Havasupai Indian Reservation. Automobiles must be left at Hualapai Hilltop; the 8-mile journey to the canyon floor and Havasu Falls can be covered on horseback/pack mule, helicopter or on foot down a precipitous trail. No day hiking is allowed.

Note: The trail is only recommended for experienced hikers in good physical condition. The return climb out of the canyon is very arduous. Summer temperatures may prohibit daytime trips; phone ahead to confirm. The canyon is subject to flash floods. Hikers must carry at least two liters of water. Camping is permitted; no open fires are allowed. Swimming is permitted. Horse/pack mule rental is available.

Hours: Office hours daily 6-6, May-Oct.; 8-5, rest of year. **Cost:** $110 (includes $100 entrance fee and $10 environmental care fee). Camping (includes all permits, fees and taxes for 3 nights/4 days) $125 (per person per weekend night); $100 (per person per weekday night). Helicopter landing fee $50 (per person, one way). Horse fee $121 (one way). Pack mule fee $400 (round trip). Reservations for horses/pack mules, hiking and camping are required. Helicopter scenic rides have limited availability; reservations are not accepted. **Phone:** (928) 448-2111, or (928) 448-2121 for camping reservations.

SUPERIOR (J-6) pop. 2,837, elev. 2,730'

Although it began as a silver-mining town, Superior owes its existence to its proximity to some of the deepest and richest copper lodes in the country. Near Superior is Apache Leap Cliff, where, according to legend, 75 Apache warriors leaped to their deaths rather than be captured by the cavalry. The town also is near the southern terminus of US 60 (Gila/Pinal Scenic Drive), which travels northward through Tonto National Forest, Salt River Canyon and the Fort Apache Indian Reservation.

Superior Chamber of Commerce: 230 Main St., P.O. Box 95, Superior, AZ 85273. **Phone:** (520) 689-0200 or (602) 625-3151.

GEM **BOYCE THOMPSON ARBORETUM STATE PARK,** 3 mi. w. on US 60 at Milepost 223, has 3 miles of walking trails and paths leading past volcanic rock formations, cliffs, forests, streams, a desert lake and hundreds of species of cacti, succulents and agaves. Plants from Africa, Asia, Australia, the Mediterranean, the Middle East and North and South America can be seen. The 1.5-mile Main Trail is made of compact gravel and soil; half of the trail is accessible to wheelchairs. **Time:** Allow 1 hour minimum. **Hours:** Daily 8-5, Oct.-Apr.; 6-3, rest of year. Last admission 1 hour before closing. Classes, workshops and guided tours are offered. Closed Christmas. Phone ahead to confirm schedule. **Cost:** $15; $5 (ages 5-12). **Phone:** (602) 827-3000. GT

SURPRISE (I-2) pop. 117,517, elev. 1,178'

• **Hotels & Restaurants map & index p. 117**
• **Part of Phoenix area — see map p. 91**

In the Sonoran desert, Surprise was founded in 1937 by Homer C. Ludden, a state legislator who named the town after his hometown in Nebraska. Surprise Stadium is the spring training center for the Kansas City Royals and the Texas Rangers. Eight miles southwest is White Tank Mountain Regional Park *(see Recreation Areas Chart)*, which offers 22 miles of trails for hiking, horseback riding and mountain biking. Ancestral Desert People petroglyphs and such wildlife as the cactus wren, the official state bird, may be seen.

Surprise Regional Chamber of Commerce: 16126 N. Civic Center Plaza, Surprise, AZ 85374. **Phone:** (623) 583-0692.

COMFORT INN & SUITES SURPRISE-PHOENIX NW 623/544-6874 7
Hotel. **Address:** 13337 W Grand Ave 85374

DAYS INN & SUITES SURPRISE 623/933-4000 9
Hotel. **Address:** 12477 W Bell Rd 85374

HAMPTON INN & SUITES BY HILTON SURPRISE 623/537-9122 4

AAA Benefit: Members save up to 15%!

Address: 14783 W Grand Ave 85374 **Location:** Jct Bell Rd, 2 mi nw. **Facility:** 100 units. 4 stories, interior corridors. **Pool:** heated outdoor. **Activities:** hot tub, exercise room. **Guest Services:** coin laundry. **Featured Amenity: full hot breakfast.**

HOLIDAY INN EXPRESS & SUITES 623/975-5540 5
Hotel. **Address:** 16540 N Bullard Ave 85374

QUALITY INN & SUITES OF SURPRISE NEAR SUN CITY 623/583-3500 10
Hotel. **Address:** 16741 N Greasewood St 85374

(See map & index p. 117.)

RESIDENCE INN BY MARRIOTT PHOENIX NW SURPRISE 623/249-6333 6

SAVE Extended Stay Hotel. **Address:** 16418 N Bullard Ave 85374

AAA Benefit: Members save 5% or more!

WINDMILL SUITES SURPRISE, AN ASCEND HOTEL COLLECTION MEMBER 623/583-0133 8

Hotel. **Address:** 12545 W Bell Rd 85378

WHERE TO EAT

AMUSE BOUCHE 623/322-8881 1

American. Casual Dining. **Address:** 17058 W Bell Rd 85374

MACAYO'S MEXICAN TABLE 623/214-5950

Mexican. Casual Dining. **Address:** 15565 W Bell Rd 85379

SAIGON KITCHEN 623/544-6400 3

Vietnamese. Casual Dining. **Address:** 14071 W Bell Rd 85374

UNI SUSHI & STEAK 623/546-7669 2

Japanese Sushi. Casual Dining. **Address:** 17191 N Litchfield Rd 85374

VOGUE BISTRO 623/544-9109 4

New American. Casual Dining. **Address:** 15411 W Waddell Rd 85379

TAYLOR pop. 4,112

RODEWAY INN-SILVER CREEK INN 928/536-2600

Motel. **Address:** 825 N Main St 85939

TEMPE (J-3) pop. 161,719, elev. 1,159'

- **Hotels p. 178 • Restaurants p. 180**
- **Hotels & Restaurants map & index p. 126**
- **Part of Phoenix area — see map p. 91**

Founded as Hayden's Ferry in 1871, Tempe originally was named for Charles Trumbull Hayden, who owned a flour mill and operated a ferry across the Salt River. The town was renamed Tempe (Tem-PEE) in 1879 for the area's alleged resemblance to the Vale of Tempe in ancient Greece.

In 1886 the dusty cow town became the home of the Arizona Territorial Normal School, later to become Arizona State University *(see attraction listing)*. Downtown Tempe has a laid-back college town feel.

ASU Gammage, one of the last major buildings designed by Frank Lloyd Wright, is a performing arts center on the campus of Arizona State University. Phone (480) 965-6912 for information about free guided tours of the center.

Twice a year, crowds head downtown for the Spring Tempe Festival of the Arts and the Tempe Fall Festival of the Arts, which feature a live entertainment stage, street performers and more than 350 artists selling handcrafted items. In October, Tempe celebrates its ties to its sister city—Regensburg, Germany—with Oktoberfest at Tempe Town Lake that's complete with beer, brats, bands and family entertainment. Sun Devil Stadium hosts a college bowl game in late November. Then Tempe residents usher in the new year at Mill Avenue's New Year's Eve.

Sports fans can go out to the ball game during spring training, which begins in late February. Fifteen Cactus League teams get ready for the season at Tempe Diablo Stadium; phone (480) 350-5205.

Tempe Tourism Office: 222 S. Mill Ave., Suite 120, Tempe, AZ 85281. **Phone:** (480) 894-8158 or (800) 283-6734.

Shopping: Specialty shops are scattered throughout downtown Tempe, the five-block segment of Mill Avenue between 3rd Street and University Drive. Arizona Mills Mall, I-10 and Baseline Road, is one of the state's largest shopping and attraction complexes. Tempe Marketplace, at McClintock Drive and Rio Salado Parkway, is a popular outdoor shopping and entertainment destination.

Nightlife: Football fans enjoy tasty food and libations as they root on ASU in the sports bars and restaurants on shady Mill Avenue. Gordon Biersch Brewery (420 S. Mill Ave., #201) pours tasty brew and has a second-floor terrace overlooking the street action below; phone (480) 736-0033. Blasted Barley Beer Co. (404 S. Mill Ave.) features craft beer and more than 40 flat-screen HDTVs and is usually packed on big game nights; phone (480) 967-5887. Postino Annex (615 S. College Ave.), set in a restored, redbrick building on the ASU campus, is the place to go before shows at the ASU Gammage auditorium; phone (480) 927-1111.

ARIZONA HISTORICAL SOCIETY/AZ HERITAGE CENTER AT PAPAGO PARK, 1300 N. College Ave., explores the history of central Arizona through interactive exhibits for children and adults. Topics include early settlements, World War II aircraft and internment camps, post-war growth of a thriving desert metropolis, copper mining and water management. Other exhibits cover Arizona history-makers such as Sandra Day O'Connor and Barry Goldwater, and a natural history exhibit of gems and minerals. Rotating displays and educational programs are offered throughout the year.

Hours: Museum Mon.-Thurs. 10-5, Fri.-Sat. 10-4. Closed major holidays. **Cost:** $12; $10 (ages 65+); $8 (ages 7-17). Prices may vary; phone ahead. **Phone:** (480) 929-0292. Center Pkwy/Washington, 24

IMAX THEATER AT ARIZONA MILLS, off I-10 Baseline Rd. exit at the mall, presents films that are based on both IMAX and IMAX 3D technology. IMAX 3D films require the use of 3D glasses. The lifelike images are projected on a screen that is six stories high. Hollywood feature films are shown. **Hours:** IMAX, IMAX 3D and feature-length films are shown daily. Phone ahead to confirm schedule. **Cost:** $15; $12 (ages 60+); $11 (ages 3-13). **Phone:** (480) 897-4629.

TEMPE HISTORY MUSEUM is off US 60 exit 174 (Rural Rd.), then .4 mi. n. to 809 E. Southern Ave. The museum has four themed areas: College Town,

(See map & index p. 126.)

Building Our Community, Living Together and Surviving in the Desert. Reading and computer stations as well as a children's gallery filled with hands-on activities provide educational opportunities. **Hours:** Tues.-Sat. 10-5, Sun. 1-5. Closed major holidays. **Cost:** Donations. **Phone:** (480) 350-5100.

AC HOTEL PHOENIX TEMPE/DOWNTOWN 480/642-6140 8

SAVE Boutique Contemporary Hotel. **Address:** 100 E Rio Salado Pkwy 85281

AAA Benefit: Members save 5% or more!

ALOFT HOTEL TEMPE 480/621-3300 6

SAVE Hotel. **Address:** 951 E Playa Del Norte Dr 85281

AAA Benefit: Members save 5% or more!

BEST WESTERN INN OF TEMPE 480/784-2233 4

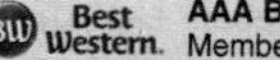

AAA Benefit: Members save up to 15% and earn bonus points!

Address: 670 N Scottsdale Rd 85281 **Location:** SR 202 (Red Mountain Frwy) exit 7 (Rural Rd S), just s. Veterans Way/College, 26. **Facility:** 103 units. 4 stories, interior corridors. *Bath:* shower only. **Activities:** hot tub, exercise room. **Guest Services:** valet laundry, area transportation. **Featured Amenity:** breakfast buffet.

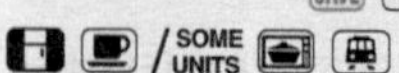

BEST WESTERN PLUS TEMPE BY THE MALL 480/820-7500 29

AAA Benefit: Members save up to 15% and earn bonus points!

Address: 5300 S Priest Dr 85283 **Location:** I-10 exit 155 (Baseline Rd), 0.4 mi e, then just s. **Facility:** 157 units. 4 stories, interior corridors. **Pool:** heated outdoor. **Activities:** hot tub, picnic facilities, exercise room. **Guest Services:** valet and coin laundry, area transportation. **Featured Amenity:** continental breakfast.

COMFORT INN & SUITES TEMPE PHOENIX SKY HARBOR AIRPORT 480/858-9898 3

Hotel. **Address:** 808 N Scottsdale Rd 85281

COMFORT SUITES PHOENIX AIRPORT 480/446-9500 16

Address: 1625 S 52nd St 85281 **Location:** I-10 exit 153B (Broadway Rd), just s, 0.5 mi e on Broadway Rd, then just n. **Facility:** 92 units. 3 stories, interior corridors. **Pool:** heated outdoor. **Activities:** hot tub, exercise room. **Guest Services:** valet and coin laundry. **Featured Amenity:** continental breakfast.

SAVE BIZ / SOME UNITS HS

100% Non-smoking Suites
Free Airport Shuttle from Sky Harbor Int'l Airport

Comfort SUITES by CHOICE HOTELS

COURTYARD BY MARRIOTT-DOWNTOWN TEMPE 480/966-2800 9

SAVE Hotel. **Address:** 601 S Ash Ave 85281

AAA Benefit: Members save 5% or more!

DOUBLETREE BY HILTON PHOENIX-TEMPE 480/967-1441 19

Hotel

DoubleTree by Hilton

AAA Benefit: Members save up to 15%!

Address: 2100 S Priest Dr 85282 **Location:** I-10 exit 153 (Broadway Rd), 0.5 mi e. **Facility:** 270 units. 3 stories, exterior corridors. **Amenities:** safes. **Pool:** heated outdoor. **Activities:** hot tub, exercise room. **Guest Services:** valet laundry, area transportation. **Featured Amenity:** breakfast buffet.

SAVE BIZ / SOME UNITS

DRURY INN & SUITES PHOENIX TEMPE 480/940-3700 33

Hotel. **Address:** 1780 W Ranch Rd 85284

EMBASSY SUITES BY HILTON PHOENIX-TEMPE 480/897-7444 24

SAVE Hotel. **Address:** 4400 S Rural Rd 85282

AAA Benefit: Members save up to 15%!

EXTENDED STAY AMERICA-PHOENIX/AIRPORT/TEMPE 480/557-8880 12

Extended Stay Hotel. **Address:** 2165 W 15th St 85281

(See map & index p. 126.)

FAIRFIELD INN & SUITES BY MARRIOTT PHOENIX TEMPE/AIRPORT 480/967-7161 **21**

Hotel

Fairfield **AAA Benefit:** Members save 5% or more!

Address: 2222 S Priest Dr 85282 **Location:** I-10 exit 153B (Broadway Rd), 0.5 mi e, then just s. **Facility:** 110 units. 5 stories, interior corridors. **Pool:** heated outdoor. **Activities:** hot tub, exercise room. **Guest Services:** valet and coin laundry, area transportation. **Featured Amenity: breakfast buffet.**

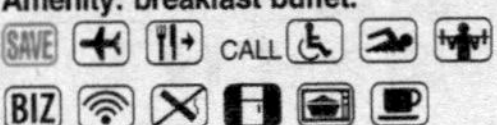

SAVE CALL BIZ

HAMPTON INN & SUITES BY HILTON PHOENIX/TEMPE-ASU AREA 480/941-3441 **2**

AAA Benefit: Members save up to 15%!

Address: 1415 N Scottsdale Rd 85281 **Location:** SR 202 Loop (Red Mountain Frwy) exit 7 (Rural Rd S), 0.5 mi n. **Facility:** 117 units. 4 stories, interior corridors. **Pool:** heated outdoor. **Activities:** hot tub, picnic facilities, exercise room. **Guest Services:** valet and coin laundry, area transportation.

HS

/ SOME UNITS

HAMPTON INN & SUITES TEMPE PHOENIX AIRPORT 480/410-6400 **14**

SAVE Hotel. **Address:** 1550 S 52nd St 85281

AAA Benefit: Members save up to 15%!

HAWTHORN SUITES BY WYNDHAM 480/633-2744 **22**

Hotel

Address: 2301 E Southern Ave 85282 **Location:** SR 101 exit 54 (Southern Ave/Baseline Rd); at southeast corner. **Facility:** 68 units, some efficiencies. 3 stories, interior corridors. **Amenities:** safes. **Pool:** heated outdoor. **Activities:** hot tub, exercise room. **Guest Services:** valet and coin laundry. **Featured Amenity: full hot breakfast.**

SAVE ECO CALL

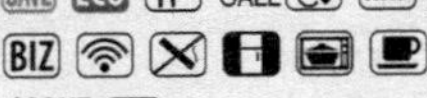

/ SOME UNITS HS

HILTON GARDEN INN PHOENIX-TEMPE ASU RESEARCH PARK 480/897-5100 **32**

SAVE Hotel. **Address:** 7290 S Price Rd 85283

AAA Benefit: Members save up to 15%!

HOLIDAY INN EXPRESS & SUITES PHOENIX TEMPE-UNIVERSITY 480/966-7202 **17**

Hotel. **Address:** 1031 E Apache Blvd 85281

HOLIDAY INN EXPRESS & SUITES TEMPE 480/831-9800 **25**

Hotel. **Address:** 1520 W Baseline Rd 85283

HOME2 SUITES BY HILTON PHOENIX-TEMPE ASU RESEARCH PARK 480/897-5200 **31**

SAVE Extended Stay Hotel. **Address:** 7200 S Price Rd 85283

AAA Benefit: Members save up to 15%!

HOTEL TEMPE PHOENIX AIRPORT INNSUITES HOTEL & SUITES 480/897-7900 **27**

Hotel. **Address:** 1651 W Baseline Rd 85283

HYATT PLACE TEMPE/PHOENIX AIRPORT 480/804-9544 **7**

Hotel

HYATT PLACE **AAA Benefit:** Members save up to 10%!

Address: 1413 W Rio Salado Pkwy 85281 **Location:** Just w of Priest Dr. Priest Dr/Washington, 23. **Facility:** 123 units. 6 stories, interior corridors. **Pool:** heated outdoor. **Activities:** exercise room. **Guest Services:** valet laundry, area transportation. **Featured Amenity: breakfast buffet.**

SAVE CALL

BIZ

/ SOME UNITS HS

MARRIOTT PHOENIX TEMPE AT THE BUTTES 602/225-9000 **20**

SAVE Resort Hotel. **Address:** 2000 Westcourt Way 85282

AAA Benefit: Members save 5% or more!

MOXY PHOENIX TEMPE/ASU AREA 480/968-3451 **18**

SAVE Hotel. **Address:** 1333 S Rural Rd 85281

AAA Benefit: Members save 5% or more!

RAMADA TEMPE AT ARIZONA MILLS MALL 480/413-1188 **26**

Hotel. **Address:** 1701 W Baseline Rd 85283

RED LION INN & SUITES PHOENIX/TEMPE 480/675-9799 **1**

Hotel

Address: 1429 N Scottsdale Rd 85281 **Location:** SR 202 Loop (Red Mountain Frwy) exit 7 (Rural Rd S), 0.5 mi n. **Facility:** 118 units, some two bedrooms and efficiencies. 1-3 stories, exterior corridors. **Pool:** heated outdoor. **Activities:** hot tub, picnic facilities, exercise room. **Guest Services:** valet and coin laundry, area transportation. **Featured Amenity: breakfast buffet.**

SAVE CALL

BIZ

/ SOME UNITS

RED ROOF PLUS+ TEMPE-PHOENIX AIRPORT 480/449-3205 **13**

Hotel

Address: 2135 W 15th St 85281 **Location:** I-10 exit 153B (Broadway Rd), just nw on S 52nd St, then just w. **Facility:** 125 units. 3 stories, interior corridors. **Amenities:** safes.

SAVE

(See map & index p. 126.)

RESIDENCE INN BY MARRIOTT TEMPE 480/756-2122 23

SAVE Extended Stay Hotel. **Address:** 5075 S Priest Dr 85282

AAA Benefit: Members save 5% or more!

RESIDENCE INN BY MARRIOTT TEMPE DOWNTOWN/ UNIVERSITY 480/967-2300 11

Extended Stay Hotel

Residence INN **AAA Benefit:** Members save 5% or more!

Address: 510 S Forest Ave 85281 **Location:** Jct University Dr, just n on Mill Ave, just e; downtown. Veterans Way/College, 26. **Facility:** 173 efficiencies, some two bedrooms. 11 stories, interior corridors. **Parking:** on-site (fee). **Terms:** check-in 4 pm. **Pool:** heated outdoor. **Activities:** hot tub, exercise room. **Guest Services:** valet and coin laundry, rental car service. **Featured Amenity: continental breakfast.**

SAVE CALL BIZ / SOME UNITS

SHERATON PHOENIX AIRPORT HOTEL TEMPE 480/967-6600 15

SAVE Hotel. **Address:** 1600 S 52nd St 85281

AAA Benefit: Members save 5% or more!

SPRINGHILL SUITES BY MARRIOTT PHOENIX TEMPE AIRPORT 480/968-8222 5

Hotel

SPRINGHILL SUITES MARRIOTT **AAA Benefit:** Members save 5% or more!

Address: 1601 W Rio Salado Pkwy 85281 **Location:** Just w of Priest Dr. Priest Dr/Washington, 23. **Facility:** 130 units. 6 stories, interior corridors. **Pool:** heated outdoor. **Activities:** hot tub, exercise room. **Guest Services:** valet and coin laundry, area transportation. **Featured Amenity: breakfast buffet.**

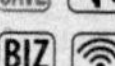

SPRINGHILL SUITES BY MARRIOTT TEMPE AT ARIZONA MILLS MALL 480/752-7979 28

Hotel

SPRINGHILL SUITES MARRIOTT **AAA Benefit:** Members save 5% or more!

Address: 5211 S Priest Dr 85283 **Location:** I-10 exit 155 (Baseline Rd), southeast corner of Baseline Rd and Priest Dr. Across from Arizona Mills Mall. **Facility:** 121 units. 3 stories, interior corridors. **Pool:** heated outdoor. **Activities:** picnic facilities, exercise room. **Guest Services:** valet and coin laundry, area transportation.

TEMPE MISSION PALMS 480/894-1400 10

Hotel

Address: 60 E 5th St 85281 **Location:** Jct University Dr, just n on Mill Ave, just e. Mill Ave/3rd St, 25. **Facility:** In the downtown area surrounded by shops and restaurants, the hotel offers newly renovated, upscale rooms and baths overlooking a beautifully landscaped courtyard with fountains. 303 units. 4 stories, interior corridors. **Parking:** on-site and valet. **Amenities:** safes. **Pool:** heated outdoor. **Activities:** hot tub, exercise room, massage. **Guest Services:** valet laundry, boarding pass kiosk, area transportation. Affiliated with Destination Hotels.

SAVE ECO CALL BIZ / SOME UNITS

TOWNEPLACE SUITES BY MARRIOTT TEMPE AT ARIZONA MILLS MALL 480/345-7889 30

SAVE Extended Stay Hotel. **Address:** 5223 S Priest Dr 85283

AAA Benefit: Members save 5% or more!

WHERE TO EAT

BYBLOS RESTAURANT 480/894-1945 15

Greek. Casual Dining. **Address:** 3332 S Mill Ave 85282

CAFE LALIBELA 480/829-1939 4

Ethiopian. Casual Dining. **Address:** 849 W University Dr 85281

CASEY MOORE'S OYSTER HOUSE 480/968-9935 6

American. Casual Dining. **Address:** 850 S Ash Ave 85281

CHOU'S KITCHEN 480/557-8888 9

Regional Chinese. Casual Dining. **Address:** 1250 E Apache Blvd 85281

THE DHABA 480/446-2824 12

Indian Casual Dining
$10-$24

AAA Inspector Notes: Savor authentic Indian cuisine while sampling such favorites as tikka masala, paneer with tamarind chutney and freshly baked naan. Be sure to check out the market next door. **Features:** beer & wine. **Address:** 1872 E Apache Blvd 85281 **Location:** Jct Rural Rd, 1.2 mi e. McClintock/Apache, 29.

L D

HAJI BABA MIDDLE EASTERN FOOD 480/894-1905 11

Middle Eastern. Casual Dining. **Address:** 1513 E Apache Blvd 85281

HOUSE OF TRICKS 480/968-1114 2

American. Casual Dining. **Address:** 114 E 7th St 85281

LA BOCCA 480/967-5244 1

Pizza. Casual Dining. **Address:** 699 S Mill Ave, Suite 115 85281

LEMON GRASS THAI CAFE 480/967-9121 14

Thai. Casual Dining. **Address:** 818 W Broadway Rd, Suite 108 85282

MACAYO'S MEXICAN TABLE 480/966-6677

Mexican. Casual Dining. **Address:** 300 S Ash Ave 85281

P.F. CHANG'S CHINA BISTRO 480/731-4600 5

Chinese. Fine Dining. **Address:** 740 S Mill Ave 85281

(See map & index p. 126.)

REPUBLIC RAMEN & NOODLES 480/388-3686 (8)

Asian Noodles. Quick Serve. **Address:** 1301 E University Dr 85281

SERRANO'S MEXICAN RESTAURANT 480/345-0044

Mexican. Casual Dining. **Address:** 6440 S Rural Rd 85283

SNOOZE AN A.M. EATERY 480/355-1934 (3)

Breakfast. Casual Dining. **Address:** 615 S College Ave 85281

SUSHI 101 480/317-0101 (7)

Sushi. Casual Dining. **Address:** 920 E University Dr, Suite 101 85281

TASTY KABOB 480/966-0260 (10)

Middle Eastern. Casual Dining. **Address:** 1250 E Apache Blvd, Suite 116 85281

TOM'S BBQ CHICAGO STYLE 480/820-0728 (16)

Barbecue. Quick Serve. **Address:** 115 E Baseline Rd, Suite 5 85283

TOP OF THE ROCK RESTAURANT 602/431-2370 (13)

American. Fine Dining. **Address:** 2000 Westcourt Way 85282

THATCHER pop. 4,865

SPRINGHILL SUITES BY MARRIOTT THATCHER 928/428-6900

Hotel

SPRINGHILL SUITES MARRIOTT **AAA Benefit:** Members save 5% or more!

Address: 2855 W Hwy 70 85552 **Location:** US 191, 2.5 mi w. **Facility:** 71 units. 3 stories, interior corridors. **Pool:** heated outdoor. **Activities:** picnic facilities, exercise room. **Guest Services:** coin laundry.

SAVE CALL BIZ HS

WHERE TO EAT

KAINOA'S HAWAIIAN GRILL 928/792-2118

Hawaiian. Quick Serve. **Address:** 3533 Hwy 70 85552

TOLLESON pop. 6,545

• Hotels & Restaurants map & index p. 117
• Part of Phoenix area — see map p. 91

BEST WESTERN TOLLESON 623/936-6000 (51)

Hotel

Best Western **AAA Benefit:** Members save up to 15% and earn bonus points!

Address: 8421 W McDowell Rd 85353 **Location:** I-10 exit 135 (83rd Ave), just n, then just w. **Facility:** 60 units, some two bedrooms. 2 stories (no elevator), interior corridors. **Pool:** outdoor. **Activities:** hot tub, exercise room. **Guest Services:** coin laundry, area transportation.

SAVE BIZ

    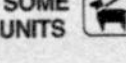

/ SOME UNITS

TOMBSTONE (G-5) pop. 1,380, elev. 4,540'

• Hotels p. 182 • Restaurants p. 182

"The town too tough to die," Tombstone was perhaps the most renowned of Arizona's old mining camps. When Ed Schieffelin came to Camp Huachuca with a party of soldiers and left the fort to prospect, his comrades told him that he would find his tombstone rather than silver. Thus, in 1877 Schieffelin named his first claim Tombstone, and rumors of rich strikes made a boomtown of the settlement that adopted this name.

Over the course of 7 years the mines produced millions of dollars in silver and gold before rising underground waters forced suspension of operations.

Days of lawlessness and violence in Tombstone climaxed with the infamous battle between Wyatt Earp and his brothers against the Clanton brothers, fought at the rear entrance to the O.K. Corral.

Many of Tombstone's historic buildings are within an area bounded by Fremont, 6th, Toughnut and 3rd streets. Among them are St. Paul's Episcopal Church, built in 1882; the Crystal Palace, one of the most luxurious saloons in the West; and the Tombstone Epitaph building, where the oldest continuously published paper in Arizona is still being printed. Western printing history exhibits in the front office are free to the public.

Tombstone Chamber of Commerce: 109 S. 4th St., P.O. Box 995, Tombstone, AZ 85638. **Phone:** (520) 457-9317 or (888) 457-3929.

BOOTHILL GRAVEYARD, at the w. city limits at 408 SR 80, contains some 250 marked graves of early citizens as well as graves of some of the town's famous and infamous residents. This is reportedly the first cemetery to be called "Boot Hill." **Time:** Allow 1 hour minimum. **Hours:** Daily 8-6. Graveyard closes at dusk. Closed Christmas. **Cost:** $3; free (ages 0-16). **Phone:** (520) 457-3300.

O.K. CORRAL, between 3rd and 4th sts. on Allen St., includes the site where the Gunfight at the O.K. Corral started on Oct. 26, 1881. Re-enactment of the gunfight takes place daily at noon, 2 and 3:30. **Time:** Allow 30 minutes minimum. **Hours:** Daily 9-5. Closed Thanksgiving and Christmas. Phone ahead to confirm schedule. **Cost:** Combination ticket with Historama (includes gunfight reenactment and Camillus Fly Photography Studio) $10; free (ages 0-5). **Phone:** (520) 457-3456.

Camillus Fly Photography Studio is between 3rd and 4th sts. on Fremont St., entered through the O.K. Corral. This is the re-created studio and boardinghouse of the pioneer photographer. Doc Holliday's room and photographs of 1880s Tombstone and Apache warrior Geronimo are displayed. **Time:** Allow 30 minutes minimum. **Hours:** Daily 9-5. Closed Thanksgiving and Christmas. **Cost:** O.K. Corral admission (includes Historama and O.K. Corral gunfight reenactment) $10; free (ages 0-5). **Phone:** (520) 457-3456.

TOMBSTONE COURTHOUSE STATE HISTORIC PARK, 223 E. Toughnut St., was built in 1882. The building contains displays pertaining to the history of Tombstone and Cochise County, using antiques and artifacts to present the lives of former citizens. **Time:** Allow 1 hour minimum. **Hours:** Daily 9-5. Closed Christmas. **Cost:** $7; $2 (ages 7-13). **Phone:** (520) 457-3311.

LANDMARK LOOKOUT LODGE 520/457-2223
Hotel. **Address:** 781 N Hwy 80 85638

THE TOMBSTONE GRAND HOTEL 520/457-9507
Hotel. **Address:** 580 W Randolph Way 85638

TOMBSTONE MONUMENT RANCH 520/457-8707
Ranch. **Address:** 895 W Monument Rd 85638

WHERE TO EAT

BIG NOSE KATE'S SALOON 520/457-3107
American. Casual Dining. **Address:** 417 E Allen St 85638

THE LONGHORN RESTAURANT 520/457-3405

American Casual Dining $7-$20

AAA Inspector Notes: This historic district corner eatery, popular with locals and tourists, serves a good selection of steak, sandwiches and Mexican entrées in an Old West decor. Desserts, such as deep-dish apple pie and the death by chocolate, are served large enough to share. **Features:** beer & wine. **Address:** 501 E Allen St 85638 **Location:** Corner of 5th St. **Parking:** street only. B L D

O.K. CAFE 520/457-3980
American. Casual Dining. **Address:** 220 E Allen St 85638

TONTO NATIONAL FOREST (H-4)

Elevations in the forest range from 1,300 ft. at Apache Junction to 7,900 ft. at the Mogollon Rim in the Payson District. Refer to AAA maps for additional elevation information.

Stretching some 90 miles south from the scenic Mogollon Rim to the city of Scottsdale, the Tonto National Forest encompasses 2.9 million acres of spectacular pine, brush and cactus country, making it one of the largest national forests. Elevations range from 1,300 feet to almost 7,900 feet in the northern pine country. Eight regions have been designated as wilderness areas; the entire forest offers more than 860 miles of trails for backpacking, hiking and horse travel.

Scenic roadways in the area include the Apache Trail (SR 88) *(see attraction listing p. 28)*, Beeline Highway (SR 87) and Young Highway (SR 288). Some unpaved roads are very rough, so phone ahead for current road condition updates. **Note:** The Apache Trail (SR 88) is a winding road and is not suitable for motor homes or vehicle-towing; nearly 25 miles of the road is unpaved.

Six lakes allow boating, swimming and fishing; Saguaro, Bartlett, Canyon, Apache and Theodore Roosevelt lakes have marina facilities. Tubing is a popular pastime in the summer on the lower Salt River. Campgrounds, picnic sites and other recreational opportunities also are available throughout the forest. A map showing roads, recreation sites and tourist services can be obtained from the local Forest Service office for $10.

For further information contact the Forest Supervisor's Office, Tonto National Forest, 2324 E. McDowell Rd., Phoenix, AZ 85006; phone (602) 225-5200. *See Recreation Areas Chart.*

TONTO NATIONAL MONUMENT (I-6)

Four miles east of Roosevelt Dam on SR 188, Tonto National Monument preserves the most accessible of south-central Arizona's prehistoric cliff dwellings. The remains of a two-story pueblo built in a natural cave are visible from the headquarters parking area. A half-mile-long (one way) paved foot trail ascends 350 feet and leads to cliff dwellings that were occupied by the Salado culture in the 13th and 14th centuries. Summer temperatures are high; wear a hat and suitable shoes and carry sufficient water.

Ranger-conducted, 3-hour tours to the less accessible 40-room Upper Cliff Dwelling are available November through April. Tours are conducted 3 or 4 days a week and are limited to 15 people per day; reservations are required. Phone (928) 467-2241, ext. 8450 for reservations.

A visitor center and museum contain artifacts from the Salado culture, including examples of the pottery and woven textiles for which they are noted. Leashed pets are allowed on the lower trail but not on the Upper Cliff Dwelling tour or in any dwellings. Allow 1 hour, 30 minutes minimum. Park and visitor center open daily 8-5; closed Christmas. Trail to the Lower Cliff Dwelling closes 1 hour before park closing. Picnic area 8-4:45. Admission $5; free (ages 0-15). Phone (928) 467-2241, ext. 8450.

TUBAC (G-4) pop. 1,191, elev. 3,200'

Tubac, meaning "sinking water," was a Pima village when Jesuit Eusebio Francisco Kino visited the area in 1691. A presidio and mission were established in 1752 (the first military base in Arizona) shortly after the Pima revolted against Spanish encroachment. Between 1752 and 1856 some 500 people lived at Tubac, but in 1776 the presidio was moved to help fortify the strategically important Tucson. With the Gadsden Purchase in 1853, the town became a part of the United States.

The Mexican War, the California gold rush of 1849 and the raiding Apaches depopulated the town throughout much of the 19th century. However, in 1859 Arizona's first newspaper was printed by a local mining company who revived the town. By 1860 Tubac was the largest town in Arizona, but the Civil War left the town unprotected, and it was deserted once again. Once the Apaches ceded control of the area in the late 1800s, Tubac began to grow, but it never regained its earlier importance.

Next to the old presidio, modern Tubac is a small community of writers and artists. Many of the shops and galleries in town sell the local art.

Tubac Chamber of Commerce: 1 Burruel Rd., Tubac, AZ 85646. **Phone:** (520) 398-2704.

TUBAC GOLF RESORT & SPA 520/398-2211

Historic Boutique Resort Hotel

Address: 1 Otero Rd 85646 **Location:** I-19 exit 40 (Chavez Siding Rd), on east side, then 2 mi s. Located in a quiet area. **Facility:** Set on more than 500 acres, the property's historic Spanish Colonial architecture and magnificent mountain views provide for a unique and tranquil getaway. A variety of guest rooms are available. 98 units, some two bedrooms and efficiencies. 1 story, exterior corridors. **Terms:** check-in 4 pm. **Amenities:** safes. **Dining:** Stables Ranch Grille, see separate listing. **Pool:** heated outdoor. **Activities:** sauna, hot tub, steamroom, regulation golf, tennis, bicycles, lawn sports, exercise room, spa. **Guest Services:** valet laundry.

SAVE ECO BIZ / SOME UNITS

WHERE TO EAT

ELVIRA'S 520/398-9421
Mexican. Casual Dining. **Address:** 2221 E Frontage Rd 85646

THE ITALIAN PEASANT 520/398-2668
Italian. Casual Dining. **Address:** 50 Avenida Goya 85646

SHELBY'S BISTRO 520/398-8075
Regional American. Casual Dining. **Address:** 19 Tubac Rd-Mercado de Baca 85646

STABLES RANCH GRILLE 520/398-2678
American. Fine Dining. **Address:** 1 Otero Rd 85646

TUBA CITY (B-4) pop. 8,611, elev. 4,936'

Tuba City was named after Tuve, a Hopi leader. Natural springs attracted generations of Hopi, Navajo and Paiute Indians to the area. In 1875 the city was laid out and settled by Mormons, who used blocks of dressed stone from nearby prehistoric sites to build structures, some of which still stand.

The town lies on US 160, 10 miles east of US 89 within Arizona's northeastern Native American country, which encompasses the Navajo and Hopi Indian reservations. A variety of Native American crafts are produced in the area, including baskets, pottery and silver products.

MOENKOPI LEGACY INN & SUITES 928/283-4500
Hotel. **Address:** 1 Legacy Ln 86045 *(See ad p. 185.)*

QUALITY INN NAVAJO NATION 928/283-4545

Hotel

Address: 10 N Main St 86045 **Location:** 1 mi n of US 160. Adjacent to historic Tuba Trading Post. **Facility:** 80 units. 2 stories (no elevator), interior corridors. **Dining:** Hogan Restaurant, see separate listing. **Activities:** exercise room. **Guest Services:** coin laundry. **Featured Amenity: full hot breakfast.**

SAVE CALL BIZ / SOME UNITS

WHERE TO EAT

HOGAN RESTAURANT 928/283-5260
Southwestern. Casual Dining. **Address:** 10 N Main St 86045

Tucson

Then & Now

Tucson is a culturally rich city that enjoys a starkly beautiful Sonoran Desert setting and reliably warm weather. It's this tourism trifecta that today draws droves of golfers, hikers, shopaholics, Mexican-food lovers and leisure-wear resort regulars to Arizona's second-largest city.

With a population above the half-million mark, Tucson has seen some unfortunate stucco-and-strip-mall suburban sprawl. But make no mistake, this is no Phoenix Junior. With the lovely Santa Catalina Mountains as a backdrop and the towering cacti of Saguaro National Park at its doorstep, Tucson feels connected to its surroundings.

Many of the city's historical adobes were bulldozed back in the 1960s. However, a good number of the low-slung Spanish and Mexican-era structures remain, especially in the Barrio Viejo neighborhood (just south of downtown) and the El Presidio Historic District in the heart of downtown.

When the summer sun isn't blazing, the latter is a nice area for a leisurely stroll, shopping at the Old Town Artisans complex and perhaps a happy hour Cadillac margarita at El Charro Cafe, the city's oldest restaurant.

Downtown's Stone Avenue is home to two of the city's most important houses of worship. The baroque St. Augustine Cathedral, completed in 1868, looks like it's been plucked straight out of a colonial Mexican town. Nearby, the historic 1910 Stone Avenue Temple was one of Arizona's first synagogues. Designed in a mix of neoclassic, Romanesque and Moorish styles, the building now houses the Jewish History Museum and Holocaust History Center.

St. Augustine Cathedral

The downtown core has long boasted some beautiful public murals and buildings, including the mosaic-tile domed, Spanish Colonial Revival-style Pima County Courthouse, completed in 1928. The Tucson Museum of Art and Historic Block in addition to two historic neighborhoods are also downtown.

Years ago some tourists complained that there's little else to entertain a non-history buff for long, but today the area is booming with dozens of restaurants—including several run by well-known chefs—and regular food truck and art gallery gatherings. Making it easy to explore Tucson's downtown, the Sun Link streetcar runs from Main Gate Square and the adjacent University of Arizona campus through the 4th Avenue shopping, dining and nightlife district, to the Mercado, Tucson's public market.

(Continued on p. 188.)

Destination Tucson

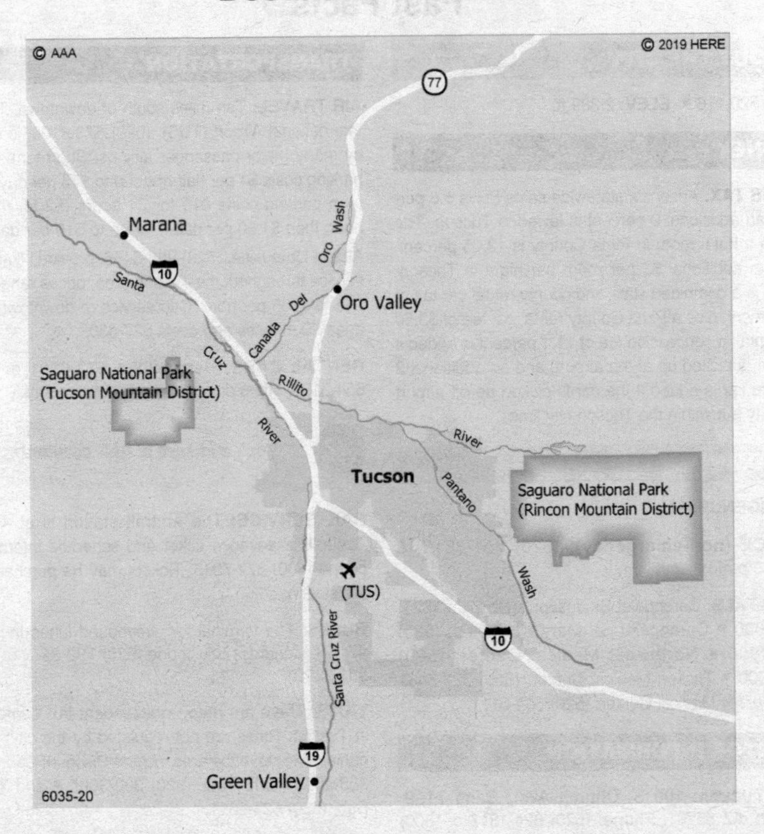

This map shows cities in the Tucson vicinity where you will find attractions, hotels and restaurants. Cities are listed alphabetically in this book on the following pages.

Fast Facts

ABOUT THE CITY

POP: 520,116 ▪ **ELEV:** 2,389 ft.

MONEY

SALES TAX: Arizona's statewide sales tax is 5.6 percent; an additional 2 percent is levied in Tucson. The tax on a hotel room in Pima County is 13.05 percent, plus an additional $2 per room per night in Tucson. There is a combined state and county rental car tax of 10 percent, plus a Pima County rental car fee of $3.50 per rental; a concession fee of 11.1 percent is added if the car is picked up at the airport, and an additional 2 percent tax is added if the car is picked up off airport property but within the Tucson city limits.

WHOM TO CALL

EMERGENCY: 911

POLICE (non-emergency): (520) 791-6813 (8 a.m.-10 p.m.)

HOSPITALS: Carondelet St. Joseph's Hospital, (520) 873-3000 ▪ Carondelet St. Mary's Hospital, (520) 872-3000 ▪ Northwest Medical Center, (520) 742-9000 ▪ Tucson Medical Center, (520) 327-5461 ▪ University Medical Center, (520) 694-0111.

VISITOR INFORMATION

Visit Tucson: 100 S. Church Ave., Suite 7199, Tucson, AZ 85701. **Phone:** (520) 624-1817 or (800) 638-8350.

A visitor information center in La Placita Village is open Mon.-Fri. 9-5, Sat.-Sun. 9-4; closed major holidays.

TRANSPORTATION

AIR TRAVEL: Ten miles south of downtown, Tucson International Airport (TUS), (520) 573-8100, is served by many major passenger airlines. Short-term airport parking costs $1 per half-hour up to $13 per day; long-term parking costs $10 for 24 hours ($2 for the first hour, then $1.50 per half-hour up to $10 per day).

Allison Limousine, (520) 888-5466, provides limousine service throughout the Tucson area; prices range from $65 to $135 per hour. Cab service to downtown averages 20 minutes and costs $27-$30.

RENTAL CARS: Hertz, (520) 573-5201 or (800) 654-3131, offers discounts to AAA members.

RAIL SERVICE: The Amtrak station is at 400 N. Toole. For advance ticket and schedule information phone (800) 872-7245. Tickets may be purchased at the station.

BUSES: The terminal for Greyhound Lines Inc. is at 471 W. Congress St.; phone (520) 792-3475 or (800) 231-2222.

TAXIS: There are many independent taxi companies in Tucson. Rates are not regulated by the city. Companies that serve the area include Discount Cab, (520) 388-9000 ▪ VIP Taxi, (520) 300-3000 ▪ and Yellow Cab, (520) 624-6611.

PUBLIC TRANSPORTATION: Sun Tran, (520) 792-9222, operates a fleet of buses running throughout the metro area as well as a streetcar line downtown. *See Getting Around, Public Transportation.*

(Continued from p. 186.)

On the east side of downtown is the lively Congress Street district. Tourists, hipsters and college students amble down sidewalks lined with early 20th-century buildings. Amtrak trains rumble into the lovingly restored Southern Pacific Railroad Depot, parts of which are more than a hundred years old. Today the depot houses a transportation museum.

After dark, indie rock fans line up under the historic Rialto Theatre's electric pink-and-purple neon marquee for a sold-out gig. It's also here you'll find the 1919 Hotel Congress, home to a hip nightclub. On the west end of Congress Street, a former silent-movie house, the Fox Tucson Theatre, is a beautifully restored venue for live shows and classic movie screenings.

Spanish, Mexican and Western heritage play big parts in the city's cultural pageant. But the constant parade of Arizona Wildcats T-shirts on the street will show you that this is a college town as well. The University of Arizona campus sits a few miles northeast of downtown.

Golf and spa resorts and modern shopping centers are ubiquitous in the foothill neighborhoods north of town. If you drive further up into the Santa Catalina Mountains, you'll find Mount Lemmon, where you can hit the slopes at one of the country's southernmost ski areas. The mountain tops out among pine trees at 9,157 feet, and from here you'll be treated to expansive views of Tucson and its surroundings. This is also the location of the Mount Lemmon SkyCenter, which takes advantage of the Tucson area's clear skies, clean air and low humidity, as do other internationally known observatories within a couple hours' drive: Kitt Peak and Whipple observatories *(see attraction listings p. 173).*

Must Do: AAA Editor's Picks

- Travel back to New Spain at **Mission San Xavier del Bac** (1950 W. San Xavier Rd.). Started in 1692 by the Rev. Eusebio Kino of the Jesuits, today's mission was built 1783-97 by the Franciscans, who continue its ministry. The atmosphere hearkens back to the 18th century, complete with arches, original statuary and mural paintings.
- Explore the diversity of Tucson's ecosystem at the **Arizona-Sonora Desert Museum** (2021 N. Kinney Rd.) where you'll find trails, gardens, animals and even an aquarium.
- Embrace the great outdoors at **Tucson Mountain Park** (W. Gates Pass Rd. & S. Kinney Rd.). No visit is complete without experiencing the stark beauty of the desert with its wide horizons and far-reaching saguaros. Whether it's hiking, taking pictures, painting or exploring the area's history, there's plenty of fun things to do.
- Indulge in flavors indigenous to Tucson and the Southwest. Thought to have been popularized by **El Charro Cafe** (311 N. Court Ave.) cheese crisps (quesadillas) and chimichangas are good bets at the family-owned restaurant, which has been open since 1922. Also featuring quesadillas, **Teresa's Mosaic Cafe** (2456 N. Silver Mosaic Dr.) is best known for huevos rancheros. Other Tucson favorites: Sonoran hot dogs (bacon-wrapped and loaded with tasty toppings) and fry bread as well as jams and candies made out of cacti.
- Unleash the kids at **Children's Museum Tucson** (200 S. 6th Ave.) where displays are geared toward your youngest family members. STEM—Science, Technology, Engineering and Mathematics—exhibits educate, and kids can get creative in themed activity areas.
- Ride the rails—or imagine you're doing so at the **Southern Arizona Transportation Museum** (414 N. Toole Ave.). Much of the West's growth came from the arrival of railroads, so you'll find the museum beside the former Southern Pacific Railroad Depot—still welcoming passengers. Highlights include a locomotive, sculpture of Doc Holiday and Wyatt Earp, and exhibits highlighting railroad culture.
- View the former site of **El Presidio San Agustin del Tucsón** (196 N. Court Ave.), an adobe established in 1775 by the Spanish. Though the last fort remnant was torn down in 1918, recent conservation efforts re-created portions. You'll see walls, a 20-foot adobe tower called a *torreón* and a mural that explains the rest of the 11-acre site.
- Browse the **Tucson Museum of Art and Historic Block** (140 N. Main Ave.), which sits on a corner of what was once the presidio. Although Art of the American West is understandably a big deal here, the museum features a range of other genres. Shop for handmade creations made by Arizona residents at the museum store and then tour the nearby historic buildings.
- Check out Tucson's many fine music venues. It's up to you whether you hang out at landmark **Hotel Congress** (311 E. Congress St.) for the party-filled ambience, or for a really unique experience, there's **Sky Bar** (536 N. 4th Ave.), a solar-powered bar that just happens to be a planetarium, too.
- March around the **Arizona Historical Society/Fort Lowell Museum** (2900 N. Craycroft Rd.) grounds to learn about frontier military life. Within the refurbished Commanding Officer's Quarters, you'll find exhibits detailing everything from the Apache Wars to everyday life for soldiers and their families.
- Refresh your memory about the indigenous history of the state and northern Mexico at the **Arizona State Museum** (1013 E. University Blvd.). One exhibit features pottery dating back hundreds of years. Other exhibits include photographs, relics and priceless textiles—but all highlight the Southwest's distinctive personality.

Hotel Congress

Tucson 1-day Itinerary

AAA editors suggest these activities for a great short vacation experience.

Morning

- The sun rising over the Sonoran Mountains provides a pleasing light that's perfect for exploring Tucson's rugged terrain. Tread carefully around the prickly saguaros—scene-stealing cacti that dot the landscape and appear on everything from salsa jars to shoot-'em-up Westerns.
- At the GEM **Arizona-Sonora Desert Museum** (2021 N. Kinney Rd.), you'll find a world-class zoo, museum and botanical garden all rolled into one. Fun things to do include investigating how saguaros provide valuable habitat for wildlife, enjoying a live-animal demonstration or walking one of the desert trails. Start early: Temperatures can climb into the 100-plus range during the summer.
- If you'd like to wander farther than the museum's trails allow, explore GEM **Tucson Mountain Park** (W. Gates Pass Rd. & S. Kinney Rd.). With approximately 20,000 acres, the park welcomes hikers, mountain bikers and equestrians alike, and no wonder—the views from Gates Pass Scenic Overlook are superb.
- Did you spot unidentified wildlife? A visit to the **International Wildlife Museum** (4800 W. Gates Pass Rd.) might clear up the mystery. Its interactive displays feature more than 400 species of preserved birds, insects and mammals in natural surroundings.
- The tile-decorated surfaces at **Teresa's Mosaic Cafe** (2456 N. Silver Mosaic Dr.) provide a colorful backdrop for plates of huevos divorciados and huevos rancheros. The latter were even featured on the Food Network's "Throwdown With Bobby Flay," where the chef tried his hand at the dish. Though the egg specialties are hard to beat, try a cheese crisp.

Afternoon

- Sure to inspire your own vacation photographs, the **Center for Creative Photography** (1030 N. Olive Rd.) offers ever-changing exhibits. It's also the museum that photographer Ansel Adams co-founded at University of Arizona, so make an appointment to survey its permanent collection.
- The GEM **Arizona State Museum** (1013 E. University Blvd.), also on campus, highlights local indigenous cultures using pottery, textiles and baskets as well as field notes and drawings.
- To explain how the state developed, the nearby **Arizona Historical Society/Arizona History Museum** (949 E. 2nd St.) delves into the Spanish and pre-territorial periods.
- Stick to **The Postal History Foundation** (920 N. First Ave.) for your fix of stamps and postal history. The structure—assembled circa 1895 from a prefabricated "post office kit"—was moved a few times before serving as a museum. Guests still can mail letters and packages from the full-service post office.

Tucson Mountain Park

- After licking envelopes and mailing presents, visit **Magpie's Gourmet Pizza** (605 N. 4th Ave.) for some finger-licking food. Made fresh to order, foodies can choose from a variety of toppings to create their own pie. Offering everything from salads and subs to calzones and oven-roasted wings, the restaurant also features delectable desserts.
- Visualize early Tucson at the **Arizona Historical Society/Downtown History Museum** (140 N. Stone Ave.). History buffs can browse through depictions of houses and other buildings, including police and fire departments, and an old-time barbershop.

Evening

- As the heat of the day settles, head toward the **Tucson Museum of Art and Historic Block** (140 N. Main Ave.) around what was once Spain's **El Presidio San Agustin del Tucsón** (196 N. Court Ave.). An on-site art museum highlights Western and Latin American art as well as rare books and manuscripts.
- The atmospheric **Main Dining Room at the Arizona Inn** (2200 E. Elm St.) awaits. Things for couples to do include ordering the pastry chef's selection of small bites or enjoying a nightcap to end the evening on a warm note.
- Or end your night at **Sky Bar** (536 N. 4th Ave.). This solar-powered bar serves galaxy-themed cocktails. Be sure to take a break from dancing to enjoy the celestial views from the telescopes on the patio.

Top Picks for Kids

Under 13

- Even the smallest kids will feel really big at **The Mini Time Machine Museum of Miniatures** (4455 E. Camp Lowell Dr.), which transports visitors to places both real and imaginary. Fairytale castles, enchanted trees and beautifully crafted miniature homes from around the world captivate young imaginations.
- Another sure bet when it comes to attractions for kids is downtown's **Children's Museum Tucson** (200 S. 6th Ave.), where educational science exhibits are cleverly disguised as fun play areas with names like Music Garden, Imaginarium Art Studio and Investigation Station.
- With hundreds of furry, feathered and funny-looking animal residents, **Reid Park Zoo** (3400 E. Zoo Ct.) sets the stage for adorable antics that will keep kids entertained while showing off our planet's biological diversity. And when it's time to cool off, head to Kenya Get Wet, the zoo's water playground.
- Too hot for a day at the zoo? Step inside the **International Wildlife Museum** (4800 W. Gates Pass Rd.), where hundreds of species of preserved mammals, birds and insects are arranged in lifelike displays. Hands-on exhibits keep young ones engaged and allow up-close encounters with wildlife that you can't get at a zoo—at least not safely.

Teens

- Explore one of the largest dry caverns in he world at **Colossal Cave Mountain Park** (16721 E. Old Spanish Trail) during a 45-minute guided tour among otherworldly rock formations. The park also features trails, a petting zoo, butterfly garden and horseback rides along with some chilling tales of outlaws who once hid out in the area and possibly left behind some stolen loot.
- Among Tucson's other great things to do with kids is the **Pima Air and Space Museum** (6000 E. Valencia Rd.), home to scores of sleek jets, World War II fighter planes and a 1960s Air Force One used by President Kennedy. Hundreds of aircraft and exhibits illustrate the history of flight, and tram tours provide an overview of the vast facility. You can even tour the nearby "Boneyard," final resting place of more than 4,000 retired aircraft.
- Take your family on a journey to the edges of the universe at **Mount Lemmon SkyCenter** (9800 E. Ski Run Rd.) atop 9,157-foot Mount Lemmon. A good attraction for kids over 7, the SkyCenter offers a wonderful evening under the stars. You can learn the names of constellations and take a peek at Saturn's rings through powerful telescopes, and the drive up the mountain alone is worth it.

Old Tucson

All Ages

- For beautiful desert scenery, **Sabino Canyon** (5900 N. Sabino Canyon Rd.) can't be beat. A natural oasis in the Santa Catalina Mountain foothills, the canyon offers spectacular views as well as a long menu of activities for the whole family including hiking, biking, horseback riding and swimming. Or, for a more relaxing journey, take a narrated tram tour, which drops visitors off at any of nine stops.
- Experience Tucson's Old West heritage during **La Fiesta de los Vaqueros** (4823 S. 6th Ave.), a 9-day festival held each February. The highlight is the Tucson Rodeo, one of the most respected in North America. The Tucson Rodeo Parade draws thousands of spectators with its horse-drawn floats, marching bands and Mexican folk dancers, and there are even rodeo events for cowboys and cowgirls under 12.
- Tucson is a great city, but it's a little disappointing when it comes to saloons, stage coaches and gunfights at high noon—unless you visit **Old Tucson** (201 S. Kinney Rd.). If you think it looks like a movie set, that's because it is! Hundreds of films and TV shows were made here, and staged gunfights, stunt shows and musical reviews are just some of the family fun offered.
- Despite the name, the Sonoran Desert is filled with life, and you should definitely explore the area's amazing landscape. But if you're pressed for time, the **Arizona-Sonora Desert Museum** (2021 N. Kinney Rd.) will give you a quick, family-friendly introduction. Part zoo, part botanical garden, part exhibition hall, this premiere Tucson attraction is perfect for kids.

Arriving

By Car

Tucson's major approach and through-route is I-10, the nation's southernmost transcontinental highway. Primarily an east-west route, it angles into the city from the southeast and the northwest. Northbound, I-10 intersects with I-19 in south Tucson and then continues along the west side of the city, providing access to the downtown area. Once I-10 leaves the city, it proceeds northwest to Phoenix, 120 miles away.

A major approach from the west is I-8, which originates in San Diego and joins with I-10 about midway between Phoenix and Tucson. Because both I-10 and I-8 traverse desert country, some of their sections are subject to dust storms, particularly in spring and early summer. Local radio stations broadcast advisories during these fluctuating weather conditions, and interstate signs with changeable messages warn motorists.

A well-known route reaching Tucson from the north is SR 77. One of the area's oldest two-lane routes, it is especially scenic. South of Tucson, I-19 leads to the Mexican border at Nogales.

Getting Around

Street System

Tucson is laid out in a grid pattern. Numbered streets run east-west to the south of Speedway Boulevard, and numbered avenues run north-south to the west of Euclid Avenue. Address numbers start at the intersection of Broadway, the north-south divider, and Stone, the east-west divider. Unless otherwise posted the speed limit on most streets is 25 to 40 mph.

Old Town Artisans

Parking

Metered parking is available on many downtown streets, but be sure to check signs and meters for restricted times and limits. There also are a number of commercial garages and lots. Rates average around $2 per hour or $5 per day.

Public Transportation

Sun Link, Tucson's modern streetcar system, began operating in 2014. The 3.9-mile system features 23 stops and connects downtown Tucson with the University of Arizona campus, Main Gate Square, the 4th Avenue Business District and the Mercado District. Several Sun Link stations are decorated with sculptures by various artists, including an eye-catching, 6-foot-tall human head made up of small, steel letters at the E. Helen Street and N. Warren Avenue station.

Riding Sun Link requires either a 1-day SunGO ticket, which costs $4, or a one-way fare of $1.50; 50c (ages 65+ with valid ID and the physically impaired). Reloadable SunGO Cards, transfers and 30-day tickets also are available. Tickets can be purchased at vending machines at each Sun Link stop, and each ticket must be validated once you are on board by tapping it against one of four validators. Phone (520) 792-9222 for more information.

Sun Tran, Tucson's bus service, operates a fleet of modern buses. The Ronstadt Transit Center, on 6th Avenue between Congress and Pennington streets, is the main downtown station. The fare to all points is $1.50; 50c (ages 65+ with valid ID and the physically impaired); free (ages 0-5). Fares can be paid to the bus driver or at self-serve ticket machines (cash only).

Shopping

If you've come to Tucson itchin' to buy turquoise, Kachina dolls and dream catchers, the world is your oyster. But Southwestern art and crafts are only part of the city's shopping picture. You can also overstuff your carry-on bag or car trunk with goods from funky boutiques, cutting-edge art galleries and high-end shopping malls.

Downtown in the El Presidio district, **Old Town Artisans,** 201 N. Court Ave., is housed in an 1850s adobe building that sits on an entire city block. The half-dozen shops and galleries deal mainly in traditional Native and Latin American crafts (pottery, carvings, blankets), but you'll also find some contemporary jewelry and art here.

The Tucson Museum of Art and Historic Block's excellent **Museum Store,** 140 N. Main Ave., carries a nice selection of works by some of the state's best artists (read: expensive), as well as art books and affordable gift items.

Surrounding downtown you'll find a sprinkling of modern art galleries, particularly in the Congress Street district; there are more galleries a few blocks north in the **Warehouse Arts District** (centered at 6th Avenue and 6th Street). For more information on galleries, check hotel brochure racks for the Central Tucson Gallery Association's Downtown Art & Lunch guide map, or phone (520) 629-9759.

Without question, downtown's most eclectic shopping and dining area is 4th Avenue (between 9th Street and University Boulevard). With the exception of a prehistoric Dairy Queen, you won't see a single chain store or restaurant (not even a Starbucks) on the entire strip, which is exactly how Tucson hipsters like it.

This is a college town, so books are big. **Antigone Books,** 411 N. 4th Ave., has a feminist bent. If you need a copy of "Eat Pray Love," there's no danger Antigone is sold out. In addition to edgy, female-focused fare and other off-beat titles, there's a selection of cute gift items. One musty whiff of **The Book Stop,** 214 N. 4th Ave., and you know you've ascended to used-book heaven.

Fashionistas will find two of the street's best clothing boutiques at **Zoe Boutique,** 3065 N. Campbell Ave., where items range from trendy to funky-casual, and **Desert Vintage,** 403 N. 6th Ave. The latter is the destination for hunting 1920s flapper dresses, bellbottoms and poodle skirts.

Tucson's Map & Flag Center, 3239 N. First Ave., is a bit off the beaten path, but a must for back-country adventurers. The store carries topographic maps for the entire state, plus travel guidebooks and detailed road maps.

As for malls, Tucson isn't in league with Phoenix, but it's no slouch, either. **Tucson Mall,** 4500 N. Oracle Rd., is the city's biggest center followed in size and variety by **Park Place Mall,** 5870 E. Broadway Blvd. Outlet fanatics can bargain hunt at the **Foothills Mall,** 7401 N. La Cholla Blvd. Shop under blue skies at **La Encantada,** 2905 E. Skyline Dr., an open-air haven with eight diverse places to eat, most of them with local roots, and high-end shops (think Brooks Brothers and Louis Vuitton); there's an Apple Store in case your iPod's on the fritz as well as year-round special events.

For a shopping courtyard filled with unique specialty boutiques, try the hacienda-style **St. Philip's Plaza,** at the southeast corner of Campbell Avenue and River Road. The plaza's **Bahti Indian Arts** specializes in Native American art and crafts. On Saturday and Sunday, the plaza hosts a farmers market; the Saturday market also includes an artisans market.

Nightlife

Tucson's nightlife is mainly concentrated in the downtown area. Whether you choose to catch a live band, sip designer cocktails or guzzle beer alongside UofA students, many spots are within walking distance of one another.

Club Congress, 311 E. Congress St., has been called one of the country's best live music clubs by *Esquire* magazine. Just off the lobby of the historic **Hotel Congress**, the venue books mostly local and regional alt-rock bands. The stage, backed with red velvet drapes and framed by Gothic-style metalwork, overlooks a dance floor that's shoulder-to-shoulder on weekends; phone (520) 622-8848.

Rialto Theatre

If you'd rather skip the club and its surprisingly high cover charge, yet still be able to hear the music, opt for the Hotel Congress' lobby bar. The décor is classic Southwest Deco, the scene is laid-back and there's a casual patio out back as well.

Across the street is the **Rialto Theatre,** 318 E. Congress St., a restored 1920 vaudeville and movie palace that now hosts mid-level touring acts (think Bon Iver, Lucinda Williams and Fleet Foxes); phone (520) 740-1000.

The miraculously rehabilitated **Fox Tucson Theatre,** 17 W. Congress St., screens classic movies just as it did back in its 1930s and '40s heyday. Also equipped with a stage and near-perfect acoustics, the Fox books live music acts and ballet performances; phone (520) 547-3040.

Downtown's tiny **The Screening Room,** 127 E. Congress St., shows a mix of recent box office smashes and indie fare; phone (520) 882-0204. Even better is **The Loft Cinema,** 3233 E. Speedway Blvd. (a few minutes east of the UofA campus), which has three screens and runs film festival standouts and theme nights like "Mondo Mondays" and "Scream-o-rama"; phone (520) 795-7777.

Fourth Avenue is loaded with casual bars and pubs popular with UofA students. On the upscale side is **Sky Bar,** 536 N. 4th Ave., a sleek space that's a chill-out café by day and a hip bar by night. DJs spin techno and house beats on weekends; there's live jazz and blues on Tuesday. Every night, flat-screen TVs show astronomical images taken from the bar's very own telescope; phone (520) 622-4300.

If it's live music you're after, **The Flycatcher,** 340 E. 6th St. (corner of 4th Ave. and 6th St.) is the neighborhood's best bet. The majority of acts playing this funky club/bar are local indie rock bands, but a quick scan of the schedule will turn up some folk, bluegrass and acoustic singer-songwriter acts as well; phone (520) 207-9251.

For country music you'll need to gas up the F-150 and head to east Tucson. Opened in 1962, **The Maverick Live Country Club,** 6622 E. Tanque Verde Rd., offers live music Tuesday through Saturday; phone (520) 298-0430.

Romantics in the mood to clink wine glasses, hear a jazz pianist and gaze out at the twinkling city lights should head for the hilltop **Hacienda del Sol Guest Ranch Resort,** 5501 N. Hacienda del Sol Rd. Both the elegant Terraza Garden Patio and Lounge and the comfy private Joesler Room are classy spots for a tête-á-tête; phone (520) 299-1501.

Big Events

In February the city boasts a superlative: the world's largest gem and mineral show with more than 40 shows across town. The focal point of the **Tucson Gem and Mineral Show** is at the **Tucson Convention Center,** which is filled with some 250 dealers selling to the public.

If you like horses and cowboys, Tucson is the destination for you mid- to late February during **La Fiesta de los Vaqueros,** held at the rodeo grounds. This classic professional rodeo event features a parade with people on foot, on horseback and in every size and shape of horse-drawn vehicle. The fiesta ends with the rodeo finals, in which some of the best riders and ropers on the circuit compete.

Pima County Fair

In March and again in December Tucson's 4th Avenue holds a huge street fair filled with artisans selling and demonstrating their crafts. Enhanced by music and food vendor booths, these weekends attract visitors and residents alike. The annual **Tucson International Mariachi Conference** and music festival comes to town in late April. Mid-month brings the **Pima County Fair.** In May, the **Tucson Folk Festival** attracts thousands of traditional music fans for a weekend of entertainment by the genre's top acts.

Tucson's fall activities begin in late September and early October with **Oktoberfest on Mount Lemmon.** In early November, a Tucson artists' organization presents the annual **All Souls Procession.** Inspired by Mexico's Día de los Muertos, thousands of people walk 2 miles through the streets of Tucson to commemorate the passing of loved ones, carrying photos of the deceased, wearing the departed's clothing or dressed in skeleton costumes.

Sports & Rec

Tucson is America's **Winter Training Capital,** and an athlete's mid-winter dream. With comfortable temperatures and abundant sunshine, it's almost impossible to lose a training day—no matter what your sport.

Tucson's city parks and Pima County parks offer facilities for almost any activity. A number of **swimming** pools and **tennis, racquetball** and **handball** courts are available as well as picnic areas, playgrounds, and **soccer** and ball fields. For information about facilities and reservations for their use contact the Pima County Parks and Recreation office at 3500 W. River Rd., (520) 724-5000, or Tucson Parks and Recreation at 900 S. Randolph Way, (520) 791-4873.

Tucson's climate is made to order for **golf** addicts. More than 60 courses are in the region—everything from world-renowned resorts to public access courses. The jaw-dropping topography and rugged desert terrain of the real Southwest have ignited the imaginations of the greatest golf course architects. Some were designed by Robert Cupp, Tom Fazio, Arthur Hill, Robert Trent Jones and Jack Nicklaus along with newcomer Notah Begay III.

Among the courses in Tucson are: Hilton Tucson El Conquistador Golf and Tennis Resort's Pusch Ridge and Cañada courses, (520) 544-5000, 10000 N. Oracle Rd. and 10555 N. La Cañada Dr.; Omni Tucson National, (520) 297-2271, 2727 W. Club Dr.; Randolph Municipal, (520) 791-4161, 600 S. Alvernon Way; and Ventana Canyon, (520) 577-1400, 6200 N. Clubhouse Ln. Also in the area is Canoa Ranch Golf Club, (520) 393-1966, at 5800 S. Camino del Sol in Green Valley.

Ranked by several elite **bicycling** publications as one of America's most bike-friendly cities, Tucson also is home to what has been called one of the premier organized rides in the United States—El Tour de Tucson attracts more than 9,000 bicyclists of all ages and abilities each November.

Hiking is probably the best way to get up close and personal with the flora and fauna of the Sonoran Desert. Tucson Mountain Park is laced with hiking trails and is among Tucson's most fun places to go. The Santa Catalina Mountains offer many areas of unspoiled beauty as well. Hiking permits are required for some areas. Empty vehicles will be fined or towed if a permit is not displayed. For more information about permits and National Forest fee areas, contact the Coronado National Forest office in Tucson; phone (520) 388-8300.

Catalina State Park *(see Recreation Areas Chart)*, (520) 628-5798, has trails that can challenge the experienced hiker but not intimidate the novice; two longer trails begin at the end of the park's paved road. For more information about hiking, phone the county's recreation office at (520) 724-5000. Hike In Tucson directs guided hiking trips along several area trails; phone (520) 477-6867 or (877) 445-3749.

Another great way to see the countryside is on a trail ride. Several stables offer half-day, full-day and overnight **horseback riding** trips into the mountains and desert. Check hotel brochure racks for stables. **Skiing** is available at Mount Lemmon Ski Valley, a scenic 30-mile drive northeast from Tucson. The southernmost ski area in the nation, Mount Lemmon offers both downhill and cross-country skiing. A scenic sky ride on the ski lift is offered during the off-season. Phone (520) 576-1400 for snow condition updates.

The University of Arizona's Wildcats excite crowds during the **football, baseball** and **basketball** seasons. Home football games are played at Arizona Stadium, baseball players batter up at Hi Corbett Field and basketball teams tip off at McKale Memorial Center.

Performing Arts

When it comes to enjoying theater during your vacation, Tucson offers many choices. Top billing is given to the **Arizona Theatre Company,** Arizona's professional state theater. This premier company performs six plays during its September through May season at the **Temple of Music and Art,** (520) 622-2823, 330 S. Scott Ave. A forum for experimental theater is **The Invisible Theatre,** (520) 882-9721, 1400 N. 1st Ave., which stages six plays between September and June.

If you're looking for things to do with kids, the **Gaslight Theatre,** (520) 886-9428, 7010 E. Broadway, offers entertainment for the entire family. The melodramas, comedies and musicals produced here encourage audience participation; reservations are required. The **University of Arizona** adds to Tucson's theater offerings. The school's resident company, (520) 621-7008, 1025 N. Olive St., presents its offerings of musicals and serious drama in spring, summer and fall, while the UA Presents series brings national touring companies to **Centennial Hall,** (520) 621-3341, 1020 E. University Blvd.

No bit players, Tucson's opera company plays a major part in the performing arts arena. Accompanied by a full orchestra from October through April, members of the **Arizona Opera,** (520) 293-4336, present five operas at **Tucson Music Hall,** 260 S. Church Ave.

Completing the cultural scene are the city's orchestras. The **Tucson Symphony Orchestra,** (520) 882-8585, plays both classical and pop music in the **Tucson Music Hall** September to May. Under the desert skies at the **DeMeester Outdoor Performance Center** in Reid Park, the **Tucson Pops Orchestra,** (520) 722-5853, entertains audiences in the spring and fall. From September through May the University of Arizona's Centennial Hall resounds with sounds from Broadway shows to jazz to chamber music performed by guest artists and musicians.

ATTRACTIONS

For a complete list of attractions, visit AAA.com/travelguides/attractions

ARIZONA HISTORICAL SOCIETY/ARIZONA HISTORY MUSEUM, 949 E. 2nd St., is in a building designed by Josias Joesler and features exhibits portraying the daily life of 1870s Tucson families; the life of Apache warrior Geronimo; and various modes of 19th- and early 20th-century transportation. Museum highlights include a walk-through, full-size replica of a 100-year-old underground copper mine, a real stagecoach and a wide variety of artifacts from the Southwest's territorial period. A research library is available.

Time: Allow 1 hour minimum. **Hours:** Museum Mon.-Thurs. 9-4, Fri. 9-8, Sat. 11-4. Library hours vary; phone ahead. Closed Jan. 1, Easter, Veterans Day, Thanksgiving and Christmas. **Cost:** $8; $6 (ages 65+); $5 (students with ID); $4 (ages 7-17). Prices may vary; phone ahead. Validated parking is available in the garage at E. 2nd Street and N. Euclid Avenue. **Phone:** (520) 628-5774.

ARIZONA HISTORICAL SOCIETY/DOWNTOWN HISTORY MUSEUM, 140 N. Stone Ave., depicts downtown Tucson's history from its origins as a Spanish presidio in 1775 to modern times. Visitors may visit a 19th-century hotel lobby and an old-time barbershop. Explore the history of downtown's police force, firefighters, schools, libraries, businesses and theaters. An exhibit about the 1934 capture of John Dillinger and his gang includes his bulletproof vest.

Time: Allow 30 minutes minimum. **Hours:** Wed.-Fri. 10-4. Closed Jan. 1, July 4, Veterans Day, Thanksgiving and Christmas. **Cost:** Donations. Validated parking is available on lower level of Wells Fargo Bank garage on E. Alameda Street. **Phone:** (520) 770-1473.

GEM **ARIZONA-SONORA DESERT MUSEUM,** 14 mi. w. in Tucson Mountain Park at 2021 N. Kinney Rd., is an interpretative center showcasing the diversity of the Sonoran Desert region, recognized as the lushest desert on earth. The museum offers a zoo, botanical garden, art gallery, natural

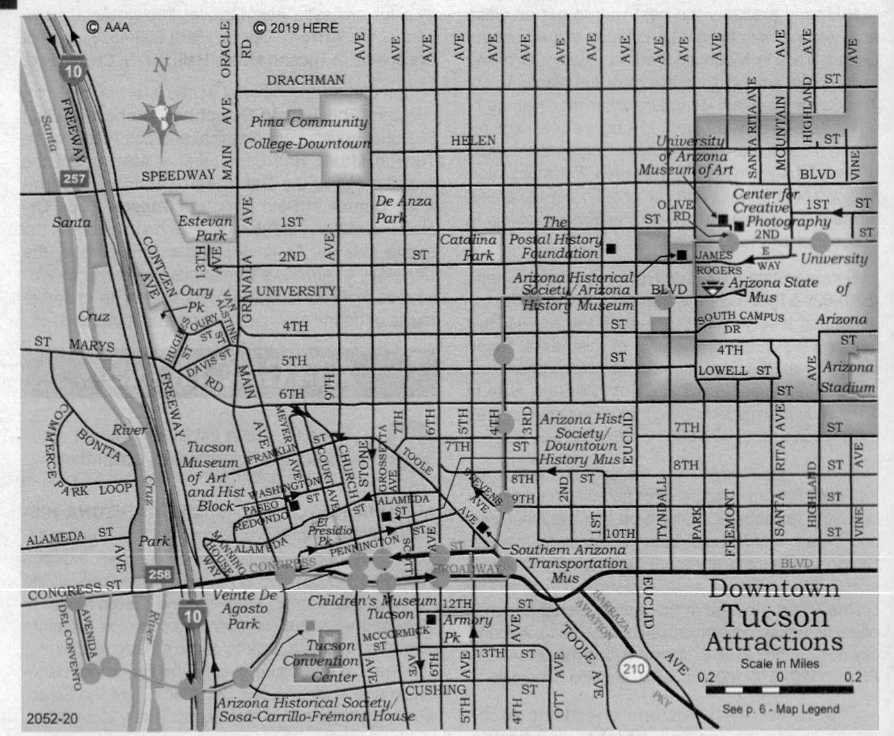

history museum and aquarium showcasing the regions' animals, plants, geology, climate and native cultures in a natural environment.

The 21-acre facility features 2 miles of walking paths and houses some 230 animal species, including coatis, javelina, road runners and Mexican gray wolves. The popular hummingbird aviary features several species of the tiny birds; visitors can see breeding and nesting activity January through May and get close enough to photograph the birds. Sixteen gardens display 1,200 types of plants and 56,000 specimens. The Earth Sciences Center, a simulated walk-through limestone cave, features a collection of regional gems and minerals. Live animal presentations include Live and (sort of) on the Loose (venomous reptiles), Raptor Free Flight (seasonal) showcasing native birds of prey, and Fur, Feathers and Fangs (mammals and birds). A stingray touch pool invites visitors to interact with cow nose stingrays from the Gulf of California.

Hours: Daily 7:30-5, Mar.-Sept.; 8:30-5, rest of year. **Cost:** $21.95; $19.95 (ages 65+); $17.95 (active and retired military with ID); $8.95 (ages 3-12). Prices may vary; phone ahead. **Phone:** (520) 883-1380. GT

GEM **ARIZONA STATE MUSEUM** is at 1013 E. University Blvd. on the University of Arizona campus. Founded in 1893, this Smithsonian affiliate reputedly has the world's largest and most comprehensive collections of Southwest Indian pottery and Native American basketry. The region's indigenous cultures are featured in exhibits, guided tours and hands-on programs.

The Paths of Life: American Indians of the Southwest exhibit highlights the origin, history and contemporary life of Apache, Hopi, Navajo, Tohono O'odham, Southern Paiute and other indigenous groups. There's a mix of prehistoric artifacts, historical objects, commissioned artwork, video interviews and dioramas.

Southwest Native American pottery and basketry are showcased. The library and archives contain photographs and archeological excavation reports.

Time: Allow 1 hour minimum. **Hours:** Museum Mon.-Sat. 10-5. Closed major holidays. **Cost:** $8; free (ages 0-17). **Phone:** (520) 621-6302. GT

CORONADO NATIONAL FOREST—see place listing p. 38.

DEGRAZIA GALLERY IN THE SUN is in the foothills of the Santa Catalina Mountains, 1 mi. n. of Sunrise Dr. at 6300 N. Swan Rd. More than 15,000 ceramics, paintings and sculptures created by Southwestern artist Ettore "Ted" DeGrazia are featured in permanent and rotating exhibits. Mission in the Sun, an open-air adobe chapel built in the 1950s by DeGrazia and his Native American friends, adjoins the gallery on the 10-acre National Historic site. The artist's final resting place is marked beside the chapel along with the first house he built. **Hours:**

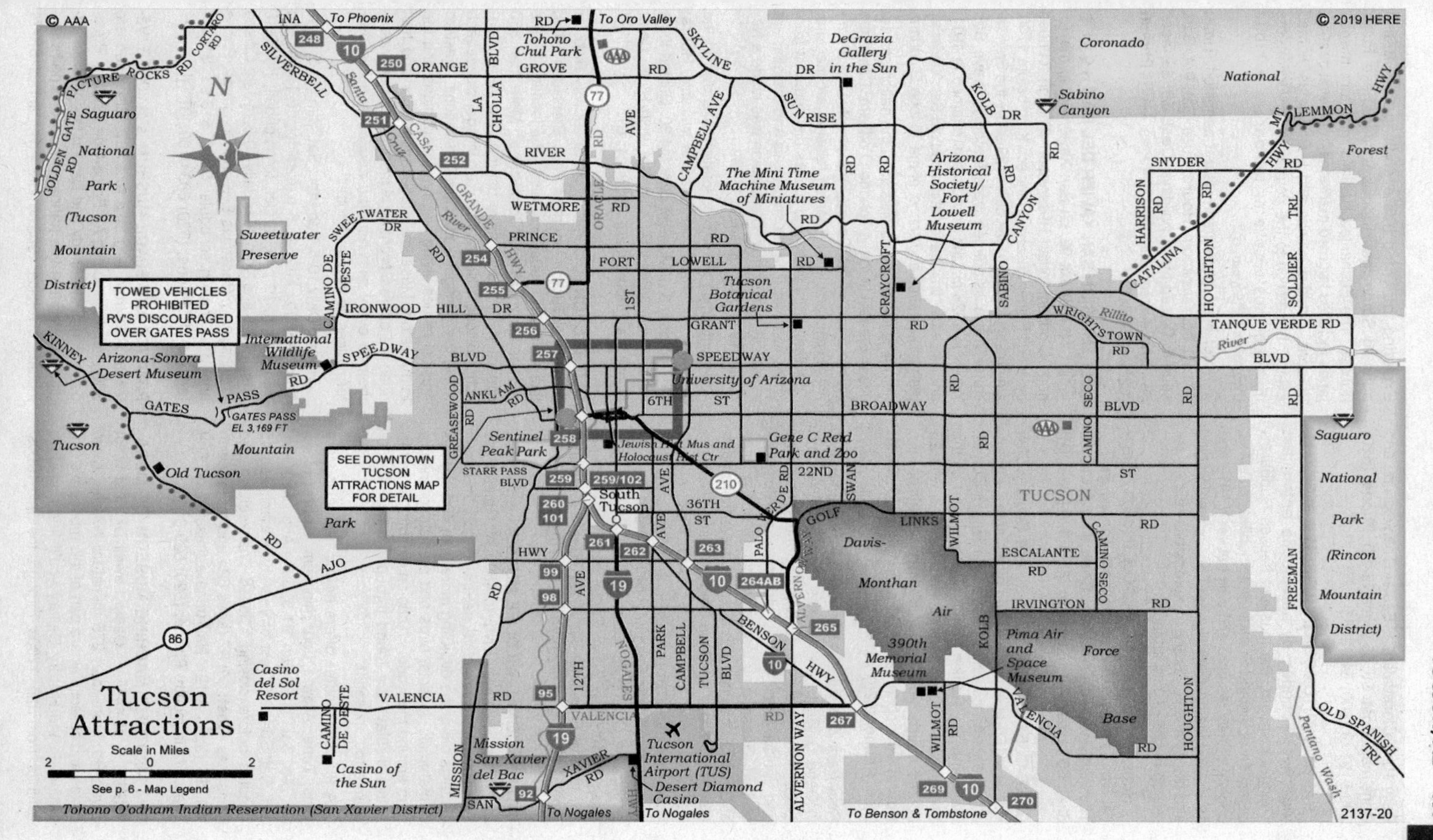

Tucson Attractions
Scale in Miles
See p. 6 - Map Legend
© AAA
© 2019 HERE
2137-20
TOWED VEHICLES PROHIBITED RV'S DISCOURAGED OVER GATES PASS
SEE DOWNTOWN TUCSON ATTRACTIONS MAP FOR DETAIL
Saguaro National Park (Tucson Mountain District)
Saguaro National Park (Rincon Mountain District)
Coronado National Forest
Tucson Mountain Park
Sweetwater Preserve
Arizona-Sonora Desert Museum
International Wildlife Museum
Old Tucson
Sabino Canyon
DeGrazia Gallery in the Sun
Tohono Chul Park
Arizona Historical Society/ Fort Lowell Museum
The Mini Time Machine Museum of Miniatures
Tucson Botanical Gardens
University of Arizona
Gene C Reid Park and Zoo
Sentinel Peak Park
Davis-Monthan Air Force Base
Pima Air and Space Museum
390th Memorial Museum
Tucson International Airport (TUS)
Desert Diamond Casino
Mission San Xavier del Bac
Casino del Sol Resort
Casino of the Sun
Tohono O'odham Indian Reservation (San Xavier District)
GATES PASS EL 3,169 FT
South Tucson
TUCSON
To Phoenix
To Oro Valley
To Benson & Tombstone
To Nogales
Pantano Wash
Santa Cruz River
Rillito River

Daily 10-4. Closed Jan. 1, Easter, Thanksgiving and Christmas. **Cost:** $8; $5 (ages 12-18). **Phone:** (520) 299-9191 or (800) 545-2185.

FRANKLIN AUTOMOBILE MUSEUM is at 3420 N. Vine Ave. Founded by automobile enthusiast Thomas Hubbard, the museum houses Hubbard's collection of vintage Franklin automobiles, all either original or fully restored and built between 1910 and 1934. Also featured are Hubbard family memorabilia and an extensive library of automobile-related research materials and artifacts.

Hours: Wed.-Sat. 10-4, mid-Oct. through Memorial Day; otherwise by appointment. Closed Jan. 1, Thanksgiving and Christmas. **Cost:** $10; $8 (ages 62+); $5 (ages 12-18). **Phone:** (520) 326-8038. GT

GENE C. REID PARK, 22nd St. and Country Club Rd., is a 160-acre park offering picnic areas, an outdoor performance center, a rose garden, Hi Corbett Field and the Reffkin Tennis Center—one of the Southwest's largest public tennis facilities with 25 lighted courts and 10 lighted racquetball courts. **Hours:** Park open daily 6:30 a.m.-10:30 p.m. **Cost:** Free. **Phone:** (520) 791-4873.

Reid Park Zoo, off 22nd St. just w. of Alvernon Rd. in Gene C. Reid Park, houses more than 500 animals, including elephants, bears, giraffes, ostriches and zebras. Each habitat and species is fully described. Guests may feed and interact with giraffes at Giraffe Encounter, ride a camel, travel the perimeter of the zoo in a train in Reid Park and cool off in Kenya Get Wet, a water playground. **Time:** Allow 2 hours minimum. **Hours:** Daily 9-4, Oct.-May; 8-3, rest of year. Giraffe Encounter daily. Closed Thanksgiving and Christmas. **Cost:** $10.50; $8.50 (ages 62+); $6.50 (ages 2-14). Camel rides $7. Carousel $3. Giraffe Encounter $2. Train rides $2. **Phone:** (520) 791-4022 or (520) 791-3204.

INTERNATIONAL WILDLIFE MUSEUM is 5 mi. w. of I-10 on Speedway Blvd. to 4800 W. Gates Pass Rd. Tucson's interactive natural history museum contains dioramas depicting more than 400 species of mammals, insects, birds and prehistoric animals from around the world. Hands-on exhibits and interactive displays are found throughout the 40,000-square-foot museum.

A 98-seat theater offers hourly natural history films. **Time:** Allow 1 hour minimum. **Hours:** Mon.-Fri. 9-5, Sat. 11-7, Sun. 11-5, June-Aug.; Mon.-Fri. 9-5, Sat.-Sun. 9-6, rest of year. Last admission 45 minutes before closing. Closed Thanksgiving and Christmas. **Cost:** $9; $7 (ages 62+ and military with ID); $4 (ages 4-12). Half-price admission on first Tues. of the month. **Phone:** (520) 629-0100.

THE MINI TIME MACHINE MUSEUM OF MINIATURES is at 4455 E. Camp Lowell Dr., just w. of Swan Rd. More than 275 miniature houses, room boxes and collectibles are part of this museum's collection. In the History Gallery you'll find miniature exhibits from the 1700s through the mid-1900s. Exploring the World has everything from British pubs to Southwest adobes to Japanese farmhouses. The Enchanted Realm's miniature miscellanea includes haunted mansions, medieval castles, dragons, pirate dioramas and a Christmas-themed exhibit. In addition to the permanent collection, the museum hosts several temporary exhibits throughout the year.

Note: Flash photography is not permitted. **Time:** Allow 1 hour minimum. **Hours:** Tues.-Sat. 9-4, Sun. noon-4. Closed major holidays. **Cost:** $9; $8 (ages 65+ and military with ID); $6 (ages 4-17). **Phone:** (520) 881-0606.

GEM **MISSION SAN XAVIER DEL BAC** is 9 mi. s. off I-19 exit 92, on San Xavier Rd. in the Tohono O'odham Indian Reservation. Though founded by Jesuit Father Eusebio Francisco Kino before 1700, the present structure was built 1783-97 by the Franciscans. The missionaries were forced to leave San Xavier in 1828 but the Franciscans returned in 1911, and since that time have maintained old San Xavier as the parish church and school of the Tohono O'odham.

This is the only Kino mission in the nation still active in preaching to the Tohono O'odham. Called the "White Dove of the Desert," the structure is an impressive example of Spanish mission architecture. The domes, carvings and arches distinguish it from other missions. The interior murals and the altar are especially noteworthy. The Mission was made a National Historic Landmark in 1963.

A continuous video presentation is shown in the museum, and a self-guiding tour is available. **Hours:** Mission daily 8-5. Museum daily 8-4:30. Guided tours depart every 30 minutes Mon.-Sat. 9:30-12:30. **Cost:** Donations. **Phone:** (520) 294-2624. GT

OLD TUCSON is 12 mi. w. via Speedway Blvd. or Ajo Way in Tucson Mountain Park. Erected in 1939, this replica of 1860s Tucson was the location for the movies "Arizona" and "Tombstone." More than 350 films and TV shows have been filmed here. Highlights include a Native American village, stagecoach rides, live gunfights, stunt demonstrations, Western musical revues, living history presentations and the Film History Museum. Stagecoach tours and trail rides are offered. Nightfall, a month-long Halloween-themed event with haunted houses and live performances, is held in October.

Hours: Daily 10-5, Feb.-Apr.; Sat.-Sun. 10-5, June 1 to mid-Aug.; Fri.-Sat. 6 p.m.-midnight, Thurs. and Sun. 6 p.m.-10 p.m. in Oct. for Nightfall; Fri.-Sun. 10-5 in May and Nov.-Dec.; daily 10-5, in Jan. Closed Thanksgiving, Christmas Eve and Christmas. Phone ahead to confirm schedule. **Cost:** $18.95; $10.95 (ages 4-11). **Phone:** (520) 883-0100. GT

PIMA AIR AND SPACE MUSEUM is at 6000 E. Valencia Rd.; from I-10 take exit 267. Displayed are 300 aircraft, including Air Force One used by Presidents John F. Kennedy and Lyndon B. Johnson. Additional aircraft in five hangars and along pathways include a replica 1903 Wright Flyer and a SR-71

Blackbird. Three hangars are dedicated to World War II. One-hour tram tours of the 80-acre facility are available, as are 75-minute bus tours of the Aircraft Boneyard/Aircraft Maintenance and Regeneration Group (AMARG) facility on Davis-Monthan Air Force Base which features more than 4,400 U.S. military aircraft on 2,600 acres.

Note: Government-issued photo ID is required to enter the base, and visitors are not permitted to leave the bus. **Hours:** Museum daily 9-5. Last admission 1 hour before closing. Tour schedules vary; phone ahead. Closed Thanksgiving and Christmas. **Cost:** Single-day museum admission (includes 390th Memorial Museum) $15.50; $12.75 (ages 65+ and military with ID); $9 (ages 5-12). Two-day museum admission $20; $16.75 (ages 65+ and military with ID); $12.50 (ages 5-12). Tram tour $6. Bus tour $7; $4 (ages 0-12). Prices may vary; phone ahead. Advance purchase is recommended for bus and tram tours. **Phone:** (520) 574-0462. GT

390th Memorial Museum is at 6000 E. Valencia Rd., at the Pima Air and Space Museum. The museum honors the men of the 390th Bombardment Group (Heavy), many of whom died while flying B-17 bombers in World War II. Exhibits include a fully restored B-17 (also known as the "Flying Fortress"), aircraft models, a one-of-a-kind nose art exhibit, flight gear, guns, photos, a Quonset hut, a World War II control tower and other memorabilia. A 54-minute video presentation includes interviews with surviving members and actual film clips from the war.

Time: Allow 30 minutes minimum. **Hours:** Daily 10-4:30. Closed Thanksgiving and Christmas. **Cost:** Pima Air and Space Museum single-day admission (includes 390th Memorial Museum) $15.50; $12.75 (ages 65+ and military with ID); $9 (ages 5-12). Two-day museum admission $20; $16.75 (ages 65+ and military with ID); $12.50 (ages 5-12). Prices may vary; phone ahead. **Phone:** (520) 574-0287.

THE POSTAL HISTORY FOUNDATION, 920 N. First Ave., features stamps, postmarks and books tracing the history of the U.S. Postal Service and caters to serious philatelists and postal historians as well as casual collectors and youth education. Original equipment from the Naco post office as well as antique file cabinets and other memorabilia from Arizona post offices are on display.

An adjacent building houses a research library of philatelic literature and a collection of Civil War memorabilia, books and documents. A working post office is on-site. **Time:** Allow 30 minutes minimum. **Hours:** Mon.-Fri. 8-3. Post Office Mon.-Fri. 8-2:30. Closed major holidays. **Cost:** Donations. **Phone:** (520) 623-6652. GT

GEM **SABINO CANYON** is at 5900 N. Sabino Canyon Rd., 17 mi. e. via Tanque Verde and Sabino Canyon rds. Part of the Coronado National Forest *(see place listing p. 38)*, this desert oasis in

Sabino Canyon

the Santa Catalina Mountains offers spectacular panoramic views and a wide range of recreational activities. Visitors can hike along a network of trails; go horseback riding; take a dip in a swimming hole or waterfall; and observe javelinas, roadrunners, white-tailed deer, numerous birds and other native wildlife.

Regional Partnering Center offers narrated excursions into the canyon aboard shuttle buses. A shuttle also transports hikers to the Bear Canyon trailhead.

Note: Beware of mountain lions and rattlesnakes within the canyon. Pets are not permitted. **Time:** Allow 1 hour minimum. **Hours:** Visitor reception area daily 9-4:30, mid-Dec. through June 30; Mon.-Fri. 9-4, Sat.-Sun. and holidays 9-4:30, rest of year. Closed Thanksgiving and Christmas. Phone ahead to confirm schedule. **Cost:** $8 (per private vehicle per day); $10 (per private vehicle per week); free (interagency pass holders and those arriving on foot or bicycle). Admission includes Sabino Canyon, Madera Canyon and Mount Lemmon picnic areas. Shuttle rides $10; $5 (ages 3-12). Bear Canyon shuttle $6; $4 (ages 3-12). Cash only. **Phone:** (520) 749-8700. GT

SAGUARO NATIONAL PARK—see place listing p. 147.

SOUTHERN ARIZONA TRANSPORTATION MUSEUM is at 414 N. Toole Ave. Exhibits at this museum and interpretive center include artifacts and memorabilia relating to the history of the railroad and transportation in southern Arizona. The former Southern Pacific Railroad Depot has been restored to its 1941 design and includes a train depot. A historic 1900 steam locomotive is on display; visitors may go inside to see it up close.

Time: Allow 30 minutes minimum. **Hours:** Tues.-Thurs. and Sun. 11-3, Fri.-Sat. 10-4. Phone ahead for guided tour schedule. **Cost:** Donations. Guided tours $5. **Phone:** (520) 623-2223. GT

GEM **TUCSON MOUNTAIN PARK,** 8 mi. w. on Speedway Blvd. and Kinney Rd., encompasses approximately 20,000 acres of the Tucson Mountains and adjoining mesa land and embraces one of the largest areas of saguaro and natural desert growth in the Southwest. Camping is available at the Gilbert Ray Campground; firewood is prohibited. Trails for hiking and horseback riding are available. **Hours:** Park open daily dawn-dusk. **Cost:** Park free. Camping $10 (tents), $20 (RV) per night. **Phone:** (520) 724-5000.

TUCSON MUSEUM OF ART AND HISTORIC BLOCK is at 140 N. Main Ave. Visitors can view collections of Latin American, Western, Asian, modern and contemporary art. The museum also comprises five homes built 1850-1907 in the El Presidio Historic District, including adobe structures housing Western and Latin American collections; the J. Knox Corbett House, a Mission Revival bungalow with Arts and Crafts *objets d'art* (open October through April); and La Casa Cordova, a Mexican-style adobe home (open November through April). A library and changing art exhibits are featured, and art lectures and classes are offered.

Hours: Museum Tues.-Sat. 10-5 (also Thurs. 5-8), Sun. noon-5. Closed major holidays. **Cost:** Museum $12; $10 (ages 65+ and veterans with ID); $7 (college students with ID); free (ages 0-18, active military and veterans with ID, and to all first Sun. of the month). Guided tours included with paid admission. **Phone:** (520) 624-2333. GT

UNIVERSITY OF ARIZONA, bounded by Euclid Ave., E. Helen St., Campbell Ave. and E. 7th St., was founded in 1885 as the state's first institution of higher learning. Today the UA is the only Arizona university with two medical schools, and it's ranked among the nation's top research universities. Campus information and a variety of guided campus walking-tours are available through the UA Visitor Center September through December and February through May. **Hours:** UA Visitor Center Mon.-Fri. 9-5; closed during winter break. Campus tours depart Wed. at 10, Feb.-May and Sept.-Dec. **Cost:** Free. Reservations are required. **Phone:** (520) 621-5130. GT

Center for Creative Photography is at 1030 N. Olive Rd., n. of 2nd St. on the University of Arizona campus. The center houses one of the world's largest collections of modern and contemporary photography. The exhibitions in the center's gallery feature works drawn from a collection of more than 90,000 photographs by more than 2,200 photographers, together with material from the archives of many leading American photographers. An additional gallery space exhibits a rotating selection of new acquisitions and collection highlights.

Metered public parking is available in the visitor section of the Park Avenue Garage, just n.e. of Speedway Blvd., with direct pedestrian access to the center's front door. **Hours:** Gallery Tues.-Fri. 9-4, Sat. 1-4. Closed major holidays. Phone ahead to confirm schedule. **Cost:** Donations. **Phone:** (520) 621-7968.

Flandrau Science Center and Planetarium, on the University of Arizona campus at 1601 E. University Blvd., is filled with hands-on, interactive exhibits geared toward school-aged children. Exhibits rotate regularly; recent ones include Puzzles, Proofs and Patterns with hands-on puzzles and games, and a mineral collection.

Time: Allow 1 hour minimum. **Hours:** Mon.-Thurs. 9-5, Fri. 9 a.m.-10 p.m., Sat. 10-10, Sun. noon-5. Phone for planetarium show options, schedule and parking information. Closed major holidays. **Cost:** (includes University of Arizona Mineral Museum and one planetarium/laser show) $16; $12 (ages 4-17, ages 55+ and college students and military with ID); $3 (each additional show). **Phone:** (520) 621-7827.

University of Arizona Mineral Museum, on the lower level of UA Science: Flandrau at 1601 E. University Blvd., displays fine gems, meteorites and mineral specimens from around the world. The museum specializes in minerals from Arizona and Mexico. Visitors can use a microscope to see micro-size specimens. **Hours:** Mon.-Thurs. 9-5, Fri. 9 a.m.-10 p.m., Sat. 10-10, Sun. 1-5. Closed major holidays. Phone ahead to confirm schedule. **Cost:** (includes Flandrau Science Center and Planetarium) $7; $5 (ages 4-17, ages 55+ and college students and military with ID). **Phone:** (520) 621-7827.

University of Arizona Museum of Art, s.e. corner of Park Ave. and Speedway Blvd. in the University of Arizona Fine Arts Complex, features more than 6,000 pieces in the museum's permanent collection comprising both European and American artwork from the 14th century to present day. Six galleries showcase changing exhibitions as well as works by such artists as Rembrandt, Pierre-Auguste Renoir, Pablo Picasso, Andy Warhol and Edward Hopper. Always on view is the 15th-century altarpiece of Ciudad Rodrigo (Spain), old master paintings from the Kress Collection and sculptor Jacques Lipchitz's sketches and models.

Time: Allow 1 hour minimum. **Hours:** Mon.-Wed. and Fri. 9-4, Thurs. 9-7, Sat. 9-5, Sun. noon-5. Closed university holidays; phone ahead to confirm schedule. **Cost:** $8; $6.50 (senior citizens); free (ages 0-18, students, military, and visitors with SNAP or Tribal ID). **Phone:** (520) 621-7567.

Sightseeing

Bus Tours

Gray Line, (520) 622-8811 or (800) 276-1528, offers sightseeing tours to Tucson's major sites as well as trips to Tombstone and the Grand Canyon. Overnight and multiple-day tours are available.

Walking Tours

For those who prefer to explore the city and its environs on their own, the *Visit Tucson Official Travel Guide*, distributed by the Visit Tucson, 100 S. Church Ave., contains walking tour information; phone (520) 624-1817 or (800) 638-8350 to have a free copy mailed to you before your trip. Visitors may also pick up a destination guide at the Tucson Visitor Center at 110 S. Church Ave., Suite 7199 (in La Placita Village), Mon.-Fri. 9-5, Sat.-Sun. 9-4 (closed weekends in summer).

Looking for other things to see in Tucson? While you're at the visitor center ask for the free Presidio Trail Historical Walking Tour brochure, which includes a map of the Presidio Trail, a bright turquoise stripe painted on the sidewalks that wind through the heart of downtown Tucson. The 2.5-mile trail begins at the intersection of Church and Washington streets and passes more than 20 numbered historical sites, including the Pima County Courthouse and the Tucson Museum of Art and Historic Block *(see attraction listings)*. If you follow the trail without the walking tour brochure and its written descriptions, don't worry; most sites on the tour are marked by plaques.

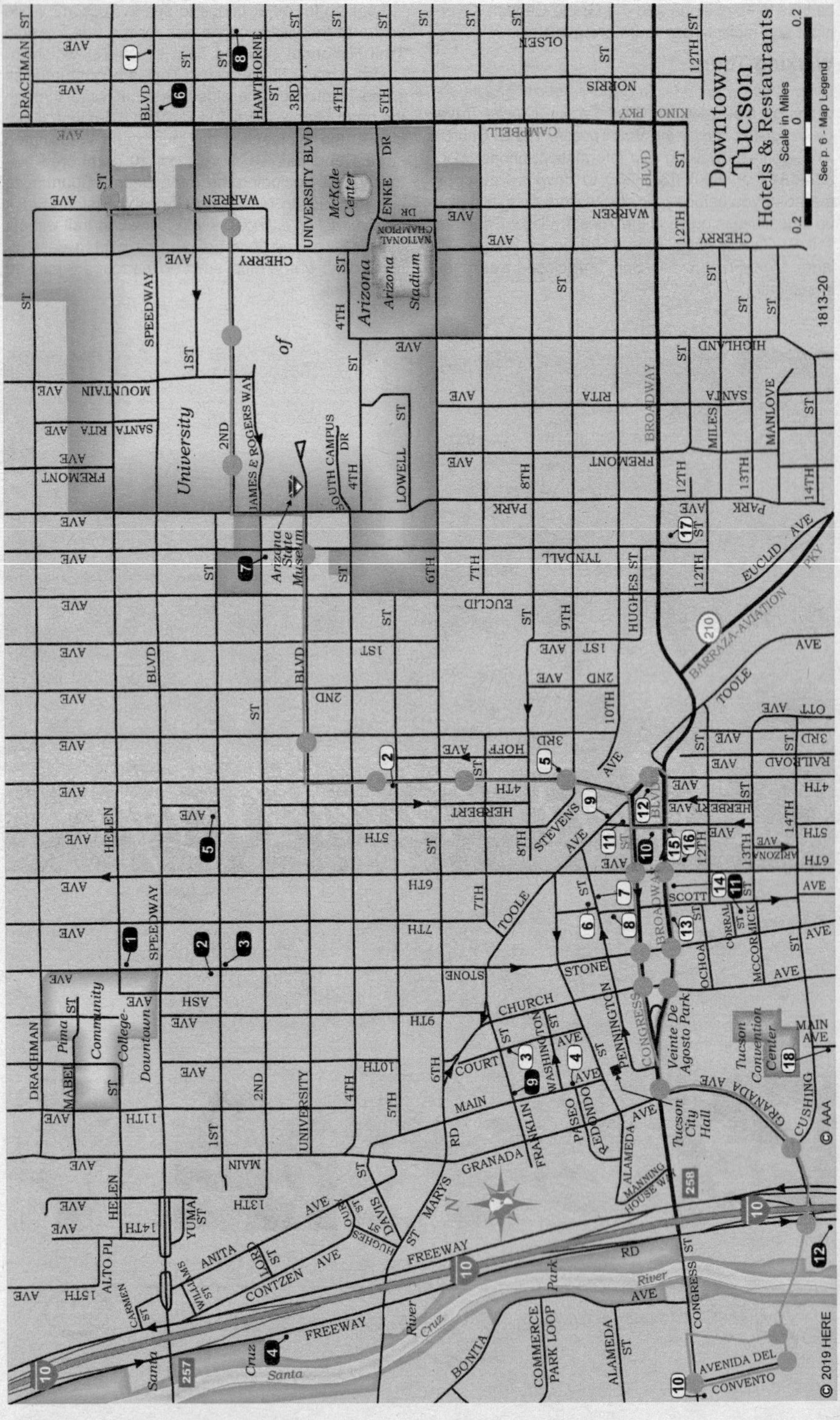

Downtown Tucson
Hotels & Restaurants
Scale in Miles
0.2 0 0.2
See p. 6 - Map Legend
1813-20
© 2019 HERE
© AAA
University of Arizona
Arizona Stadium
McKale Center
Arizona State Museum
Pima Community College-Downtown
Tucson Convention Center
Tucson City Hall
Veinte De Agosto Park
SPEEDWAY BLVD
BROADWAY BLVD
UNIVERSITY BLVD
EUCLID AVE
STONE AVE
CONGRESS ST
CAMPBELL AVE
CHERRY AVE
FREEWAY
BARRAZA-AVIATION PKY
TOOLE AVE
GRANADA AVE
MAIN AVE
CHURCH AVE
Santa Cruz River

Downtown Tucson

This index helps you "spot" where approved hotels and restaurants are located on the corresponding detailed maps. Restaurant price range is a combination of lunch and/or dinner. Turn to the listing page for more information and consult display ads for special promotions.

For more details, rates and reservations: AAA.com/travelguides/hotels

DOWNTOWN TUCSON

Map Page	Hotels	Diamond Rated	Member Savings	Page
1 p. 202	Econo Lodge University	◆		213
2 p. 202	**Best Western Royal Sun Inn & Suites**	◆◆◆	✔	213
3 p. 202	**University Inn**	◆◆	✔	213
4 p. 202	**Country Inn & Suites by Radisson-Tucson City Center**	◆◆◆	✔	213
5 p. 202	Catalina Park Inn Bed and Breakfast	◆◆◆		213
6 p. 202	**Aloft Tucson University**	◆◆◆	✔	212
7 p. 202	**Tucson Marriott University Park Hotel**	◆◆◆	✔	213
8 p. 202	Adobe Rose Inn	◆◆◆		212
9 p. 202	El Presidio Bed & Breakfast Inn	◆◆◆		213
10 p. 202	AC Hotel by Marriott Tucson Downtown	◆◆◆	✔	212
11 p. 202	The Blenman House Inn	◆◆◆		213
12 p. 202	Ramada by Wyndham Tucson	◆◆		213

Map Page	Restaurants	Diamond Rated	Cuisine	Price Range	Page
1 p. 202	Trident Grill	◆◆	American	$11-$21	213
2 p. 202	Magpie's Gourmet Pizza	◆	Pizza	$8-$28	213
3 p. 202	El Charro Cafe	◆◆	Mexican	$11-$20	213
4 p. 202	Café a la C'Art	◆◆	American	$11-$25	213
5 p. 202	Ermanos Craft Beer & Wine Bar	◆◆	American	$11-$24	213
6 p. 202	Reilly Craft Pizza and Drink	◆◆	Italian	$12-$19	213
7 p. 202	Cafe Poca Cosa	◆◆	Mexican	$13-$25	213
8 p. 202	47 Scott	◆◆	American	$12-$22	213
9 p. 202	Maynards Market & Kitchen	◆◆◆	New American	$19-$43	213
10 p. 202	Augustin Kitchen	◆◆◆	New American	$14-$28	213
11 p. 202	Cup Cafe	◆◆	American	$12-$25	213
12 p. 202	Obon Sushi Bar Ramen	◆◆	Japanese	$12-$16	213
13 p. 202	Penca	◆◆◆	Regional Mexican	$8-$23	213
14 p. 202	MiAn Sushi & Modern Asian Cuisine	◆◆	Asian	$13-$38	213
15 p. 202	Charro Steak	◆◆◆	Steak	$18-$38	213
16 p. 202	DOWNTOWN Kitchen + Cocktails	◆◆◆	American	$21-$32	213
17 p. 202	Welcome Diner	◆◆	American	$12-$16	213
18 p. 202	El Minuto Cafe	◆◆	Mexican	$8-$18	213

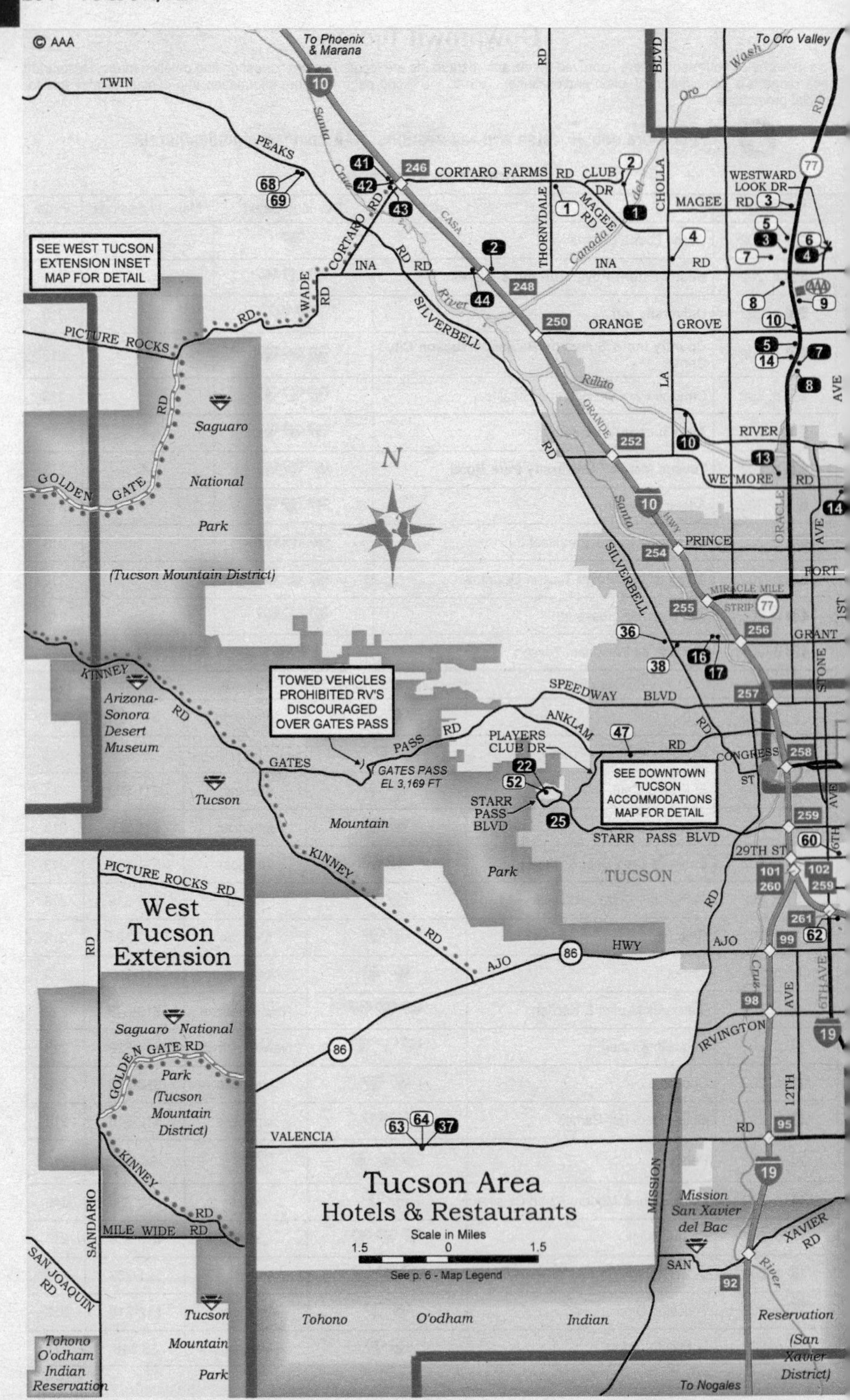

© AAA
To Phoenix & Marana
To Oro Valley
TWIN PEAKS
CORTARO FARMS RD
CLUB DR
MAGEE RD
WESTWARD LOOK DR
THORNYDALE RD
CHOLLA BLVD
SEE WEST TUCSON EXTENSION INSET MAP FOR DETAIL
CORTARO RD
CASA
INA RD
WADE RD
SILVERBELL RD
ORANGE GROVE
PICTURE ROCKS RD
LA
RIVER
WETMORE RD
Saguaro National Park
(Tucson Mountain District)
GOLDEN GATE
PRINCE
ORACLE
FORT
MIRACLE MILE STRIP
GRANT
STONE AVE
1ST AVE
KINNEY RD
Arizona-Sonora Desert Museum
TOWED VEHICLES PROHIBITED RV'S DISCOURAGED OVER GATES PASS
SPEEDWAY BLVD
ANKLAM RD
PLAYERS CLUB DR
GATES PASS RD
GATES PASS EL 3,169 FT
CONGRESS ST
SEE DOWNTOWN TUCSON ACCOMMODATIONS MAP FOR DETAIL
STARR PASS BLVD
Tucson Mountain Park
29TH ST
6TH AVE
TUCSON
AJO HWY
West Tucson Extension
IRVINGTON
12TH AVE
VALENCIA RD
Tucson Area Hotels & Restaurants
Scale in Miles
1.5 0 1.5
See p. 6 - Map Legend
MISSION
Mission San Xavier del Bac
SAN XAVIER RD
SANDARIO RD
MILE WIDE RD
SAN JOAQUIN RD
Tohono O'odham Indian Reservation
Reservation (San Xavier District)
To Nogales

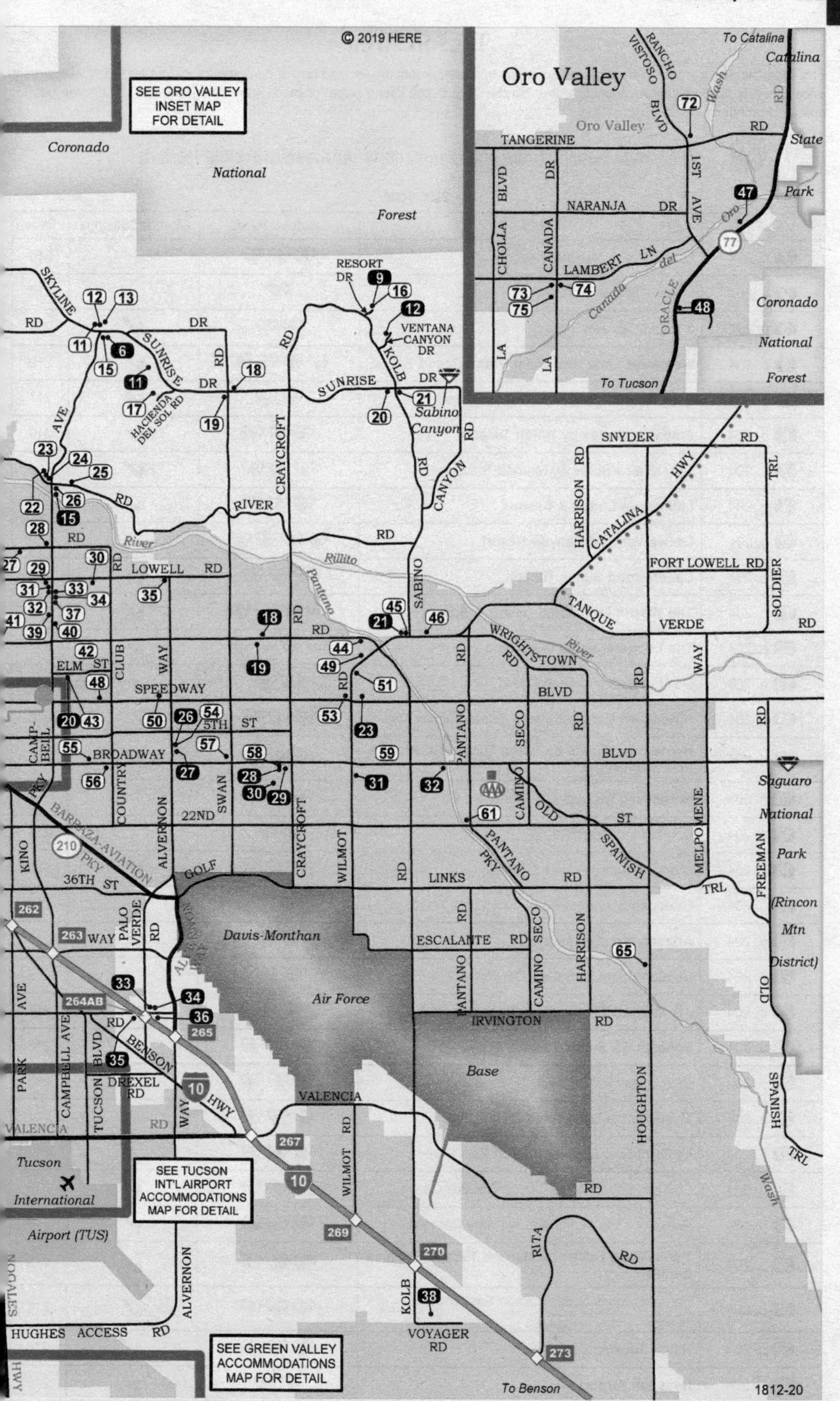
© 2019 HERE
SEE ORO VALLEY INSET MAP FOR DETAIL
Coronado
National
Forest
Oro Valley
To Catalina
Catalina
State
Park
TANGERINE
RD
RANCHO VISTOSO BLVD
1ST AVE
NARANJA DR
LAMBERT LN
CHOLLA BLVD
CANADA DR
LA CANADA
Canada del Oro
ORACLE
To Tucson
Coronado
National
Forest
SKYLINE
RD
DR
SUNRISE DR
HACIENDA DEL SOL RD
AVE
RESORT DR
VENTANA CANYON DR
KOLB RD
SUNRISE DR
Sabino Canyon
SABINO CANYON RD
CRAYCROFT RD
RIVER RD
Rillito River
Pantano
SNYDER RD
HARRISON RD
CATALINA HWY
TRL
FORT LOWELL RD
TANQUE VERDE RD
SOLDIER
WRIGHTSTOWN RD
River
LOWELL RD
CLUB
ELM ST
WAY
SPEEDWAY BLVD
5TH ST
CAMPBELL
BROADWAY BLVD
COUNTRY
SWAN
22ND ST
ALVERNON
WILMOT RD
PANTANO RD
SECO
CAMINO SECO
OLD SPANISH TRL
MELPOMENE WAY
Saguaro National Park (Rincon Mtn District)
KINO PKY
BARRAZA-AVIATION PKY
210
36TH ST
GOLF LINKS RD
PANTANO PKY
FREEMAN RD
262
263
WAY
PALO VERDE RD
ALVERNON WAY
Davis-Monthan
Air Force
Base
ESCALANTE RD
CAMINO SECO
HARRISON RD
IRVINGTON RD
OLD SPANISH TRL
264AB
265
PARK AVE
CAMPBELL AVE
TUCSON BLVD
BENSON HWY
DREXEL RD
10
VALENCIA RD
HOUGHTON RD
267
WILMOT RD
Tucson International Airport (TUS)
SEE TUCSON INT'L AIRPORT ACCOMMODATIONS MAP FOR DETAIL
269
270
RITA RD
KOLB
Wash
NOGALES HWY
HUGHES ACCESS RD
VOYAGER RD
SEE GREEN VALLEY ACCOMMODATIONS MAP FOR DETAIL
273
To Benson
1812-20

Tucson Area

This index helps you "spot" where approved hotels and restaurants are located on the corresponding detailed maps. Restaurant price range is a combination of lunch and/or dinner. Turn to the listing page for more information and consult display ads for special promotions.

For more details, rates and reservations: AAA.com/travelguides/hotels

TUCSON

Map Page	Hotels	Diamond Rated	Member Savings	Page
1 p. 204	Omni Tucson National Resort	◆◆◆		218
2 p. 204	Motel 6 Tucson North #1127	◆		217
3 p. 204	**3 Palms Tucson**	◆◆	✔	214
4 p. 204	**Westward Look Wyndham Grand Resort & Spa**	◆◆◆◆	✔	219
5 p. 204	**Best Western InnSuites Tucson Foothills**	◆◆	✔	214
6 p. 204	**Embassy Suites by Hilton Tucson**	◆◆◆	✔	216
7 p. 204	TownePlace Suites by Marriott Tucson	◆◆◆	✔	218
8 p. 204	**La Posada Lodge & Casitas**	◆◆◆	✔	217
9 p. 204	**Loews Ventana Canyon Resort**	◆◆◆◆	✔	217
10 p. 204	**Candlewood Suites Tucson**	◆◆◆	✔	215
11 p. 204	**The Westin La Paloma Resort & Spa**	◆◆◆◆	✔	218
12 p. 204	**The Lodge at Ventana Canyon**	◆◆◆◆	✔	217
13 p. 204	Comfort Suites at Tucson Mall	◆◆		215
14 p. 204	Holiday Inn Express Hotel & Suites-Tucson Mall	◆◆◆		216
15 p. 204	**Homewood Suites by Hilton Tucson/St. Philip's Plaza University**	◆◆◆	✔	216
16 p. 204	Holiday Inn Express & Suites-Grant Rd	◆◆◆		216
17 p. 204	Comfort Inn-Grant Rd	◆◆		215
18 p. 204	Sheraton Tucson Hotel & Suites	◆◆◆	✔	218
19 p. 204	Extended Stay America-Tucson Grant Road	◆◆		216
20 p. 204	**Arizona Inn** *(See ad p. 214.)*	◆◆◆◆	✔	214
21 p. 204	Comfort Suites at Sabino Canyon	◆◆		215
22 p. 204	**JW Marriott Tucson Starr Pass Resort & Spa**	◆◆◆◆	✔	217
23 p. 204	**Sonesta ES Suites Tucson**	◆◆◆	✔	218
25 p. 204	Starr Pass Golf Suites	◆◆◆		218
26 p. 204	Lodge on the Desert	◆◆◆		217
27 p. 204	La Quinta Inn & Suites Tucson Reid Park	◆◆◆		217
28 p. 204	Courtyard by Marriott-Tucson Williams Centre	◆◆◆	✔	215
29 p. 204	Residence Inn by Marriott Williams Centre	◆◆◆	✔	218
30 p. 204	**TownePlace Suites by Marriott Tucson Williams Centre**	◆◆◆	✔	218
31 p. 204	Hampton Inn & Suites Tucson East/Williams Center	◆◆◆	✔	216
32 p. 204	**Hilton Tucson East**	◆◆◆	✔	216
33 p. 204	**Days Inn Airport**	◆◆	✔	216

TUCSON (cont'd)

Map Page	Hotels (cont'd)	Diamond Rated	Member Savings	Page
34 p. 204	Comfort Inn & Suites	◆◆		215
35 p. 204	Studio 6 Extended Stay #6002	◆◆		218
36 p. 204	**Red Roof Inn-Tucson South**	◆◆	✔	218
37 p. 204	**Casino Del Sol**	◆◆◆◆	✔	215
38 p. 204	Voyager Hotel & RV Resort	◆◆		218

Map Page	Restaurants	Diamond Rated	Cuisine	Price Range	Page
1 p. 204	Colt's Taste of Texas	◆◆	Steak	$9-$33	219
2 p. 204	Bob's Steak & Chop House	◆◆◆	Steak	$29-$59	219
3 p. 204	Bottega Michelangelo	◆◆◆	Italian	$9-$28	219
4 p. 204	Mosaic Cafe Dos	◆◆	Mexican	$8-$14	220
5 p. 204	Saffron Indian Bistro	◆◆◆	Indian	$11-$19	220
6 p. 204	**Gold**	◆◆◆	American	$22-$42	219
7 p. 204	Tohono Chul Park Garden Bistro	◆◆	American	$12-$17	220
8 p. 204	Wildflower Tucson	◆◆◆	American	$12-$35	221
9 p. 204	Hi Falutin Western Grill	◆◆	American	$14-$36	219
10 p. 204	Sushi on Oracle	◆◆	Sushi	$10-$22	220
11 p. 204	Firebirds Wood Fired Grill	◆◆◆	American	$12-$36	219
12 p. 204	North Italia	◆◆◆	New Italian	$13-$38	220
13 p. 204	Vivace Restaurant	◆◆◆	Italian	$13-$47	221
14 p. 204	Mr. An's Teppan Steak & Sushi	◆◆	Japanese	$10-$30	220
15 p. 204	Fleming's Prime Steakhouse & Wine Bar	◆◆◆	Steak	$34-$57	219
16 p. 204	Flying V Bar & Grill	◆◆◆	Regional Southwestern	$18-$45	219
17 p. 204	**The Grill at Hacienda del Sol**	◆◆◆◆	Southwestern	$28-$50	219
18 p. 204	Bazil's	◆◆◆	Regional Italian	$15-$40	219
19 p. 204	Trattoria Pina	◆◆	Italian	$10-$38	221
20 p. 204	Risky Business	◆◆	American	$8-$23	220
21 p. 204	Commoner & Co.	◆◆◆	New American	$14-$28	219
22 p. 204	Sullivan's Steakhouse	◆◆◆	Steak	$14-$69	220
23 p. 204	P.F. Chang's China Bistro	◆◆◆	Chinese	$10-$28	220
24 p. 204	Zinburger	◆◆	Burgers	$10-$16	221
25 p. 204	El Corral Steakhouse	◆◆	Steak	$20-$31	219
26 p. 204	Reforma Cocina & Cantina	◆◆◆	Regional Mexican	$9-$23	220
27 p. 204	Guadalajara Original Grill	◆◆	Mexican	$8-$22	219
28 p. 204	Ghini's French Caffe	◆◆	French	$8-$13	219
29 p. 204	Rosa's Mexican Food	◆◆	Mexican	$8-$15	220
30 p. 204	Cody's Beef 'n Beans	◆◆	Steak	$9-$27	219

Map Page	Restaurants (cont'd)	Diamond Rated	Cuisine	Price Range	Page
31 p. 204	Prep & Pastry	◆◆	American	$7-$13	220
32 p. 204	Pastiche Modern Eatery	◆◆◆	American	$15-$30	220
33 p. 204	Beyond Bread	◆◆	American	$6-$13	219
34 p. 204	Lovin' Spoonfuls	◆◆	Vegetarian	$6-$15	220
35 p. 204	Le Rendez-vous	◆◆◆	French	$10-$34	220
36 p. 204	Teresa's Mosaic Cafe	◆◆	Mexican	$9-$18	220
37 p. 204	Sauce	◆◆	Italian	$7-$11	220
38 p. 204	Rusty's Family Restaurant & Sports Grille	◆◆	American	$8-$20	220
39 p. 204	India Oven	◆◆	Indian	$8-$14	219
40 p. 204	Blue Willow Restaurant Bakery	◆◆	American	$9-$18	219
41 p. 204	Sher-E-Punjab	◆◆	Indian	$8-$13	220
42 p. 204	Kingfisher	◆◆◆	Seafood	$14-$33	219
43 p. 204	**Main Dining Room at the Arizona Inn**	◆◆◆◆	Continental	$12-$40	220
44 p. 204	Prep & Pastry	◆◆	American	$11-$15	220
45 p. 204	The Eclectic Cafe	◆◆	American	$7-$14	219
46 p. 204	Zona 78	◆◆	Italian	$11-$27	221
47 p. 204	Daisy Mae's Steakhouse	◆◆	Steak	$16-$36	219
48 p. 204	Choice Greens	◆	Specialty	$6-$10	219
49 p. 204	Pinnacle Peak Restaurant	◆	Steak	$8-$27	220
50 p. 204	Feast	◆◆◆	American	$12-$30	219
51 p. 204	Jonathan's Cork	◆◆◆	Southwestern Steak	$12-$42	219
52 p. 204	Primo	◆◆◆◆	Regional Italian	$25-$45	220
53 p. 204	Casa Molina	◆◆	Mexican	$8-$20	219
54 p. 204	Cielos	◆◆◆	American	$11-$32	219
55 p. 204	Zemam's	◆◆	Ethiopian	$9-$14	221
56 p. 204	Bisbee Breakfast Club Broadway	◆◆	Breakfast	$10-$12	219
57 p. 204	The Hungry Fox Restaurant and Country Store	◆◆	American	$7-$14	219
58 p. 204	Pita Jungle	◆◆	Mediterranean	$7-$16	220
59 p. 204	New Delhi Palace	◆◆	Indian	$9-$14	220
60 p. 204	Mi Nidito Family Restaurant	◆◆	Mexican	$7-$13	220
61 p. 204	Casa del Rio	◆◆	Mexican	$8-$12	219
62 p. 204	Silver Saddle Steakhouse	◆◆	Steak	$8-$33	220
63 p. 204	Tequila Factory	◆◆	Mexican	$5-$19	220
64 p. 204	PY Steakhouse	◆◆◆	Steak	$19-$44	220
65 p. 204	McGraw's Cantina	◆◆	American	$8-$28	220

MARANA

Map Page	Hotels	Diamond Rated	Member Savings	Page
41 p. 204	Comfort Inn & Suites	◆◆◆		77
42 p. 204	La Quinta Inn & Suites NW Tucson Marana	◆◆◆		78
43 p. 204	Holiday Inn Express & Suites Tucson North-Marana	◆◆◆		78
44 p. 204	**Best Western Gold Poppy Inn**	◆◆	✔	77

Map Page	Restaurants	Diamond Rated	Cuisine	Price Range	Page
68 p. 204	La Olla Mexican Cafe	◆◆	Mexican	$9-$17	78
69 p. 204	Li'l Abner's Steakhouse	◆◆	Steak	$16-$45	78

ORO VALLEY

Map Page	Hotels	Diamond Rated	Member Savings	Page
47 p. 204	Holiday Inn Express Hotel & Suites Oro Valley-Tucson North	◆◆◆		84
48 p. 204	Fairfield Inn & Suites by Marriott Tucson North/Oro Valley	◆◆◆	✔	84

Map Page	Restaurants	Diamond Rated	Cuisine	Price Range	Page
72 p. 204	Dragon Village Restaurant	◆◆	Chinese	$6-$13	84
73 p. 204	Harvest	◆◆◆	Regional American	$9-$21	84
74 p. 204	GMG Chinese Bistro	◆◆	Chinese	$10-$26	84
75 p. 204	Caffe Torino Ristorante Italiano	◆◆	Italian	$12-$24	84

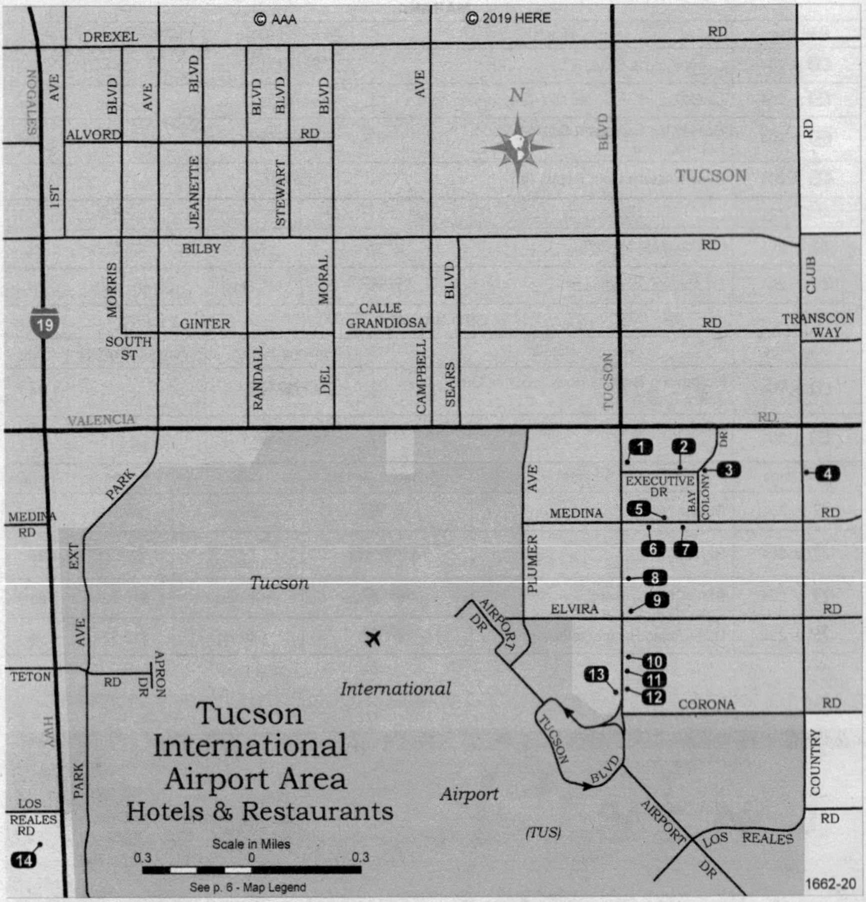

Tucson International Airport Area
Hotels & Restaurants

Scale in Miles 0.3 0 0.3

See p. 6 - Map Legend

1662-20

Airport Hotels

Map Page	TUCSON INTERNATIONAL (Maximum driving distance from airport: 1.6 mi)	Diamond Rated	Member Savings	Page
8 this page	**Best Western Tucson Int'l Airport Hotel & Suites, 0.8 mi**	♦♦♦	✔	214
5 this page	**Country Inn & Suites by Radisson-Tucson Airport, 1.1 mi**	♦♦	✔	215
1 this page	**Courtyard by Marriott Tucson Airport, 1.1 mi**	♦♦♦	✔	215
12 this page	**DoubleTree Suites by Hilton Tucson Airport, 0.5 mi**	♦♦♦	✔	216
13 this page	Four Points by Sheraton Tucson Airport, 0.7 mi	♦♦♦	✔	216
10 this page	Hampton Inn Tucson Airport, 0.6 mi	♦♦♦	✔	216
4 this page	Hilton Garden Inn Tucson Airport, 1.6 mi	♦♦♦	✔	216
6 this page	Holiday Inn Express Tucson Airport, 1.0 mi	♦♦♦		216
9 this page	**Hyatt Place Tucson Airport, 0.7 mi**	♦♦♦	✔	217

Map Page	**TUCSON INTERNATIONAL** (Maximum driving distance from airport: 1.6 mi) (cont'd)	Diamond Rated	Member Savings	Page
11 p. 210	La Quinta Inn & Suites Tucson Airport, 0.6 mi	◆◆		217
7 p. 210	**Residence Inn by Marriott Tucson Airport, 1.1 mi**	◆◆◆	✔	218
2 p. 210	Staybridge Suites Tucson Airport, 1.2 mi	◆◆◆		218
3 p. 210	**TownePlace Suites by Marriott Tucson Airport, 1.3 mi**	◆◆◆	✔	218

Tucson International Airport

This index helps you "spot" where approved hotels and restaurants are located on the corresponding detailed maps. Restaurant price range is a combination of lunch and/or dinner. Turn to the listing page for more information and consult display ads for special promotions.

For more details, rates and reservations: AAA.com/travelguides/hotels

TUCSON

Map Page	Hotels	Diamond Rated	Member Savings	Page
1 p. 210	**Courtyard by Marriott Tucson Airport** *(See ad p. 215.)*	◆◆◆	✔	215
2 p. 210	Staybridge Suites Tucson Airport	◆◆◆		218
3 p. 210	**TownePlace Suites by Marriott Tucson Airport**	◆◆◆	✔	218
4 p. 210	Hilton Garden Inn Tucson Airport	◆◆◆	✔	216
5 p. 210	**Country Inn & Suites by Radisson-Tucson Airport**	◆◆	✔	215
6 p. 210	Holiday Inn Express Tucson Airport	◆◆◆		216
7 p. 210	**Residence Inn by Marriott Tucson Airport**	◆◆◆	✔	218
8 p. 210	**Best Western Tucson Int'l Airport Hotel & Suites**	◆◆◆	✔	214
9 p. 210	**Hyatt Place Tucson Airport**	◆◆◆	✔	217
10 p. 210	Hampton Inn Tucson Airport	◆◆◆	✔	216
11 p. 210	La Quinta Inn & Suites Tucson Airport	◆◆		217
12 p. 210	**DoubleTree Suites by Hilton Tucson Airport**	◆◆◆	✔	216
13 p. 210	Four Points by Sheraton Tucson Airport	◆◆◆	✔	216
14 p. 210	**Desert Diamond Casino & Hotel**	◆◆◆	✔	216

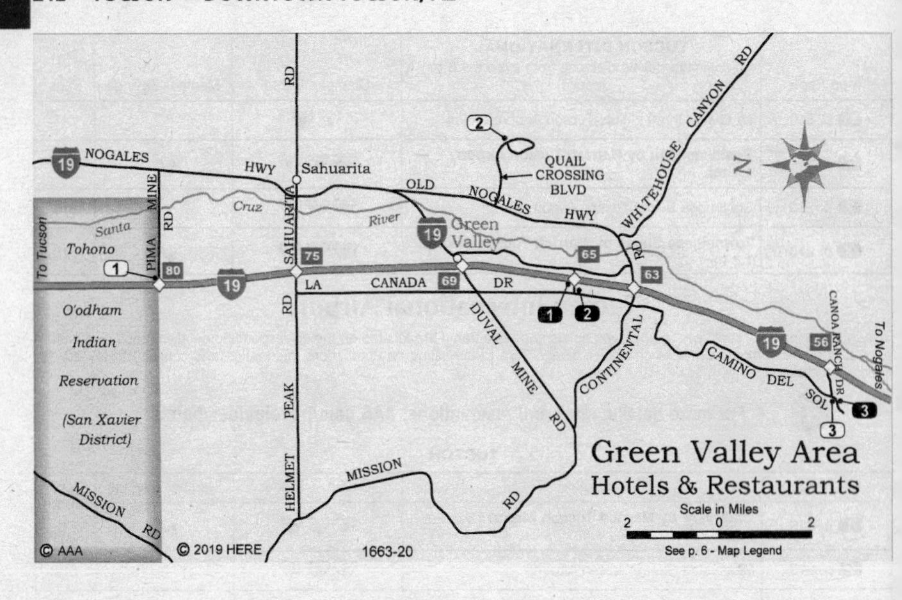

Green Valley Area

This index helps you "spot" where approved hotels and restaurants are located on the corresponding detailed maps. Restaurant price range is a combination of lunch and/or dinner. Turn to the listing page for more information and consult display ads for special promotions.

For more details, rates and reservations: AAA.com/travelguides/hotels

GREEN VALLEY

Map Page	Hotels	Diamond Rated	Member Savings	Page
1 this page	**Comfort Inn**	♦♦	✔	68
2 this page	**Best Western Green Valley Inn**	♦♦♦	✔	68
3 this page	**Canoa Ranch Golf Resort**	♦♦♦	✔	68

Map Page	Restaurants	Diamond Rated	Cuisine	Price Range	Page
1 this page	Agave at Desert Diamond Casino	♦♦	Regional American	$10-$28	68
2 this page	Grill at Quail Creek	♦♦	American	$8-$29	68
3 this page	Grill on the Green at Canoa Ranch Golf Club	♦♦♦	American	$10-$30	68

DOWNTOWN TUCSON

• Hotels & Restaurants map & index p. 202

AC HOTEL BY MARRIOTT TUCSON DOWNTOWN 520/385-7111 10

♦♦♦ SAVE Hotel. **Address:** 151 E Broadway Blvd 85701

AAA Benefit: Members save 5% or more!

ADOBE ROSE INN 520/318-4644 8

♦♦♦ Bed & Breakfast. **Address:** 940 N Olsen Ave 85719

ALOFT TUCSON UNIVERSITY 520/908-6800 6

Hotel

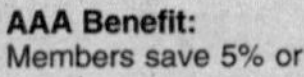

Address: 1900 E Speedway Blvd 85719 **Location:** Southeast corner of Speedway Blvd and Campbell Ave. **Facility:** 154 units. 7 stories, interior corridors. *Bath:* shower only. **Parking:** on-site (fee). **Amenities:** safes. **Pool:** heated outdoor. **Activities:** exercise room. **Guest Services:** valet and coin laundry.

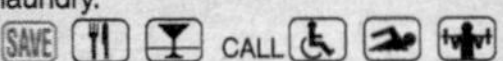

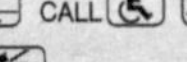

(See map & index p. 202.)

BEST WESTERN ROYAL SUN INN & SUITES 520/622-8871 2

Hotel

AAA Benefit: Members save up to 15% and earn bonus points!

Address: 1015 N Stone Ave 85705 **Location:** I-10 exit 257 (Speedway Blvd), 0.8 mi e, then just s. **Facility:** 79 units. 2 stories (no elevator), exterior corridors. **Pool:** heated outdoor. **Activities:** hot tub, exercise room. **Guest Services:** valet laundry. **Featured Amenity: breakfast buffet.**

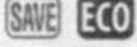

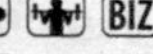

THE BLENMAN HOUSE INN 520/670-9022 11

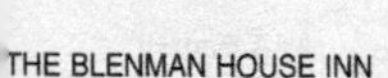

Historic Bed & Breakfast. **Address:** 204 S Scott Ave 85701

CATALINA PARK INN BED AND BREAKFAST 520/792-4541 5

Bed & Breakfast. **Address:** 309 E 1st St 85705

COUNTRY INN & SUITES BY RADISSON-TUCSON CITY CENTER 520/867-6200 4

Hotel

Address: 705 N Freeway 85745 **Location:** I-10 exit 257 (Speedway Blvd), just w, then just s. **Facility:** 79 units. 3 stories, interior corridors. **Pool:** heated outdoor. **Activities:** hot tub, exercise room. **Guest Services:** valet and coin laundry. **Featured Amenity: full hot breakfast.**

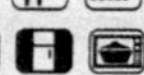

ECONO LODGE UNIVERSITY 520/622-6714 1

Motel. **Address:** 1136 N Stone Ave 85705

EL PRESIDIO BED & BREAKFAST INN 520/623-6151 9

Classic Historic Bed & Breakfast. **Address:** 297 N Main Ave 85701

RAMADA BY WYNDHAM TUCSON 520/239-2300 12

Hotel. **Address:** 777 W Cushing St 85745

TUCSON MARRIOTT UNIVERSITY PARK HOTEL 520/792-4100 7

Hotel

AAA Benefit: Members save 5% or more!

Address: 880 E 2nd St 85719 **Location:** I-10 exit 257 (Speedway Blvd), 1.2 mi e to Euclid Ave, then just s. **Facility:** 250 units. 9 stories, interior corridors. **Parking:** on-site (fee) and valet. **Pool:** heated outdoor. **Activities:** hot tub, exercise room. **Guest Services:** valet laundry, boarding pass kiosk.

UNIVERSITY INN 520/791-7503 3

Motel

Address: 950 N Stone Ave 85705 **Location:** Jct Stone Ave and 1st St, 1 blk s of Speedway Blvd. **Facility:** 38 units. 2 stories (no elevator), exterior corridors. **Pool:** outdoor. **Guest Services:** coin laundry. **Featured Amenity: continental breakfast.**

WHERE TO EAT

47 SCOTT 520/624-4747 8

American. Gastropub. **Address:** 47 N Scott Ave 85701

AUGUSTIN KITCHEN 520/398-5382 10

New American. Casual Dining. **Address:** 100 S Avenida del Convento 85745

CAFÉ A LA C'ART 520/628-8533 4

American. Casual Dining. **Address:** 150 N Main Ave 85701

CAFE POCA COSA 520/622-6400 7

Mexican. Casual Dining. **Address:** 110 E Pennington St 85701

CHARRO STEAK 520/485-1922 15

Steak. Casual Dining. **Address:** 188 E Broadway Blvd 85701

CUP CAFE 520/798-1618 11

American. Casual Dining. **Address:** 311 E Congress St 85701

DOWNTOWN KITCHEN + COCKTAILS 520/623-7700 16

American. Casual Dining. **Address:** 135 S 6th Ave 85701

EL CHARRO CAFE 520/622-1922 3

Mexican. Casual Dining. **Address:** 311 N Court Ave 85701

EL MINUTO CAFE 520/882-4145 18

Mexican. Casual Dining. **Address:** 354 S Main Ave 85701

ERMANOS CRAFT BEER & WINE BAR 520/445-6625 5

American. Gastropub. **Address:** 220 N Fourth Ave 85705

MAGPIE'S GOURMET PIZZA 520/628-1661 2

Pizza. Casual Dining. **Address:** 605 N 4th Ave 85705

MAYNARDS MARKET & KITCHEN 520/545-0577 9

New American. Fine Dining. **Address:** 400 E Toole Ave 85701

MIAN SUSHI & MODERN ASIAN CUISINE 520/882-0001 14

Asian. Casual Dining. **Address:** 88 E Broadway 85701

OBON SUSHI BAR RAMEN 520/485-3590 12

Japanese. Casual Dining. **Address:** 350 E Congress St 85701

PENCA 520/203-7681 13

Regional Mexican. Casual Dining. **Address:** 50 E Broadway 85701

REILLY CRAFT PIZZA AND DRINK 520/882-5550 6

Italian. Casual Dining. **Address:** 101 E Pennington St 85701

TRIDENT GRILL 520/795-5755 1

American. Casual Dining. **Address:** 2033 E Speedway Blvd 85719

WELCOME DINER 520/622-5100 17

American. Casual Dining. **Address:** 902 E Broadway Blvd 85719

TUCSON

• Restaurants p. 219
• Hotels & Restaurants map & index p. 204, 210

3 PALMS TUCSON 520/575-9255 **3**

Hotel

Address: 7411 N Oracle Rd 85704 **Location:** SR 77 (Oracle Rd), just n of Ina Rd. **Facility:** 155 units, some efficiencies. 2-3 stories, exterior corridors. **Pool:** heated outdoor. **Activities:** hot tub, picnic facilities. **Guest Services:** coin laundry. **Featured Amenity: breakfast buffet.**

SAVE CALL BIZ / SOME UNITS

ARIZONA INN 520/325-1541 **20**

Historic Boutique Hotel

Address: 2200 E Elm St 85719 **Location:** I-10 exit 257 (Speedway Blvd), 2.5 mi e, 0.5 mi n on Campbell Ave, then just e. Located in a quiet residential area. **Facility:** This historic property, complete with elegant appointments and lush expansive gardens, has kept the integrity of the early 1900s in the style of its rooms. 90 units, some two bedrooms and houses. 1-2 stories (no elevator), interior/exterior corridors. **Parking:** on-site and valet. **Amenities:** safes. **Dining:** Main Dining Room at the Arizona Inn, see separate listing, entertainment. **Pool:** heated outdoor. **Activities:** sauna, tennis, bicycles, lawn sports, exercise room, massage. **Guest Services:** valet laundry. *(See ad this page.)*

SAVE CALL BIZ HS / SOME UNITS

BEST WESTERN INNSUITES TUCSON FOOTHILLS 520/297-8111 **5**

Hotel

AAA Benefit: Members save up to 15% and earn bonus points!

Address: 6201 N Oracle Rd 85704 **Location:** I-10 exit 250 (Orange Grove Rd), 4 mi e, then just s. **Facility:** 158 units, some efficiencies. 2 stories (no elevator), exterior corridors. **Pool:** heated outdoor. **Activities:** hot tub, picnic facilities, exercise room. **Guest Services:** coin laundry, area transportation. **Featured Amenity: breakfast buffet.**

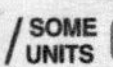

SAVE BIZ / SOME UNITS HS

BEST WESTERN TUCSON INT'L AIRPORT HOTEL & SUITES 520/746-3932 **8**

Hotel

AAA Benefit: Members save up to 15% and earn bonus points!

Address: 6801 S Tucson Blvd 85756 **Location:** Just n of Tucson International Airport. **Facility:** 167 units. 2 stories, interior corridors. **Amenities:** *Some:* safes. **Pool:** heated outdoor. **Activities:** hot tub, exercise room. **Guest Services:** valet and coin laundry, area transportation. **Featured Amenity: full hot breakfast.**

SAVE BIZ

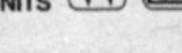

/ SOME UNITS

(See maps & indexes p. 204, 210.)

CANDLEWOOD SUITES TUCSON 520/373-5799 10

Extended Stay Hotel

Address: 1995 W River Rd 85704 **Location:** I-10 exit 250 (Orange Grove Rd), 0.4 mi e to River Rd, then 2.7 mi se. **Facility:** 89 efficiencies. 4 stories, interior corridors. **Pool:** heated outdoor. **Activities:** hot tub, picnic facilities, exercise room. **Guest Services:** complimentary and valet laundry.

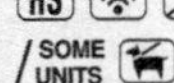

SOME UNITS

CASINO DEL SOL 520/324-9000 37

Resort Hotel

Address: 5655 W Valencia Rd 85757 **Location:** I-19 exit 95 (Valencia Rd), 5.8 mi w. **Facility:** Located in a scenic area with Sonoran desert and mountain views, this expansive property is a combined upscale resort and entertainment complex. 215 units. 10 stories, interior corridors. **Parking:** on-site and valet. **Terms:** check-in 4 pm. **Amenities:** safes. **Dining:** 5 restaurants, also, PY Steakhouse, Tequila Factory, see separate listings. **Pool:** heated outdoor. **Activities:** hot tub, regulation golf, exercise room, spa. **Guest Services:** valet laundry.

SOME UNITS

COMFORT INN & SUITES 520/747-7474 34

Hotel. **Address:** 4850 S Hotel Dr 85714

COMFORT INN-GRANT RD 520/547-1755 17

Hotel. **Address:** 1560 W Grant Rd 85745

COMFORT SUITES AT SABINO CANYON 520/298-2300 21

Hotel. **Address:** 7007 E Tanque Verde Rd 85715

COMFORT SUITES AT TUCSON MALL 520/888-6676 13

Hotel. **Address:** 515 W Auto Mall Dr 85705

COUNTRY INN & SUITES BY RADISSON-TUCSON AIRPORT 520/741-9000 5

Hotel

Address: 6681 S Tucson Blvd 85756 **Location:** 0.4 mi n of Tucson International Airport entrance. **Facility:** 83 units. 3 stories, interior corridors. **Pool:** heated outdoor. **Activities:** hot tub, exercise room. **Guest Services:** valet and coin laundry. **Featured Amenity: breakfast buffet.**

SOME UNITS

COURTYARD BY MARRIOTT TUCSON AIRPORT 520/573-0000 1

Hotel

COURTYARD **AAA Benefit:** Members save 5% or more!

Address: 2505 E Executive Dr 85756 **Location:** On Tucson Blvd, 0.7 mi n of Tucson International Airport entrance. **Facility:** 149 units. 3 stories, interior corridors. **Pool:** heated outdoor. **Activities:** hot tub, exercise room. **Guest Services:** valet and coin laundry, boarding pass kiosk, area transportation. *(See ad this page.)*

SOME UNITS

COURTYARD BY MARRIOTT-TUCSON WILLIAMS CENTRE 520/745-6000 28

Hotel. **Address:** 201 S Williams Blvd 85711

AAA Benefit: Members save 5% or more!

What's for dinner?

AAA.com/travelguides/restaurants

▼ *See AAA listing this page* ▼

(See maps & indexes p. 204, 210.)

DAYS INN AIRPORT 520/747-8988 (33)

Hotel

Address: 4855 S Palo Verde Blvd 85714 **Location:** I-10 exit 264 westbound; exit 264B eastbound, just n. **Facility:** 65 units. 2 stories (no elevator), exterior corridors. **Pool:** outdoor. **Activities:** hot tub. **Guest Services:** coin laundry. **Featured Amenity:** continental breakfast.

SAVE BIZ HS

DESERT DIAMOND CASINO & HOTEL 520/342-3100 (14)

Hotel

Address: 7350 S Nogales Hwy 85756 **Location:** I-19 exit 95 (Valencia Rd), 1.4 mi e, then 1 mi s. **Facility:** The property boasts renovated upscale guest rooms and public areas, which are removed from the hustle and bustle of the casino. A fire pit near the pool offers a cozy spot to unwind. 148 units. 4 stories, interior corridors. **Amenities:** safes. **Dining:** 3 restaurants. **Pool:** heated outdoor. **Activities:** hot tub, exercise room. **Guest Services:** valet laundry.

SAVE CALL BIZ HS / SOME UNITS

DOUBLETREE SUITES BY HILTON TUCSON AIRPORT 520/225-0800 (12)

Hotel

AAA Benefit: Members save up to 15%!

Address: 7051 S Tucson Blvd 85756 **Location:** At entrance to Tucson International Airport. **Facility:** 204 units. 3 stories, exterior corridors. **Amenities:** safes. **Pool:** heated outdoor. **Activities:** hot tub, exercise room. **Guest Services:** valet and coin laundry, area transportation.

SAVE CALL BIZ / SOME UNITS

EMBASSY SUITES BY HILTON TUCSON 520/352-4000 (6)

Hotel

AAA Benefit: Members save up to 15%!

Address: 3110 E Skyline Dr 85718 **Location:** Jct Sunrise and Skyline drs; southeast corner. **Facility:** 120 units. 2-3 stories, interior corridors. **Amenities:** safes. **Pool:** heated outdoor. **Activities:** hot tub, exercise room. **Guest Services:** valet and coin laundry, area transportation. **Featured Amenity:** full hot breakfast.

EXTENDED STAY AMERICA-TUCSON GRANT ROAD 520/795-9510 (19)

Extended Stay Hotel. **Address:** 5050 E Grant Rd 85712

FOUR POINTS BY SHERATON TUCSON AIRPORT 520/746-0271 (13)

SAVE Hotel. **Address:** 7060 S Tucson Blvd 85756

AAA Benefit: Members save 5% or more!

HAMPTON INN & SUITES TUCSON EAST/WILLIAMS CENTER 520/514-0500 (31)

SAVE Hotel. **Address:** 251 S Wilmot Rd 85711

AAA Benefit: Members save up to 15%!

HAMPTON INN TUCSON AIRPORT 520/918-9000 (10)

SAVE Hotel. **Address:** 6971 S Tucson Blvd 85756

AAA Benefit: Members save up to 15%!

HILTON GARDEN INN TUCSON AIRPORT 520/741-0505 (4)

SAVE Hotel. **Address:** 6575 S Country Club Rd 85706

AAA Benefit: Members save up to 15%!

HILTON TUCSON EAST 520/721-5600 (32)

Hotel

Hilton HOTELS & RESORTS

AAA Benefit: Members save up to 15%!

Address: 7600 E Broadway Blvd 85710 **Location:** 0.5 mi e of Kolb Rd. **Facility:** 232 units. 7 stories, interior corridors. **Amenities:** safes. **Pool:** heated outdoor. **Activities:** hot tub, exercise room. **Guest Services:** valet laundry, area transportation.

SAVE CALL BIZ

HOLIDAY INN EXPRESS & SUITES-GRANT RD 520/624-3200 (16)

Hotel. **Address:** 1564 W Grant Rd 85745

HOLIDAY INN EXPRESS HOTEL & SUITES-TUCSON MALL 520/202-5000 (14)

Hotel. **Address:** 620 E Wetmore Rd 85705

HOLIDAY INN EXPRESS TUCSON AIRPORT 520/889-6600 (6)

Hotel. **Address:** 2548 E Medina Rd 85756

HOMEWOOD SUITES BY HILTON TUCSON/ST. PHILIP'S PLAZA UNIVERSITY 520/577-0007 (15)

AAA Benefit: Members save up to 15%!

Address: 4250 N Campbell Ave 85718 **Location:** I-10 exit 254 (Prince Rd), 4 mi e, then 1 mi n. **Facility:** 122 efficiencies. 3 stories, interior corridors. **Pool:** heated outdoor. **Activities:** hot tub, picnic facilities, exercise room. **Guest Services:** valet and coin laundry, area transportation. **Featured Amenity:** breakfast buffet.

SAVE BIZ

(See maps & indexes p. 204, 210.)

HYATT PLACE TUCSON AIRPORT 520/295-0405 9

Hotel

HYATT PLACE **AAA Benefit:** Members save up to 10%!

Address: 6885 S Tucson Blvd 85756 **Location:** Just n of Tucson International Airport. **Facility:** 120 units. 5 stories, interior corridors. **Amenities:** safes. **Pool:** heated outdoor. **Activities:** exercise room. **Guest Services:** valet laundry, area transportation. **Featured Amenity:** breakfast buffet.

SAVE CALL BIZ / SOME UNITS HS

JW MARRIOTT TUCSON STARR PASS RESORT & SPA 520/792-3500 22

Resort Hotel

JW MARRIOTT **AAA Benefit:** Members save 5% or more!

Address: 3800 W Starr Pass Blvd 85745 **Location:** I-10 exit 259 (Starr Pass Blvd), 4.8 mi w. **Facility:** Carved out of the hillside overlooking the valley, the elegant setting complements the hotel's comfortable upscale rooms and spacious baths. 575 units. 6 stories, interior corridors. **Parking:** on-site (fee) and valet. **Terms:** check-in 4 pm. **Amenities:** safes. **Dining:** 6 restaurants, also, Primo, see separate listing. **Pool:** heated outdoor. **Activities:** hot tub, steamroom, regulation golf, recreation programs, kids club, bicycles, trails, health club, spa. **Guest Services:** complimentary and valet laundry, boarding pass kiosk, area transportation.

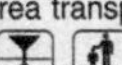

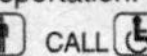

SAVE CALL BIZ

$HS

LA POSADA LODGE & CASITAS 520/887-4800 8

Hotel

Address: 5900 N Oracle Rd 85704 **Location:** 0.5 mi s of Orange Grove Rd. **Facility:** 72 units. 3 stories, exterior corridors. *Bath:* shower only. **Pool:** heated outdoor. **Activities:** hot tub, exercise room. **Featured Amenity:** full hot breakfast.

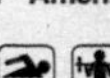

SAVE

/ SOME UNITS

LA QUINTA INN & SUITES TUCSON AIRPORT 520/573-3333 11

Hotel. **Address:** 7001 S Tucson Blvd 85706

LA QUINTA INN & SUITES TUCSON REID PARK 520/795-0330 27

Hotel. **Address:** 102 N Alvernon Way 85711

THE LODGE AT VENTANA CANYON 520/577-1400 12

Boutique Resort Hotel

Address: 6200 N Clubhouse Ln 85750 **Location:** I-10 exit 256 (Grant Rd), 8.6 mi e, 0.6 mi e on Tanque Verde Rd, 2 mi n on Sabino Canyon Rd, then 3.2 mi n on Kolb Rd. Located in a residential resort area. **Facility:** This boutique-style resort, set at the foot of the Santa Catalina Mountains, has spacious rooms and baths, all provided in an intimate setting with full resort facilities. 50 efficiencies, some two bedrooms. 2 stories, interior/exterior corridors. **Parking:** on-site and valet. **Terms:** check-in 4 pm. **Amenities:** safes. **Dining:** 3 restaurants. **Pool:** heated outdoor. **Activities:** sauna, hot tub, steamroom, regulation golf, tennis, recreation programs, exercise room, spa. **Guest Services:** complimentary and valet laundry, area transportation.

SAVE CALL BIZ

/ SOME UNITS

LODGE ON THE DESERT 520/320-2000 26

Hotel. **Address:** 306 N Alvernon Way 85711

LOEWS VENTANA CANYON RESORT 520/299-2020 9

Resort Hotel

Address: 7000 N Resort Dr 85750 **Location:** I-10 exit 256 (Grant Rd), 8.6 mi e, 0.6 mi ne on Tanque Verde Rd, 2 mi n on Sabino Canyon Rd, then 3.5 mi n on Kolb Rd. Located in a quiet area. **Facility:** The elegant building, reminiscent of a Frank Lloyd Wright design, sits at the base of the Santa Catalina Mountains and is surrounded by full resort facilities. Guest rooms were recently renovated. 398 units. 3-4 stories, interior/exterior corridors. **Parking:** on-site and valet. **Terms:** check-in 4 pm. **Amenities:** safes. **Dining:** 3 restaurants, also, Flying V Bar & Grill, see separate listing. **Pool:** heated outdoor. **Activities:** sauna, hot tub, steamroom, regulation golf, tennis, recreation programs, playground, trails, health club, spa. **Guest Services:** valet laundry, area transportation.

SAVE ECO CALL BIZ / SOME UNITS

MOTEL 6 TUCSON NORTH #1127 520/744-9300 2

Hotel. **Address:** 4630 W Ina Rd 85741

(See maps & indexes p. 204, 210.)

OMNI TUCSON NATIONAL RESORT 520/297-2271 **1**

Resort Hotel. **Address:** 2727 W Club Dr 85742

RED ROOF INN-TUCSON SOUTH 520/571-1400 **36**

Hotel

Address: 3704 E Irvington Rd 85714 **Location:** I-10 exit 264 westbound; exit 264B eastbound. **Facility:** 118 units. 2 stories, exterior corridors. **Amenities:** safes. **Pool:** heated outdoor. **Guest Services:** coin laundry.

/ SOME UNITS

RESIDENCE INN BY MARRIOTT TUCSON AIRPORT 520/294-5522 **7**

Extended Stay Hotel

Residence INN **AAA Benefit:** Members save 5% or more!

Address: 2660 E Medina Rd 85756 **Location:** 0.5 mi n of airport entrance on Tucson Blvd, just e. **Facility:** 124 efficiencies. 3 stories, interior corridors. **Pool:** heated outdoor. **Activities:** hot tub, picnic facilities, exercise room. **Guest Services:** valet and coin laundry, area transportation. **Featured Amenity: full hot breakfast.**

SAVE BIZ HS / SOME UNITS

RESIDENCE INN BY MARRIOTT WILLIAMS CENTRE 520/790-6100 **29**

SAVE Extended Stay Hotel. **Address:** 5400 E Williams Cir 85711

AAA Benefit: Members save 5% or more!

SHERATON TUCSON HOTEL & SUITES 520/323-6262 **18**

SAVE Hotel. **Address:** 5151 E Grant Rd 85712

AAA Benefit: Members save 5% or more!

SONESTA ES SUITES TUCSON 520/721-0991 **23**

Extended Stay Hotel

Address: 6477 E Speedway Blvd 85710 **Location:** Just e of Wilmot Rd. **Facility:** 128 units, some two bedrooms, efficiencies and kitchens. 2 stories (no elevator), exterior corridors. **Terms:** check-in 4 pm. **Pool:** heated outdoor. **Activities:** hot tub, picnic facilities, exercise room. **Guest Services:** valet and coin laundry. **Featured Amenity: breakfast buffet.**

SAVE BIZ / SOME UNITS

STARR PASS GOLF SUITES 520/670-0500 **25**

Condominium. **Address:** 3645 W Starr Pass Blvd 85745

STAYBRIDGE SUITES TUCSON AIRPORT 520/807-1004 **2**

Extended Stay Hotel. **Address:** 2705 E Executive Dr 85756

STUDIO 6 EXTENDED STAY #6002 520/746-0030 **35**

Extended Stay Motel. **Address:** 4950 S Outlet Center Dr 85706

TOWNEPLACE SUITES BY MARRIOTT TUCSON 520/292-9697 **7**

SAVE Extended Stay Hotel. **Address:** 405 W Rudasill Rd 85704

AAA Benefit: Members save 5% or more!

TOWNEPLACE SUITES BY MARRIOTT TUCSON AIRPORT 520/294-6677 **3**

Extended Stay Hotel

TOWNEPLACE SUITES MARRIOTT **AAA Benefit:** Members save 5% or more!

Address: 6595 S Bay Colony Dr 85756 **Location:** 0.7 mi n of Tucson International Airport. **Facility:** 91 efficiencies. 3 stories, interior corridors. **Pool:** heated outdoor. **Activities:** picnic facilities, exercise room. **Guest Services:** valet and coin laundry.

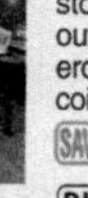

SAVE CALL BIZ / SOME UNITS

TOWNEPLACE SUITES BY MARRIOTT TUCSON WILLIAMS CENTRE 520/747-0720 **30**

Extended Stay Hotel

TOWNEPLACE SUITES MARRIOTT **AAA Benefit:** Members save 5% or more!

Address: 384 S Williams Blvd 85711 **Location:** Jct Campbell Ave, 3.8 mi e on Broadway Blvd, just s. **Facility:** 124 efficiencies. 3-4 stories, interior corridors. **Pool:** heated outdoor. **Activities:** picnic facilities, exercise room. **Guest Services:** valet and coin laundry. **Featured Amenity: full hot breakfast.**

SAVE CALL BIZ HS / SOME UNITS

VOYAGER HOTEL & RV RESORT 520/574-5000 **38**

Hotel. **Address:** 8701 S Kolb Rd 85756

THE WESTIN LA PALOMA RESORT & SPA 520/742-6000 **11**

Resort Hotel

WESTIN HOTELS & RESORTS **AAA Benefit:** Members save 5% or more!

Address: 3800 E Sunrise Dr 85718 **Location:** SR 77 (Oracle Rd), 4.6 mi e on Ina Rd via Skyline and Sunrise drs, then just s on Via Palomita. **Facility:** In an attractive desert setting, the resort features large rooms with balconies or patios. Guests will enjoy the beautiful pool area with a waterfall, pond, swim-up bar and waterslide. 487 units. 3 stories, exterior corridors. **Parking:** on-site and valet. **Terms:** check-in 4 pm. **Amenities:** safes. **Dining:** 6 restaurants. **Pool:** heated outdoor. **Activities:** sauna, hot tub, steamroom, regulation golf, tennis, recreation programs, kids club, lawn sports, trails, health club, spa. **Guest Services:** valet laundry, area transportation.

SAVE ECO CALL BIZ SHS / SOME UNITS

(See maps & indexes p. 204, 210.)

WESTWARD LOOK WYNDHAM GRAND RESORT & SPA
520/297-1151 (4)

Resort Hotel

Address: 245 E Ina Rd 85704 **Location:** I-10 exit 248 (Ina Rd), 6 mi e, then left on Westward Look Dr. **Facility:** Nestled on 80 acres of lush desert terrain, the resort boasts fabulous views of the Santa Catalina mountains, multiple pools, gardens and nature trails, and oversized casita-style guest rooms. 241 units. 1-2 stories (no elevator), exterior corridors. **Parking:** on-site and valet. **Terms:** check-in 4 pm. **Amenities:** safes. **Dining:** 2 restaurants, also, Gold, see separate listing. **Pool:** heated outdoor. **Activities:** hot tub, tennis, recreation programs, bicycles, lawn sports, trails, exercise room, spa. **Guest Services:** valet laundry, boarding pass kiosk, rental car service, area transportation.

WHERE TO EAT

BAZIL'S 520/577-3322 (18)
Regional Italian. Casual Dining. **Address:** 4777 E Sunrise Dr, Suite 119 85718

BEYOND BREAD 520/322-9965 (33)
American. Quick Serve. **Address:** 3026 N Campbell Ave 85719

BISBEE BREAKFAST CLUB BROADWAY 520/327-0029 (56)
Breakfast. Casual Dining. **Address:** 2936 E Broadway Blvd 85716

BLUE WILLOW RESTAURANT BAKERY 520/327-7577 (40)
American. Casual Dining. **Address:** 2616 N Campbell Ave 85719

BOB'S STEAK & CHOP HOUSE 520/877-2377 (2)
Steak. Fine Dining. **Address:** 2727 W Club Dr 85742

BOTTEGA MICHELANGELO 520/297-5775 (3)
Italian. Casual Dining. **Address:** 420 W Magee Rd 85704

CASA DEL RIO 520/308-6896 (61)
Mexican. Casual Dining. **Address:** 1060 S Pantano Rd 85710

CASA MOLINA 520/886-5468 (53)
Mexican. Casual Dining. **Address:** 6225 E Speedway Blvd 85712

CHOICE GREENS 520/319-2467 (48)
Specialty. Quick Serve. **Address:** 2829 E Speedway Blvd 85716

CIELOS 520/325-3366 (54)
American. Casual Dining. **Address:** 306 N Alvernon Way 85711

CODY'S BEEF 'N BEANS 520/322-9475 (30)
Steak. Casual Dining. **Address:** 2708 E Fort Lowell Rd 85716

COLT'S TASTE OF TEXAS 520/572-5968 (1)
Steak. Casual Dining. **Address:** 8310 N Thornydale Rd 85741

COMMONER & CO. 520/257-1177 (21)
New American. Casual Dining. **Address:** 6960 E Sunrise Dr 85750

DAISY MAE'S STEAKHOUSE 520/792-8888 (47)
Steak. Casual Dining. **Address:** 2735 W Anklam Rd 85745

THE ECLECTIC CAFE 520/885-2842 (45)
American. Casual Dining. **Address:** 7053 E Tanque Verde Rd 85715

EL CORRAL STEAKHOUSE 520/299-6092 (25)
Steak. Casual Dining. **Address:** 2201 E River Rd 85718

FEAST 520/326-9363 (50)
American. Casual Dining. **Address:** 3719 E Speedway Blvd 85712

FIREBIRDS WOOD FIRED GRILL 520/577-0747 (11)
American. Casual Dining. **Address:** 2985 E Skyline Dr 85718

FLEMING'S PRIME STEAKHOUSE & WINE BAR
520/529-5017 (15)
Steak. Fine Dining. **Address:** 6360 N Campbell Ave 85718

FLYING V BAR & GRILL 520/299-2020 (16)
Regional Southwestern. Fine Dining. **Address:** 7000 N Resort Dr 85750

GHINI'S FRENCH CAFFE 520/326-9095 (28)
French. Casual Dining. **Address:** 1803 E Prince Rd 85719

GOLD 520/917-2930 (6)

American
Fine Dining
$22-$42

AAA Inspector Notes: *Classic.* The view over the valley below, which is particularly breathtaking at night, complements the fine-dining experience. Sonoran Desert spices and flavors infuse classic and contemporary cuisine. The pastry chef's creations are delectable and unique. **Features:** full bar, patio dining. **Reservations:** suggested. **Address:** 245 E Ina Rd 85704 **Location:** I-10 exit 248 (Ina Rd), 6 mi e, then left on Westward Look Dr; in Westward Look Wyndham Grand Resort & Spa. **Parking:** on-site and valet. (B) (L) (D)

THE GRILL AT HACIENDA DEL SOL 520/529-3500 (17)

Southwestern
Fine Dining
$28-$50

AAA Inspector Notes: Both in the main dining room and on the patio, the charming ambience of old Tucson is apparent in this restaurant's décor. Seasonal menu offerings, presented by accomplished servers, are prepared with the freshest ingredients and feature innovative flavor combinations. **Features:** full bar, patio dining, Sunday brunch, happy hour. **Reservations:** suggested. **Address:** 5601 N Hacienda del Sol Rd 85718 **Location:** Jct SR 77 (Oracle Rd), 5.4 mi e on Ina Rd/Skyline and Sunrise drs, 0.6 mi s to Via Alcalde, then just nw; in Hacienda del Sol Guest Ranch Resort. **Parking:** on-site and valet. (D)

GUADALAJARA ORIGINAL GRILL 520/323-1022 (27)
Mexican. Casual Dining. **Address:** 1220 E Prince Rd 85719

HI FALUTIN WESTERN GRILL 520/297-0518 (9)
American. Casual Dining. **Address:** 6780 N Oracle Rd 85704

THE HUNGRY FOX RESTAURANT AND COUNTRY STORE
520/326-2835 (57)
American. Casual Dining. **Address:** 4637 E Broadway Blvd 85711

INDIA OVEN 520/326-8635 (39)
Indian. Casual Dining. **Address:** 2727 N Campbell Ave 85719

JONATHAN'S CORK 520/296-1631 (51)
Southwestern Steak. Casual Dining. **Address:** 6320 E Tanque Verde Rd 85715

KINGFISHER 520/323-7739 (42)
Seafood. Casual Dining. **Address:** 2564 E Grant Rd 85716

(See maps & indexes p. 204, 210.)

LA PARRILLA SUIZA

Mexican. Casual Dining.

LOCATIONS:

Address: 2720 N Oracle Rd 85705 **Phone:** 520/624-4300
Address: 4250 W Ina Rd 85741 **Phone:** 520/572-7200

LE RENDEZ-VOUS 520/323-7373 (35)

French. Fine Dining. **Address:** 3844 E Fort Lowell Rd 85716

LOVIN' SPOONFULS 520/325-7766 (34)

Vegetarian. Casual Dining. **Address:** 2990 N Campbell Ave 85719

MAIN DINING ROOM AT THE ARIZONA INN
520/325-1541 (43)

Continental Fine Dining $12-$40

AAA Inspector Notes: Decorated as it might have been when the inn first opened in 1929, the restaurant is a nice spot for refined dining. Tall windows overlook the landscaped courtyard, with mirrors and soft lighting creating a refined atmosphere. Diners can savor preparations of seafood, beef and lamb or select from the ever-changing chef's tasting menu. **Features:** full bar, patio dining, Sunday brunch. **Reservations:** suggested. **Address:** 2200 E Elm St 85719 **Location:** I-10 exit 257 (Speedway Blvd), 2.5 mi e, 0.5 mi n on Campbell Ave, then just e; in Arizona Inn. **Parking:** on-site and valet. B L D

MAMA'S FAMOUS PIZZA & HEROS

Pizza. Casual Dining.

LOCATIONS:

Address: 50 S Houghton Rd 85748 **Phone:** 520/751-4600
Address: 6996 E 22nd St 85710 **Phone:** 520/750-1919
Address: 7965 N Oracle Rd 85704 **Phone:** 520/297-3993
Address: 4500 E Speedway Blvd 85712 **Phone:** 520/319-8856

MCGRAW'S CANTINA 520/885-3088 (65)

American. Casual Dining. **Address:** 4110 S Houghton Rd 85730

MI NIDITO FAMILY RESTAURANT 520/622-5081 (60)

Mexican. Casual Dining. **Address:** 1813 S 4th Ave 85713

MOSAIC CAFE DOS 520/297-8470 (4)

Mexican. Casual Dining. **Address:** 7350 N La Cholla Blvd 85741

MR. AN'S TEPPAN STEAK & SUSHI 520/797-0888 (14)

Japanese. Casual Dining. **Address:** 6091 N Oracle Rd 85704

NEW DELHI PALACE 520/296-8585 (59)

Indian. Casual Dining. **Address:** 6751 E Broadway Blvd 85710

NORTH ITALIA 520/299-1600 (12)

New Italian. Casual Dining. **Address:** 2995 E Skyline Dr 85718

OREGANO'S PIZZA BISTRO

Italian Pizza. Casual Dining.

LOCATIONS:

Address: 4900 E Speedway Blvd 85712 **Phone:** 520/327-8955
Address: 100 W Orange Grove Rd 85704 **Phone:** 520/229-9999

PASTICHE MODERN EATERY 520/325-3333 (32)

American. Casual Dining. **Address:** 3025 N Campbell Ave 85719

P.F. CHANG'S CHINA BISTRO 520/615-8788 (23)

Chinese. Fine Dining. **Address:** 1805 E River Rd, Suite 100 85718

PINNACLE PEAK RESTAURANT 520/296-0911 (49)

Steak. Casual Dining. **Address:** 6541 E Tanque Verde Rd 85715

PITA JUNGLE 520/207-6873 (58)

Mediterranean. Casual Dining. **Address:** 5340 E Broadway Blvd 85711

PREP & PASTRY 520/326-7737 (31)

American. Casual Dining. **Address:** 3073 N Campbell Ave 85719

PREP & PASTRY 520/838-0809 (44)

American. Casual Dining. **Address:** 6450 E Grant Rd 85715

PRIMO 520/792-3500 (52)

Regional Italian. Fine Dining. **Address:** 3800 W Starr Pass Blvd 85745

PY STEAKHOUSE 520/324-9350 (64)

Steak. Fine Dining. **Address:** 5655 W Valencia Rd 85757

RA SUSHI BAR RESTAURANT 520/615-3970

Japanese Sushi. Casual Dining. **Address:** 2905 E Skyline Dr, Suite 289 85718

REFORMA COCINA & CANTINA 520/867-4134 (26)

Regional Mexican. Casual Dining. **Address:** 4310 N Campbell Ave 85718

RISKY BUSINESS 520/577-0021 (20)

American. Casual Dining. **Address:** 6866 E Sunrise Dr 85750

ROSA'S MEXICAN FOOD 520/325-0362 (29)

Mexican. Casual Dining. **Address:** 1750 E Fort Lowell Rd 85719

RUSTY'S FAMILY RESTAURANT & SPORTS GRILLE
520/623-3363 (38)

American. Casual Dining. **Address:** 2075 W Grant Rd 85745

SAFFRON INDIAN BISTRO 520/742-9100 (5)

Indian. Casual Dining. **Address:** 7607 N Oracle Rd 85704

SAUCE 520/297-8575

Italian. Quick Serve. **Address:** 7117 N Oracle Rd 85718

SAUCE 520/514-1122

Italian. Casual Dining. **Address:** 5285 E Broadway, Suite 101 85711

SAUCE 520/795-0344 (37)

Italian. Quick Serve. **Address:** 2990 N Campbell Ave, #110 85719

SHER-E-PUNJAB 520/624-9393 (41)

Indian. Casual Dining. **Address:** 853 E Grant Rd 85719

SILVER SADDLE STEAKHOUSE 520/622-6253 (62)

Steak. Casual Dining. **Address:** 310 E Benson Hwy 85713

SULLIVAN'S STEAKHOUSE 520/299-4275 (22)

Steak. Fine Dining. **Address:** 1785 E River Rd 85718

SUSHI ON ORACLE 520/297-3615 (10)

Sushi. Casual Dining. **Address:** 6449 N Oracle Rd 85704

TEQUILA FACTORY 520/838-6626 (63)

Mexican. Casual Dining. **Address:** 5655 W Valencia Rd 85757

TERESA'S MOSAIC CAFE 520/624-4512 (36)

Mexican. Casual Dining. **Address:** 2455 N Silverbell Rd 85745

TOHONO CHUL PARK GARDEN BISTRO 520/742-6455 (7)

American. Casual Dining. **Address:** 7366 N Paseo Del Norte 85704

(See maps & indexes p. 204, 210.)

TRATTORIA PINA 520/577-6992 (19)

♦♦ Italian. Casual Dining. **Address:** 5541 N Swan Rd 85718

VIVACE RESTAURANT 520/795-7221 (13)

♦♦♦ Italian. Fine Dining. **Address:** 6440 N Campbell Ave 85718

WILDFLOWER TUCSON 520/219-4230 (8)

♦♦♦ American. Casual Dining. **Address:** 7037 N Oracle Rd 85718

ZEMAM'S 520/323-9928 (55)

♦♦ Ethiopian. Casual Dining. **Address:** 2731 E Broadway Blvd 85716

ZINBURGER 520/299-7799 (24)

♦♦ Burgers. Casual Dining. **Address:** 1865 E River Rd 85718

ZONA 78 520/296-7878 (46)

♦♦ Italian. Casual Dining. **Address:** 7301 E Tanque Verde Rd 85715

GEM TUMACÁCORI NATIONAL HISTORICAL PARK (G-4)

Approximately 19 miles north of Nogales off I-19 exit 29, Tumacácori National Historical Park preserves the abandoned Mission San Jose de Tumacácori. Once a Pima Indian village, Tumacácori was visited by Jesuit Eusebio Francisco Kino in 1691. In 1767 the Jesuits were expelled from Tumacácori by the King of Spain and replaced by Franciscans. The Franciscans began building the present massive adobe church about 1800, but it was never completed. Apache raids, neglect and a terrible winter contributed to its abandonment in 1848, yet afterward people continued to visit the site.

The area became a national monument in 1908. The 1990 addition of two Spanish mission sites, Guevavi and Calabazas, increased the total acreage to 47. It later was expanded again to include a mile of the Santa Cruz River riparian corridor and mesquite bosque (forest) and now encompasses 360 acres. Guevavi and Calabazas can be visited by reservation only. A historic museum distinguished by architectural features of the Sonora missions unfolds local history and describes mission life.

A self-guiding tour includes the church and cemetery, mortuary chapel, the convent area, a patio garden and a visitor center/museum. Picnic facilities are available. Allow 1 hour minimum. Daily 9-5; closed Thanksgiving and Christmas. Admission, valid for 7 days, $5; free (ages 0-15). Prices may vary; phone ahead. Inter-agency passes are accepted. Phone (520) 398-2341.

GEM TUZIGOOT NATIONAL MONUMENT (C-3)

About 2 miles northwest of Cottonwood via Main Street to Tuzigoot Road, Tuzigoot National Monument preserves the remains of a pueblo that was occupied by Ancestral Puebloan people referred to as the Sinagua culture from about A.D. 1000 until the early 1400s. From more than 110 rooms archeologists have recovered stone and bone tools, textiles, pottery, shell beads and bracelets, which are displayed in the visitor center.

Allow 1 hour minimum. Daily 8-4. Admission $10 (includes admission to Montezuma Castle National Monument); free (ages 0-15). Prices may vary; phone ahead. Federal Recreation passes are accepted. Phone (928) 634-5564.

VALLE (B-3) pop. 832, elev. 5,994'

PLANES OF FAME AIR MUSEUM is at the Valle Airport near jct. SR 64 and US 180 at 755 Mustang Way. Covering aviation history from World War I through the supersonic jet age, the museum's collection includes Gen. Douglas MacArthur's personal transport plane *Bataan,* a Lockheed C-121A Constellation. Other aircraft include a Grumman F-11F Tiger formerly used by the Navy's Blue Angels and a 1944 Messerschmitt BF109G-10. A flyby/fly-in is held in August.

Time: Allow 1 hour minimum. **Hours:** Daily 9-5. Closed Thanksgiving and Christmas. Phone ahead to confirm schedule. **Cost:** $10; $8 (active military with ID); $5 (ages 5-11). **Phone:** (928) 635-1000.

VERMILION CLIFFS NATIONAL MONUMENT (A-3)

Bounded on the east by Glen Canyon National Recreation Area, on the west by Kaibab National Forest, to the north by the Utah border and to the south by SR 89A, remote Vermilion Cliffs National Monument contains 293,000 acres of unspoiled plateaus, canyons and cliffs. Elevations range from 3,100 to 7,100 feet.

Ancestral Puebloan villages and geologic formations can be found on the monument lands, which were traversed by Spanish explorers and Mormon pioneers. Animal inhabitants include desert bighorn sheep, mule deer, pronghorn and mountain lions. For further information contact the Arizona Strip Field Office, Bureau of Land Management; 345 E. Riverside Dr., St. George, UT 84790; phone (435) 688-3200.

GEM WALNUT CANYON NATIONAL MONUMENT (C-4)

Off I-40 exit 204, 7.5 miles east of Flagstaff, Walnut Canyon National Monument preserves the remains of more than 300 pre-Columbian dwellings built on a series of ledges in the 400-foot-deep gorge. Inhabited by the Walnut Canyon community (archeologists are uncertain of what these inhabitants called themselves) about 1000-1200, the single-family dwellings are visible from the visitor center on the canyon rim.

The self-guiding Island Trail, which descends 185 feet over the course of a half mile, is an interesting but arduous paved path that leads past 25 of the cliff dwelling rooms. The Rim Trail, a pleasant .75-mile round trip, features two overlooks into the canyon as well as access to a small pueblo and pit house. Snow and ice might close both trails at times in winter and spring.

Interpretive programs within the backcountry are available by reservation from Memorial Day through Labor Day. Other ranger-led programs include short hikes and patio talks, which are available year-round, depending on staffing. A museum and picnic facilities are available; however, food is not available. Pets are not allowed on park trails, in buildings or tied to fixed objects.

Note: The Island Trail includes descending/ascending 240 steps and might be cumbersome for the physically challenged and those with heart conditions.

Allow 1 hour, 30 minutes minimum. Daily 9-5; closed Christmas. Last admittance to main trail is 1 hour before closing. Admission (valid 7 days) $15 per person; free (ages 0-15). Prices may vary; phone ahead. For further information contact the Superintendent, Walnut Canyon National Monument, 6400 N. SR 89, Flagstaff, AZ 86004; phone (928) 526-3367.

WICKENBURG (G-1) pop. 6,363, elev. 2,093'

Nineteen miles southwest of Wickenburg is the Vulture Gold Mine, which yielded more than $20 million in gold during the hectic period following its discovery by Henry Wickenburg in 1863. Allegedly Wickenburg found the gold in one of the rocks he was hurling at his escaping mule.

The gold rush that ensued reached such proportions that by 1866 Wickenburg was the third largest city in Arizona and missed becoming the territorial capital by only two votes. Still standing in the center of town is the old mesquite jail tree to which lawmen chained their prisoners during the early boom years; no one wanted to take time from mining to build a proper jail.

The Hassayampa River, running through town, was called "the river which flows upside down" by Native Americans because it flows 20 feet below ground for most of its length. Along its banks is one of the last and greatest natural riparian areas in the state. The Nature Conservancy's Hassayampa River Preserve protects a portion of this endangered habitat.

Wickenburg, known for its Old West atmosphere and many dude ranches, brings the past to life in February during Gold Rush Days, when the Desert Caballeros ride into the Bradshaw Mountains to spend several days under the stars; the whole town gathers to bid the horsemen farewell as they ride off into the mountains.

Wickenburg Chamber of Commerce: 216 N. Frontier St., Wickenburg, AZ 85390. **Phone:** (928) 684-5479 or (800) 942-5242.

DESERT CABALLEROS WESTERN MUSEUM, 21 N. Frontier St., contains American Western fine art, dioramas depicting the town's history, a re-creation of an early Wickenburg street scene, ancient native artifacts, and a collection of gems and minerals. A bolo tie collection is on display along with works by such noted Western artists as Frederic Remington and Charles Russell. Exhibitions include the annual Cowgirl Up! Art from the Other Half of the West. Complimentary narrated tours via headsets are available.

Time: Allow 1 hour minimum. **Hours:** Mon.-Sat. 10-5, Sun. noon-4, Sept.-May; Tues.-Sat. 10-5, Sun. noon-4, rest of year. Closed Jan. 1, Memorial Day, July 4, Labor Day, Thanksgiving and Christmas. **Cost:** $12; $10 (ages 60+); free (ages 0-17, and active military with guest). **Phone:** (928) 684-2272.

BEST WESTERN RANCHO GRANDE 928/684-5445

Hotel

AAA Benefit: Members save up to 15% and earn bonus points!

Address: 293 E Wickenburg Way 85390 **Location:** On US 60; center. **Facility:** 76 units, some efficiencies and kitchens. 1-2 stories (no elevator), exterior corridors. **Pool:** heated outdoor. **Activities:** picnic facilities. **Guest Services:** valet laundry. **Featured Amenity:** breakfast buffet.

/ SOME UNITS

LOS VIAJEROS INN 928/684-7099

Hotel. **Address:** 1000 N Tegner Rd 85390

QUALITY INN WICKENBURG 928/684-5461

Hotel. **Address:** 850 E Wickenburg Way 85390

RANCHO DE LOS CABALLEROS 928/684-5484

Historic Ranch. **Address:** 1551 S Vulture Mine Rd 85390

SUPER 8 WICKENBURG 928/684-0808

Motel. **Address:** 1021 N Tegner St 85390

WHERE TO EAT

ANITA'S COCINA MEXICAN RESTAURANT 928/684-5777

Mexican. Casual Dining. **Address:** 57 N Valentine St 85390

WILLCOX (F-5) pop. 3,757, elev. 4,156'

Willcox grew from a small cow town into one of the country's major cattle-shipping centers. In days past the large cattle ranches in the surrounding hills and valleys were notorious as refuges for fugitive gunslingers, who often brought their business to town: Wyatt Earp's brother Warren was killed at Headquarters Saloon in 1900. Saloons and other buildings from the late 1800s can be seen in or near the historic district, bounded by Railroad and Haskell avenues and Maley and Stewart streets.

Rex Allen was born and raised in Willcox. Tributes to the cowboy actor include the Rex Allen Arizona-Cowboy Museum and Cowboy Hall of Fame on Railroad Avenue and a bronze statue in a park across from the museum. A bronze heart embedded in the statue at Allen's request represents his enduring love for his hometown. The Friends of Marty Robbins Museum has joined Rex Allen on Railroad Avenue and pays tribute to the late singer/actor.

Cattle raising is still important, but added to the contemporary economic mix are the cultivation of apples, peaches, pistachios, onions and tomatoes. At a variety of "U-pick" farms northwest via Fort Grant Road, visitors can pluck fresh produce straight from the orchards and fields July through October.

Thanks to its high desert climate, Willcox also is known for its vineyards, which produce Syrah, Petite Sirah, Zinfandel and Cabernet Sauvignon among several other grape varieties. Maps for a self-guiding wine country tour are available at the Willcox Regional Visitor Center.

Birding is a popular diversion in Sulphur Springs Valley, a mecca for migrating waterfowl and shorebirds as well as wintering raptors. Sandhill cranes arrive in October and stay through February.

Southeast of town at Apache Pass is the isolated Fort Bowie National Historic Site. The fort was built in 1862 to guard the Butterfield Overland Trail and to protect pioneers from Apache raids and skirmishes with Native Americans led by Cochise and Geronimo. The site can only be reached by traveling the last 1.5 miles on foot. The high elevation and temperature extremes might make this hike unsuitable for some. Water is available at the fort, but hikers should bring their own canteen. Beware of flash floods, mountain lions and rattlesnakes. All historic items and natural features are strictly protected; metal detectors, digging tools, guns and hunting are prohibited. Phone (520) 847-2500.

Willcox Regional Visitor Center and Chamber of Commerce: 1500 N. Circle I Rd., Willcox, AZ 85643. **Phone:** (520) 384-2272 or (800) 200-2272.

Self-guiding tours: Brochures for a self-guiding walking tour of the historic district and a self-guiding tour of the surrounding wine country are available from the visitor center.

DAYS INN 520/384-4222

Motel. **Address:** 724 N Bisbee Ave 85643

HOLIDAY INN EXPRESS & SUITES WILLCOX 520/384-3333

Hotel. **Address:** 1251 N Virginia Ave 85643

WILLIAMS (C-3) pop. 3,023, elev. 6,752'

- **Hotels p. 223 • Restaurants p. 226**
- **Part of Grand Canyon National Park area — see map p. 57**

Williams was named after William (Bill) Shirley Williams, the early mountain man who guided trapping parties and expeditions through the wilderness.

Primarily a resort town, Williams marks the beginning of the major entrance route to Grand Canyon National Park *(see place listing p. 57)*. The town is at the base of Bill Williams Mountain and boasts an 18-hole golf course and a ski area offering both downhill and cross-country skiing. In the surrounding Kaibab National Forest *(see place listing p. 70)*, cross-country skiing and hiking are popular. Kaibab Dogtown and White Horse lakes offer camping, picnicking and fishing, while Cataract Lake is open for day use only.

Williams and Forest Service Visitor Center: 200 West Railroad Ave., Williams, AZ 86046. **Phone:** (928) 635-4061.

BEARIZONA, off I-40 exit 165 at 1500 E. SR 66, is a drive-through wildlife park set in a 160-acre forest. During the 3-mile drive you'll see bison, black bears, deer, elk, American burros, bighorn sheep, Rocky Mountain goats, wolves and other animals in natural habitats. Afterward you can park your car and walk through Fort Bearizona, an area that's home to young foxes, black bear cubs, bobcats and javelinas. The Wild Ride is a guided bus tour through the park. A birds of prey show is presented several times daily.

Time: Allow 2 hours minimum. **Hours:** Daily 8 a.m.-dusk (last admission at 6 p.m.), June 1-Aug. 15; hours may vary, rest of year. Wild Ride daily at 10, noon, 2 and 4. Birds of Prey Show daily at 11, 1 and 3, Mar.-Dec. Phone ahead to confirm schedule. **Cost:** $25; $23 (ages 62+); $15 (ages 4-12). Maximum per private vehicle $120. **Phone:** (928) 635-2289.

GEM **GRAND CANYON RAILWAY,** .5 mi. s. of I-40 exit 163 (Grand Canyon Blvd.), offers round-trip excursions through grassy plains and pine forests to the South Rim of the Grand Canyon aboard 1950s-era passenger cars powered by vintage diesel locomotives. Strolling musicians, Western characters and a mock train robbery provide entertainment during the ride.

Passengers arrive at the 1910 Grand Canyon Depot, in the historic district at the South Rim; the depot is the only working log depot in the country. A Wild West show takes place daily at 9. Six classes of train service are available. For an additional fee, bus tours of the South Rim with lunch are available.

Refreshments are available in some cars. **Hours:** Train departs daily at 9:30 (also at 10:30, Memorial Day-Labor Day) and returns at 5:45 (at 6:45 p.m., Memorial Day-Labor Day) with a 3.5-hour stopover at the canyon. Closed Christmas Eve and Christmas. Phone ahead to confirm schedule.

Cost: Round-trip coach fare $82; $51 (ages 2-15). Round-trip first-class fare $159; $121 (ages 2-15). One-way fare available; upgraded seats are available for an additional fee. Fare does not include admission to Grand Canyon National Park. Fares may vary; phone ahead. Reservations are recommended. **Phone:** (800) 843-8724. GT

AMERICAS BEST VALUE INN 928/635-4085
Motel. **Address:** 302 E Route 66 86046

BEST WESTERN PLUS INN OF WILLIAMS 928/635-4400

Hotel

AAA Benefit: Members save up to 15% and earn bonus points!

Address: 2600 W Route 66 86046 **Location:** I-40 exit 161, south on Route 66. **Facility:** 79 units. 2 stories, interior corridors. **Dining:** Western View Steakhouse, see separate listing, entertainment. **Pool:** heated outdoor. **Activities:** hot tub, trails, exercise room. **Guest Services:** coin laundry. **Featured Amenity: breakfast buffet.** *(See ad this page.)*

SAVE CALL BIZ / SOME UNITS

COMFORT INN NEAR GRAND CANYON 928/635-4045
Hotel. **Address:** 911 W Route 66 86046

DAYS INN OF WILLIAMS 928/635-4051
Motel. **Address:** 2488 W Route 66 86046

GRAND CANYON RAILWAY & HOTEL 928/635-4010

Hotel

Address: 235 N Grand Canyon Blvd 86046 **Location:** I-40 exit 163, 0.5 mi s. Located at historic Williams Depot. **Facility:** 298 units. 2 stories, interior corridors. **Dining:** 2 restaurants, entertainment. **Pool:** heated indoor. **Activities:** hot tub, playground, game room, exercise room. **Guest Services:** coin laundry, area transportation.

SAVE CALL BIZ / SOME UNITS

HOLIDAY INN EXPRESS & SUITES 928/635-2221
Hotel. **Address:** 1150 W Cataract Lake Rd 86046

HOWARD JOHNSON EXPRESS INN 928/635-9561

Hotel

Address: 511 N Grand Canyon Blvd 86046 **Location:** I-40 exit 163, just s. **Facility:** 54 units. 2 stories (no elevator), interior corridors. **Amenities:** safes. **Pool:** heated indoor. **Activities:** hot tub. **Featured Amenity: continental breakfast.**

SAVE CALL

LA QUINTA INN & SUITES 928/635-0033
Hotel. **Address:** 1100 W Cataract Lake Rd 86046

THE LODGE ON ROUTE 66 928/635-4534
Motel. **Address:** 200 E Route 66 86046

RODEWAY INN & SUITES DOWNTOWNER MOTEL 928/635-4041
Motel. **Address:** 201 E Route 66 86046

TRAVELODGE WILLIAMS 928/635-2651

Motel

Address: 430 E Route 66 86046 **Location:** I-40 exit 163, 0.5 mi s, then just e. **Facility:** 41 units, some two bedrooms. 2 stories (no elevator), exterior corridors. **Pool:** heated outdoor. **Activities:** hot tub. **Guest Services:** coin laundry. **Featured Amenity: continental breakfast.**

SAVE CALL BIZ / SOME UNITS

▼ See AAA listing p. 31 ▼

WHERE TO EAT

ANNA'S PLACE GRAND CANYON COFFEE & CAFE 928/635-4907

Breakfast Burgers. Casual Dining. **Address:** 137 W Railroad Ave 86046

CRUISER'S ROUTE 66 BAR & GRILL 928/635-2445

American. Casual Dining. **Address:** 233 W Route 66 86046

DARA THAI CAFE 928/635-2201

Thai. Casual Dining. **Address:** 145 W Route 66 86046

HISTORIC BREWING BARREL & BOTTLE HOUSE 928/635-5325

American. Brewpub. **Address:** 141 W Railroad Ave 86046

KICKS ON ROUTE 66 928/635-2052

American. Casual Dining. **Address:** 2550 W Route 66 86046

PINE COUNTRY RESTAURANT 928/635-9718

American. Casual Dining. **Address:** 107 N Grand Canyon Blvd 86046

ROD'S STEAK HOUSE 928/635-2671

Steak
Casual Dining
$8-$29

AAA Inspector Notes: *Classic.* Serving travelers along Historic Route 66 since 1946, the restaurant has specialty steaks-as well as seafood and chicken dishes. A must-try is the sugar-dipped charred steak, a surprising delight. **Features:** full bar. **Address:** 301 E Route 66 86046 **Location:** Center. L D

STATION 66 ITALIAN BISTRO 928/635-3992

Italian. Casual Dining. **Address:** 144 W Historic Route 66 86046

WESTERN VIEW STEAKHOUSE 928/635-4400

Steak
Casual Dining
$17-$45

AAA Inspector Notes: This small restaurant is located off the hotel lobby and offers an upscale menu featuring Prime steaks, halibut and lamb chops. The portions are large, but the dessert cart is tempting even if guests are full. **Features:** full bar, patio dining. **Address:** 2600 W Route 66 86046 **Location:** I-40 exit 161, south on Route 66; in Best Western Plus Inn of Williams. D CALL

Relaxed dining, forest views, steakhouse & Mexican food

WINDOW ROCK (B-6) pop. 2,712, elev. 6,890'

Window Rock is the capital of the Navajo nation and seat of its tribal government. The elected tribal council meets in the council house at least four times a year. Window Rock also contains the U.S. government's Bureau of Indian Affairs, Navajo Area Office. The headquarters of the Navajo Arts and Crafts Enterprises is just east of the junction of SR 264 and Navajo Route 12.

NAVAJO NATION MUSEUM, at jct. SR 264 and Post Office Loop Rd., contains photographs, jewelry, textiles and other items relating to the history and culture of the Navajo people. One exhibit describes the arduous 1864 ordeal known as the "Long Walk," in which the Navajo were removed from tribal lands and marched some 300 miles to a Fort Sumner, N.M., prison camp. **Hours:** Mon. 8-5, Tues.-Fri. 8-6, Sat. 9-5. Closed Easter. **Cost:** Donations. **Phone:** (928) 871-7941.

QUALITY INN NAVAJO NATION CAPITAL 928/871-4108

Hotel

Address: 48 W Hwy 264 86515 **Location:** Center. **Facility:** 56 units. 2 stories (no elevator), exterior corridors. **Dining:** Diné Restaurant, see separate listing. **Activities:** exercise room. **Guest Services:** coin laundry. **Featured Amenity:** full hot breakfast.

SAVE BIZ / SOME UNITS

WHERE TO EAT

DINÉ RESTAURANT 928/871-4108

Regional American. Casual Dining. **Address:** 48 W Hwy 264 86515

WINKELMAN (E-5) pop. 353, elev. 1,928'

A mining and agricultural center, Winkelman is near the 8.5-mile Aravaipa Canyon, a wilderness retreat that was once the headquarters of the Apache Indians. The canyon's abundant vegetation, nourished by the year-round flow of Aravaipa Creek, contrasts with the surrounding desert terrain.

Off SR 77, then 13 miles east on a paved and gravel road, the canyon is within the 4,044-acre Aravaipa Canyon Primitive Area. Permits are required to enter the area; contact the Bureau of Land Management's District Office in Safford; phone (928) 348-4400. Visitation to the area is limited; reservations are required.

WINSLOW (C-5) pop. 9,655, elev. 4,856'

Winslow was named after Gen. Edward Francis Winslow, a president of the Atlantic and Pacific Railroad. This railroad center is an important shipping and trading site. A two-story mural and bronze statue at Standin' on the Corner Park in downtown Winslow illustrate the Eagles' song "Take It Easy" and its well-known reference to the town. The Apache-Sitgreaves National Forests *(see place listing p. 29)* lie south of town.

Winslow Chamber of Commerce: 523 W. Second St., Winslow, AZ 86047. **Phone:** (928) 289-2434.

LA POSADA is off I-40 exit 253, then 1 mi. s. to Second St., just e. to 303 E. Second St. (Rte. 66).

Designed by Mary Elizabeth Jane Colter and considered her masterpiece, La Posada attracted such luminaries as Howard Hughes, Albert Einstein and Bob Hope. Constructed in 1929 in the style of an 1869 Spanish hacienda, the building has stone and tile floors, glass murals, original furnishings and gardens. Antiques and art from around the globe decorate this working hotel. **Time:** Allow 1 hour, 30 minutes minimum. **Hours:** Daily 7 a.m.-10 p.m. **Cost:** Free. **Phone:** (928) 289-4366.

GEM **METEOR CRATER,** 22 mi. w. on I-40, then 6 mi. s. off exit 233, was formed nearly 50,000 years ago by a meteorite; the crater is 550 feet deep, 2.4 miles in circumference and nearly 1 mile across.

The meteor, estimated to have been 90 feet across and traveling 26,000 mph, slammed into the rocky plain and left a crater that was originally 700 feet deep and more than 4,000 feet across. Because the terrain of the crater is very similar to the moon, NASA once trained Apollo astronauts here, and an Apollo test capsule is on display.

The Discovery Center provides information and films about the formation of the crater and features interactive exhibits about meteorites and asteroids. Visitors can explore the crater from numerous locations on the rim and an indoor viewing area, and take a journey into space on the STS Barringer in a 4D experience (additional fee).

Guided rim tours of the crater depart daily. **Note:** Inquire about weather policies. **Time:** Allow 2 hours minimum. **Hours:** Daily 7-7, Memorial Day-Labor Day; 8-5, rest of year. Closed Christmas. Phone ahead to confirm schedule. **Cost:** $18; $16 (ages 60+); $9 (ages 6-17 and veterans with ID); $5 (military dependents ages 6-17); free (ages 0-5 and active military with ID). **Phone:** (928) 289-5898 or (800) 289-5898. ***(See ad p. 42.)*** GT

ROCK ART RANCH is off I-40 exit 286, 1.5 mi. s. on SR 77 to McLaws Rd., 10.7 mi. w. to Territorial Rd., 7.5 mi. w. to Rock Art Ranch Rd., then 2.2 mi. s.w. to ranch entrance. The working cattle ranch consists of more than 7,000 acres. The restored bunkhouse of the Hashknife Cattle Company, a large 19th-century ranching operation, is featured. Ancestral Puebloan and Hohokam artifacts and pots, some dating to 7,500 years old, are displayed in a barn-like building. Visitors may drive 2 miles with a guide to Chevelon Canyon and examine more than 3,000 petroglyphs, many more than 6,000 years old, on canyon walls.

Note: A descent into a 50-foot-deep canyon is required to view the petroglyphs; appropriate attire and footwear are strongly recommended. The climb and descent are not recommended for the physically impaired, elderly guests and small children. **Time:** Allow 2 hours, 30 minutes minimum. **Hours:** Mon.-Sat. by appointment. Closed major holidays. **Cost:** $35; free (ages 0-12). Prices may vary depending on the number of people on a tour. Reservations for all activities are recommended 2 to 3 days in advance. Reservations are required. **Phone:** (928) 386-5047.

BEST WESTERN PLUS WINSLOW INN 928/289-2960

Hotel

AAA Benefit: Members save up to 15% and earn bonus points!

Address: 816 Transcon Ln 86047 **Location:** I-40 exit 255, just n. **Facility:** 54 units. 2 stories, interior corridors. **Pool:** heated indoor. **Activities:** exercise room. **Guest Services:** coin laundry. **Featured Amenity: breakfast buffet.**

SAVE CALL BIZ

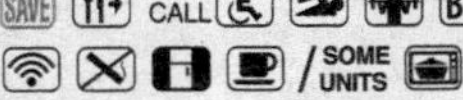

LA POSADA HOTEL 928/289-4366

Historic Hotel. **Address:** 303 E 2nd St 86047

WHERE TO EAT

MOJO COFFEEHOUSE & CAFE 928/289-6656

Coffee/Tea. Quick Serve. **Address:** 1700 N Park Dr 86047

THE TURQUOISE ROOM 928/289-2888

Southwestern. Fine Dining. **Address:** 303 E 2nd St 86047

GEM WUPATKI NATIONAL MONUMENT (B-4)

Lying about 33 mi. n. of Flagstaff and reached via US 89, 35,253-acre Wupatki National Monument contains more than 2,600 archeological sites, including some 1,000 structures. Thanks to increased rainfall and the water-retaining layer of ash and cinders covering the ground after the late 11th-century eruption of Sunset Crater Volcano (south of the monument), farming became productive enough that at one time the region may have been one of the more densely populated sections of northern Arizona. The original inhabitants of Wupatki are believed to have been ancestors of the Hopi Indians.

The largest and one of the most impressive sites is Wupatki, or "Long-cut House," containing more than 100 rooms. Nearby are a ceremonial amphitheater, ball court and "blow hole." Other important ruins are the Citadel, Nalakihu, Lomaki and the three-story Wukoki, all reachable by short, self-guiding trails. Most of the ruins were inhabited from about 1100-1225. Picnicking is available. Visitors must stay on the trails; the backcountry is closed to unguided travel in order to protect the cultural resources.

Allow 1 hour minimum. Visitor center open daily 9-5; closed Christmas. Ruins and trails open daily dawn-dusk. Admission $25 (per private vehicle); $20 (per motorcycle); $15 (per person arriving by foot or bicycle); free ages 0-15. Admission includes Sunset Crater Volcano National Monument *(see place listing p. 175)*. Phone (928) 679-2365.

YOUNGTOWN pop. 6,156

• Hotels & Restaurants map & index p. 117
• Part of Phoenix area — see map p. 91

QUALITY INN & SUITES PHOENIX NW-SUN CITY
623/933-8211 36

Hotel

Address: 11201 Grand Ave 85363 **Location:** On US 60, just se of 113th Ave. **Facility:** 96 units, some efficiencies. 2 stories (no elevator), interior/exterior corridors. **Terms:** check-in 4 pm. **Pool:** heated outdoor. **Activities:** picnic facilities. **Guest Services:** coin laundry. **Featured Amenity: full hot breakfast.**

YUMA (E-1) pop. 93,064, elev. 200'

• Hotels p. 230 • Restaurants p. 230

Tucked into Arizona's southwestern corner, Yuma is on the Arizona-California state line not far from the Mexican border. The town occupies a historically important spot on the Colorado River where it narrows between two granite outcroppings, creating the easiest crossing for many miles.

Although he was not the first white man to visit the area, Father Eusebio Francisco Kino was the first to recognize the Yuma Crossing as the gateway to California. Yet Kino's discovery would not be used for almost a century until Juan Bautista de Anza, presidial captain of Tubac, arrived in search of an overland route to California through Yuma in 1774. The Anza expedition reached Mission San Gabriel, near present-day Los Angeles, in March of that year.

In 1779 two missions were founded at the crossing by Father Francisco Garcés, who, along with all the colonists, was later killed during the last major uprising of the Quechan Indians in 1781. The Spanish retreated and never again tried to dominate the Quechan or control the Yuma Crossing.

After Mexico won its independence from Spain in 1821, the area became part of the new nation's northern territories, but the Mexican government's control over these territories was compromised by economic decline and internal conflict. At the same time, mountain men—American trappers and explorers who acted as guides for settlers heading west—began blazing new trails into the region.

During the Mexican-American War (1846-48), the U.S. Army organized a unit of Mormon volunteers that set out on a difficult march covering nearly 2,000 miles between Council Bluffs, Iowa, and San Diego. In doing so, they blazed a wagon trail that crossed the Colorado River at Yuma. A bronze statue in Yuma's West Wetlands Park, 2200 W. Water St., commemorates the Mormon Battalion's historic trek across the Southwest.

Gold seekers by the thousands poured through Yuma during the California gold rush of 1849, using a rope ferry at present-day Main Street to cross the Colorado River. It wouldn't be until 1873, however, that the city was formally named Yuma, having previously been called Colorado City and later Arizona City.

Pivot Point Interpretative Plaza, 200 N. Madison Ave., preserves the last remnants of the pivoting railroad bridge that once allowed trains to cross the river but also could swing wide to let steamboats pass. The plaza includes a landscaped park with interpretive panels; a 1907 Baldwin steam locomotive; an audio installation re-creating sounds of a train, a steamboat and the bridge swinging aside; and at night, a light display with twin laser beams tracing the old bridge's route across the river. A pedestrian pathway links the plaza to Gateway Park.

The Yuma Art Center & Historic Yuma Theatre, 245 S. Main St., is a downtown cultural center and performing arts venue featuring four visual art galleries and a 650-seat theater. Built in 1911 for vaudeville shows and movies, the theater today hosts a range of events including community theater performances, jazz festivals, film screenings and art lectures. Phone (928) 373-5202.

Yuma is host to a number of outdoor events. The city becomes flooded with dove hunters when hunting season opens September 1 and the population nearly doubles during the winter months as snowbirds arrive to enjoy the sunshine. Golf is a popular pastime with 13 lush golf courses from which to choose. The visitors bureau offers field-to-feast agriculture tours of the area's number one industry, while the Yuma Lettuce Days Festival takes place in late March or early April.

Yuma Visitors Bureau: 201 N. 4th Ave., Yuma, AZ 85364. **Phone:** (928) 783-0071 or (800) 293-0071.

Shopping: Yuma Palms Regional Center, at 16th St. and I-8, is anchored by Dillard's and JCPenney.

IMPERIAL NATIONAL WILDLIFE REFUGE encompasses 25,768 acres along the lower Colorado River. The Arizona section of the refuge is 40 mi. n. off US 95 via Martinez Lake Rd., following signs. The remainder of the refuge can be reached best by boat or four-wheel-drive vehicle. Canada geese, ducks, egrets and eagles gather at the refuge. Hiking, hunting, fishing and boating are permitted in designated areas. Maps and public-use regulations are available upon request.

Hours: Daily dawn-dusk. Visitor center open Mon.-Fri. 8-4:30, Sat.-Sun. 9-4, Nov. 15-Mar. 31; Mon.-Fri. 7:30-4, rest of year. Closed Thanksgiving and Christmas. Phone ahead to confirm schedule. **Cost:** Free. **Phone:** (928) 783-3371.

YUMA QUARTERMASTER DEPOT STATE HISTORIC PARK, I-8 4th Ave. exit to 201 N. 4th Ave., is on a 10-acre site on the s. side of the Colorado River. The park salutes 5 centuries of transportation across the Colorado River. From 1864 through 1883 the U.S. Army Quartermaster Depot stored and distributed supplies for military posts throughout the Southwest. Five restored buildings stand on the site that once comprised the depot. The depot office was built in 1872. **Hours:** Tues.-Sun. 9-4:30 (also Mon. 9-4:30, Oct.-May). Closed Thanksgiving and Christmas. **Cost:** $4; $2 (ages 7-13 and active military with ID). **Phone:** (928) 783-0071.

BAYMONT INN & SUITES YUMA 928/539-9000

Hotel. **Address:** 1731 S Sunridge Dr 85365

BEST WESTERN INNSUITES YUMA MALL HOTEL & SUITES 928/783-8341

Hotel

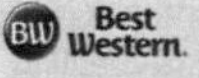

AAA Benefit: Members save up to 15% and earn bonus points!

Address: 1450 Castle Dome Ave 85365 **Location:** I-8 exit 2 (16th St/US 95), just e to Yuma Palms Pkwy, just n, then just w. **Facility:** 166 units, some efficiencies. 2-3 stories (no elevator), exterior corridors. **Pool:** heated outdoor. **Activities:** hot tub, picnic facilities, exercise room. **Guest Services:** valet and coin laundry, area transportation. **Featured Amenity:** breakfast buffet.

SOME UNITS

CANDLEWOOD SUITES 928/726-2800

Extended Stay Hotel. **Address:** 2036 S Ave 3 E 85365

DAYS INN YUMA 928/329-7790

Motel

Address: 1671 E 16th St 85365 **Location:** I-8 exit 2 (16th St/US 95), just e. **Facility:** 64 units. 2 stories (no elevator), exterior corridors. **Pool:** outdoor. **Activities:** hot tub. **Guest Services:** coin laundry. **Featured Amenity: breakfast buffet.**

CALL SOME UNITS

FAIRFIELD INN & SUITES BY MARRIOTT 928/345-1800

Hotel. **Address:** 1801 S Sunridge Dr 85365

AAA Benefit: Members save 5% or more!

HAMPTON INN & SUITES BY HILTON YUMA 928/329-5600

Hotel

AAA Benefit: Members save up to 15%!

Address: 1600 E 16th St 85365 **Location:** I-8 exit 2 (16th St/US 95), just e, then just n. Adjacent to Yuma Palms Shopping Center. **Facility:** 90 units. 4 stories, interior corridors. *Bath:* shower only. **Pool:** heated outdoor. **Activities:** hot tub, exercise room. **Guest Services:** valet and coin laundry. **Featured Amenity: breakfast buffet.**

CALL

HILTON GARDEN INN YUMA/PIVOT POINT 928/783-1500

Hotel. **Address:** 310 N Madison Ave 85364

AAA Benefit: Members save up to 15%!

HISTORIC CORONADO MOTOR HOTEL 928/783-4453

Classic Hotel. **Address:** 233 4th Ave 85364

HOLIDAY INN 928/782-9300

Hotel. **Address:** 1901 E 18th St 85365

HOLIDAY INN EXPRESS & SUITES 928/317-1400

Hotel. **Address:** 2044 S Ave 3 E 85365

HOMEWOOD SUITES BY HILTON YUMA 928/782-4100

Extended Stay Hotel. **Address:** 1955 E 16th St 85365

AAA Benefit: Members save up to 15%!

LA FUENTE INN & SUITES 928/329-1814

Hotel

Address: 1513 E 16th St 85365 **Location:** I-8 exit 2 (16th St/US 95), just e. **Facility:** 96 units. 2 stories (no elevator), exterior corridors. **Pool:** heated outdoor. **Activities:** hot tub, picnic facilities, exercise room. **Guest Services:** coin laundry. **Featured Amenity: breakfast buffet.**

SOME UNITS

RADISSON HOTEL YUMA 928/783-8000

Hotel. **Address:** 1501 S Redondo Center Dr 85365

SPRINGHILL SUITES BY MARRIOTT 928/783-7853

Hotel. **Address:** 1825 E 18th St 85365

AAA Benefit: Members save 5% or more!

TOWNEPLACE SUITES BY MARRIOTT 928/783-6900

Extended Stay Hotel. **Address:** 1726 S Sunridge Dr 85365

AAA Benefit: Members save 5% or more!

WINGATE BY WYNDHAM YUMA 928/783-1400

Hotel

Address: 1760 S Sunridge Dr 85365 **Location:** I-8 exit 2 (16th St/US 95), just e to Sunridge Dr, then just s. **Facility:** 76 units. 3 stories, interior corridors. **Amenities:** safes. **Pool:** outdoor. **Activities:** hot tub, game room, picnic facilities, exercise room. **Guest Services:** coin laundry. **Featured Amenity: breakfast buffet.**

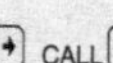

CALL

WHERE TO EAT

AH-SO SUSHI & STEAK RESTAURANT 928/329-7442

Japanese. Casual Dining. **Address:** 1325 S Yuma Palms Pkwy, Suite B5 85365

BURGERS & BEER 928/783-3987

American. Casual Dining. **Address:** 321 W 20th St 85364

DA BOYZ ITALIAN CUISINE 928/783-8383

Italian. Casual Dining. **Address:** 284 S Main St 85364

THE GARDEN CAFE 928/783-1491

American. Casual Dining. **Address:** 250 Madison Ave 85364

HUNTER STEAKHOUSE 928/783-1166

Steak. Casual Dining. **Address:** 2355 S 4th Ave 85364

JULIEANNA'S PATIO CAFE 928/317-1961
American. Casual Dining. **Address:** 1951 W 25th St 85364

KNEADERS BAKERY & CAFE 928/783-4099
Deli. Quick Serve. **Address:** 1651 E Castle Dome Ave 85364

LA FONDA TORTILLA FACTORY 928/783-6902
Mexican. Casual Dining. **Address:** 1095 S 3rd Ave 85364

LUTES CASINO 928/782-2192
American. Casual Dining. **Address:** 221 S Main St 85364

MARKET GRILL STEAK & SEAFOOD 928/783-8000
American. Casual Dining. **Address:** 1501 S Redondo Center Dr 85365

MOSTLY MUFFINS BAKERY & CAFE 928/783-7484
Breads/Pastries Sandwiches. Quick Serve. **Address:** 2451 W 16th St 85364

NINJA SUSHI 928/782-4000
Sushi. Casual Dining. **Address:** 1400 E 16th St 85365

PRISON HILL BREWING COMPANY 928/276-4001
American. Casual Dining. **Address:** 278 S Main St 85364

RIVER CITY GRILL 928/782-7988
Seafood. Casual Dining. **Address:** 600 W 3rd St 85364

YUMA LANDING BAR & GRILL 928/782-7427
American. Casual Dining. **Address:** 195 S 4th Ave 85364

Bandelier National Monument

New Mexico

Welcome to New Mexico, deemed the home of the world's finest chile peppers, where you can fire up your taste buds with 10-plus varieties—most in the "extra hot" category.

Ristras, colorful strings of sun-dried chile peppers, drape café entryways and residential doorways. They're said to ward off evil, welcome visitors and alert guests to the fiery delicacies served there.

But chile isn't the only thing that heats things up. The radiant symbol that has come to represent New Mexico (found on its license plate and flag) is the Zia Pueblo sign for sun. Four rays extend from the center, signifying directions, seasons, periods of the day and stages of life.

Hundreds of rainbow-colored gentle giants fill the sunny sky with hot air during balloon festivals held statewide. The selection is anything but ordinary at the Albuquerque International Balloon Fiesta: It's common to see such diverse shapes as a castle, parrot, cola can and corncob. And if you can't make it in time for a festival, local companies offer the chance to take to the skies year-round on a hot-air balloon ride.

Ristras

From the basket of a balloon you can glimpse centuries-old, flat-roofed houses and cliff dwellings constructed of adobe—sun-dried bricks of earth, sand, charcoal and grass. This mixture served as the primary building material for pueblos, communal settlements established by the Spanish in the 16th century.

Working pueblos remain at Taos and elsewhere in north-central New Mexico. Each retains an independent government, social order and religious practice. Artisans produce traditional art individual to their own pueblo: Turquoise jewelry, storyteller dolls, pottery, drums, carvings, Navajo rugs and weavings are coveted by visitors and collectors alike.

Some pueblos welcome guests to experience their heritage at annual festivals held in honor of the pueblo's patron saint. Corn, deer or buffalo dances are executed according to strict standards, culminating in a flamboyant display of colorful costumes.

While native traditions at the pueblos continue, only stark stone and adobe walls remain at the uninhabited Chaco Culture National Historical Park, and at Aztec Ruins and Bandelier national monuments. Explore what were once thriving Ancestral Puebloan communities; multistory cliff dwellings with remnants of hundreds of rooms, kivas (ceremonial meeting halls) and petroglyphs offer a warm welcome into the state's rich history.

Sizzling Secrets

Southeastern New Mexico was a hotbed of controversy when, in 1947, a farmer discovered exotic metal debris on a sheep ranch. Some say it was the wreckage of a flying saucer, while others believe it to be the result of tests performed by the U.S. Air Force.

The mysteries surrounding what was dubbed the "Roswell Incident" make the International UFO Museum & Research Center in Roswell all the more intriguing. Don't miss the annual Roswell UFO Festival—held in the summer—where aliens are the hot ticket.

Or you can learn more about another top-secret scientific development—the Manhattan Project. Los Alamos was chosen as the hot spot for a weapons laboratory that developed and tested the atomic bomb during World War II. Visit the Bradbury Science Museum and peruse artifacts from the project.

If you can't stand the heat, pack a jacket and head for the cool solace of Carlsbad Caverns. At 830 feet below ground, the three-level Big Room begs exploration. Arguably one of the world's biggest underground chambers, it encompasses 8 acres—and at 56 F, it's definitely cool.

Recreation

From snow-clad mountains and sandy desert lowlands to rusty looking canyons and verdant timbered forests, the New Mexico landscape is a tapestry of colors and shapes that can be enjoyed in any season.

North-central New Mexico is *the* place for snow skiing. Sandia Peak Ski Area, just east of Albuquerque in the Cibola National Forest, packs a variety of trails, bowls and catwalks into a wedge of mountain.

Ski Santa Fe, north of Santa Fe, attracts families and first-timers to its groomed slopes for downhill skiing. With runs for beginning, intermediate and advanced skiers as well as freestyle areas for both snowboarding and skiing, Angel Fire Resort, east of Taos, is another family favorite.

Alpine skiing is the winter sport of choice at Taos Ski Valley, where snowfall averages more than 300 inches per year—the most in the state—and the vertical drop exceeds 2,600 feet.

Enchanted Forest, east of Red River; Sugarite Canyon State Park, on the Colorado border near Raton; and Manzano Mountains State Park, southeast of Albuquerque, welcome cross-country skiers.

When the snow melts, shift gears and explore the state by bicycle. Trails in southern New Mexico are as varied as the terrain. Fresnal Canyon Loop traverses the Sacramento Mountains foothills, just northeast of Alamogordo, passing through villages and orchards. Race the jackrabbits on a 4.5-mile loop around Tortugas Mountain, 1 mile southeast of Las Cruces. This desert area's riding surface comes in three textures: rocky, sandy and smooth.

Bicycling on paved surfaces can be a family event at Chaco Culture National Historical Park, in the northwest. An easy 9-mile circle tour begins at the visitor center and offers stops at several archeological ruins. The king of the road-rides may well be a 70-mile round-trip excursion via state and forest roads from Carlsbad to Sitting Bull Falls, in Lincoln National Forest.

With some 1,500 miles of trails, Gila National Forest, in the southwest, invites camping, hiking and backpacking. State parks, too, cater to this trinity of outdoor activities. Strike camp beside Elephant Butte Lake in that state park; walk among the aspens in Hyde Memorial; or press deep into primitive Morphy Lake State Park's backwoods.

The spring thaw creates a flood of whitewater rafting opportunities in northern New Mexico, especially on the Rio Grande and Rio Chama.

Sandia Peak Aerial Tramway, Albequerque

Historic Timeline

- **1598** Conquistador Juan de Oñate takes possession of New Mexico for Spain.
- **1680** The victorious Pueblo Rebellion expels Spanish rule.
- **1850** New Mexico becomes a U.S. territory.
- **1862** Key Civil War battles are waged at Glorieta Pass and Valverde.
- **1864** Col. Kit Carson forces more than 8,000 Navajos to make the 300-mile Long Walk to Bosque Redondo.
- **1912** New Mexico is admitted to the Union as the 47th state.
- **1916** The United States invades Mexico after Pancho Villa attacks Columbus.
- **1945** The United States tests the first atomic bomb at Trinity Site.

- **1947** Reports of a crashed UFO spark media interest in Roswell.
- **1986** The United States' deepest limestone cave is discovered in Carlsbad Caverns National Park.
- **2010** Santa Fe celebrates its 400th anniversary.

What To Pack

Temperature Averages Maximum/Minimum	JANUARY	FEBRUARY	MARCH	APRIL	MAY	JUNE	JULY	AUGUST	SEPTEMBER	OCTOBER	NOVEMBER	DECEMBER
Albuquerque	47/26	53/30	61/36	69/43	79/53	88/62	90/67	87/65	81/58	69/46	56/34	46/27
Carlsbad	58/28	63/32	70/38	79/46	87/56	95/64	95/68	93/67	87/59	78/48	67/36	58/28
Clayton	49/22	51/24	59/30	67/38	76/47	85/56	89/61	86/60	79/52	69/41	57/30	48/22
Las Cruces	59/29	64/33	70/38	78/45	87/54	95/62	95/68	92/67	88/60	79/47	67/36	58/29
Roswell	55/26	61/31	68/37	77/45	85/55	93/63	94/67	92/66	86/59	76/47	64/34	55/26
Santa Fe	44/18	48/22	56/26	65/32	74/41	84/49	86/55	83/53	78/47	67/36	53/25	43/18

From the records of The Weather Channel Interactive, Inc.

Good Facts To Know

ABOUT THE STATE

POPULATION: 2,059,179.

AREA: 121,590 square miles; ranks 5th.

CAPITAL: Santa Fe.

HIGHEST POINT: 13,161 ft., Wheeler Peak.

LOWEST POINT: 2,842 ft., Red Bluff Reservoir.

TIME ZONE(S): Mountain. DST.

GAMBLING

MINIMUM AGE FOR GAMBLING: 21.

REGULATIONS

TEEN DRIVING LAWS: No more than one passenger under the age of 21 is permitted (family members exempt). Driving is not permitted midnight-5 a.m. The minimum age for an unrestricted driver's license is 16 years, 6 months. Phone (888) 683-4636 for more information about New Mexico's driver's license regulations.

SEAT BELT/CHILD RESTRAINT LAWS: Seat belts required for driver and all passengers 18 and older. Children ages 7 through 17 must use child restraints or seat belts. Appropriate child restraints are required for children under age 7 or under 60 pounds. AAA recommends the use of seat belts and appropriate child restraints for the driver and all passengers.

CELLPHONE RESTRICTIONS: All drivers are prohibited from text messaging while driving. Instruction and provisional license holders may not use any wireless device while driving. In some cities, including Santa Fe and Las Cruces, drivers are also prohibited from using hand-held cellphones.

HELMETS FOR MOTORCYCLISTS: Required for riders under 18.

RADAR DETECTORS: Permitted for passenger vehicles; prohibited for commercial vehicles.

MOVE OVER LAW: Driver is required to slow down and vacate the lane nearest stopped police, fire and recovery or repair vehicles, including tow trucks, using audible or flashing signals.

FIREARMS LAWS: Vary by state or county. Contact New Mexico Department of Public Safety, 6301 Indian School Rd. N.E., Suite 310, Albuquerque, NM 87110; phone (505) 841-8053.

HOLIDAYS

HOLIDAYS: Jan. 1 ▪ Martin Luther King Jr. Day, Jan. (3rd Mon.) ▪ Memorial Day, May (last Mon.) ▪ July 4 ▪ Labor Day, Sept. (1st Mon.) ▪ Columbus Day, Oct. (2nd Mon.) ▪ Veterans Day, Nov. 11 ▪ Thanksgiving, Nov. (4th Thurs.) ▪ Presidents Day (observed day after Thanksgiving) ▪ Christmas, Dec. 25.

MONEY

TAXES: New Mexico has a 5.13 percent gross receipts tax, with a local option for additional increments of up to 3.7 percent.

VISITOR INFORMATION

INFORMATION CENTERS: State welcome centers that provide maps, weather information, brochures and information about attractions, accommodations, historic sites, parks and events are at I-10W near Anthony ▪ US 64/84 at Chama ▪ I-40 exit 22 at Gallup ▪ I-40W near Glenrio ▪ I-10E exit 20 at Lordsburg ▪ I-25 exit 451 near Raton ▪ I-25 mile marker 269, 17 miles south of Santa Fe, near the Santo Domingo Indian Reservation ▪ at 491 Old Santa Fe Tr. in downtown Santa Fe ▪ and at US 60/70/84 near Texico.

ROAD CONDITIONS: The State Department of Transportation provides current information about road closures and conditions; phone (800) 432-4269.

SPECIAL NOTE: Plague bacilli, a condition promoted by fleas, is endemic to New Mexico. Pet owners are advised to provide flea protection for their animals.

FURTHER INFORMATION FOR VISITORS:
New Mexico Department of Tourism
Lamy Building
491 Old Santa Fe Tr.
Santa Fe, NM 87501-2753
(505) 827-7336

NATIONAL FOREST INFORMATION:
Southwestern Region
333 Broadway Blvd. S.E.
Albuquerque, NM 87102
(505) 842-3293
(877) 444-6777
TTY (505) 842-3198 (reservations)

FISHING AND HUNTING REGULATIONS:
Department of Game and Fish
1 Wildlife Way
Santa Fe, NM 87507
(505) 476-8000
(888) 248-6866 (license and permits)

RECREATION INFORMATION:
State Parks Division
1220 S. St. Francis Dr.
Santa Fe, NM 87505
(505) 476-3200
(505) 476-3325 (state forestry)
(888) 667-2757 (state parks)

New Mexico Annual Events

Please call ahead to confirm event details.

Visit AAA.com/travelguides/events to find AAA-listed events for every day of the year

WINTER

Dec. - WinterFest / Los Alamos / 505-661-4844
- New Mexico Bowl / Albuquerque 505-925-5626
- Old-Fashioned Christmas / Truth Or Consequences / 575-740-3902

Jan. - New Year's Day Celebration / Taos 505-758-1028
- Souper Bowl / Albuquerque 505-349-2052
- Chama Chile Ski Classic and Winter Fiesta / Chama / 575-756-2294

Feb. - For the Love of Art Month / Las Cruces / 575-523-6403
- Mount Taylor Winter Quadrathlon Grants / 505-285-3542
- Community Arts Party / Socorro 575-835-5688

SPRING

Mar. - Rockhound Roundup / Deming 575-544-9019
- National Fiery Foods and Barbecue Show / Albuquerque / 505-873-8680
- Rio Grande Arts and Crafts Festival Albuquerque / 505-292-7457

Apr. - American Indian Week / Albuquerque 505-843-7270
- Gathering of Nations Powwow Albuquerque / 505-836-2810
- Park 'N the Park / Rio Rancho / 505-891-5015

May - Cathedral Park Arts and Crafts Fair Santa Fe / 505-473-5590
- Truth or Consequences Fiesta / Truth Or Consequences / 505-740-7542
- Blessing of the Fields / Las Cruces / 505-522-4100

SUMMER

June - Art & Wine Festival / Red River / 575-754-2366, ext. 1
- Rodeo de Santa Fe / Santa Fe / 505-471-4300

July - Fiestas de Taos / Taos 800-732-8267
- Freedom Days / Farmington 505-326-7602
- Santa Fe International Folk Art Market / Santa Fe / 505-467-1197

Aug. - Hot Chili Days, Cool Mountain Nights Red River / 254-968-8505
- The Great Southwestern Antique & Vintage Show / Albuquerque 505-255-4054
- Inter-Tribal Indian Ceremonial Gallup / 505-863-3896

FALL

Sept. - New Mexico State Fair / Albuquerque 505-222-9700
- Santa Fe Wine and Chile Fiesta Santa Fe / 505-438-8060
- Northern New Mexico Fine Arts and Crafts Guild Cathedral Park Show Santa Fe / 505-473-5590

Oct. - Lincoln County Cowboy Symposium Ruidoso Downs / 575-378-4431
- Harvest Festival / Santa Fe / 505-471-2261
- International Balloon Fiesta Albuquerque / 505-821-1000

Nov. - Renaissance ArtsFaire / Las Cruces / 575-523-6403
- Christmas on the Pecos / Carlsbad 575-887-6516
- River of Lights / Albuquerque 505-768-2000

San Miguel Chapel, Santa Fe

International Balloon Fiesta, Albuquerque

Anderson Museum of Contemporary Art, Roswell

Snowshoeing

Railyard District, Santa Fe

Index: Great Experience for Members

AAA editor's picks of exceptional note

Carlsbad Caverns National Park

Chimney Rock

New Mexico History Museum

Aztec Ruins National Monument

See Orientation map on p. 246 for corresponding grid coordinates, if applicable.

* Indicates the GEM is temporarily closed.

New Mexico
Atlas Section

Use these detailed driving maps to plan your stops and find your way. For complete route planning, purchase the latest AAA Road Atlas at participating AAA/CAA offices, and use the free online TripTik Travel Planner at AAA.com/maps

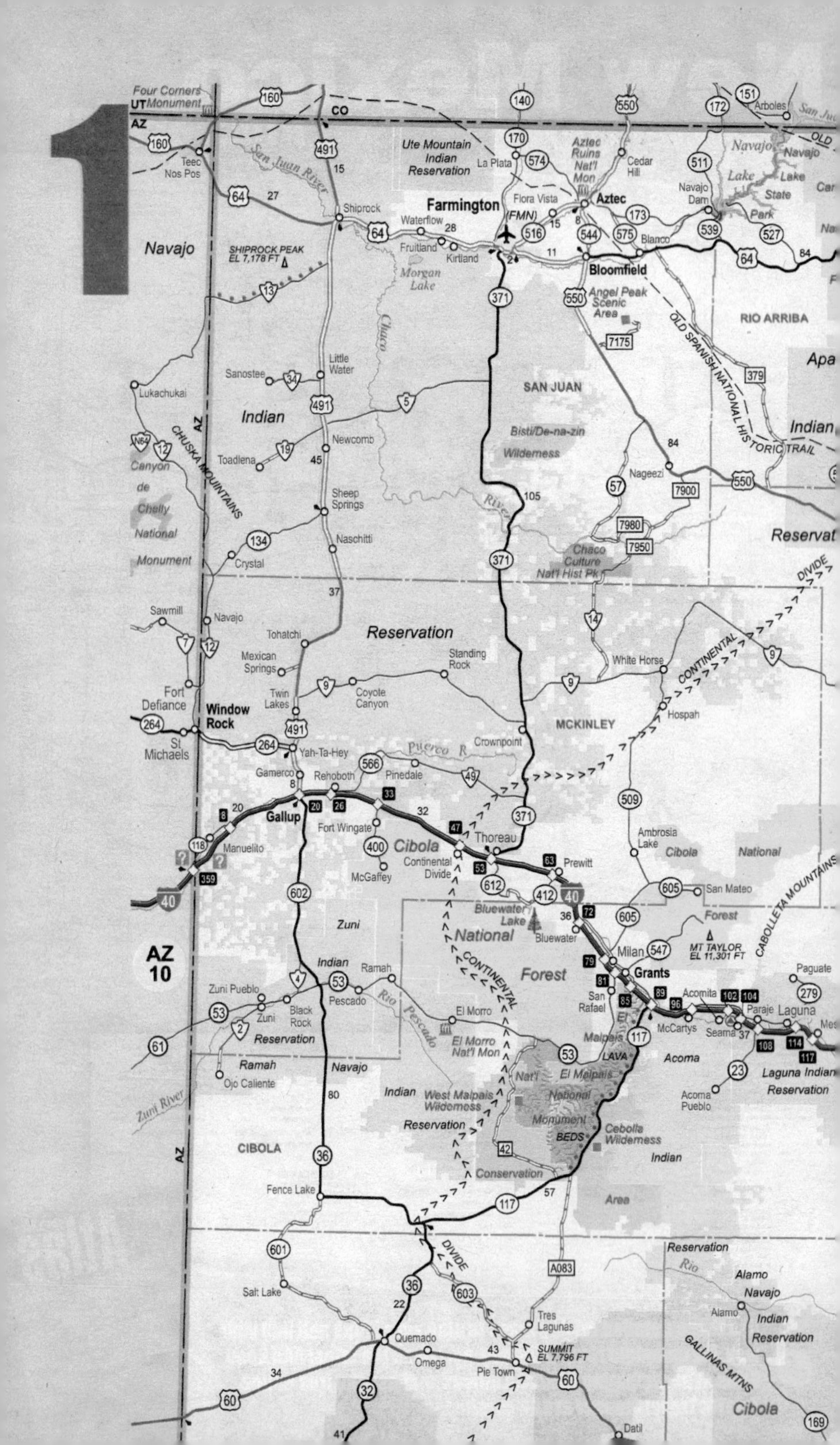
1
Four Corners Monument
UT
CO
AZ
Teec Nos Pos
San Juan River
Shiprock
Ute Mountain Indian Reservation
La Plata
Aztec Ruins Nat'l Mon
Cedar Hill
Aztec
Farmington
(FMN)
Flora Vista
Waterflow
Fruitland
Kirtland
Bloomfield
Blanco
Navajo Dam
Navajo Lake State Park
Arboles
Navajo
Morgan Lake
SHIPROCK PEAK EL 7,178 FT
Angel Peak Scenic Area
RIO ARRIBA
OLD SPANISH NATIONAL HISTORIC TRAIL
Chaco
Little Water
Sanostee
Lukachukai
Indian
SAN JUAN
Bisti/De-na-zin Wilderness
CHUSKA MOUNTAINS
Canyon de Chelly National Monument
Toadlena
Newcomb
Sheep Springs
Naschitti
Crystal
Nageezi
Chaco Culture Nat'l Hist Pk
Reservation
Sawmill
Navajo
Tohatchi
Mexican Springs
Standing Rock
White Horse
CONTINENTAL DIVIDE
Fort Defiance
Window Rock
Twin Lakes
Coyote Canyon
Hospah
MCKINLEY
St Michaels
Yah-Ta-Hey
Crownpoint
Puerco R
Gamerco
Rehoboth
Pinedale
Gallup
Manuelito
Fort Wingate
Cibola
Thoreau
Continental Divide
McGaffey
Prewitt
Ambrosia Lake
Cibola National Forest
San Mateo
CABOLLETA MOUNTAINS
Bluewater Lake
Bluewater
Zuni
National Forest
Milan
MT TAYLOR EL 11,301 FT
Grants
San Rafael
AZ 10
Indian
Ramah
Zuni Pueblo
Zuni
Black Rock
Pescado
Rio Pescado
El Morro
El Morro Nat'l Mon
Acomita
McCartys
Seama
Paraje
Laguna
Paguate
Reservation
El Malpais
LAVA
Acoma
Laguna Indian Reservation
Ramah
Navajo
Ojo Caliente
Zuni River
Indian
West Malpais Wilderness
Nat'l El Malpais National Monument
Acoma Pueblo
BEDS
Cebolla Wilderness
Reservation
CIBOLA
Indian
Conservation
Area
Fence Lake
Reservation
Rio
Alamo
Navajo
Alamo
Indian Reservation
Salt Lake
DIVIDE
Tres Lagunas
Quemado
Omega
SUMMIT EL 7,796 FT
Pie Town
GALLINAS MTNS
Cibola
Datil
160
140
550
172
151
170
574
491
511
64
516
544
575
173
539
527
13
371
550
7175
379
34
5
12
19
57
7900
134
7980
7950
14
7
9
264
566
49
8
20
26
33
32
47
118
359
40
400
53
612
412
63
72
605
602
547
79
81
89
96
102
104
279
4
85
117
108
114
61
2
23
36
42
601
603
A083
60
32
22
43
34
41
169
105
84
45
37
80
57
27
15
28
11

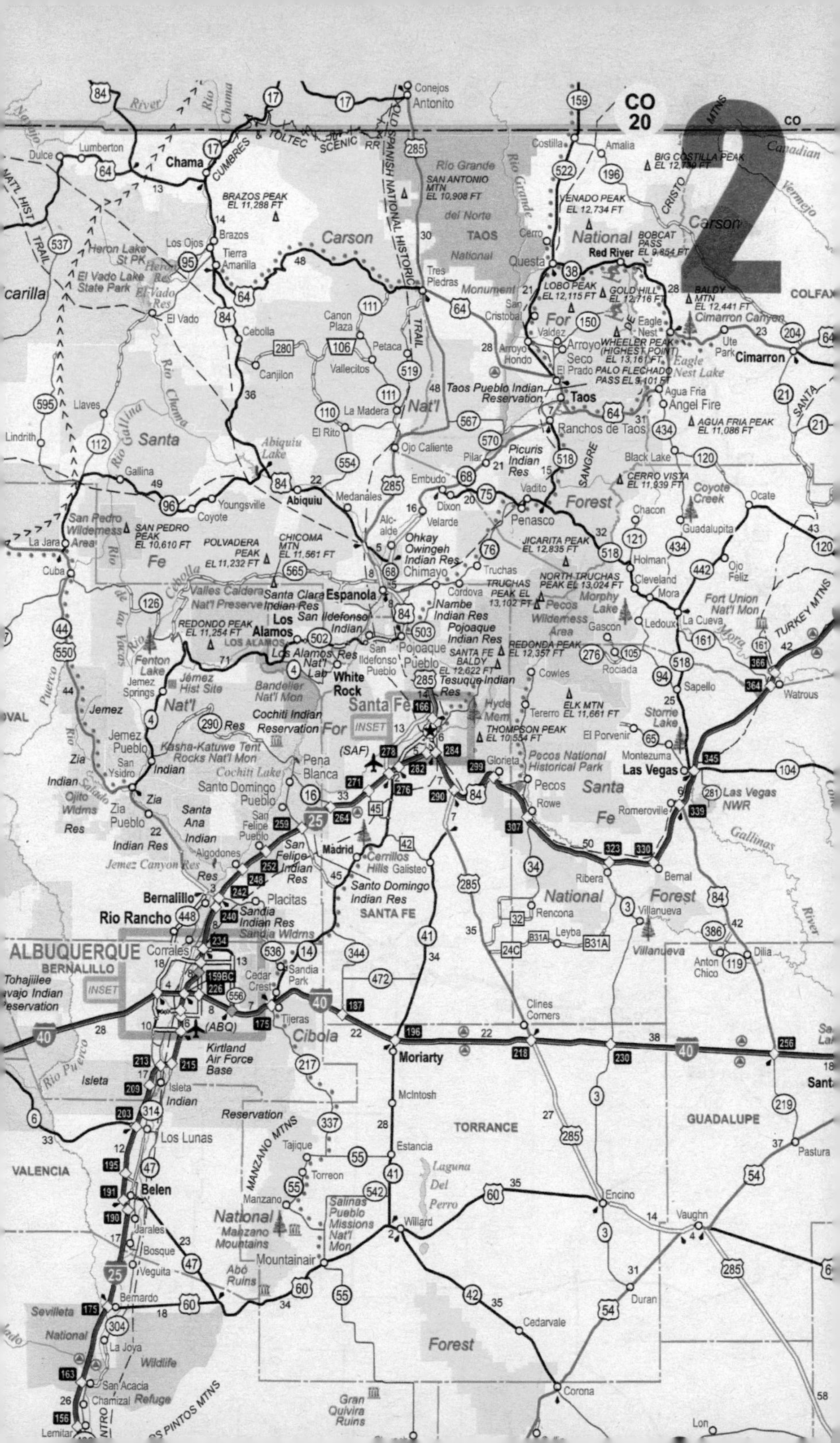

CO
20
2
CO
Conejos
Antonito
OLD SPANISH NATIONAL HISTORIC TRAIL
CUMBRES & TOLTEC SCENIC RR
Chama
Dulce
Lumberton
Rio Grande del Norte
SAN ANTONIO MTN EL 10,908 FT
BRAZOS PEAK EL 11,288 FT
Costilla
Amalia
BIG COSTILLA PEAK EL 12,739 FT
VENADO PEAK EL 12,734 FT
Canadian
Vermejo
Carson
Los Ojos
Brazos
Tierra Amarilla
Heron Lake St PK
El Vado Lake State Park
Heron Res
El Vado Res
El Vado
Carson
TAOS
National Monument
Cerro
Questa
National
Red River
BOBCAT PASS EL 9,854 FT
Tres Piedras
LOBO PEAK EL 12,115 FT
GOLD HILL EL 12,716 FT
BALDY MTN EL 12,441 FT
COLFAX
San Cristobal
Canon Plaza
Cebolla
Petaca
Vallecitos
Canjilon
Valdez
Arroyo Hondo
Arroyo Seco
El Prado
Taos
Eagle Nest
WHEELER PEAK (HIGHEST POINT) EL 13,161 FT
PALO FLECHADO PASS EL 9,101 FT
Eagle Nest Lake
Cimarron Canyon
Ute Park
Cimarron
Taos Pueblo Indian Reservation
Agua Fria
Angel Fire
Llaves
La Madera
Nat'l
El Rito
Ranchos de Taos
AGUA FRIA PEAK EL 11,086 FT
Lindrith
Santa
Abiquiu Lake
Ojo Caliente
Picuris Indian Res
Pilar
SANGRE
Black Lake
Gallina
Embudo
Dixon
Vadito
CERRO VISTA EL 11,939 FT
Coyote Creek
Ocate
Abiquiu
Medanales
Velarde
Forest
Youngsville
Coyote
Penasco
Chacon
Guadalupita
San Pedro Wilderness Area
SAN PEDRO PEAK EL 10,610 FT
Alcalde
Ohkay Owingeh Indian Res
CHICOMA MTN EL 11,561 FT
POLVADERA PEAK EL 11,232 FT
JICARITA PEAK EL 12,835 FT
Holman
La Jara
Cuba
Fe
Chimayo
Truchas
Cleveland
Ojo Feliz
Mora
NORTH TRUCHAS PEAK EL 13,024 FT
TRUCHAS PEAK EL 13,102 FT
Valles Caldera Nat'l Preserve
Santa Clara Indian Res
Espanola
Cordova
Fort Union Nat'l Mon
TURKEY MTNS
San Ildefonso Indian
Nambe Indian Res
Pecos Wilderness Area
Morphy Lake
La Cueva
Los Alamos
Pojoaque Indian Res
Gascon
Ledoux
REDONDO PEAK EL 11,254 FT
LOS ALAMOS
Los Alamos Nat'l Lab
San Ildefonso Pueblo
Pojoaque Pueblo
SANTA FE BALDY EL 12,622 FT
REDONDA PEAK EL 12,357 FT
Rociada
Fenton Lake
Jemez Springs
Jemez Hist Site
White Rock
Tesuque Indian Res
Cowles
Sapello
Watrous
Bandelier Nat'l Mon
Santa Fe
ELK MTN EL 11,661 FT
Storrie Lake
Jemez
Nat'l
Cochiti Indian Reservation
For
INSET
Hyde Mem
Tererro
Res
THOMPSON PEAK EL 10,554 FT
El Porvenir
Jemez Pueblo
Kasha-Katuwe Tent Rocks Nat'l Mon
(SAF)
Glorieta
Pecos National Historical Park
Montezuma
Las Vegas
San Ysidro
Indian
Cochiti Lake
Pena Blanca
Pecos
Santa
Zia
Santo Domingo Pueblo
Las Vegas NWR
Indian
Zia
Rowe
Romeroville
Ojito Wldrns
Zia Pueblo
Santa Ana Indian
San Felipe Pueblo
Fe
Res
Indian Res
Madrid
Gallinas
Algodones
San Felipe Indian Res
Cerrillos Hills
Galisteo
Jemez Canyon Res
Res
Ribera
Bernal
Santo Domingo Indian Res
National
Forest
Bernalillo
Placitas
SANTA FE
Villanueva
Rio Ranchos
Sandia Indian Res
Sandia Wldrns
Rencona
Leyba
Villanueva
River
ALBUQUERQUE
Corrales
BERNALILLO
Tohajiilee Navajo Indian Reservation
INSET
Cedar Crest
Sandia Park
Anton Chico
Dilia
Clines Corners
Tijeras
(ABQ)
Cibola
Moriarty
Kirtland Air Force Base
Rio Puerco
Isleta
Isleta Indian
Reservation
McIntosh
TORRANCE
GUADALUPE
Los Lunas
MANZANO MTNS
Tajique
Estancia
Pastura
VALENCIA
Torreon
Laguna Del Perro
Belen
Manzano
Encino
National
Manzano Mountains
Salinas Pueblo Missions Nat'l Mon
Willard
Vaughn
Jarales
Bosque
Veguita
Mountainair
Abo Ruins
Duran
Bernardo
Sevilleta
National
La Joya
Wildlife
Forest
Cedarvale
San Acacia
Chamizal
Refuge
Corona
LOS PINTOS MTNS
Gran Quivira Ruins
Lemitar

3
CO
OK
OK
92
TX
W
TX
108
RATON PASS
EL 7,834 FT
Sugarite Canyon
Raton
River
TRAIL
COLFAX
Maxwell NWR
Maxwell
Springer
Miami
SANTA
FE
Levy
Wagon
Mound
MORA
River
Watrous
Folsom
Capulin Volcano
Nat'l Mon
Capulin
Des
Moines
Dry
Cimarron
River
Kenton
Moses
Kiowa
Seneca
National
Grasslands
MOUNTAIN TIME
CENTRAL TIME
Grenville
CUT-OFF
Clayton
Lake
Mt Dora
CIMARRON
TRAIL
UNION
Clayton
Texline
Farley
Gladstone
Yates
Kiowa
National
Grasslands
Canadian
Mills
Roy
Solano
HARDING
Bueyeros
Sedan
Stead
Amistad
Mosquero
Gallegos
Nara Visa
Sabinoso
Wilderness
SAN MIGUEL
Bell
Ranch
Trujillo
Trementina
Conchas
Lake
Conchas
Lake
Conchas
Variadero
River
Canadian
Ute
Lake
Ute Lake
Logan
Tucumcari
Montoya
Newkirk
Cuervo
Santa
Rosa
Lake
Santa Rosa
Lake
Santa Rosa
Puerto
de Luna
Pastura
Pecos
Sumner
Lake
Sumner Lake
Fort
Sumner
Yeso
DE BACA
CONEJOS MESA
Taiban
Melrose
QUAY
San Jon
Bard
Glenrio
Quay
Ragland
Forrest
McAlister
House
Field
CURRY
Ranchvale
St Vrain
Portair
Cannon
AFB
Clovis
Farwell
Grady
Broadview
Bellview
Pleasant
Hill
Oasis
Floyd
Portales
Arch
Melrose
Air Force
Range
N

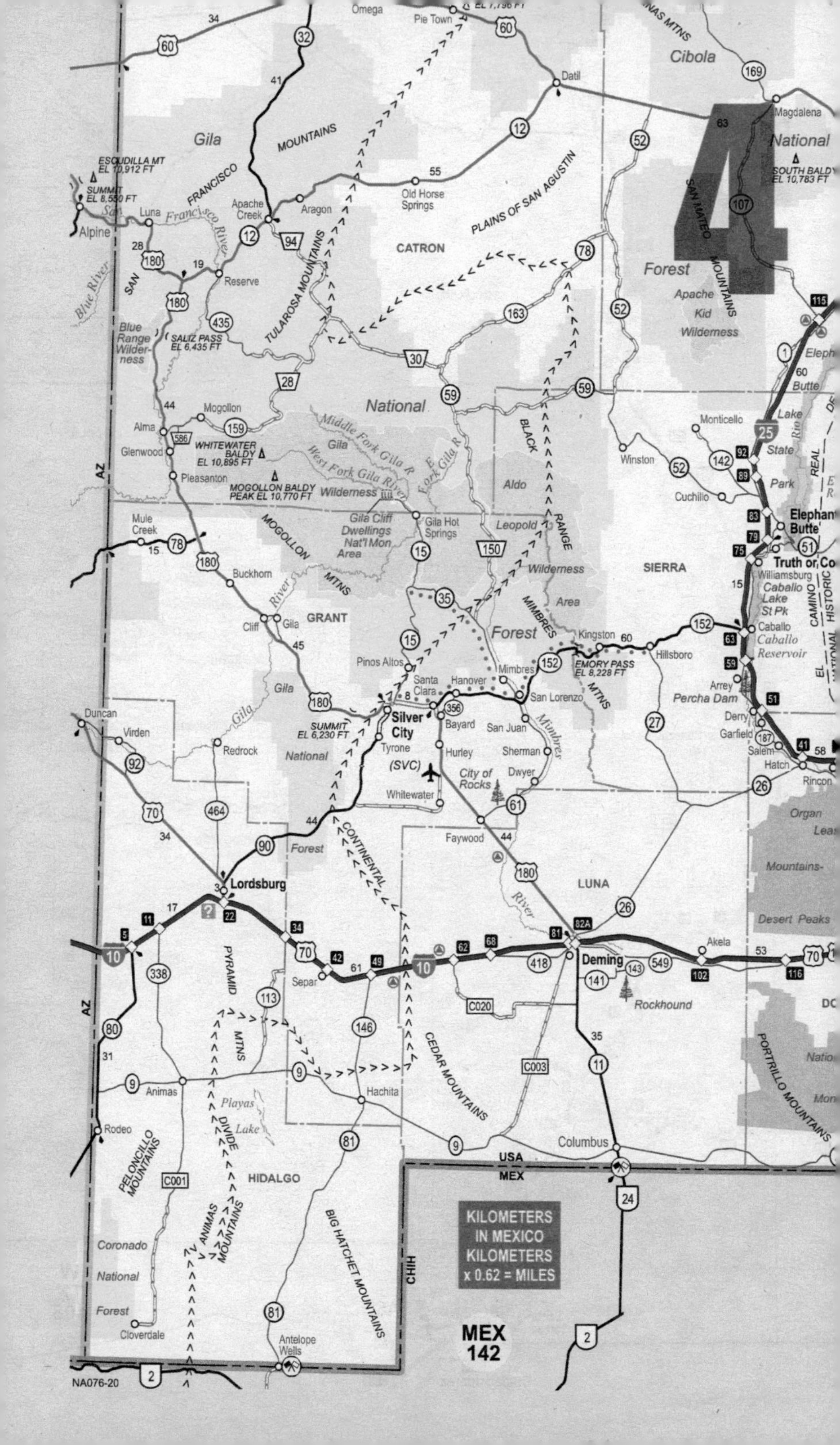

Omega
Pie Town
Datil
Magdalena
Cibola
National
Forest
SOUTH BALDY EL 10,783 FT
SAN MATEO MOUNTAINS
Apache Kid Wilderness
4
Gila
MOUNTAINS
ESCUDILLA MT EL 10,912 FT
SUMMIT EL 8,550 FT
FRANCISCO
Luna
Alpine
Apache Creek
Aragon
Old Horse Springs
PLAINS OF SAN AGUSTIN
CATRON
Reserve
Blue River
SAN
TULAROSA MOUNTAINS
Blue Range Wilderness
SALIZ PASS EL 6,435 FT
National
Mogollon
Alma
Glenwood
Pleasanton
WHITEWATER BALDY EL 10,895 FT
MOGOLLON BALDY PEAK EL 10,770 FT
Middle Fork Gila R
West Fork Gila River
E. Fork Gila R
Gila Wilderness
BLACK RANGE
Aldo Leopold Wilderness
Area
Winston
Monticello
Cuchillo
Elephant Butte
Truth or Co
Williamsburg
Caballo Lake St Pk
Caballo
Caballo Reservoir
Lake State Park
SIERRA
AZ
Mule Creek
Gila Cliff Dwellings Nat'l Mon Area
Gila Hot Springs
MOGOLLON MTNS
Buckhorn
Cliff
Gila
GRANT
Forest
MIMBRES MTNS
Kingston
Hillsboro
EMORY PASS EL 8,228 FT
Pinos Altos
Santa Clara
Hanover
Mimbres
San Lorenzo
Silver City
Bayard
San Juan
Hurley
Sherman
Tyrone
(SVC)
City of Rocks
Dwyer
Whitewater
SUMMIT EL 6,230 FT
Duncan
Virden
Redrock
National
Forest
Faywood
CONTINENTAL
Lordsburg
LUNA
Deming
Akela
Rockhound
Separ
Arrey
Percha Dam
Derry
Garfield
Salem
Hatch
Rincon
Organ Mountains-Desert Peaks
PYRAMID MTNS
CEDAR MOUNTAINS
Animas
Playas Lake
DIVIDE
Hachita
Rodeo
PELONCILLO MOUNTAINS
HIDALGO
Columbus
USA
MEX
PORTRILLO MOUNTAINS
ANIMAS MOUNTAINS
BIG HATCHET MOUNTAINS
Coronado National Forest
Cloverdale
Antelope Wells
CHIH
KILOMETERS IN MEXICO
KILOMETERS x 0.62 = MILES
MEX 142
NA076-20

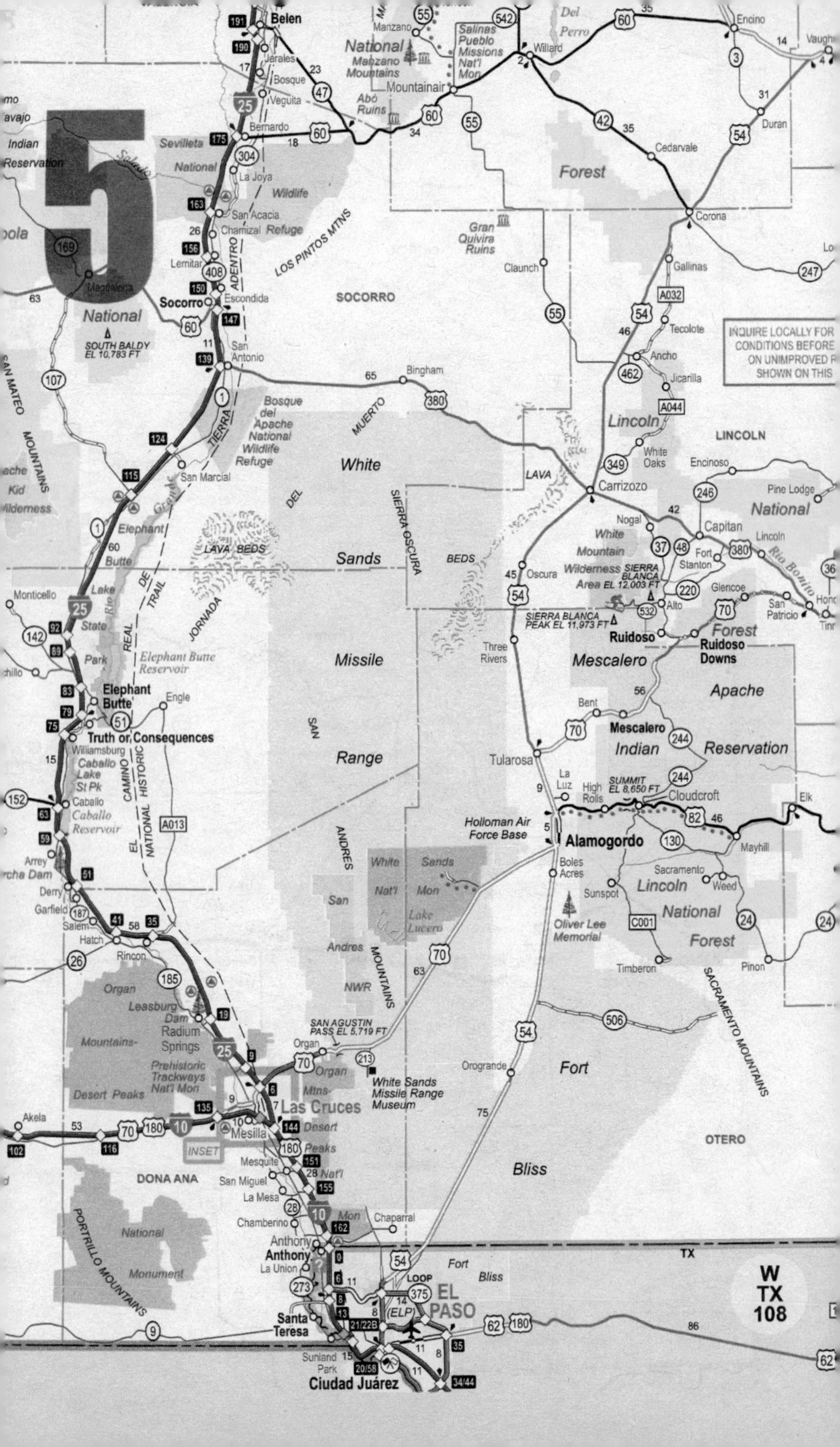

5
Belen
Jarales
Bosque
Veguita
Bernardo
Sevilleta
National
Wildlife
Refuge
La Joya
San Acacia
Chamizal
Lemitar
Socorro
Escondida
San Antonio
Magdalena
National
SOUTH BALDY EL 10,783 FT
SAN MATEO MOUNTAINS
Apache Kid Wilderness
Navajo Indian Reservation
LOS PINTOS MTNS
SOCORRO
Manzano
National
Manzano Mountains
Mountainair
Abó Ruins
Salinas Pueblo Missions Nat'l Mon
Willard
Del Perro
Encino
Vaughn
Duran
Cedarvale
Forest
Corona
Gran Quivira Ruins
Claunch
Gallinas
Tecolote
Ancho
Jicarilla
INQUIRE LOCALLY FOR CONDITIONS BEFORE ON UNIMPROVED R SHOWN ON THIS
Bingham
Bosque del Apache National Wildlife Refuge
San Marcial
JORNADA DEL MUERTO
White Sands Missile Range
LAVA BEDS
SIERRA OSCURA
Lincoln
White Oaks
LINCOLN
Encinoso
Pine Lodge
National
Carrizozo
Nogal
Capitan
Lincoln
Fort Stanton
Rio Bonito
White Mountain Wilderness Area
SIERRA BLANCA EL 12,003 FT
SIERRA BLANCA PEAK EL 11,973 FT
Oscura
Alto
Glencoe
San Patricio
Hondo
Ruidoso
Ruidoso Downs
Forest
Three Rivers
Mescalero Apache Indian Reservation
Bent
Mescalero
Tularosa
La Luz
High Rolls
SUMMIT EL 8,650 FT
Cloudcroft
Elk
Holloman Air Force Base
Alamogordo
Boles Acres
Mayhill
Sacramento
Weed
Sunspot
Lincoln National Forest
Oliver Lee Memorial
Timberon
Pinon
SACRAMENTO MOUNTAINS
White Sands Nat'l Mon
Lake Lucero
San Andres
San Andres NWR
SAN ANDRES MOUNTAINS
SAN AGUSTIN PASS EL 5,719 FT
White Sands Missile Range Museum
Orogrande
Fort Bliss
OTERO
Monticello
Elephant Butte Lake State Park
Elephant Butte Reservoir
EL CAMINO REAL DE TIERRA ADENTRO NATIONAL HISTORIC TRAIL
Rio Grande
Elephant Butte
Engle
Truth or Consequences
Williamsburg
Caballo Lake St Pk
Caballo
Caballo Reservoir
Arrey
Derry
Garfield
Salem
Hatch
Rincon
Organ Mountains-Desert Peaks Nat'l Mon
Leasburg Dam
Radium Springs
Prehistoric Trackways Nat'l Mon
Organ
Las Cruces
Mesilla
INSET
Akela
DONA ANA
Mesquite
San Miguel
La Mesa
Chamberino
Chaparral
Anthony
La Union
PORTRILLO MOUNTAINS
Santa Teresa
Sunland Park
Ciudad Juárez
EL PASO
LOOP
(ELP)
Fort Bliss
TX
W TX 108

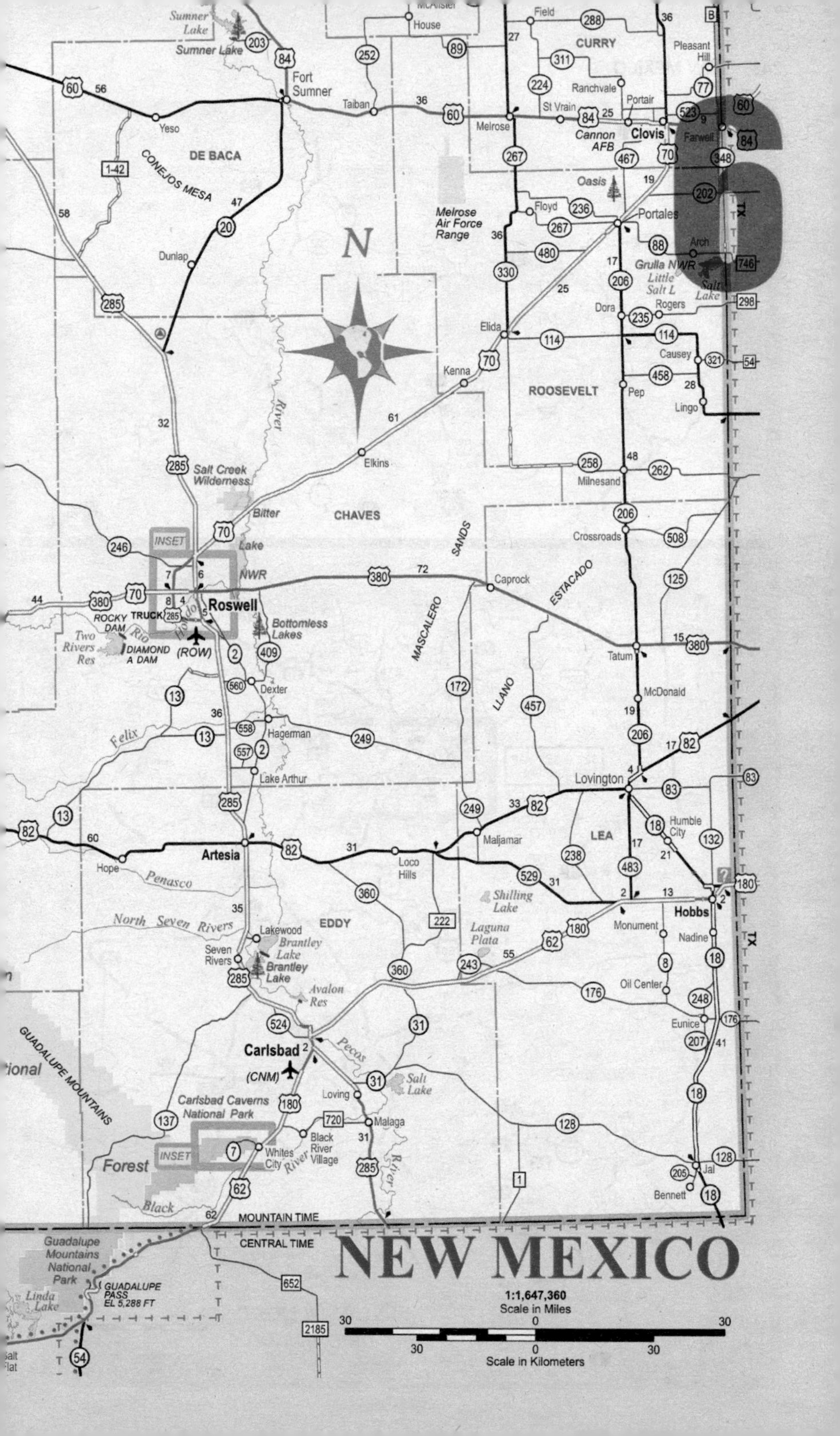

NEW MEXICO
Sumner Lake
Fort Sumner
Taiban
Yeso
DE BACA
CONEJOS MESA
Dunlap
CURRY
Field
House
Pleasant Hill
Ranchvale
Portair
St Vrain
Melrose
Cannon AFB
Clovis
Farwell
Oasis
Floyd
Portales
Melrose Air Force Range
Arch
Grulla NWR
Little Salt L
Salt Lake
Dora
Rogers
Elida
Causey
Kenna
ROOSEVELT
Pep
Lingo
Elkins
Milnesand
Salt Creek Wilderness
Bitter Lake NWR
CHAVES
SANDS
Crossroads
Caprock
ESTACADO
MASCALERO
INSET
TRUCK
Roswell
ROCKY DAM
Two Rivers Res
DIAMOND A DAM
(ROW)
Bottomless Lakes
Dexter
Hagerman
Lake Arthur
Felix
LLANO
Tatum
McDonald
Lovington
Humble City
LEA
Maljamar
Artesia
Hope
Penasco
Loco Hills
Shilling Lake
Hobbs
North Seven Rivers
EDDY
Lakewood
Brantley Lake
Seven Rivers
Laguna Plata
Monument
Nadine
Oil Center
Avalon Res
Eunice
Carlsbad
(CNM)
Pecos
Salt Lake
Loving
Malaga
GUADALUPE MOUNTAINS
Carlsbad Caverns National Park
Whites City
Black River Village
River
Forest
Black
Jal
Bennett
MOUNTAIN TIME
CENTRAL TIME
Guadalupe Mountains National Park
GUADALUPE PASS EL 5,288 FT
Linda Lake
TX
1:1,647,360
Scale in Miles
Scale in Kilometers

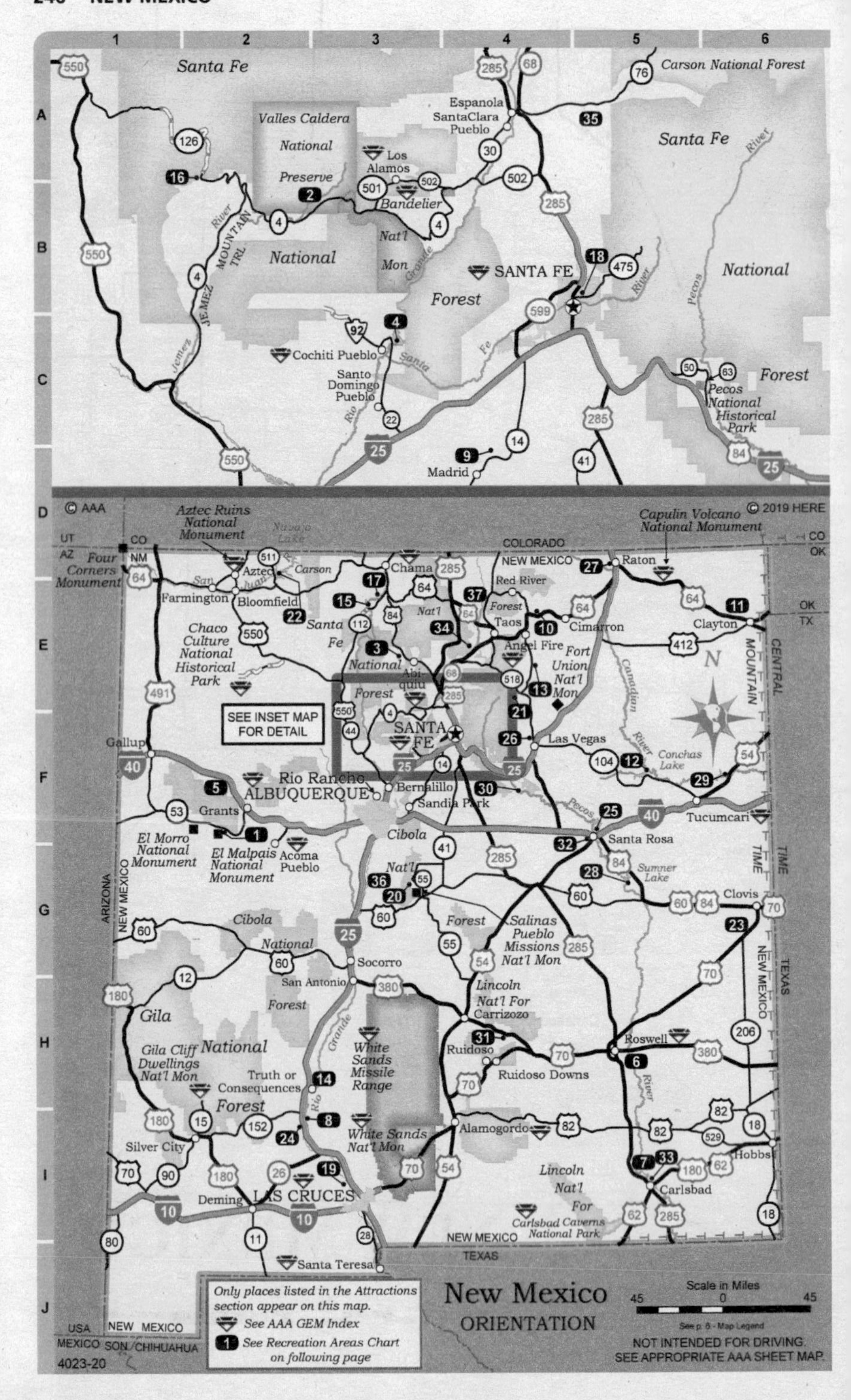
Santa Fe
Valles Caldera National Preserve
Los Alamos
Bandelier Nat'l Mon
Espanola
SantaClara Pueblo
Carson National Forest
Santa Fe National Forest
SANTA FE
Cochiti Pueblo
Santo Domingo Pueblo
Pecos National Historical Park
Madrid
JEMEZ MOUNTAIN TRL
© AAA
© 2019 HERE
Aztec Ruins National Monument
Capulin Volcano National Monument
Four Corners Monument
Farmington
Bloomfield
Aztec
Chama
Red River
Taos
Cimarron
Raton
Clayton
Angel Fire
Fort Union Nat'l Mon
Chaco Culture National Historical Park
SEE INSET MAP FOR DETAIL
Abiquiu
Gallup
Las Vegas
Rio Rancho
ALBUQUERQUE
Bernalillo
Sandia Park
Grants
El Morro National Monument
El Malpais National Monument
Acoma Pueblo
Tucumcari
Santa Rosa
Sumner Lake
Conchas Lake
Clovis
Salinas Pueblo Missions Nat'l Mon
Socorro
San Antonio
Lincoln Nat'l For
Carrizozo
Gila Cliff Dwellings Nat'l Mon
Gila National Forest
Truth or Consequences
White Sands Missile Range
Ruidoso
Ruidoso Downs
Roswell
Alamogordo
White Sands Nat'l Mon
Silver City
Deming
LAS CRUCES
Santa Teresa
Carlsbad
Carlsbad Caverns National Park
Hobbs
ARIZONA
NEW MEXICO
TEXAS
COLORADO
MOUNTAIN
CENTRAL
TIME
Only places listed in the Attractions section appear on this map.
See AAA GEM Index
See Recreation Areas Chart on following page
New Mexico
ORIENTATION
Scale in Miles
45 0 45
See p. 8 - Map Legend
NOT INTENDED FOR DRIVING.
SEE APPROPRIATE AAA SHEET MAP.
4023-20

Recreation Areas Chart

The map location numerals in column 2 show an area's location on the preceding map.

Find thousands of places to camp at AAA.com/campgrounds

	MAP LOCATION	CAMPING	PICNICKING	HIKING TRAILS	BOATING	BOAT RAMP	BOAT RENTAL	FISHING	SWIMMING	PET FRIENDLY	BICYCLE TRAILS	WINTER SPORTS	VISITOR CENTER	LODGE/CABINS	FOOD SERVICE
NATIONAL PARKS *(See place listings.)*															
Chaco Culture (E-2) 33,974 acres. Northwest New Mexico.		●	●	●						●	●		●		
NATIONAL FORESTS *(See place listings.)*															
Carson (D-2) 1,500,000 acres. North-central New Mexico.		●	●	●				●		●	●	●	●		
Cibola (G-2) 1,625,542 acres. Central New Mexico.		●	●	●				●	●	●	●	●	●		
Gila (H-1) 3,321,000 acres. Southwestern New Mexico.		●	●	●	●	●		●	●	●	●	●	●		
Lincoln (H-4) 1,103,441 acres. South-central New Mexico. Horse rental.		●	●	●				●		●	●	●			●
Santa Fe (A-5) 1,600,000 acres. North-central New Mexico between the San Pedro Mountains and the Sangre de Cristo Mountains. Nonmotorized boats only.		●	●	●	●			●		●	●	●	●		
NATIONAL CONSERVATION AREAS															
El Malpais (F-2) 231,230 acres 23 mi. s. of I-40 exits 81 or 89 via SRs 53 or 117. Caving, horseback riding.	1		●	●						●	●	●	●		
Valles Caldera (B-2) 89,000 acres 18 mi. w. of Los Alamos off SR 4.	2		●	●				●			●	●	●		
ARMY CORPS OF ENGINEERS															
Abiquiu Lake (E-3) 4,015 acres 7 mi. n.w. of Abiquiu via US 84. Water skiing.	3	●	●	●	●	●		●	●	●	●		●		
Cochiti Lake (C-3) 1,200 acres 5 mi. n. of Pea Blanca on SR 22. Golfing, sailing, windsurfing.	4	●	●	●	●	●	●	●	●	●			●		
STATE															
Bluewater Lake (F-2) 3,000 acres 28 mi. n.w. of Grants off I-40.	5	●	●	●	●	●		●	●	●		●	●		
Bottomless Lakes (H-5) 1,400 acres 12 mi. s.e. of Roswell via US 380, then 3 mi. s. on SR 409. Hand-propelled craft and small gas or electric motors only.	6	●	●	●	●		●	●	●	●	●		●		
Brantley Lake (I-5) 3,000 acres 19 mi. n. of Carlsbad off US 285.	7	●	●		●	●		●	●	●	●		●		
Caballo Lake (I-3) 11,610 acres 16 mi. s. of Truth or Consequences off I-25. Bird-watching; horse trails.	8	●	●	●	●	●		●	●	●			●		
Cerrillos Hills (D-4) 1,116 acres 4 mi. n. of Madrid on CR 59. Mountain biking; horse rental.	9		●	●						●	●	●	●		
Cimarron Canyon (E-4) 33,000 acres 12 mi. w. of Cimarron via US 64.	10	●	●	●				●		●		●			
Clayton Lake (E-6) 471 acres 12 mi. n. of Clayton on SR 370.	11	●	●	●	●	●		●		●	●		●		
Conchas Lake (F-5) 290 acres 34 mi. n.w. of Tucumcari via SR 104.	12	●	●		●	●		●	●	●			●	●	
Coyote Creek (E-4) 80 acres 17 mi. n.e. of Mora on SR 434.	13	●	●	●				●		●			●		
Elephant Butte Lake (H-3) 40,056 acres 5 mi. n. of Truth or Consequences off I-25.	14	●	●	●	●	●	●	●	●	●		●	●		
El Vado Lake (E-3) 1,730 acres 4 mi. n.e. of El Vado off SR 112.	15	●	●	●	●	●		●	●	●	●				
Fenton Lake (A-1) 700 acres 38 mi. w. of Los Alamos via SRs 4 and 126. Canoeing, cross-country skiing; horse trails. Boats with electric motors only.	16	●	●	●	●	●		●		●	●	●			
Heron Lake (E-3) 4,107 acres 11 mi. w. of Tierra Amarilla via US 84 and SR 95.	17	●	●	●	●	●		●	●	●		●	●		
Hyde Memorial (B-5) 350 acres 8 mi. n.e. of Santa Fe on Hyde Park Rd.	18	●	●	●						●		●	●		●
Leasburg Dam (I-3) 240 acres 1 mi. w. of Radium Springs. Canoeing; playground. Non-motorized boats only.	19	●	●	●	●			●	●	●	●		●		
Manzano Mountains (G-3) 160 acres 16 mi. n.w. of Mountainair via SR 55.	20	●	●	●						●	●	●	●		
Morphy Lake (F-4) 30 acres 25 mi. n. of Las Vegas off SR 518.	21	●	●	●	●	●		●		●					
Navajo Lake (E-2) 21,000 acres 23 mi. n.e. of Bloomfield on SR 511.	22	●	●	●	●	●	●	●	●	●	●	●	●		
Oasis (G-6) 193 acres 6.5 mi. n. of Portales off SR 467.	23	●	●	●				●		●	●		●		
Percha Dam (I-2) 84 acres 21 mi. s. of Truth or Consequences via I-25. Playground.	24	●	●					●	●	●			●		

Recreation Areas Chart

The map location numerals in column 2 show an area's location on the preceding map.

Find thousands of places to camp at AAA.com/campgrounds

	MAP LOCATION	CAMPING	PICNICKING	HIKING TRAILS	BOATING	BOAT RAMP	BOAT RENTAL	FISHING	SWIMMING	PET FRIENDLY	BICYCLE TRAILS	WINTER SPORTS	VISITOR CENTER	LODGE/CABINS	FOOD SERVICE
Santa Rosa Lake (F-5) 500 acres 7 mi. n. of Santa Rosa via SR 91. Water skiing; nature trail.	25	●	●	●	●	●		●	●	●	●		●		
Storrie Lake (F-4) 83 acres 4 mi. n. of Las Vegas off SR 518. Windsurfing.	26	●	●	●	●	●		●	●	●			●		
Sugarite Canyon (D-5) 3,600 acres 10 mi. n.e. of Raton via SR 72. Historic. Canoeing, cross-country skiing, mountain climbing, snowmobiling; horse trails.	27	●	●	●	●	●		●		●	●	●	●		
Sumner Lake (G-5) 6,700 acres 16 mi. n.w. of Fort Sumner on US 84.	28	●	●	●	●	●		●	●	●	●		●		
Ute Lake (F-6) 1,500 acres 2 mi. s.w. of Logan on SR 540.	29	●	●	●	●	●	●	●	●	●			●		
Villanueva (F-4) 1,679 acres 31 mi. s.w. of Las Vegas via I-25 and SR 3.	30	●	●	●				●	●	●			●		
OTHER															
Fort Stanton (H-4) 24,000 acres 7.7 mi. w. of Lincoln on US 380, then 1 mi. s. on SR 220. Caving; horse trails.	31	●	●	●							●				
Janes-Wallace Memorial (G-4) 1 mi. s. of Santa Rosa on SR 91.	32	●	●					●			●				
Lake Carlsbad (I-5) In Carlsbad on Park Dr. Water skiing.	33	●	●		●	●		●	●		●				
Orilla Verde (E-4) 2,840 acres 6 mi. n of Pilar on SR 570. Canoeing, kayaking.	34	●	●	●	●			●		●	●		●		
Santa Cruz Lake (A-5) 2,543 acres 14 mi. e. of Española via SRs 76 and 4.	35	●	●	●	●	●		●		●					
Sen. Willie M. Chavez (G-3) 150 acres on the Rio Grande at Belen.	36	●	●	●				●		●	●				
Wild Rivers (E-4) 20,300 acres 5 mi. w. of Questa off SR 378.	37	●	●	●	●	●		●		●	●		●		

ABIQUIU (E-3) pop. 231, elev. 6,063'

In the mid-18th century Abiquiu (AH-be-cue) was one of several settlements the Spanish government provided for *Genízaros,* people of mixed blood who were either the Spaniards' own prisoners or captives ransomed from the Comanches or Apaches and later released from slavery. By 1778 the community was a stop on the Old Spanish Trail, which led westward to an infant coastal hamlet called Los Angeles.

Abiquiu was the birthplace of Padre Antonio José Martínez, the priest credited with the establishment of the Southwest's first coeducational school. His lifelong crusade to educate his people took him to Taos in 1826, then into politics.

The area is known for its colorful, rugged rock formations and other scenic features. Abiquiu Lake *(see Recreation Areas Chart)*, 7 miles northwest via US 84, provides opportunities for water sports while controlling downstream flooding and sedimentation. The Carson and Santa Fe national forests surround the lake.

As anyone who has seen her landscapes would conclude, artist Georgia O'Keeffe spent winters and springs in Abiquiu and summers and autumns at nearby Ghost Ranch. The artist's ashes were scattered at Pedernal, the flat-topped mountain to the south of Ghost Ranch. Along US 84 are views O'Keeffe captured in her work.

Guided tours of the Georgia O'Keeffe Home and Studio are available March through November by reservation only; advance payment is required. Tours accommodate up to 12 people and depart from the nearby Abiquiu Inn. For more information phone (505) 946-1000.

GHOST RANCH is 12 mi. n.w. on US 84; watch for the signed turnoff. Georgia O'Keeffe owned a summerhouse and painted familiar scenes at this 21,000-acre former ranch, now a Presbyterian education and retreat center. In addition to the spectacular climb to Chimney Rock, hikers can tackle Box Canyon (a 4-mile round trip that reaches elevations of 6,900 feet) and the more difficult Kitchen Mesa trail, a 5-mile trek that takes several hours to complete.

Also at the site are a meditation labyrinth, a Zen garden, a medicine wheel and two museums. O'Keeffe Landscape Trail Rides are offered year-round; reservations are required. Georgia O'Keeffe at Ghost Ranch Landscape Tours are given mid-March through Thanksgiving weekend. **Hours:** Ranch open daily at 8. O'Keeffe Trail Ride departs daily at 10 and 2 (sunset trail rides depart Tues. and Thurs.; departure times vary by month). Landscape Tours are given Tues.-Sun. at 1:30 and 3. **Cost:** Grounds and conservation fee $5. Landscape tour $37. Walking tour $49. O'Keefe Trail Ride $95. **Phone:** (505) 685-1000 or (877) 804-4678.

GEM **Chimney Rock** is 12 mi. n.w. on US 84; watch for the signed turnoff. The signed trailhead is located at the arroyo behind the Ghost Ranch museums and past the Corral Block complex.

This is the most popular of several hiking trails at Ghost Ranch, and deservedly so; it's a stunner. The wide dirt trail starts out at a level pace, with tall, spire-shaped Chimney Rock in the distance. The sere landscape beckons. You'll see drought-tolerant vegetation like cholla, prickly pear cactus, saltbush and piñon pine, brightened in spots by wildflowers growing in sheltered rock crevices.

Soon the trail begins ascending a ridge to the top of a red rock mesa that is within striking distance of Chimney Rock. The climb is moderately strenuous; watch your footing and keep an eye out for the designated markers painted on rocks in order to stay on the trail. After reaching the top of the mesa hikers approach Chimney Rock from behind, getting close enough for a dizzying look at the valley floor below.

Spectacular 360-degree vistas take in the Piedra Lumbre basin, Mt. Pedernal on the western horizon and an array of multicolored sandstone and gypsum formations. The views as you climb from 6,500 to 7,100 feet are absolutely splendid.

Note: The round-trip distance is 3 miles. Hikers should check in at the Ghost Ranch Welcome Center office before and after hiking. Wear hiking boots or non-slip athletic shoes and a hat (there's no shade) and bring water. Do not attempt to climb any of the rock formations or get close to the soft rock edges at the top of the mesa. **Time:** Allow 2 hours minimum. **Hours:** Daily 8-5. **Cost:** $5 conservation fee. **Phone:** (505) 685-1000 or (877) 804-4678.

Florence Hawley Ellis Museum of Anthropology is located at the Ghost Ranch Education and Retreat Center, 12 mi. n.w. on US 84. It features exhibits depicting 12,000 years of civilization within the Chama-Rio Grande region. Contemporary Southwestern art also is displayed. **Time:** Allow 30 minutes minimum. **Hours:** Mon.-Sat. 9-5, Sun. 1-5. **Cost:** $5 conservation fee (includes Ruth Hall Museum of Paleontology). **Phone:** (505) 685-1000, ext. 4118.

Ruth Hall Museum of Paleontology is at the Ghost Ranch Education and Retreat Center, 12 mi. n.w. on US 84. It documents the area's rich fossil record, including the 1947 discovery of a small, predatory dinosaur named *Coelophysis,* the state fossil. Also on display is a complete and remarkably well-preserved skeleton of the dinosaur *Tawa hallae,* a T. Rex relative that lived in North America during the late Triassic period. **Time:** Allow 30 minutes minimum. **Hours:** Mon.-Sat. 9-5, Sun. 1-5. **Cost:** $5 conservation fee (includes Florence Hawley Ellis Museum of Anthropology). **Phone:** (505) 685-1000.

ACOMA PUEBLO (G-2) elev. 6,550'

One of the oldest continuously inhabited settlements in the country—evidence dates it from A.D. 1150—Acoma was well established when Francisco

Vázquez de Coronado explored New Mexico in 1540. Inhabitants of Sky City, as the pueblo was known, worked fields on the plains 357 feet below their village and climbed back atop the mesa each night. Acoma afforded protection through decades of warfare, but the numerical superiority of the Spaniards proved too much. A final battle in 1599 vanquished the community.

Today only a few dozen Acomans live year-round on the mesa top; others live in nearby villages but return to Sky City for cultural observances. Visitors must register at the Sky City Cultural Center and Haak'u Museum at the base of the mesa, where permits and guided tours are available.

About 3 miles northeast is Enchanted Mesa, which looms 430 feet above the surrounding plain. According to Acoma tribal folklore, this was an ancestral settlement, but access to it was wiped out by a violent storm, leaving several Acoma women and children to starve on the mesa top.

GEM **ACOMA PUEBLO (SKY CITY)** is off I-40 exit 102, then about 16 mi. s. on R.R. 30/32 following signs to the Sky City Cultural Center at 1232 E. Haak'u Rd. Occupied by the Acomans since the second century, this 367-foot-high mesa is topped by one of the largest adobe structures in North America, the 1629 Spanish mission San Esteban del Rey. Building materials, including great log beams hand cut on Mount Taylor some 30 miles north, were manually carried to the summit by Acoman laborers.

The first Native American site to be designated as such by the National Trust for Historic Preservation, Acoma Pueblo is the 28th National Trust Historic Site. More than 15 Acoma families live on the mesa in dwellings without running water or electricity while observing the customs and traditions of their ancestors. Pottery makers showcasing their works for sale outside their homes are observed on guided walking tours featuring the pueblo, the plaza and the mission church, with its ecclesiastic art, tapestries and hand-carved woodwork.

Visits to the mesa must be arranged through a guide at the Sky City Cultural Center and Haak'u Museum, located at the base of the pueblo. Video filming is prohibited; obtain a permit for still photography at the cultural center. The 1.5-hour guided walking tour traverses areas of uneven and rough terrain; comfortable walking shoes are recommended. Revealing clothing and cellphones are not permitted.

Time: Allow 3 hours minimum. **Hours:** Daily 9-5, late Mar.-Oct. 31; Sat.-Sun. 9-4, rest of year. Guided tours given on the half hour 9:30-3:30, late Mar.-Oct. 31; 9:30-2:30, rest of year. Closed June 24 and 29, July 9-14 and 25, first or second weekend in Oct., first Sat. of Dec. and other days without notice. Phone ahead to confirm schedule. **Cost:** Guided tour fee $25; $22 (ages 60+ and active military and college students with ID); $17 (ages 6-17); still-camera photography fee without tour $15. **Phone:** (800) 747-0181.

Sky City Cultural Center and Haak'u Museum is at the base of the Acoma Pueblo, off I-40 exit 102, then 16 mi. s. to 1232 E. Haak'u Rd. It contains two galleries offering rotating displays.

Time: Allow 1 hour minimum. **Hours:** Daily 9-5, Mar.-Oct.; Sat.-Sun. 9-4, rest of year. Guided tours are given on the half hour 9:30-3:30. Closed June 19, 24 and 29, July 9-14 and 25, first or second weekend in Oct., first Sat. in Dec. and other days without notice. Phone ahead to confirm schedule. **Cost:** Guided tours $25; $22 (ages 60+, active military and college students with ID); $17 (ages 6-17); still-camera photography permit fee (does not include tour fee) $15. **Phone:** (800) 747-0181.

ALAMOGORDO (I-4) pop. 30,403, elev. 4,335'

A ready water supply from the looming Sacramento Mountains prompted the town's founding as a railroad terminal in 1898. Alamogordo—Spanish for "fat cottonwood"—grew quickly as ranching, lumber production, farming and tourism were added to its assets. Nevertheless, modern development has been due primarily to the Holloman Air Force Base. Diversified industry, much of it related to space, also contributes to the economy.

Tularosa Basin Museum of History, 1004 N. White Sands Blvd., focuses on local and regional history; phone (575) 434-4438. Leading eastward to Cloudcroft, US 82 passes through the state's only highway tunnel.

The Southern New Mexico Festival of Quilts takes place in June.

Alamogordo Chamber of Commerce and Aubrey L. Dunn Sr. Visitor Center: 1301 N. White Sands Blvd., Alamogordo, NM 88310. **Phone:** (575) 437-6120 or (800) 826-0294.

GEM **NEW MEXICO MUSEUM OF SPACE HISTORY** is 2 mi. e. of US 54/70 via Indian Wells Rd. to Scenic Dr., left on Scenic Dr. to SR 2001, then right to 3198 SR 2001. This large complex includes the museum, Stapp Air and Space Park, the Astronaut Memorial Garden, the International Space Hall of Fame and the Daisy Track. Exhibits honor pioneers from many nations and include international space program items. A special display chronicles the pivotal role that New Mexico plays in the ongoing race to space. A Smithsonian affiliate, the museum serves as the archive for Spaceport America.

Featuring a state-of-the-art 4K laser planetarium projection system, the New Horizons Dome Theater and Planetarium presents giant-screen films, digital planetarium shows and live star talks. The Air & Space Park feature a high-speed sled, rocket engines and missiles.

Time: Allow 2 hours minimum. **Hours:** Mon., Wed.-Sat. 10-5, Sun. noon-5. Phone ahead to confirm film schedule and showtimes. Closed Thanksgiving and Christmas. **Cost:** Museum $8; $7 (ages

60+, active military with ID and New Mexico residents); $6 (ages 4-12). Theater admission $8; $7 (ages 60+, active military with ID and New Mexico residents); $6 (ages 4-12). Planetarium $6; $5 (ages 60+, ages 4-12, active military with ID and New Mexico residents). Combination tickets are available. Theater admission may be higher for certain films. **Phone:** (575) 437-2840 or (877) 333-6589.

OLIVER LEE MEMORIAL STATE PARK is 12 mi. s. on US 54 to jct. CR A16, then e. on A16/Dog Canyon Rd. to 409 Dog Canyon Rd. A green oasis flourishes here around the springs of Dog Canyon, a deep ravine on the west-facing flank of the Sacramento Mountains. The park features historical exhibits and the restored 19th-century house of rancher Oliver Milton Lee. **Hours:** Park daily 24 hours. Visitor center daily 9-4. One-hour ranch house tours are given Sat.-Sun. at 3. **Cost:** $5 (per private vehicle). **Phone:** (575) 437-8284.

HOLIDAY INN EXPRESS HOTEL & SUITES 575/434-9773

Hotel. **Address:** 100 Kerry Ave 88310

QUALITY INN & SUITES 575/434-4200

Hotel

Address: 1020 S White Sands Blvd 88310 **Location:** 1.6 mi e of jct US 82/70 and 54. **Facility:** 90 units, some efficiencies and kitchens. 2 stories (no elevator), exterior corridors. **Pool:** heated outdoor. **Activities:** hot tub, exercise room. **Guest Services:** coin laundry. **Featured Amenity: full hot breakfast.**

WHITE SANDS MOTEL 575/437-2922

Vintage Motel

Address: 1101 S White Sands Blvd 88310 **Location:** 1.6 mi s of jct US 54/70 and 82. **Facility:** This is a nice little motel in a central location in Alamogordo. All guest rooms have updated bedding and flat-panel TVs. The family suites are very spacious. 24 units. 1 story, exterior corridors. **Featured Amenity: continental breakfast.**

WHERE TO EAT

MARGO'S MEXICAN FOOD 575/434-0689

Regional Mexican. Casual Dining. **Address:** 504 1st St 88310

ALBUQUERQUE (F-3) pop. 545,852, elev. 4,957'

- **Hotels p. 266 • Restaurants p. 268**
- **Attractions map p. 254**
- **Hotels & Restaurants map & index p. 258, 260**

The Duke City. Burque. ABQ. They're all nicknames for New Mexico's largest city, and etymologically speaking, you wonder if it isn't because the full name (pronounced "AL-buh-kur-kee") isn't a bit of a tongue twister. While Burque and ABQ are simply shorter versions, the Duke City is a tribute to Don Francisco Fernández de la Cueva, the 8th Duke of Alburquerque of Spain—and somewhere along the way the first "r" got dropped.

Albuquerque was founded in 1706 as a Spanish colonial outpost and farming community along the Rio Grande. The town was laid out in traditional Spanish fashion: a central plaza bordered by a church on one side and government buildings on the other. Following the Mexican War in 1846-47 the U.S. government established a federal garrison to protect American settlers during the period of westward expansion, and the town became a major supply depot.

The arrival of the Atchison, Topeka and Santa Fe Railroad in 1880 ushered in a more modern era. The plaza, however, was bypassed; the rail yards were built 2 miles to the east. The area languished, but fortunately for the benefit of future visitors it didn't lose its trademark Spanish character; today Old Town is a tourist hot spot offering a variety of fun things to do.

The city fills a wide valley between the Sandia Mountains to the east and the sweeping plateau country paralleling the north-south flowing Rio Grande to the west. It's a big city that doesn't look like one. The modest downtown skyline is no match for the twin summits of the Sandias (10,678-foot Sandia Crest and 9,702-foot South Sandia Peak). This small mountain range—running about 17 miles north to south and 4 to 8 miles east to west—is nevertheless steep and rugged, and gives Albuquerque a prominent backdrop. *Sandia* is the Spanish word for watermelon, and dramatic Southwestern sunsets often cast a pinkish hue over the mountains. The ponderosa pines growing along the top of the range even suggest (if you have an active imagination) a watermelon's green rind.

Adding a great deal more color are the fanciful shapes of hot-air balloons. Balloonists from all over the world come here to fly, especially during the 9-day Albuquerque International Balloon Fiesta held the first full weekend of October, which is one of the area's most spectacular things to see. Not only are morning temperatures cool at this time of year, but an atmospheric effect known as the "Albuquerque Box" makes precision flying possible. The "box" is a set of predictable wind patterns that balloon navigators can take advantage of to change direction by varying their altitude, thus staying within a confined area.

The most dramatic sight at this major annual event is the mass ascensions, hundreds of spherical, brilliantly hued balloons taking to the air at once in coordinated flights. The spectacle is a photographer's dream. Also popular is the Special Shape Rodeo, when cows, pigs, soft drink cans and other nontraditional balloon shapes have their turn aloft. During evening Balloon Glows, pilots fire up their propane burners and masses of balloons are illuminated from within. The Anderson-Abruzzo Albuquerque International Balloon Museum in Balloon Fiesta Park is a great place to learn more about hot-air ballooning.

(See maps & indexes p. 258, 260.)

Other big events celebrate the state's cultural heritage: Some 3,000 Native American dancers and singers participate in the Gathering of Nations Powwow, held at the New Mexico State Fairgrounds in April, while the Traditional Winter Spanish Market in late November shares Hispanic heritage through art, music and dance.

The high desert landscape in and around Albuquerque is a study in shades of brown. This region averages a meager 9 inches of rain a year, so the predominant vegetation is drought-tolerant sagebrush, which forms distinctive silvery-green clumps. Desert plants like yucca and juniper thrive. The sunlight is piercing, the sky huge. The wind often blows.

But it's hardly desolate. Wildlife abounds in the wetlands bordering the Rio Grande, as do cottonwood trees, which form a green ribbon along the river's course. Cottonwoods like water; their presence was a welcome sight to 19th-century pioneers traveling across the Great Plains, since a grove of cottonwoods meant shade, wood and a water supply.

Mexican heritage is evident in the prevalence of terra cotta and turquoise; the two colors even adorn concrete abutments along I-25. But New Mexican cuisine is more of a state affair. It's not Tex-Mex, and it's not California-style Mexican. The chief difference boils down to chile peppers.

New Mexico chiles come in two varieties, green and red (the color depends on the stage of ripeness when picked). They're served roasted or chopped, but usually as a sauce—and at many restaurants in town you're more likely to be asked "Green or red?" than "Sweet or unsweet tea?" If you want both, the proper response is "Christmas." A green chile-slathered cheeseburger is a local delicacy, along with blue corn enchiladas and sopaipillas, puffy pieces of fried bread that should be drizzled liberally with honey.

East-west Central Avenue navigates downtown Albuquerque, passes the University of New Mexico and runs through the funky Nob Hill district. The avenue is better known to out-of-towners as Historic Route 66, an icon for American auto travel.

During its golden era in the 1930s and '40s a slew of whimsically designed motels, diners and service stations opened along Route 66, beckoning motorists to stop. The completion of I-40 in 1959 was a blow, allowing drivers to zip along without being bogged down by stop signs and traffic lights. Most of the roadside architecture is gone, although you'll still see the occasional pueblo-inspired building and Art Deco storefront, reminders of the Duke City's good old days.

Albuquerque Convention and Visitors Bureau: 20 First Plaza N.W., Suite 601, Albuquerque, NM 87102. **Phone:** (505) 842-9918 or (800) 284-2282.

Self-guiding tours: Brochures of driving tours through Albuquerque and nearby communities are available from the convention and visitors bureau.

Shopping: The most interesting shopping isn't in chain stores; it's at places where you can immerse yourself in the distinctive culture of the Southwest. And there's no better place to start than Old Town's enticing collection of shops, galleries and artist studios, which is one of Albuquerque's most fun places to go.

You'll find Native American pottery, weavings, turquoise and silver jewelry, *retablos* (religious paintings), tinwork, custom-made furniture and more. The Aceves Old Town Basket & Rug Shop (301 Romero St. in Plaza Don Luis) is a treasure trove of ceramic figures, decorative tiles, knickknacks and hand-woven textiles; items are literally packed to the rafters here. Southwestern Handcrafts & Gifts (1919 Old Town Rd. in Plaza Hacienda) is a general store that carries everything from stoneware, Kachina dolls and decorated vases to Route 66 and Roswell alien souvenirs.

The Penfield Gallery of Indian Arts (22-B San Felipe St. N.W.) has Navajo rugs, sand paintings, and fetish and storyteller figures. Oaxacan wood carvings and finely crafted turquoise earrings are on display at the Tanner Chaney Gallery (323 Romero St. N.W. in Plazuela Sombra).

No shopping trip to Old Town is complete without a stop at The Candy Lady (424 San Felipe St. NW, near The Albuquerque Museum of Art & History). Chile brittle, homemade fudge, a wall devoted to black licorice—it's all here at this destination for dessert lovers, including sugar-free chocolate truffles for those feeling a bit guilty.

Nob Hill-Highland is another area with an offbeat selection of shops lining Central Avenue (Route 66). Antiques and collectibles dealers display their wares at the Antique Specialty Mall (4516 Central Ave. S.E.). As the name implies, Cowboys and Indians Antiques (4000 Central Ave. S.E.) features Indian baskets, Zuni fetishes, spurs, horse figure clocks and turquoise jewelry. Lilly Barrack (3205 Central Ave. N.E.) specializes in contemporary silver jewelry, often in designs paired with uncut gemstones.

Astro-Zombies (3100 Central Ave. S.E.) has a huge collection of comics (DC, Marvel, Dark Horse, Japanese manga), graphic novels and collectible toys from Star Wars characters to Godzilla. Next door is Masks Y Mas (Masks and More), where much of the merchandise revolves around Mexico's Day of the Dead celebration—skeleton figures, bizarre-looking masks and lots of original art. Even if you don't buy anything, the wildly colorful wall murals at both of these establishments are worth a look.

In downtown Albuquerque, Patrician Design (216 Gold Ave. S.W.) sells paintings, painted furniture and pet portraits, plus unusual jewelry and decorative home and office accessories. A block north, Skip Maisel's Indian Jewelry & Crafts (510 Central Ave. S.W.) is in a historic building complete with a neon Indian chief sign. This large emporium is crammed with pottery, rugs, Hopi dolls, opal jewelry and cool items like the feather-bedecked charms called dream catchers. You also can observe Native American crafters at work in the store.

(See maps & indexes p. 258, 260.)

Another one-stop destination for quality arts and crafts is the Bien Mur Indian Market Center at Sandia Pueblo (I-25 to exit 234, then east on Tramway Road to Rainbow Road). The circular building's kiva-shaped showroom displays authentic Native American items like war bonnets, moccasins, musical instruments (flutes, rattles, drums), Zuni fetishes, Hopi and Navajo jewelry, Kachina carvings, rugs and pottery. An added attraction is the 107-acre buffalo preserve established by the pueblo—a section of which borders the parking lot—where you can observe these magnificent beasts in a natural setting.

Albuquerque's mall of choice is ABQ Uptown (Louisiana Boulevard and Indian School Road), an outdoor mix of retailers and local restaurants that includes the usual suspects (Anthropologie, Eddie Bauer, Pottery Barn). Nearby at Louisiana and Menaul boulevards is the Coronado Center, with anchors JCPenney, Macy's and Kohl's as well as some 130 additional stores and places to eat.

Nightlife: The KiMo Theatre (423 Central Ave. N.W. at 5th Street) opened in 1927 as a movie palace, boasting an architectural style dubbed "Pueblo Deco." This is one of only a handful of theaters in the country that incorporate Native American design motifs (ceiling beams that resemble logs, rows of buffalo skulls with glowing eyes), all carefully restored since the theater was rescued from the brink of demolition in the 1970s. Performances run the gamut from music to film showings to special events; for event information phone (505) 768-3522.

Shows at the Launchpad, 618 Central Ave. S.W. (look for the silver sputnik above the door), lean toward punk, hardcore and metal, with occasional appearances by national bands; phone (505) 764-8887. Blues, blues-rock and country-rock musicians take the stage for shows at Low Spirits, 2823 2nd St. N.W. (two blocks north of Menaul Boulevard in the Near North Valley neighborhood). The bar has an open mic happy hour weekdays from 4-8. For ticket information phone (505) 344-9555.

Q Bar, in the Hotel Albuquerque at Old Town (800 Rio Grande Blvd. N.W.), is a swanky lounge with a piano bar, plush seating areas and a billiards room. The cocktails here are pricey but expertly made. There's live music—mostly jazz—Tuesday through Saturday evenings; for table reservations phone (505) 225-5928. More casual is O'Niell's Irish Pub (4310 Central Ave. S.E. in Nob Hill), where local musicians play on Sunday at 4. Phone (505) 255-6782.

Vernon's Black Diamond Lounge is an intimate lounge that seats just 50 and aims to replicate the speakeasies of the Prohibition era, at least in ambience (subdued lighting, black walls, red stage curtains). It's the kind of atmosphere that will appeal to serious jazz fans, and it's perfect if you're looking for things for couples to do. There's a cover charge of $10 and a one-drink minimum per set. The club is inside Vernon's Hidden Valley Steakhouse, 6855 4th St. N.W. (in the northern suburb of Los Ranchos). Patrons are urged to "dress well." Reservations are recommended; phone (505) 341-0831.

Sandia Resort & Casino (north on I-25 to exit 234, then east a quarter mile on Tramway Road) provides the necessary sparkle for a glitzy evening out. This expansive resort sits on Sandia Pueblo land and has outstanding views of the Sandia Mountains. The casino features more than 2,300 slots, a bevy of table games (blackjack, craps, roulette, mini baccarat), live keno and a nonsmoking poker room. Big-name concerts take place at the resort's outdoor amphitheater from late May to mid-September; for ticket and schedule information phone (800) 745-3000.

ABQ BIOPARK AQUARIUM AND BOTANIC GARDEN are at 2601 Central Ave. N.W. Marine habitats of the Gulf of Mexico and other ecosystems are presented at the aquarium. Tanks contain stingrays, jellyfish, eels, sharks and other aquatic life. The botanic garden features Mediterranean and desert conservatories, a children's fantasy garden, water and plant exhibits, demonstration gardens, the BUGarium insect exhibit, the Rio Grande Heritage Farm and the Sasebo Japanese Garden.

Time: Allow 1 hour, 30 minutes minimum. **Hours:** Daily 9-5 (also Sat.-Sun. 5-6, June-Aug. and some holidays). Last admission 30 minutes before closing. Closed Jan. 1, Thanksgiving and Christmas. **Cost:** $14.50; $10 (New Mexico residents); $7.50 (ages 65+); $5.50 (New Mexico residents ages 65+); $6 (ages 3-12); $5 (New Mexico residents ages 3-12). Combination ticket with ABQ BioPark Zoo (Tues.-Sun. and holidays 9-noon) $22; $16 (New Mexico residents); $12 (ages 65+); $9 (New Mexico residents ages 65+); $8 (ages 3-12); $7 (New Mexico residents ages 3-12). Ages 0-12 must be with an adult. **Phone:** (505) 768-2000.

GEM **ABQ BIOPARK ZOO** is at 903 Tenth St. S.W. The zoo houses more than 1,000 animals representing some 250 species in a variety of naturalistic habitats. Popular residents include chimpanzees, gorillas, elephants, polar bears, giraffes, hippos, Komodo dragons, jaguars and zebras. Tropical America features toucans, spider monkeys, tamarins, tarantulas and colorful bromeliads.

The 6-acre Africa exhibit is home to warthogs, cheetahs, rhinos and Marabou storks. Seal and sea lion feedings take place daily in a 350,000-gallon tank. Youngsters will enjoy the Colores Kids Playground, which has a jungle gym for ages 3-12 and a splash pad that's open in summer.

Note: Some habitats are closed for renovations; the rest of the zoo will remain open. Phone ahead for updates. **Hours:** Daily 9-5 (also Sat.-Sun. 5-6, June -Aug. and some holidays). Last admission 30 minutes before closing. Closed Jan. 1, Thanksgiving and Christmas. **Cost:** $14.50; $10 (New Mexico residents); $7.50 (ages 65+); $5.50 (New Mexico residents ages 65+); $6 (ages 3-12); $5 (New Mexico residents ages 3-12). Combination ticket with ABQ BioPark Aquarium and Botanic Garden (Tues.-Sun. and holidays 9-noon) $22; $16 (New

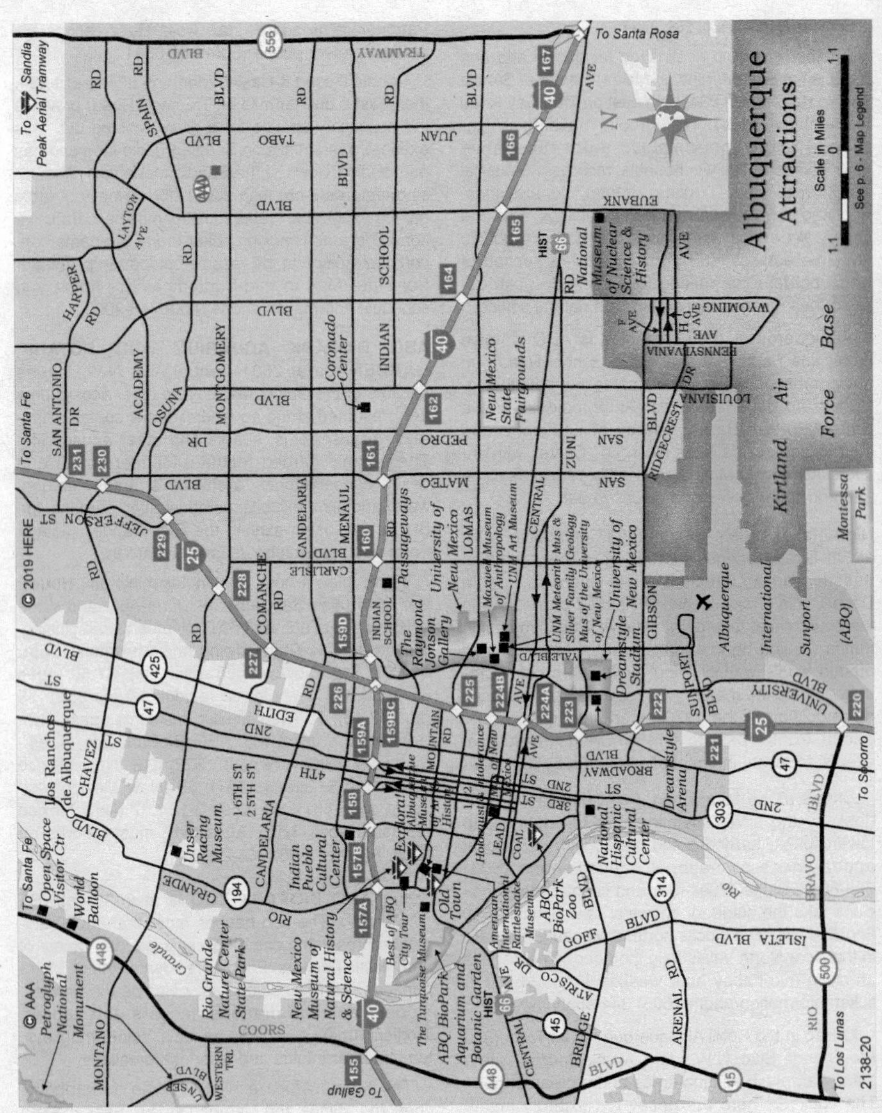

(See maps & indexes p. 258, 260.)

Mexico residents); $12 (ages 65+); $9 (New Mexico residents ages 65+); $8 (ages 3-12); $7 (NewMexico residents ages 3-12). Ages 0-12 must be with an adult. **Phone:** (505) 768-2000.

THE ALBUQUERQUE MUSEUM OF ART & HISTORY is at 2000 Mountain Rd. N.W. The museum features national and international exhibits and art of the Southwest and explores 400 years of Albuquerque history through permanent displays, exhibitions and guided walking tours of Old Town. The collection includes works from major New Mexican artists from the early 20th century to the present. A sculpture garden also is featured.

Time: Allow 2 hours minimum. **Hours:** Tues.-Sun. 9-5. Thirty-minute gallery tours depart Tues.-Sun. at 2. Sculpture garden tours depart Tues.-Sat. at 10, Apr.-Nov. Old Town walking tours depart Tues.-Sun. at 11, mid-Mar. to mid-Dec. Closed Jan. 1, Thanksgiving and Christmas. Phone ahead to confirm schedule. **Cost:** $4; $3 (ages 13-18); $2 (ages 65+); $1 (ages 4-12); free (Sun. 9-1, first Wed. of the month and 5-8:30 third Thurs. of the month). Special fees may apply. **Phone:** (505) 243-7255. GT

GEM **ANDERSON-ABRUZZO ALBUQUERQUE INTERNATIONAL BALLOON MUSEUM** is at 9201 Balloon Museum Dr. N.E. Embrace the spirit of adventure through interactive exhibits about balloon flight, which dates to the early 1700s. In addition

(See maps & indexes p. 258, 260.)

to highlighting the history of ballooning, exhibits also reveal the many uses of balloons in the scientific realm, from weather forecasting to the development of Project Strato-Lab, a U.S. Navy program designed to gather data about human physiology in the stratosphere and a precursor to space exploration.

Other exhibit topics include recreational ballooning and lighter-than-air craft used in conflicts ranging from the Civil War to World War II. Colorful balloons of all shapes and sizes are suspended throughout the two-story grand hall, and some can be viewed up close from a catwalk. Collections include gondolas, balloon systems, books, ephemera and decorative arts.

The museum is named after pioneering balloonists and Albuquerque natives Maxie Anderson and Ben Abruzzo, who, along with a third pilot, were the first to cross the Atlantic Ocean in a gas balloon.

Time: Allow 1 hour minimum. **Hours:** Tues.-Sun. 9-5. Closed Jan. 1, Thanksgiving and Christmas. Phone ahead to confirm schedule. **Cost:** $4; $3 (New Mexico residents with ID); $2 (ages 4-12 and 65+); free (to all Sun. 9-1 and first Fri. of the month). **Phone:** (505) 768-6020.

BEST OF ABQ CITY TOUR departs from the Hotel Albuquerque at 800 Rio Grande N.W. Narrated 1.75-hour tours aboard an open-air trolley include such sights as Old Town, Route 66, historic neighborhoods, Museum Row, the Railyards, the University of New Mexico and the ABQ BioPark Zoo.

Note: Sunscreen or a light jacket may be necessary in some months. **Time:** Allow 1 hour, 30 minutes minimum. **Hours:** Tours depart Tues.-Sun. at 10, noon and 2. Hours vary seasonally and on holidays. Phone ahead to confirm schedule. **Cost:** $25-$35; $15 (ages 0-12). **Phone:** (505) 200-2642.

GEM **EXPLORA!** is at 1701 Mountain Rd. N.W. Visitors wander through a maze of activity areas at this innovative science center and children's museum featuring hands-on science, technology, engineering, math and art exhibits. Giant bubbles, a laminar-flow fountain and activities involving electricity, light, sound, water and more engage children and adults alike while encouraging independent thinking, exploration and experimentation. **Time:** Allow 1 hour minimum. **Hours:** Mon.-Sat. 10-6, Sun. noon-6 (closes at 2 on Christmas Eve and Dec. 31). Closed Jan. 1, July 4, week after Labor Day, Thanksgiving and Christmas. **Cost:** $8; $5 (ages 65+ and students and military with ID); $4 (ages 1-11). **Phone:** (505) 224-8323.

INDIAN PUEBLO CULTURAL CENTER is at 2401 12th St. N.W. The center depicts the history, art and culture of New Mexico's 19 Native American pueblos. The main museum features interactive exhibits, an extensive collection of artifacts and an intergenerational learning classroom. Events and programs offer hands-on learning about the Pueblo people, and traditional dances take place weekly. An exhibit gallery highlights the work of traditional and contemporary artists.

Time: Allow 30 minutes minimum. **Hours:** Daily 9-5. Closed Jan. 1, Memorial Day, July 4, Labor Day, Thanksgiving and Christmas. **Cost:** $8.40; $6.40 (ages 62+, military with ID and New Mexico residents); $5.40 (ages 5-17 and college students with ID). **Phone:** (505) 843-7270 or (866) 855-7902.

NATIONAL MUSEUM OF NUCLEAR SCIENCE & HISTORY is at 601 Eubank Blvd. S.E. The nation's official museum for the history and science of the Nuclear Age features replicas of the world's first two atomic weapons, Little Boy and Fat Man. Exhibits cover such topics as atomic theory, the Cold War, pioneers in nuclear science, uranium processing, radiation facts and the testing of the first atomic bomb. A hands-on physics lab for children also is available. Numerous airplanes and other large artifacts are installed in Heritage Park. Films relating to the history of nuclear development are shown daily.

Time: Allow 2 hours minimum. **Hours:** Daily 9-5. Phone ahead for holiday schedule. Closed Jan. 1, Easter, Thanksgiving and Christmas. **Cost:** $12; $10 (ages 6-17 and 60+); $8 (retired military with ID); $7 (active military with ID). **Phone:** (505) 245-2137.

GEM **NEW MEXICO MUSEUM OF NATURAL HISTORY & SCIENCE** is .5 mi. s. of I-40 on Rio Grande Blvd., then 2 blks. e. to 1801 Mountain Rd. N.W. The origins and geological history of the Southwest are explored through full-scale dinosaur models, a walk-through volcano model, an ice age cave replica, a time machine and a fossil preparation area. A saltwater tide pool, a hands-on naturalist center, botanical exhibits and planetarium shows also are offered. The Lockheed Martin DynaTheater presents giant-screen film adventures to exotic locales.

Time: Allow 1 hour minimum. **Hours:** Daily 9-5 (also first Fri. 5:30-9). DynaTheater films are shown on the hour 10-4; other show schedules vary. Closed Jan. 1, Thanksgiving and Christmas. **Cost:** Museum $8; $7 (ages 60+); $5 (ages 3-12). Planetarium show $7; $6 (ages 60+); $4 (ages 3-12). DynaTheater $7; $6 (ages 60+); $5 (ages 3-12). Combination tickets are available. **Phone:** (505) 841-2800.

GEM **OLD TOWN** is .5 mi. s. of I-40 exit 157A via Rio Grande Blvd. to 303 Romero St. N.W. Albuquerque began where Old Town stands today, and the focal point of community life in the city's beginnings remains a place where people come to meet, sightsee and above all, shop. It doesn't look much like it did some 3 centuries ago, but Old Town's narrow streets, winding brick walkways, hidden patios and wrought-iron benches do invite visitors to relax and stay awhile.

The focal point of this village-like setting is a tree-shaded plaza with a gazebo, the scene of frequent impromptu musical performances. Standing on the plaza's north side is the San Felipe de Neri Church, founded in 1706 by Fray Manuel Moreno, a Franciscan priest. The original church building collapsed during the very rainy summer of 1792; the present adobe structure, in the shape of a cross and with

(See maps & indexes p. 258, 260.)

walls 5 feet thick, dates from 1793. The church's rose garden is a lovely, quiet spot to relax.

Surrounding the plaza is a pedestrian-friendly district (bounded north/south by Mountain Road and Central Avenue and east/west by Rio Grande Boulevard and 19th Street) containing more than 150 shops, boutiques, galleries and artist studios. Browsers will find all things Southwestern, of course, but Old Town shops offer everything from handmade Native American jewelry, Oaxacan woodcarvings and Mata Ortiz pottery to painted ponies, Christmas ornaments and Route 66 memorabilia.

Across from the plaza's east side, in the 200 block of San Felipe Road, vendors and local artists display their wares on blankets under the building *portal* (porch). And it's a sure bet that before you leave you'll see a couple of *ristras,* those hanging strings of dried red chile peppers that all but shout out "New Mexico."

Pick up a free Old Town map at the information center in Plaza Don Luis (303 Romero St.). **Hours:** Guided 75-minute public historical walking tours depart daily at noon, private history tours depart at 10, 2 and 4 from the ticket window at Plaza Don Luis. Ghost tour departs nightly at 8 p.m. (and at 10 p.m. on full moon nights). Pre-paid reservations are required 2-hours in advance of all tours. **Cost:** Tour fee $20; $18 (ages 55+ and active military and college students with ID); $16 (ages 13-17); $10 (ages 6-12). **Phone:** (505) 246-8687. GT

OPEN SPACE VISITOR CENTER is at 6500 Coors Blvd., N.W. The center offers information and resources about Albuquerque's Open Space Division with exhibits interpreting the natural and cultural resources protected by the city-wide program. An art gallery, agricultural fields that draw a variety of wildlife and beautiful views of the Sandia Mountains are offered. Comfortable indoor and outdoor viewing areas are available to watch sandhill cranes and other migratory birds during their fall and winter migratory season. The 16-mile, multiuse Paseo del Bosque trail is accessible from the visitor center. **Time:** Allow 1 hour minimum. **Hours:** Tues.-Sun. 9-5. Closed major holidays. Phone ahead to confirm schedule. **Cost:** Free. **Phone:** (505) 897-8831.

PETROGLYPH NATIONAL MONUMENT is at 6510 Western Trail N.W. Boca Negra Canyon, Rinconada Canyon and Piedras Marcadas Canyon all afford opportunities for viewing petroglyphs by way of self-guiding trails. A visitor center offers general park information only. **Time:** Allow 1 hour minimum. **Hours:** Daily 8:30-4:30. Closed Jan. 1, Thanksgiving and Christmas. **Cost:** Free. **Parking:** $2 (Sat.-Sun.); $1 (Mon.-Fri.) at Boca Negra Canyon. **Phone:** (505) 899-0205, ext. 335.

SANDIA CREST—see Cibola National Forest p. 281.

GEM **SANDIA PEAK AERIAL TRAMWAY** is off I-25 exit 234 (Tramway Road), then 6 mi. e. to 30 Tramway Rd. N.E. The 2.7-mile tramway, one of the world's longest, takes passengers above the deep canyons and spectacular terrain of the western Sandia Mountains in the Cibola National Forest. A Forest Service visitor center is in the upper tram terminal. Restaurants operate at the base and summit.

Sandia Peak is a popular recreation spot. Skiers frequent the 10,378-foot peak from mid-December to mid-March. In summer 24 miles of trails are available for mountain biking. Bicycle rentals are available weekends and holidays, early July through Labor Day, and in October during the Albuquerque International Balloon Fiesta.

Hours: Trams depart every 20-30 minutes daily 9-9, Memorial Day weekend-Labor Day and during the Albuquerque International Balloon Fiesta; every 20-30 minutes Wed.-Mon. 9-8, Tues. 5-8, rest of year. The tram is closed for 10 to 12 days in Apr. and Nov. for maintenance; phone for details. **Cost:** Round-trip tram fare $25; $20 (ages 13-20 and 62+); $15 (ages 5-12). **Phone:** (505) 856-7325.

THE TURQUOISE MUSEUM is at 400 2nd St. S.W. A castle is the setting for this museum, which features rare turquoise specimens from around the world. **Hours:** Mon.-Sat. 10-5. Closed major holidays. **Cost:** $20; $15 (ages 5-17 and 55+). Reservations are required. **Phone:** (505) 247-8650.

UNIVERSITY OF NEW MEXICO is 2 mi. e. on US 66/Central Ave. to 2301 Central Ave. N.E. New Mexico's flagship research university occupies an 800-acre campus with buildings featuring Pueblo Revival-style architecture, and the grounds are designated a National College Arboretum. Of particular interest are several museums and libraries as well as Popejoy Hall, 1 University of New Mexico. Home to the New Mexico Philharmonic, Popejoy Hall also presents lectures, musicals, ballet and concerts by nationally known artists. For schedule information or to purchase tickets for individual events, phone (505) 925-5858 or (877) 664-8661 Mon.-Fri. 10-4.

In December the GEM New Mexico Bowl takes place at Dreamstyle Stadium; teams representing the Mountain West and Western Athletic conferences compete for a 20-inch Zia Pueblo pottery trophy. **Hours:** Academic buildings open Mon.-Fri. 8-5. **Phone:** (505) 277-1989.

Maxwell Museum of Anthropology is on the University of New Mexico campus at 500 University Blvd. N.E. Exhibits explore world cultures, with a special emphasis on the heritage of the Southwest. Permanent exhibits include People of the Southwest and Ancestors. Changing exhibits also are presented. **Hours:** Tues.-Sat. 10-4. Closed major holidays. **Cost:** Donations. **Phone:** (505) 277-4405.

Silver Family Geology Museum of the University of New Mexico is at 221 Yale Blvd. (Northrop Hall) in the Earth and Planetary Sciences Building. Various types of minerals, the geology of the Earth and New Mexico fossils are depicted in more than 20 exhibits. **Time:** Allow 30 minutes minimum. **Hours:** Mon.-Fri.

(See maps & indexes p. 258, 260.)

7:30-noon and 1-4:30. Closed major holidays. **Cost:** Donations. **Phone:** (505) 277-4204.

UNM Art Museum is on the University of New Mexico campus at 203 Cornell Dr. N.E., in the Center for the Arts complex. The permanent collection includes some 30,000 pieces of photography, prints and paintings spanning the 16th through the 21st centuries. **Time:** Allow 1 hour minimum. **Hours:** Tues.-Fri. 10-4, Sat. 10-8. Closed major holidays. **Cost:** Donations. **Phone:** (505) 277-4001.

UNM Meteorite Museum, part of the Institute of Meteoritics, is on the first floor of the Earth and Planetary Sciences Building, 221 Yale Blvd. (106 Northrop Hall) on the University of New Mexico campus. The institute is a center for the teaching and research of space and planetary sciences, and is the home of one of the world's largest collections of meteorites. Hundreds of meteorites discovered throughout the world are displayed, including the 1,000 kg Norton County stony meteorite. **Hours:** Tues. and Thurs. 10-noon and 2-3; Mon. and Wed. 11-2. Closed major and university holidays. Phone ahead to confirm schedule. **Cost:** Free. **Phone:** (505) 277-2747.

UNSER RACING MUSEUM is at 1776 Montano N.W. The museum traces the history of the Unser family in racing from the early 1900s to the present. Exhibits—some interactive—include antique cars, trophies and uniforms. The Indy simulator is sure to get your engine going. Changing exhibits also are offered. **Time:** Allow 1 hour minimum. **Hours:** Daily 10-4. **Cost:** $10; $6 (ages 60+ and military with ID); free (ages 0-16 with adult). **Phone:** (505) 341-1776.

RECREATIONAL ACTIVITIES

Hot Air Ballooning

- **Rainbow Ryders, Inc. Hot Air Balloon Ride Co.** departs from various locations for flights over the Rio Grande Valley. **Hours:** Daily at dawn. **Phone:** (505) 823-1111 or (800) 725-2477. ***(See ad this page.)***

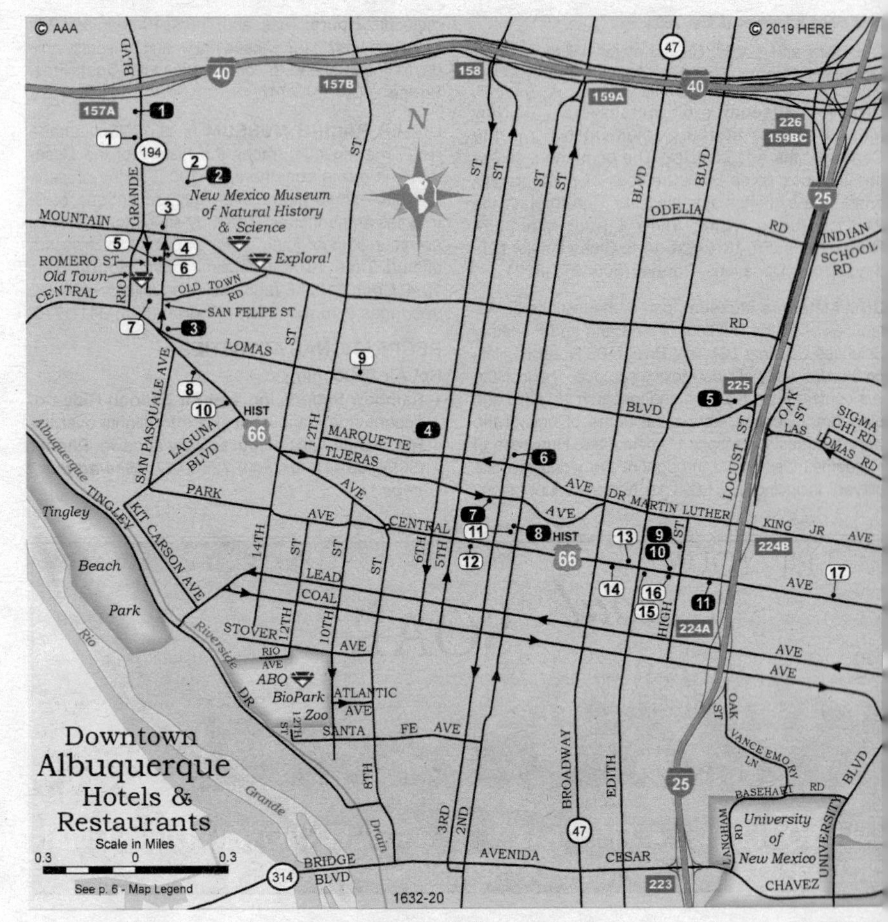

Downtown Albuquerque

This index helps you "spot" where approved hotels and restaurants are located on the corresponding detailed maps. Restaurant price range is a combination of lunch and/or dinner. Turn to the listing page for more information and consult display ads for special promotions.

For more details, rates and reservations: AAA.com/travelguides/hotels

DOWNTOWN ALBUQUERQUE

Map Page	Hotels	Diamond Rated	Member Savings	Page
1 this page	**Best Western Plus Rio Grande Inn** *(See ad p. 267.)*	◆◆◆	✔	266
2 this page	Hotel Chaco	◆◆◆◆		268
3 this page	Bottger Mansion of Old Town	◆◆◆		266
4 this page	Mauger Estate Bed & Breakfast	◆◆◆		268
5 this page	Embassy Suites by Hilton Albuquerque	◆◆◆	✔	266
6 this page	**DoubleTree by Hilton Albuquerque** *(See ad p. 268.)*	◆◆◆	✔	266
7 this page	**Hyatt Regency Albuquerque**	◆◆◆	✔	268
8 this page	**Hotel Andaluz Albuquerque, Curio Collection by Hilton**	◆◆◆◆	✔	268

DOWNTOWN ALBUQUERQUE (cont'd)

Map Page	Hotels (cont'd)	Diamond Rated	Member Savings	Page
9 p. 258	**Albuquerque Downtown Historic Bed & Breakfast**	3 diamonds	✔	266
10 p. 258	Days Inn Albuquerque Downtown	2 diamonds		266
11 p. 258	**Hotel Parq Central**	4 diamonds	✔	268

Map Page	Restaurants	Diamond Rated	Cuisine	Price Range	Page
1 p. 258	D.H. Lescombes Winery & Bistro	2 diamonds	American	$10-$28	269
2 p. 258	Level 5	3 diamonds	American	$12-$54	269
3 p. 258	Seasons Rotisserie & Grill	3 diamonds	American	$8-$32	269
4 p. 258	La Crepe Michel	3 diamonds	French	$8-$23	269
5 p. 258	High Noon Restaurant & Saloon	2 diamonds	Regional American	$11-$37	269
6 p. 258	**Church Street Cafe**	2 diamonds	Mexican	$10-$22	269
7 p. 258	Antiquity Restaurant	3 diamonds	Continental	$20-$32	268
8 p. 258	Vinaigrette	2 diamonds	Natural/Organic	$11-$18	269
9 p. 258	The Cellar	3 diamonds	Spanish Small Plates	$12-$28	268
10 p. 258	Amore Neapolitan Pizzeria	2 diamonds	Pizza	$8-$15	268
11 p. 258	Mas Tapas y Vino	3 diamonds	Spanish	$14-$42	269
12 p. 258	Brixens	2 diamonds	American	$12-$28	268
13 p. 258	The Artichoke Cafe	3 diamonds	New American	$14-$39	268
14 p. 258	Standard Diner	2 diamonds	American	$10-$20	269
15 p. 258	Farina Pizzeria	2 diamonds	Pizza	$8-$19	269
16 p. 258	The Grove Cafe & Market	2 diamonds	Breakfast Sandwiches	$7-$12	269
17 p. 258	66 Diner	2 diamonds	Burgers Desserts	$7-$14	268

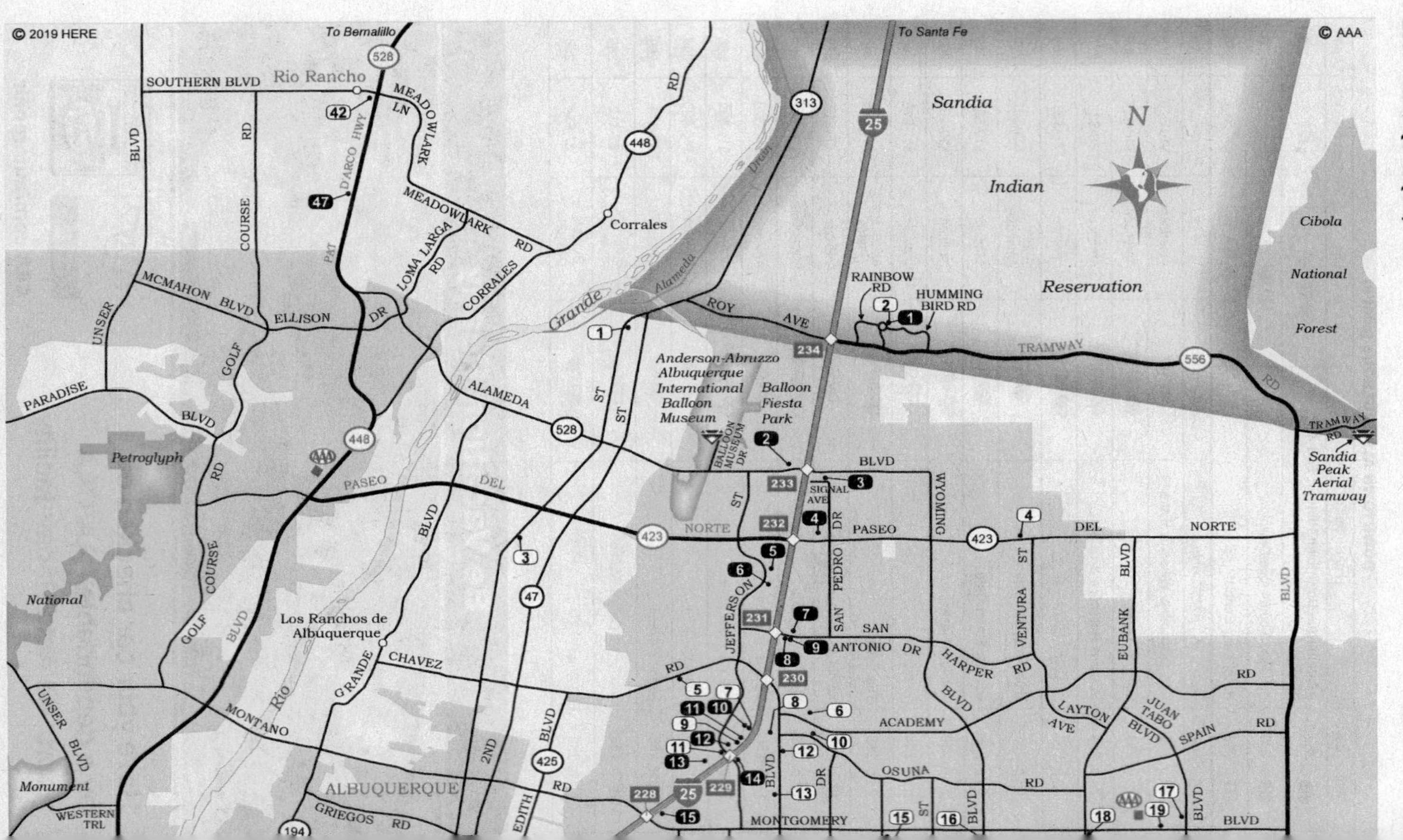

© 2019 HERE
To Bernalillo
To Santa Fe
© AAA
528
Rio Rancho
SOUTHERN BLVD
MEADOWLARK
LN
42
D'ARCO HWY
PAT
47
COURSE
RD
BLVD
MEADOWLARK
RD
LOMA LARGA
RD
CORRALES
Corrales
448
RD
313
25
Sandia
Indian
Reservation
N
Cibola
National
Forest
Drain
Alameda
Grande
RAINBOW
RD
HUMMING
BIRD RD
ROY
AVE
234
TRAMWAY
556
RD
TRAMWAY
RD
Sandia
Peak
Aerial
Tramway
MCMAHON
BLVD
ELLISON
DR
UNSER
GOLF
PARADISE
BLVD
ALAMEDA
528
ST
Anderson-Abruzzo
Albuquerque
International
Balloon
Museum
Balloon
Fiesta
Park
BALLOON
MUSEUM
DR
BLVD
233
SIGNAL
AVE
WYOMING
Petroglyph
PASEO
DEL
NORTE
423
232
PASEO
DR
DEL
NORTE
ST
VENTURA
EUBANK
BLVD
COURSE
GOLF
BLVD
3
47
JEFFERSON
SAN
PEDRO
231
SAN
ANTONIO
DR
HARPER
RD
National
Los Ranchos de
Albuquerque
CHAVEZ
GRANDE
Rio
RD
230
ACADEMY
LAYTON
AVE
JUAN
TABO
BLVD
SPAIN
RD
UNSER
BLVD
MONTANO
2ND
BLVD
425
OSUNA
RD
Monument
WESTERN
TRL
ALBUQUERQUE
GRIEGOS
RD
194
EDITH
228
229
MONTGOMERY
BLVD

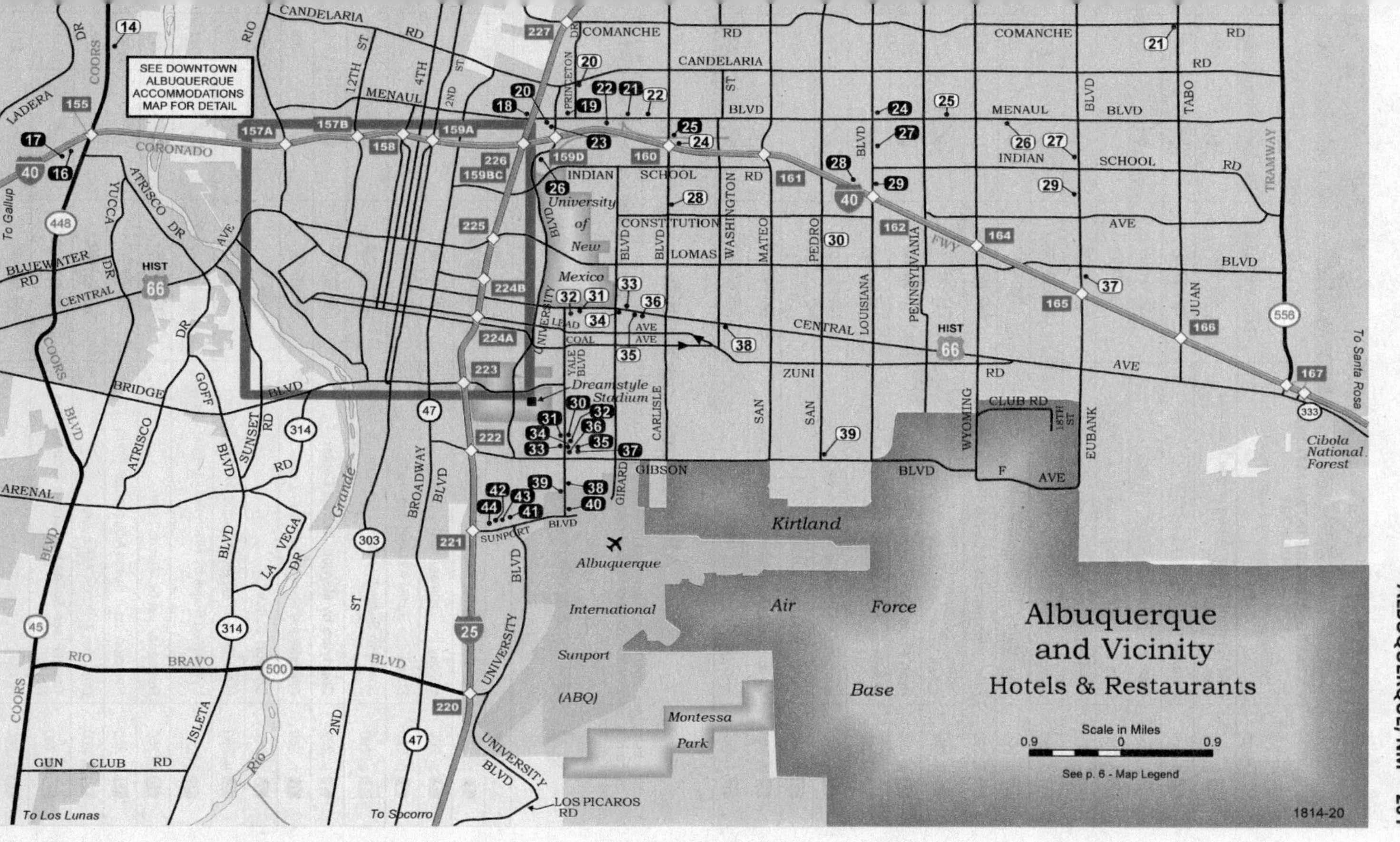
Albuquerque and Vicinity
Hotels & Restaurants
Scale in Miles
0.9 0 0.9
See p. 6 - Map Legend
1814-20
SEE DOWNTOWN ALBUQUERQUE ACCOMMODATIONS MAP FOR DETAIL
To Gallup
To Santa Rosa
To Los Lunas
To Socorro
Cibola National Forest
Kirtland Air Force Base
Albuquerque International Sunport (ABQ)
Montessa Park
University of New Mexico
Dreamstyle Stadium
Rio Grande

Airport Hotels

Map Page	**ALBUQUERQUE INTERNATIONAL SUNPORT** (Maximum driving distance from airport: 1.6 mi)	Diamond Rated	Member Savings	Page
38 p. 260	**Best Western Airport Albuquerque InnSuites Hotel & Suites, 1.0 mi**	◆◆	✔	269
31 p. 260	**Comfort Inn Airport, 1.5 mi**	◆◆◆	✔	269
34 p. 260	Courtyard by Marriott Airport, 1.4 mi	◆◆◆	✔	270
35 p. 260	Days Inn & Suites Albuquerque Airport, 1.5 mi	◆◆		270
36 p. 260	Fairfield Inn & Suites by Marriott Airport, 1.4 mi	◆◆◆	✔	270
44 p. 260	Hampton Inn & Suites Albuquerque Airport, 1.6 mi	◆◆◆	✔	270
39 p. 260	Hilton Garden Inn Albuquerque Airport, 1.0 mi	◆◆	✔	270
33 p. 260	Holiday Inn Express & Suites, 1.4 mi	◆◆◆		270
41 p. 260	Homewood Suites by Hilton Albuquerque Airport, 1.4 mi	◆◆◆	✔	271
43 p. 260	**Hyatt Place Albuquerque Airport, 1.4 mi**	◆◆◆	✔	271
30 p. 260	Residence Inn by Marriott Albuquerque Airport, 1.5 mi	◆◆◆	✔	271
40 p. 260	Sheraton Albuquerque Airport Hotel, 0.7 mi	◆◆◆	✔	272
32 p. 260	Sleep Inn Airport Albuquerque, 1.5 mi	◆◆		272
42 p. 260	Staybridge Suites Albuquerque Airport, 1.5 mi	◆◆◆		272
37 p. 260	TownePlace Suites by Marriott, 1.5 mi	◆◆◆	✔	272

Albuquerque and Vicinity

This index helps you "spot" where approved hotels and restaurants are located on the corresponding detailed maps. Restaurant price range is a combination of lunch and/or dinner. Turn to the listing page for more information and consult display ads for special promotions.

For more details, rates and reservations: AAA.com/travelguides/hotels

ALBUQUERQUE

Map Page	Hotels	Diamond Rated	Member Savings	Page
1 p. 260	**Sandia Resort & Casino**	◆◆◆◆	✔	272
2 p. 260	Holiday Inn Express Hotel & Suites	◆◆◆		270
3 p. 260	Staybridge Suites Albuquerque North	◆◆◆		272
4 p. 260	SpringHill Suites by Marriott Albuquerque Journal Center North	◆◆◆	✔	272
5 p. 260	**Courtyard by Marriott Journal Center**	◆◆◆	✔	270
6 p. 260	Albuquerque Marriott Pyramid North	◆◆◆	✔	269
7 p. 260	**Comfort Suites**	◆◆	✔	269
8 p. 260	Hilton Garden Inn Albuquerque Journal Center	◆◆◆	✔	270
9 p. 260	Homewood Suites by Hilton-Albuquerque Journal Center	◆◆◆	✔	271
10 p. 260	Residence Inn by Marriott North	◆◆◆	✔	271
11 p. 260	Hampton Inn & Suites Albuquerque North I-25	◆◆◆	✔	270
12 p. 260	Drury Inn & Suites-Albuquerque	◆◆◆		270
13 p. 260	**TownePlace Suites by Marriott Albuquerque North**	◆◆◆	✔	272
14 p. 260	Holiday Inn Hotel & Suites	◆◆◆		271

ALBUQUERQUE (cont'd)

Map Page	Hotels (cont'd)	Diamond Rated	Member Savings	Page
15 p. 260	**Best Western Plus Executive Suites**	♦♦♦	✔	269
16 p. 260	Days Inn West Albuquerque	♦		270
17 p. 260	**Hampton Inn & Suites**	♦♦♦	✔	270
18 p. 260	Quality Inn & Suites	♦♦		271
19 p. 260	La Quinta Inn & Suites Albuquerque Midtown	♦♦♦		271
20 p. 260	**Fairfield by Marriott Albuquerque-University Area**	♦♦♦	✔	270
21 p. 260	Candlewood Suites	♦♦		269
22 p. 260	Holiday Inn Express Albuquerque Midtown	♦♦♦		270
23 p. 260	Crowne Plaza Albuquerque	♦♦♦		270
24 p. 260	Sheraton Albuquerque Uptown Hotel *(See ad p. 266.)*	♦♦♦	✔	272
25 p. 260	**Hampton Inn University-Midtown**	♦♦♦	✔	270
26 p. 260	Home2 Suites by Hilton Albuquerque Downtownn	♦♦♦	✔	271
27 p. 260	**Hyatt Place Albuquerque Uptown**	♦♦♦	✔	271
28 p. 260	Hilton Garden Inn Albuquerque Uptown	♦♦♦	✔	270
29 p. 260	**Albuquerque Marriott Hotel**	♦♦♦	✔	269
30 p. 260	Residence Inn by Marriott Albuquerque Airport	♦♦♦	✔	271
31 p. 260	**Comfort Inn Airport**	♦♦♦	✔	269
32 p. 260	Sleep Inn Airport Albuquerque	♦♦		272
33 p. 260	Holiday Inn Express & Suites	♦♦♦		270
34 p. 260	Courtyard by Marriott Airport	♦♦♦	✔	270
35 p. 260	Days Inn & Suites Albuquerque Airport	♦♦		270
36 p. 260	Fairfield Inn & Suites by Marriott Airport	♦♦♦	✔	270
37 p. 260	TownePlace Suites by Marriott	♦♦♦	✔	272
38 p. 260	**Best Western Airport Albuquerque InnSuites Hotel & Suites**	♦♦	✔	269
39 p. 260	Hilton Garden Inn Albuquerque Airport	♦♦	✔	270
40 p. 260	Sheraton Albuquerque Airport Hotel	♦♦♦	✔	272
41 p. 260	Homewood Suites by Hilton Albuquerque Airport	♦♦♦	✔	271
42 p. 260	Staybridge Suites Albuquerque Airport	♦♦♦		272
43 p. 260	**Hyatt Place Albuquerque Airport** *(See ad p. 271.)*	♦♦♦	✔	271
44 p. 260	Hampton Inn & Suites Albuquerque Airport	♦♦♦	✔	270

Map Page	Restaurants	Diamond Rated	Cuisine	Price Range	Page
1 p. 260	El Pinto	♦♦	Mexican	$8-$30	272
2 p. 260	Bien Shur Restaurant	♦♦♦	International	$26-$50	272
3 p. 260	Casa de Benavidez New Mexican Restaurant	♦♦	Mexican	$9-$22	272
4 p. 260	Jinja Bar & Bistro	♦♦	Asian	$10-$18	272
5 p. 260	Vic's Daily Cafe	♦♦	American	$6-$10	273
6 p. 260	**Trombino's Bistro Italiano**	♦♦♦	Italian	$13-$30	273
7 p. 260	P.F. Chang's China Bistro	♦♦♦	Chinese	$8-$25	273

Map Page	Restaurants (cont'd)	Diamond Rated	Cuisine	Price Range	Page
8 p. 260	Saigon Restaurant	◆◆	Vietnamese	$8-$20	273
9 p. 260	Pars Cuisine	◆◆◆	Mediterranean	$10-$29	273
10 p. 260	Monroe's Restaurant	◆◆	Mexican	$9-$22	273
11 p. 260	Nick & Jimmy's Restaurant & Bar	◆◆	Mediterranean	$12-$30	273
12 p. 260	Siam Cafe	◆◆	Thai	$8-$11	273
13 p. 260	Azuma	◆◆	Japanese	$9-$30	272
14 p. 260	Mimmo's Ristorante & Pizzeria	◆◆	Italian	$8-$18	273
15 p. 260	Weck's	◆◆	American	$8-$10	273
16 p. 260	Range Cafe	◆◆	American	$8-$18	273
17 p. 260	Flying Star Cafe	◆◆	American	$9-$15	272
18 p. 260	Scarpa's Brick Oven Pizza	◆◆	Italian	$9-$15	273
19 p. 260	Savoy Bar & Grill	◆◆◆	American	$9-$38	273
20 p. 260	Milly's Restaurant	◆◆	American	$5-$10	273
21 p. 260	Garcia's Kitchen	◆◆	Mexican	$5-$15	272
22 p. 260	Richard's Mexican Restaurant	◆◆	Mexican	$6-$10	273
24 p. 260	AMORE Neapolitan Pizzeria	◆	Italian Pizza	$6-$15	272
25 p. 260	Krung Thai	◆◆	Thai	$7-$13	273
26 p. 260	Los Cuates del Norte	◆◆	Mexican	$9-$20	273
27 p. 260	Paisano's Italian Restaurant	◆◆	Italian	$11-$30	273
28 p. 260	Taj Mahal Cuisine of India	◆◆	Indian	$10-$18	273
29 p. 260	Ming Dynasty	◆◆	Chinese	$7-$12	273
30 p. 260	Christy Mae's	◆◆	American	$9-$11	272
31 p. 260	Frontier Restaurant	◆	Mexican	$4-$9	272
32 p. 260	Salt And Board	◆◆	American	$10-$24	273
33 p. 260	Zinc Wine Bar & Bistro	◆◆◆	American	$17-$32	273
34 p. 260	Mannie's	◆◆	American	$10-$12	273
35 p. 260	Nob Hill Bar & Grill	◆◆	American	$11-$25	273
36 p. 260	Kelly's Brewery & Restaurant	◆◆	American	$10-$14	272
37 p. 260	The Owl Cafe	◆◆	American	$5-$12	273
38 p. 260	Loyola's Family Restaurant	◆◆	Mexican	$7-$13	273
39 p. 260	**Cervantes Restaurant & Lounge**	◆◆	Regional Mexican	$9-$26	272

RIO RANCHO

Map Page	Hotel	Diamond Rated	Member Savings	Page
47 p. 260	Hilton Garden Inn Albuquerque North/Rio Rancho	◆◆◆	✔	296

Map Page	Restaurant	Diamond Rated	Cuisine	Price Range	Page
42 p. 260	O'Hare's Grille & Pub	◆◆	American	$7-$22	296

▼ *See AAA listing p. 272* ▼

DOWNTOWN ALBUQUERQUE

- Restaurants p. 268
- Hotels & Restaurants map & index p. 258

ALBUQUERQUE DOWNTOWN HISTORIC BED & BREAKFAST

505/842-0223 **9**

Historic Bed & Breakfast

Address: 207 & 209 High St NE 87102 **Location:** I-25 exit 224A northbound; exit 224B southbound, just w, then just n. **Facility:** The property is comprised of beautifully restored homes and cottages nestled in what was once Albuquerque's first subdivision. The Spy House offers a glimpse of historic national intrigue. 10 units, some kitchens and cottages. 1-2 stories (no elevator), interior corridors. **Parking:** on-site and street. **Activities:** hot tub. **Guest Services:** complimentary and valet laundry. **Featured Amenity: full hot breakfast.**

SAVE | BIZ | HS | / SOME UNITS

BEST WESTERN PLUS RIO GRANDE INN

505/843-9500 **1**

Hotel

AAA Benefit: Members save up to 15% and earn bonus points!

Address: 1015 Rio Grande Blvd NW 87104 **Location:** I-40 exit 157A, just s. **Facility:** 173 units. 4 stories, interior corridors. **Amenities:** *Some:* safes. **Pool:** heated outdoor. **Activities:** hot tub, exercise room. **Guest Services:** valet and coin laundry, area transportation. *(See ad p. 267.)*

SAVE

BIZ | HS | / SOME UNITS

BOTTGER MANSION OF OLD TOWN

505/243-3639 **3**

Historic Bed & Breakfast. **Address:** 110 San Felipe St NW 87104

DAYS INN ALBUQUERQUE DOWNTOWN

505/247-8897 **10**

Motel. **Address:** 615 Central Ave NE 87102

DOUBLETREE BY HILTON ALBUQUERQUE

505/247-3344 **6**

Hotel

AAA Benefit: Members save up to 15%!

Address: 201 Marquette Ave NW 87102 **Location:** I-25 exit 224B (Central Ave), 0.8 mi w to 2nd St, then just n. **Facility:** 295 units. 15 stories, interior corridors. **Parking:** on-site (fee). **Amenities:** video games, safes. **Pool:** outdoor. **Activities:** exercise room. **Guest Services:** valet laundry. *(See ad p. 268.)*

SAVE

CALL | BIZ

/ SOME UNITS

EMBASSY SUITES BY HILTON ALBUQUERQUE

505/245-7100 **5**

SAVE Hotel. **Address:** 1000 Woodward Pl NE 87102

AAA Benefit: Members save up to 15%!

Rio Grande Inn

Old Town Charm

Enjoy your Albuquerque experience at our ideal location, within walking distance of Old Town Plaza, five museums, and dozens of restaurants, shops, and galleries. Just minutes away are the Albuquerque Zoo, and Bio Park, Indian Pueblo Cultural Center and Downtown Business District. Exit 157A off I-40 at Rio Grande Blvd.

The Zia Lounge is a great gathering place for good conversation, savory food and local brews.

All guestrooms have custom hand-carved furnishings, free Wi-Fi, 42" flat screen TV, mini-fridge and coffee maker.

Lounge by our outdoor pool and hot tub after a long day of sightseeing. Enjoy year round swimming when they are both enclosed for the winter.

free local shuttle | free parking | free wireless Internet
satellite TV w/ 150+ HD channels | Albuquerque Bar & Grill restaurant onsite

riograndeinn.com • 800.959.4726
1015 Rio Grande Blvd NW Albuquerque, New Mexico 87104 • 505.843.9500

(See map & index p. 258.)

HOTEL ANDALUZ ALBUQUERQUE, CURIO COLLECTION BY HILTON 505/242-9090 8

Historic Hotel

CURIO A COLLECTION BY HILTON **AAA Benefit:** Members save up to 15%!

Address: 125 2nd St NW 87102 **Location:** I-25 exit 224A northbound; exit 224B southbound; jct Copper Ave. Located in a commercial area. **Facility:** This historic hotel boasts stylish Andalusian-influenced décor throughout. Guest rooms feature contemporary, upscale appointments and amenities. 107 units. 10 stories, interior corridors. **Parking:** valet only. **Amenities:** safes. **Activities:** health club. **Guest Services:** valet laundry.

SAVE BIZ HS / SOME UNITS

HOTEL CHACO 505/246-9989 2

Hotel. **Address:** 2000 Bellamah Ave NW 87104

HOTEL PARQ CENTRAL 505/242-0040 11

Historic Boutique Resort Hotel

Address: 806 Central Ave SE 87102 **Location:** I-25 exit 224B southbound; exit 224A northbound, just w. **Facility:** In a renovated 1926 hospital, the property reflects a blend of historic elegance and contemporary comfort with chic stylish décor. The trendy rooftop bar has incredible sunset views over downtown. 74 units. 4 stories, interior corridors. **Amenities:** safes. **Activities:** hot tub, exercise room, massage. **Guest Services:** valet and coin laundry, area transportation. **Featured Amenity: continental breakfast.**

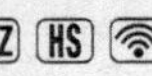

HYATT REGENCY ALBUQUERQUE 505/842-1234 7

Hotel

AAA Benefit: Members save up to 10%!

Address: 330 Tijeras Ave NW 87102 **Location:** I-25 exit 224B, 0.5 mi w on Dr Martin Luther King Jr Ave, just s on 3rd St, then just w. **Facility:** 382 units. 20 stories, interior corridors. **Parking:** on-site (fee) and valet. **Amenities:** *Some:* safes. **Dining:** 4 restaurants. **Pool:** heated outdoor. **Activities:** sauna, hot tub, recreation programs, exercise room, massage. **Guest Services:** valet laundry.

MAUGER ESTATE BED & BREAKFAST 505/242-8755 4

Historic Bed & Breakfast. **Address:** 701 Roma Ave NW 87102

WHERE TO EAT

66 DINER 505/247-1421 17

Burgers Desserts. Casual Dining. **Address:** 1405 Central Ave NE 87106

AMORE NEAPOLITAN PIZZERIA 505/312-8784 10

Pizza. Casual Dining. **Address:** 1700 Central Ave SW 87104

ANTIQUITY RESTAURANT 505/247-3545 7

Continental. Fine Dining. **Address:** 112 Romero St NW 87104

THE ARTICHOKE CAFE 505/243-0200 13

New American. Fine Dining. **Address:** 424 Central Ave SE 87102

BRIXENS 505/242-2400 12

American. Gastropub. **Address:** 400 Central Ave SW 87102

THE CELLAR 505/242-3117 9

Spanish Small Plates. Casual Dining. **Address:** 1025 Lomas Blvd NW 87102

▼ See AAA listing p. 266 ▼

(See map & index p. 258.)

CHURCH STREET CAFE 505/247-8522 (6)

Mexican Casual Dining $10-$22

AAA Inspector Notes: *Historic.* This 1706 adobe house also contains an art gallery. Tasty Mexican dishes, such as tamales, chiles rellenos and burritos, as well as a selection of sandwiches, are served in the dining room and on the patio. **Features:** beer & wine, patio dining. **Address:** 2111 Church St NW 87104 **Location:** I-40 exit 157A (Rio Grande Blvd), 0.5 mi s to Mountain Rd, then just e; in Old Town. **Parking:** street only. B L D

D.H. LESCOMBES WINERY & BISTRO 505/243-9916 (1)

American. Casual Dining. **Address:** 901 Rio Grande Blvd NW, Suite B-100 87104

FARINA PIZZERIA 505/243-0130 (15)

Pizza. Casual Dining. **Address:** 510 Central Ave SE 87102

THE GROVE CAFE & MARKET 505/248-9800 (16)

Breakfast Sandwiches. Quick Serve. **Address:** 600 Central Ave SE 87102

HIGH NOON RESTAURANT & SALOON 505/765-1455 (5)

Regional American. Casual Dining. **Address:** 425 San Felipe NW 87104

LA CREPE MICHEL 505/242-1251 (4)

French. Casual Dining. **Address:** 400 San Felipe St NW, Unit C-2 87104

LEVEL 5 505/246-9989 (2)

American. Casual Dining. **Address:** 2000 Bellamah Ave NW 87104

MAS TAPAS Y VINO 505/923-9080 (11)

Spanish. Casual Dining. **Address:** 125 Second St NW 87102

SEASONS ROTISSERIE & GRILL 505/766-5100 (3)

American. Fine Dining. **Address:** 2031 Mountain Rd NW 87104

STANDARD DINER 505/243-1440 (14)

American. Casual Dining. **Address:** 320 Central Ave SE 87102

VINAIGRETTE 505/842-5507 (8)

Natural/Organic. Casual Dining. **Address:** 1828 Central Ave SW 87104

ALBUQUERQUE

- Restaurants p. 272
- Hotels & Restaurants map & index p. 260

ALBUQUERQUE MARRIOTT HOTEL 505/881-6800 (29)

AAA Benefit: Members save 5% or more!

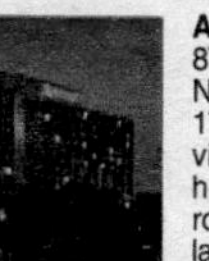

Address: 2101 Louisiana Blvd NE 87110 **Location:** I-40 exit 162, just n; in Northeast Heights. **Facility:** 411 units. 17 stories, interior corridors. **Amenities:** video games. **Pool:** heated outdoor, heated indoor. **Activities:** exercise room. **Guest Services:** valet and coin laundry, area transportation.

ALBUQUERQUE MARRIOTT PYRAMID NORTH 505/821-3333 (6)

SAVE Hotel. **Address:** 5151 San Francisco Rd NE 87109

AAA Benefit: Members save 5% or more!

BEST WESTERN AIRPORT ALBUQUERQUE INNSUITES HOTEL & SUITES 505/242-7022 (38)

Hotel

AAA Benefit: Members save up to 15% and earn bonus points!

Address: 2400 Yale Blvd SE 87106 **Location:** I-25 exit 222 (Gibson Blvd) northbound; exit 222A southbound, 1 mi e, then just s. **Facility:** 109 units, some kitchens. 2 stories (no elevator), interior corridors. **Pool:** heated outdoor. **Activities:** hot tub, exercise room. **Guest Services:** valet and coin laundry, area transportation. **Featured Amenity:** breakfast buffet.

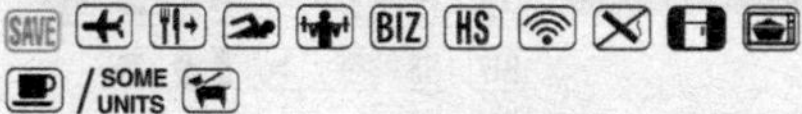

/ SOME UNITS

BEST WESTERN PLUS EXECUTIVE SUITES 505/830-0900 (15)

AAA Benefit: Members save up to 15% and earn bonus points!

Address: 4630 Pan American Frwy NE 87109 **Location:** I-25 exit 228, just ne on Montgomery Blvd/Montano Rd NE. **Facility:** 89 units. 3 stories, interior corridors. **Pool:** heated indoor. **Activities:** hot tub, exercise room. **Guest Services:** coin laundry. **Featured Amenity:** breakfast buffet.

CANDLEWOOD SUITES 505/888-3424 (21)

Extended Stay Hotel. **Address:** 3025 Menaul Blvd NE 87107

COMFORT INN AIRPORT 505/242-0036 (31)

Address: 1801 Yale Blvd SE 87106 **Location:** I-25 exit 222A; exit 222 northbound, 1 mi e on Gibson Blvd, then just n. **Facility:** 72 units. 3 stories, interior corridors. **Pool:** heated indoor. **Activities:** hot tub, exercise room. **Guest Services:** valet and coin laundry, area transportation. **Featured Amenity:** full hot breakfast.

SAVE CALL BIZ

/ SOME UNITS

COMFORT SUITES 505/797-0850 (7)

Address: 5251 San Antonio Dr NE 87109 **Location:** I-25 exit 231, just e. **Facility:** 70 units. 3 stories, interior corridors. **Pool:** heated indoor. **Activities:** hot tub, exercise room. **Guest Services:** coin laundry. **Featured Amenity:** breakfast buffet.

(See map & index p. 260.)

COURTYARD BY MARRIOTT AIRPORT 505/843-6600 34

SAVE Hotel. **Address:** 1920 Yale Blvd SE 87106

AAA Benefit: Members save 5% or more!

COURTYARD BY MARRIOTT JOURNAL CENTER 505/823-1919 5

Hotel

COURTYARD **AAA Benefit:** Members save 5% or more!

Address: 5151 Journal Center Blvd NE 87109 **Location:** I-25 exit 232, just s on Pan American Frwy NE. **Facility:** 150 units. 1-4 stories, interior corridors. *Bath:* some shared. **Terms:** check-in 4 pm. **Pool:** heated indoor. **Activities:** exercise room. **Guest Services:** valet and coin laundry.

SAVE CALL BIZ HS

/ SOME UNITS

CROWNE PLAZA ALBUQUERQUE 505/884-2500 23

Hotel. **Address:** 1901 University Blvd NE 87102

DAYS INN & SUITES ALBUQUERQUE AIRPORT 505/247-1500 35

Hotel. **Address:** 2331 Centre Ave SE 87106

DAYS INN WEST ALBUQUERQUE 505/836-3297 16

Motel. **Address:** 6031 Iliff Rd NW 87121

DRURY INN & SUITES-ALBUQUERQUE 505/341-3600 12

Hotel. **Address:** 4310 The 25 Way NE 87109

FAIRFIELD BY MARRIOTT ALBUQUERQUE-UNIVERSITY AREA 505/889-4000 20

Hotel

Fairfield **AAA Benefit:** Members save 5% or more!

Address: 1760 Menaul Blvd NE 87102 **Location:** I-40 exit 159D, just n. **Facility:** 189 units. 3 stories, interior corridors. **Pool:** heated indoor. **Activities:** sauna, hot tub, exercise room. **Guest Services:** valet and coin laundry. **Featured Amenity: breakfast buffet.**

SAVE CALL BIZ

/ SOME UNITS

FAIRFIELD INN & SUITES BY MARRIOTT AIRPORT 505/247-1621 36

SAVE Hotel. **Address:** 2300 Centre Ave SE 87106

AAA Benefit: Members save 5% or more!

HAMPTON INN & SUITES 505/833-3700 17

Hotel

AAA Benefit: Members save up to 15%!

Address: 6150 Iliff Rd NW 87121 **Location:** I-40 exit 155, 0.6 mi s, then just w. **Facility:** 88 units. 4 stories, interior corridors. **Pool:** heated indoor. **Activities:** hot tub, exercise room. **Guest Services:** coin laundry.

SAVE CALL BIZ

HAMPTON INN & SUITES ALBUQUERQUE AIRPORT 505/246-3574 44

SAVE Hotel. **Address:** 1300 Woodward Rd SE 87106

AAA Benefit: Members save up to 15%!

HAMPTON INN & SUITES ALBUQUERQUE NORTH I-25 505/345-4500 11

SAVE Hotel. **Address:** 4412 The 25 Way 87109

AAA Benefit: Members save up to 15%!

HAMPTON INN UNIVERSITY-MIDTOWN 505/837-9300 25

Hotel

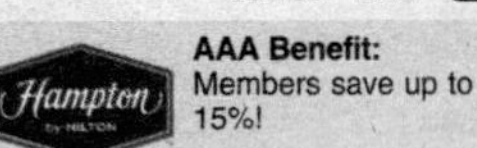

AAA Benefit: Members save up to 15%!

Address: 2300 Carlisle Blvd NE 87110 **Location:** I-40 exit 160, just w, then just n. **Facility:** 126 units. 4 stories, interior corridors. **Pool:** heated outdoor. **Activities:** hot tub, exercise room. **Guest Services:** coin laundry. **Featured Amenity: full hot breakfast.**

SAVE CALL BIZ

HILTON GARDEN INN ALBUQUERQUE AIRPORT 505/765-1000 39

SAVE Hotel. **Address:** 2601 Yale Blvd SE 87106

AAA Benefit: Members save up to 15%!

HILTON GARDEN INN ALBUQUERQUE JOURNAL CENTER 505/314-0800 8

SAVE Hotel. **Address:** 5320 San Antonio Dr NE 87109

AAA Benefit: Members save up to 15%!

HILTON GARDEN INN ALBUQUERQUE UPTOWN 505/944-0300 28

SAVE Hotel. **Address:** 6510 Americas Pkwy 87110

AAA Benefit: Members save up to 15%!

HOLIDAY INN EXPRESS ALBUQUERQUE MIDTOWN 505/881-0544 22

Hotel. **Address:** 2500 Menaul Blvd NE 87107

HOLIDAY INN EXPRESS & SUITES 505/338-5255 33

Hotel. **Address:** 1921 Yale Blvd SE 87106

HOLIDAY INN EXPRESS HOTEL & SUITES 505/797-2291 2

Hotel. **Address:** 5401 Alameda Blvd NE 87113

(See map & index p. 260.)

HOLIDAY INN HOTEL & SUITES 505/944-2222 14

Hotel. **Address:** 5050 Jefferson St NE 87109

HOME2 SUITES BY HILTON ALBUQUERQUE DOWNTOWNN 505/242-0002 26

SAVE Extended Stay Hotel. **Address:** 1660 University Blvd NE 87102

AAA Benefit: Members save up to 15%!

HOMEWOOD SUITES BY HILTON ALBUQUERQUE AIRPORT 505/944-4663 41

SAVE Extended Stay Hotel. **Address:** 1520 Sunport Pl SE 87106

AAA Benefit: Members save up to 15%!

HOMEWOOD SUITES BY HILTON-ALBUQUERQUE JOURNAL CENTER 505/998-4663 9

SAVE Extended Stay Hotel. **Address:** 5400 San Antonio Dr NE 87109

AAA Benefit: Members save up to 15%!

HYATT PLACE ALBUQUERQUE AIRPORT 505/242-9300 43

Hotel

HYATT PLACE **AAA Benefit:** Members save up to 10%!

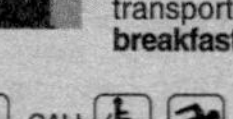

Address: 1400 Sunport Pl SE 87106 **Location:** I-25 exit 221, 0.3 mi e to University Blvd exit, then just n to Woodward Rd. **Facility:** 127 units. 6 stories, interior corridors. **Amenities:** safes. **Pool:** heated outdoor. **Activities:** exercise room. **Guest Services:** valet laundry, area transportation. **Featured Amenity:** breakfast buffet. *(See ad this page.)*

SAVE CALL BIZ

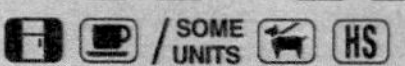

/ SOME UNITS HS

HYATT PLACE ALBUQUERQUE UPTOWN 505/872-9000 27

Hotel

HYATT PLACE **AAA Benefit:** Members save up to 10%!

Address: 6901 Arvada Ave NE 87110 **Location:** I-40 exit 162, 0.7 mi n. **Facility:** 126 units. 6 stories, interior corridors. **Amenities:** safes. **Pool:** heated outdoor. **Activities:** exercise room. **Guest Services:** valet laundry. **Featured Amenity: breakfast buffet.**

SAVE CALL BIZ

/ SOME UNITS HS

ISLETA RESORT & CASINO 505/724-3800

Resort Hotel. **Address:** 11000 Broadway SE 87105

LA QUINTA INN & SUITES ALBUQUERQUE MIDTOWN 505/761-5600 19

Hotel. **Address:** 2011 Menaul Blvd 87107

QUALITY INN & SUITES 505/345-0010 18

Hotel. **Address:** 1315 Menaul Blvd NE 87107

RESIDENCE INN BY MARRIOTT ALBUQUERQUE AIRPORT 505/242-2844 30

SAVE Extended Stay Hotel. **Address:** 2301 International Dr SE 87106

AAA Benefit: Members save 5% or more!

RESIDENCE INN BY MARRIOTT NORTH 505/761-0200 10

SAVE Extended Stay Hotel. **Address:** 4331 The Lane at 25 NE 87109

AAA Benefit: Members save 5% or more!

ROUTE 66 CASINO HOTEL 505/352-7866

Hotel. **Address:** 14500 Central Ave SW 87121

▼ *See AAA listing this page* ▼

(See map & index p. 260.)

SANDIA RESORT & CASINO 505/796-7500 **1**

Resort Hotel

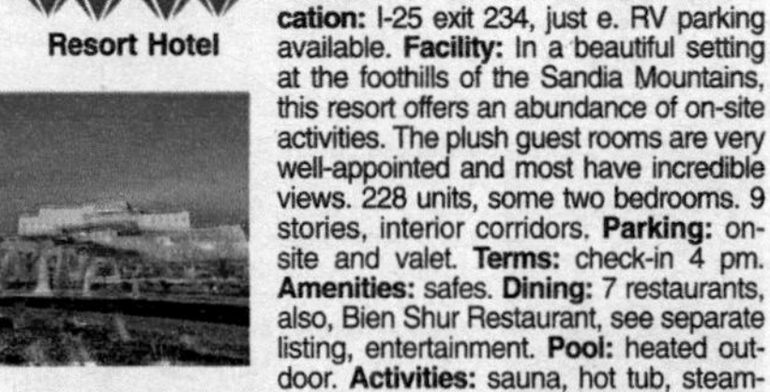

Address: 30 Rainbow Rd NE 87113 **Location:** I-25 exit 234, just e. RV parking available. **Facility:** In a beautiful setting at the foothills of the Sandia Mountains, this resort offers an abundance of on-site activities. The plush guest rooms are very well-appointed and most have incredible views. 228 units, some two bedrooms. 9 stories, interior corridors. **Parking:** on-site and valet. **Terms:** check-in 4 pm. **Amenities:** safes. **Dining:** 7 restaurants, also, Bien Shur Restaurant, see separate listing, entertainment. **Pool:** heated outdoor. **Activities:** sauna, hot tub, steamroom, regulation golf, recreation programs, exercise room, spa. **Guest Services:** valet laundry, area transportation.

SAVE CALL BIZ HS

SHERATON ALBUQUERQUE AIRPORT HOTEL 505/843-7000 **40**

SAVE Hotel. **Address:** 2910 Yale Blvd SE 87106

AAA Benefit: Members save 5% or more!

SHERATON ALBUQUERQUE UPTOWN HOTEL 505/881-0000 **24**

AAA Benefit: Members save 5% or more!

SAVE Hotel. **Address:** 2600 Louisiana Blvd NE 87110 ***(See ad p. 266.)***

SLEEP INN AIRPORT ALBUQUERQUE 505/244-0423 **32**

Hotel. **Address:** 2300 International Ave SE 87106

SPRINGHILL SUITES BY MARRIOTT ALBUQUERQUE JOURNAL CENTER NORTH 505/856-5910 **4**

SAVE Hotel. **Address:** 5910 Holly Ave NE 87109

AAA Benefit: Members save 5% or more!

STAYBRIDGE SUITES ALBUQUERQUE AIRPORT 505/338-3900 **42**

Extended Stay Hotel. **Address:** 1350 Sunport Pl SE 87106

STAYBRIDGE SUITES ALBUQUERQUE NORTH 505/266-7829 **3**

Extended Stay Hotel. **Address:** 5817 Signal Ave NE 87113

TOWNEPLACE SUITES BY MARRIOTT 505/232-5800 **37**

SAVE Extended Stay Hotel. **Address:** 2400 Centre Ave SE 87106

AAA Benefit: Members save 5% or more!

TOWNEPLACE SUITES BY MARRIOTT ALBUQUERQUE NORTH 505/345-3131 **13**

Extended Stay Hotel

TOWNEPLACE SUITES MARRIOTT **AAA Benefit:** Members save 5% or more!

Address: 5511 Office Blvd NE 87109 **Location:** I-25 exit 229 (Jefferson St), just s. **Facility:** 91 units, some two bedrooms, efficiencies and kitchens. 4 stories, interior corridors. **Pool:** heated outdoor. **Activities:** exercise room. **Guest Services:** valet and coin laundry.

SAVE CALL BIZ HS / SOME UNITS

WHERE TO EAT

AMORE NEAPOLITAN PIZZERIA 505/554-1967 **24**

Italian Pizza. Quick Serve. **Address:** 3600 Cutler Ave NE 87110

AZUMA 505/880-9800 **13**

Japanese. Casual Dining. **Address:** 4701 San Mateo Blvd NE 87109

BIEN SHUR RESTAURANT 505/796-7500 **2**

International. Fine Dining. **Address:** 30 Rainbow Rd NE 87113

CASA DE BENAVIDEZ NEW MEXICAN RESTAURANT 505/898-3311 **3**

Mexican. Casual Dining. **Address:** 8032 4th St NW 87114

CERVANTES RESTAURANT & LOUNGE 505/262-2253 **39**

Regional Mexican Casual Dining

$9-$26

AAA Inspector Notes: *Classic.* This restaurant has been a local favorite since 1973. Traditional fare is prepared using family recipes. Tasty New Mexican dishes include carne adovada, chile rellenos and tamales. Their salsa is outstanding and can be purchased if you'd like to take some home. The restaurant is very near to Kirtland Air Force Base. **Features:** full bar. **Address:** 5801 Gibson Rd SE 87108 **Location:** Jct San Pedro Dr.

L D

CHRISTY MAE'S 505/255-4740 **30**

American. Casual Dining. **Address:** 1400 San Pedro Dr NE 87110

EL PINTO 505/898-1771 **1**

Mexican. Casual Dining. **Address:** 10500 4th St NW 87114

FLYING STAR CAFE 505/275-8311 **17**

American. Casual Dining. **Address:** 4501 Juan Tabo Blvd NE 87111

FRONTIER RESTAURANT 505/266-0550 **31**

Mexican. Quick Serve. **Address:** 2400 Central Ave SE 87106

GARCIA'S KITCHEN 505/275-5812 **21**

Mexican. Casual Dining. **Address:** 3601 Juan Tabo Blvd NE 87111

JINJA BAR & BISTRO 505/856-1413 **4**

Asian. Casual Dining. **Address:** 8900 Holly Ave NE, Suite B 87122

KELLY'S BREWERY & RESTAURANT 505/262-2739 **36**

American. Casual Dining. **Address:** 3222 Central Ave SE 87106

(See map & index p. 260.)

KRUNG THAI 505/292-9319 (25)

Thai. Casual Dining. **Address:** 7923 Menaul Blvd NE 87110

LOS CUATES DEL NORTE 505/237-2800 (26)

Mexican. Casual Dining. **Address:** 8700 Menaul Blvd NE 87112

LOYOLA'S FAMILY RESTAURANT 505/268-6478 (38)

Mexican. Casual Dining. **Address:** 4500 Central Ave SE 87108

MANNIE'S 505/265-1669 (34)

American. Casual Dining. **Address:** 2900 Central Ave SE 87106

MILLY'S RESTAURANT 505/884-0707 (20)

American. Casual Dining. **Address:** 2100 Candelaria Rd NE 87107

MIMMO'S RISTORANTE & PIZZERIA 505/831-4191 (14)

Italian. Casual Dining. **Address:** 3301 Coors Blvd NW 87120

MING DYNASTY 505/296-0298 (29)

Chinese. Casual Dining. **Address:** 1551 Eubank Blvd NE 87112

MONROE'S RESTAURANT 505/881-4224 (10)

Mexican. Casual Dining. **Address:** 6051 Osuna Rd NE 87109

NICK & JIMMY'S RESTAURANT & BAR 505/344-9169 (11)

Mediterranean. Casual Dining. **Address:** 5021 S Pan American West Frwy 87109

NOB HILL BAR & GRILL 505/266-4455 (35)

American. Casual Dining. **Address:** 3128 Central Ave SE 87106

THE OWL CAFE 505/291-4900 (37)

American. Casual Dining. **Address:** 800 Eubank Blvd NE 87123

PAISANO'S ITALIAN RESTAURANT 505/298-7541 (27)

Italian. Casual Dining. **Address:** 1935 Eubank Blvd NE 87112

PAPPADEAUX SEAFOOD KITCHEN 505/345-0240

Seafood. Casual Dining. **Address:** 5011 Pan American Frwy NE 87109

PARS CUISINE 505/345-5156 (9)

Mediterranean. Casual Dining. **Address:** 4320 The 25 Way NE, Suite 100 87109

P.F. CHANG'S CHINA BISTRO 505/344-8282 (7)

Chinese. Fine Dining. **Address:** 4440 The 25 Way NE 87109

RANGE CAFE 505/293-2633 (16)

American. Casual Dining. **Address:** 4401 Wyoming Blvd NE 87111

RICHARD'S MEXICAN RESTAURANT 505/881-1039 (22)

Mexican. Casual Dining. **Address:** 3301 Menaul Blvd NE, Suite 1 87107

RUDY'S COUNTRY STORE AND BAR-B-QUE

Barbecue. Quick Serve.

LOCATIONS:

Address: 2321 Carlisle Blvd NE 87110 **Phone:** 505/884-4000
Address: 10136 Coors Blvd NW 87114 **Phone:** 505/890-7113

SAIGON RESTAURANT 505/884-0706 (8)

Vietnamese. Casual Dining. **Address:** 6001 San Mateo Blvd NE, Suite D4 87109

SALT AND BOARD 505/219-2001 (32)

American. Gastropub. **Address:** 115 Harvard Dr SE 87106

SANDIAGO'S GRILL AT THE TRAM 505/856-6692

Regional American. Casual Dining. **Address:** 40 Tramway Rd NE 87122

SAVOY BAR & GRILL 505/294-9463 (19)

American. Fine Dining. **Address:** 10601 Montgomery Blvd NE 87111

SCARPA'S BRICK OVEN PIZZA 505/323-0222 (18)

Italian. Casual Dining. **Address:** 9700 Montgomery Blvd NE 87111

SIAM CAFE 505/883-7334 (12)

Thai. Casual Dining. **Address:** 5500 San Mateo Blvd NE, Suite 101 87109

TAJ MAHAL CUISINE OF INDIA 505/255-1994 (28)

Indian. Casual Dining. **Address:** 1430 Carlisle Blvd NE 87110

THUNDER ROAD STEAKHOUSE & CANTINA 505/352-7888

Southwestern Steak. Casual Dining. **Address:** 14500 Central Ave SW 87121

TROMBINO'S BISTRO ITALIANO 505/821-5974 (6)

Italian
Casual Dining
$13-$30

AAA Inspector Notes: Well-prepared and delicious entrées-including pasta, veal, poultry, seafood and aged steaks-are served in this locally popular restaurant's Mediterranean atmosphere. Fresh ingredients, tasty homemade breads, sauces, pizza and tempting desserts complete the menu. **Features:** full bar, happy hour. **Reservations:** suggested. **Address:** 5415 Academy Rd NE 87109 **Location:** I-25 exit 230 (Osuna Rd), just s on San Mateo Blvd to Academy Rd, then just e. D

VIC'S DAILY CAFE 505/341-9710 (5)

American. Casual Dining. **Address:** 3600 Osuna Rd NE, Unit 105 87109

WECK'S 505/881-0019 (15)

American. Casual Dining. **Address:** 3913 Louisiana Blvd NE 87110

ZINC WINE BAR & BISTRO 505/254-9462 (33)

American. Fine Dining. **Address:** 3009 Central Ave NE 87106

ANGEL FIRE (E-4) pop. 1,216, elev. 8,415'

Tucked into the Moreno Valley and surrounded by the imposing Sangre de Cristo Mountains, Angel Fire gained its name from two different natural phenomena—bright afternoon sunlight reflecting off alpine peaks, and (according to 19th-century mountain man and Indian fighter Kit Carson) early morning winter sunlight glinting on ice-covered tree branches. At different points in time this ruggedly scenic region has been home to Moache Ute Indians, miners, ranchers, trappers, pioneers and cowboys.

Angel Fire was a filming location for the 1989 TV mini-series "Lonesome Dove," and you can still visit the cabin built for this critically acclaimed and immensely popular Western starring Robert Duvall and Tommy Lee Jones, in which New Mexico stood in for Montana.

A year-round outdoor activity mecca, Angel Fire offers summer boating, fishing, hunting, golfing, hiking, mountain biking and horseback riding. Torchlight parades, races and a web of runs (from beginner to advanced) keep boarders, skiers and snowshoe enthusiasts busy during the winter months.

Duffers looking to improve their game will find that golf balls travel up to 10 percent farther due to the high altitude. Angel Fire Resort Golf Course, N. Angel Fire Road and Miller Lane, is one of the area's premier public courses; phone (800) 633-7463.

Culturally, the Music from Angel Fire festival brings chamber music to the mountain community from late August to early September.

Angel Fire Chamber of Commerce: 3407 Mountain View Blvd., Centro Plaza, P.O. Box 547, Angel Fire, NM 87710. **Phone:** (575) 377-6353 or (800) 446-8117.

GEM **VIETNAM VETERANS MEMORIAL STATE PARK** is at 34 Country Club Rd. This curvilinear structure originally was built as one family's memorial to a young son killed in an enemy ambush in Vietnam. President Ronald Reagan proclaimed it "a memorial of national significance" in November 1987. The chapel is dedicated to Vietnam War casualties. Its hilltop vantage affords views of the Sangre de Cristo Mountains and the broad Moreno Valley. **Hours:** Chapel and grounds are open daily 24 hours. Visitor center daily 9-5 Apr.-Oct.; Thurs.-Mon. 9-5 rest of year. Closed Thanksgiving and day after Thanksgiving. **Cost:** Donations. **Phone:** (575) 377-2293 (park office), or (575) 377-6900 (foundation).

ARTESIA pop. 11,301, elev. 3,379'

ARTESIA INN 575/746-9801

Motel. **Address:** 1820 S 1st St 88210

BEST WESTERN PECOS INN 575/748-3324

Hotel

AAA Benefit: Members save up to 15% and earn bonus points!

Address: 2209 W Main St 88210 **Location:** 1.5 mi w on US 82. **Facility:** 82 units, some two bedrooms and kitchens. 2 stories (no elevator), interior corridors. **Pool:** heated indoor. **Activities:** hot tub, picnic facilities, exercise room. **Guest Services:** valet and coin laundry. **Featured Amenity: full hot breakfast.**

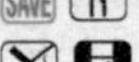

/ SOME UNITS HS

COMFORT INN & SUITES ARTESIA 575/616-2000

Hotel. **Address:** 115 N 26th St 88210

HAMPTON INN & SUITES 575/746-0707

Hotel

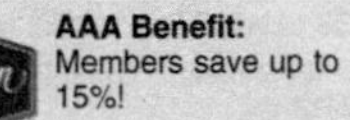

AAA Benefit: Members save up to 15%!

Address: 2501 S Permian Pavilion Loop 88210 **Location:** 1.5 mi w on US 82, then just n. **Facility:** 81 units. 4 stories, interior corridors. **Pool:** heated indoor. **Activities:** picnic facilities, exercise room. **Guest Services:** coin laundry. **Featured Amenity: breakfast buffet.**

SAVE CALL BIZ / SOME UNITS HS

HOTEL ARTESIA 575/746-2066

Hotel. **Address:** 203 N 2nd St 88210

LA QUINTA INN & SUITES ARTESIA 575/736-2400

Hotel. **Address:** 2207 W Main St 88210

WHERE TO EAT

ADOBE ROSE RESTAURANT 575/746-6157

Southwestern. Casual Dining. **Address:** 1614 N 13th St 88210

LA FONDA RESTAURANT 575/746-9411

Mexican. Casual Dining. **Address:** 210 W Main St 88210

AZTEC (D-2) pop. 6,763, elev. 5,623'

Nearby Aztec Ruins National Monument is a popular day trip. The Aztec Arches were considered sacred by the Puebloan Indians. One of the most impressive of these natural sandstone features is the Cox Canyon Arch, which has an estimated span of 43 feet. While the rock formations are uniformly amazing, they're not all easy to find. The Aztec Visitor Center, 110 N. Ash St., can provide driving directions to some of the more accessible arches; phone (505) 334-9551.

Aztec Chamber of Commerce: 110 N. Ash St., Aztec, NM 87410. **Phone:** (505) 334-7646.

Self-guiding tours: Information on walking tours of the city's historic sites is available from the Aztec Museum & Pioneer Village.

GEM AZTEC RUINS NATIONAL MONUMENT (D-2)

In the northwest corner of New Mexico, just north of Aztec on US 516 to Ruins Road, is one of the best preserved Ancestral Pueblo ruins in the Southwest. The misnomer Aztec was given by early settlers who incorrectly identified the builders of these sandstone pueblos.

Although smaller than the site preserved at Chaco Culture National Historical Park, the structures here make up for that in terms of detail. Especially noteworthy is the Great Kiva, a ceremonial building that is the only reconstruction of its kind in North America.

The largest of these sandstone pueblos, the West Ruin, was built about 1110; it contained more than 500 rooms, some of which remain intact. Several smaller structures adjoin the main ruin. Among the architectural features are original roofs that have amazingly withstood the test of time.

The visitor center displays artifacts uncovered during excavations, and a 15-minute video offers background information and historical context. Monument open daily 8-6, Memorial Day-Labor Day; 8-5, rest of year. Closed Jan. 1, Thanksgiving and Christmas. Admission, valid for 7 days, $5; free (ages 0-15). Phone (505) 334-6174.

GEM BANDELIER NATIONAL MONUMENT (B-3)

About 50 miles northwest of Santa Fe via US 285 to Pojoaque, then west on SR 502 and south on SR 4, this 50-square-mile site sits on the Pajarito Plateau in northern New Mexico's rugged canyon and mesa country. Pueblo and cliff dwellings constitute the remnants of an Ancestral Puebloan community established 7 to 8 centuries ago.

The most accessible sites consist of cave rooms hewn out of the soft tuff rock, houses built on the talus slopes and a circular community village. Bandelier also contains more than 33,000 acres of designated wilderness, including some 70 miles of hiking trails. Offering views of archeological sites, the 1.2-mile round-trip paved Main Loop Trail starts at the visitor center. Free permits, required for overnight back-country travel, can be obtained at the White Rock Visitor Center. Pets or bicycles are not permitted on any trails in the monument.

In summer a variety of ranger-led activities are offered, including guided walks, interpretive programs and craft demonstrations. The Nightwalk tour of archeological sites is conducted largely in silence, which emphasizes the sense of solitude. An introductory slide program and a small museum in the visitor center provide background orientation. One- and 2-hour self-guiding walking tours of the principal sites start at the visitor center.

Note: From mid-May to mid-October, visitors are required to take a shuttle bus from the visitor center to the most frequently visited sites between 9 a.m. and 3 p.m. Buses run approximately every 30 minutes Mon.-Fri., every 20 minutes Sat.-Sun.

Monument open daily dawn-dusk, except during heavy snow days. Visitor center open daily 9-6, mid-May to mid-Oct.; 9-4:30, rest of year. Closed Jan. 1 and Christmas. Admission $20 (per private vehicle), $15 (per motorcycle, up to two riders), $10 (for individuals arriving on foot or bicycle). Visitor center free. Nightwalk tours free; reservations are required. Visitors are advised to phone ahead for current road conditions before visiting the site. Phone (505) 672-3861, ext. 517.

BELÉN pop. 7,269, elev. 4,808'

BAYMONT BY WYNDHAM BELEN 505/861-5000

Hotel. **Address:** 2110 Camino del Llano 87002

BERNALILLO (F-3) pop. 8,320, elev. 5,052'

Bernalillo's (bern-a-LEE-oh) first settlers arrived at the turn of the 18th century and were descendants of Bernal Díaz del Castillo, who chronicled Hernando Cortés' conquest of Mexico. Reminders of times past include the pueblo of Santa Ana and the Spanish-American village of San Ysidro, both northwest of town.

The Santa Ana Pueblo Mission, one of the oldest missions in the United States, is open to visitors on feast day, July 26. It is believed to have been built by Spanish missionary Fray Juan de Rosas, who accompanied Spanish explorer Juan de Oñate on his expedition to New Mexico in 1598.

Sandoval County Visitor Center: 264 S. Camino del Pueblo, P.O. Box 40, Bernalillo, NM 87004. **Phone:** (505) 867-8687 or (800) 252-0191.

DAYS INN BERNALILLO 505/771-7000

Hotel

Address: 107 N Camino del Pueblo 87004 **Location:** I-25 exit 242, just w. **Facility:** 56 units. 3 stories, interior corridors. **Amenities:** safes. **Pool:** heated indoor. **Activities:** hot tub, exercise room. **Guest Services:** coin laundry. **Featured Amenity: full hot breakfast.**

SAVE CALL BIZ HS / SOME UNITS

HOLIDAY INN EXPRESS-BERNALILLO 505/867-1600

Hotel. **Address:** 119 Bell Ln 87004

HYATT REGENCY TAMAYA RESORT AND SPA 505/867-1234

Resort Hotel

AAA Benefit: Members save up to 10%!

Address: 1300 Tuyuna Tr 87004 **Location:** I-25 exit 242, 1 mi w on US 550 to Tamaya Blvd, then 1 mi n, follow signs. **Facility:** This upscale resort in a tranquil setting offers a strong Native American feel and incredible views. Activities for the entire family include a luxurious spa, 18-hole golf course and Camp Hyatt. 350 units. 4 stories, interior/exterior corridors. **Parking:** on-site and valet. **Terms:** check-in 4 pm. **Amenities:** safes. **Dining:** 4 restaurants. **Pool:** heated outdoor. **Activities:** sauna, hot tub, steamroom, regulation golf, tennis, recreation programs, kids club, bicycles, playground, trails, exercise room, spa. **Guest Services:** valet laundry, area transportation.

SAVE ECO CALL BIZ / SOME UNITS

WHERE TO EAT

ABUELITA'S NEW MEXICAN RESTAURANT 505/867-9988

Mexican. Casual Dining. **Address:** 621 S Camino del Pueblo 87004

PRAIRIE STAR 505/867-3327

Northern American. Fine Dining. **Address:** 288 Prairie Star Rd 87004

THE RANGE CAFE 505/867-1700

American. Casual Dining. **Address:** 925 Camino del Pueblo 87004

BLOOMFIELD (E-2) pop. 8,112, elev. 5,453'

Bloomfield was settled around 1876 and quickly morphed into an all-but-lawless Wild West town, complete with a gang of rustlers headed by the ex-sheriff. The brazen gang operated openly, marketing stolen beef through its own butcher shop. Blancett's Saloon was a hangout for gunslingers from every corner of the San Juan Basin.

By the early 20th century, however, residents were more interested in stimulating agriculture through irrigation, an endeavor that persists in this arid region. The Navajo Reservoir, 25 miles northeast via US 64 and SR 511, is the source of much of the area's water. Navajo Lake State Park surrounds the reservoir and offers recreational opportunities, including world-class fly fishing *(see Recreation Areas Chart).*

Bloomfield Chamber of Commerce: 224 W. Broadway, Bloomfield, NM 87413. **Phone:** (505) 632-0880.

BEST WESTERN TERRITORIAL INN & SUITES 505/632-9100

AAA Benefit: Members save up to 15% and earn bonus points!

Address: 415 S Bloomfield Blvd 87413 **Location:** Just s of jct US 64 and 550. **Facility:** 65 units. 3 stories, interior corridors. **Pool:** heated indoor. **Activities:** hot tub, exercise room. **Guest Services:** coin laundry. **Featured Amenity: breakfast buffet.**

SUPER 8 505/632-8886

Motel. **Address:** 525 W Broadway Blvd 87413

CAPULIN VOLCANO NATIONAL MONUMENT (D-5)

Three miles north of US 64/87 and Capulin on SR 325, Capulin Volcano National Monument contains one of the best examples of a volcanic cinder cone in the nation. About 60,000 years ago ash, cinders and lava erupted and formed a classic cinder cone that stands more than 1,000 feet above the surrounding prairie. Today, a 2-mile road winds up the volcano, and five trails lead into the crater and around the rim. The view from the summit includes the Rocky Mountains, volcanic features of the Raton-Clayton Volcanic Field, and the distant horizons of Colorado, Oklahoma and Texas. Ranger-led programs are offered in summer.

The visitor center offers information and a 10-minute video program. Pets are not allowed on trails. The road to the crater rim, park and visitor center is open daily 8-5:30, mid-June through Labor Day; 8-4:30, rest of year. Last vehicle admission to rim 10 minutes before closing. Phone ahead to confirm schedule. Closed Jan. 1, Thanksgiving and Christmas. Admission, valid for 7 days, $15 (per private vehicle), $10 (per motorcycle). Phone (575) 278-2201.

CARLSBAD (I-5) pop. 26,138, elev. 3,111'

The fields of cotton, alfalfa and veggies that surround Carlsbad are made possible by the U.S. Bureau of Reclamation's system of dams and canals, which irrigates 25,000 acres. Carlsbad Caverns National Park is nearby, and Lake Carlsbad *(see Recreation Areas Chart)* offers fishing, boating and water sports.

Homeowners along the Pecos River decorate their houses, yards and docks with Christmas lights for Christmas on the Pecos, an annual celebration lasting from Thanksgiving weekend through New Year's Eve. Nighttime pontoon boat tours make it impossible to *not* get into the holiday spirit.

Carlsbad Chamber of Commerce: 302 S. Canal St., Carlsbad, NM 88220. **Phone:** (575) 887-6516.

CANDLEWOOD SUITES CARLSBAD SOUTH 575/941-3711

Extended Stay Contemporary Hotel. **Address:** 3711 San Jose Blvd 88220

COMFORT SUITES 575/689-2222

Hotel. **Address:** 2600 W Pierce St 88220

FAIRFIELD INN & SUITES BY MARRIOTT 575/887-8000

Hotel

Fairfield **AAA Benefit:** Members save 5% or more!

Address: 2525 S Canal St 88220 **Location:** 1.5 mi s on US 62, 180 and 285. **Facility:** 91 units. 3 stories, exterior corridors. **Pool:** heated outdoor. **Activities:** hot tub, picnic facilities, exercise room. **Guest Services:** coin laundry. **Featured Amenity: continental breakfast.**

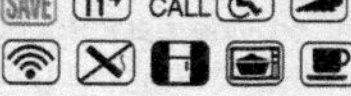

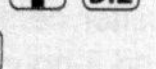

HAMPTON INN & SUITES 575/725-5700

SAVE Hotel. **Address:** 120 Esperanza Cir 88220

AAA Benefit: Members save up to 15%!

HOLIDAY INN EXPRESS & SUITES 575/234-1252

Address: 2210 W Pierce St 88220 **Location:** N on US 285. **Facility:** 80 units. 3 stories, interior corridors. **Pool:** heated indoor. **Activities:** hot tub, exercise room. **Guest Services:** coin laundry.

LA QUINTA INN & SUITES 575/236-1010

Hotel

Address: 4020 National Parks Highway 88220 **Location:** 1.5 mi s on US 62, 180 and 285. **Facility:** 96 units. 4 stories, interior corridors. **Pool:** heated outdoor. **Activities:** hot tub, picnic facilities, exercise room. **Guest Services:** coin laundry.

SAVE CALL BIZ HS / SOME UNITS

SLEEP INN & SUITES 575/941-2300

Hotel

Address: 3825 National Parks Hwy 88220 **Location:** 2 mi s of jct US 62 and 180. **Facility:** 64 units. 3 stories, interior corridors. **Pool:** heated indoor. **Activities:** exercise room. **Guest Services:** coin laundry.

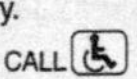

SAVE CALL BIZ

HS

STEVENS INN 575/887-2851

Hotel

Address: 1829 S Canal St 88220 **Location:** 1 mi s on US 62, 180 and 285. **Facility:** 223 units, some kitchens. 1-2 stories (no elevator), exterior corridors. **Dining:** The Flume Restaurant, see separate listing, entertainment. **Pool:** outdoor. **Activities:** exercise room. **Guest Services:** valet and coin laundry. **Featured Amenity: breakfast buffet.**

SAVE BIZ / SOME UNITS

TOWNEPLACE SUITES BY MARRIOTT 575/689-8850

SAVE Extended Stay Hotel. **Address:** 311 Pompa St 88220

AAA Benefit: Members save 5% or more!

THE TRINITY HOTEL 575/234-9891

Historic Boutique Country Inn. **Address:** 201 S Canal St 88220

U.S. TRAVELERS INN & SUITES 575/887-1994

Hotel. **Address:** 2429 W Pierce St 88220

WHERE TO EAT

THE FLUME RESTAURANT 575/887-2851

American. Casual Dining. **Address:** 1829 S Canal St 88220

RED CHIMNEY PIT BAR-B-Q 575/885-8744

Barbecue. Casual Dining. **Address:** 817 N Canal St 88220

THE TRINITY RESTAURANT 575/234-9891

American. Casual Dining. **Address:** 201 S Canal St 88220

YELLOW BRIX RESTAURANT 575/941-2749

American. Casual Dining. **Address:** 201 N Canal St 88220

GEM CARLSBAD CAVERNS NATIONAL PARK (I-4)

Elevations in the park range from 3,596 ft. in the southeastern corner to 6,368 ft. in the southwestern region. Refer to AAA maps for additional elevation information.

Carlsbad Caverns National Park is 20 miles southwest of Carlsbad off US 62/180. The park covers 46,776 acres in the rugged foothills of the Guadalupe Mountains, with miles of caves cutting through a Permian-age fossil reef. Among more than 117 known caves is Lechuguilla, thought to be the nation's deepest limestone cavern. The park's showpiece is Carlsbad Cavern, a series of enormous rooms that make up one of the world's largest caves.

Unlike most limestone caves that form when surface water flows through cracks in the rock, these passageways in the Guadalupe Mountains are the rare product of sulfuric acid. A hydrogen sulfide gas solution rose from petroleum deposits thousands of feet below the surface and mixed with the water table to create an aggressive chemical that dissolved holes in the subterranean limestone. As the mountains rose over a period of 20 million years, ground water drained from the caves, revealing the wonders of Carlsbad.

A steep, paved trail leads into the cavern's natural entrance, which measures 90 feet wide and 40 feet high. The cavern has more than 30 miles of surveyed subterranean corridors and great chambers. Formations range from small, delicate growths resembling plants to massive stalagmites, stalactites and columns. Many are tinted by iron and other minerals present in the limestone. Highlights include Bat Cave, Devil's Spring, Iceberg Rock, Green Lake Overlook and the Boneyard, a maze of limestone rock reminiscent of Swiss cheese.

The 8-acre Big Room, one of the most impressive chambers, has a 255-foot ceiling. Its clear pools contain limestone masses resembling lily pads. Other formations evoke an atmosphere of snow-banked forests, adding to the tranquil beauty of the cavern.

Every summer hundreds of thousands of bats emerge from Carlsbad Cavern's uppermost chamber at dusk to feed on flying insects. From Memorial Day to late October (weather permitting), park rangers give a pre-flight talk in an amphitheater at the mouth of the cave. The flight outward lasts a half-hour to 2 hours; the bats return near dawn. Cameras, cellular phones and other electronic devices are prohibited. During the day, bats hang head down from the walls and ceilings of a portion of the cavern not open to visitors. At the GEM Dawn of the Bats in mid-summer, visitors gather at the park just before dawn to watch the bats' spectacular return flight.

General Information and Activities

The park is open all year, except Jan. 1, Thanksgiving and Christmas. The visitor center is open daily 8-7 (cave tours are offered 8:30-5), Memorial Day weekend-Labor Day; 8-5 (cave tours are offered

8:30-3:30), rest of year. Last cave entry via natural entrance is 1 hour, 30 minutes before closing. Visitors may explore Carlsbad Cavern on two self-guiding routes, the Natural Entrance and the Big Room, and return to the surface by elevator. The Big Room route is recommended for visitors who are short on time or who prefer a less strenuous walk.

A brief orientation is presented prior to tours. Interpretive signs explain cavern features, history and geology, and an audio guide providing descriptive commentary is available to rent. Additional activities include ranger talks, self-guiding nature trails and a desert automobile drive.

Guided cave tours are led by park rangers and range from easy walks to difficult crawls and climbs. These tours fill quickly in the summer and are available by reservation only.

The visitor center includes educational exhibits about the area's geology, biology, history and archeology; works of art depicting cave features; and original Ansel Adams photographs. A half-mile self-guiding desert nature trail begins near the cave entrance.

The 9.5-mile Walnut Canyon Desert Drive, a one-way loop drive over a graded gravel road, offers views of Rattlesnake Canyon and upper Walnut Canyon; the loop is not maintained for low-clearance vehicles. A permit is required for overnight back-country trips; inquire at the visitor center for hiking information. *See Recreation Areas Chart.*

The temperature underground is a constant 56 F. A sweater and flat-heeled shoes with rubber soles are recommended. Baby strollers are not permitted inside the caves. Flash and time-exposure photography is allowed, but all photographs must be taken from paved trails. Food is available but is not permitted on cave trails. **Note:** To prevent the spread of fungus that causes a deadly disease to bats, visitors entering park caves may be screened; some clothing and equipment may not be permitted or disinfection may be required.

ADMISSION to the park area and the visitor center without entrance to the caves is free. Cave admission, valid for 3 days (includes the Natural Entrance and Big Room self-guiding routes), $10; free (ages 0-15). Ranger-led tours $7-$20; $3.50-$10 (ages 4-15); age restrictions may apply. Audio guide rental $4.

PETS (except service dogs) are not permitted inside caves. The visitor center provides kennels for $10 per pet.

ADDRESS inquiries to the Superintendent, Carlsbad Caverns National Park, 3225 National Parks Hwy., Carlsbad, NM 88220; phone (575) 785-2232.

CARLSBAD CAVERNS GUIDED TOURS depart from various sites in Carlsbad Caverns National Park. Offered in addition to the Natural Entrance and Big Room self-guiding tours of Carlsbad Cavern are four guided tours led by park rangers. Tours range from easy to difficult, and participants must supply batteries for some routes. **Note:** Sturdy hiking boots are required. Tours fill quickly in the summer. **Hours:** Departure times and tour lengths vary. Closed Jan. 1, Thanksgiving and Christmas. **Cost:** Cavern admission, valid for 3 days, $12; free (ages 0-15). Fees, group sizes and age restrictions vary. Reservations are required for guided tours. **Phone:** (575) 785-2232 for more information, or (877) 444-6777 for reservations.

Hall of the White Giant Tour departs from the Carlsbad Caverns Visitor Center at 727 Carlsbad Caverns Hwy., 7 mi. off US 62/180. This strenuous, 4-hour guided tour leads to a remote chamber. Participants must crawl long distances, squeeze through crevices such as the tight Matlock's Pinch and climb a slippery passage.

Note: The tour is temporarily closed; phone ahead for updates. Hiking boots or other sturdy shoes, knee-pads, gloves and three new AA batteries are required; a long-sleeved shirt and long pants are recommended. Backpacks are not permitted. Headlamps are provided. The tour is limited to eight participants. **Hours:** Tours depart Wed. at 8:30 a.m., June 1 to mid-Aug. Guests should arrive 15 minutes prior to departure. Closed Jan. 1, Thanksgiving and Christmas. **Cost:** (in addition to cavern admission fee) $20; $10 (ages 12-15). Ages 0-11 are not permitted. Cavern admission, valid for 3 days, $12; free (ages 0-15). Reservations are required. **Phone:** (877) 444-6777.

King's Palace Tour departs from the underground rest area in Carlsbad Cavern. This 1.5-hour tour covers 1 mile and descends to the deepest part of the cavern open to the public, 830 feet below the surface. Cave formations include helictites, draperies, columns and soda straws. Park rangers conduct blackouts during the tour, turning off the artificial lights briefly to underscore the cavern's natural darkness. **Note:** The tour is limited to a maximum of 40 participants and requires walking up a very steep hill at the conclusion. **Hours:** Tours depart daily at 10:30. Closed Jan. 1, Thanksgiving and Christmas. **Cost:** (in addition to cavern admission fee) $8; $4 (ages 4-15). Ages 0-3 are not permitted. Cavern admission, valid for 3 days, $12; free (ages 0-15). Reservations are required. **Phone:** (877) 444-6777.

Left Hand Tunnel Tour departs from the Carlsbad Caverns Visitor Center at 727 Carlsbad Caverns Hwy., 7 mi. off US 62/180. This 2-hour lantern tour highlights cavern history and geology along a half-mile route. Sights along this easy tour include cave pools and fossils. **Note:** Closed-toe shoes are required. Backpacks are not permitted. Lanterns are provided. The tour is limited to 15 participants. **Hours:** Tours depart daily at 1. Closed Jan. 1, Thanksgiving and Christmas. **Cost:** (in addition to cavern admission fee) $7; $3.50 (ages 6-15). Ages 0-5 are not permitted. Cavern admission, valid for 3 days, $12; free (ages 0-15). Reservations are required. **Phone:** (877) 444-6777.

Lower Cave Tour departs from the Carlsbad Caverns Visitor Center at 727 Carlsbad Caverns Hwy., 7 mi. off US 62/180. Entered by descending 10 feet, walking down a slope using a rope and 50 feet of ladders, this area of the cavern contains beautiful formations and evidence of early exploration. The Rookery is a showcase for cave pearls.

Note: The 3-hour tour involves ladder climbing and heights and is moderately strenuous. Hiking boots and three new AA batteries are required; gloves, helmets and headlamps are provided. Backpacks are not permitted. The tour is limited to 12 participants. **Hours:** Tours depart Tues., Thurs., Sat.-Sun. at 8:30 a.m., early April to Dec. 31. Closed Jan. 1, Thanksgiving and Christmas. **Cost:** (in addition to cavern admission fee) $20; $10 (ages 12-15). Ages 0-11 are not permitted. Cavern admission, valid for 3 days, $12; free (ages 0-15). Reservations are required. **Phone:** (877) 444-6777.

Slaughter Canyon Cave Tour departs from the Carlsbad Caverns Visitor Center at 727 Carlsbad Caverns Hwy., 7 mi. off US 62/180, to CR 418, following signs to the cave entrance. Dramatic formations in this undeveloped cave include the 89-foot-high Monarch, the sparkling Christmas Tree column and the delicate Chinese Wall.

Note: An unpaved, half-mile trail leads from the parking area to the cave, climbing 500 feet; allow 45 minutes to make this steep and strenuous climb. Hiking boots or other sturdy shoes, two C-cell flashlights with new batteries and water are required. The 2-hour tour is limited to 25 participants. **Hours:** Tours depart Mon., Wed. and Fri. at 8:30 a.m., early April to late May and Sept. 4-Dec. 31; Fri. at 8:30 a.m. late May-Sept. 3. Closed Jan. 1, Thanksgiving and Christmas. **Cost:** $15; $7.50 (ages 8-15). Ages 0-7 are not permitted. Reservations are required. **Phone:** (877) 444-6777.

Spider Cave Tour departs from the Carlsbad Caverns Visitor Center at 727 Carlsbad Caverns Hwy., 7 mi. off US 62/180. This three-dimensional maze includes tight crawlways, canyonlike passages and bizarre formations. Highlights include the Mace and Medusa rooms and Cactus Spring.

Note: The tour is temporarily closed; phone ahead for updates. Hiking boots or other sturdy shoes, gloves, kneepads and four new AA batteries are required for this strenuous tour; a long-sleeved shirt, long pants and water are recommended. Backpacks are not permitted. Helmets and headlamps are provided. The 4-hour tour is limited to eight participants. **Hours:** Tours depart Sun. at 8:30 a.m., June 1 to mid-Aug. Guests should arrive 15 minutes prior to departure. Closed Jan. 1, Thanksgiving and Christmas. **Cost:** Fee $20; $10 (ages 12-15). Ages 0-11 are not permitted. Reservations are required. **Phone:** (877) 444-6777.

CARRIZOZO (H-4) pop. 996, elev. 5,426'

Once a shipping and commercial center for area ranches, Carrizozo now is a busy county seat and tourist center. In addition to its own parks and recreational facilities, it offers easy access to the northern portion of Lincoln National Forest *(see place listing p. 292)*. Established in 1899 as a division point on the El Paso & Northeastern Railroad, the community takes its name from *carrizo*, a regional grass.

Nine miles northeast via US 54 and SR 349 is the ghost town of White Oaks. For 20 years after the original gold strike on nearby Baxter Mountain in 1879, White Oaks was a substantial community with stone buildings, two banks, four churches, four newspapers and more than 50 established businesses. Although White Oaks faded with the gold market in the 20th century, one of the first strikes—the Old Abe Mine—produced $3 million in gold until it closed around 1960.

Carrizozo Chamber of Commerce: P.O. Box 567, Carrizozo, NM 88301. **Phone:** (575) 648-2732.

CARSON NATIONAL FOREST (D-2)

Elevations in the forest range from 6,000 ft. in the Pinon Juniper Tree region to 13,161 ft. at Wheeler Peak. Refer to AAA maps for additional elevation information.

In north central New Mexico, Carson National Forest encompasses 1,500,000 acres. Its scenic and recreational focus is in the districts that encompass the Sangre de Cristo and the San Juan mountains flanking the upper Rio Grande Valley.

The Wheeler Peak, Latir Peak, Cruces Basin and Pecos wilderness areas preserve the region's pristine beauty. The Enchanted Circle Scenic Byway is an 84-mile drive offering panoramic views of the southern Rocky Mountains, including Wheeler Peak. It loops from Taos east to Eagle Nest, then north to Questa via SR 38, and south on SR 522 back to Taos.

The curved cliff side of Echo Amphitheater, 9 miles south of Canjilon on US 84, is a prime spot for photography. Summer and winter recreation is available. Trails for bicycling, hiking, horseback riding, snowmobiling and cross-country skiing traverse the forest.

For further information contact Carson National Forest, 208 Cruz Alta Rd., Taos, NM 87571; phone (575) 758-6200. *See Recreation Areas Chart.*

GEM CHACO CULTURE NATIONAL HISTORICAL PARK (E-2)

Located in northwestern New Mexico, Chaco Culture National Historical Park preserves the remains of 13 major great houses, or public buildings, and several thousand smaller sites representing the culture of the Ancestral Puebloan people between A.D. 850 and 1250. It is one of the most impressive cultural sites in the Southwest.

By about A.D. 500 the Ancestral Puebloan people had gradually replaced a nomadic existence with an agricultural lifestyle revolving around permanent settlements. During the mid-9th century they began to construct Pueblo Bonito at the base of the northern wall of Chaco Canyon. By the late 12th century this great house had attained a height of more than four stories in some portions and contained more than 600 kivas (ceremonial rooms).

Numerous smaller village sites along Chaco Canyon attest to the once-sizable population of the greater settlement. In addition to building monumental structures as well as an elaborate irrigation system of gates and canals that diverted runoff from summer thunderstorms into their cornfields, the Chacoans also built a vast road network. Straight, 30-foot-wide corridors linked the canyon settlements with more far-flung sites, some as distant as locations in the present-day states of Arizona, Colorado and Utah.

Another major achievement was a highly sophisticated solstice marker. High on isolated Fajada Butte, a sliver of noontime sunlight shines between stone slabs onto two spiral petroglyphs. The marker precisely timed equinoxes and solstices on which the Chacoans based crop planting times and ceremonial observances. **Note:** The butte is closed to the public due to its fragile condition.

As Chaco's influence waned, ceremonial centers emerged at nearby Aztec and Mesa Verde, and by 1250 only the wind whistled through the colossal and deserted masonry walls of Pueblo Bonito and its sister cities. The Chacoans were assimilated into existing Zuni, Hopi, Acoma and Rio Grande pueblo populations, but their descendants return to honor these sacred places.

The recommended park access is from the north via the US 550 exit at CR 7900; park entry is about 3 miles southeast of Nageezi and approximately 50 miles west of Cuba. Follow signs 21 miles to the park boundary. This route consists of 8 miles of paved road (CR 7900 and CR 7950), then 8 miles of gravel and 5 miles of rough dirt road (CR 7950). The road is only lightly maintained, and may be impassable during or after inclement weather.

Visitors with motor homes should make sure their interior items are secured. Phone the park visitor center at (505) 786-7014, ext. 221 for current road conditions.

Major sites are located within walking distance of 9-mile Canyon Loop Drive. The most important site, and a must-see for visitors, is Pueblo Bonito, about 4.5 miles from the visitor center. The self-guiding gravel trail through the pueblo is a little over half a mile round trip and negotiates several short but steep rises. This monumental ruin was constructed from sandstone blocks held together by adobe mortar, rising from an arid canyon floor with no natural protection from the elements. Today only standing walls and doorways remain.

Self-guiding trails explore six other major sites: Chetro Ketl, Pueblo del Arroyo, Casa Rinconada and three village sites. Allow 1 hour minimum per site. Four other back-country trails for day hiking lead to more distant sites; free permits, which can be obtained at the visitor center and at trailheads, are required.

Due to the remote location and extensive ruins and trails, it may be worthwhile to plan 2 or even 3 days for a visit. A full day is required for travel and to see just a portion of the park; a second or third day is necessary to explore the entire site. Wear sturdy shoes and bring drinking water and sun protection for any extended explorations.

There are no lodgings or food service facilities within the park. Gallo Campground, which is open year-round, is located 1 mile east of the park visitor center and has 49 campsites (15 for tent camping) available for $15 per night (maximum of 14 days). This is primitive camping with no shade; each site has a picnic table and fire grate, but gathering wood is prohibited and no firewood is available in the park. There are no showers or hook-ups; drinking water is available in the visitor center parking area. Trailers and RVs more than 35 feet in length may not be accommodated. April through October are the busiest months. Advance reservations are required; phone (877) 444-6777.

Because points of interest are accessible only over dirt roads that are rough, towing trailers more than 35 feet long is not advised. There are no gas stations or other services within the park. Campers must bring their own wood or charcoal. Drinking water and dump station facilities are available year round.

Ranger-led walking tours of Pueblo Bonito are offered year-round, and other activities are offered April through October. The Chaco Night Sky Program occasionally features astronomy programs, daytime solar viewing and telescope viewing of the night sky. Obtain schedules at the visitor center; for current program information phone (505) 786-7014. Picnicking is permitted in designated areas.

The park is open daily 7 a.m.-sunset; closed Jan. 1, Thanksgiving and Christmas. Park entrance fee, valid for 7 days, $20 (per private vehicle), $15 (for motorcyclists); $10 (for individuals arriving on foot or bicycle). *See Recreation Areas Chart.*

CHACO CULTURE NATIONAL HISTORICAL PARK VISITOR CENTER is 2.5 mi. from the park entrance. A short film about the region is shown. **Hours:** Visitor Center open daily 8-5. Canyon Loop Road open daily 7-sunset. Closed Jan. 1, Thanksgiving and Christmas. **Cost:** Visitor center free. Park entrance fee, valid for 7 days, $25 (per private vehicle), $20 (for motorcyclists); $15 (for individuals arriving on foot or bicycle). **Phone:** (505) 786-7014, ext. 221.

CHAMA (D-3) pop. 1,022, elev. 7,875'

Like the railroad that is its most popular attraction, Chama sprang up during the silver mining boom of the 1880s. Old railroad yards, shops, a roundhouse and one of the last coal tipples in the nation remain as relics of that era.

Chama Valley Chamber of Commerce: P.O. Box 306-RB, Chama, NM 87566. **Phone:** (575) 756-2306 or (800) 477-0149.

GEM CUMBRES & TOLTEC SCENIC RAILROAD departs from 500 S. Terrace Ave. (SR 17). The 64-mile railroad, built in 1880, is jointly owned by New Mexico and Colorado, with trips between Chama and Antonito, Colo. Excursions on the vintage, narrow-gauge, coal-burning trains feature spectacular views of the rugged San Juan and Sangre de Cristo mountain ranges.

Osier, an old stagecoach stop, is the transfer and lunch point. Passengers have the option of traveling to Antonito by motor coach and returning to Chama by train, traveling to Antonito by train and returning to Chama by motor coach, or traveling to Osier and returning to Chama by train. Half-day trips to Cumbres by train and returning to Chama by motor coach also are offered.

AAA offices in New Mexico and Colorado can make reservations. **Hours:** Train departs daily at 10 a.m., motor coach departs daily at 8:30, Memorial Day weekend-late Oct. Half-day excursions depart Mon., Wed. and Fri. at 10 a.m., early July-early Aug. Phone ahead to confirm schedule. **Cost:** Fares (includes lunch) range $79.75-$205.75; $32.25-$79.75 (ages 2-12). Reservations are recommended. **Phone:** (575) 756-2151 in N.M. or (888) 286-2737. ***(See ad this page.)***

VISTA DEL RIO LODGE 575/756-2138

Motel

Address: 2595 US Hwy 84/64 87520 **Location:** 0.5 mi s of SR 17. Located in a quiet area. **Facility:** 19 units. 1 story, exterior corridors. **Activities:** fishing.

SAVE / SOME UNITS

WHERE TO EAT

HIGH COUNTRY RESTAURANT AND SALOON 575/756-2384

American. Casual Dining. **Address:** 2281 Hwy 17 87520

CIBOLA NATIONAL FOREST (G-2)

Elevations in the forest range from 5,000 ft. in the Magdalena district to 11,301 ft. at Mt. Taylor. Refer to AAA maps for additional elevation information.

The forest comprises scattered mountain ranges rising from the desert east and south of Albuquerque and stretching west to Arizona. Cibola National Forest's 1,625,542 acres encompass four ranger districts: Sandia, Mt. Taylor, Mountainair and Magdalena. Recreational opportunities include camping, fishing and hiking. *See Recreation Areas Chart.*

The rugged Canadian River Canyon west of Roy provides another type of beauty within Kiowa National Grassland. The forest also administers Black Kettle National Grassland, in neighboring western Oklahoma and the Texas panhandle. Camping and fishing center on the grassland's five lakes. In some areas, hunting is available in season, and there is skiing at Sandia Peak Ski Area.

A chairlift carries visitors to the northeastern face of Sandia Peak. The lift may be accessed via the Sandia Peak Aerial Tramway *(see attraction listing p. 256)* or by automobile, taking I-40 exit 175 north to SR 536. The tram operates daily 9-9, Memorial Day weekend through Labor Day and during the Albuquerque International Balloon Fiesta; Wed.-Mon. 9-8, Tues. 5-8, rest of year. It is closed for 10 to 12 days in April and November for maintenance. The tram also transports mountain bikes for cyclists exploring the peak's upper trails. Phone (505) 856-7325.

SANDIA CREST is 16 mi. e. of Albuquerque on I-40, 6 mi. n. on SR 14, then 14 mi. n.w. on the Sandia Crest National Scenic Byway (SR 536) to 1 SR 536. At the observation deck atop the 10,678-foot crest, the panorama encompasses 15,000 square miles. A self-guiding nature trail begins here and loops for a half-mile. The byway is a 14-mile spur of the Turquoise Trail, a scenic stretch of SR 14 that links Albuquerque and Santa Fe. Volcanic formations, mountains, desert landscapes and the Rio Grande are visible.

Snowboarding and downhill and cross-country skiing are available in winter; hiking and mountain biking are popular in summer. Equipment can be rented in both seasons. Food is available at the top of the crest. **Cost:** $3 recreation amenity fee. **Parking:** $1 at the base of the tramway. **Phone:** (505) 281-3304, (505) 856-1532 for the tram, or (505) 242-9052 for the ski area.

SANDIA PEAK AERIAL TRAMWAY—see Albuquerque p. 256.

CIMARRON (E-4) pop. 1,021, elev. 6,428'

Meaning "wild" or "untamed," Cimarron was fitting for both the brawling stream and the settlement that developed on its banks. Although Eagle Nest Lake ultimately tamed the river, nothing could contain the activities in town from the late 1860s to about 1880. The Las Vegas *Gazette* once reported, "Things are quiet in Cimarron; nobody has been killed in three days."

Clay Allison, Billy the Kid, Bob Ford and Black Jack Ketchum were among notorious part-time residents. Gunfights killed 26 men, and New Mexico's first printing press was dumped into the Cimarron River before the range wars ended and the town ceased to be a magnet for every outlaw in the Southwest.

Cimarron languished after losing the county seat to Springer in 1880 but revived in the early 1900s with the arrival of two railroads and the lumber industry. The modern-day city serves nearby ranches, some logging operations and a lively tourist trade. Standing as reminders of a boisterous past are the old jail and the St. James Hotel at 617 S. Collison St., where Annie Oakley joined Buffalo Bill Cody's Wild West Show. Four miles south on SR 21 is Philmont Scout Ranch, a high-adventure camp for members of the Boy Scouts.

Sizable populations of eagles, hawks and falcons inhabit the 3,700-acre Maxwell National Wildlife Refuge, 30 miles east off I-25. Part of Carson National Forest, Valle Vidal offers 100,000 acres of rugged back country for backpacking, hunting and fishing. It is 4 miles north on scenic US 64, then 21 miles northwest on Valle Vidal Road, following signs. Cimarron Canyon State Park, 12 miles west on US 64, offers brown trout fishing, hiking and camping *(see Recreation Areas Chart).*

Cimarron Chamber of Commerce: 104 N. Lincoln Ave., P.O. Box 604, Cimarron, NM 87714. **Phone:** (575) 376-2417 or (888) 376-2417.

Self-guiding tours: A walking tour map available from the chamber of commerce describes 14 historic buildings in the old town of Cimarron.

CASA DEL GAVILAN 575/376-2246

Historic Bed & Breakfast. **Address:** 570 Hwy 21 S 87714

WHERE TO EAT

ST. JAMES RESTAURANT 575/376-2664

American Casual Dining
$6-$32

AAA Inspector Notes: In the historic St James Hotel, this dining room features Western décor and many antiques related to the local ranching community. Patio dining is available in season. **Features:** full bar, patio dining. **Reservations:** suggested. **Address:** 617 S Collison Ave 87714 **Location:** Center; in Express St. James Hotel. B L D

CLAYTON (E-6) pop. 2,980, elev. 5,053'

So numerous were the herds of cattle driven through this small farming community in the mid-1880s that the Denver & Fort Worth Railroad established the settlement as a division point. As a railhead and trading center, Clayton underwent a Wild West phase. Celebrated train robber Black Jack Ketchum was hanged from a gallows enclosed in a stockade to foil yet another rescue by his gang.

Clayton, at the foot of the Rabbit Ear Mountains, is still a cattle town; some of the largest feedlots in the region are just to the north. It also is one of the world's largest producers of carbon dioxide, which is used for recovering oil in the Permian Basin in New Mexico and Texas.

Livestock studies are conducted at Clayton Livestock Research Center, 5 miles east in the Kiowa and Rita Blanca National Grasslands. The University of New Mexico and the U.S. Forest Service investigate problems related to the health, nutrition and management of cattle. Phone (575) 374-2566.

Recreational opportunities abound at Clayton Lake State Park *(see Recreation Areas Chart)*, known for its excellent trout, catfish, walleye and bass fishing. Dinosaur tracks were first discovered on the spillway of the dam in 1982; since then more than 500 tracks have been plotted.

Clayton-Union County Chamber of Commerce: 1103 S. First St., P.O. Box 476, Clayton, NM 88415. **Phone:** (575) 374-9253 or (800) 390-7858.

BEST WESTERN KOKOPELLI LODGE 575/374-2589

Hotel

AAA Benefit: Members save up to 15% and earn bonus points!

Address: 702 S 1st St 88415 **Location:** US 87, 0.5 mi se of jct US 56 and 64. **Facility:** 50 units. 2 stories (no elevator), exterior corridors. **Pool:** heated outdoor. **Activities:** exercise room. **Featured Amenity: breakfast buffet.**

QUALITY INN & SUITES 575/374-0133

Hotel. **Address:** 1120 S 1st St 88415

CLOVIS (G-6) pop. 37,775, elev. 4,266'

On the high plains of eastern New Mexico in the heart of cattle country, Clovis is a ranching, farming and dairy center. Six miles west is Cannon Air Force Base, a major contributor to the local economy.

Buddy Holly recorded his 1957 hit "Peggy Sue" at the Norman Petty Recording Studio, 1313 W. 7th St. The facility contains original recording equipment and music memorabilia; a visit will take you back to the glory days of early rock 'n roll. Guided tours are available by appointment only and must be made at least 1 month in advance; phone (575) 763-3435.

Clovis/Curry County Chamber of Commerce: 105 E. Grand Ave., Clovis, NM 88101. **Phone:** (575) 763-3435 or (800) 261-7656.

Shopping: North Plains Mall (2809 N. Prince St.) is an indoor, fashion/specialty mall with some 50 stores anchored by Dillard's, JCPenney and Sears. In addition to typical retailers selling such items as apparel, bath and beauty products, electronics and housewares, you'll find chain restaurants and a movie theater.

Traci's Greenhouse (2600 Mabry Dr.) is a one-stop shopping experience offering garden plants and accessories, clothes, New Mexico gifts and jewelry as well as home décor. Take a break from browsing at the adjacent coffee bistro.

COMFORT INN & SUITES 575/762-4536

Hotel. **Address:** 201 Schepps Blvd 88101

FAIRFIELD INN & SUITES BY MARRIOTT 575/762-1411

Hotel

Fairfield

AAA Benefit: Members save 5% or more!

Address: 4305 N Prince St 88101 **Location:** Jct US 60/84, 2.0 mi n. **Facility:** 69 units. 3 stories, interior corridors. **Pool:** heated outdoor. **Activities:** hot tub, exercise room. **Guest Services:** valet and coin laundry.

HAMPTON INN BY HILTON 575/763-3300

SAVE Hotel. **Address:** 2212 Mabry Dr 88101

AAA Benefit: Members save up to 15%!

LA QUINTA INN & SUITES CLOVIS 575/763-8777

Hotel. **Address:** 4521 N Prince St 88101

TOWNEPLACE SUITES BY MARRIOTT 575/265-7400

SAVE Extended Stay Hotel. **Address:** 4612 N Prince St 88101

AAA Benefit: Members save 5% or more!

WHERE TO EAT

COTTON PATCH CAFE 575/762-2233

American. Casual Dining. **Address:** 2604 N Prince St 88101

RIB CRIB BBQ AND GRILL 575/742-0200

Barbecue. Casual Dining. **Address:** 4020 N Prince St 88101

COCHITÍ PUEBLO (C-3) pop. 528, elev. 5,258'

West of the Rio Grande and a few miles southwest of Cochiti Dam, this ancient Keresan pueblo retains few of its old landmarks. The mission church, San Buenaventura de Cochiti, was built in 1628. The tribe leases land to the community of Cochiti Lake, where a recreation area offers boating, camping, fishing, sailing, windsurfing and nature trails *(see Recreation Areas Chart)*. Visitors to the pueblo are welcome dawn to dusk. Drawing, painting, photography or tape recording is not permitted.

GEM **KASHA-KATUWE TENT ROCKS NATIONAL MONUMENT** is roughly midway between Albuquerque and Santa Fe. From Albuquerque, take I-25 n. to exit 259, then SR 22 w. to Cochiti Pueblo and follow signs to the national monument. From Santa Fe, take I-25 s. to exit 264, then SR 16 w. about 8 mi. to SR 22 and follow signs. Located on north-central New Mexico's Pajarito Plateau, Tent Rocks is a remarkable wonderland of cone-shaped rock formations, the product of volcanic eruptions that occurred millions of years ago. The pumice, ash and tuff deposits left behind were subsequently shaped by wind, water and erosion.

Boulder caps perch precariously atop many of these tapering formations—which range in height from a few to more than 90 feet—protecting the softer rock below. Narrow, twisting passageways carved over time by wind and rushing water through slot canyon, also are fascinating geologic features. Ponderosa and piñon pines grow along with desert plants like Indian paintbrush and Apache plume.

The area's austere beauty can be explored on two hikes. The 1.2-mile Cave Loop Trail is an easy trek that leads to an above-ground cave. The more strenuous Canyon Trail (3 miles round-trip) ascends a narrow canyon with a steep 630-foot elevation gain. The trail ends atop a mesa that offers breathtaking 360-degree views of the tent rocks below, the Rio Grande Valley and the Sangre de Cristo, Jémez and Sandia mountains looming in the distance.

Note: The trailhead is 4 miles from the Monument entrance gate along a paved road. The trail is rated moderate with some more difficult areas toward the end of Slot Canyon trail; steps built into the trail help facilitate the ascent. Wear sturdy hiking shoes, a hat and sunscreen, and bring drinking water. Stay on the designated trail; climbing on the rock formations or off trail is prohibited. There are parking areas and restrooms at the trailhead. The Veteran's Memorial Overlook and Trail can be accessed along a gravel access road that passes through private and Bureau of Land Management land. This area is open seasonally; phone ahead to confirm schedule. Dogs and drones are not permitted.

Time: Allow 2 hours, 30 minutes minimum. **Hours:** Daily 8-4. Increased visitation in summer may cause 30 to 90 minute entrance delays starting at 9. As parking becomes available, new visitors will be allowed entry. Closing begins at 3:30 from the top of slot canyon trail. Visitors must be in their vehicles by 4:30 and exit the Monument gated area by 5. Closed Jan. 1, Jan. 6, Fri. before Easter, Easter, Mon. after Easter, May 3, July 13-14, July 25, Nov. 1, Thanksgiving and Christmas. **Cost:** $100 (more than 25 people); $25 (9-25 people); $5 (up to 8 people). **Phone:** (505) 331-6259 for the fee booth.

DEMING (I-2) pop. 14,855, elev. 4,337'

Fields of chiles flourish in the river valley around Deming, along with secondary crops cotton, onions, pecans, grapes and sorghum. The water that sustains them is the subsurface flow of the Mimbres River, which vanishes underground north of the city and reappears at the surface as a lake in the Mexican state of Chihuahua. Southeast of this growing retirement center the Little Florida (flo-REE-da) Mountains yield agates, fire opals, jasper and semiprecious stones.

Deming-Luna County Chamber of Commerce and Visitors Center: 800 E. Pine St., P.O. Box 8, Deming, NM 88030. **Phone:** (575) 546-2674.

Self-guiding tours: A walking-tour brochure listing 16 historic buildings and sites is available from the Deming-Luna County Chamber of Commerce and Visitors Center.

BEST WESTERN DEMING SOUTHWEST INN 575/546-4544

Hotel

AAA Benefit: Members save up to 15% and earn bonus points!

Address: 1500 W Pine St 88030 **Location:** I-10 exit 81, just e. **Facility:** 40 units. 1 story, exterior corridors. **Pool:** outdoor. **Guest Services:** coin laundry. **Featured Amenity: breakfast buffet.**

SOME UNITS

DAYS INN DEMING 575/546-8813

Motel

Address: 1601 E Pine St 88030 **Location:** I-10 exit 85, 2 mi w on business loop; exit 81 eastbound, 1 mi e on business loop. **Facility:** 57 units. 2 stories (no elevator), exterior corridors. **Pool:** outdoor. **Guest Services:** coin laundry. **Featured Amenity: breakfast buffet.**

SOME UNITS

HAMPTON INN BY HILTON DEMING 575/546-2022
Hotel. **Address:** 3751 E Cedar St 88030

AAA Benefit: Members save up to 15%!

HOLIDAY INN EXPRESS & SUITES 575/545-6500
Hotel. **Address:** 3801 E Cedar St 88030

WHERE TO EAT

RANCHER'S GRILL 575/546-8883
American. Casual Dining. **Address:** 316 E Cedar St 88030

ELEPHANT BUTTE pop. 1,431

ELEPHANT BUTTE INN 575/297-4990
Hotel. **Address:** 401 Hwy 195 87935

EL MALPAIS NATIONAL MONUMENT

El Malpais National Monument is south of Grants via I-40 to SRs 53 and 117. It preserves and protects 114,106 acres of a landscape shaped by volcanic action that over time created lava flows and lava tube caves. Visitors can hike trails, embark on scenic drives and explore caves (a free permit is required) in a setting that is remarkable for its unspoiled solitude. **Note:** Wear sturdy boots and exercise extreme caution when hiking on the sharp lava formations.

Caving permits and information about recreational activities and cave exploration can be obtained at the El Malpais Visitor Center, just south of I-40 exit 85 at 1900 E. Santa Fe Ave. in Grants. Monument open daily 24 hours. Visitor center open daily 8-5; closed Jan. 1, Thanksgiving and Christmas. Admission is free. Phone (505) 876-2783 to speak with a park ranger.

EL MALPAIS NATIONAL CONSERVATION AREA is within El Malpais National Monument via I-40 exit 89 (CR 117) or I-40 exit 81 (CR 53). Encompassing 231,230 acres of public lands, the conservation area offers numerous recreational opportunities, including hiking, mountain biking, primitive camping, cave exploration (bring your own equipment) and horseback riding.

Marked trails traversing designated wilderness areas explore the region's natural features. The Armijo Canyon Trail is a sandy trek that winds among piñon pine and juniper trees. The La Ventana Arch Trail passes dramatic sandstone cliff formations and offers a good view of La Ventana Natural Arch; this impressive geological formation is New Mexico's second tallest arch.

The Bureau of Land Management Ranger Station, 9 miles south of I-40 exit 89 via CR 117, contains exhibits about the historical and cultural aspects of El Malpais and has information about the region's natural history, geology and indigenous animals and plants. A short hiking trail beginning at the parking area leads to impressive vistas of the surrounding countryside. *See Recreation Areas Chart.*

Hours: Conservation area open daily 24 hours. Ranger station open daily 8:30-4:30; closed Jan. 1, Thanksgiving and Christmas. **Cost:** Free. **Phone:** (505) 280-2918 for the BLM ranger station.

EL MORRO NATIONAL MONUMENT (F-2)

El Morro National Monument is 43 miles southwest of Grants via SR 53. The central features of the 1,278-acre monument are 200-foot-high Inscription Rock and the water hole fed by snowmelt and rainfall pouring off the rock. The Spanish called the sandstone mesa *El Morro,* meaning "the bluff" or "the headland."

Carved into the soft rock are centuries-old petroglyphs. The first known European inscription was left in 1605 by Juan de Oñate, governor and colonizer of New Mexico. Others include those of Gov. Manuel de Silva Nieto in 1629; a soldier in 1632; Don Diego de Vargas, leader of the 1692 reconquest; and Lt. Edward Beale, who passed by with a camel caravan in 1857. Other soldiers and settlers making their way west added their names and dates.

Two Ancestral Puebloan villages once thrived atop this mesa. Remains of an 875-room dwelling from about the 13th century have been partly excavated.

Self-guiding tours are available. A half-mile trail and a 2-mile trail take about 45 minutes and 1.5 hours, respectively. A 15-minute video presentation in the visitor center offers a glimpse into the cultural and natural history of the area. A small campground is available on a first-come, first-served basis. For further information contact the Superintendent, El Morro National Monument, HC 61, Box 43, Ramah, NM 87321.

Visitor center daily 9-5. Hiking trails daily 9-4. Closed Jan. 1, Thanksgiving and Christmas. Last admittance to Headland Trail 1 hour before closing. Phone ahead to confirm schedule. Phone (505) 783-4226.

ESPAÑOLA (A-4) pop. 10,224, elev. 5,589'

In the northern Rio Grande Valley between the Jémez Mountains and Truchas Peaks, Española was founded in 1598 by the Spaniards as the first capital of New Mexico. It grew into a trading and distribution center when the Denver and Rio Grande Western Railroad built its Chili Line between Española and Antonito, Colo., in the late 1870s.

In late summer garlands of *ristras*—strings of scarlet chile peppers dried in the sun—decorate houses and fences. Española is a central point for visits to surrounding pueblo villages where arts and crafts are sold, including Nambé, Picurís, Pojoaque, San Ildefonso, Ohkay Owingeh, Santa Clara, Taos and Tesuque.

Española Valley Chamber of Commerce: 1 Calle de las Españolas, Suites F and G, P.O. Box 190, Española, NM 87532-0190. **Phone:** (505) 753-2831.

FARMINGTON (E-2) pop. 45,877, elev. 5,292'

• Hotels p. 286 • Restaurants p. 286

Apple orchards replaced saloons and coal miners ousted card sharks as Farmington evolved into the major commerce and industrial center of the Four Corners region in northwestern New Mexico.

Navajo Mine, west of town, is one of the largest coal mining operations in the world. Its output fuels the adjacent Four Corners Power Plant, which in turn heats the waters used by windsurfers on nearby Morgan Lake. Anglers favor the San Juan River and Farmington and Jackson lakes.

West of town the vast Navajo Nation Reservation extends into Arizona. The convention and visitors bureau distributes a list of trading posts.

Forty miles south via SR 371 is the Bisti/De-Na-Zin Wilderness, an area of weirdly eroded hoodoos and slate-topped *mesitas*—geological formations made up of sandstone and shale that have become eroded by wind and rain. Angel Peak Scenic Area lies 30 miles southeast via SR 550. Once considered by the Navajos as the dwelling place of sacred ones, the colorful sandstone formations crowning the peak were shaped over millions of years.

Changing exhibits by area artists are displayed at the San Juan College Henderson Fine Arts Center Art Gallery. Outdoor theatrical performances are offered mid-June to mid-August in the Lions Wilderness Park, a natural sandstone amphitheater.

Farmington Convention and Visitors Bureau: 3041 E. Main St., Farmington, NM 87402. **Phone:** (505) 326-7602 or (800) 448-1240.

BEST WESTERN PLUS THE FOUR CORNERS INN 505/564-8100

AAA Benefit: Members save up to 15% and earn bonus points!

Address: 4751 Cortez Way 87402 **Location:** On US 550 at Cortez Way. **Facility:** 66 units. 3 stories, interior corridors. **Pool:** heated indoor. **Activities:** hot tub, exercise room. **Guest Services:** coin laundry. **Featured Amenity: breakfast buffet.**

SOME UNITS

COMFORT INN 505/325-2626

Address: 555 Scott Ave 87401 **Location:** 1 mi e on SR 516 (Main St), just s. **Facility:** 59 units. 2 stories (no elevator), interior corridors. **Pool:** heated outdoor. **Guest Services:** valet laundry. **Featured Amenity: full hot breakfast.**

SOME UNITS

COMFORT SUITES 505/325-9414
Hotel. **Address:** 1951 Cortland Dr 87401

COURTYARD BY MARRIOTT FARMINGTON 505/325-5111
SAVE Hotel. **Address:** 560 Scott Ave 87401
AAA Benefit: Members save 5% or more!

FAIRFIELD INN & SUITES BY MARRIOTT FARMINGTON 505/324-0777
SAVE Hotel. **Address:** 2850 E Main St 87402
AAA Benefit: Members save 5% or more!

HOLIDAY INN EXPRESS & SUITES 505/325-2545
Hotel. **Address:** 2110 Bloomfield Blvd 87401

HOME2 SUITES BY HILTON 505/325-1500
SAVE Extended Stay Contemporary Hotel. **Address:** 777 S Browning Pkwy 87401
AAA Benefit: Members save up to 15%!

TOWNEPLACE SUITES BY MARRIOTT 505/327-2442
SAVE Extended Stay Hotel. **Address:** 4200 Sierra Vista Dr 87402
AAA Benefit: Members save 5% or more!

WHERE TO EAT

BLUE MOON DINER 505/324-0001
American. Casual Dining. **Address:** 1819 E 20th St 87401

D.H. LESCOMBES WINERY & BISTRO 505/325-0711
American. Casual Dining. **Address:** 5150 E Main St, Suite 101 87401

KB DILLON'S BAR & GRILLE 505/325-0222
American. Casual Dining. **Address:** 101 W Broadway 87401

LOS HERMANITOS RESTAURANT 505/326-5664
Mexican. Casual Dining. **Address:** 3501 E Main St 87401

LOS RIOS CAFE 505/325-5699
Mexican. Casual Dining. **Address:** 915 Farmington Ave 87401

PIZZA 9 505/325-6463
Pizza Sandwiches. Quick Serve. **Address:** 685 Scott Ave 87401

SI SEÑOR RESTAURANT 505/324-9050
Southwestern. Casual Dining. **Address:** 4015 E 30th St 87402

THREE RIVERS EATERY AND BREW HOUSE 505/324-2187
American. Casual Dining. **Address:** 101 E Main St 87401

TRATTORIA DI BERNARDONE 505/325-0303
Italian. Casual Dining. **Address:** 5520 E Main St 87402

FORT UNION NATIONAL MONUMENT (E-4)

Eight miles northwest of Watrous on SR 161 (off I-25 exit 366), ranks of chimneys are stark reminders of the days when Fort Union was one of the largest military posts on the Southwestern frontier. From 1851 until 1891 Fort Union was the chief quartermaster depot for all garrisons throughout the region as well as the primary station for troops assigned to protect settlers and Santa Fe Trail travelers.

The site was well chosen, for the two branches of the Santa Fe Trail—the Mountain Branch and the Cimarron—pass through the Fort Union Valley. In addition, the remote location put the soldiers closer to the tribes and farther from towns that might distract them from their duties.

A group of log buildings west of Wolf Creek constituted the first Fort Union. For a decade it served as a way station on the Santa Fe Trail and as a headquarters for battling the Utes, Jicarilla Apaches, Comanches and Kiowas.

The outbreak of the Civil War abruptly turned the Army's attention away from these conflicts. The second Fort Union, an earthwork defense bastion, was built east of the creek in late 1861. It was constructed by local volunteers just before Confederate forces from Texas, eager to control Colorado's mineral resources and Fort Union's supplies, swept up the Rio Grande Valley. After their supply train was destroyed in the Battle of Glorieta, the Confederate troops retreated and headed for home.

The third fort dates from the mid-1860s; its garrison, quartermaster depot and arsenal still stand today. For the next 15 years the Indian wars occupied the military, while tons of goods flowed through the depot. Gradually local tribes were subdued. The Santa Fe Railway reached New Mexico in 1879, making travel safer. Fort Union was abandoned in 1891.

Interpretive signs relay the history of the fort and the local area. A self-guiding 1.25-mile interpretive trail explores 100 acres of adobe ruins. A half-mile trail also is an option. A visitor center containing a museum relates fort history. Living-history demonstrations and other events are offered during summer. Daily 8-5, Memorial Day-Labor Day; 8-4, rest of year. Closed Jan. 1, Thanksgiving and Christmas. Free. Phone (505) 425-8025.

GALLUP (F-1) pop. 21,678, elev. 6,508'

The Atchison, Topeka & Santa Fe Railway pushed into this red rock mesa region in 1881 to use area coal deposits for its engines. Until then mostly stockmen had lived in the area; Gallup was a stage stop with nothing more than a saloon/general store called the Blue Goose. Coal mining and the presence of the railroad attracted settlers from other nations, giving the city an unusually cosmopolitan heritage.

The city is best known as the principal Navajo trading center—their vast reservation extends north and west into Arizona—as well as for the residents of nearby Zuni Pueblo. Gallup has more than 100 trading posts, shops and galleries; at many trading posts handmade articles ranging from rugs and baskets to turquoise jewelry are sold.

Gallup Chamber of Commerce and Convention and Visitors Bureau: 106 W. Hwy. 66, Gallup, NM 87301. **Phone:** (505) 722-2228.

BEST WESTERN PLUS GALLUP INN & SUITES 505/726-5380

Hotel

AAA Benefit: Members save up to 15% and earn bonus points!

Address: 910 E Aztec Ave 87301 **Location:** I-40 exit 22; jct Ford Dr, just s. **Facility:** 69 units, some kitchens. 4 stories, interior corridors. **Amenities:** safes. **Pool:** heated indoor. **Activities:** hot tub, exercise room. **Guest Services:** valet and coin laundry. **Featured Amenity:** full hot breakfast.

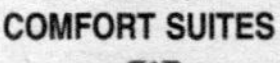

COMFORT SUITES 505/863-3445

Hotel

Address: 3940 E Hwy 66 87301 **Location:** I-40 exit 26, just e. **Facility:** 66 units. 3 stories, interior corridors. **Amenities:** *Some:* safes. **Pool:** heated indoor. **Activities:** hot tub, exercise room. **Guest Services:** valet and coin laundry. **Featured Amenity:** full hot breakfast.

FAIRFIELD INN & SUITES BY MARRIOTT 505/863-0900

Hotel. **Address:** 3510 Route 66 87301

AAA Benefit: Members save 5% or more!

HAMPTON INN & SUITES 505/726-0900

Hotel. **Address:** 1460 W Maloney Ave 87301

AAA Benefit: Members save up to 15%!

HILTON GARDEN INN 505/722-9600

Hotel. **Address:** 1530 W Maloney Ave 87301

AAA Benefit: Members save up to 15%!

HOLIDAY INN EXPRESS & SUITES 505/722-7500

Hotel. **Address:** 3850 E Hwy 66 87301

LA QUINTA INN & SUITES GALLUP 505/722-2233

Hotel. **Address:** 3880 E Hwy 66 87301

SPRINGHILL SUITES BY MARRIOTT GALLUP 505/726-9940

Hotel

SPRINGHILL SUITES MARRIOTT **AAA Benefit:** Members save 5% or more!

Address: 1105 W Lincoln Ave 87301 **Location:** I-40 exit 20, just n. **Facility:** 95 units. 4 stories, interior corridors. **Pool:** heated indoor. **Activities:** hot tub, exercise room. **Guest Services:** valet and coin laundry. **Featured Amenity:** full hot breakfast.

TOWNEPLACE SUITES BY MARRIOTT 505/722-6500

Extended Stay Hotel. **Address:** 3920 E Historic Hwy 66 87301

AAA Benefit: Members save 5% or more!

WHERE TO EAT

ANGELA'S CAFE 505/722-7526

American. Casual Dining. **Address:** 201 E Hwy 66 87301

BADLANDS GRILL 505/722-5157

Steak. Casual Dining. **Address:** 2201 W Hwy 66 87301

DON DIEGO'S RESTAURANT & LOUNGE 505/722-5517

Mexican. Casual Dining. **Address:** 801 W Historic Hwy 66 87301

EARL'S FAMILY RESTAURANT 505/863-4201

American Casual Dining

$8-$17

AAA Inspector Notes: *Classic.* Since 1947, this landmark family restaurant has served a wide variety of American and Mexican dishes. The favorite steak and enchiladas is a blend of the two cuisines. A long held tradition allows Native American artists to sell jewelry and crafts directly to dining patrons inside and at tables outside the eatery. **Address:** 1400 E Hwy 66 87301 **Location:** I-40 exit 22, just s to US 66, then e. B L D

EL SOMBRERO 505/863-4554

Mexican. Casual Dining. **Address:** 1201 W US 66 87301

KING DRAGON 505/863-6300

Chinese. Casual Dining. **Address:** 1212 N Hwy 491 87301

GILA CLIFF DWELLINGS NATIONAL MONUMENT (H-2)

Gila Cliff Dwellings National Monument is a minimum 2-hour drive 44 miles north of Silver City via SR 15, at 26 Jim Bradford Trail in Mimbres. Vehicles pulling trailers 20 feet or longer should take SR 35 from Mimbres or SR 152 through Hillsboro, and then SR 15. In this rough and desolate country near the west fork of the Gila (HEE-la) River, seven natural cavities indent the face of a cliff some 175 feet above the canyon floor. Five of these hollows contain rooms constructed during the late 13th century by people of the Mogollon culture—these remain the focus of the monument.

A 1-mile hiking trail loops from the contact station to the dwellings. The Gila Visitor Center is 2 miles south of the monument entrance. Guided 1-hour tours of the cliff dwellings depart Fri.-Sun., April to Veterans Day (tour dates and times may vary; phone ahead) from the dwellings themselves. Allow 30 minutes to walk from the trailhead. Pets are not permitted on the monument trails; free kennels are available.

Trail to dwellings open daily 9-5 (last entry 1 hour before closing). Visitor center open daily 8-4:30. Admission $5-$10; free (ages 0-15 and Federal Recreational Lands Pass holders); $10 (family). Exact change is required and may be obtained at the visitor center. Self-guiding trail pamphlets and travel guide brochures are available at no cost. Phone (575) 536-9461.

GILA NATIONAL FOREST (H-1)

Elevations in the forest range from 4,000 ft. in the desert to 11,000 ft. at Whitewater Baldy. Refer to AAA maps for additional elevation information.

In southwestern New Mexico, Gila (HEE-la) National Forest occupies 3,321,000 acres of forest and rangeland. The smaller of its two units extends north from Lordsburg along the Big Burro Mountains. The main unit, north of Silver City *(see place listing p. 319)*, embraces the Black, Mogollon, Tularosa and Diablo mountains. These wild ranges and remote canyons were the stronghold of such Apache warriors as Geronimo and Mangas Coloradas.

Much of the Mogollon Mountains lies within the Gila Wilderness, the first area in the nation to be so designated. Instrumental in its 1924 establishment was Aldo Leopold, the forester and naturalist whose "Sand County Almanac" and other writings have become classics of environmental literature.

A plaque 9 miles south of Glenwood on US 180 at the Aldo Leopold Overlook marks the Leopold Vista Historical Monument. The Gila, Blue Range and Aldo Leopold wilderness areas as well as Gila Cliff Dwellings National Monument are north of Silver City.

In the 1870s the region was the center of a mining boom, of which ghost towns and old mine structures are silent reminders. The half-mile-long Catwalk National Recreation Trail passes through the steep walls of Whitewater Canyon. A metal suspension bridge carries hikers across a creek that once provided water to a nearby mill. Now a popular recreation area, it is reached via SR 174 from US 180. A $3 fee per private vehicle is charged to access the Catwalk National Recreation Area.

The 110-mile Trail of the Mountain Spirits Scenic Byway travels from Silver City east to San Lorenzo, through the Mimbres Valley, down Sapillo Creek, past Clinton P. Anderson Vista to Gila Cliff Dwellings National Monument, and returns to Silver City over the Pinos Altos Range. Overlooks along the byway provide perspective on the magnitude of the cliffs and the surrounding countryside.

There are numerous developed recreation areas in the forest. Stream and lake fishing and big game hunting are available in season. *See Recreation Areas Chart.*

GILA VISITOR CENTER is 3.5 mi. n. of Gila Hot Springs via SR 15; vehicles pulling trailers 20 feet or longer should use SR 35 north from San Lorenzo. It contains displays of cultural artifacts and exhibits about the Apache and Mogollon people and the Gila Wilderness. A 15-minute video is shown. You can also pick up information about all Gila National Forest recreational activities. **Hours:** Daily 8-4:30. Phone ahead during winter months for road condition updates. **Cost:** $5; free (ages 0-15); $10 (family). **Phone:** (575) 536-9461.

GRANTS (F-2) pop. 9,182, elev. 6,450'

Operated by the Cibola County Historical Society, the Western New Mexico Aviation Heritage Museum honors the pioneer aviators who flew the then-remote Amarillo to Los Angeles stretch of the Mid-continental Airway, established by Charles Lindbergh for Transcontinental Air Transport. The route was equipped with generator-powered beacon towers spaced approximately every 10 to 15 miles to aid pilots flying mail delivery planes at night. A 30-minute guided walking tour of the restored airway beacon at the Grants-Milan Airport is offered Sat. 9-1; from I-40, take exits 79 or 81 to Airport Road.

Grants/Cibola County Chamber of Commerce: 100 N. Iron Ave., P.O. Box 297, Grants, NM 87020. **Phone:** (505) 287-4802.

EL CAFECITO 505/285-6229

New Mexican. Casual Dining. **Address:** 820 E Santa Fe Ave 87020

LA VENTANA STEAKHOUSE 505/287-9393

Steak. Casual Dining. **Address:** 110 1/2 Geis St 87020

HOBBS (I-6) pop. 34,122, elev. 3,621'

Oil and water mix in the economy of Hobbs, a modern city on the western edge of the flat Llano

Estacado. Grasslands first attracted farmers and cattlemen to this region in the early 20th century; one of them, James Hobbs, gave his name to the community. A vast underground reserve of water provided irrigation for bountiful crops of cotton, alfalfa, vegetables and grain.

In 1928, however, the discovery of another kind of well changed pastoral Hobbs into a boomtown. Within a decade the city was the home of some 10,000 citizens, most associated with tapping the oil field that still produces 90 percent of the state's petroleum. Many oil companies operating in the area have headquarters in Hobbs.

History buffs will want to check out the Thelma A. Webber Southwest Heritage Room in the Scarborough Memorial Library at the University of the Southwest, 6610 Lovington Hwy. It has a small exhibit of prehistoric Native American artifacts, art pieces and pioneer collectibles; phone (800) 530-4400.

Hobbs Chamber of Commerce: 400 N. Marland Blvd., Hobbs, NM 88240. **Phone:** (575) 397-3202.

BAYMONT INN & SUITES 575/964-8400
Hotel. **Address:** 3510 N Central Ave 88240

BEST WESTERN EXECUTIVE INN 575/397-7171

Hotel

AAA Benefit: Members save up to 15% and earn bonus points!

Address: 309 N Marland Blvd 88240 **Location:** US 62, 180 and Snyder St. **Facility:** 62 units. 2 stories (no elevator), exterior corridors. **Amenities:** safes. **Pool:** outdoor. **Activities:** picnic facilities. **Featured Amenity: breakfast buffet.**

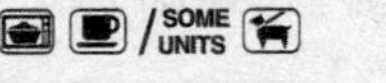

COMFORT SUITES-HOBBS 575/492-1000
Hotel. **Address:** 2708 W Scenic Dr 88240

COUNTRY INN & SUITES BY RADISSON HOBBS NEW MEXICO 575/391-0282
Hotel. **Address:** 5220 N Lovington Hwy 88240

FAIRFIELD INN BY MARRIOTT 575/393-0667
SAVE Hotel. **Address:** 1350 W Joe Harvey Blvd 88240
AAA Benefit: Members save 5% or more!

HAMPTON INN & SUITES BY HILTON 575/492-6000
SAVE Hotel. **Address:** 5420 N Lovington Hwy 88242
AAA Benefit: Members save up to 15%!

HILTON GARDEN INN HOBBS 575/393-5645
SAVE Hotel. **Address:** 4620 N Lovington Hwy 88240
AAA Benefit: Members save up to 15%!

HOLIDAY INN EXPRESS & SUITES 575/391-8777
Hotel. **Address:** 4000 N Lovington Hwy 88240

LA QUINTA INN & SUITES BY WYNDHAM HOBBS 575/397-8777
Hotel. **Address:** 3312 N Lovington Hwy 88240

QUALITY INN & SUITES 575/392-8777
Hotel. **Address:** 3610 N Lovington Hwy 88240

SLEEP INN & SUITES 575/393-3355
Hotel. **Address:** 4630 N Lovington Hwy 88240

TOWNEPLACE SUITES BY MARRIOTT HOBBS 575/964-8900
SAVE Extended Stay Hotel. **Address:** 3811 N Central Ave 88240
AAA Benefit: Members save 5% or more!

WHERE TO EAT

CATTLE BARON STEAK & SEAFOOD 575/393-2800
American. Casual Dining. **Address:** 1930 N Grimes St 88240

PACIFIC RIM 575/392-0030
Pacific Rim. Casual Dining. **Address:** 1309 Joe Harvey Blvd 88240

SAXONY STEAK ROOM 575/397-3251
Steak. Casual Dining. **Address:** 501 N Marland Blvd 88240

TIA JUANA'S MEXICAN GRILLE & CANTINA 575/392-0500
Mexican. Casual Dining. **Address:** 3510 N Lovington Hwy 88240

TOKYO JAPANESE STEAKHOUSE AND SUSHI BAR 575/964-8522
Japanese. Casual Dining. **Address:** 915 E Bender Blvd 88240

LAGUNA PUEBLO (C-2) elev. 5,807'

Rich in history, Laguna Pueblo consists of six villages; Old Laguna Village has served as the capital since the early 1300s. Casa Blanca is a tourist and commercial center for the reservation, which is known for its traditional crafts, pottery and jewelry.

After the completion of the mission church, the Spanish government recognized the pueblo as one of the largest Keresan pueblos. Completed in 1699, the Mission of the Pueblo of Laguna is a long, narrow stone structure notable for its bright and unusual interior design.

The pueblo can be visited 8-4:30 weekdays; weekend religious ceremonies are closed to the public. Photographing, sketching, painting or recording pueblo ceremonies is not permitted.

Shopping: Browse for pottery and traditional Indian crafts at the Dancing Eagle Supermarket, off I-40.

LAS CRUCES (I-3) pop. 97,618, elev. 3,908'

• **Hotels p. 291 • Restaurants p. 291**

A little forest of crosses marking the graves of members of a caravan ambushed by Mescalero Apaches soon came to identify this spot on El Camino Real at the foot of the Organ Mountains. By the mid-19th century Las Cruces—the crosses—was a major supply point for mining operations and forts that protected the trade routes to

Santa Fe and points west. The largest of these posts was Fort Selden in nearby Radium Springs.

The Mesquite Street Historic District, east of Main Street, preserves 22 blocks of the original town site, which was plotted out in 1849 using rawhide ropes. Many of the small adobe houses, painted vibrant shades of pink, blue and green, are at least a century old.

Irrigated by the Rio Grande, the surrounding Mesilla Valley is a leading producer of alfalfa, chile peppers, onions, corn, cotton and pecans. About 25 miles northeast of town on US 70/82, then 4 miles south, is White Sands Missile Range *(see place listing p. 327)*, where experimental rockets are tested.

In mid-May crowds gather for the GEM Blessing of the Fields, a colorful procession around the grounds of the New Mexico Farm & Ranch Heritage Museum with folklorico dancing, bread-baking demonstrations and other festivities. In early November thousands flock to Young Park, 1905 Nevada Ave., for the GEM Renaissance ArtsFaire. In addition to spotlighting the creativity of local and regional artists, this popular event offers live entertainment, food and an appearance by Magellan the dragon.

Surrounding Las Cruces is the Organ Mountains-Desert Peaks National Monument. Designated in 2014, it encompasses 466,330 acres and includes four distinct geologic areas: the Organ Mountains, the Desert Peaks, the Potrillo Mountains and the Doña Ana Mountains.

The Potrillo Mountains, the most remote section, is a volcanic landscape of cinder cones, lava flows and craters pockmarking broad desert plains. The Desert Peaks include the Doña Ana Mountains, an isolated cluster of steep and jagged peaks; they offer an extensive network of hiking, mountain biking and equestrian trails as well as rock climbing areas.

The Robledo Mountains cover a much larger area characterized by peaks that rise sharply from the flat desert plain. Farther to the northwest are the Sierra de las Uvas, masses of volcanic rock punctuated by cliffs. For day visitors the Organ Mountains region is not only the most developed portion, but the easiest to reach.

For more information about Organ Mountains-Desert Peaks National Monument, contact the Bureau of Land Management's Las Cruces District office, 1800 Marquess St., Las Cruces, NM 88005; phone (575) 525-4300.

Visit Las Cruces: 211 N. Water St., Las Cruces, NM 88001. **Phone:** (575) 541-2444.

GEM **NEW MEXICO FARM & RANCH HERITAGE MUSEUM** is off I-25 exit 1, then 1.5 mi. e. to 4100 Dripping Springs Rd. New Mexico's rural life and 4,000-year-old farming history are explored via interactive displays and demonstrations. The 47-acre site includes a working cattle ranch where milking and blacksmith techniques are demonstrated. Horses, donkeys, goats and sheep also live on the ranch. A greenhouse, gardens and a theater are on the premises.

Hours: Mon.-Sat. 9-5, Sun. noon-5. Closed Jan. 1, Thanksgiving and Christmas. **Cost:** $5; $4 (ages 60+); $3 (ages 4-17); $2 (active military and U.S. veterans with ID). **Phone:** (575) 522-4100. ***(See ad this page.)***

ORGAN MOUNTAINS-DESERT PEAKS NATIONAL MONUMENT surrounds Las Cruces. Visitors wishing to check out the nation's newest national monument should head to the Organ Mountains, the

▼ *See AAA listing this page* ▼

most easily accessible of its four areas. The name refers to the needle-like spires resembling organ pipes that jut dramatically from the Chihuahuan Desert floor and reach heights of up to 9,000 feet. Other features of this ruggedly scenic environment are narrow canyons and open woodlands. The Organ Mountains offer numerous opportunities for hiking, horseback riding, mountain biking, camping, wildlife viewing and landscape photography.

Dripping Springs Natural Area is one of several designated recreation areas within the national monument. More than 4 miles of easy hiking trails wind past desert scrub and woods of juniper and oak trees. Bird watchers will spot red-tailed hawks, golden eagles and Gambel's quail, among other species; wildlife includes desert mule deer, coyotes and the occasional mountain lion.

The Dripping Springs Visitor Center is about 10 miles east of Las Cruces; from I-25 exit 1, take University Avenue/Dripping Springs Road east to the end. Interpretive displays provide information about the Organ Mountains. **Hours:** Entrance gate open daily 8-7, Apr.-Sept.; 8-5, rest of year. Visitor center open daily 8-5; closed Jan. 1, Thanksgiving and Christmas. **Cost:** Day use fee $5 (per private vehicle). **Phone:** (575) 522-1219.

BEST WESTERN MISSION INN 575/524-8591

AAA Benefit: Members save up to 15% and earn bonus points!

Address: 1765 S Main St 88005 **Location:** I-10 exit 142 (University Ave), 1 mi n. **Facility:** 68 units. 2 stories (no elevator), exterior corridors. **Pool:** outdoor. **Featured Amenity: breakfast buffet.**

COMFORT INN & SUITES DE MESILLA 575/527-1050
Hotel. **Address:** 1300 Avenida de Mesilla 88005

COMFORT SUITES OF LAS CRUCES I-25 NORTH 575/521-1030
Hotel. **Address:** 236 N Telshor Blvd 88011

DAYS INN LAS CRUCES 575/526-8311
Hotel. **Address:** 755 Avenida de Mesilla 88005

DRURY INN & SUITES LAS CRUCES 575/523-4100
Hotel. **Address:** 1631 Hickory Loop 88005

HAMPTON INN & SUITES I-25 575/527-8777
Hotel. **Address:** 2350 E Griggs Ave 88001
AAA Benefit: Members save up to 15%!

HAMPTON INN & SUITES LAS CRUCES I-10 575/541-8777
Hotel. **Address:** 1641 Hickory Loop 88001
AAA Benefit: Members save up to 15%!

HILTON GARDEN INN LAS CRUCES 575/522-0900
Hotel. **Address:** 2550 S Don Roser Dr 88011
AAA Benefit: Members save up to 15%!

HOLIDAY INN EXPRESS & SUITES NORTH 575/522-0700
Hotel. **Address:** 2142 Telshor Ct 88011

HOLIDAY INN EXPRESS HOTEL & SUITES LAS CRUCES 575/527-9947
Hotel. **Address:** 2635 S Valley Dr 88005

HOME2 SUITES BY HILTON LAS CRUCES 575/527-6491
Extended Stay Hotel. **Address:** 1120 N Telshor Blvd 88011
AAA Benefit: Members save up to 15%!

HOTEL ENCANTO DE LAS CRUCES 575/522-4300

Address: 705 S Telshor Blvd 88011 **Location:** I-25 exit 3 (Lohman Ave), just e, then just s. **Facility:** 202 units. 7 stories, interior corridors. **Pool:** heated outdoor. **Activities:** hot tub, exercise room. **Guest Services:** valet laundry, area transportation.

LA QUINTA INN & SUITES LAS CRUCES ORGAN MOUNTAIN 575/523-0100
Hotel. **Address:** 1500 Hickory Dr 88005

LUNDEEN INN OF THE ARTS 575/526-3326
Historic Bed & Breakfast. **Address:** 618 S Alameda Blvd 88005

RAMADA PALMS DE LAS CRUCES 575/526-4411
Hotel. **Address:** 201 E University Ave 88005

SPRINGHILL SUITES BY MARRIOTT 575/541-8887
Hotel. **Address:** 1611 Hickory Loop 88005
AAA Benefit: Members save 5% or more!

STAYBRIDGE SUITES 575/521-7999
Extended Stay Hotel. **Address:** 2651 Northrise Dr 88011

TOWNEPLACE SUITES BY MARRIOTT LAS CRUCES 575/532-6500
Extended Stay Hotel. **Address:** 2143 Telshor Ct 88011
AAA Benefit: Members save 5% or more!

WHERE TO EAT

BOBA CAFE 575/647-5900
Sandwiches Soup. Casual Dining. **Address:** 1900 S Espina St, Suite 8 88001

CATTLE BARON STEAK & SEAFOOD 575/522-7533
American. Casual Dining. **Address:** 790 S Telshor Blvd 88011

CHILITOS 575/526-4184
Mexican. Casual Dining. **Address:** 2405 S Valley Dr 88005

D.H. LESCOMBES WINERY & BISTRO 575/524-0390
American. Casual Dining. **Address:** 1720 Avenida de Mesilla 88004

EL SOMBRERO PATIO CAFE 575/524-9911
Mexican. Casual Dining. **Address:** 363 S Espina St 88001

FARLEY'S 575/522-0466
American. Casual Dining. **Address:** 3499 Foothills Rd 88011

HIGH DESERT BREWING CO. 575/525-6752
American. Casual Dining. **Address:** 1201 W Hadley Ave 88005

INTERNATIONAL DELIGHTS CAFE 575/647-5956
Mediterranean. Quick Serve. **Address:** 1245 El Paseo Rd 88001

LORENZO'S 575/521-3505
Italian. Casual Dining. **Address:** 1753 E University Ave 88001

LUNA ROSSA WINERY & PIZZERIA 575/526-2484
Italian. Casual Dining. **Address:** 1321 Avenida de Mesilla 88005

MIX PACIFIC RIM CUISINE 575/532-2042
Asian. Casual Dining. **Address:** 1001 E University Ave, Suite D4 88001

OLD MESILLA PASTRY CAFE-THE SHED RESTAURANT 575/525-2636
American. Casual Dining. **Address:** 810 S Valley Dr 88005

PECAN GRILL & BREWERY 575/521-1099
American. Brewpub. **Address:** 500 S Telshor Blvd 88011

SAKURA JAPANESE HIBACHI GRILL & SUSHI BAR 575/522-0678
Japanese. Casual Dining. **Address:** 3961 E Lohman Ave 88011

SALUD! DE MESILLA 575/323-3548
New American. Casual Dining. **Address:** 1800 Avenida de Mesilla 88005

SI SEÑOR RESTAURANT 575/527-0817
Mexican. Casual Dining. **Address:** 1551 Amador Ave 88001

ZEFFIRO PIZZERIA NAPOLETANA 575/525-6757
Pizza. Casual Dining. **Address:** 136 N Water St 88001

LAS VEGAS (F-4) pop. 13,753, elev. 6,430'

The faint wagon wheel ruts still visible outside Las Vegas attest to the town's era as a mercantile center on the Santa Fe Trail. Las Vegas also was a military post until Fort Union *(see Fort Union National Monument p. 286)* was built. During the 1880s it was known as one of the roughest towns on the frontier, frequented by such desperadoes as Billy the Kid and Doc Holliday. The arrival of the Santa Fe Railroad in 1879 brought commercial prosperity, and hundreds of historic buildings still stand.

Recreational activities can be enjoyed at Storrie Lake State Park, 4 miles north off SR 518 *(see Recreation Areas Chart)*; Morphy Lake State Park, 25 miles north off SR 518 *(see Recreation Areas Chart)*; and in the Sangre de Cristo Mountains, which rise to the west *(see Santa Fe National Forest p. 317)*.

City of Las Vegas Visitors Center: 500 Railroad Ave., Las Vegas, NM 87701. **Phone:** (505) 425-3707 or (800) 832-5947.

Self-guiding tours: A brochure describing walking and driving tours is available from the visitors center.

BEST WESTERN PLUS MONTEZUMA INN & SUITES 505/426-8000

AAA Benefit: Members save up to 15% and earn bonus points!

Address: 2020 N Grand Ave 87701 **Location:** I-25 exit 347, just sw. **Facility:** 67 units. 3 stories, interior corridors. **Pool:** heated indoor. **Activities:** sauna, hot tub, exercise room. **Guest Services:** valet and coin laundry. **Featured Amenity: breakfast buffet.**

HOLIDAY INN EXPRESS HOTEL & SUITES 505/426-8182
Hotel. **Address:** 816 S Grand Ave 87701

WHERE TO EAT

DICK'S RESTAURANT 505/454-8084
American. Casual Dining. **Address:** 705 Douglas Ave 87701

LINCOLN NATIONAL FOREST (H-4)

Elevations in the forest range from 4,440 ft. at Grapevine Canyon to 11,580 ft. at Lookout Mountain. Refer to AAA maps for additional elevation information.

In south central New Mexico, most of the Sacramento, Jicarilla, Guadalupe and Capitan mountains lie within the three districts of Lincoln National Forest. Covering 1,103,441 acres of pine, juniper and fir timber lands, the terrain in this vast region ranges from desert to subalpine.

Within the Smokey Bear Ranger District are two wilderness areas offering unspoiled back country for hikes and horseback rides. The district office is located in Ruidoso *(see place listing p. 298)*, a popular recreation center and resort.

The Smokey Bear Ranger District also was home to the original Smokey Bear, the living symbol of fire prevention. The Smokey Bear Historical Park in Capitan, north of Ruidoso, displays memorabilia about the tiny cub and information about wildfire prevention along with the town's original train depot. In fire season from April through July, campfires and charcoal grills may be prohibited. Points of interest and a bevy of scenic vistas along Billy the Kid National Scenic Byway make it a drive well worth exploring.

The Sacramento Ranger District is located in and around the mountain community of Cloudcroft. Shaded by tall pines, it's a haven for those wishing to escape the desert heat below. At an elevation of 9,000 feet, the nine-hole golf course at The Lodge Resort & Spa is not only one of the highest courses in the nation but offers challenging terrain as well (picture a 150-foot vertical drop at the first hole tee-off). The course is open April through October, and calling ahead for a tee time is recommended; phone (800) 395-6343.

In addition to golf, the area around Cloudcroft offers camping, hiking, fishing, horseback riding, hunting, skiing and off-road ATV trails. Take a drive along the Sunspot Scenic Highway (SR 6563) and marvel at spectacular views of the Tularosa Basin and the dunes of White Sands National Monument *(see place listing p. 328)*.

The southern Guadalupe Ranger District encompasses the relatively less-traveled Guadalupe Mountains. A 150-foot waterfall, an uncommon feature in this semi-arid region, is the scenic centerpiece of an oasis in the otherwise desert-like environment at Sitting Bull Falls Recreation Area, 49 miles southwest of Carlsbad via US 285, SR 137 and CR 409. The area is open daily 8:30-6; last admittance is 1 hour before closing. Phone ahead to confirm hours. Admission $5 (per private vehicle; exact change is required), free for Federal Recreational Lands Pass holders. Phone (575) 885-4181.

Numerous caves can be explored; permits are issued on a first-come, first-served basis. For further information contact the Lincoln Forest Supervisor's Office, 3463 Las Palomas Rd., Alamogordo, NM 88310. It's advisable to check current road and trail conditions before planning a visit, especially during the winter months; phone (575) 434-7200. *See Recreation Areas Chart.*

LORDSBURG pop. 2,797

COMFORT INN & SUITES 575/542-3355

Hotel

Address: 400 W Wabash St 88045 **Location:** I-10 exit 22, just n, then w. **Facility:** 64 units. 3 stories, interior corridors. **Pool:** heated indoor. **Activities:** sauna, hot tub, exercise room. **Guest Services:** coin laundry. **Featured Amenity: full hot breakfast.**

SOME UNITS

HAMPTON INN 575/542-8900

Hotel. **Address:** 412 W Wabash St 88045

AAA Benefit: Members save up to 15%!

MOTEL-6 LORDSBURG 575/542-8807

Motel

Address: 1303 S Main St 88045 **Location:** I-10 exit 22, just s. **Facility:** 40 units. 1 story, exterior corridors. **Pool:** outdoor. **Guest Services:** coin laundry.

SOME UNITS

WHERE TO EAT

KRANBERRY'S FAMILY RESTAURANT 575/542-9400

American. Casual Dining. **Address:** 1405 S Main St 88045

LOS ALAMOS (A-3) pop. 12,019, elev. 7,320'

• Hotels p. 294 • Restaurants p. 294

In 1943 the federal government selected Los Alamos Ranch School as the top-secret, maximum security site for the Manhattan Project, an atomic bomb research and testing program where "Little Boy" and "Fat Man"—the atomic bombs that ended World War II—were built. By 1945, when the first atomic device was detonated at Trinity Site *(see White Sands Missile Range p. 327)*, more than 3,000 civilian and military personnel were working at the laboratory.

Los Alamos National Laboratory continues to apply science to issues of national security, economic strength and energy security. Its staff of 11,000 conducts extensive research about technology associated with nuclear weapons, deterrence and other defense applications, energy production, health, safety and environmental concerns, astrophysics and life sciences.

Explosions of another sort created the rugged setting that was so essential for maintaining the secrecy of the Manhattan Project. About a million years ago the volcanic vents that had built the Jémez Mountains issued 100 cubic miles of ash and pumice and then collapsed. The result is Valle Grande, one of the largest measured calderas on Earth. Covering 148 square miles, the depression has a rim that averages some 500 feet in height above its floor.

SR 4, about 15 miles west of Los Alamos, follows the crater's southern curve and makes it possible to view the vast, grassy bowl. Over time erupting ash hardened into a layer of tuff, the Pajarito Plateau, which seems even more remote because it is protected by a series of finger-like canyons serrating its edges.

Within the plateau is Bandelier National Monument *(see place listing p. 275)*, the site of extensive Ancestral Puebloan ruins. Guided hiking trips and van tours of Valles Caldera National Preserve *(see Recreation Areas Chart)* offer opportunities to explore the region's geology, archeology and wildlife; phone (575) 829-4100 for information.

Los Alamos Chamber of Commerce and Visitor Center: 109 Central Park Sq., Los Alamos, NM 87544. **Phone:** (505) 662-8105, (505) 661-4816 for the chamber or (800) 444-0707.

Self-guiding tours: A guidebook available at the visitor center and the Los Alamos County Historical Museum (1050 Bathtub Row) outlines a walking tour of local historical sites. A virtual tour app provided by the Manhattan Project National Historical Park guides users on a walking tour past more than a dozen sites used during the Manhattan Project. The

Los Alamos Visitor Contact Station (475 20th St.) can provide more information about the virtual tour app; phone (505) 661-6277.

GEM **BRADBURY SCIENCE MUSEUM** is at 1350 Central Ave. It features films and interactive exhibits interpreting Los Alamos National Laboratory's contributions to modern science, research and technology, including its role in the Manhattan Project and current mission in national security. **Hours:** Tues.-Sat. 10-5, Sun.-Mon. 1-5. Closed Jan. 1, Thanksgiving and Christmas. **Cost:** Free. **Phone:** (505) 667-4444.

HOLIDAY INN EXPRESS & SUITES 505/661-2646

Hotel. **Address:** 60 Entrada Dr 87544

WHERE TO EAT

THE BLUE WINDOW BISTRO 505/662-6305

International. Casual Dining. **Address:** 813 Central Ave 87544

MADRID (D-4) pop. 204, elev. 6,020'

Amiable little Madrid couldn't be more different from the Spanish capital it shares a name with, starting with its pronunciation (say "MAH-drid"). This spot of a hamlet in the high desert country of central New Mexico has had several incarnations over the course of approximately 2 centuries: coal mining boomtown, home of the Madrid Miners minor league baseball team, all-but-deserted "ghost town," offbeat artists' collective. The last one describes Madrid today and is one reason why it's one of the state's most distinctive small communities.

The nearby, mineral-rich Ortiz Mountains ensured Madrid's early success. By 1892 coal was being extracted from mines with shafts as deep as 2,500 feet. A company town of wood-framed cabins rose up, supplying coal for the Santa Fe Railway and the U.S. Government. Beginning in the early 1920s, Madrid became famous for its big Fourth of July parade and a lavish Christmastime display of lights, powered by electricity provided by coal-fed generators. Baseball games were played in the first lighted ballpark in the West.

But the development of cheaper and cleaner fuels brought about Madrid's decline. By the end of the 1950s the mines had closed and only a handful of people were left. Rebirth began in the early 1970s, when artists and craftspeople who didn't mind roughing it started converting old miners' cabins into funky little galleries and shops.

Today there are reminders of Madrid's past in names like the Mine Shaft Tavern and the Ghost Town Trading Post. There's a definite hippie sensibility—a stone gargoyle here, a whiff of incense there. And more recently a biker contingent has made its presence known. The 2007 hit movie "Wild Hogs," a comedy about a group of suburbanites (led by Will Ferrell and Tim Allen) turned wannabe bikers, was partially filmed in town; Maggie's Diner, built specifically for the film, was left standing.

Another blink-and-you'll-miss-it town is Cerrillos, a couple of miles north of Madrid off SR 14 (watch for the signed turnoff). As early as 1,000 B.C., prehistoric people using stone axes and antler picks worked the surrounding region for turquoise, that beautifully hued mineral long prized as a gem and ornamental stone. Cerrillos turquoise even ended up adorning the crown jewels of Spain. Gold, silver, lead and zinc also were extracted from area mines that reached their peak in the 1880s, when the town boasted four hotels and more than 20 saloons.

Today's Cerrillos is a far cry from its boisterous past, but there's still a rustic Old West look to the cottonwood-shaded dirt streets and adobe houses. While "sleepy" is an accurate description, there are a couple of shops and artist studios for visitors to explore. The Cerrillos Turquoise Mining Museum (17 Waldo St.; watch for the signs) has an interesting collection of rocks, Cerrillos turquoise, bottles, curios, tools, coffee cans, hand grinders and antiques amassed by the owners, plus an adjacent fenced enclosure where you can feed llamas, goats and chickens. The museum is open daily 9-5; phone (505) 438-3008.

The stretch of SR 14 between I-40 exit 175 and I-25 exit 278 is called the Turquoise Trail National Scenic Byway. Tijeras is the gateway to this popular alternate route between Albuquerque and Santa Fe. The natural setting is grand—forests of juniper and piñon pine, sagebrush-speckled hills, rolling prairies, vistas of the Sandia Mountains. The Turquoise Trail scenery is particularly spectacular from the village of Golden north to Madrid. Just north of Cerrillos is the Garden of the Gods, a grouping of vertical sandstone and mudstone rocks. While not as large, impressive or famous as the towering red sandstone formations at Garden of the Gods Park in Colorado Springs, they were shaped by the same geological forces.

Shopping: Narrow, winding SR 14, Madrid's main—and only—drag, is lined with an eclectic collection of art galleries and little shops housed in fancifully decorated wooden houses. Parking is a do-it-yourself affair; in other words, grab a spot wherever you can along the road or in one of the few gravel lots. Some establishments are open seasonally or have reduced hours during the winter months.

Galleries like the Chumani Gallery (2839 SR 14), Spirit in Art (just off SR 14 on Firehouse Road), Johnsons of Madrid (2843 SR 14) and Indigo (2854 SR 14) deal in contemporary paintings, Navajo jewelry, Mata Ortiz pottery, Cerrillos turquoise and fiber art. Cowgirl Red (2865 SR 14) has Wild West art, antiques and vintage cowboy boots. Heaven Boutique (2853 SR 14) is a Victorian-style boutique selling clothing, jewelry, hats and gifts.

Madrid's meeting place is the Java Junction (2855 SR 14), where you can mingle with the locals over coffee or a smoothie before checking out the kitschy array of novelty coffee mugs, kitchen magnets and T-shirts, as well as a killer selection of hot sauces and regional salsas.

MINE SHAFT TAVERN 505/473-0743

American. Casual Dining. **Address:** 2846 SR 14 87010

MESCALERO pop. 1,338, elev. 6,600'

INN OF THE MOUNTAIN GODS RESORT & CASINO 575/464-7777

Resort Hotel

Address: 287 Carrizo Canyon Rd (Rt 4) 88340 **Location:** Jct Sudderth Dr, 3.4 mi w, follow signs. **Facility:** This combination resort-casino on the Mescalero Apache Reservation features a breathtaking view of the lake and a pristine natural setting. The spacious guest rooms feature modern amenities. 273 units. 6 stories, interior corridors. **Parking:** on-site and valet. **Amenities:** safes. **Dining:** 5 restaurants, also, Wendell's, see separate listing. **Pool:** heated indoor. **Activities:** sauna, hot tub, steamroom, self-propelled boats, fishing, regulation golf, downhill skiing, snowboarding, recreation programs, playground, game room, trails, exercise room, spa. **Guest Services:** valet laundry.

HS

WHERE TO EAT

WENDELL'S 575/464-7777

Steak. Fine Dining. **Address:** 287 Carrizo Canyon Rd 88340

MORIARTY pop. 1,910

AMERICAS BEST VALUE INN 505/832-4457

Hotel

Address: 1316 Route 66 W 87035 **Location:** I-40 exit 194, 0.5 mi se on US 66 and I-40 business loop. Located in a commercial area. **Facility:** 26 units. 2 stories (no elevator), interior corridors. **Featured Amenity: continental breakfast.**

SAVE

/ SOME UNITS

BEST WESTERN MORIARTY HERITAGE INN 505/832-5000

Hotel

AAA Benefit: Members save up to 15% and earn bonus points!

Address: 111 Anaya Blvd 87035 **Location:** I-40 exit 194, 0.4 mi e. **Facility:** 70 units. 2 stories, interior corridors. **Pool:** heated indoor. **Activities:** hot tub, exercise room. **Guest Services:** coin laundry. **Featured Amenity: full hot breakfast.**

QUALITY INN 505/832-6666

Hotel. **Address:** 119 Route 66 E 87035

SUPER 8 505/832-6730

Hotel

Address: 1611 W Old Route 66 87035 **Location:** I-40 exit 194, 0.5 mi e on Central Ave. **Facility:** 66 units. 2 stories (no elevator), interior corridors. **Guest Services:** coin laundry. **Featured Amenity: continental breakfast.**

/ SOME UNITS

PECOS NATIONAL HISTORICAL PARK (C-5)

Two miles south of Pecos on SR 63, Pecos National Historical Park preserves the ruins of one of the state's largest ancient pueblos as well as two mission churches built by Franciscans in the 17th and 18th centuries. After famine, diseases and emigration contributed to a population decline over the years, in 1838 the remaining Pecos people moved to Jémez Pueblo.

Visitors can explore the ruins via a 1.2-mile self-guiding trail or the 2.25-mile Civil War Battle of Glorieta Pass Trail. Guided 1.5- to 2-hour walking tours and narrated van tours also are offered. The visitor center has displays of hand-carved furniture, artifacts from excavations, tin chandeliers and original artwork. You can also watch a film about Pecos history.

Picnicking is permitted. Allow 1 hour, 30 minutes minimum. Trails open daily 8-6, Memorial Day weekend-Labor Day; 8-4, rest of year. Phone ahead to confirm winter hours. Closed Jan. 1, Thanksgiving and Christmas. Admission $7; free (ages 0-15 and Federal Recreational Lands pass holders). Van tour $2. Phone (505) 757-7241.

RATON (D-5) pop. 6,885, elev. 6,680'

• Hotels p. 296 • Restaurants p. 296

In 1866 Uncle Dick Wootton, an enterprising local, completed 27 miles of road over Raton Pass, set up a tollgate at his ranch near the summit and charged $1.50 per wagon to use his Santa Fe Trail improvement. As the trail was the main route to the Southwest, Wootton fared well; his bank deposits were allegedly whiskey kegs full of silver dollars.

By 1880 the stopover 7 miles south of the summit of Raton (ra-TONE) Pass had evolved into a full-fledged community. Surviving Victorian-style buildings along First Street are a reminder of Raton's late 19th-century mining and railroad heyday; one example is the 1890s-era Palace Hotel is at First and Cook streets.

Sugarite Canyon State Park *(see Recreation Areas Chart)*, 10 miles northeast via SR 72, offers lakes and picnic sites.

Raton Chamber of Commerce: 100 Clayton Rd., Raton, NM 87740. **Phone:** (575) 445-3689.

Self-guiding tours: Brochures detailing tours of the city's historic district are available from the chamber and economic development council.

BEST WESTERN PLUS RATON HOTEL 575/445-8501

AAA Benefit: Members save up to 15% and earn bonus points!

Address: 473 Clayton Rd 87740 **Location:** I-25 exit 451, just w. **Facility:** 75 units. 2 stories, interior/exterior corridors. **Dining:** Mulligan's, see separate listing. **Pool:** heated indoor. **Activities:** exercise room. **Guest Services:** coin laundry. **Featured Amenity: breakfast buffet.**

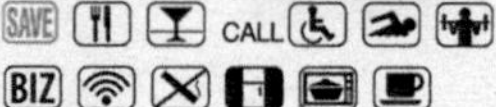

CALL

BIZ

/ SOME UNITS HS

HOLIDAY INN EXPRESS HOTEL & SUITES 575/445-1500

Hotel. **Address:** 101 Card Ave 87740

WHERE TO EAT

K-BOB'S STEAKHOUSE 575/445-2548

Steak. Casual Dining. **Address:** 1228 S 2nd St 87740

MULLIGAN'S 575/445-8501

American. Casual Dining. **Address:** 473 Clayton Rd 87740

RED RIVER (E-4) pop. 477, elev. 8,650'

Gold drew early settlers to this former frontier town on the northeastern face of Wheeler Peak. Today's visitors are drawn by the prospect of fun; skiing and snowmobiling are popular winter pursuits, with hiking, fishing and mountain biking taking over in the summer.

Red River Visitor Center: 101 W. River St., P.O. Box 870, Red River, NM 87558. **Phone:** (575) 754-3030.

BEST WESTERN RIVERS EDGE 575/754-1766

AAA Benefit: Members save up to 15% and earn bonus points!

Address: 301 W River St 87558 **Location:** 1 blk s of W Main St (SR 38); center. **Facility:** 31 units, some kitchens. 2 stories (no elevator), exterior corridors. **Parking:** winter plug-ins. **Activities:** hot tub, fishing, downhill & cross country skiing, snowmobiling, picnic facilities, trails. **Guest Services:** coin laundry. **Featured Amenity: continental breakfast.**

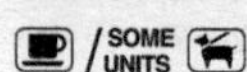

/ SOME UNITS

WHERE TO EAT

CAPO'S 575/754-6297

Italian. Casual Dining. **Address:** 110 Pioneer Rd 87558

RIO RANCHO (F-3) pop. 87,521, elev. 5,550'

• **Hotels & Restaurants map & index p. 260**

J&R VINTAGE AUTO MUSEUM is off I-25 exit 242, 2.4 mi. w. on US 550, then .5 mi. s. to 3650A SR 528. More than 65 restored vintage cars are displayed, including several that have competed in the Great American Race. Highlights include a 1917 Marmon, a 1928 Model A Ford and a 1932 Packard. **Time:** Allow 30 minutes minimum. **Hours:** Mon.-Sat. 10-5. Closed major holidays. **Cost:** $6; $5 (ages 55+); $3 (ages 6-12). **Phone:** (505) 867-2881.

HILTON GARDEN INN ALBUQUERQUE NORTH/RIO RANCHO 505/896-1111 (47)

SAVE Hotel. **Address:** 1771 Rio Rancho Blvd 87124

AAA Benefit: Members save up to 15%!

WHERE TO EAT

O'HARE'S GRILLE & PUB 505/896-0123 (42)

American. Casual Dining. **Address:** 4100 Southern Blvd SE 87124

ROSWELL (H-5) pop. 48,366, elev. 3,573'

• **Restaurants p. 298**

Roswell's economy is based on agriculture, manufacturing, oil production—and little green men. Long fueled by reports of flying saucers, tourism is big business. The city's primary intergalactic port, the International UFO Museum & Research Center, showcases a variety of exhibits documenting what has come to be known as the "Roswell Incident"—the military's supposed recovery (and subsequent cover-up) of extraterrestrial debris from a local ranch in 1947.

Additionally, each July the Roswell UFO Festival attracts curious earthlings with 4 days of alien-inspired activities, including a costume contest, a parade, and lectures given by UFO investigators and witnesses.

While it's *possible* you'll have your own close encounter of the third kind in the self-proclaimed "Alien Capital of the World," you're more likely to meet a few undergrads than a bug-eyed space creature. Roswell is home to a branch of Eastern New Mexico University as well as the prestigious New Mexico Military Institute, a 4-year high school and 2-year junior college founded in 1891. The latter institution boasts such alumni as journalists Sam Donaldson and Chuck Roberts, founder of the Hilton Hotels chain Conrad Hilton and Pulitzer Prize-winning author Paul Horgan.

The Roswell Symphony Orchestra contributes to the cultural scene. Many performances take place at Pearson Auditorium, 426 N. Main St. For schedule information, phone (575) 623-5882.

While your eyes will likely be fixed on the skies much of the time, be sure to take a breather from stargazing to explore some of the region's alluring Blue Planet landscapes. A handful of bicycle trails highlight scenic views, including the 1.5-mile HondoRiver Recreation Trail, accessed via the western terminus just east of Hendricks and S. Main streets or the eastern terminus off E. Second Street.

The 5-mile Spring River Recreation Trail runs between Enchanted Lands Park, 306 N. Sycamore

Ave., and Spring River Park and Zoo. There are pretty, tree-lined 1- and 2-mile bicycle paths at Cielo Grande Recreational Area, off W. College Boulevard.

Established in 1933, Bottomless Lakes State Park *(see Recreation Areas Chart)* is 15 miles southeast via US 380 and SR 409. New Mexico's first state park comprises a series of water-filled sinkholes ranging in depth from 17 to 90 feet and bordered by high red bluffs. The deepest, Lea Lake, is suitable for swimming and scuba diving. It's stocked with rainbow trout in winter, and in summer you can traverse the lake's greenish-blue waters aboard a rented paddleboat. Other recreational pursuits at the park include camping, hiking and wildlife viewing.

Roswell Chamber of Commerce: 131 W. 2nd St., Roswell, NM 88201. **Phone:** (575) 623-5695.

ANDERSON MUSEUM OF CONTEMPORARY ART is at 409 E. College Blvd. The museum displays work from the Roswell Artist-In-Residence Program, which attracts visual artists from around the world. The permanent collection includes more than 400 paintings, sculptures, photographs and mixed-media pieces. **Time:** Allow 1 hour minimum. **Hours:** Mon.-Fri. 9-4, Sat.-Sun. 1-5. Closed major holidays. **Cost:** Free. **Phone:** (575) 623-5600.

INTERNATIONAL UFO MUSEUM & RESEARCH CENTER is at 114 N. Main St. The center is dedicated to the study of Unidentified Flying Objects (UFOs) thought to be from other planets. Exhibits include paintings, murals and dioramas depicting the purported 1947 crash of a UFO in Roswell along with other alleged sightings of alien beings and their spacecraft. On the premises is a research library with extensive works dealing with UFOs. **Time:** Allow 1 hour, 30 minutes minimum. **Hours:** Daily 9-5. Closed Jan. 1, Thanksgiving and Christmas. **Cost:** $5; $3 (ages 65+ and military with ID); $2 (ages 5-15). **Phone:** (575) 625-9495.

GEM **ROSWELL MUSEUM AND ART CENTER** is in the Civic Center Plaza at 11th and Main sts. Known for its New Mexico modernism collection, the museum showcases Southwestern culture through historical artifacts and fine art. Highlights include works by Andrew Dasburg, Stuart Davis, Marsden Hartley, Victor Higgins, Georgia O'Keeffe, Roswell landscape artist Peter Hurd and the Rogers and Mary Ellen Aston Collection of the American West.

The Goddard wing has a re-creation of Dr. Robert Goddard's early laboratory with displays about rocketry and space. The Robert H. Goddard Planetarium presents monthly astronomy programs and multimedia presentations. **Hours:** Tues.-Sat. 9-5, Sun. and holidays 1-5. Closed Jan. 1, Thanksgiving and Christmas. **Cost:** Donations. A fee is charged for special events. **Phone:** (575) 624-6744.

BAYMONT INN & SUITES ROSWELL 575/208-0536

Hotel. **Address:** 2300 N Main St 88201

BEST WESTERN EL RANCHO PALACIO 575/622-2721

Hotel

Best Western **AAA Benefit:** Members save up to 15% and earn bonus points!

Address: 2205 N Main St 88201 **Location:** Jct US 70 and 285, 1.8 mi n. **Facility:** 45 units. 2 stories (no elevator), exterior corridors. **Pool:** outdoor. **Featured Amenity: continental breakfast.**

SAVE / SOME UNITS

CANDLEWOOD SUITES ROSWELL 575/623-4300

Extended Stay Hotel. **Address:** 4 Military Heights Dr 88201

COMFORT SUITES ROSWELL 575/623-5501

Hotel. **Address:** 3610 N Main St 88201

DAYS INN 575/623-4021

Hotel

Address: 1310 N Main St 88201 **Location:** Jct US 70 and 285, 0.8 mi n. **Facility:** 62 units. 2 stories (no elevator), exterior corridors. **Pool:** outdoor. **Activities:** exercise room. **Featured Amenity: breakfast buffet.**

SAVE BIZ HS

/ SOME UNITS

FAIRFIELD BY MARRIOTT 575/624-1300

Hotel

Fairfield **AAA Benefit:** Members save 5% or more!

Address: 1201 N Main St 88201 **Location:** Jct US 380 and 285, 0.7 mi n. **Facility:** 67 units. 3 stories, interior corridors. **Pool:** heated outdoor. **Activities:** hot tub, picnic facilities, exercise room. **Guest Services:** valet and coin laundry.

SAVE CALL BIZ

HS

HAMPTON INN & SUITES BY HILTON 575/623-5151

Hotel

AAA Benefit: Members save up to 15%!

Address: 3607 N Main St 88201 **Location:** Jct US 70 and 285 N, 1 mi s. **Facility:** 70 units. 3 stories, interior corridors. **Pool:** heated indoor. **Activities:** sauna, hot tub, exercise room. **Guest Services:** valet and coin laundry. **Featured Amenity: full hot breakfast.**

SAVE CALL BIZ

HS

HOLIDAY INN 575/623-3216

Hotel. **Address:** 3620 N Main St 88201

LA QUINTA INN & SUITES BY WYNDHAM ROSWELL 575/622-8000

Hotel. **Address:** 200 E 19th St 88201

QUALITY INN & SUITES 575/623-4567

Hotel

Address: 3595 N Main St 88201 **Location:** Jct US 70 and 285, 3 mi n. **Facility:** 55 units. 2 stories (no elevator), interior corridors. **Amenities:** safes. **Pool:** heated indoor. **Activities:** hot tub. **Guest Services:** valet and coin laundry. **Featured Amenity: continental breakfast.**

TOWNEPLACE SUITES BY MARRIOTT 575/622-5460

Extended Stay Hotel

TOWNEPLACE SUITES MARRIOTT **AAA Benefit:** Members save 5% or more!

Address: 180 E 19th St 88201 **Location:** Jct Main St, just e. **Facility:** 71 kitchen units, some two bedrooms. 3 stories, interior corridors. **Terms:** check-in 4 pm. **Pool:** heated outdoor. **Activities:** picnic facilities, exercise room. **Guest Services:** valet and coin laundry.

HS

/SOME UNITS

WHERE TO EAT

BIG D'S DOWNTOWN DIVE 575/627-0776

American. Quick Serve. **Address:** 505 N Main St 88201

CATTLE BARON STEAK & SEAFOOD 575/622-2465

American. Casual Dining. **Address:** 1113 N Main St 88201

LEMON GRASS THAI CUISINE 575/208-0411

Thai. Casual Dining. **Address:** 610 S Main St 88201

LOS CERRITOS MEXICAN KITCHEN 575/622-4919

Mexican. Casual Dining. **Address:** 2103 N Main St 88201

PASTA CAFE ITALIAN BISTRO 575/624-1111

Italian. Casual Dining. **Address:** 1208 N Main St 88201

PECOS FLAVORS WINERY & BISTO 575/622-2031

Deli. Casual Dining. **Address:** 412 W 2nd St 88201

PEPPERS GRILL & BAR 575/623-1700

American. Casual Dining. **Address:** 500 N Main St 88201

RIB CRIB BBQ AND GRILL 575/625-1200

Barbecue. Casual Dining. **Address:** 4495 N Main St 88202

TIA JUANA'S MEXICAN GRILLE & CANTINA 575/627-6113

Mexican. Casual Dining. **Address:** 3601 N Main St 88201

RUIDOSO (H-4) pop. 8,029, elev. 6,720'

With skiing in winter, golfing, horseback riding, camping, hiking and fishing in spring and summer and the fall foliage beauty of aspen trees highlighting autumn, Ruidoso is among New Mexico's premier year-round mountain playgrounds. It's such a popular destination, in fact, that making travel reservations several months in advance is advisable for holiday weekends.

The natural backdrop—the heavily forested Sacramento Mountains within Lincoln National Forest*(see place listing p. 292)*—is sublime. The resort community that now extends for 10 miles along the Ruidoso River had inauspicious beginnings in the 1890s as a trading post, and an old waterwheel from that era still stands on Main Street.

Ruidoso Valley Chamber of Commerce Visitors Center: 720 Sudderth Dr., Ruidoso, NM 88345. **Phone:** (575) 257-7395 or (877) 784-3676.

BEST WESTERN PLUS RUIDOSO INN 575/257-3600

Hotel

Best Western PLUS **AAA Benefit:** Members save up to 15% and earn bonus points!

Address: 97 Camelot Dr 88345 **Location:** US 70, just w of jct Sudderth Dr, just n. **Facility:** 57 units. 3 stories, interior corridors. **Terms:** check-in 4 pm. **Pool:** heated indoor. **Activities:** hot tub, playground, picnic facilities, exercise room. **Guest Services:** coin laundry. **Featured Amenity: breakfast buffet.**

CROWN POINT CONDOMINIUMS 575/257-7641

Condominium. **Address:** 220 Crown Dr 88355

HOTEL RUIDOSO-MIDTOWN 575/257-2007

Hotel

Address: 110 Chase Dr 88345 **Location:** Just s of jct Sudderth Dr. **Facility:** 55 units. 3 stories, interior corridors. **Pool:** heated indoor. **Activities:** hot tub, picnic facilities, exercise room. **Guest Services:** coin laundry. **Featured Amenity: breakfast buffet.**

MCM ELEGANTÉ LODGE & RESORT 575/258-5500

Hotel. **Address:** 107 Sierra Blanca Dr 88345

WHISPERING PINE CABINS 575/257-4311

Cabin. **Address:** 422 Main Rd 88345

WHERE TO EAT

CAFE RIO 575/257-7746

Italian. Casual Dining. **Address:** 2547 Sudderth Dr 88345

CASA BLANCA 575/257-2495

Mexican. Casual Dining. **Address:** 501 Mechem Dr 88345

CATTLE BARON STEAK & SEAFOOD 575/257-9355

American. Casual Dining. **Address:** 657 Sudderth Dr 88345

CORNERSTONE BAKERY CAFE 575/257-1842

Breads/Pastries. Casual Dining. **Address:** 359 Sudderth Dr 88345

GRILL CALIENTE 575/630-0224

Southwestern. Casual Dining. **Address:** 2800 Sudderth Dr 88345

K-BOB'S STEAKHOUSE 575/378-0025

Steak. Casual Dining. **Address:** 157 W Hwy 70 88345

LINCOLN COUNTY GRILL 575/257-7669

American. Casual Dining. **Address:** 2717 Sudderth Dr 88345

THE RANCHERS STEAK AND SEAFOOD 575/257-7540

Steak Seafood. Casual Dining. **Address:** 2823 Sudderth Dr 88345

TEXAS CLUB 575/258-3325

Steak. Casual Dining. **Address:** 212 Metz Dr 88345

TINA'S CAFE 575/257-8930

American. Casual Dining. **Address:** 522 Sudderth Dr 88345

THE VILLAGE BUTTERY 575/257-9251

Sandwiches Soup. Quick Serve. **Address:** 2107 Sudderth Dr 88345

RUIDOSO DOWNS (H-4) pop. 2,815, elev. 6,420'

From humble origins in a mountain field in 1947, Ruidoso Downs Race Track—also the site of the Racehorse Hall of Fame—is a premier facility for quarter horse and Thoroughbred racing. The All-American Futurity is held on Labor Day, the final day of the racing season. Famed as the world's richest quarter horse race (the purse exceeds $3 million), it is the final leg of quarter horse racing's Triple Crown. It is preceded by the Ruidoso Quarter Horse Futurity and the Rainbow Futurity, which take place in June and July, respectively. For more information phone (575) 378-4431.

The 84-mile-long Billy the Kid National Scenic Byway more than lives up to its name in terms of impressive mountain vistas. Maps and information are available from the scenic byway interpretive center on US 70, next to the Hubbard Museum of the American West.

Events at the Lincoln County Cowboy Symposium, held the second full weekend in October, include cowboy poetry readings, musical performances, roping demonstrations, a chuck wagon cook-off and displays of Western arts and crafts.

BEST WESTERN PINE SPRINGS INN 575/378-8100

Hotel

AAA Benefit: Members save up to 15% and earn bonus points!

Address: 111 Pine Springs Dr 88346 **Location:** On US 70, 1.2 mi e of SR 48. Across from racetrack. **Facility:** 98 units. 2 stories (no elevator), exterior corridors. **Terms:** check-in 4 pm. **Pool:** heated outdoor. **Activities:** hot tub, picnic facilities. **Guest Services:** coin laundry. **Featured Amenity: breakfast buffet.**

HAMPTON INN & SUITES BY HILTON RUIDOSO DOWNS 575/378-1199

SAVE Hotel. **Address:** 26141 US Hwy 70 E 88346

AAA Benefit: Members save up to 15%!

SALINAS PUEBLO MISSIONS NATIONAL MONUMENT (G-3)

Salinas Pueblo Missions National Monument is the site of three geographically and historically related pueblos and 17th-century Spanish Franciscan missions. The park includes the former Gran Quivira National Monument and two former state monuments, Abó and Quarai.

Because there was no further resettlement after the Spaniards and the Tompiro and Tewa Indians abandoned the site in the late 17th century, the masonry ruins are remarkably intact. A visitor center is near Mountainair, on US 60 a block west of SR 55, and is open daily 8-5. All three pueblo sites open daily 9-6, Memorial Day weekend-Labor Day; 9-5, rest of year. Sites closed Jan. 1, Thanksgiving and Christmas. Free. Phone (505) 847-2585.

ABÓ RUINS are 9 mi. w. of Mountainair on US 60, then .7 mi. n. on SR 513. Once a large pueblo, this Tompiro Indian village was abandoned in the 1670s. The ruins of San Gregorio de Abó, a medieval-style church built in 1620 that has a 40-foot-tall buttressed curtain wall, rise curiously from the desert floor. **Time:** Allow 1 hour minimum. **Hours:** Open daily 9-6, Memorial Day-Labor Day; 9-5, rest of year. Closed Jan. 1, Thanksgiving and Christmas. **Cost:** Free. **Phone:** (505) 847-2585.

GRAN QUIVIRA RUINS are 26 mi. s. of Mountainair off SR 55. Historians estimate that at its height the Gran Quivira pueblo was home to more than 2,000 people. Some 20 limestone house mounds date from 1300 to about 1670; approximately 300 rooms and six kivas can be explored. Also preserved are the 17th-century ruins of San Isidro and San Buenaventura. **Time:** Allow 1 hour minimum. **Hours:** Ruins daily 9-6, Memorial Day-Labor Day; 9-5, rest of year. Closed Jan. 1, Thanksgiving and Christmas. **Phone:** (505) 847-2585.

QUARAI RUINS are 8 mi. n. of Mountainair on SR 55, then 1 mi. w. on a hard-surfaced road. At the site are 10 large unexcavated pueblo house mounds. The remains of the 1630 church and convent of Nuestra Señora de La Purísma Concepción de Cuarac include impressive sandstone walls nearly 40 feet tall. The ruins of another, smaller church dating from before 1820 also can be seen. **Hours:** Ruins daily 9-6, Memorial Day-Labor Day; 9-5, rest of year. Closed Jan. 1, Thanksgiving and Christmas. **Phone:** (505) 847-2585.

SAN ANTONIO (H-3) pop. 165, elev. 4,568'

Founded in 1629 as a mission, San Antonio is a trading center for nearby farms and ranches. Corn and alfalfa thrive in the fields along the Rio Grande Valley. But to the southeast, beyond the river valley, lies a 35-mile-wide, 90-mile-long stretch of merciless desert. In the days when settlers trudged westward along the El Camino Real—The Royal Road—the desert earned the name Jornada del Muerto, or Journey of the Dead.

Some 21 miles south across the Rio Grande from San Marcial is Valverde Battlefield, scene of the first Civil War engagement in New Mexico. Confederate forces led by Gen. H.H. Sibley beat back Union troops from nearby Fort Craig in a daylong battle in February 1862, and went on to occupy Albuquerque. Eroded remnants of the fort survive and are accessible by way of a 5-mile gravel road; the battlefield, however, is not.

San Antonio is the birthplace of famed hotelier Conrad Hilton. The ruins of the Hilton family's mercantile boardinghouse and home are at Sixth and Main streets, west of SR 1 and 1 mile south of US 380.

BOSQUE DEL APACHE NATIONAL WILDLIFE REFUGE is 8 mi. s. of I-25 exit 139 at US 380 and SR 1. It features a 12-mile auto tour route along which are six observation decks, seven hiking trails and a scenic overlook providing access to marsh, grassland and desert upland habitats.

A visitor center contains exhibits pertaining to wildlife that inhabit or visit the refuge, including sandhill cranes, snow geese and more than 380 other bird species as well as coyotes, mountain lions, deer, elk, javalina, turkeys and rattlesnakes. Bird-watching is best from early November to mid-February.

The Laura Jean Deal Desert Arboretum has one of the Southwest's most complete collections of cacti, succulents and native trees and plants. The peak bloom period is April through August.

Fishing and hunting are permitted in designated areas during regulated seasons. **Time:** Allow 2 hours minimum. **Hours:** Refuge daily 1 hour before dawn-1 hour after dusk. Visitor center daily 8-4, Sept.-May; Thurs.-Mon 8-4. rest of year. Closed Jan. 1, July 4, Thanksgiving and Christmas. **Cost:** Auto tour route $5 (per private vehicle). **Phone:** (575) 835-1828.

SANDIA PARK (F-3) pop. 237, elev. 7,159'

Sandia Park, about 25 miles east of Albuquerque, is on the Turquoise Trail National Scenic Byway, a desert highland route that runs past Sandia Mountain and winds through the Cibola National Forest *(see place listing p. 281)*.

TINKERTOWN MUSEUM is 1 mi. w. on SR 536 to 121 Sandia Crest Rd. The museum displays the life's work of New Mexican folk artist Ross Ward, whose carved and hand-painted miniatures include an animated Western town and a three-ring circus. A wall made of more than 50,000 glass bottles surrounds the museum. **Hours:** Daily 9-6, Apr.-Oct. Last admission 30 minutes before closing. **Cost:** $3.50; $3 (ages 62+); $1 (ages 4-16). **Phone:** (505) 281-5233.

SANTA CLARA PUEBLO (A-4) elev. 5,605'

In the 12th century, ancestors of the present-day Santa Clara Pueblo carved primitive dwellings into the cliffs above Santa Clara Canyon, where they hunted and farmed. Today visitors can view the Puye Cliff Dwellings, two levels of cliff and cave dwellings. The tribe migrated east to the Rio Grande Valley and the present pueblo site around 1600.

PUYE CLIFF DWELLINGS TOUR is at SR 30 and Santa Clara Canyon Rd. Located atop the Pajarito Plateau at an elevation of nearly 7,000 feet is the ancestral home of the Santa Clara Pueblo people. This was once a multi-story complex built around a large central plaza. The southern portion contained 173 rooms on the ground floor. Guided tours offer both breathtaking views and an in-depth cultural and spiritual appreciation of pueblo life. The Harvey House displays pueblo-related exhibits, and during the summer local artisans display their work.

The tour requires walking on steep slopes at a high elevation. Allow 15 minutes to drive from the Welcome Center to the tour site. **Time:** Allow 1 hour minimum. **Hours:** Daily 9-6, mid-Apr. through Sept. 30; 9-3, rest of year (weather permitting). Closed the week before Easter, June 13, Aug. 12 and Christmas. **Cost:** Tour fees range $20-$35; $18-$33 (ages 0-14 and 55+). Harvey House $7; $5 (ages 0-14 and 55+). Reservations are recommended. **Phone:** (505) 917-6650. GT

SANTA FE (F-4) pop. 67,947, elev. 6,989'

- **Hotels p. 313 • Restaurants p. 314**
- **Attractions map p. 305**
- **Hotels & Restaurants map & index p. 308, 311**

Having celebrated its 400th birthday in 2010, you'd think Santa Fe would stop, take a deep breath and rest on that considerable achievement. Not a chance. While this city treats preservation of the past as paramount, there are always new things to see. You can return a dozen times and still leave with new discoveries and experiences under your belt.

The high desert country that surrounds New Mexico's capital city, however, is timeless. Undulating hills that stretch to the horizon in all directions are a study in shades of buff, beige and brown. The landscape is speckled with clumps of *Artemisia tridentate*—more commonly known as sagebrush—a hardy shrub with silvery-gray leaves, a pungent fragrance and a tolerance for arid conditions. In the distance, mountains stand like sentinels—the Jemez range to the northwest, the Sangre de Cristos to the northeast. It's an austere but awesome natural setting heightened by remarkably clear air and the intense azure blue of the vast New Mexico sky.

Surely it's a setting that captivated Spanish explorer Juan de Oñate. In 1598 he led the initial effort to colonize the region that was claimed for the Spanish Crown as the province of Santa Fé de Nuevo México. Ten years later the newly appointed Spanish governor, Don Pedro de Peralta, founded a city that was to be the seat of power for all imperial holdings north of the Rio Grande. Peralta lived up to the Spanish penchant for cumbersome titles, naming it La Villa Real de la Santa Fé de San Francisco de Asis—the Royal Town of the Holy Faith of St. Francis of Assisi.

(See maps & indexes p. 308, 311.)

In 1610 Santa Fe became the provincial capital. It's a designation the city has retained ever since, except for a brief period during the Pueblo Revolt of 1680 when Indian villages banded together to expel the colonizers. That same year a mission was established to serve as headquarters for a second power in the region: the church. Franciscan fathers fanned out to usher the Indians into the Christian fold; according to a 1617 report, 14,000 souls had been converted. Four hundred years later the sturdy walls of the San Miguel Mission Church are still intact.

Spanish colonists adopted a tried-and-true method of construction for their own churches, government buildings and other structures. The Pueblo Indians used adobe, a mixture of earth, straw and water that was shaped into bricks and dried in the sun. The bricks were stacked and bonded together with more adobe. Pueblo walls were frequently several feet thick, with entry to their dwellings through an opening in the rooftop accessed via ladder. These walls efficiently kept the interiors cool in summer and warm in winter.

Innovations like mud-brick fireplaces and *hornos* (outdoor ovens) were added. A few buildings from this era survive today. The Oldest House on E. De Vargas Street (across from the San Miguel Mission Church) was built around 1646; although the "oldest" title also is claimed by houses in Connecticut, Florida and Massachusetts, this is the only one made of adobe. Another place to see adobe dwellings in their original state (minus doors and windows that were added later) is at Taos Pueblo *(see attraction listing p. 323).*

Question: What's a non-authentic adobe? Answer: Most of the buildings in town. In 1912 a code was passed requiring the use of a style called Spanish Pueblo Revival. It incorporated the defining features of local architecture, which included earth-toned, flat-topped buildings, wood-beamed ceilings *(vigas),* and door and window frames painted white or turquoise. But the majority of houses and commercial structures in the city have stucco surfaces that mimic adobe, referred to amusingly as "Santa Fake" and faux-dobe (foe-dough-bee).

Authentic adobe or not, Santa Fe still looks like no other place in the country. "The City Different" prides itself on the cultivation of "Santa Fe style." It's a term that goes beyond decorative details like clay pots, cow skulls, Southwestern blankets and Native American artifacts (there are plenty of those).

Santa Fe style embraces the use of natural materials to enhance the stark natural beauty of the landscape. That's why you'll see, along with the omnipresent adobe, weathered stone walls and picturesque fences made from tree branches lashed together. And everything is suffused with the elusive quality of light that has long attracted painters and photographers, a constant interplay between piercing sun and flickering shadow that's downright mesmerizing.

By Spanish decree the original town was laid out around a central square, bordered on one side by the seat of government (the Palace of the Governors, which looks much the same now as it did 4 centuries ago), and on the other by a church (the present-day Cathedral Basilica of St. Francis of Assisi). A grid of narrow streets and alleyways radiated out from this central point. Today, of course, these streets are lined with shops, local restaurants, art galleries and museums, forming a compact downtown core that's best experienced on foot.

A magnet for residents and visitors alike, The Plaza is a popular destination morning, noon and evening. It has tree-shaded green lawns and plenty of benches where you can relax and take in the scene. Street musicians contribute a frequent soundtrack. In summer flower baskets hang from the ornamental wrought-iron lampposts, and during the Christmas holidays walkways and rooftops glow with the soft light from *farolitos,* small paper bags holding sand and a single lit candle. The Plaza is Santa Fe's heart, a perfect starting point for exploring a city that's different in the most delightful way.

Guided downtown walking tours, led by docents from the New Mexico History Museum, depart from the blue gate at the Palace of the Governors April to October; phone (505) 476-5200. Historic Walks of Santa Fe also offer guided walking tours departing from various hotels; phone (505) 986-8388.

Given all this history and culture, it's no surprise that the city's events calendar is packed. GEM Rodeo de Santa Fe, which takes place in late June, draws big crowds who cheer on hundreds of cowboys and cowgirls competing in barrel racing, bull riding, calf roping and steer wrestling.

The Fiestas de Santa Fe has been observed since 1712. Always taking place the weekend after Labor Day, it features mariachi concerts, an arts and crafts festival at The Plaza, lectures, entertainment and traditional mass services. The festivities culminate with the ritual burning of Zozobra, a 50-foot-tall marionette effigy known as Old Man Gloom, in order to dispel the travails of the previous year (it's advised not to bring young children to this particular event).

Celebrate Santa Fe's culinary side at the Santa Fe Wine and Chile Fiesta. Dozens of local restaurants and West Coast wineries participate in this foodie extravaganza. Activities include wine seminars, cooking demos and guest chef tours, which combine a visit to attractions like El Rancho de las Golondrinas or Georgia O'Keeffe's former home in the town of Abiquiu with a chef-prepared gourmet lunch. The Grand Tasting, the fiesta's keynote event, is a delicious treat.

Search out high-quality keepsakes at the GEM Santa Fe International Folk Art Market; this July event showcases the work of artists from more than 80 countries. The GEM Traditional Spanish Summer Market in late July celebrates Hispanic heritage through art, music and dance. The Indian Market in late August is Santa Fe's oldest and largest market, celebrating emerging and established artists from some 100 tribes.

Tourism Santa Fe: 201 W. Marcy St., Santa Fe, NM 87501. **Phone:** (505) 955-6200 or (800) 777-2489.

Shopping:

Shopping is a favorite way to while away the time in Santa Fe, but where you go depends on your vacation agenda. Downtown is shopping central, with stores and boutiques catering to just about every taste (and disposable income level). Serious art collectors for whom money is no object head for Canyon Road, while the up-and-coming Railyard District offers additional shopping opportunities.

Many shops traffic in the usual T-shirts and Southwestern-themed souvenirs, but you also can find more offbeat and specialized merchandise. The mini-malls are as good a place as any to start. Plaza Mercado (entrances on San Francisco, Galisteo and Water streets) has more than 30 specialty retailers.

The Santa Fe Arcade (60 E. San Francisco St. on the south side of The Plaza) is a sleek three-level indoor mall with trendy shops specializing in stylish Western wear, custom-made boots, home accessories and gold and silver jewelry. Malouf on the Plaza specializes in pricey, high-end clothing and accessories: designer fashions, handbags, jewelry and shoes for her; shirts, ties, sportswear and tailored apparel for him.

Art galleries are scattered throughout downtown. POP Gallery (125 Lincoln Ave., next to the New Mexico History Museum) displays photography, jewelry and modern art and sculpture in varied media. Most of the items are expensive, but there are some reasonable deals to be had. D R Fine Art Santa Fe (123 Galisteo St.) sells contemporary Southwest landscape paintings by David Rothermel. Moon Rabbit Toys (112 W. San Francisco St.) stocks toys from all over the world, an eclectic array of stuffed animals, high-quality jigsaw puzzles and the latest must-owns for serious gamers.

The Shops at La Fonda at the La Fonda Hotel (100 E. San Francisco St.) offer clothing, designer jewelry, handmade textiles, folk art and kitchen accessories. Also at the hotel is Señor Murphy's candy shop, where you can sample goodies like chocolate piñon nut clusters. Across the street is the O'Farrell Hat Company, selling customized cowboy hats and "Santa Fe sticks," locally handcrafted canes and walking sticks made from fine hardwoods.

The buildings surrounding Sena Plaza (125 E. Palace Ave. opposite The Plaza) were once part of one big single-family residence, with multiple rooms for family members as well as various tradesmen. The shops here sell pottery, ceramics and touristy gifts. A courtyard (accessible only through two narrow entryways on Palace Avenue) has shade trees, benches, a fountain and an arbor; it's a secluded little spot to relax for a spell.

Few cities in the country offer a better selection of Native American art. Ortega's on the Plaza (101 W. San Francisco St.) carries Navajo weavings, Zuni fetishes, traditional turquoise jewelry, silver-studded belts, pottery and other treasures, along with a beautiful array of beadwork.

(See maps & indexes p. 308, 311.)

For a more personalized shopping experience, wander among the displays of traditional and contemporary jewelry, arts and crafts, pottery, sand paintings and other handmade items sold under the *portal* (porch) of the Palace of the Governors (105 W. Palace Ave.). Vendors spread their wares on blankets on the sidewalk outside this long adobe building. Although the casual setting might imply that haggling is acceptable, prices are usually fixed (though often a bargain compared with many shops). And it's fun to meet the artists and learn about their work.

Within walking distance of downtown, Canyon Road (between East Alameda Street and Acequia Madre) is the upscale center of the Santa Fe art scene. The 10 or so blocks between Paseo de Peralta and Palace Avenue constitute a "gallery row" of festively decorated adobes trading in all manner of fine art, from paintings and sculpture to rugs, jewelry and custom-designed furniture.

Galleries dealing in contemporary works include Patricia Carlisle Fine Art (554 Canyon Rd.) and the Waxlander Gallery & Sculpture Garden (622 Canyon Rd.). At the Wiford Gallery (403 Canyon Rd.) there's an outdoor garden with Utah artist Lyman Whitaker's contemporary wind sculptures, delicate-looking copper and stainless steel creations that twirl whenever there's a breeze. Western-themed paintings by artists representing the early Taos and Santa Fe schools are displayed at the Nedra Matteucci Galleries (1075 Paseo de Peralta).

The Railyard District (along Guadalupe Street between Paseo de Peralta and Montezuma Avenue) is also worth investigating. Casa Nova (530 S. Guadalupe St.) has a little bit of everything—vibrantly colorful furniture, dinnerware, baskets, wall decorations and handicrafts, mostly created by African artists.

For Southwestern agricultural specialties like locally grown white corn, cactus honey and an incredible variety of heirloom tomatoes and dried chiles, check out the Santa Fe Farmers Market in the Railyard (Guadalupe Street at Paseo de Peralta). The Saturday market sets up 7-1 during the summer months, 8-1 the rest of the year; a Tuesday market is open 7-1 from June through September and 8-1 in May, October and November. Everything from pottery to hand-blown glass can be found at the Railyard Artisan Market, held in the Farmers Market Pavilion building Sundays 10-4, year-round.

Nightlife:

Given Santa Fe's close relationship with the fine arts, it's no surprise that highbrow cultural events top the social calendar. First and foremost is the Santa Fe Opera, where classics like "Madame Butterfly," contemporary works and world premieres are performed in a state-of-the-art, open-air venue that has the Sangre de Cristo and Jemez mountains as a backdrop. This may be the only opera company in the world that has to compete with a spectacular sunset for the audience's attention. The show actually begins a couple of hours earlier, when opera goers begin arriving with lavish tailgate picnics in tow. Attendees also can take advantage of a preview buffet set up on the landscaped rehearsal grounds.

Some 40 performances are offered in July and August. Single ticket prices range $32-$225, depending on the seating section and performance date, and are nonrefundable. A roof covers all seating areas, but evenings can occasionally be cool, rainy or both. The facility is located 7 miles north of downtown Santa Fe on the west side of US 84/285 (exit 168). The box office is open Mon.-Fri. 9-5 (Mon.-Sat. 9-5 during the season); phone (505) 986-5900 or (800) 280-4654.

A variety of events—from the Santa Fe Chamber Music Festival, performances by the Santa Fe Symphony Orchestra and the Aspen Santa Fe Ballet, and popular music headliners to theater, ballet and classic film festivals—take place at the Lensic Performing Arts Center (211 W. San Francisco St.). The Lensic opened in 1931 as a movie palace and vaudeville theater; a major renovation in 2001 retained the building's distinctive Spanish-style facade and rooftop line of undulating sea serpents. Phone (505) 988-1234 for the box office.

The Pink Adobe (406 Old Santa Fe Tr. across from the San Miguel Mission Church) has been around since 1944, when Rosalea Murphy opened the doors of her restaurant. Locals refer to it as "the Pink," and the restaurant's Dragon Room Lounge is a popular hangout with the artsy crowd. The ambience is classy: dim lighting, walls decorated with carved wood dragons, and a bar with elm trees growing through the roof. Live music runs to jazz, salsa and flamenco, and the specialty margaritas pack a potent punch. Phone (505) 983-7712.

More raucous is dive bar Evangelo's (200 W. San Francisco St.). In the basement (Underground at Evangelo's) local rock and reggae bands tear it up several nights a week. The mahogany bar dispenses a variety of imported brews. Cowgirl BBQ (319 S. Guadalupe St.) has a big outdoor patio with a lantern-festooned tree, country bands, Cowgirl Karaoke nights and—parents take note—a Kid Corral to keep the young 'uns happy.

Or among the other nice things to do downtown, you could take an evening stroll. Weather permitting (meaning if it isn't too chilly), The Plaza is a pretty, peaceful spot to relax on a bench, enjoy an ice cream cone and people watch. You may even be treated to an impromptu concert by a couple of jamming musicians.

INSIDER INFO:
Pueblo Etiquette

When Spanish conquistadors arrived in northern New Mexico in the 1500s, they encountered a vast network of Indian villages dating back centuries. The Spaniards referred to Native Americans as Pueblo Indians, after the Spanish word for town. About 25 pueblos remain today, and many of the people who live on these lands still adhere to traditional ways and speak the Tewa language in addition to Spanish or English.

(See maps & indexes p. 308, 311.)

If you're wondering what to do on your New Mexico vacation, visiting a pueblo is a wonderful way to experience a different culture. One of the most accessible for tourists is Taos Pueblo, right outside of Taos. The ceremonial village—the only section of the pueblo open to visitors—is considered sacred, and about 150 Taos Indians choose to live here as their ancestors did, without benefit of conveniences like electricity and plumbing.

Primitive-looking yet ingenious devices are scattered throughout the village. Lattice-like drying racks were used for harvested corn, pumpkin, squash and bean crops, and to cure wild game meat for food and animal hides for clothing. Beehive-shaped, outdoor adobe ovens called *hornos* are still used to bake Indian fry bread.

Most pueblos celebrate annual feast days coinciding with a Catholic patron saint designated by the early Spanish missionaries. A blend of ancient harvest traditions and Catholic religious practices, they combine traditional dances with singing and drumming; some also incorporate private ceremonies, processions and masses.

Taos Pueblo celebrates the San Geronimo Feast Day on Sept. 30 with traditional pole climbing. The Buffalo and Deer Dance is performed on the Jan. 23 feast day at San Ildefonso Pueblo. One of the smallest pueblos, but one with a very rich heritage, is Tesuque Pueblo, where the Corn Dance takes place the first weekend in June and the Feast Day of San Diego is celebrated on Nov. 12.

Nambé Pueblo, about 18 miles north of Santa Fe, sits at the base of the Sangre de Cristo Mountains; the Nambé Falls Ceremonial on July 4, which includes dances and an arts and crafts fair, is a popular event with both pueblo residents and tourists. Some pueblos also hold celebrations on Christmas Day, and most celebrate Día de El Rey (King's Day) on Jan. 6.

Many pueblos are open to the public, and visitors are usually welcome on feast days. It's advisable to confirm if the pueblo is open on the day you plan to visit; contact the Eight Northern Indian Pueblos Council at (505) 747-1593, or inquire at Tourism Santa Fe.

Feast day or not, it's important to follow commonsense etiquette. Most pueblos have strict rules regarding photography, filming and even sketching, so ask regarding what type of cameras are allowed and if fees are required. Ignoring these rules could result in the confiscation of your equipment.

Laptops, iPads and cellphones are usually not welcome on pueblo grounds. Refrain from photographing religious sites (chapels or kivas), and always ask if you can photograph tribal members or their personal property before doing so. If you happen to receive an invitation to someone's home accept graciously, but refrain from offering payment or a tip.

Ceremonial dances are no different than any religious rite. The participants are in a prayerful state, and quiet, respectful behavior is expected. Refrain from loud talking, clapping, dancing along or wandering around during a dance. If photographing dancers, keep a respectful distance during the ceremony and between dances.

You are a guest while on pueblo land; do not enter or peek into a resident's home unless a sign on the door welcomes visitors. Children should not climb on walls or look into windows. Kivas and cemeteries are generally off limits; also heed all signs that designate restricted access areas. Different pueblos have different rules (for example, wading is forbidden in Red Willow Creek at Taos Pueblo), so make sure you're familiar with them before you set off exploring.

CATHEDRAL BASILICA OF ST. FRANCIS OF ASSISI is 1 blk. e. of The Plaza on Cathedral Pl. Built to serve the fledgling settlement's Catholic community, this became the first church in New Mexico to attain the status of cathedral basilica. The parish was founded in 1610; the present church, built in 1869, is one of Santa Fe's most widely recognized landmarks.

Bordered by a lovely tree-shaded park, it's also one of the few downtown buildings that isn't an adobe. The cathedral's sharp, French Romanesque lines provide a striking contrast to the rounded contours of its neighbors, making it a popular subject to photograph.

Archbishop J.B. Lamy, who inspired Willa Cather's novel "Death Comes for the Archbishop," is buried beneath the main altar beside missionary priests Fray Zarate and Fray Gerónimo de la Lama. When services are not being held visitors may view a display of ecclesiastical art in the sanctuary. **Hours:** Mon.-Thurs. 8:30-11:30 and 12:30-4:30, Fri. 8:30-noon. Services are held daily. **Cost:** Free. **Phone:** (505) 982-5619.

GEORGIA O'KEEFFE MUSEUM is at 217 Johnson St. The artist's best-known works include many pieces inspired by New Mexico's stark beauty and by the objects, places and experiences that informed her life. The museum's series of thematic galleries include O'Keeffe's first American abstract artworks, paintings depicting the wonders of the natural world and the artist's iconic New Mexico landscapes.

Time: Allow 1 hour minimum. **Hours:** Daily 9-5 (also Fri. 5-7). Closed Jan. 1, Easter, Thanksgiving, Christmas and between exhibit installations. Phone ahead to confirm schedule. **Cost:** $13; $11 (students 18 and over with ID); free (ages 0-17 and first Fri. of the month for New Mexico residents with ID). Audio tour rental fee $5. **Phone:** (505) 946-1000.

LORETTO CHAPEL is at 211 Old Santa Fe Tr. The "Miraculous Staircase" to the chapel's choir loft has two 360-degree turns and no visible means of support. An anonymous carpenter is said to have fashioned the spiral steps in 1878 using only wooden pegs. Legend suggests that St. Joseph, the patron saint of carpenters, inspired the work.

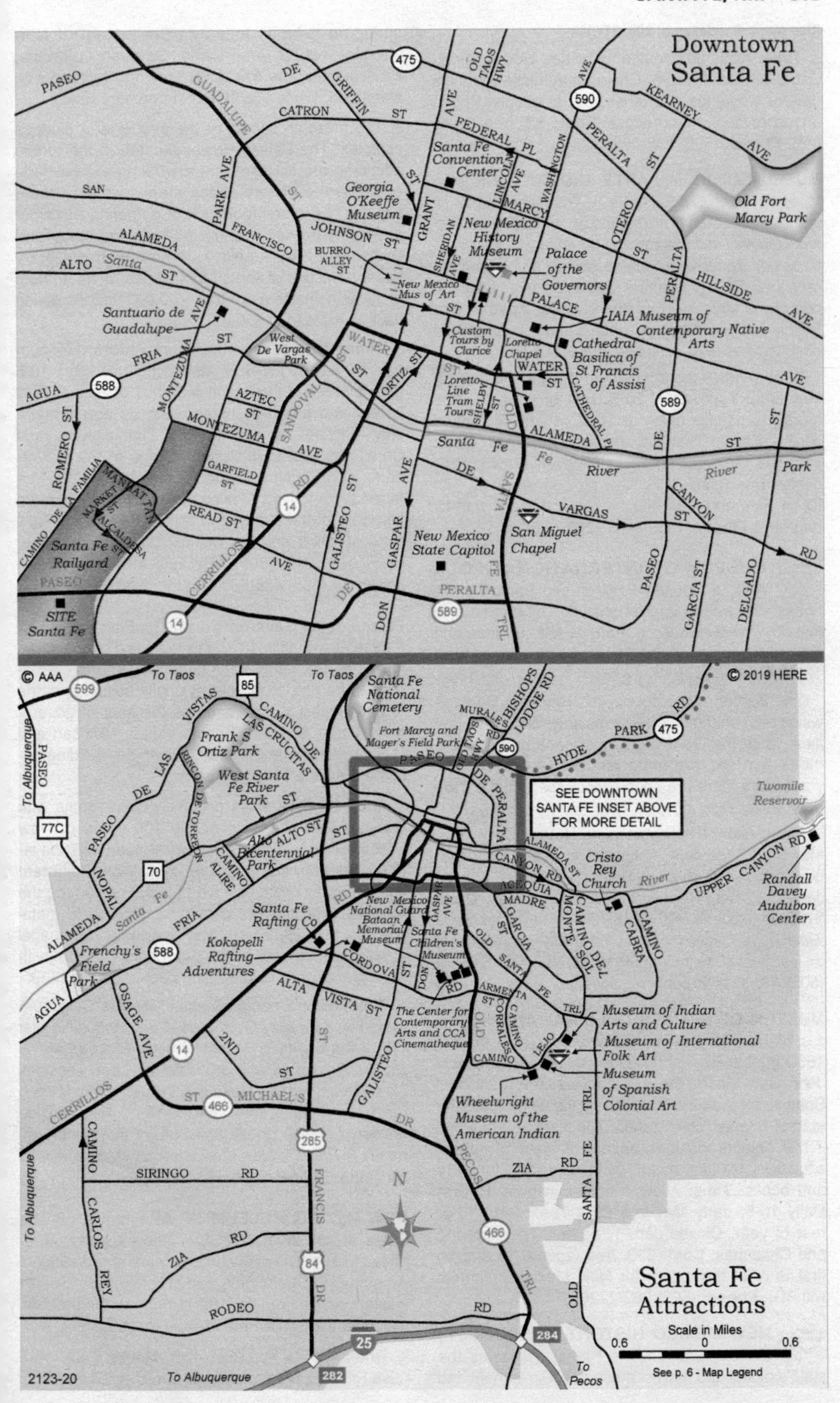
Downtown Santa Fe
Georgia O'Keeffe Museum
Santa Fe Convention Center
New Mexico History Museum
Palace of the Governors
New Mexico Mus of Art
Santuario de Guadalupe
West De Vargas Park
Custom Tours by Clarice
Loretto Chapel
Cathedral Basilica of St Francis of Assisi
IAIA Museum of Contemporary Native Arts
Loretto Line Tram Tours
Old Fort Marcy Park
Santa Fe Railyard
SITE Santa Fe
New Mexico State Capitol
San Miguel Chapel
© AAA
© 2019 HERE
SEE DOWNTOWN SANTA FE INSET ABOVE FOR MORE DETAIL
Santa Fe National Cemetery
Fort Marcy and Mager's Field Park
Frank S Ortiz Park
West Santa Fe River Park
Alto Bicentennial Park
Twomile Reservoir
Cristo Rey Church
Randall Davey Audubon Center
Santa Fe Rafting Co
Kokopelli Rafting Adventures
New Mexico National Guard Bataan Memorial Museum
Santa Fe Children's Museum
The Center for Contemporary Arts and CCA Cinematheque
Frenchy's Field Park
Museum of Indian Arts and Culture
Museum of International Folk Art
Museum of Spanish Colonial Art
Wheelwright Museum of the American Indian
To Taos
To Albuquerque
To Pecos
Santa Fe Attractions
Scale in Miles
0.6 0 0.6
See p. 6 - Map Legend
2123-20

(See maps & indexes p. 308, 311.)

Time: Allow 30 minutes minimum. **Hours:** Mon.-Sat. 9-5, Sun. 10:30-5. Chapel may close part of a day for weddings and other special events. Phone ahead to confirm schedule. **Cost:** $3; free (ages 0-6). **Phone:** (505) 982-0092.

MUSEUM OF INDIAN ARTS AND CULTURE is on Museum Hill off Old Santa Fe Tr. The museum has an inclusive collection of New Mexican and Southwestern archeological and anthropological artifacts. Objects include pottery, basketry, textiles, jewelry and contemporary arts. One permanent exhibition examines the comprehensive story of the Navajo, Apache and Pueblo peoples in their own words and voices, and the other focuses on 4 centuries of pueblo pottery.

Time: Allow 1 hour minimum. **Hours:** Daily 10-5, May-Oct.; Tues.-Sun. 10-5, rest of year. Guided tours are usually given at 10:30, 1 and 3. Closed Jan. 1, Easter, Thanksgiving and Christmas. **Cost:** $12; $11 (students with ID); $7 (New Mexico residents); free (ages 0-16, New Mexico residents with ID on Sun. and New Mexico senior citizens with ID on Wed.). **Phone:** (505) 476-1269. GT

GEM **MUSEUM OF INTERNATIONAL FOLK ART,** on Museum Hill off Old Santa Fe Tr., houses the world's largest collection of international folk art. The Girard Wing features folk art, toys and miniature scenes of marketplaces and villages from 100 countries.

The Bartlett, Neutrogena and Hispanic Heritage wings offer changing exhibitions and hands-on activities, while the Gallery of Conscience presents exhibits that explore important social issues. For youngsters there are special activities and the Tree of Life play area.

Time: Allow 1 hour minimum. **Hours:** Daily 10-5, May-Oct.; Tues.-Sun. 10-5, rest of year. Docent-led guided tours are given at 10:30, 11:30 and 2. Closed Jan. 1, Easter, Thanksgiving and Christmas. **Cost:** $12; $11 (students with ID); $7 (New Mexico residents with ID); free (ages 0-16 and to New Mexico residents on first Sun. of the month). **Phone:** (505) 476-1200, or (505) 476-1217 to confirm guided tour times.

MUSEUM OF SPANISH COLONIAL ART is 2 mi. s.e. of The Plaza at 750 Camino Lejo. Housed in a 1930 Pueblo Revival building designed by architect John Gaw Meem, the museum presents traditional Spanish art produced throughout the world since the start of Spanish colonization. The collection of some 3,700 objects includes painted images of saints, sculpture, textiles, metal work, ceramics, furniture and books. **Time:** Allow 1 hour minimum. **Hours:** Daily 10-5, early May-late Oct.; Tues.-Sun. 10-5, rest of year. Closed Jan. 1, Easter, Thanksgiving and Christmas. **Cost:** $10; free (ages 0-15 and on first Sun. of the month for New Mexico residents with ID). **Phone:** (505) 982-2226.

GEM **NEW MEXICO HISTORY MUSEUM,** 113 Lincoln Ave. on The Plaza, combines the state's oldest and newest museums. Permanent and changing exhibits focus on the history of New Mexico—Native Americans, Spanish colonists, Mexican rule, the Santa Fe Trail, the railroad era, statehood, World War II and the present day.

The museum serves as the anchor of a campus complex. The Palace Press, situated in the rooms adjoining the courtyard, is a working exhibit dedicated to the history of the state's printing techniques. The *portal* (porch) is a gathering place for artisans who sell jewelry, pottery, weavings and crafts. The Fray Angelico Chavez History Library has a collection of some 40,000 titles, while a photo archives contains more than 750,000 images dating back to the early 1850s.

Time: Allow 3 hours minimum. **Hours:** Museum daily 10-5 (also Fri. 5-7), May-Oct.; Tues.-Sun. 10-5 (also first Fri. of the month 5-7), rest of year. History library and photo archives open by appointment only. Closed Jan. 1, Easter, Thanksgiving and Christmas. **Cost:** (includes Palace of the Governors) $12; $7 (New Mexico residents with ID); free (ages 0-16, to New Mexico residents with ID on the first Sun. of the month and on Fri. 5-7, and to New Mexico senior citizens with ID on Wed.). **Phone:** (505) 476-5200, (505) 476-5026 for the photo archives, or (505) 476-5090 for the history library. GT

Palace of the Governors is on The Plaza at 105 W. Palace Ave. Built in 1610, this long, low adobe structure is a National Historic Landmark and is considered to be one of the oldest public buildings in the United States. It functioned as the seat of government under Spanish, Pueblo Indian, Mexican and U.S. territorial rule until 1909, when the building became the state history museum.

Four-foot-thick walls enclose period rooms with displays that chronicle nearly 400 years of New Mexico History. There are several open-pit excavation sites showing layers of foundations, different types of wall constructions and middens. Among the artifacts exhibited are ceramics, glassware, metal utensils, buttons, jewelry and weapons. The chapel room is a replica of a mid-19th century chapel with a simple, brightly colored altarpiece made in 1830.

Time: Allow 2 hours minimum. **Hours:** Daily 10-5 (also Fri. 5-7), May-Oct.; Tues.-Sun. 10-5 (also first Fri. of the month 5-7), rest of year. Closed Jan. 1, Easter, Thanksgiving and Christmas. **Cost:** (includes New Mexico History Museum) $12; $7 (New Mexico residents with ID); free (ages 0-16, to New Mexico residents with ID on the first Sun. of the month and on Fri. 5-7, and to New Mexico senior citizens with ID on Wed.). **Phone:** (505) 476-5100. GT

NEW MEXICO MUSEUM OF ART is just off The Plaza at 107 W. Palace Ave. The museum, completed in 1917, houses contemporary and traditional American art. Changing exhibits focus on Southwestern artists from the 19th century to the present, including the Santa Fe and Taos masters.

Time: Allow 1 hour minimum. **Hours:** Daily 10-5 (also Fri. 5-8), Memorial Day-Labor Day; Tues.-Sun.

See maps & indexes p. 308, 311.)

10-5 (also Fri. 5-8), rest of year. Closed Jan. 1, Easter, Thanksgiving and Christmas. **Cost:** $12; free (ages 0-16). Combination tickets are available with the Museum of Indian Arts and Culture, the Museum of International Folk Art and the New Mexico History Museum/Palace of the Governors. **Phone:** (505) 476-5072.

NEW MEXICO STATE CAPITOL is at 490 Old Santa Fe Tr. at the jct. of Paseo de Peralta, 4 blks. s. of The Plaza. The capitol building is designed in the shape of the state's official emblem, the Zia sun symbol, and features a permanent collection of contemporary artwork and furnishings handcrafted by New Mexicans. Galleries on the second floor permit views of the house and senate chambers. **Hours:** Self-guiding tours Mon.-Fri. 7-6. Guided tours are given Mon.-Fri. by appointment. Closed Jan. 1, Easter, Labor Day, Thanksgiving, Christmas Eve and Christmas. **Cost:** Free. **Phone:** (505) 986-4589.

GEM **SAN MIGUEL CHAPEL** is 3 blks. s. of The Plaza at 401 Old Santa Fe Tr. (at E. De Vargas St.). A feeling of timelessness emanates from this simple mission church, built by Tlaxcala Indians under the direction of Franciscan *padres* (priests). Constructed around 1610, it is thought to be the nation's oldest active church. Records of its early history were burned during the Pueblo Indian Rebellion of 1680, but the thick, sturdy adobe walls remained unscathed; stone buttresses were subsequently added to strengthen the walls and bell tower.

The sanctuary has wooden pews and massive timber roof beams *(vigas)*. The hand-carved wooden *reredos* (altar screen) dates from 1798. Paintings of saints and Christ the Nazarene surround a gilded and painted wooden statue of St. Michael the Archangel, brought from Mexico in the early 18th century. In the rear of the church is a painting of Our Lady of Guadalupe. The 780-pound San Jose Bell that once hung in the bell tower now is displayed in the gift shop, and visitors are welcome to ring it; according to legend, those who do are destined to return to Santa Fe.

Hours: Mon.-Sat. 10-4. The church is occasionally closed for special events; phone ahead to confirm. Closed Christmas. **Cost:** $1; free (ages 0-6). **Phone:** (505) 983-3974.

WHEELWRIGHT MUSEUM OF THE AMERICAN INDIAN is 2 mi. s.e. of The Plaza at 704 Camino Lejo on Museum Hill. Reminiscent of an eight-sided Navajo hogan, the museum offers historic and contemporary art exhibits with emphasis on the Southwest. Displays include pottery, jewelry, rugs and baskets. **Hours:** Daily 10-5. Closed Jan. 1, Thanksgiving and Christmas. **Cost:** $5; free (ages 0-11 and students and active military with ID). **Phone:** (505) 982-4636 or (800) 607-4636. GT

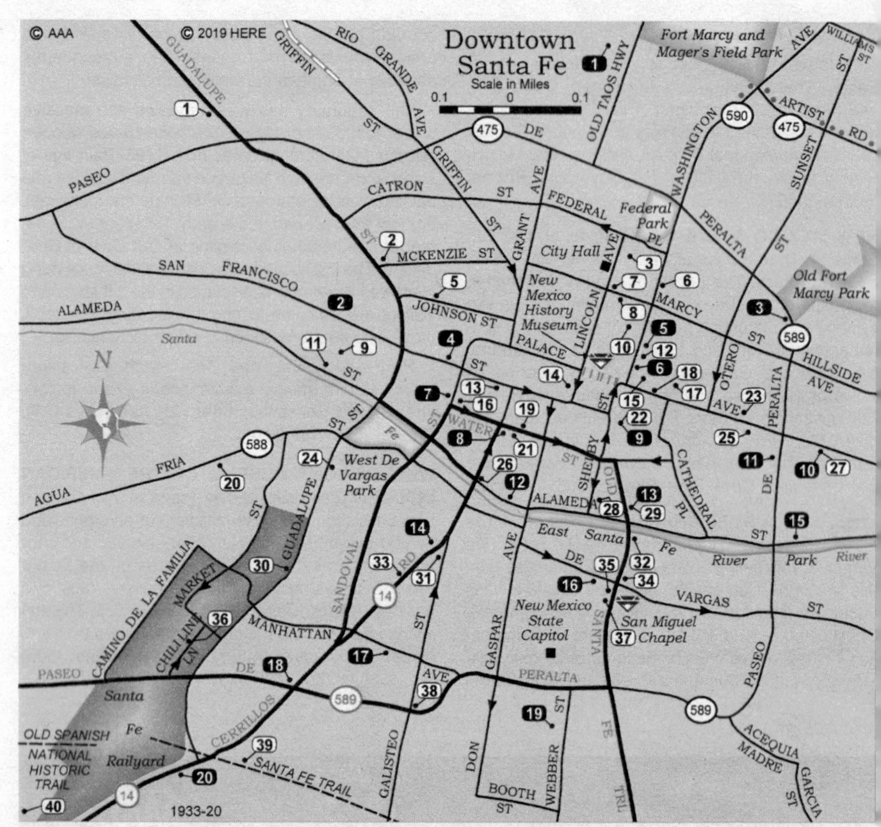

Downtown Santa Fe

This index helps you "spot" where approved hotels and restaurants are located on the corresponding detailed maps. Restaurant price range is a combination of lunch and/or dinner. Turn to the listing page for more information and consult display ads for special promotions.

For more details, rates and reservations: AAA.com/travelguides/hotels

DOWNTOWN SANTA FE

Map Page	Hotels	Diamond Rated	Member Savings	Page
1 this page	Casa Cuma Bed & Breakfast	♦♦♦		313
2 this page	Las Palomas	♦♦♦		314
3 this page	Inn on the Paseo	♦♦♦		314
4 this page	**Eldorado Hotel & Spa**	♦♦♦♦	✔	313
5 this page	**Hotel Chimayó de Santa Fe**	♦♦♦	✔	313
6 this page	Rosewood Inn of the Anasazi	♦♦♦♦		314
7 this page	**Hilton Santa Fe Historic Plaza**	♦♦♦♦	✔	313
8 this page	Otra Vez en Santa Fe	♦♦♦		314
9 this page	**La Fonda On the Plaza**	♦♦♦♦	✔	314
10 this page	**La Posada de Santa Fe Resort & Spa, Tribute Portfolio**	♦♦♦♦	✔	314
11 this page	Drury Plaza Hotel in Santa Fe	♦♦♦		313
12 this page	Inn of the Governors	♦♦♦		313

DOWNTOWN SANTA FE (cont'd)

Map Page	Hotels (cont'd)	Diamond Rated	Member Savings	Page
13 p. 308	**The Inn & Spa at Loretto**	♦♦♦♦	✔	313
14 p. 308	**Old Santa Fe Inn**	♦♦♦	✔	314
15 p. 308	**Inn On The Alameda**	♦♦♦	✔	313
16 p. 308	The Inn of The Five Graces	♦♦♦♦		313
17 p. 308	The Parador	♦♦♦		314
18 p. 308	Hotel Santa Fe, The Hacienda & Spa	♦♦♦		313
19 p. 308	Four Kachinas Inn	♦♦♦		313
20 p. 308	**Santa Fe Sage Inn & Suites**	♦♦	✔	314

Map Page	Restaurants	Diamond Rated	Cuisine	Price Range	Page
1 p. 308	Jinja Bar & Bistro	♦♦	Asian	$9-$21	314
2 p. 308	Bumble Bee's Baja Grill	♦	Regional Mexican	$7-$16	314
3 p. 308	**Osteria d'Assisi**	♦♦♦	Northern Italian	$10-$35	315
5 p. 308	Shohko Cafe	♦♦♦	Japanese	$15-$38	315
6 p. 308	El Meson	♦♦♦	Spanish	$22-$44	314
7 p. 308	Il Piatto	♦♦♦	Italian	$13-$38	314
8 p. 308	La Boca	♦♦♦	International Small Plates	$12-$49	315
9 p. 308	Vanessie	♦♦♦	American	$16-$65	315
10 p. 308	The Bull Ring	♦♦♦	Steak	$10-$48	314
11 p. 308	Bouche French Bistro	♦♦♦	French	$16-$38	314
12 p. 308	Anasazi Restaurant	♦♦♦	Regional American	$12-$45	314
13 p. 308	Tia Sophia's	♦♦	Southwestern	$7-$12	315
14 p. 308	Plaza Cafe	♦♦	American	$12-$25	315
15 p. 308	The Burrito Company	♦	Regional Mexican	$6-$9	314
16 p. 308	Blue Corn Cafe & Brewery	♦♦	Southwestern	$9-$22	314
17 p. 308	La Casa Sena Restaurant	♦♦♦	Regional American	$12-$42	315
18 p. 308	The Shed	♦♦	Regional Mexican	$8-$20	315
19 p. 308	Cafe Pasqual's	♦♦	Regional American	$13-$39	314
20 p. 308	Radish & Rye	♦♦♦	New American	$12-$48	315
21 p. 308	Coyote Cafe	♦♦♦	Southwestern	$28-$43	314
22 p. 308	La Plazuela at La Fonda	♦♦♦	Regional American	$11-$33	315
23 p. 308	Chez Mamou French Cafe & Bakery	♦♦	French	$10-$32	314
24 p. 308	Cowgirl Bar and Grill	♦♦	Regional American	$8-$23	314
25 p. 308	Eloisa	♦♦♦	New Southwestern	$13-$42	314
26 p. 308	L'Olivier	♦♦♦	French	$19-$45	315
27 p. 308	Julia, a Spirited Restaurant & Bar	♦♦♦	Continental	$13-$39	314
28 p. 308	**Sazon**	fyi	New World	$12-$45	315

Map Page	Restaurants (cont'd)	Diamond Rated	Cuisine	Price Range	Page
29 p. 308	Luminaria Restaurant & Patio	♦♦♦	New American	$20-$45	315
30 p. 308	Tomasita's Restaurant	♦♦	Regional Mexican	$7-$22	315
31 p. 308	Saveur	♦♦	French	$6-$22	315
32 p. 308	315 Restaurant & Wine Bar	♦♦♦	French	$24-$36	314
33 p. 308	Yin Yang	♦♦	Chinese	$8-$26	315
34 p. 308	Upper Crust Pizza	♦	Pizza	$4-$23	315
35 p. 308	The Pink Adobe	♦♦♦	American	$18-$40	315
36 p. 308	Second Street Brewery at the Railyard	♦♦	American	$9-$15	315
37 p. 308	Rio Chama	♦♦♦	Steak	$11-$40	315
38 p. 308	Restaurant Martin	♦♦♦	New American	$17-$46	315
39 p. 308	Vinaigrette	♦♦	Natural/Organic	$10-$20	315
40 p. 308	La Choza	♦♦	Regional Mexican	$9-$23	315

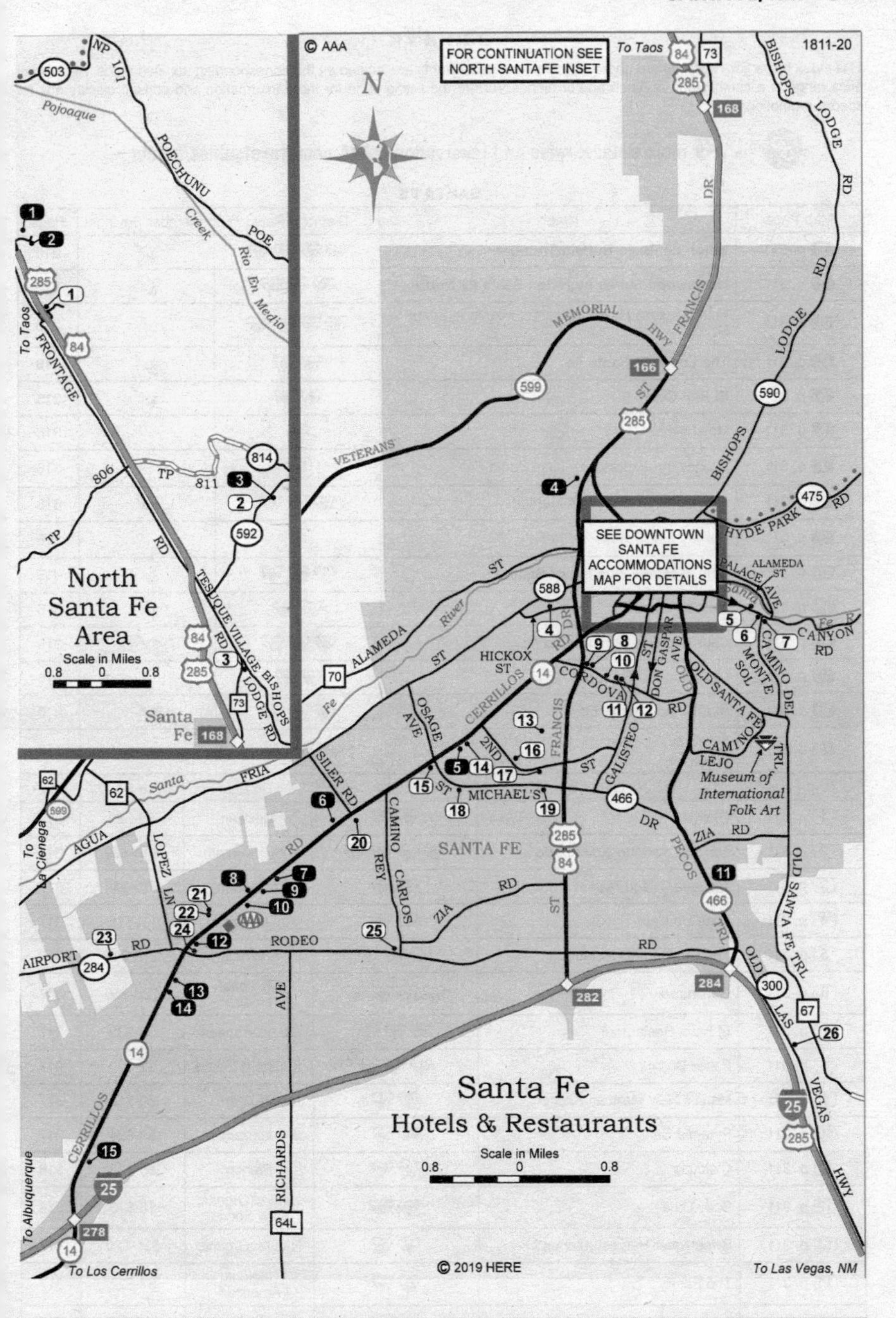

FOR CONTINUATION SEE NORTH SANTA FE INSET
SEE DOWNTOWN SANTA FE ACCOMMODATIONS MAP FOR DETAILS
North Santa Fe Area
Scale in Miles
Santa Fe
Hotels & Restaurants
SANTA FE
Museum of International Folk Art
To Taos
To Albuquerque
To Los Cerrillos
To La Cienega
To Las Vegas, NM
© AAA
© 2019 HERE
1811-20

Santa Fe

This index helps you "spot" where approved hotels and restaurants are located on the corresponding detailed maps. Restaurant price range is a combination of lunch and/or dinner. Turn to the listing page for more information and consult display ads for special promotions.

For more details, rates and reservations: AAA.com/travelguides/hotels

SANTA FE

Map Page	Hotels	Diamond Rated	Member Savings	Page
1 p. 311	**Hilton Santa Fe Buffalo Thunder**	◆◆◆◆	✔	316
2 p. 311	**Homewood Suites by Hilton Santa Fe North**	◆◆◆	✔	316
3 p. 311	Four Seasons Resort Rancho Encantado Santa Fe	◆◆◆◆		316
4 p. 311	**The Lodge at Santa Fe**	◆◆	✔	316
5 p. 311	**El Rey Court**	◆◆	✔	315
6 p. 311	Motel 6-150	◆		316
7 p. 311	Holiday Inn Express & Suites Santa Fe	fyi		316
8 p. 311	Fairfield Inn & Suites by Marriott	◆◆◆	✔	316
9 p. 311	Holiday Inn Express-Santa Fe	fyi		316
10 p. 311	**Best Western Plus Inn of Santa Fe**	◆◆◆	✔	315
11 p. 311	**Pecos Trail Inn**	◆◆	✔	316
12 p. 311	DoubleTree by Hilton Santa Fe	◆◆◆	✔	315
13 p. 311	La Quinta Inn Santa Fe	◆◆		316
14 p. 311	**Hyatt Place Santa Fe**	◆◆◆	✔	316
15 p. 311	SureStay Collection by Best Western - Inn at Santa Fe	◆◆		316

Map Page	Restaurants	Diamond Rated	Cuisine	Price Range	Page
1 p. 311	Gabriel's	◆◆	Mexican	$9-$20	317
2 p. 311	**Terra at Rancho Encantado**	◆◆◆◆	Southwestern	$18-$39	317
3 p. 311	Tesuque Village Market	◆◆	American	$10-$40	317
4 p. 311	Tune-Up Cafe	◆◆	International	$9-$15	317
5 p. 311	The Compound Restaurant	◆◆◆	American	$18-$49	317
6 p. 311	**Geronimo**	◆◆◆◆	Regional International	$28-$50	317
7 p. 311	El Farol Restaurant	◆◆◆	Mediterranean	$8-$39	317
8 p. 311	Paper Dosa	◆◆◆	Southern Indian	$9-$20	317
9 p. 311	Maria's New Mexican Kitchen	◆◆	Mexican	$9-$18	317
10 p. 311	Pyramid Cafe	◆◆	Mediterranean	$9-$24	317
11 p. 311	Clafoutis	◆◆	French	$5-$13	316
12 p. 311	Body Cafe	◆◆	Natural/Organic Raw Foods	$8-$15	316
13 p. 311	Sweetwater Harvest Kitchen	◆◆	Natural/Organic	$11-$20	317
14 p. 311	The Pantry	◆◆	Regional American	$7-$22	317
15 p. 311	Jambo Cafe	◆◆	African	$10-$17	317
16 p. 311	Midtown Bistro	◆◆◆	Northern Mexican	$12-$42	317
17 p. 311	Chocolate Maven Bakery & Cafe	◆◆	American	$10-$15	316
18 p. 311	Pizzeria Espiritu	◆◆	Italian	$10-$25	317

Map Page	Restaurants (cont'd)	Diamond Rated	Cuisine	Price Range	Page
19 p. 311	Chow's Asian Bistro	◆◆	Asian	$9-$20	316
20 p. 311	Dr. Field Goods Kitchen	◆◆	Regional American	$8-$15	317
21 p. 311	Santa Fe Capitol Grill	◆◆	International	$8-$27	317
22 p. 311	Cleopatra's Cafe	◆	Mediterranean	$6-$16	317
23 p. 311	Puerto Penasco	◆◆	Mexican Seafood	$7-$15	317
24 p. 311	Blue Corn Cafe & Brewery	◆◆	Southwestern	$9-$30	316
25 p. 311	Joe's Diner and Pizza	◆◆	American	$9-$32	317
26 p. 311	Harry's Roadhouse	◆◆	American	$10-$30	317

DOWNTOWN SANTA FE

- **Restaurants p. 314**
- **Hotels & Restaurants map & index p. 308**

CASA CUMA BED & BREAKFAST 505/216-7516 **1**

◆◆◆ Bed & Breakfast. **Address:** 105 Paseo de la Cuma 87501

DRURY PLAZA HOTEL IN SANTA FE 505/424-2175 **11**

◆◆◆ Hotel. **Address:** 828 E Paseo de Peralta 87501

ELDORADO HOTEL & SPA 505/988-4455 **4**

◆◆◆◆ Hotel

Address: 309 W San Francisco St 87501 **Location:** Just w of The Plaza; at Sandoval St. **Facility:** This property's public areas feature contemporary Southwestern décor. The guest rooms are comfortable and nicely decorated; some rooms have balconies and views of the Sangre de Cristo Mountains. 219 units. 5 stories, interior corridors. **Parking:** valet only. **Terms:** check-in 4 pm. **Amenities:** safes. **Dining:** 2 restaurants. **Pool:** heated outdoor. **Activities:** sauna, hot tub, steamroom, health club, spa. **Guest Services:** valet laundry.

FOUR KACHINAS INN 505/988-1631 **19**

◆◆◆ Bed & Breakfast. **Address:** 512 Webber St 87505

HILTON SANTA FE HISTORIC PLAZA 505/988-2811 **7**

◆◆◆◆ Hotel

Hilton HOTELS & RESORTS **AAA Benefit:** Members save up to 15%!

Address: 100 Sandoval St 87501 **Location:** Just sw of The Plaza; between San Francisco and W Alameda sts. **Facility:** The hotel is built around the historic former home of a prominent Santa Fe family. Guest rooms feature comfortable beds, plush bedding and Southwest accents. 158 units, some two bedrooms. 3 stories, interior/exterior corridors. **Parking:** on-site (fee). **Amenities:** safes. **Pool:** heated outdoor. **Activities:** hot tub, health club, massage. **Guest Services:** valet laundry.

HOTEL CHIMAYÓ DE SANTA FE 505/988-4900 **5**

◆◆◆ Hotel

Address: 125 Washington Ave 87501 **Location:** Just ne of The Plaza; center. **Facility:** 56 units, some efficiencies. 2-3 stories, interior/exterior corridors. **Parking:** on-site (fee). **Terms:** check-in 4 pm. **Guest Services:** valet laundry, area transportation.

HOTEL SANTA FE, THE HACIENDA & SPA 505/982-1200 **18**

◆◆◆ Hotel. **Address:** 1501 Paseo de Peralta 87501

THE INN & SPA AT LORETTO 505/988-5531 **13**

◆◆◆◆ Hotel

Address: 211 Old Santa Fe Tr 87501 **Location:** Just s of The Plaza. Located in the historic district. **Facility:** This is a cozy retreat after a day spent museum hopping, sightseeing and shopping, all available just a short walk away. Rooms feature tasteful Southwest style; some have fireplaces or balconies. 136 units, some kitchens. 5 stories, interior corridors. **Parking:** valet only. **Terms:** check-in 4 pm. **Amenities:** safes. **Dining:** Luminaria Restaurant & Patio, see separate listing. **Pool:** heated outdoor. **Activities:** exercise room, spa. **Guest Services:** valet laundry.

THE INN OF THE FIVE GRACES 505/992-0957 **16**

◆◆◆◆ Historic Boutique Country Inn. **Address:** 150 E DeVargas St 87501

INN OF THE GOVERNORS 505/982-4333 **12**

◆◆◆ Hotel. **Address:** 101 W Alameda St 87501

INN ON THE ALAMEDA 505/984-2121 **15**

◆◆◆ Hotel

Address: 303 E Alameda St 87501 **Location:** Just e of The Plaza; jct Paseo de Peralta. **Facility:** 72 units. 1-3 stories, interior/exterior corridors. **Terms:** check-in 4 pm. **Amenities:** safes. **Activities:** hot tub, exercise room, massage. **Guest Services:** valet and coin laundry, area transportation. **Featured Amenity:** breakfast buffet.

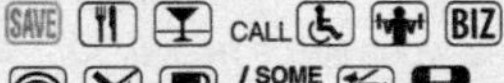

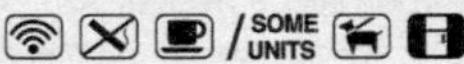

(See map & index p. 308.)

INN ON THE PASEO 505/984-8200 3

Boutique Bed & Breakfast. **Address:** 630 Paseo de Peralta 87501

LA FONDA ON THE PLAZA 505/982-5511 9

Historic Hotel

Address: 100 E San Francisco St 87501 **Location:** On The Plaza. **Facility:** This stunning inn maintains its historic charm but with modern conveniences. The guest rooms feature a chic, contemporary Southwest style. 180 units. 5 stories, interior corridors. **Parking:** on-site (fee) and valet. **Amenities:** safes. **Dining:** 3 restaurants, also, La Plazuela at La Fonda, see separate listing, entertainment. **Pool:** heated outdoor. **Activities:** hot tub, steamroom, exercise room, spa. **Guest Services:** valet laundry.

SOME UNITS

LA POSADA DE SANTA FE RESORT & SPA, TRIBUTE PORTFOLIO 505/986-0000 10

Resort Hotel

TRIBUTE PORTFOLIO **AAA Benefit:** Members save 5% or more!

Address: 330 E Palace Ave 87501 **Location:** Jct Paseo de Peralta and E Palace Ave. **Facility:** This classic Santa Fe resort blends Old World New Mexico style with elegant contemporary luxury amenities. Rooms feature typical plastered walls and custom wood furniture; some have fireplaces. 157 units, some two bedrooms. 1-2 stories (no elevator), exterior corridors. **Parking:** valet only. **Terms:** check-in 4 pm. **Amenities:** safes. **Dining:** 3 restaurants, also, Julia, a Spirited Restaurant & Bar, see separate listing. **Pool:** heated outdoor. **Activities:** hot tub, steamroom, recreation programs, exercise room, spa. **Guest Services:** valet laundry, area transportation.

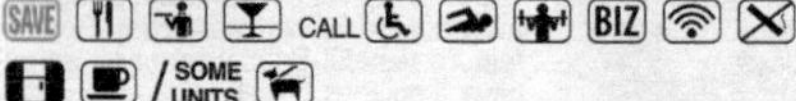

SOME UNITS

LAS PALOMAS 505/982-5560 2

Boutique Hotel. **Address:** 460 W San Francisco St 87501

OLD SANTA FE INN 505/995-0800 14

Motel

Address: 201 Montezuma Ave 87501 **Location:** Just sw of The Plaza; center. **Facility:** 58 units. 1-2 stories (no elevator), interior/exterior corridors. **Amenities:** safes. **Activities:** exercise room. **Featured Amenity: breakfast buffet.**

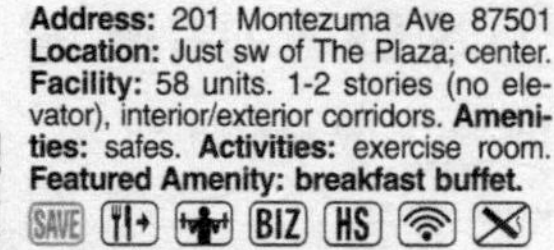

OTRA VEZ EN SANTA FE 505/988-2244 8

Condominium. **Address:** 202 Galisteo St 87501

THE PARADOR 505/988-1177 17

Historic Bed & Breakfast. **Address:** 220 W Manhattan Ave 87501

ROSEWOOD INN OF THE ANASAZI 505/988-3030 6

Hotel. **Address:** 113 Washington Ave 87501

SANTA FE SAGE INN & SUITES 505/982-5952 20

Hotel

Address: 725 Cerrillos Rd 87505 **Location:** 0.4 mi ne of St. Francis Dr (US 84). **Facility:** 145 units. 2 stories (no elevator), exterior corridors. **Parking:** on-site (fee). **Terms:** check-in 4 pm. **Pool:** heated outdoor. **Activities:** exercise room. **Guest Services:** coin laundry, area transportation. **Featured Amenity: full hot breakfast.**

SAVE CALL BIZ

SOME UNITS

WHERE TO EAT

315 RESTAURANT & WINE BAR 505/986-9190 32

French. Fine Dining. **Address:** 315 Old Santa Fe Tr 87501

ANASAZI RESTAURANT 505/988-3236 12

Regional American. Fine Dining. **Address:** 113 Washington Ave 87501

BLUE CORN CAFE & BREWERY 505/984-1800 16

Southwestern. Casual Dining. **Address:** 133 W Water St 87501

BOUCHE FRENCH BISTRO 505/982-6297 11

French. Fine Dining. **Address:** 451 W Alameda St 87501

THE BULL RING 505/983-3328 10

Steak. Fine Dining. **Address:** 150 Washington Ave 87501

BUMBLE BEE'S BAJA GRILL 505/820-2862 2

Regional Mexican. Quick Serve. **Address:** 301 Jefferson St 87501

THE BURRITO COMPANY 505/982-4453 15

Regional Mexican. Quick Serve. **Address:** 111 Washington Ave 87501

CAFE PASQUAL'S 505/983-9340 19

Regional American. Casual Dining. **Address:** 121 Don Gaspar Ave 87501

CHEZ MAMOU FRENCH CAFE & BAKERY 505/216-1845 23

French. Casual Dining. **Address:** 217 E Palace Ave 87501

COWGIRL BAR AND GRILL 505/982-2565 24

Regional American. Casual Dining. **Address:** 319 S Guadalupe St 87501

COYOTE CAFE 505/983-1615 21

Southwestern. Casual Dining. **Address:** 132 W Water St 87501

EL MESON 505/983-6756 6

Spanish. Casual Dining. **Address:** 213 Washington Ave 87501

ELOISA 505/982-0083 25

New Southwestern. Casual Dining. **Address:** 228 E Palace Ave 87501

IL PIATTO 505/984-1091 7

Italian. Casual Dining. **Address:** 95 W Marcy St 87501

JINJA BAR & BISTRO 505/982-4321 1

Asian. Casual Dining. **Address:** 510 N Guadalupe St, Suite P 87501

JULIA, A SPIRITED RESTAURANT & BAR 505/986-0000 27

Continental. Fine Dining. **Address:** 330 E Palace Ave 87501

(See map & index p. 308.)

LA BOCA 505/982-3433 (8)
Three Diamond International Small Plates. Casual Dining. **Address:** 72 W Marcy St 87501

LA CASA SENA RESTAURANT 505/988-9232 (17)
Three Diamond Regional American. Fine Dining. **Address:** 125 E Palace Ave 87501

LA CHOZA 505/982-0909 (40)
Two Diamond Regional Mexican. Casual Dining. **Address:** 905 Alarid St 87505

LA PLAZUELA AT LA FONDA 505/982-5511 (22)
Three Diamond Regional American. Casual Dining. **Address:** 100 E San Francisco St 87501

L'OLIVIER 505/989-1919 (26)
Three Diamond French. Fine Dining. **Address:** 229 Galisteo St 87501

LUMINARIA RESTAURANT & PATIO 505/984-7915 (29)
Three Diamond New American. Fine Dining. **Address:** 211 Old Santa Fe Tr 87501

OSTERIA D'ASSISI 505/986-5858 (3)

Three Diamond
Northern Italian Casual Dining
$10-$35

AAA Inspector Notes: This busy restaurant, near both the business and cultural centers of the city, serves up delicious Northern Italian cuisine to tourists and locals in comfortable surroundings. Some gluten-free pasta dishes are available. **Features:** full bar, patio dining, Sunday brunch, happy hour. **Reservations:** suggested. **Address:** 58 S Federal Pl 87501 **Location:** 1 blk n of The Plaza. **Parking:** on-site and street.
L D

THE PINK ADOBE 505/983-7712 (35)
Three Diamond American. Casual Dining. **Address:** 406 Old Santa Fe Tr 87501

PLAZA CAFE 505/982-1664 (14)
Two Diamond American. Casual Dining. **Address:** 54 Lincoln Ave 87501

RADISH & RYE 505/930-5325 (20)
Three Diamond New American. Casual Dining. **Address:** 548 Agua Fria St 87501

RESTAURANT MARTIN 505/820-0919 (38)
Three Diamond New American. Fine Dining. **Address:** 526 Galisteo St 87501

RIO CHAMA 505/955-0765 (37)
Three Diamond Steak. Casual Dining. **Address:** 414 Old Santa Fe Tr 87501

SAVEUR 505/989-4200 (31)
Two Diamond French. Casual Dining. **Address:** 204 Montezuma Ave 87501

SAZON 505/983-8604 (28)

fyi
New World Fine Dining
$12-$45

Under major renovation, call for details. **Last rated:** Four Diamond **AAA Inspector Notes:** Just off The Plaza, this hidden gem is where the foodies go to immerse themselves in contemporary Mexican cuisine. The chef prepares a variety of moles daily and incorporates them in the ever-changing menu. After dinner, be sure to save room for one of the delicious house-made desserts. Try one of the many margaritas made with mescal. **Features:** full bar. **Reservations:** suggested. **Address:** 221 Shelby St 87501 **Location:** Just s of Water St. **Parking:** street only. D

SECOND STREET BREWERY AT THE RAILYARD 505/989-3278 (36)
Two Diamond American. Brewpub. **Address:** 1607 Paseo de Peralta, Suite 10 87501

THE SHED 505/982-9030 (18)
Two Diamond Regional Mexican. Casual Dining. **Address:** 113 &1/2 E Palace Ave 87501

SHOHKO CAFE 505/982-9708 (5)
Three Diamond Japanese. Casual Dining. **Address:** 321 Johnson St 87501

TIA SOPHIA'S 505/983-9880 (13)
Two Diamond Southwestern. Casual Dining. **Address:** 210 W San Francisco St 87501

TOMASITA'S RESTAURANT 505/983-5721 (30)
Two Diamond Regional Mexican. Casual Dining. **Address:** 500 S Guadalupe St 87501

UPPER CRUST PIZZA 505/982-0000 (34)
One Diamond Pizza. Quick Serve. **Address:** 329 Old Santa Fe Tr 87501

VANESSIE 505/982-9966 (9)
Three Diamond American. Fine Dining. **Address:** 427 W Water St 87501

VINAIGRETTE 505/820-9205 (39)
Two Diamond Natural/Organic. Casual Dining. **Address:** 709 Don Cubero Alley 87505

YIN YANG 505/986-9279 (33)
Two Diamond Chinese. Casual Dining. **Address:** 418 Cerrillos Rd 87501

SANTA FE

- **Restaurants p. 316**
- **Hotels & Restaurants map & index p. 311**

BEST WESTERN PLUS INN OF SANTA FE 505/438-3822 (10)

Three Diamond
Hotel

Best Western PLUS **AAA Benefit:** Members save up to 15% and earn bonus points!

Address: 3650 Cerrillos Rd 87507 **Location:** I-25 exit 278, 2.8 mi n. **Facility:** 95 units. 3 stories, interior corridors. **Pool:** heated indoor. **Activities:** hot tub, exercise room. **Guest Services:** valet and coin laundry. **Featured Amenity:** **breakfast buffet.**

SAVE CALL BIZ HS
/ SOME UNITS

DOUBLETREE BY HILTON SANTA FE 505/473-4646 (12)
Three Diamond SAVE Hotel. **Address:** 4048 Cerrillos Rd 87507

AAA Benefit: Members save up to 15%!

EL REY COURT 505/982-1931 (5)

Two Diamond
Classic Historic Motel

Address: 1862 Cerrillos Rd 87505 **Location:** 1.5 mi s of jct St Francis Rd. **Facility:** Built in 1936, this property captures Santa Fe's charm with its white adobe buildings and lush landscaping, including several hidden gardens. Each room has unique Southwestern décor. 86 units, some two bedrooms, efficiencies and kitchens. 1-2 stories (no elevator), exterior corridors. **Terms:** check-in 4 pm. **Pool:** heated outdoor. **Activities:** sauna, hot tub, playground, exercise room. **Guest Services:** coin laundry.

SAVE BIZ

/ SOME UNITS

(See map & index p. 311.)

FAIRFIELD INN & SUITES BY MARRIOTT 505/474-3900 8

SAVE Hotel. **Address:** 3625 Cerrillos Rd 87507

AAA Benefit: Members save 5% or more!

FOUR SEASONS RESORT RANCHO ENCANTADO SANTA FE 505/946-5700 3

Resort Hotel. **Address:** 198 State Road 592 87506

HILTON SANTA FE BUFFALO THUNDER 505/455-5555 1

Resort Hotel

AAA Benefit: Members save up to 15%!

Address: 20 Buffalo Thunder Tr 87506 **Location:** US 84/285 exit 177, just ne. **Facility:** The luxurious resort property has activities for all interests, from a golf course, casino, spa and shopping to fine dining. Guest rooms feature custom furniture and upscale amenities. 393 units. 6 stories, interior corridors. **Parking:** on-site and valet. **Terms:** check-in 4 pm. **Amenities:** safes. **Dining:** 7 restaurants, nightclub, entertainment. **Pool:** heated outdoor, heated indoor. **Activities:** sauna, hot tub, steamroom, regulation golf, tennis, recreation programs in season, game room, health club, spa. **Guest Services:** valet laundry.

SAVE CALL BIZ / SOME UNITS

HOLIDAY INN EXPRESS & SUITES SANTA FE 505/473-9004 7

fyi Hotel. Under major renovation, call for details. **Last Rated:** **Address:** 3348 Cerrillos Rd 87507

HOLIDAY INN EXPRESS-SANTA FE 505/474-7570 9

fyi Hotel. Under major renovation, call for details. **Last Rated:** **Address:** 3450 Cerrillos Rd 87507

HOMEWOOD SUITES BY HILTON SANTA FE NORTH 505/455-9100 2

Extended Stay Hotel

AAA Benefit: Members save up to 15%!

Address: 10 Buffalo Thunder Tr 87506 **Location:** US 84/285 exit 177, just ne. **Facility:** 81 units, some two bedrooms, efficiencies and kitchens. 3 stories, interior/exterior corridors. **Amenities:** video games. **Pool:** heated outdoor. **Activities:** regulation golf, picnic facilities, exercise room. **Guest Services:** valet and coin laundry, area transportation. **Featured Amenity: continental breakfast.**

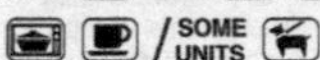

SAVE CALL BIZ / SOME UNITS

HYATT PLACE SANTA FE 505/474-7777 14

Hotel

HYATT PLACE **AAA Benefit:** Members save up to 10%!

Address: 4320 Cerrillos Rd 87507 **Location:** I-25 exit 278, 2 mi e. **Facility:** 92 units. 3 stories, interior corridors. **Pool:** heated indoor. **Activities:** hot tub, exercise room. **Guest Services:** valet and coin laundry, area transportation. **Featured Amenity: breakfast buffet.**

SAVE CALL BIZ / SOME UNITS

LA QUINTA INN SANTA FE 505/471-1142 13

Hotel. **Address:** 4298 Cerrillos Rd 87507

THE LODGE AT SANTA FE 505/992-5800 4

Hotel

Address: 750 N St. Francis Dr 87501 **Location:** Jct of Cerrillos Rd and St. Francis Dr (US 84/285), 1.1 mi nw to Alamo Dr, just w, then just n. **Facility:** 128 units. 1-3 stories, interior/exterior corridors. **Terms:** check-in 4 pm. **Pool:** heated outdoor. **Activities:** hot tub, exercise room. **Guest Services:** coin laundry, area transportation.

SAVE BIZ / SOME UNITS

MOTEL 6-150 505/473-1380 6

Motel. **Address:** 3007 Cerrillos Rd 87507

PECOS TRAIL INN 505/982-1943 11

Motel

Address: 2239 Old Pecos Tr 87505 **Location:** I-25 exit 284, 0.8 mi n on CR 466. **Facility:** 23 units, some two bedrooms and kitchens. 1 story, exterior corridors. **Pool:** heated outdoor.

SAVE CALL / SOME UNITS

SURESTAY COLLECTION BY BEST WESTERN - INN AT SANTA FE 505/474-9500 15

Hotel. **Address:** 8376 Cerrillos Rd 87507

WHERE TO EAT

BLUE CORN CAFE & BREWERY 505/438-1800 24

Southwestern. Casual Dining. **Address:** 4056 Cerrillos Rd 87505

BODY CAFE 505/986-0362 12

Natural/Organic Raw Foods. Casual Dining. **Address:** 333 W Cordova Rd 87505

CHOCOLATE MAVEN BAKERY & CAFE 505/984-1980 17

American. Casual Dining. **Address:** 821 W San Mateo Rd, Suite C 87505

CHOW'S ASIAN BISTRO 505/471-7120 19

Asian. Casual Dining. **Address:** 720 St. Michael's Dr 87501

CLAFOUTIS 505/988-1809 11

French. Casual Dining. **Address:** 333 W Cordova Rd 87505

(See map & index p. 311.)

CLEOPATRA'S CAFE 505/474-5644 (22)

Mediterranean. Quick Serve. **Address:** 3482 Zafarano Dr 87507

THE COMPOUND RESTAURANT 505/982-4353 (5)

American. Fine Dining. **Address:** 653 Canyon Rd 87501

DR. FIELD GOODS KITCHEN 505/471-0043 (20)

Regional American. Casual Dining. **Address:** 2860 Cerrillos Rd 87505

EL FAROL RESTAURANT 505/983-9912 (7)

Mediterranean. Casual Dining. **Address:** 808 Canyon Rd 87501

GABRIEL'S 505/455-7000 (1)

Mexican. Casual Dining. **Address:** US 285/84 87501

GERONIMO 505/982-1500 (6)

Regional International Fine Dining
$28-$50

AAA Inspector Notes: *Classic.* Whether you choose to dine on the porch to watch the art gallery aficionados pass by, inside in the lounge or in the quietly elegant dining room, the polished and attentive service staff will provide a smooth dining experience. The menu highlights Southwestern-style cuisine at its best with favorites being the green miso sea bass, mesquite grilled Maine lobster tail and the tellicherry rubbed elk tenderloin. Don't plan to skip dessert—the coffee crème brûlée is not to be missed. **Features:** full bar, patio dining. **Reservations:** suggested. **Address:** 724 Canyon Rd 87501 **Location:** 0.5 mi e of jct Paseo de Peralta. **Parking:** on-site and valet. [D]

HARRY'S ROADHOUSE 505/989-4629 (26)

American. Casual Dining. **Address:** 96B Old Las Vegas Hwy 87505

IZANAMI IZAKAYA 505/982-9304

Japanese. Casual Dining. **Address:** 3451 Hyde Park Rd 87501

JAMBO CAFE 505/473-1269 (15)

African. Casual Dining. **Address:** 2010 Cerrillos Rd 87505

JOE'S DINER AND PIZZA 505/471-3800 (25)

American. Casual Dining. **Address:** 2801 Rodeo Rd 87507

MARIA'S NEW MEXICAN KITCHEN 505/983-7929 (9)

Mexican. Casual Dining. **Address:** 555 W Cordova Rd 87505

MIDTOWN BISTRO 505/820-3121 (16)

Northern Mexican. Fine Dining. **Address:** 901 W San Mateo, Suite A 87501

THE PANTRY 505/986-0022 (14)

Regional American. Casual Dining. **Address:** 1820 Cerrillos Rd 87505

PAPER DOSA 505/930-5521 (8)

Southern Indian. Casual Dining. **Address:** 551 W Cordova Rd 87505

PIZZERIA ESPIRITU 505/424-8000 (18)

Italian. Casual Dining. **Address:** 1722-A St. Michael's Dr 87505

PUERTO PENASCO 505/438-6622 (23)

Mexican Seafood. Casual Dining. **Address:** 4681 Airport Rd, Suite 1 87507

PYRAMID CAFE 505/989-1378 (10)

Mediterranean. Casual Dining. **Address:** 505 W Cordova Rd 87505

SANTA FE CAPITOL GRILL 505/471-6800 (21)

International. Casual Dining. **Address:** 3462 Zafarano Dr 87507

SWEETWATER HARVEST KITCHEN 505/795-7383 (13)

Natural/Organic. Casual Dining. **Address:** 1512 Pacheco St, Bldg B 87505

TERRA AT RANCHO ENCANTADO 505/946-5800 (2)

Southwestern Fine Dining
$18-$39

AAA Inspector Notes: This upscale restaurant has a contemporary ambience that leads to the start of a memorable dining experience. A beautiful roaring gas stone fireplace sits at the back of the dining room. Their menu has such creative choices as buffalo bistro steak, chile-roasted chicken breast and mushroom ragu strudel. Consider one of their creatively prepared desserts to end your meal. **Features:** full bar, patio dining, Sunday brunch. **Reservations:** suggested. **Address:** 198 SR 592 87506 **Location:** US 285/84 exit 172 (CR 73/Tesuque), 0.5 mi se to SR 592, then 2 mi ne; in Four Seasons Resort Rancho Encantado Santa Fe. **Parking:** on-site and valet. [B] [L] [D]

TESUQUE VILLAGE MARKET 505/988-8848 (3)

American. Casual Dining. **Address:** 138 Tesuque Village Rd 87506

TUNE-UP CAFE 505/983-7060 (4)

International. Casual Dining. **Address:** 1115 Hickox St 87505

SANTA FE NATIONAL FOREST (A-5)

Elevations in the forest range from 5,300 ft. to 13,103 ft. at Truchas Peak. Refer to AAA maps for additional elevation information.

In the north central part of the state, some 1,600,000 acres of forest and rangeland lie within Santa Fe National Forest. The southern Sangre de Cristo Range, with several 12,000- to 13,000-foot peaks, dominates the eastern half. Within the forest are Pecos Wilderness, the headwaters of the Pecos River and the Santa Fe Basin winter sports area. The 18-mile trip along SR 63 between Cowles and Pecos provides outstanding views of the forest's eastern section.

In the portion west of the Rio Grande are the Jémez Mountains, San Pedro Parks Wilderness, Chama River Canyon Wilderness and Dome Wilderness. Developed recreation sites and day-use picnic areas are near streams, trailheads and other scenic highlights. Recreational opportunities include hiking, fishing, horseback riding and such winter sports as cross-country skiing and snowshoeing. Fees are required for some developed areas.

For information and maps contact the Supervisor, Santa Fe National Forest, 11 Forest Ln., Santa Fe, NM 87508; phone (505) 438-5300 (Public Information Officer). *See Recreation Areas Chart.*

SANTA ROSA (F-5) pop. 2,848, elev. 4,599'

• Hotels p. 318 • Restaurants p. 318

Santa Rosa is surrounded by parcels of land with property lines that were established by Spanish land grants. Many residents are descended from the exploration party that accompanied Francisco Vázquez de Coronado in 1540.

Ironically, this semi-desert region also has artesian springs and spring-fed lakes. Blue Hole, an artesian spring 81 feet deep, is a half-mile west of Park Lake. Scuba divers can explore the 64-degree water; a diving permit is required. Fishing and scuba diving are also good at Perch Lake.

Other nearby lakes, such as Park Lake and the lake in Janes-Wallace Memorial Park *(see Recreation Areas Chart)*, yield catches of trout, crappie and walleye. Anglers fish for channel catfish in the Pecos River. Rock Lake State Fish Hatchery, 2 miles south of town on River Road, raises rainbow trout and walleye.

Scenic SR 91 follows the Pecos River south for 10 miles to Puerto de Luna, one of several abandoned Spanish settlements in this region. A marker indicates where Coronado camped while a makeshift bridge was built so the river could be crossed. Another scenic is SR 91; 7 miles north of Santa Rose is Santa Rosa Lake State Park *(see Recreation Areas Chart)*. A nature trail and recreational facilities are adjacent to the dam and reservoir.

Santa Rosa Visitors Information Center: 1085 Blue Hole Rd., P.O. Box 429, Santa Rosa, NM 88435. **Phone:** (575) 472-3763.

BEST WESTERN SANTA ROSA INN 575/472-5877

AAA Benefit: Members save up to 15% and earn bonus points!

Address: 2491 Historic Route 66 88435 **Location:** I-40 exit 277, 0.5 mi w. **Facility:** 44 units. 1 story, exterior corridors. **Pool:** heated outdoor. **Guest Services:** coin laundry. **Featured Amenity: full hot breakfast.**

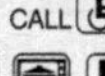

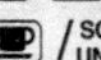

DAYS INN & SUITES 575/472-3446

Address: 2255 Historic Route 66 88435 **Location:** I-40 exit 275, just w. **Facility:** 58 units. 1-2 stories (no elevator), exterior corridors. **Pool:** outdoor. **Guest Services:** coin laundry. **Featured Amenity: continental breakfast.**

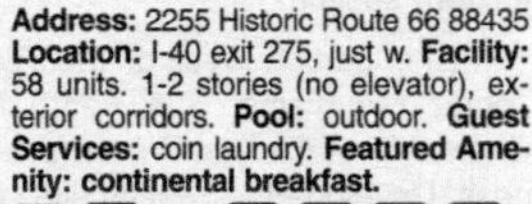

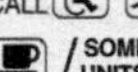

HAMPTON INN 575/472-2300

AAA Benefit: Members save up to 15%!

Address: 2475 Historic Route 66 88435 **Location:** I-40 exit 277, 1 mi w. **Facility:** 64 units. 3 stories, interior corridors. **Pool:** heated indoor. **Activities:** hot tub, game room, exercise room. **Guest Services:** coin laundry. **Featured Amenity: full hot breakfast.**

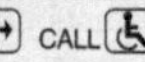

HOLIDAY INN EXPRESS 575/472-5411

Hotel. **Address:** 2516 Historic Route 66 88435

SUPER 8-SANTA ROSA 575/472-5388

Motel. **Address:** 2075 Historic Route 66 88435

WHERE TO EAT

JOSEPH'S BAR & GRILL 575/472-3361

Southwestern. Casual Dining. **Address:** 1775 Historic Route 66 88435

SANTA FE GRILLE 575/472-5568

American. Casual Dining. **Address:** 2249 Historic Route 66 88435

SANTA TERESA (J-3) pop. 4,258, elev. 4,100'

Santa Teresa is on the western edge of the El Paso/Ciudad Juárez metropolitan area. Since it bypasses Ciudad Juárez, Santa Teresa is the recommended crossing point for tourists and other travelers who are driving to Chihuahua and beyond or otherwise headed for interior Mexico. Banjercito offices at this border crossing and at the 30-kilometer (19-mile) mark on Mex. 45 (the Juárez-Chihuahua Highway) can process the paperwork necessary for vehicle travel into the interior.

Dollars or pesos are accepted when entering or departing Mexico or the United States. Baggage may be inspected at the customs offices. Both Mexican and U.S. Customs and Border Protection offices are open daily 24 hours at Ciudad Juárez; daily 6 a.m.-midnight at Santa Teresa. AAA/CAA members can obtain Mexican automobile insurance at AAA Texas offices.

GEM **WAR EAGLES AIR MUSEUM** is off I-10 exit 8, 7.5 mi. w. on Airport Rd. to Santa Teresa Airport. The museum features restored aircraft from the World War II era and jet fighters used in the Korean Conflict. Fighters include the P-51 Mustang, the P-38 Lightning, the P-40 Warhawk, a twin-engine Invader bomber and a Fieseler Storch.

Among the 1950s jets are a T-33 Silver Star and MiG-15. Additional displays feature women aviators, flight equipment and 46 vintage automobiles. **Time:** Allow 1 hour minimum. **Hours:** Tues.-Sun. 10-4. Last admission 30 minutes before closing. Closed major holidays. **Cost:** $5; $4 (ages 65+ and military with ID); free (ages 0-11 and students with ID). **Phone:** (575) 589-2000.

TRAVELODGE 575/589-0552

Hotel. **Address:** 2680 Airport Rd 88008

SANTO DOMINGO PUEBLO (C-3) pop. 2,456, elev. 5,185'

Santo Domingo received its name in 1691 when missionaries began renaming New Mexican pueblos for Catholic saints. Keresan people had inhabited the site since the 1200s. The pueblo's actual location has changed over the years with flooding of the Rio

Grande. The town of Domingo became a stopover on the way to Peña Blanca during Spanish colonial times; it later served as a stage stop on the road between Albuquerque and Santa Fe. The 1883 Santo Domingo Trading Post is one of the largest in the area.

SANTO DOMINGO PUEBLO is off I-25 exit 259, then 2.5 mi. w. Because of their proximity to the ancient Cerrillos turquoise mines, the Keresan artisans of Santo Domingo earned a reputation for fine jewelry, beadwork and mosaics. Their *heishe* beads are prized today. A community center offers visitors a glimpse into tribal life and traditions. Some 350 artists gather for an arts and crafts festival on Labor Day weekend.

The Church of the Pueblo of Santo Domingo dates from 1886 and replaced a mission that was carried away by Rio Grande floodwaters. Visitors can see historical records and paintings by Native American artists. Photography, sketching and painting are not permitted. **Hours:** Daily 8-5. Phone ahead to confirm schedule. **Cost:** Donations. **Phone:** (505) 465-2214.

SILVER CITY (I-2) pop. 10,315, elev. 5,938'

The discovery of silver in the late 1860s led to the founding of appropriately named Silver City, while the establishment of Western New Mexico University in 1893—the same year the bottom dropped out of the silver market—ensured its continued existence. This was also the boyhood home of one William Bonney, who achieved notoriety at a young age as outlaw Billy the Kid.

Mining processes can be viewed from an open pit copper mine 15 miles east on SR 152. The huge pit, 1.7 miles across and 1,000 feet deep, has produced mountains of ore since the discovery of the deposits in 1800. One of the largest operations of its type in the United States, Chino Mine shows evidence of Spanish and Mexican workings. Chino Mines Co. provides an observation point and a picnic area.

Twelve miles south on SR 90, another vast open-pit mine yields some 50,000 tons of copper ore a day from the original site of Tyrone. Built in 1915 by Phelps-Dodge Corp. to house miners and their families, it was a beautifully designed city until declining markets caused the closure of the mine in 1921. Reactivation in the mid-1960s resulted in a new Tyrone 4.5 miles south of Silver City.

Silver City provides access to the 110-mile Trail of the Mountain Spirits, which leads to Gila Cliff Dwellings National Monument *(see place listing p. 288)* via US 180 and SRs 152, 35 and 15, then crosses the Pinos Altos Range back to Silver City. Contact the visitor center at Gila National Forest *(see place listing p. 288)* at (575) 536-9461.

Silver City/Grant County Chamber of Commerce: 500 18th St., Silver City, NM 88061. **Phone:** (575) 538-3785 or (800) 548-9378.

Self-guiding tours: Pocket guides describing walking tours of three historic neighborhoods—Capilla, Gospel Hill and the historic business district—can be purchased at the Silver City Museum.

COMFORT INN 575/534-1883

Hotel. **Address:** 1060 E Hwy 180 88061

HOLIDAY INN EXPRESS 575/538-2525

Hotel. **Address:** 1103 Superior St 88061

QUALITY INN 575/534-1111

Hotel. **Address:** 1120 Hwy 180 E 88061

WHERE TO EAT

ADOBE SPRINGS CAFE 575/538-3665

Regional American. Casual Dining. **Address:** 1617 Silver Heights Blvd 88061

DIANE'S RESTAURANT 575/538-8722

International. Fine Dining. **Address:** 510 N Bullard St 88061

JALISCO CAFE 575/388-2060

Mexican. Casual Dining. **Address:** 103 S Bullard St 88061

REVEL 575/388-4920

New American. Casual Dining. **Address:** 304 N Bullard St 88061

SOCORRO (G-3) pop. 9,051, elev. 4,605'

• Hotels p. 320 • Restaurants p. 320

Socorro was the largest—and wildest—city in New Mexico during the 1880s. After the Panic of 1893 sent silver prices plunging, local mines produced zinc and other ores until these reserves became depleted. The mining era also produced the New Mexico School of Mines, founded in 1889 and later renamed the New Mexico Institute of Mining and Technology.

Socorro County Chamber of Commerce: 101 Plaza St., P.O. Box 743, Socorro, NM 87801. **Phone:** (575) 835-0424.

Self-guiding tours: A brochure outlining a walking tour of historic buildings and places, most within walking distance of the central plaza, is available from the chamber.

EL CAMINO REAL HISTORIC TRAIL SITE is about 35 mi. s. of Socorro off I-25S exit 115, then 1.5 mi. s. on SR 1, then 3 mi. e. on CR 1598 (just past marker 24). Used by traders, settlers and Native Americans for some 300 years, El Camino Real de Tierra Adentro (The Royal Road to the Interior) brought the first Spanish and Mexican colonists to what is now New Mexico. The trail not only provided a means of travel through a vast region but served as a means of introducing livestock, agricultural products, cultural ideas, religion and literature.

Exhibits at the visitor center include a re-creation of the main plaza in Zacatecas, Mexico, a hand-hewn *carreta* (cart) that carried people and their belongings along the trail, a *tienda* (store) and such artifacts as tools and leather water jugs. **Time:** Allow 1 hour minimum. **Hours:** Wed.-Sun. 8:30-5. Closed Jan. 1, Easter, Thanksgiving and Christmas. **Cost:** $5; free (ages 0-16, military with ID, New Mexico residents with ID on first Sun. of the month and New Mexico senior citizens with ID on Wed.). **Phone:** (575) 854-3600.

SAN MIGUEL MISSION is n. of the plaza at 403 El Camino Real. Its long history dates back to 1598, when Franciscan priest Juan de Oñate lead a band of several hundred colonists north from Mexico; the mission he founded was named Nuestra Señora del Socorro (Our Lady of Perpetual Help). The twin-towered adobe church, built in the early 19th century, remains an active parish; the original church was abandoned following the Pueblo Rebellion of 1680 and fell into ruins.

Changes to the building over the years include the addition of stained-glass windows and a side chapel. Hand-carved ceiling beams highlight the newly restored main sanctuary. The church celebrated its 400th anniversary in 2015. A collection of artifacts is displayed in the adjoining office. **Hours:** Church daily 8-6. Office Mon.-Thurs. 8:30-4:30, Fri. 8:30-noon. Mass is held Sat. at 5, Sun. at 8 and 10 a.m. **Cost:** Donations. **Phone:** (575) 835-2891.

BEST WESTERN SOCORRO HOTEL & SUITES 575/838-0556

AAA Benefit: Members save up to 15% and earn bonus points!

Address: 1100 California Ave NE 87801 **Location:** I-25 exit 150, just s. **Facility:** 120 units. 2 stories (no elevator), interior/exterior corridors. **Pool:** heated indoor. **Activities:** hot tub, exercise room. **Guest Services:** coin laundry. **Featured Amenity: continental breakfast.**

/ SOME UNITS

COMFORT INN & SUITES 575/838-4400

Hotel. **Address:** 1259 Frontage Rd NW 87801

ECONO LODGE INN & SUITES 575/835-1500

Address: 713 California St NW 87801 **Location:** I-25 exit 150, 1 mi s. **Facility:** 65 units. 1-2 stories (no elevator), exterior corridors. **Pool:** outdoor. **Activities:** sauna, hot tub, exercise room. **Featured Amenity: full hot breakfast.**

/ SOME UNITS

HOLIDAY INN EXPRESS 575/838-4600

Hotel. **Address:** 1040 N California St 87801

WHERE TO EAT

FRANK & LUPE'S EL SOMBRERO 575/835-3945

Mexican. Casual Dining. **Address:** 210 Mesquite St 87801

SOCORRO SPRINGS RESTAURANT AND BREWERY 575/838-0650

American. Casual Dining. **Address:** 1012 N California St 87801

TAOS (E-4) pop. 5,716, elev. 6,952'

• Hotels p. 326 • Restaurants p. 326
• Hotels & Restaurants map & index p. 324

Originally named Don Fernando de Taos by the Spanish, this northeastern New Mexico jewel has long been a lure. The natural setting in the shadow of the lofty Sangre de Cristo Mountains is glorious. There's a mystical quality that finds its most evocative expression through art. And how many other towns can you name that have a history embracing the Athabascans, Kit Carson and Dennis Hopper?

The Athabascan people (now referred to as Apaches and Navajos) began settling this area almost a thousand years ago. Adobe dwellings were constructed as early as 1350 A.D. at Taos Pueblo, which has the distinction of being considered the nation's oldest continuously inhabited community as well as being the only UNESCO Living World Heritage Site in the United States. The pueblo's two largest structures appear today much as they did in 1540, when the first Spanish explorers arrived. Searching for the "seven cities of gold" that supposedly contained unlimited riches, the Spaniards unfortunately came face to face with a very early urban legend.

Christopher Houston "Kit" Carson is a major figure in Taos lore. The Missouri-born frontiersman was a fur trapper before gaining renown as the guide for John C. Frémont's successful 1840s exploration of the Continental Divide—a trek that set off a flurry of expeditions charting the American West.

Carson later became a Taos rancher and a U.S. Army general who was instrumental in quelling a Navajo uprising in New Mexico. His legendary status grew from the publication of many dime store novels and pulp magazine stories. You can brush up on the "fighting trapper's" life at the Kit Carson Home and Museum and visit his grave in Kit Carson Park.

Flash back to a more recent time—the 1960s—when hippie communes began springing up in the region's spectacular high desert country. Actor/filmmaker Dennis Hopper came to New Mexico to scout locations for "Easy Rider," a 1969 cult classic that vividly depicts the counterculture vibe of the time, partially filmed in and around Taos. He returned and lived here for 12 years. A 2010 memorial service for the two-time Oscar nominee was held at the historic San Francisco de Asis Church in Ranchos de Taos. Hopper is buried nearby.

What always has attracted people is the sheer beauty of the land. Adventurous sketch and watercolor

(See map & index p. 324.)

artists in search of inspiration arrived along with railroad survey teams in the 1870s. The proposed Río del Norte and Santa Fe Railroad never came to fruition, and later efforts to bring rail service to town also failed. This has left Taos somewhat delightfully isolated despite the inevitable presence of modern highways.

It was illustrator Ernest Blumenschein who really got the town's artistic ball rolling. On a covered wagon trip to the Southwest in 1898, he and colleague Bert Phillips were forced to stop in Taos to repair a broken wheel. They became enthralled with the surroundings during their brief stay, and both eventually settled in permanently. In 1915 Blumenschein helped form the Taos Society of Artists, which established the town as an artists' colony with a bent for the eccentric; creative types have gravitated here ever since.

The heart of Taos is Taos Plaza, just off Paseo del Pueblo Norte between Kit Carson Road and Camino de la Placita. It dates back to the late 18th century and has long been a local meeting place. A big cottonwood tree stands in the center of this small plaza; in spring and summer its shiny green leaves flutter in the slightest breeze and then turn bright yellow in the fall, providing a lovely contrast to the azure blue sky.

The plaza's gazebo was donated by Mabel Dodge, a transplanted New York socialite and art connoisseur who came to town in 1918, married Taos Indian Tony Luhan and championed New Mexico's Indian culture and natural beauty to contemporaries like Georgia O'Keeffe, D.H. Lawrence and Ansel Adams. This is a perfect spot to relax and set your internal clock to a more laid-back rhythm.

Taos also provides plenty of outdoor action for active types who aren't content to sit and contemplate. The nearby Rio Grande makes the area a popular starting point for river rafting excursions. During high-water season, from late April to mid-June, the thrills range from relatively gentle to pulse pounding (the latter courtesy of the infamous Taos Box, 16 miles of wilderness gorge and physically demanding rapids). Outfitters are based in town and in Santa Fe.

Mountain bikers and hikers meet their match on the trails that traverse 13,161-foot Wheeler Peak, and Wheeler Peak Wilderness Area offers summer fishing and camping. Winter sports enthusiasts flock to Taos Ski Valley's world-class downhill facilities; phone (575) 586-0520 for snow conditions and year-round recreational activities.

SRs 522 and 38 and US 64—the Enchanted Circle Scenic Byway—encircle Wheeler Peak, offering a multitude of spectacular vistas. About a half hour's drive north of Taos via SR 522 is the tiny, historic village of Questa, one of a long string of villages scattered up the Rio Grande into southern Colorado. Founded in 1842, the isolated settlement was subject to Ute raids for generations. The location still feels remote, and thankfully its beauty remains unspoiled.

The focal point of the community is a thick-walled adobe church that gave the village its original name, San Antonio del Río Colorado. "Questa" was an Anglo attempt at simplification that became an official misspelling of the Spanish *cuesta,* or ridge, where the church plaza was built.

Lovely scenery surrounds Questa. Hiking trails descend into the Rio Grande Gorge and wind around lakes nestled in the Sangre de Cristo Mountains. Thanks to a location between the Carson National Forest and the Rio Grande del Norte National Monument, this region offers outdoor recreation galore, from mountain biking and fishing to horseback riding excursions and hiking treks with a llama-riding guide.

The Questa Visitor Center, in the center of the village on SR 38 just after the SR 522 turn-off, is open Thurs.-Sun. 9:30-5 (also holiday and mid-summer Mondays), Memorial Day-Labor Day; phone (575) 613-2852. For information about recreational opportunities within Rio Grande del Norte National Monument contact the Bureau of Land Management Taos field office; phone (575) 758-8851.

Taos Visitor Center: 1139 Paseo del Pueblo Sur, Taos, NM 87571. **Phone:** (575) 758-3873 or (800) 348-0696.

Self-guiding tours: A walking tour map of the city's historic district and Taos Plaza is available from the visitor center.

Shopping: Many shops at Taos Plaza veer more toward souvenirs, T-shirts and knickknacks than fine art, but it's such a relaxed hangout that you'll want to poke around anyway. Indulge your sweet tooth at the Rocky Mountain Chocolate Factory (next to LaFonda Hotel) before browsing the merchandise at places like the Taos Trading Co. or Mesa's Edge Jewelry.

There's more browsing at the John Dunn House Shops, a tree-shaded, open-air lane of shops between Taos Plaza and Bent Street. Monet's Kitchen has Southwest table and kitchen accessories; Leatherwerks sells handmade belts, hats and jackets. Rock hounds should check out the La Tierra Mineral Gallery (fossils, crystals, jewelry). Moby Dickens Bookshop has a good Southwest selection.

Taos Blue (101 Bent St., just off Paseo del Pueblo Norte) offers finely handcrafted Southwestern and northern New Mexico art—pottery, jewelry, beadwork, medicine bags, Kachina dolls and the like. The gallery also sells fetishes, which are small carvings of animals made from turquoise, mother of pearl and other materials. Created by the Zuni for ceremonial purposes, they're prized by collectors of contemporary Native American art.

The town's thriving art scene, in fact, lures collectors from around the country. Ledoux Street, a block southwest of the plaza, is lined with galleries like 203 Fine Art (203 Ledoux St.), the Inger Jirby Gallery (207 Ledoux St.) and the R.C. Gorman Navajo Gallery (210 Ledoux St.). Local merchants usher in the holiday season with Lighting Ledoux, held in early December.

There are more galleries along Kit Carson Road just east of the plaza. Parsons Gallery of the West

(See map & index p. 324.)

(122-D Kit Carson Rd.) features vintage Western art; the Thom Wheeler Studio Gallery (939 Kit Carson Rd.) has paintings and sculptures. Cowboy collectibles and Western-style furnishings are on display at Horse Feathers (109 Kit Carson Rd. next to the Kit Carson Home and Museum).

Take home a bit of Taos history from the El Rincón Trading Post (114 Kit Carson Rd.). Established in 1909, it actually was a trading post back in the day. In addition to Indian pottery, baskets and rugs, this is a great place to hunt for old turquoise jewelry pawned more than a century ago. The store also has a museum with a collection of Western and Indian artifacts—everything from buckskin britches to peyote fans (used for powwow ceremonial dances).

Ancient traditions live on at Taos Pueblo. Tourism contributes to the local livelihood, and many of the adobe dwellings contain gift shops that sell items like clay pottery, tanned buckskin moccasins and handcrafted pipes. Family-run Wahleah's Taos Pueblo Gallery has five rooms filled with rugs, deerskin drums, beautiful turquoise jewelry and traditional crafts. Even Wahleah's T-shirts, imprinted with lovely nature scenes and cool-looking Indian symbols, are works of art. And don't leave without trying some Indian fry bread, baked in an outdoor adobe oven.

Nightlife: Taos isn't known for frenetic nightlife; options here are mellow and mostly revolve around live music. The Adobe Bar (125 Paseo del Pueblo Norte in The Historic Taos Inn), fondly known as "the living room of Taos," is *the* place to go if you want to mingle with Taoseños. There's live music every night of the week—everything from jazz, bluegrass and alt-country to flamenco, Celtic and native folk music. Better yet, there's no cover charge. The list of creative margaritas includes the inn's famous "Cowboy Buddha."

The Alley Cantina (just off the plaza at 121 Teresina Ln.) is a lively restaurant and bar where singles congregate at happy hour and diners scarf down the highly regarded fish and chips. This is said to be the oldest building in Taos, although only parts of the walls can make that claim. Legend also has it that Teresina Bent, daughter of 19th-century territorial governor Charles Bent, haunts the premises. Local bands play several nights a week.

More local talent—from guitarists to oboe players to stand-up comics—takes the stage on open mic nights (Mondays beginning at 6:30 at the Adobe Bar, Wednesdays at 9:30 at the Alley Cantina). Caffe Tazza (122 Kit Carson Rd.) has weekend open mic nights that bring young performers and mostly acoustic music to this cozy coffeehouse.

Another popular nightspot is the Anaconda Bar (317 Kit Carson Rd. in the El Monte Sagrado Resort), where the decor includes a snake sculpture slithering across the ceiling and a massive saltwater aquarium. Live entertainment takes place Friday and Saturday evenings beginning at 10.

Or you could just hang out in Taos Plaza. When the weather's warm the plaza becomes a magnet for locals and tourists alike. But it's Taos Plaza Live (every Thursday evening from late May to early September) that brings out the crowds. Two bands perform at each show, and the musical lineup is eclectic: rock, jazz, blues, country, traditional New Mexican and Native American. Performances start at 6; admission is free.

E.L. BLUMENSCHEIN HOME AND MUSEUM is 2 blks. w. of historic Taos Plaza on Ledoux St. The artist and co-founder of the original Taos Society of Artists made this his permanent home in 1919. Portions of the adobe house were built in 1797; other sections were purchased by Blumenschein. The restored 13-room house contains original furnishings and serves as a showcase for works by Ernest and Mary Blumenschein, their daughter, Helen, and other Taos painters. **Hours:** Mon.-Sat. 10-5, Sun. noon-5, Apr.-Sept. (Blumenschein Museum is closed Wed. and Thurs.) Phone for winter hours. **Cost:** $8; $7 (seniors); $4 (ages 5-15). Combination ticket with Martinez Hacienda $12. **Phone:** (575) 758-0505.

HARWOOD MUSEUM OF ART is at 238 Ledoux St. Taos art from the late 18th century to the present includes paintings, sculpture and Hispanic religious art. The Agnes Martin Gallery presents seven paintings by this foremost American abstract artist. Changing exhibits focus on Taos artists. **Hours:** Tues.-Sat. 10-5, Sun. noon-5 (also first Fri. of the month 5-7, June-Sept.). Closed Jan. 1, Thanksgiving and Christmas. **Cost:** $10; $8 (ages 65+ and students with ID); free (ages 0-18 and military with ID and their families). **Phone:** (575) 758-9826.

KIT CARSON HOME AND MUSEUM is at 113 Kit Carson Rd. Located within the home of Christopher Houston "Kit" Carson and his wife Josefa and their children, the museum focuses on the history of the Carson family. Kit Carson was a well-known mountain man, guide, army officer and Mason. Exhibits reflect the life of the home's occupants during the mid-1800s. A 20-minute video presentation about Carson also is shown. **Time:** Allow 1 hour minimum. **Hours:** Daily 10-5:30, Mar.-Oct.; 10-4:30, rest of year. Closed Jan. 1, Thanksgiving and Christmas. Phone ahead to confirm schedule. **Cost:** $7; $6 (ages 62+); $5 (ages 13-19 and Veterans with ID); free (ages 0-12 and active military with ID). **Phone:** (575) 758-4945.

MILLICENT ROGERS MUSEUM is 4 mi. n. of Taos Plaza near US 64. The adobe house contains displays relating to the art, history and culture of the Southwest. Emphasis is given to the Indian, Hispanic and Anglo art of Taos and northern New Mexico. A highlight among the 20 galleries is the collection of pottery by Maria Martinez, a San Ildefonso Pueblo potter whose career spanned some 85 years. **Time:** Allow 1 hour minimum. **Hours:** Daily 10-5, Apr.-Oct.; Tues.-Sun. 10-5, rest of year. Closed Jan. 1, Martin Luther King Jr. Day, Presidents Day, Easter, July 4, Labor Day, San Geronimo Day, Thanksgiving and Christmas. **Cost:** $10; $8

(See map & index p. 324.)

(ages 60+); $6 (students and active and retired military with ID); $2 (ages 6-16). Rates may vary; phone ahead. **Phone:** (575) 758-2462.

RIO GRANDE GORGE BRIDGE is 10 mi. w. of Taos on US 64. Built in 1965, this continuous steel deck truss bridge is 1,272 feet long and spans the gorge some 650 feet above the Rio Grande. A raised sidewalk allows daredevils to walk out to the mid-span observation deck for a dizzying look down—the gorge is spectacularly deep at this point—with rugged cliff walls zigzagging to the water far below. If you suffer from acrophobia even hanging on to the guardrail for dear life won't be enough, but the views still are spectacular (and not as vertigo-inducing) from the side of the highway.

There are parking areas on both sides of the highway at the east end of the bridge, and vendors set up tables to sell jewelry, T-shirts and other items. The 20-minute drive from Taos is a scenic one, running through a flat, sagebrush-speckled valley framed by the Sangre de Cristo Mountains to the east and the San Juan range to the northwest. **Hours:** Daily 24 hours. **Cost:** Free.

TAOS ART MUSEUM AT FECHIN HOUSE is at 227 Paseo del Pueblo Norte. Housed in the historic home of Russian-born artist Nicolai Fechin, the permanent collection includes paintings by the Taos Society of Artists and the Taos Moderns. The Fechin House, designed and reconstructed in the 1930s, is considered an architectural masterpiece. It is filled with Fechin's hand-carved doors, windows, furniture and art. **Time:** Allow 30 minutes minimum. **Hours:** Tues.-Sun. 10-5, May-Oct.; Tues.-Sun. 10-4, rest of year. Phone ahead to confirm schedule. **Cost:** $10; $9 (ages 65+ and military with ID); $6 (students with ID). **Phone:** (575) 758-2690.

TAOS PUEBLO is 2 mi. n. of the plaza via Paseo del Pueblo Norte, then about half a mile n. on the entrance road to the parking/registration area. Located at the base of Taos Mountain, this is one of the oldest continuously inhabited communities in North America.

Stepping onto pueblo land is like taking a big step backward in time. Buildings are constructed entirely of adobe; roofs are supported by *vigas* (large wood timbers). The only modern additions are simple doors and windows. The two largest structures are composed of individual dwellings with common walls but no connecting doorways. About 150 Taos Indians choose to live in the sacred village as their ancestors did, without conveniences like electricity or plumbing; drinking water comes from Red Willow Creek, which flows through the center of the pueblo.

A cemetery with primitive wood crosses contains a bell tower, all that remains of the original San Geronimo Church, erected in the early 17th century by Spanish priests overseeing Indian labor. The present church dates from 1850 and has a simple dignity; a central altar figure of the Virgin Mary also represents Mother Nature in the blend of Catholic and native religious iconography.

Registration is required to enter the pueblo. Visitors must heed all signs designating restricted access. **Time:** Allow 1 hour minimum. **Hours:** Mon.-Sat. 8-4:30, Sun. 8:30-4:30, late Apr.-Oct. 31; Mon.-Sat. 8-4, Sun. 8:30-4, rest of year. Closed for approximately 10 weeks from late winter to early spring. Phone ahead to confirm schedule. **Cost:** $16; $14 (students with ID); free (ages 0-10). **Phone:** (575) 758-1028. GT

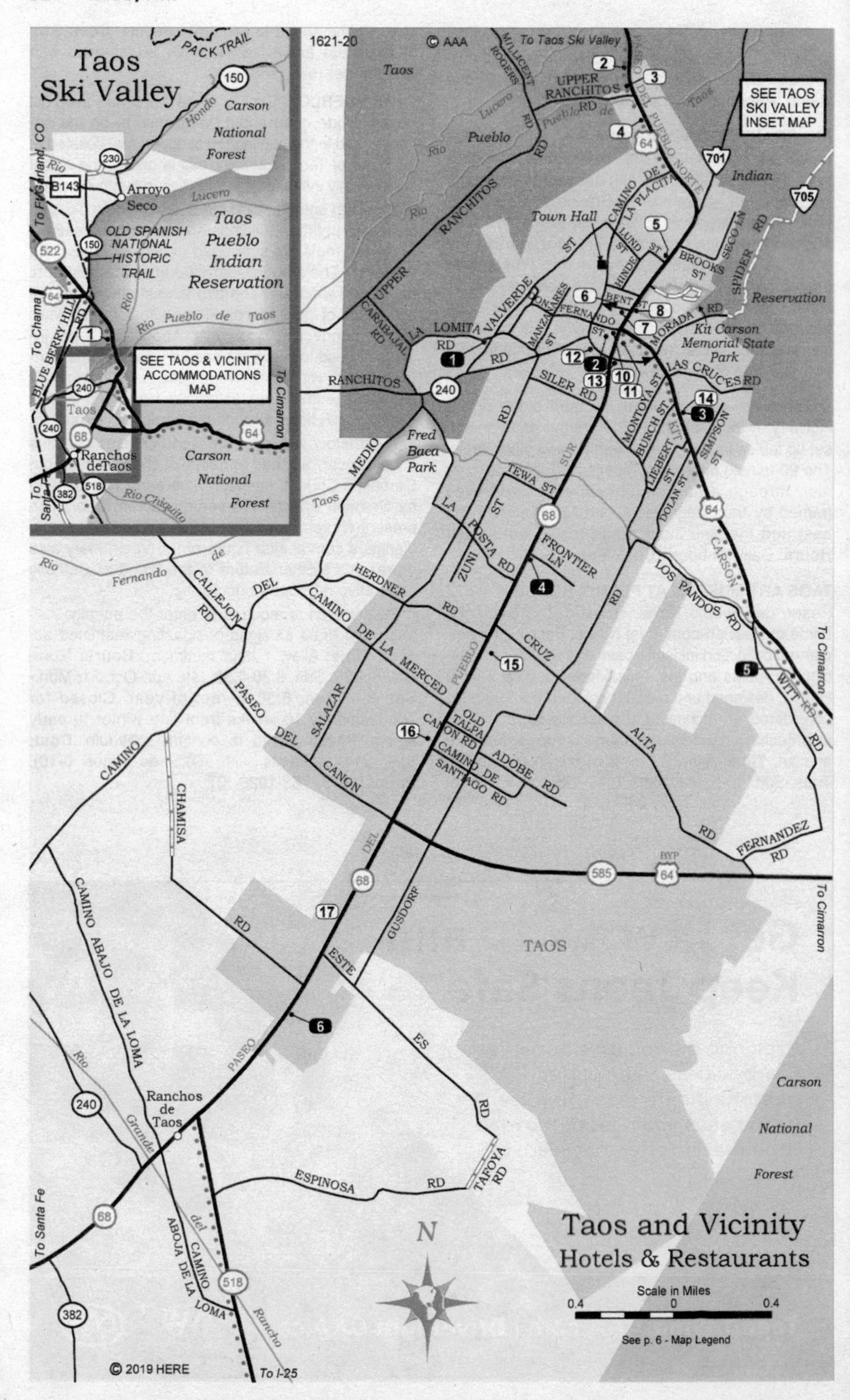

Taos and Vicinity
Hotels & Restaurants
Taos Ski Valley
SEE TAOS SKI VALLEY INSET MAP
SEE TAOS & VICINITY ACCOMMODATIONS MAP
Taos Pueblo Indian Reservation
Carson National Forest
Kit Carson Memorial State Park
Fred Baca Park
Town Hall
Ranchos de Taos
Arroyo Seco
OLD SPANISH NATIONAL HISTORIC TRAIL
TAOS
To Taos Ski Valley
To Cimarron
To Santa Fe
To I-25
To Chama
To Ft Garland, CO
Scale in Miles
0.4 0 0.4
See p. 6 - Map Legend
1621-20
© AAA
© 2019 HERE

Taos and Vicinity

This index helps you "spot" where approved hotels and restaurants are located on the corresponding detailed maps. Restaurant price range is a combination of lunch and/or dinner. Turn to the listing page for more information and consult display ads for special promotions.

For more details, rates and reservations: AAA.com/travelguides/hotels

TAOS

Map Page	Hotels	Diamond Rated	Member Savings	Page
1 p. 324	Dreamcatcher Bed & Breakfast	♦♦♦		326
2 p. 324	Hotel La Fonda De Taos	♦♦♦		326
3 p. 324	El Monte Sagrado	♦♦♦♦		326
4 p. 324	American Artists Gallery House Bed & Breakfast	♦♦♦		326
5 p. 324	Inn On The Rio	♦♦♦		326
6 p. 324	Hampton Inn by Hilton New Mexico-Paseo del Pueblo Sur	♦♦♦	✔	326

Map Page	Restaurants	Diamond Rated	Cuisine	Price Range	Page
1 p. 324	Orlando's New Mexican Cafe	♦♦	Mexican	$8-$17	326
2 p. 324	Guadalajara Grill	♦	Mexican	$5-$16	326
3 p. 324	Gutiz	♦♦	French	$8-$16	326
4 p. 324	Taos Pizza Outback	♦♦	Italian	$4-$29	326
5 p. 324	Michael's Kitchen	♦♦	American	$7-$10	326
6 p. 324	Lambert's of Taos	♦♦♦	American	$10-$40	326
7 p. 324	Bent Street Deli & Cafe	♦♦	American	$4-$12	326
8 p. 324	Caffe Renato	♦♦	Italian	$12-$20	326
10 p. 324	The Gorge Bar and Grill	♦♦	American	$9-$26	326
11 p. 324	Eske's Brew Pub & Eatery	♦♦	American	$8-$14	326
12 p. 324	Byzantium	♦♦♦	New American	$16-$28	326
13 p. 324	Taos Mesa Brewing Taos Tap Room	♦♦	American	$11-$24	326
14 p. 324	De la Tierra Restaurant	♦♦♦	Southwestern	$9-$39	326
15 p. 324	El Taoseno Restaurant	♦♦	Mexican	$6-$13	326
16 p. 324	5 Star Burgers	♦♦	American	$9-$14	326
17 p. 324	Guadalajara Grill	♦	Mexican	$7-$16	326

(See map & index p. 324.)

AMERICAN ARTISTS GALLERY HOUSE BED & BREAKFAST 575/758-4446 (4)
Bed & Breakfast. **Address:** 132 Frontier 87571

DREAMCATCHER BED & BREAKFAST 575/758-0613 (1)
Bed & Breakfast. **Address:** 416 La Lomita Rd 87571

EL MONTE SAGRADO 575/758-3502 (3)
Resort Hotel. **Address:** 317 Kit Carson Rd 87571

HAMPTON INN BY HILTON NEW MEXICO-PASEO DEL PUEBLO SUR 575/737-5700 (6)
SAVE Hotel. **Address:** 1515 Paseo del Pueblo Sur 87571

AAA Benefit: Members save up to 15%!

HOTEL LA FONDA DE TAOS 575/758-2211 (2)
Historic Hotel. **Address:** 108 S Taos Plaza 87571

INN ON THE RIO 575/758-7199 (5)
Bed & Breakfast. **Address:** 910 Kit Carson Rd 87571

WHERE TO EAT

5 STAR BURGERS 575/758-8484 (16)
American. Casual Dining. **Address:** 1032 Paseo Del Pueblo Sur 87571

BENT STREET DELI & CAFE 575/758-5787 (7)
American. Casual Dining. **Address:** 120-M Bent St 87571

BYZANTIUM 575/751-0805 (12)
New American. Casual Dining. **Address:** 112 Camino de la Placitas 87571

CAFFE RENATO 575/758-0244 (8)
Italian. Casual Dining. **Address:** 133 Paseo Del Pueblo Norte 87571

DE LA TIERRA RESTAURANT 575/758-3502 (14)
Southwestern. Fine Dining. **Address:** 317 Kit Carson Rd 87571

EL TAOSENO RESTAURANT 575/758-4142 (15)
Mexican. Casual Dining. **Address:** 819 Paseo Del Pueblo Sur 87571

ESKE'S BREW PUB & EATERY 575/758-1517 (11)
American. Brewpub. **Address:** 106 Des Georges Ln 87571

THE GORGE BAR AND GRILL 575/758-8866 (10)
American. Casual Dining. **Address:** 103-I E Plaza 87571

GUADALAJARA GRILL 575/751-0063 (17)
Mexican. Quick Serve. **Address:** 1384 Paseo del Pueblo Sur 87571

GUADALAJARA GRILL 575/737-0816 (2)
Mexican. Quick Serve. **Address:** 822 Paseo Del Pueblo Norte 87571

GUTIZ 575/758-1226 (3)
French. Casual Dining. **Address:** 812B Paseo Del Pueblo Norte 87571

LAMBERT'S OF TAOS 575/758-1009 (6)
American. Fine Dining. **Address:** 123 Bent St 87571

MICHAEL'S KITCHEN 575/758-4178 (5)
American. Casual Dining. **Address:** 304C Paseo del Pueblo Norte 87571

ORLANDO'S NEW MEXICAN CAFE 575/751-1450 (1)
Mexican. Casual Dining. **Address:** 1114 Don Juan Valdez Ln 87571

TAOS MESA BREWING TAOS TAP ROOM 575/758-1900 (13)
American. Brewpub. **Address:** 201 Paseo Del Pueblo Sur 87571

TAOS PIZZA OUTBACK 575/758-3112 (4)
Italian. Casual Dining. **Address:** 712 Paseo de Pueblo Norte 87571

TRUTH OR CONSEQUENCES (H-3)

pop. 6,475, elev. 4,242'

Playing host to a live broadcast of the radio program "Truth or Consequences" changed not only Hot Springs' future but also its name. So pleased were residents with the publicity engendered by Ralph Edwards' popular show that they adopted the program's name in 1950.

The fire of the chile peppers—one of the Rio Grande Valley's major crops—is nearly matched by the thermal springs that bubble to the surface in Truth or Consequences (their average temperature is 110 F). The Apaches took advantage of the water's legendary curative properties, and bathhouses operated in the vicinity of the springs in the early 20th century.

Both Elephant Butte Lake State Park in Elephant Butte and Caballo Lake State Park in Caballo offer water-oriented recreation. *See Recreation Areas Chart.*

Geronimo Trail Scenic Byway Interpretive Visitors Center: 301 S. Foch St., Truth or Consequences, NM 87901. **Phone:** (575) 894-1968.

SPACEPORT AMERICA visitor center is at 301 S. Foch St. Spaceport America is the world's first purpose-built commercial space launch facility, equipped with such basic infrastructure as an airfield, launch pads and hangars. The visitor center, housed in a historic adobe building in Truth or Consequences, contains educational and interactive space travel-related exhibits. The remote Spaceport America site, situated in the midst of stark high desert country, can be toured and is reached via a rolling multimedia theater shuttle.

At the site visitors can engage in interactive exhibits, experience the thrill of rapid acceleration courtesy of a G-Shock simulator, meet Spaceport America crew members and view the futuristic Gateway to Space terminal/hangar. **Time:** Allow 5 hours minimum. **Hours:** Visitor center open daily 8:30-4:30. Morning tours to the spaceport site depart Mon. and Thurs.-Sun. at 9 (boarding begins at 8:45) and return to the visitor center at 1. Afternoon tours depart Fri.-Sun. at 1:30, May-Sept. (boarding begins at 1:15) and return to the visitor center at 5:30. All tours are subject to change or cancellation. **Cost:** Visitor center free. Spaceport America tour fee $49.99; $29.99 (ages 0-17). Tour reservations must be made at least 24 hours in advance. **Phone:** (844) 727-7223.

HOLIDAY INN EXPRESS & SUITES 575/894-3900
Hotel. **Address:** 2201 FG Amin St 87901

SIERRA GRANDE LODGE & SPA 575/894-6976

Boutique Hotel. **Address:** 501 McAdoo St 87901

WHERE TO EAT

LA COCINA RESTAURANT 575/894-6499

Mexican. Casual Dining. **Address:** 1 Lakeway Dr 87901

LATITUDE 33 575/740-7804

Asian Fusion. Casual Dining. **Address:** 304 S Pershing St 87901

LOS ARCOS 575/894-6200

Steak. Casual Dining. **Address:** 1400 N Date St 87901

TUCUMCARI (F-5) pop. 5,363, elev. 4,086'

Tucumcari, named for 4,999-foot Tucumcari Mountain—utilized by Comanche Indians as a lookout point, or *tucumcari*—is another town that came into being by way of a rail line (in this case, the Rock Island Railroad). Legend traces the origin of the name to an ill-fated romance between the warrior Tocom and Kari, the daughter of a chief. When Tocom died in a fight for Kari's hand she stabbed the victor, then herself. Witnessing the tragedy, her father also ended his life with a dagger, crying out "Tocom-Kari."

In the 1920s Tucumcari became the first New Mexico stop for westbound travelers on new federal highway Route 66. Stretching 2,448 miles from Chicago to Los Angeles, it played a major role in early transcontinental auto travel. The interstate highway system eventually supplanted Route 66, and it was officially decertified in 1985.

You'll still see a few neon-lit motor courts, kitschy reminders of a bygone era, along the Tucumcari stretch of Route 66. Another local landmark is Tee Pee Curios, known for its teepee-shaped entrance and elaborate neon sign. It opened in 1944 as a Gulf gas station and souvenir shop.

Two Canadian River reservoirs not only provide necessary irrigation but opportunities for outdoor recreation. Conchas Lake is 34 miles northwest of town via SR 104; Ute Lake is 23 miles northeast via SR 54 to Logan. *See Recreation Areas Chart.*

Tucumcari-Quay County Chamber of Commerce: 404 W. Rte. 66, P.O. Drawer E, Tucumcari, NM 88401. **Phone:** (575) 461-1694.

MESALANDS COMMUNITY COLLEGE'S DINOSAUR MUSEUM AND NATURAL SCIENCES LABORATORY is at 222 E. Laughlin Ave. The Exhibit Hall showcases original and replicated fossils and skeletons from the Mesozoic era, the "Age of Dinosaurs." The centerpiece is a 40-foot-long skeleton of a Torvosaurus, a rare carnivorous relative of the Tyrannosaurus rex. **Time:** Allow 1 hour minimum. **Hours:** Tues.-Sat. 10-6, Mar. 1-Labor Day; Tues.-Sat. noon-5, rest of year. Closed Jan. 1, Thanksgiving and Christmas. **Cost:** $6.50; $5.50 (ages 65+); $4.50 (students with ID); $4 (ages 5-11). **Phone:** (575) 461-3466.

BEST WESTERN DISCOVERY INN 575/461-4884

Hotel

Best Western **AAA Benefit:** Members save up to 15% and earn bonus points!

Address: 200 E Estrella Ave 88401 **Location:** I-40 exit 332, just n. **Facility:** 80 units. 2 stories (no elevator), exterior corridors. **Pool:** outdoor. **Activities:** exercise room. **Guest Services:** coin laundry. **Featured Amenity: breakfast buffet.**

SAVE CALL BIZ

/SOME UNITS

DAYS INN 575/461-3158

Hotel. **Address:** 2623 S 1st St 88401

HOLIDAY INN EXPRESS HOTEL & SUITES 575/461-3333

Hotel

Address: 2624 S Adams St 88401 **Location:** I-40 exit 332, just n. **Facility:** 80 units. 3 stories, interior corridors. **Pool:** heated indoor. **Activities:** sauna, hot tub, game room, exercise room. **Guest Services:** coin laundry. **Featured Amenity: full hot breakfast.**

SAVE CALL  BIZ

HS

LA QUINTA INN & SUITES TUCUMCARI 575/461-2233

Hotel. **Address:** 2516 S Adams St 88401

WHERE TO EAT

DEL'S RESTAURANT 575/461-1740

American. Casual Dining. **Address:** 1202 E Route 66 88401

KIX ON 66 COFFEE SHOP & EATERY 575/461-1966

American. Casual Dining. **Address:** 1102 E Route 66 Blvd 88401

WHITE ROCK pop. 5,725

HAMPTON INN & SUITES LOS ALAMOS 505/672-3838

SAVE Hotel. **Address:** 124 SR 4 87544

AAA Benefit: Members save up to 15%!

WHITE SANDS MISSILE RANGE (H-3) elev. 4,295'

On July 16, 1945, in a remote section of White Sands Missile Range, the first man-made atomic explosion sent a huge multicolored cloud surging to an altitude of 40,000 feet. The resultant sloping crater at Trinity Site is evidence of the beginning of the Atomic Age.

The desert environment proved ideal for rocket testing and, in the 1960s, testing for the lunar module engines that propelled Apollo astronauts off the moon's surface. Today the world-class test facilities are used by the U.S. Army as well as private industry and foreign nations for laser, radar and flight research.

Vehicle passes are issued at the main gate; a valid driver's license, registration and proof of insurance are required. A photo ID is required for all vehicle occupants over age 16. Trinity Site is open the first Saturday in April and October. For more information contact the Public Affairs Office, Bldg. 1782, White Sands Missile Range, NM 88002; phone (575) 678-1134 or (575) 437-6120 (Alamogordo Chamber of Commerce).

GEM **WHITE SANDS MISSILE RANGE MUSEUM** is 19 mi. n.e. of Las Cruces on US 70/80, then 4 mi. s. to just inside the main gate. The history of the Frontier Army in southern New Mexico, as well as nation's missile program and the Atomic Age, is chronicled via artifacts, displays and photographs depicting early rocket launches and the first atomic bomb test at Trinity Site.

An outdoor park displays some 60 rockets and missiles, including a restored German V-2 rocket exhibited horizontally to reveal its interior. There also are exhibits about Paleo-Indian culture as well as 19th-century mining and ranching. **Time:** Allow 30 minutes minimum. **Hours:** Mon.-Fri. 8-4, Sat. 10-3. Missile park open daily dawn-dusk. Closed major holidays. **Cost:** Free. **Phone:** (575) 678-3358.

GEM WHITE SANDS NATIONAL MONUMENT (I-3)

About 15 miles southwest of Alamogordo on US 70, White Sands National Monument is the source of rare gypsum sands that form snow-white dunes rising up to 60 feet above the Tularosa Basin floor.

Covering 275 square miles, the massive dunes are created when rain and melting snow dissolve gypsum from the surrounding mountains and carry it into Lake Lucero, a seasonal lake, or *playa.* Desert heat evaporates the water, causing gypsum crystals to form. Dry winds expose the crystals, eroding them into sand-sized particles that are blown into the dune field.

Much of this wide sea of dunes is bare of vegetation. A few species of plants exhibit remarkable adaptation to the shifting sands; the stem of the soaptree yucca stretches up to 30 feet to keep the plant from being buried.

Drinking water is available only at the visitor center; covered picnic sites and restrooms are in the heart of the dunes area. Interactive exhibits at the visitor center describe the origin and history of White Sands, and a video is shown every half hour.

Ranger-guided sunset strolls are offered daily 1 hour before sunset, except on Christmas. There are several hiking trails; brochures describing desert hiking safety can be obtained at the visitor center. On full-moon nights from May through October, the park remains open until 11 p.m. so visitors can witness celestial light reflecting off the dunes. Music and educational programs pertaining to New Mexico's heritage and the monument's geology, plants and animals also are presented on full-moon nights.

Scenic, 16-mile round-trip Dunes Drive can be entered daily 7 a.m.-8 p.m., Memorial Day weekend-Labor Day; 7 a.m.-dusk, rest of year. It is subject to closures of up to 3 hours during missile testing. Visitors must exit the park by 1 hour after dusk, except on full-moon nights May-Oct. Visitor center open daily 9-5; phone for extended summer hours. Closed Christmas. Admission, valid for 7 days, $5; free (ages 0-15). Phone (575) 479-6124, ext. 236.

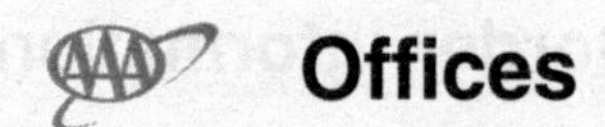

Offices

Main office listings are shown in **BOLD TYPE** and toll-free member service numbers appear in *ITALIC TYPE.*
All are closed Saturdays, Sundays and holidays unless otherwise indicated.
The addresses, phone numbers and hours for any AAA/CAA office are subject to change.
The type of service provided is designated below the name of the city where the office is located:

- ✚ Auto travel services, including books and maps, and on-demand TripTik® routings.
- ● Auto travel services, including selected books and maps, and on-demand TripTik® routings.
- ■ Books/maps only, no marked maps or on-demand TripTik® routings.
- ▲ Travel Agency Services, cruise, tour, air, car and rail reservations; domestic and international hotel reservations; passport photo services; international and domestic travel guides and maps; travel money products; and International Driving Permits. In addition, assistance with travel related insurance products including trip cancellation, travel accident, lost luggage, trip delay and assistance products.
- ✪ Insurance services provided. If only this icon appears, only insurance services are provided at that office.
- ◐ Car Care Plus Facility provides car care services.
- ▣ Electric vehicle charging station on premises.

AAA NATIONAL OFFICE: 1000 AAA DRIVE, HEATHROW, FLORIDA 32746-5063, (407) 444-7000

ARIZONA

CHANDLER—AAA ARIZONA, 301 N ARIZONA AVE, 85225. WEEKDAYS (M-F) 7:00-6:00, SAT 8:00-4:00. (602) 230-3690 ◐

CHANDLER—AAA ARIZONA, 4040 W RAY RD STE 2, 85226. WEEKDAYS (M-F) 8:30-5:30. (602) 230-3601 ✚ ▲ ✪ ▣

CHANDLER—AAA ARIZONA, 6205 W CHANDLER BLVD, 85226. WEEKDAYS (M-F) 7:00-6:00, SAT 8:00-4:00. (602) 230-3600 ◐

GILBERT—AAA ARIZONA, 2786 S SANTAN VILLAGE PKY, 85295. WEEKDAYS (M-F) 7:00-6:00, SAT 8:00-4:00. (480) 857-3200 ◐

GILBERT—AAA ARIZONA, 2786 S.SANTAN VILLAGE PKY, 85295. WEEKDAYS (M-F) 8:30-5:30, SAT 9:00-3:00. (480) 812-8500, *(800) 922-8228.* ✚ ▲ ✪ ◐

GOODYEAR—AAA ARIZONA, 14175 W INDIAN SCH RD A-8, 85395. WEEKDAYS (M-F) 8:30-5:30. (602) 230-3170 ✚ ▲ ✪

MESA—AAA ARIZONA, 4126 E VALLEY AUTO DR, 85206. WEEKDAYS (M-F) 7:00-6:00, SAT 8:00-4:00. (602) 241-3900 ◐

MESA—AAA ARIZONA, 4126 E VALLEY AUTO DR, 85206. WEEKDAYS (M-F) 8:30-5:30, SAT 9:00-3:00 (MAPS & TOURBOOKS ONLY). (602) 241-3901 ✚ ▲ ✪

PEORIA—AAA ARIZONA, 7422 W THUNDERBIRD RD, 85381. WEEKDAYS (M-F) 7:00-6:00, SAT 8:00-4:00. (602) 230-3100 ◐ ▣

PEORIA—AAA ARIZONA, 7422 W THUNDERBIRD RD, 85381. WEEKDAYS (M-F) 8:30-5:30, SAT 9:00-3:00 (MAPS & TOURBOOKS ONLY). (602) 230-3101 ✚ ▲ ✪ ▣

PHOENIX—AAA ARIZONA, 1050 E CAMELBACK RD, 85014. WEEKDAYS (M-F) 7:00-6:00, SAT 8:00-4:00. (602) 230-3401 ◐ ▣

PHOENIX—AAA ARIZONA, 15439 N 40TH ST, 85032. WEEKDAYS (M-F) 7:00-6:00, SAT 8:00-4:00. (602) 230-3200 ◐

PHOENIX—AAA ARIZONA, 4046 E GREENWAY RD, 85032. WEEKDAYS (M-F) 8:30-5:30. (602) 230-3201 ✚ ▲ ✪ ▣

PHOENIX—AAA ARIZONA, 4101 E BELL RD, 85032. WEEKDAYS (M-F) 7:00-6:00, SAT 8:00-4:00. (602) 230-3250 ◐

PHOENIX—AAA ARIZONA, 742 E GLENDALE AVE #182, 85020. WEEKDAYS (M-F) 8:30-5:30. (602) 285-6241 ✚ ▲ ✪

PRESCOTT—AAA ARIZONA, 172 E SHELDON ST #C-100, 86301. WEEKDAYS (M-F) 8:30-5:30. (928) 541-8600 ✚ ▲ ✪

SCOTTSDALE—AAA ARIZONA, 14850 N FRANK LLOYDWRIGHT, 85260. WEEKDAYS (M-F) 8:30-5:30. (602) 248-3701 ✚ ▲ ✪

SCOTTSDALE—AAA ARIZONA, 15509 N HAYDEN RD, 85260. WEEKDAYS (M-F) 7:00-6:00, SAT 8:00-4:00. (602) 248-3700 ◐

SCOTTSDALE—AAA ARIZONA, 7520 E MCDOWELL RD, 85257. WEEKDAYS (M-F) 7:00-6:00, SAT 8:00-4:00. (602) 248-3750 ◐

SCOTTSDALE—AAA ARIZONA, 7520 E MCDOWELL RD, 85257. WEEKDAYS (M-F) 8:30-5:30. (602) 230-3750 ● ▲ ✪

SUN CITY WEST—AAA ARIZONA, 19802 R H JOHNSON BL #141, 85375. WEEKDAYS (M-F) 8:30-5:30. (602) 230-3301 ✚ ▲ ✪

TUCSON—AAA ARIZONA, 3870 W RIVER RD STE 102, 85741. WEEKDAYS (M-F) 7:00-6:00, SAT 8:00-4:00. (520) 258-7708 ◐

TUCSON—AAA ARIZONA, 6950 N ORACLE RD, 85704. WEEKDAYS (M-F) 8:30-5:30. (520) 258-0505 ✚ ▲ ✪ ▣

TUCSON—AAA ARIZONA, 7060 E SPEEDWAY, 85710. WEEKDAYS (M-F) 7:00-6:00, SAT 8:00-4:00. (520) 290-1000 ◐

TUCSON—AAA ARIZONA, 8204 E BROADWAY, 85710. WEEKDAYS (M-F) 8:30-5:30. (520) 258-0504 ✚ ▲ ✪

NEW MEXICO

ALBUQUERQUE—AAA NEW MEXICO, 10501 MONTGOMERY BLVD NE, 87111. WEEKDAYS (M-F) 9:00-5:30, SAT 10:00-2:00. (505) 291-6611, *(877) 222-1020.* ✚ ▲ ✪

ALBUQUERQUE—AAA NEW MEXICO, 9231 COORS RD NW STE 5&6, 87114. WEEKDAYS (M-F) 9:00-5:30, SAT 10:00-2:00. (505) 792-1938, *(877) 222-1020.* ✚ ▲ ✪

LAS CRUCES—AAA NEW MEXICO, 3991 E LOHMAN AVE STE #A, 88011. WEEKDAYS (M-F) 9:00-5:30, SAT 10:00-2:00. (575) 523-5681, *(877) 222-1020.* ✚ ▲ ✪

SANTA FE—AAA NEW MEXICO, 3517 ZAFARANO DR STE D, 87507. WEEKDAYS (M-F) 9:00-5:30, SAT 10:00-2:00. (505) 471-6620, *(877) 222-1020.* ✚ ▲ ✪

Border Information

Traveling to Mexico

FOR U.S. AND CANADIAN RESIDENTS TRAVELING TO MEXICO

AAA recommends that travelers consult U.S. State Department travel advisories when planning travel abroad. Find this information online at travel.state.gov/content/passports/english/alertswarnings/mexico-travel-warning.html.

Border crossing requirements: Travelers are required to present proper travel documents for travel to Mexico and to return to the United States.

Air travel: U.S. and Canadian citizens traveling between the United States and Mexico by air are required to show a valid passport.

Land or sea travel: A passport or passport card, or other U.S. official ID (not including a state-issued driver's license), is required to enter Mexico by land or sea. U.S. citizens returning to the United States from Mexico by land or sea are required to present proper travel documents according to the Western Hemisphere Travel Initiative. Approved documents include a passport or passport card, Enhanced Driver's License or Trusted Traveler program card; for more information refer to the U.S. Department of State website. Canadian citizens should refer to the Canada Border Services Agency website for requirements to re-enter Canada; cbsa-asfc.gc.ca.

Children: Minors under age 18 traveling alone or with someone other than a parent or legal guardian are required to present a notarized letter of consent from at least one absent parent giving permission to travel only if the minor is departing (not entering) Mexico, is traveling by air or sea or is using Mexican documents to travel. However, because airline or Mexican immigration officials may request a notarized letter of consent under other circumstances as well, the U.S. Embassy in Mexico City recommends that any minor traveling without both parents carry a notarized consent letter at all times. For more information contact the embassy, a Mexican consulate office or the Mexican National Immigration Institute (INM).

Automobile insurance: Full coverage from a reliable Mexican insurance company is required, including property damage and public liability. AAA offices in border states, Nevada and Utah can provide Mexican automobile insurance to members. U.S. or Canadian automobile insurance is not valid in Mexico.

Tourist permits: When traveling to Mexico as a tourist you must obtain an FMM tourist permit. A valid passport or passport card is required in order to obtain a permit.

Permits are issued online and at Mexican immigration offices at official points of entry. You must have a valid tourist permit if you remain within the border zone—the area within 20 to 30 kilometers (12 to 19 miles) of the U.S. border, depending on the Mexican state—for more than 72 hours, or if you travel beyond the border zone. **Note:** In the state of Baja California the border "free zone" is no longer valid and every visitor must have a tourist permit regardless of the length of his or her stay.

The permit costs 500 pesos (approximately $26.32 U.S.), which must be paid at a Mexican bank (see the list of banks on the back of the permit form) or at a bank window at the border. You are required to show the "Fee Paid" stamp on your tourist permit when leaving Mexico.

If traveling by air, the permit is distributed on the flight and the fee is included in the airline ticket price. If arriving by cruise ship, the fee is collected when disembarking or is included in the cruise fare if the stay is longer than 72 hours.

Tourist permit exemptions:

- Visitors traveling by sea, staying less than 72 hours and remaining in the seaport.
- Visitors traveling by land to destinations within the border zone (except Baja California) and staying less than 72 hours.
- Visitors traveling by land beyond the border zone, staying less than 72 hours and limiting their visit to the following destinations/tourist corridors: Sonoyta to Puerto Peñasco, Sonora; Ciudad Juárez to Paquime, Chihuahua; Piedras Negras to Santa Rosa, Coahuila; and Reynosa to Presa Cuchillo, Nuevo León.
- Business travelers with a business visa; students (as defined by Mexican immigration laws) with a student visa (contact a Mexican consulate for business/student visa information).

Tourist permit validity:

- The permit is valid for up to 180 days.
- A multiple-entry permit allows unlimited visits into and out of Mexico within the 180-day period.
- A tourist permit not used within 90 days of issue becomes void.
- Visitors should carry their tourist permit with them at all times while in Mexico.
- If you lose your permit while in Mexico, a duplicate can be obtained from a local immigration office (write down your tourist permit number and keep it separate from the permit to expedite the paperwork involved).
- Permits must be turned in to Mexican immigration officials at the border when you depart the country by land, except in Baja California (following the permit expiration date it can be shredded or discarded). If departing by air, the permit must be turned in to immigration officials at the airport.
- If you wish to remain in Mexico beyond the permit validity period an extension must be requested from immigration authorities prior to the expiration date.
- Violation of the laws governing tourist permits may result in subsequently being refused entry into Mexico and/or incurring a substantial fine.

Vehicle travel beyond the border zone requires a government-issued temporary vehicle importation permit and a promise to return vehicle form. These two documents are not required in Baja California unless the vehicle is put on a ferry bound for the mainland. They also are not required for travel to the following destinations in the state of Sonora: Rocky Point (Puerto Peñasco), Guaymas, San Carlos, Bahía Kino and other locations west of Mex. 15, as well as cities along Mex. 15 (Magdalena, Santa Ana, Hermosillo).

An Only Sonora permit is acceptable if driving is confined within the state east of Mex. 15 as well as south of Empalme (about 350 miles south of the U.S. border). The permit can be obtained at Banjercito offices in Agua Prieta (opposite Douglas, Ariz.), Cananea (on Mex. 2 southwest of Agua Prieta) and Empalme (on Mex. 15 at Km marker 98, just south of the Guaymas bypass).

The temporary vehicle importation permit and promise to return vehicle form can be purchased at the Banjercito office at an official point of entry (immigration checkpoint). The vehicle owner must present a valid (unexpired) tourist permit and a current vehicle license/registration receipt (the original and two copies). Information on the application for temporary vehicle importation and on the promise to return form must match; the same requirements apply to both.

An administration fee (approximately $51 U.S.) plus applicable IVA tax must be paid with a major international credit card (American Express, Mastercard or Visa) in order to receive a temporary importation permit windshield sticker. The credit card must be in the vehicle owner's name and issued by a U.S. or Canadian bank or lending institution. Vehicle owners who don't have a major credit card must post a bond ($200 to $400 based on vehicle value) with a Mexican bonding firm (Afianzadora) at the point of entry. Cash, checks, money orders or credit cards issued by a Mexican bank are not accepted.

More about temporary importation permits:

- Generally issued for 180 days, the same length as the tourist permit.
- Only one permit will be issued per person, for one motorized vehicle at a time.
- Carry the permit with you; do not leave it in the vehicle.
- Return permit, promise to return vehicle form and windshield sticker to Mexican

customs officials at the Banjercito office at the border before or on the expiration date shown on the form, or be subject to a fine.

- If the permit or form is lost or stolen, Mexican customs offices can issue replacement documentation provided you obtain a certified document attesting to the loss from your homeland (U.S. or Canada) embassy or consulate.
- If you remain in Mexico beyond the authorized time period and without the proper documentation, your car will be immediately confiscated.

Pets: U.S. visitors may bring a dog, cat or bird into Mexico with government approval. A pet health certificate signed not more than 15 days before the animal enters Mexico and a pet vaccination certificate showing proof of treatment for rabies, hepatitis and leptospirosis are required at the border for each animal. A pet permit fee is charged at the time of entry.

Leaving Mexico

FOR U.S. AND CANADIAN RESIDENTS LEAVING MEXICO

When leaving the country:

- FMM tourist permits, temporary vehicle importation permits, promise to return vehicle forms and windshield stickers must be returned to Mexican immigration and customs officials at the departure or border checkpoint (or at an interior inspection point).

- Those entering Mexico with a motor vehicle must leave the country with the vehicle.
- At highway stations near the U.S. border, Mexican agricultural officials will inspect vehicles traveling north that are carrying any fruits, vegetables, houseplants and other plant matter.
- You must have an export certificate to take official cultural artifacts (excluding handicrafts) out of the country.
- Religious or archeological artifacts may not be taken out of the country.

Returning to the United States or Canada:

U.S. citizens returning from Mexico by land or sea are required to present proper travel documents; refer to the U.S. Department of State website for the most current information. Canadian citizens entering the United States are subject to the rules governing entry to the U.S. by foreign nationals; refer to the Canadian Border Services Agency website for requirements to re-enter Canada.

U.S. exemptions:

- You may bring back duty-free articles not exceeding $800 in retail value.
- The exemption is allowed once every 30 days.
- A family (related persons living in the same household) may combine exemptions; i.e., a family of six would be entitled to $1,600 worth of goods duty-free on one declaration, even if the articles claimed by one member exceed that individual's $800 amount.
- Duty must be paid on all items in excess of the exemption amount.
- Payment of duty is required upon arrival.
- Gifts taken across the U.S./Mexico border are considered to be for personal use and are included in the $800 exemption.
- Articles purchased and left behind for alterations or other reasons do not qualify for the $800 exemption when shipped at a later date.
- The $800 exemption may include no more than 1 liter of alcoholic beverages and no more than 200 cigarettes and 100 cigars.

Restricted or prohibited articles: An agricultural quarantine bans the importation of certain fruits, vegetables, plants, livestock, poultry and meats. All food products brought into the United States must be declared. The U.S. Department of Agriculture also prohibits bringing back any type of pet. Visit the